Photo by Philip Fein

Mark Schorer has been studying Blake for ten years and has actually been at work on this book since 1941 when he was awarded a Guggenheim Fellowship to undertake it, a grant which was renewed in 1942.

He is the author of two novels, A HOUSE TOO OLD (1935), and THE HERMIT PLACE (1941), of many critical articles, and of over thirty short stories which have appeared in magazines and anthologies. These are being collected in book form.

Mark Schorer was born in 1908, in Wisconsin, was educated at the University of Wisconsin and Harvard. He has taught at his Alma Mater, at Dartmouth, and at Harvard University where he was the Briggs-Copeland Instructor in Composition. He is now Associate Professor of English at the University of California at Berkeley. Mr. Schorer is married and has two children.

WILLIAM BLAKE

✲

The Politics of Vision

"Newton"

By courtesy of the trustees of the Tate Gallery

"All that we saw was owing to your metaphysics."

WILLIAM BLAKE

The Politics of Vision

MARK SCHORER

NEW YORK: HENRY HOLT AND COMPANY

First printing

PRINTED IN THE UNITED STATES OF AMERICA

Once again,

to RUTH

Contents

Contents

List of Illustrations

Preface

THE MOTIVE behind this book is the belief that William Blake, about whom many other books have been written, has never yet been examined in detail as a man in the world, as a poet with a particular temperamental bias, coming out of a particular tradition, in a particular period of history. He was a visionary poet deeply immersed in radical religious and political movements of the eighteenth century, aware of and keenly interested in the major currents of opinion of his time. To reveal the extent of this interest I have largely ignored archaic systems of thought and symbolism from which Blake drew. He was an eighteenth-century poet who wrapped himself in the mantles of a curious antiquity which are paraphernalia useful both to expression and disguise; but they are paraphernalia still, and Blake critics before now have given this paraphernalia perhaps all the attention that it needs.

The book has three parts. The first is largely concerned with definitions, and I have made full use here of Blake's casual writings, his fragments, letters, notes, and recorded conversations, in the hope that the reader may hear the voice of the man as he was, genial and angry, and infer, with the aid of such technical definition as I can give, the supremely important fact of personality, and the intellectual and aesthetic paradoxes into which Blake's temperament plunged him. The second part of the book, after a biographical introduction and a summary of eighteenth-century radical opinion, examines Blake's poetry as the expression and the correction of French Revolutionary ideas. The third part of the book considers Blake's development as a poet, and relates his poetic evolution and his consequent attitudes toward art and poetry to his personal dilemma and, more than that, to the particular ideas which it led him to.

Throughout the book appear various paintings by Blake which are intended as amplifications or illustrations of points made about the poems. For the sake of this connection, I have added to Blake's titles quotations from the writings. This book is concerned with Blake's graphic art only when it is a direct aid to the understanding of his poems.

Some readers may feel that the proportions of the book do not indicate that I have a very high regard for poetry as an art. That is to say, the extended attention which the book gives to historical and intellectual considerations and the relatively brief attention which it gives to technical matters may suggest that I find a poet's value to exist in what he believes rather than in what his poetry is. This is not at all the case. The primary problem in Blake criticism, because Blake is an obscure poet, has always been with what he believed and what he meant to say, and it remains so, and what Blake's poetry *is,* in its merits as in its defects, and certainly in its development as a whole, has an unusually direct, in fact, a nearly one-to-one, relation with what it says, and with what Blake believed about the world and about himself as a poet in the world. I do not think that he was a *great* poet because he preached tirelessly a doctrine of human liberty; but I think that he was the *kind* of poet he was because he did.

An exposition of Blake may be conducted in one of at least two ways. There is the way of Mr. Middleton Murry, in his book *William Blake,* which attempts a "pure" account of Blake's doctrine—that is, an effort to understand Blake from his own page alone, without reference to history or recourse to similarities in other writers, who are, it is perfectly true, not Blake. Another way is the way of this book, which not only invokes historical considerations at every turn, but constantly calls in as witness the work of other writers. I do not have Mr. Murry's temerity in boldly entering Blake's mind, and I have taken the more halting approach to his genius. Whether I have reproduced anything like a semblance of his mind the reader must judge, but I am confident that I have at any rate not merely reproduced my own. Shelley, among Blake's contemporaries, is constantly useful as a reference, and, among modern poets, Yeats. Yeats is an accessible poet, and yet what he says is often so very close to what Blake said at his most inaccessible that comparison has been irresistible. I trust that a great many such allusions have not strained unduly the limits of my discussion.

I have tried to avoid denunciation of Blake's excesses; this seems as useless as the kind of adulation to which, since Swinburne, Blake has usually been subject. It is easy enough to see where he is deficient, but it is not quite so easy to see the reasons, in himself and in his age, for his deficiencies. And it is quite as possible, for example, that had he had a better education, as a number of good critics have wished, he might have become no artist or poet at all, as it is that he might have become a better one. "Do not," warned Coleridge, "let us introduce an Act of Uniformity against poets." The fact is that there Blake is, larger today than ever, in all his eccentricity and perverseness and beauty and power and ugliness, and to lump these under the misused term of "mysticism," as most critics have done, and praise him in a cultish spirit, seems as uncritical as it is to lump them under the easy term of "madness," as his contemporaries and the older critics did, and damn him for differing from the world.

In the course of preparing to write this book, I have, with a few exceptions, read the more than fifty books about Blake and the vast number of essays and articles. To most of these I have had no recourse since, but some of them have been invaluable. I should mention first of all Mr. Geoffrey Keynes's magnificent edition of Blake's writings, to which all students of Blake are indebted; I have used the third, one-volume edition (1932). To Mr. S. Foster Damon's book, *William Blake: His Philosophy and Symbols,* which is a landmark in Blake criticism, the second part of my book is especially indebted, for this work fixed, with as much finality as they are capable of, the meanings of Blake's symbols, and in the future, divagation from Mr. Damon's concrete interpretations need be only minor. I depart from him not in specific matters but in his over-all view of Blake as a traditional mystic, and this difference plays some part, of course, in the evaluation of particulars, as it does in that of sources. For my treatment of mysticism, I am indebted, in spite of the great disparity in our evaluation of mysticism, to Miss Helen C. White's *The Mysticism of William Blake,* which was the first and remains nearly the only book about Blake not to view him as a traditional mystic; I am indebted, too, to many conversations with Miss White, who has been both my teacher and my friend, and has always been tolerant of moods which must have seemed to her either merely brash or else heretical. My debt to books on specific problems, such as Mr. Wicksteed's study of the *Songs of Innocence and Experience* and Miss Lowery's of the *Poetical Sketches,* as well as to articles and essays and chapters in books on larger subjects, is acknowledged in the notes. (Notes which amplify the text usually appear at the bottom of the proper page; the notes at the back of the book are mainly references. I have exercised a personal preference and listed these under chapter, page, and line numbers in order to avoid superior numerals in the text.) I wish to mention especially a very good book indeed, called *The Man without a Mask,* and published last year by Jacob Bronowski in England. Mr. Bronowski's point of view and mine are much alike, and we deal with some of the same material, but since my book was nearly finished when I first saw his, I have made almost no changes because of it.

My indebtedness of a more personal sort is vast. First of all, I wish to thank the trustees of the Guggenheim Memorial Foundation and especially the secretary, Mr. Henry Allen Moe, from whom I twice received a grant to work on this book, and except for whom I should be working at it still; then to the Mary L. Adams Fellowship of the University of Wisconsin, which relieved me from teaching duties as a graduate student when I first began work on Blake; and to the Clark Bequest of Harvard University, from which I received a generous grant that relieved me of the most onerous duties in the preparation of the manuscript. I am indebted to the librarians of various institutions, whose courtesy and help have been unfailing: to those of the University of Wisconsin, of the Newberry Library in Chicago and of the Morgan Library in New York, of Dartmouth College, and of Harvard College, especially to Mr. William Jackson of the Houghton Library, and of the Huntington Library in California, especially to Mr. Louis B. Wright. To the Huntington Library I am indebted for permission to print for the first time in its entirety a letter from Blake to William Hayley (catalogued HM 20063), and to the Houghton Library for permission to print for the first time two letters of Hayley's which concern Blake. I wish to acknowledge the courtesy of several museums for permission to reproduce pictures in their possession, and of the editors of *Hemispheres,* of the *Kenyon Review,* of *Modern Philology* and the University of Chicago Press, of the *Sewanee Review,* and of the *Yale Review* for their permission to use again, although often in a considerably different form, material which first appeared in those periodicals.

To attempt to express my indebtedness to individuals would be to attempt a history of my education. Their help has varied from the most specific kind of assistance, such as finding for me an elusive reference, to the most general kind of enthusiasm and encouragement which, in the dark night of composition, is of such immeasurable comfort to a writer. I should not be happy if I did not mention Miss Agnes and Miss Elizabeth Mongan, Miss Ethel M. Thornbury, Albert Guerard, Jr., Howard Mumford Jones, I. A. Richards, George Sherburn, Morton Downey Zabel, and Philip Wheelwright; Eleanor and Kenneth Murdock, for more than friendship; Mr. Damon for his general interest and for permission to quote from a letter; Miss Zea Zinn, an authority on the condition of her sex in her own time no less than in that of Mary Wollstonecraft's; Miss Ruth Wallerstein and John Gaus, to whom I owe perhaps the crucial segment in my education; F. O. Matthiessen, who read a great portion of the manuscript and made invaluable suggestions; Mrs. Elizabeth C. Moore, who made the index for the book; William Sloane, for his early and sustained interest in this project, and Ralph Bates, my editor, the kind of critic most writers are never fortunate enough to find. Finally, there is that gift of love which willingly meets a daily demand in patience and fortitude and understanding, the gift which one has not earned and which, as the gesture of a dedication reminds one, cannot possibly be repaid.

M. S.

Cambridge, Massachusetts
July 1945

Chronology

(According to the third edition of Geoffrey Keynes's *Poetry and Prose of William Blake*)

	Composed	Printed or Engraved
Poetical Sketches	1769-1778	1783
An Island in the Moon	1787	—
There is no Natural Religion, I and II	1788	1788
All Religions Are One	1788	1788
Songs of Innocence	1787-1789	1789
The Book of Thel	1789	1789
Tiriel	c. 1789	—
The French Revolution	1791	1791
The Gates of Paradise	1793; 1818	1793; 1818
The Marriage of Heaven and Hell	1793	1793
Songs of Experience	1789-1794	1794
Visions of the Daughters of Albion	1793	1793
America	1793	1793
Europe: A Prophecy	1794	1794
The First Book of Urizen	1794	1794
The Book of Ahania	1795	1795
The Book of Los	1795	1795
The Song of Los	1795	1795
Vala, or The Four Zoas	1795-1804	—
Auguries of Innocence	c. 1803	—
Milton	1804-1808	1804-1808
Jerusalem	1804-1820	1804-1820
A Descriptive Catalogue	1809	1809
"*Public Address*" and *Additions to A Descriptive Catalogue*	1810	—
The Everlasting Gospel	1818	—
The Ghost of Abel	1822	1822

"Where man is not, nature is barren."

—William Blake, *The Marriage of Heaven and Hell*

PART ONE

Mythology and Mysticism

☼

"We have come to give you metaphors for poetry."

—The spirits to W. B. YEATS, in "A Vision"

CHAPTER ONE

The Mask of William Blake

I

WILLIAM BLAKE, of all poets perhaps the most single-minded, with the most stubborn integrity, remains also the poet of strangest mixtures, both grand transmutations and partial compounds. His attempt to achieve a poetic content that would, through an original mythology, synthesize the contraries of a visionary temperament and a social intelligence, and would not only relate but equate his two fundamental impulses—the evangelical and the humanitarian—is the root of his problem as a poet. He sought to dramatize the *singleness* of salvation—spiritual and social, inner and outer, the problem in which most modern thinkers still find only irredeemable polarities.

To trace the dialectic of innocence and experience, he tried to express (and to correct) the ideas of political thinkers like Paine and Godwin in the vocabulary of religious thinkers like Boehme and Swedenborg. The product of this effort is sometimes beautiful, sometimes merely grotesque, and often both grotesque and beautiful. The alternations spring from the anarchistic position to which his effort impelled him, an anarchism of spirit that inevitably encompassed the body and institutions; for the position was developed in opposition to the impulse to power ("Attempting to be more than Man We become less"), but it overlooked the important fact that in attempting to be more than poets, poets become at least something different.

William Blake

In its effort to account for Blake's difference from other poets, the traditional view of him commits itself to this curious contradiction: a body of complex and difficult work produced by a simple personality and an untutored intelligence. Such an interpretation defies nearly everything that we know of the nature of man and of the history of art, and it may be time for the expression of a view somewhat less anomalous. Blake's personality was single, but it was hardly simple; and his intelligence was untrained, but hardly, for that reason, untouched.

Obviously, the personality of the poet was at least as complex as his poetry, and was formed by identical or analogous conflicts. The difficulty seems to have come about because most critics of Blake have given at least tacit acceptance to his own view of himself: that of an unlettered poet in whom Divinity found utterance. It is a view that was partially required by the necessities of temperament, partially fabricated to meet the necessities of history. Divinity there is in this poet, but let us give him the credit that he sometimes failed to give himself and assume that it is divinity which he was wholly capable of construing. And if it is unjust to Blake to attribute his beauties to Deity, it is no less unjust to attribute to Deity Blake's blemishes—" . . . cannot the spirit parse and spell?" demanded Emerson.

In an age when poets were notoriously solemn about themselves, Blake had the temerity to be humorous, even perversely so, about himself. The perfect juxtaposition, perhaps, is Shelley's remark "I am convinced that there can be no entire regeneration of mankind until laughter is put down!" with Blake's "I hate scarce smiles: I love laughing." His laughter extended to his own gift. Thus, it amused him to let the gullible and the respectably literal think of him as outrageously mad or as preternaturally wise, as they wished. When he wrote, "A man may lie for his own pleasure, but if any one is hurt by his lying will confess his lie," he was perhaps justifying his own public exploitation of his genius. The visionary heads that he drew for the eager astrologist Varley, and the conversations with the startled Crabb Robinson, are examples, as is the well-known conversation at a dinner party: "Did you ever see a fairy's funeral, madam?"

Yet it is to be remembered that when he was asked where he

saw such extraordinary phenomena, he was usually prompt to answer, *"Here,* madam," and point to his head. And that is, of course, where most of his visions took place. But he did not admit that all of them were there. As far as one can tell, Blake's term "vision" indicates at least three different forms.

> Now I a fourfold vision see,
> And a fourfold vision is given to me;
> 'Tis fourfold in my supreme delight
> And threefold in soft Beulah's night
> And twofold Always. May God us keep
> From Single Vision & Newton's sleep!

Examination would yield a number of meanings in these lines, but for present purposes we need only observe that Blake himself distinguished between several varieties of vision. Whether or not these lines in themselves intend a particular set of distinctions, one must yet make them to get at the most fundamental fact about Blake as artist and poet; for the distinctions exist in the work itself. What did he mean by "vision"?

Newton's single vision is simple sensation, the perception of objective reality, of the material universe, seeing "with the eye." Twofold vision is seeing "through the eye," the perception of spiritual forms in material objects. This Blake apparently practiced at will, as most of us in some degree could. It is essentially a matter of autosuggestion, even of self-hypnosis.

> For double the vision my Eyes do see,
> And a double vision is always with me.
> With my inward Eye 'tis an old Man grey;
> With my outward, a Thistle across my way.

It is this double vision that perceives Swedenborgian correspondence, cabalistic analogy, in all things—a world in a grain of sand, heaven in a wild flower. And by the nature of Blake's mystagogical view, the spiritual forms of things were almost always perceived as in some sense human. Thus he saw not the sun rising but "an Innumerable company of the Heavenly host crying, 'Holy, Holy, Holy is the Lord God Almighty.' " When his "Eyes did Expand," he saw not land and ocean flooded with sunshine, but numberless "particles" of light, each in the form of a man; and then:

My Eyes more and more
Like a Sea without shore
Continue Expanding,
The Heavens commanding,
Till the Jewels of Light,
Heavenly Men beaming bright,
Appear'd as One Man.

It is to be remembered that Blake and his wife made a practice of staring into the fire until they saw forms there, and that Blake once said that he could gaze at a knot of wood until he was frightened by it. This kind of vision, then, is a variety of autosuggestion that derives from the object itself. Therefore it cannot be this kind that Blake has in mind when he insists that "Nature and Fancy are Two Things & can Never be joined," or that "Natural Objects always did & now do weaken, deaden & obliterate Imagination in Me." For to double vision, natural objects are essential, as Blake elsewhere explains: ". . . I know that This World Is a World of Imagination & Vision. I see Every thing I paint in This World, but Every body does not see alike . . . to the Eyes of the Man of Imagination, Nature is Imagination itself. As a man is, so he sees. As the Eye is formed, such are its Powers. You certainly Mistake, when you say that the Visions of Fancy are not to be found in This World. To Me This World is all One continued Vision of Fancy or Imagination, & I feel Flatter'd when I am told so." The discrepancy in Blake's attitude toward the material universe points toward the most enduring and the most extensive conflict in his personality and poetry.

To the third order of vision, which resembles hallucination, nature may indeed have been a hindrance. Here an image in the mind is projected in space and observed as if it possessed objective reality. Of this sort, surely, were those childhood visions when God's face at the window set the four-year-old screaming and when Ezekiel sat placidly under a tree. Such was the vision of Christ and his Apostles to the dreaming boy in Westminster. Such, it is possible, was the vision of his brother's soul rising to heaven from the deathbed, "clapping its hands." Such was the single ghost that Blake saw, "scaly, speckled, very awful," coming down the stairs at him; and such was the vision of the Ancient of Days—which became one of his most striking paintings—hovering in the air at the top of the staircase.

But when the dead brother, Robert, came to Blake in the night and explained to him the method of illuminated printing that he was to make his own, Blake was not experiencing hallucination. This, the final and most frequent order of vision, was simply an extremely vivid mental impression that had no external representation at all. From this kind of vision most of his poetry and his pictures derive, and it differs from the image-making capacity of other poets only in its burden of emotional intensity, in its uncontrolled spontaneity, and in its particular preternatural content and persistent symbolical quality. Most important, it was the vividness of his mental conceptions that gave the poet the conviction of revelation, which laid upon him the obligation of working as a "literalist of the imagination." This is the quality which separates him most sharply from other modern poets; for he conceived of his material as sanctified, hence not to be tampered with, but copied directly. In reality, Blake's gift was a high degree of visual imagination, always desired and sometimes induced by prayer,* which could function with or without the immediate stimulus of natural objects. He could retain the images within the mind or project them with equal vividness into space.†

* " 'What do we do, Kate, when the visions forsake us?' 'We kneel down and pray, Mr. Blake.' "—Arthur Symons, *William Blake,* Dutton, 1907, p. 233.

† ". . . Blake was supereminently endowed with the power of disuniting all other thoughts from his mind, whenever he wished to indulge in thinking of any particular subject; and so firmly did he believe, by this abstracting power, that the objects of his compositions were before him in his mind's eye, that he frequently believed them to be speaking to him."—J. T. Smith, *Biographical Sketch of Blake,* London, 1828, reprinted by Symons, p. 363.

"He thinks all men partake of it [vision], but it is lost by not being cultivated, and he eagerly assented to a remark I made that all men have all faculties to a greater or less degree."—Henry Crabb Robinson, *On Books and Their Writers,* ed. by Edith Morley, 3 vols., London, 1938, Vol. I, p. 330.

Blake's only test of true vision, of whatever order, was its exactness, the degree of articulation: "The connoisseurs and artists who have made objections to Mr. B.'s mode of representing spirits with real bodies, would do well to consider that the Venus, the Minerva, the Jupiter, the Apollo, which they admire in Greek statues are all of them representations of spiritual existences, of Gods immortal, to the mortal perishing organ of sight; and yet they are embodied and organized in solid marble. Mr. B. requires the same latitude. . . . The Prophets describe what they saw in Vision as real and existing men, whom they saw with their imaginative and immortal organs; the Apostles the same; the clearer the organ the more distinct the object. A Spirit and a Vision are not, as the modern philosophy supposes, a cloudy vapour, or a nothing: they are organized and minutely articulated beyond all that the mortal and perishing nature can produce. . . . The painter of this work asserts that all his imaginations appear to him infinitely more perfect and more minutely organized than any thing seen by his mortal eye."

This gift Blake could treat fancifully ("The Prophets Isaiah and Ezekiel dined with me, and I asked them how they dared so roundly to assert" . . .), or earnestly ("I am really drunk with intellectual vision"). But he never lost sight of it as his peculiar talent, his genius, and he never failed to respect it as divine. It is the first feature in his picture of himself, and "perception," as a result, is the real subject of most of his poems. Blake's longest work, *Jerusalem,* is a poem about perception and reality; its most frequently repeated line is "They became what they beheld." At the very peak of the narrative he exclaims:

. . . & every Word & every Character
Was Human according to the Expansion or Contraction, the Translucence or
Opakeness of Nervous fibres: such was the variation of Time & Space
Which vary according as the Organs of Perception vary.

"Perception," likewise, is the subject of much of the poetry of Blake's contemporaries. Coleridge's lines, in "Dejection"—

> O Wordsworth! we receive but what we give,
> And in our life alone does Nature live—

have more than a merely fortuitous value to the understanding of Blake's vision. They suggest a fairly complete analogy between Blake's four kinds of perception and Coleridge's theory of the imagination as he outlined this at the end of the first volume of the *Biographia Literaria.* The analogy may be useful in suggesting mundane terms that account for or at least elucidate experiences that to Blake were ethereal.

Single vision, that "Newton's sleep" which Blake scorned, corresponds to Coleridge's Primary Imagination—the perception of the everyday world by the senses as these are conceived in such a psychology as Locke's, of

> . . . that inanimate cold world allowed
> To the poor loveless ever-anxious crowd.

But twofold, threefold, and fourfold vision all pertain to the Secondary Imagination, a function which, unsatisfied by mere sense experience of objective reality, *feels* about it, and in doing so reorganizes it. In developing this conception, Coleridge had to pass from the psychology of Locke and Hartley into that of another school. Precisely because Blake rejected the first conception as any part of art and gave his whole fealty to the second, he could never admit the ultimate validity of the sensationalist school, and he vilified Locke tirelessly throughout his lifetime. "The mind is not a *tabula rasa.* It is not 'conditioned' by outer circumstances. On the contrary, the perceptive organs are themselves creative. It is not the mind, but the world, which is 'conditioned.' "

Of the three kinds of true vision, the first, twofold, seems to correspond to Coleridge's first doctrine of the life of nature, and the second and third kinds with the second, or projective. These doctrines, as formulated by I. A. Richards, are:

"1. The mind of the poet at moments, penetrating 'the film of familiarity and selfish solicitude,' gains an insight into reality, reads Nature as a symbol of something behind or within Nature not ordinarily perceived.

"2. The mind of the poet creates a Nature into which his own feelings, his aspirations and apprehensions, are projected."

When Blake's "Eyes did Expand" and, by seeing through them rather than with them, he observed old men in thistles and multitudes in sunbeams, he seems to have been practicing the first mode, to which the object itself is essential, and the vision is within it and derived from it. When he found nature an obstruction, and his vision consisted of his own creations, which were either thrust into space or retained in the mind, then he seems to have been practicing the second mode. The three forms of Blake's vision provide extreme illustrations of Coleridge's two doctrines, extreme both in their religious portent and in their sometimes terrible concreteness. But they are illustrations and, what is more, they seem to substantiate Dr. Richards's claim that the two doctrines are not discrete at all, but complementary. "The colours of Nature are a suffusion from the light of the mind," he says, "but the light of the mind in its turn, the shaping spirit of Imagination, comes from the Mind's response to Nature." ". . . The subject is what it is through the objects it has been."

One may apply this generalization to Blake in these terms: As a child he seems to have had an even more insistent and compelling visual capacity than most children, and he was early habituated to what we can only call hallucinations. This visual capacity did not dim and fade as he grew up, as it does in most children. And when he began to regard himself as an artist and a poet—this was before he was fifteen—he came to regard his visions as some sort of divine favor. Finally, having become accustomed to peopling the world about him with objects that were not there, it was easy enough to see "people" in the objects that were. The two modes became co-operative agents that sustained one another. That is, the mind which began by projecting into nature the objects that it wished to see presently saw what it wished in the real objects of nature itself. And because the two modes are actually interdependent, it is very likely that Blake himself did not realize that when he formulated them in general statements about nature and matter, they came into linguistic and metaphysical conflict, and at least the theoretical substructure of his work became self-contradictory.

II

WE MUST PROCEED at once to a further complexity. Blake made no distinction between the visual and the verbal. It is a peculiar mark of his genius that image and intuition are nearly identical, and this is perhaps the precise intent of his phrase "intellectual vision." We have heard much in the last two decades of the "felt thought" of the English metaphysical poets, but the "direct sensuous apprehension of thought" of these poets is different from Blake's "intellectual vision." Blake's habit of mind may be described, in the sense of C. E. Douglas, as apocalyptic, "thinking visually. The Apocalyptist thinks in pictures, not 'true' in themselves, but indicative of the truth which lies behind." The difference is that between ideas which come to the poet in the form of images and images in which the poet later discovers ideas. Intellect and sense are fused in both methods, but the control in the first is exercised by intellect, in the second by sense.

The first method results in a relatively systematic arrangement of images within the poem, the second, in a kaleidoscopic lack of arrangement, if it is a poem of any length. The second method is characteristic of Blake. His ideas, even the wonderfully generalized aphorisms, came to him as images; and his images, on the other hand, are invariably symbolical. "Prayers plow not! Praises reap not!" His paintings are always descriptive and usually literary. His poems are pictorial. Thus his pictures are not to be regarded as illustrations to the poems so much as restatements of them. This is *ut pictura poesis* with a vengeance, the sister arts joined at birth. To be granted heavenly sights meant necessarily to hear heavenly sounds; to see "visions of eternity" meant that he became the repositor of eternal wisdom. To see was immediately to know.

It was no difficult step for Blake, then, to move from the conception of himself as a visionary to the further conception of himself as a poet who wrote under divine dictate; that is, in a sense, automatically. In some sense all creative activity is by nature automatic. But this is only to say that art tends to arise from extrarational levels of consciousness and that during its composition rational controls are more or less relaxed. It is only accidentally, however, that art comes about when rational controls are relaxed completely, as in writing such as "Kubla Khan." The temperament of the poet and the fashion of his age determine his place in the scale, and Blake, who never questioned his temperament and had no interest in fashions, went as far in the direction of the automatic as it is possible for poetry to go and remain poetry.

Blake is that curious kind of poet of whom it can almost never be said that this or that is a *bad* poem; for when his poetry is not first-rate, it is not poetry at all but something else, and something that is sometimes nearly monstrous. Of this something else there is a generous amount, because Blake submitted more eagerly than most poets to the dictates of what is called inspiration, a word he understood literally as afflatus. "And tho' I call them Mine [his designs, in this instance], I know that they are not Mine, being of the same opinion with Milton when he says That the Muse visits his slumbers & awakes & governs his song." But Milton's "heavenly muse" was metaphorical, an ancient literary convention adjusted to his religion; whereas the spirits and angels of Blake, who tended always to eliminate the distinction between the literal and the metaphorical, were not quite so. There is literalness here: "I have written this Poem from immediate Dictation, twelve or sometimes twenty or thirty lines at a time, without Premeditation & even against my Will; the Time it has taken in writing was thus render'd Non Existent, & an immense Poem Exists which seems to be the Labour of a long Life, all produc'd without Labour or Study." And here again, although mixed with fancy: "I may praise it, since I dare not pretend to be any other than the Secretary; the Authors are in Eternity." It is a literalness that would seem less bald were we to consider now the exact nature of Blake's religion, more particularly of his religion of art; and one may argue for this literalness in spite of the fact that Blake, like any other poet, gave thought to his prosody and sometimes made extensive revisions. But verbally, at least, Blake's divine dictation is not so close to literary convention as to the habit of those stages in religious mysticism which identify inspiration with revelation. Perhaps Jakob Boehme, the hierophantic cobbler, best represents this habit: "Art has not wrote here, neither was there any Time to consider how to set it punctually down . . . the Reason was this, that the burning Fire often forced forward with Speed, and the Hand and Pen must hasten directly after it; *for it comes and goes as a sudden Shower.*"

Blake's words, like his visions, would seem frequently to have come with an uncontrolled spontaneity, and as he gave in ever more and more to vision, so he gave in more and more to the "sudden Shower" of words. The passive agency of revelation became his view of his genius and he defended the view with the familiar zeal of the primitive artist. The Swiss theologian Lavater had written, "Intuition of truth, not preceded by perceptible meditation, is genius," and, "He knows himself greatly who never opposes his genius." Blake underlined both comments in his copy of the *Aphorisms,* and to the second he added "Most Excellent!" To obstruct one's genius was to deny God and to destroy oneself: ". . . if we fear to do the dictates of our Angels, & tremble at the Tasks set before us; if we refuse to do Spiritual Acts because of Natural Fears or Natural Desires! Who can describe the dismal torments of such a state!"

But again, as another conflict arises, this is precisely what Blake does—he opposes his genius in the dialectic of the self. For the primitive on the one hand believes in the accessibility of art to everyone, being himself a man of open simplicity; and on the other hand, he tends to view himself as the appointed receptacle of the divine mysteries. Once more, Boehme is the best example. He wrote: "My Beloved Reader, if you would understand the *High Mysteries,* you need not first put an *Academy* upon your nose, nor use any such *Spectacles*"; but also, "Loving Reader, I had need have an angelical Tongue . . . and thou an angelical Mind, and then we should well understand one another." Thus Blake liked to think that his works were perfectly comprehensible to the innocent, to minds not blunted by education and fashion, especially children. "The Beauty of the Bible is that the most Ignorant & Simple Minds Understand it Best," he declared; but also: "What is Grand is necessarily obscure to Weak men. That which can be made Explicit to the Idiot is not worth my care. The wisest of the Ancients consider'd what is not too Explicit as the fittest for Instruction, because it rouzes the faculties to act."

The Blake who wrote "The Lamb" is not quite the same Blake who wrote *Jerusalem;* there is a sharp difference in the poet's conception of his function. Yet the difference between an open simplicity and gnostic wisdom is not necessarily one of kind. These are the extremes which tend to meet in the artist who submits to the concept of original genius, who grants complete authority to the compulsions of that genius. And the answer to any objection is always the same, and perhaps must be; Blake said, "I could not do otherwise; it was out of my power!" *

A form of automatism, then, is the second feature of Blake's mask, and it is important to observe how the man persuades himself that the mask is real: ". . . every genius, every hero, is a prophet," was still another observation in Lavater that Blake underscored. The proper qualification is Spinoza's: ". . . prophecy never rendered the prophet wiser than he was before"; or Locke's: "God, when he makes the prophet, does not unmake the man." Blake, like Boehme or any other, was reordering his reading and his experience; but in an important sense he declined to recognize the result as quite his own.

* Rosamund Harding, in *An Anatomy of Inspiration,* Cambridge, Eng., 1940, pp. 13-16, has conveniently catalogued a whole mass of remarks on the subject of literary possession and compulsion, even from such mundane writers as Thackeray and Meredith. Almost always the religious language is a *façon de parler* only. For of course one is "possessed"; one is possessed by the unusual awareness of the principle of coherence, as one's sensible and intellectual experience falls abruptly into pattern, and what was "many" becomes for the moment "one." It is demonstrably difficult to avoid the language of mystical experience in describing this state of affairs, but actually, the contents of the creative and of the mystical experience are, as will presently be shown, quite opposite.

III

If Blake came to think of his purpose as prophetic, his motive was not to isolate himself among the select but to find company that would break down his isolation. Indeed, his definition of the prophet is extremely generous. In that extraordinary series of annotations in which he all but defended the deism of Thomas Paine against the bitter Anglican orthodoxy of Bishop Watson, Blake argued that prophets in the modern sense—that is, prognosticators—had never existed, and cited Jonah's prophecy of Nineveh. "Every honest man is a Prophet; he utters his opinion both of private & public matters. Thus: If you go on So, the result is So. He never says, such a thing shall happen let you do what you will. A Prophet is a Seer, not an Arbitrary Dictator." This is an even more inclusive definition than that of *The Age of Reason,* but obviously derives from it. Paine, working in the established tradition of Biblical criticism on historical principles, declared that the Bible mentioned neither poets nor poetry, and that prophets and prophecy, "to which later times have affixed a new idea," denominated exactly these. His argument inevitably suggests that famous, fanciful dinner party at which Blake asked of Isaiah and Ezekiel how they "dared so roundly to assert that God spoke to them. . . .

"Isaiah answer'd: 'I saw no God, nor heard any, in a finite organical perception; but my senses discover'd the infinite in everything, and as I was then perswaded, & remain confirm'd, that the voice of honest indignation is the voice of God, I cared not for consequences, but wrote.'

"Then I asked: 'does a firm perswasion that a thing is so, make it so?'

"He replied: 'All poets believe that it does, & in ages of imagination this firm perswasion removed mountains; but many are not capable of a firm perswasion of any thing.' "

We must separate the elements here. The first and basic attraction of prophecy to Blake is nothing more than the fact that it provided a sanction, unassailable in its sources, for complete independence of judgment. (One recalls that, after an argument, Yeats's spirits said to him, "You have said what we wanted to have said," precisely as "The Spirit said to him: 'Blake, be an artist and nothing else. In this there is felicity.' ") A similar assurance was a need more dear to Blake than one can well say. He was born into a Nonconformist's household, and from childhood was familiar with the extreme of that antiauthoritarianism which characterizes the English sects. The significance to his career as a poet of the deep vein of religious independence in Blake can never be exaggerated. It is the very root of the man. Observe, for example, the striking similiarity between a typical utterance of Blake's and Cotton Mather's complaint against the Quakers in Massachusetts Bay. Blake wrote:

The Vision of Christ that thou dost see
Is my Vision's Greatest Enemy . . .
Both read the Bible day & night,
But thou read'st black where I read white.

Mather said: ". . . it was very enraging . . . to hear these wretches ordinarily saying among the people, 'We deny thy Christ! We deny thy God! Thy Bible is the word of the devil!' " The attitude the elder Blakes took toward William's education could have prevailed only in a dissenter's house.

Because as a child he could not brook discipline, and especially the indignity of whippings, William was not sent to school at all.

Thank God, I never was sent to school
To be Flog'd into following the Style of a Fool.

At an early age, and at his own desire, he was given instruction in drawing, apprenticed to an engraver, and allowed to educate himself as he wished. His attitude toward churches was identical with his attitude toward schools. Except for a brief attachment to a Swedenborgian community, he seems in his youth, as in his age, to have kept himself free from the claims of all the current dogmas: a sectarian without a sect. No less were his social relations determined by the need of independence. The restrictions of conventions and manners quickly drove him out of polite society, into which he was early introduced and congenially received.*

From the time he was fifteen, Blake had been writing verses that in their extreme statement of the conventional humanitarian attitudes indicated that he would find congenial company among political radicals, whose tradition was never remote from English religious dissent. That company he found in the years when the zealotry of the French Revolution achieved wide public expression in England, and late in life he declared that he had always been a "Liberty Boy." This remark separates Blake from those of his contemporaries among the English poets who changed their minds after 1791 and began the defense of orthodoxy. All through the terrorized reaction in England and the Napoleonic ascendancy, the radicals were dispersed: hunted and hounded, publicly execrated, imprisoned, and their dwelling places burned. Blake went underground with them and his poetry in a very real way went underground with him.

By 1800, poverty forced him to accept the patronage of a stupid and stubborn poetaster, William Hayley. For three years poverty forced him to live under that indignity. This is the one occasion in Blake's life when he allowed his art to submit to commercial order, or his judgment to that of another. Two letters, dated 1799, to the Reverend Doctor Trusler, author of *Hogarth Moralized,* are eloquent of Blake's situation. In the first he wrote: "I attempted every morning for a fortnight together to follow your Dictate . . . here I counted without my host. I now find my mistake . . . being also in the predicament of that prophet who says: 'I cannot go beyond the command of

* " 'Don't you think I have something of the Goat's face?' says he.

" 'Very like a Goat's face,' she answer'd.

" 'I think your face,' said he, 'is like that noble beast the Tyger. Oh, I was at Mrs. Sicknacker's, & I was speaking of my abilities, but their nasty hearts, poor devils, are eat up with envy. They envy me my abilities, & all the women envy your abilities.'

" 'My dear, they hate people who are of higher abilities than their nasty, filthy selves. But do you outface them, & then strangers will see that you have an opinion.' "—*Poetry and Prose of William Blake,* ed. by Geoffrey Keynes, Random House, 1932, p. 887.

the Lord.'" In the second he wrote: "I feel very sorry that your Ideas & Mine on Moral Painting differ so much as to have made you angry with my method of study. If I am wrong, I am wrong in good company." The result of this sort of impossible commercial relationship was that he fled eagerly into the no less impossible embrace of Hayley.*

Hayley seemed sympathetic, and his letters show that as far as he was capable of understanding them, he did have Blake's interests at heart. He wrote to Mr. Evans, a bookseller: ". . . send me your full & frank opinion concerning the adventure of my worthy Friend Blake, in the Ballads, that I gave Him in a sanguine Hope of putting a little money in his pocket.—He suspended their publication, that He might proceed, without any Interruption, in his plates for the Life of Cowper, which have engrossed much of his time even to this Hour, as He and his good industrious Wife together take all the Impressions from the various Engravings in their own domestic press.—Do you think it will answer to Him to resume the Series of the Ballads? . . . I

* A number of Blake's letters testify to his expectations. One, Number Twelve in Keynes' *Poetry and Prose,* has been available until now only in extracts from a sale catalogue. The original is in the possession of the Huntington Library, and reads as follows:

Leader of My Angels

My dear & too careful & overjoyous Woman has exhausted her strength to such a degree with expectation and gladness added to labour in our removal that I fear it will be Thursday before we can get away from this — City. I shall not be able to avail myself of the assistance of Brunos fairies. But I Invoke the Good Genii that Surround Miss Pooles Villa to shine upon my journey thru the Petworth road which by your fortunate advice I mean to take but whether I come on Wednesday or Thursday that Day shall be marked on my calendar with a Star of the first magnitude.

Eartham will be my first temple & altar. My Wife is like a flame of many colours of precious jewels whenever she hears it named. Excuse my haste & recieve my hearty Love & Respect.

I am Dear Sir
Your Sincere
William Blake

H B Lambeth
Sept 16. 1800

My fingers Emit sparks of fire with Expectation of my future labours.

am very desirous of not leading Him into an *unprofitable adventure*. . . . What Cash have you for him?—He is an excellent creature, but not very fit to manage pecuniary concerns to his own advantage. . . . Favour me with all your Ideas on this subject! & assist me, as far as you properly can, in my cordial wish to serve a very ingenious worthy Man, who is devoted to a Life of Industry & Retirement!"

What chafing drudgery it must have been for Blake, who had himself written of lambs and tigers, to put his talents as an artist to the service of Hayley's stupid little ballads about animals. What a waste of his energies it must have seemed to engrave plates for Hayley's pious life of Cowper when Blake himself was living out a spiritual biography of proportion and vehemence utterly beyond the range of poor Cowper. What could have been more offensive to Blake than yielding to the peculiar ignorance of that patronage? ". . . I send you," wrote Hayley to Lady Hesketh, "a neat copy (on the other side of the paper) from the Kind Hand of the friendly Zealous Engraver, who daily works by my side, & who flatters me so far as to say . . ."

But if for three years he had to trim his sails, Blake, whose drawings were subject to the dictates of his patron, yet had his poetry into which to retreat. This Hayley did not need to see. And there was always that last stand of the badgered artist, the notebook:

> I Write the Rascal Thanks till he & I
> With Thanks & Compliments are quite drawn dry.

And:

> Thy Friendship oft has made my heart to ake:
> Do be my Enemy for Friendship's sake.

The Hayley relationship was doomed to a wretched end: "I regard Fashion in Poetry as little as I do in Painting . . . but Mr. H. approves of My Designs as little as he does of my Poems, and I have been forced to insist on his leaving me in both to my own Self Will; for I am determin'd to be no longer Pester'd with his Genteel Ignorance & Polite Disapprobation. I know myself both Poet & Painter, & it is not his affected Contempt that can move me to any thing but a more assiduous pursuit of both Arts." For the last twenty-five years of his life, Blake never again compromised with his convictions.

The result was a spectacularly unsuccessful career, and the results of that, a very bitter resentment and an increasing insistence on the triviality of worldly rewards. If at forty-three he still felt hope of success and could write "tho' [I] laugh at Fortune, I am perswaded that She Alone is the Governor of Worldly Riches, & when it is Fit she will call on me; till then I wait with Patience, in hopes that She is busied among my Friends," his tone is conspicuously without any such moderateness in the last years of his life, when he was nearly seventy. On one of his illustrations to Dante he wrote then of the same fickle deity: "The hole of a Shit-house. The Goddess Fortune is the devil's servant, ready to Kiss any one's Arse." More and more as his years passed he distinguished in his casual writings between "corporeal" and "spiritual" bread. When his opinions kept the former from him, as they frequently did, they seemed more and more to reward him with the latter, and he asserted, even in exasperation, that he was satisfied. Not only did his insistence on independent judgment drive him irremediably into the role of prophet, but also, and relentlessly, into that special role of the prophet without honor.

> For meditations upon unknown thought
> Make human intercourse grow less and less.

The role of prophet had deeper beguilements. Isaiah identified the prophet and the man who insists on the truth of a "firm perswasion." But by implication he also identified all those true poets whose senses, like this Isaiah's own, discover the infinite in everything. These are the poets of at least twofold vision, who write "spiritual allegory" in some way like Blake's poems. "This is to be understood as unusual in our time, but common in ancient," said Blake. Thus Milton was something of an exception, but the Bible—and Ossian!—were the rule. Hebraic prophets and Gaelic bards were one to Blake, and exercised an almost equally powerful influence.* Spinoza's analysis of prophecy is useful to the understanding of this curious identification: ". . . the power of prophecy implies not a peculiarly perfect mind, but a peculiarly vivid imagination . . . the prophets perceived nearly everything in parables and allegories, and clothed spiritual truths in bodily forms, for such is the usual method of imagination." Blake, searching for historical examples of symbolical writing like his own, found them in the prophets and the available bards.† These poets were congenial to the sort of poetry he himself wrote in greatest abundance. The early poems were not prophecies in the sense of the later Prophetic Books, it is true, yet this is only further evidence of the argument that, giving in to his genius as he conceived it, the poet persuaded himself of the mask.

But the historical function of prophets is not to write a certain kind of poetry so much as to order social wisdom toward a desired conduct of life. The bard is the tribal poet, the singer of myth and the maker of it; and although his language is symbolical, his wisdom is public. Blake, who stated most glowingly the major piece of social wisdom of his day ("All deities reside in the human breast") and many another of less importance, had some sense of the public function of prophecy, but one cannot be certain how abidingly. Many points in his writing reveal this sense, as: "Visions of these eternal principles or characters of human life appear to poets, in all ages; the Grecian gods . . . are visions of the eternal attributes, or divine names, which,

* Blake was not the first poet to make this identification. See Ronald Crane, "An Early Eighteenth-Century Enthusiast for Primitive Poetry: John Husbands," *Modern Language Notes,* Vol. XXXVII (January 1922), p. 35: "To bring Hebrew Scripture, Lapland songs, Runic and Welsh Odes together, under the general concept of 'natural' or primitive poetry, and to proclaim them, in certain qualities at least, equal or even superior to the Greek or Roman classics—this was to do something essentially new. . . . Husbands deserves to be remembered among the critics and scholars who in the heart of the 'classical' age were helping to prepare men's minds for the coming transformation of literary taste and ideas."

† "I Believe both Macpherson & Chatterton, that what they say is Ancient Is so. I own myself an admirer of Ossian equally with any other Poet whatever, Rowley & Chatterton also."—*Poetry and Prose,* p. 1025.

when erected into gods, become destructive to humanity. They ought to be the servants, and not the masters of man, or of society. They ought to be made to sacrifice to Man, and not man compelled to sacrifice to them; for when separated from man or humanity . . . they are destroyers." Our gods are our motives writ large, "eternal principles or characters of *human* life," the vast images of universal qualities and quarrels. "As the interest of man, so his God—as his God, so he," declared Lavater; and Blake replied, "All gold!" The poet, the prophet ("every genius, every hero"), has the power of intuition to perceive these qualities and conflicts in their actuality, in their undying reality as ideas; it is his function to reveal them to man in a fashion so persuasive that man may order them in the interests of his own best order. But man's world and man's order is here, in this transitory sphere, where we are always enchaining ourselves and always submitting to illusion; not there, where ideas prevail in themselves, where there is no illusion and no slavery.

IV

Now ALL THE ANTINOMIES in Blake appear, and if they prove to be not only personal but mainly historical, that indicates that he followed his genius with good reason; for most of the men of his time, certainly most of the poets, had no sense whatever of these conflicts in the historical situation to which Blake's intuitions immediately led him. If he assumed a mask, as a counter to himself, it was perhaps to encompass, to resolve, conflicts that most men were anxious merely to suppress or conquer. Blake's proverb "The cistern contains: the fountain overflows," together with that other, "Exuberance is Beauty," suggests an admirable comment by I. A. Richards: "People who are always winning victories over themselves might equally well be described as always enslaving themselves. Their lives become unnecessarily narrow. The minds of many saints have been like wells; they should have been like lakes or like the sea." The problem in this difficult historical moment was not to conquer one, but to reconcile both the public and the private interest, the intellect and the sensibility, and every poet of this period can be observed caught in the struggle. Coleridge's poetic faculty was apparently not robust enough ever to grasp the public interest, and he became an admirable writer of prose. Wordsworth did the inverse, and more and more wrote prose in the form of poetry—which is hardly a solution. We like to think that if Keats had lived, he would have adjusted the attractions of sensuosity and the impulse to a normal ethical response to society; but it is unlikely that Shelley, whose mind was prevailingly theoretical, could have bulwarked with any real social wisdom his increasingly febrile pursuit of a static intellectual beauty, his pseudo-Platonics. Byron puts the case in lighter terms, as a conflict between social conservatism, a private aristocratic snobbery, and an explicit political liberalism. The tension here between the resultant eighteenth-century forms and the nineteenth-century content produced comic verse that retains much of its original attraction; but one can hardly regard Byron the lyrist very seriously, for here the intellectual term has been utterly dismissed.

F. O. Matthiessen recently called Blake (and he is the first to do so) the greatest of these poets; and as the period continues to shake down, this opinion will probably gain general acceptance. We are beginning to see that Blake alone had an intuitive grasp of the essential conflict; and that he alone established a dialectical formula by means of which he hoped to deal with it. "Without Contraries is no progression" was his reiterated demand on life. This is the basis of that potent attraction of Blake for Yeats, one of the few poets since Blake who achieved an adjustment of the contraries, whose sensibility, deplorable when isolated, was successfully encompassed in the rich severity of his work as "a sixty-year-old smiling public man." Blake, like Yeats, found metaphorical support for his dialectical view in such curious, even outrageous, places as the system of correspondence of Swedenborg and Boehme, in the analogical pursuits of the cabalists, and in the alchemy of Paracelsus and Agrippa. He found support also in the works on magic and religion attributed to that collective figure, Hermes Trismegistus, who said that "all things must needs be composed of opposites and contraries" and spoke of "the ıendship of contraries." Blake, like Yeats, is a clear example of the axiom—Mr. Eliot's dogma to the contrary—that no poet can be discredited by his sources.

Blake's work alone formulates the conflict in its basic historical terms, as a conflict between those forces which Kierkegaard later called Civilization and Christianity, and T. E. Hulme, the Humanist and the Religious views; between the desire for man's improvement here and the desire for his salvation in another life—progress versus grace. In Blake, this conflict takes many forms. His early work, for example, may be regarded as a kind of externalization of the conflict, a series of alternate statements of one interest and the other. Thus, if *Songs of Innocence* seems to be on one side, clearly *Songs of Experience* is on the other. The little *Tractates on Natural Religion* may be opposed to *Tiriel; The Book of Thel* to *The French Revolution;* and *The Gates of Paradise* to *The Marriage of Heaven and Hell.* The question, then, is whether the later works, the Prophetic Books, resolve the antithesis; that they were intended to do so is beyond question. Furthermore, when one looks back at the early work from the vantage point of the later, it is apparent that the separation we have just made is an oversimplification, that it is a matter of emphasis only and of varying symbols, and that one group is necessary to an understanding of the other, as in any dialectical proceeding; for these are, as Blake called them, "the two contrary states of the human soul," and one term cannot be defined without its opposite.

The conflict begins in Blake's attitude toward nature. Is he rejecting the material universe, or is he rejecting a particular materialistic theory of the universe? If the former, what can he mean by such a line as this? "I'll . . . shew you all alive the world"; if the latter, by this?

> Of the Sleep of Ulro! and of the passage through
> Eternal Death! and of the awaking to Eternal Life.

Did he want it both ways? Crabb Robinson reports, ". . . he did not believe in the omnipotence of God—the language of the Bible on that subject is only poetical or allegorical. Yet soon after he denied that the natural world is anything." If at thirty-six he wrote, "Man has no Body distinct from his Soul; for that call'd Body is a portion of Soul discern'd by the five Senses, the chief inlets of Soul in this age," at sixty-three he wrote, "The Natural Body is an Obstruction to the Soul or Spiritual Body." And yet in the same late document he also said that "Form must be apprehended by Sense or the Eye of Imagination."

In other terms, the conflict is present in the quarrel between gnosis and simplicity, in the conception of the prophet as both the recipient of esoteric and the dispenser of exoteric wisdom, of spiritual knowledge for natural uses. In still other terms, the conflict is contained in the opposition between the idea of the sacred individual judgment and the idea of necessary social harmony, the conflict between anarchy and order, liberty and fraternity, which again finds externalization in the very form of Blake's long works, where a vision of order climaxes considerable literary disorder. The conflict lay deep in the tradition in which Blake grew up. The stubborn tendency to transform the principle of religious freedom into its political analogues ("the rights of man's mind" into "the rights of man") is the characteristic quality of seventeenth-century dissent. There is a significant connection between the evangelical mood in religion and morals and the prevailing humanitarian attitudes in the second half of the eighteenth century. The tendency, gaining strength in French rationalism, crystallized in the Revolution, which Tocqueville described as operating in the manner of a religious rather than a political revolution. Such eighteenth-century dissenting preachers as Price and Priestley were not radicals with passionate sympathy for the revolutionary effort by mere reason of accident. Godwin himself had been a minister, and a pamphlet of 1791 called *Christianity Consistent with the Love of Freedom* argued that "Christianity is not a negation of the privileges of man but an institution for his improvement." Such an argument, like Blake's poetry, involved a violent reorganization of orthodoxy, but in no other way could a synthesis of these contrary ends be attained. "The progress of religion is defined by the denunciation of Gods," says Whitehead; which says what we have been saying if it is understood that denunciation is not destruction, and with gods can never be.

The essential conflict in Blake, then, and a major intellectual crisis of his time, is between an ethical response to man and, in Kierkegaard's words, "the teleological suspension of ethics," the counterphrase to Hegel's disparaging "moral form of evil." We may state it in brief if not in easy terms as the quarrel between politics and mysticism. Most critics of Blake have devoted their energies to the elucidation of his system, which they have termed mystical. Mystagogical I believe we must call it, but it is mystical in a sense so special that the term here is useless. This system is the rhetorical result of the mask of Blake, the metaphorical enlargement in terms of which contraries can be resolved. No such systematic conception as Yeats worked out in his doctrine of the mask is intended here; merely the informal and usual notion of an assumed role that in many features varies from the features it covers. And yet, like Yeats, Blake might have said:

> I made my song a coat
> Covered with embroideries
> Out of old mythologies
> From heel to throat.

And one may argue that in Blake, as in Yeats, the central problem involves essentially not mysticism at all, but mythology—a mythology for the materials of which both turned to a wide variety of documents, some of which are mystical—and that when Blake seems to be a mystic, he is usually only mistaking the embroideries for the coat itself.

The distinction is fundamental and the argument necessary; labels are the agents of a simultaneous diffusion and delimitation of meaning. If we say that Blake is a mystic, we associate him with a particular order of experience that when we examine his work we find to be but feebly represented there; but at the same time we disassociate him sharply from a vast range of ideas and experiences that is there firmly and crucially.

CHAPTER TWO

The Necessity of Myth

I

THE DEFINITION OF MYSTICISM, to be useful at all, must be stringent, for mysticism is in itself a highly specialized experience. But the definition of myth, if the term is to be used in the discussion of modern poets, particularly of William Blake, must be both broad and loose, for myth operates universally and diversely. The term must include such varying manifestations as the sharply formed figures of classic fable and the malformations of delusion and neurosis. Even a loose definition does not include, however, the current journalistic sense of falsehood, nor does it imply anti-intellectualism or any other such pejorative. The term denotes, in fact, neither the negation nor the contrary of ideas, but their basis and their structure, the element by which they are activated. "The doctrines which men ostensibly hold," wrote Leslie Stephen, "do not become operative upon their conduct until they have generated an imaginative symbolism."

Myths are the instruments by which we continually struggle to make our experience intelligible to ourselves. A myth is a large, controlling image that gives philosophical meaning to the facts of ordinary life; that is, which has organizing value for experience. A mythology is a more or less articulated body of such images, a pantheon. Without such images, experience is chaotic, fragmentary and merely phenomenal. It is the chaos of experience that creates them, and they are intended to rectify it. All real convictions involve a mythology, either in its usual, broad sense or in a private sense. In the first case it is embodied in literature or in ritual or in both, in which it has application to the whole of a society and tends to be religious. In the second, it remains in the realm of fantasy, in which it tends to be obsessive and fanatical. This is not to say that sound myths of general application necessarily support religions; rather that they perform the historical functions of religion—they unify experience in a way that is satisfactory to the whole culture and to the whole personality. Philip Wheelwright, from the point of view of an uncommon philosophical theism, argues understandably that "the very essence of myth" is "that haunting awareness of transcendental forces peering through the cracks of the visible universe." Durkheim pointed out that myth suggests the sacred rather than the profane; that is, the enormous area of experience into which technology cannot usefully enter rather than the relatively small area into which it does. Yet this does not make religious experience proper more than a portion of the larger area. That myth cannot be so limited is made clear by our own civilization, which seems to be struggling toward a myth that will be explicitly ethical, even political. Today, Thomas Mann has said, "the question of the human conscience . . . is presented to us essentially in its political form; perhaps more than in any other epoch of history, it wears a political face." Wars may be described as the clash of mythologies; and a basically disorganized society such as ours is the result of a number of antithetical and competing mythologies that fail to adjust themselves.

Rational belief is secondary. We habitually tend to overlook the fact that as human beings we are rational creatures not first of all but last of all, and that civilization emerged only yesterday from a primitive past that is at least relatively timeless. Belief organizes experience not because it is rational but because all belief depends on a controlling imagery, and rational belief is the intellectual formalization of that imagery. As a basic set of images, Christianity has commanded the unanimous faith of millions; as a system of belief capable of a wide variety of dogmas, it has commanded the intellectual assent of hostile sectarian groups. Such a more recent mythology as socialism, which as a faith presents an international hope for the full development of democratic man, is rent by schisms as dogma.

All those systems of abstractions which we call ideologies acttivate our behavior, when they do, only because they are themselves activated by images, however submerged. An abstraction is a generalization, and the essential antecedents of generalizations are *things*. Jung, writing of language, has made the useful observation that "Speech is a storehouse of images founded in experience, and therefore concepts which are too abstract do not easily take root in it, or quickly die out again for lack of contact with reality." Are not ideas, like language itself, supported by the "submerged metaphor"? In this sense, myth is indispensable to any form of belief. And in this sense, one may even concur with Hume's offensive remark that "there is no such passion in human minds, as the love of mankind, merely as such"; for this passion, like all others, must have an image, real or ideal, as its correlative. Myth is fundamental, the dramatic representation of our deepest instinctual life, of a primary awareness of man in the universe, capable of many configurations, upon which all particular opinions and attitudes depend. Wallace Stevens writes: ". . . we live in an intricacy of new and local mythologies, political, economic, poetic, which are asserted with an ever-enlarging incoherence." Even when, as in modern civilization, myths multiply and separate and tend to become abstract so that the images themselves recede and fade, even then they are still the essential substructure of all human activity.

Most profoundly they apply in literature. Great literature is impossible without a previous imaginative consent to a ruling mythology that makes intelligible and unitive the whole of that experience from which particular fables spring and from which they, in turn, take their meaning. Literature ceases to be perceptual and tends to degenerate into mere description without adequate myth; for, to cite Malinowski, myth, continually modified and renewed by the modifications of history, is in some form an "indispensable ingredient of all culture." Thus, for example, the prevailing and tiresome realism of modern fiction. When we feel that we are no longer in a position to say what life means, we must content ourselves with telling how it looks. Those of our novelists who have transcended realism have done so by a boot-strap miracle, by supplying the myth themselves. Mann has made a possibly artificial use of literary myth. Joyce attempted to distil their mythical essences from specifically modern developments such as psychology. Kafka disturbingly dramatized neurosis. In a disintegrating society such as this, before it can proceed with other business, literature must become the explicit agent of coherence. In the realm of the imagination serious artists must be like Hart Crane's tramps in their cross-country freight cars: "They know a body under the wide rain." All readers are aware that the chief energies of modern poets have been expended not simply in writing poetry but in employing poetry to discover its indispensable substructure. They have been compelled to build a usable mythology, one that will account for and organize our competing and fragmentary myths. T. S. Eliot is the most familiar example; here excursions into anthropology and Orientalism preceded and enriched the final embrace of Christian orthodoxy. The example of Yeats is no less spectacular and is even more systematic: Years devoted to the exploration of magic and spiritualism and all the disreputable purlieus of mysticism were combined with the results of a late interest in politics, and the curious mixture seems to have served its purpose. Americans generally have found the material for their myths nearer at hand than have modern Europeans. Hart Crane ingeniously but unsuccessfully utilized a combination of American Indian legend and modern American industrialism in the construction of his single sustained work. Older poets and poets less given to self-questioning, like Robert Frost, were apparently quite comfortable in employing the available myth of the independent American democrat for which younger men no longer find historical sanction. Among younger men, the quest is apparent in such diverse examples as W. H. Auden, Delmore Schwartz, and Karl Shapiro, and one could multiply the instances. The hunt for the essential image goes on everywhere today—but the problem is hardly new.

II

The Elizabethans, who seem to have enjoyed an intellectual flexibility denied to men since the middle of the seventeenth century,* employed an enormous variety of myth, both classical and Christian. But on the merely decorative level they ransacked and temporarily exhausted the myths of Greece and Rome, and throughout the seventeenth century poetry began to move away from classical mythology altogether. It is no accident that this movement began rather abruptly with Donne, who was among the first of the poets to reflect the developments of science explicitly. In this he followed a critical mood first expressed by Bacon, who is the fountainhead of these developments. (The historical irony here is that when the same impulse was applied to language itself, as it was by Hobbes, the poetic style of Donne became an impossibility.) The measure of Dryden and Pope may be taken up to a point in these terms: Dryden has majesty because the pagan and the Christian myths are still moderately available to him; Pope—a shallower spirit who contented himself with the new and inadequate myth—has a sustained elegance only, and moments of superb refinement; for when he employs the older myths at all, they are now available to comedy alone. The history of epic is instructive. The old epic formula involved supernatural machinery, in practice usually derived from pagan myth. Its many critics did not foresee that when the formula was demolished, the epic itself would vanish; the discredited machinery became the vehicle of *mock* epic. Nor have we yet effected a substitute for the old heroic reference, the supernatural. Within the new reference, presumably a social one, too many myths are still competing, and there is no certainty. Many

* It is here, when "man became passive before a mechanized nature," that Yeats repeatedly located the crisis of modern intellectual life. See the Introduction to *The Oxford Book of Modern Verse,* Oxford University Press, 1936, p. xxvii, and the passage in the *Autobiography,* Macmillan, 1938, p. 226, where Yeats contrasts the sensationalism of Locke with Henry More's faith in the *anima mundi.*

modern men of refined intellect would say that there is no substitute.

If epic poetry is impossible without an adequate and explicit mythology, so too is the greatest lyric poetry. Compare such moderns as Hardy and the later Yeats with their contemporary, Bridges. The recurrent triviality of this last poet ("I love beauty, and was born to rhyme") results from the fact that he does not really regard poetry seriously, but as a mere ornament to life. Such a view tends to reduce the composition of poetry to the arrangement of ornaments. Very pretty, even grave things may result, but they would hardly satisfy the demands the greatest lyric poets place upon themselves. The difference is eloquently embodied in this contrast: While Yeats was struggling to break down the barriers of mind—that is, of modern positivism—by associating himself with societies for psychical research, Bridges was attempting to impose barriers on language by founding and operating a society to purify English. On the other hand, didactic and informative poetry can do well enough with nearly any mythical material—as witness the eclecticism of *The Testament of Beauty,* which has been called "the expression not of one mind but of several"—or even with myth that has not been articulated. This will explain the prevailing temper of eighteenth-century poetry, most of which we must designate not as poetry at all, for, in spite of its increasing solemnity, it fails in an important kind of seriousness. Solemnity has of course nothing to do with seriousness; many of Blake's lyrics are light verse, but they are more "serious" than Wordsworth at his pompous norm or Shelley at his frenetic. The poems of Prior, minor as they may be, are yet more "serious" than those of Addison. And in this respect, too, Yeats's Crazy Jane songs surpass Bridges' sonnets on "The Growth of Love." Everyone will agree that as the decades passed eighteenth-century poetry became solemn enough, but few will contend that it became more serious than Prior, or Pope at his most vindictive and comic. Employing the myth of contemporary science, eighteenth-century poetry more and more took to itself the *functions* of science, which are exposition and description. These are not the functions of major poetry, but they justify the tag "the age of prose." Thus in the eighteenth century poetry at its best was elegant, like Pope's; impressively severe, like Johnson's; stunningly vituperative, like Churchill's. At its second level, it was sometimes worthily prosaic, like Thomson's and Dyer's; more often merely prosaic, like Blair's, Young's, Akenside's, and so on. It was all these things and other things besides, but one thing it was not—it was not grand. And it was a fashion of the time, in the unfelt modesty of "progress" odes like those of Gray and Collins, to declare the poetry of the century—including theirs—inferior. Blake took them at their word and cried, "Indeed!"

A recent series of lectures by a well-known scholar, Professor Pottle, attempts to explain this lack of grandeur in the eighteenth century and its presence nearly everywhere in the nineteenth (as he thinks) and, indeed, all the conflicting fashions of poetry from age to age, in terms of poetic idiom alone. Idiom, in this usage, is the direct expression of the peculiar sensibility of an age. This argument commits Professor Pottle to a complete relativism in theory and if pursued, reduces the practice of criticism to the drier varieties of scholarship. And it does not go far enough to be of much use. Idiom is determined by sensibility, to be sure; but sensibility, which is the form of aesthetic response, is itself determined by the indispensable cultural ingredient, myth. Pushing the argument this far, one attains to at least a limited absolutism, an absolutism to be applied to culture in general and to all of its products. The myths of one age are better than those of another; that is, some myths include more of the total experience of a culture than others, and in the great ages, ages of amplitude and spaciousness, they include everything. Then poetry attains its full stature: its vitality is not lessened by shifts of sensibility, because it has achieved density, strata of various meaning. The great limitation of most eighteenth-century poetry is that it is thin; it means no more than it intends to mean.

Did Coleridge, translating Schiller, perceive the problem?

The intelligible forms of ancient poets,
The fair humanities of old religion,
The Power, the Beauty, and the Majesty,

That had their haunts in dale, or piny mountain,
Or forest by slow stream, or pebbly spring,
Or chasms and wat'ry depths: all these have vanished.
They live no longer in the faith of reason!
But still the heart doth need a language, still
Doth the old instinct bring back the old names.*

William Blake, who cried with malice,

Lo the Bat with Leathern wing,
Winking & blinking,
Winking & blinking,
Winking & blinking,
Like Doctor Johnson,

certainly did perceive the problem. Writing at the end of a century whose poetic product seemed with very few exceptions unutterably dreary to him, he wanted above everything to return grandeur to poetry; and to this effect alone, he knew, myth was indispensable.

III

UNLIKE SOME POETS of his time, Blake attempted almost no use of the figures and conventions of classical mythology. They were not, and in that age he felt could not have been, used in any organic fashion; for these myths were, in Coleridge's term, "exploded." As Douglas Bush points out, only Collins seemed to have any inclination to use them more significantly than as decoration. Decoration did not interest Blake, and the classical mythology enters his work at only four or five points, most of these in his juvenile efforts. His verses on the decline of poetry in the eighteenth century are properly addressed "To the

* It is interesting to recall Leslie Stephen's remark on Wordsworth's sonnet, "The World Is Too Much with Us." "The nostalgia for a pagan condition," says Stephen, represents "the loss of a system of symbols which could enable him to express readily and vigorously every mood produced by the vicissitudes of human life."—*History of English Thought in the Eighteenth Century*, 2 vols., Putnam, 1927, Vol. I, p. 16.

Muses"—the "Fair Nine." Half a dozen characters from the Greek and Roman pantheon appear in "Imitation of Spenser," again appropriately enough. Once he mentions Pandora, and a few times, "Phebus." Mars makes a symbolical appearance, in strange company, in the Prophetic Book *America;* and the several appearances of Bacchus and Venus, jointly with Thor and Frigga, in *Jerusalem,* are perhaps no more incongruous than the appearance of various historical figures. These few instances comprise Blake's total use of the ancient myths, for he was wholly aware of their degraded place in the decor of the seventeenth and eighteenth centuries: "Bloated Gods, Mercury, Juno, Venus, & the rattle traps of Mythology & the lumber of an awkward French Palace are thrown together around Clumsy & Ricketty Princes & Princesses higgledy piggledy."

Under the circumstances Blake found it a mythology without meaning, first petrified and now corroded, of possible use to the poet interested in "delicate conceits," but of no use whatever to one busy "with the terrors of thought." It might be supposed that the naturalistic basis of Greek myth would have indisposed Blake to it in any situation; but this is not true. He was fully acquainted with its naturalistic basis ("The ancient Poets animated all sensible objects with Gods or Geniuses" . . .) but his objection was to its systematization (". . . thus began Priesthood; Choosing forms of worship from poetic tales"). His most frequent image for systematization was petrifaction, and a good image this is for a condition that is intended to suggest the impossibility of further intuitional activity. A fundamental reason for Blake's rejecting an older mythology and insisting on his own was to disassociate his utterance from the literalness and the externality to which older myths had been subjected, and which had rendered them unadaptable to fresh historical situations. The example of Keats and Shelley, who found the old mythology still quite limber, did not alter Blake's point of view; as he was more robust, so he was also more brash than they.

Coleridge argued that the agent which destroyed the classic myths was "the mechanical system of philosophy," and this is true enough; but it is not all of the truth. For the mechanical philosophy shook, just as clearly, the established Christian mythology. It is important to see that both Christianity and the mechanical system of philosophy entailed their own myths, Milton adequately representing one, Pope or Thomson the other. But vital remnants of the Christian myth remained, and these, working in terms of politics—for this was the necessary compromise if anything was to be saved from Christianity—co-operated with the antithetical myth of contemporary science until by the time of the French Revolution a new adjustment had been attained. Blake's problem was to find the metaphorical terms that would articulate and encompass both the Christian and the scientific myth, as well as those new terms which were the terms of the synthesis itself.

The Christian mythology, never so generally useful to English poetry as the pagan, was last successfully employed by John Milton. By deliberately turning his back on the new science, Milton managed to retain a nearly orthodox view of a universe interpenetrated by God and his interests, and of man in immediate relation to God and answerable to him. Blake was not alone among his contemporaries in having the enormous good sense to admire Milton (but in the major poems rather than in the minor), and while he was the only one among them who possessed genius, it was perhaps not plastic enough to assimilate that terrific influence. He took the Christian mythology as Milton had employed it, with the emphasis on the creation and the resurrection—paradise lost and paradise regained—and with the help of certain semimystical writings and his own highly personal responses to the leading ideas of his age (responses capable of extraordinary transvaluations), manipulated it to his inclusive purposes. And in a sense he solved a problem that had existed throughout the whole literature of the century.

For the literature of the eighteenth century is curious in that it constantly reflects two worlds and never brings them together. There is the world of affairs, of reason, of ethical notions, the world of mechanistic philosophy and of natural religion—all of which had its myth. And then there is that curious half-world of morbid fancy, of Gothic titillation and unkempt bards, of garden ruins and Tahitian dinner guests and chinoiserie and every manner of restless exoticism—all of which was an attempt to enrich the inadequate myth of the former. Often enough these two spheres appear in the same writer, as they do in Thomas Gray, and even in the same work, but they never merge. One never helps to explain the other; they continue to involve their separate responses.

No one in the century recognized the trouble, although a good many writers observed the symptoms. That nearly unknown figure John Husbands declared in 1731, "'Tis too true indeed, that *the Poetical* character has of late been separated from the *religious,*" which is as exact a statement of the *symptom* as one could wish for. But no one went further. Writers like Dennis, Addison, and Thomson, like Edward Young, Horace Walpole, Bishop Hurd, and the Wartons, asserted in one way or another the superiority of primitive genius and resisted the prevailing neoclassicism. But all these still conceived of genius as operating rather on the plane of fancy than on the plane of imagination, which integrates sensibility and intellect. In one sense these writers were not wrong; for it is the primitive—Blake, Whitman, Lawrence—who brings these two realms of experience together most vigorously, if not usually most satisfactorily.

The failure of the eighteenth-century worthies to make a distinction that was not explicitly made until the time of Coleridge—the distinction between a function that is external, decorative, static, and a function that is organic and organizing, "esemplastic" in Coleridge's big word—was not theirs but that of the century, or of the condition of contemporary metaphysics. Failure it was, however, for it is exactly fancy that retains this separation between ordinary life and the life of the imagination. Yet their discussion and that Gothic world of sensibility glued together by poets and novelists comprised the century's rather feeble, if protracted, attempt to fill the chasm of a departed mythology. ". . . The gradual ebbing of an ancient faith leaves a painful discord between the imagination and the reason," wrote Stephen, and the eighteenth-century attempt to bridge the gap by fancy was of course unsuccessful; for true and useful myth does not titillate, but assimilates and modifies the facts of experience by means of the imagination, which takes reason into account.

Juliet's moving fears of the tomb echo in all the charnel-house poetry of the age, and in Blake too, but how weakly, how theatrically! For they are lath-and-plaster fears of an experience that, because it is deprived in the imagination of its full consequences, is nearly meaningless and can only titillate.

The myth that the eighteenth century could seriously employ was the austere—indeed, in its first manifestations, the barren myth of Newton, the myth of the mechanical universe, with its religious, ethical, and social ramifications. This is the picture that Milton was still able to reject, of a universe created by a God but from which that God, a mechanist, had withdrawn after his work was completed. It was a universe that operated on fixed and changeless principles that man could, to a point, understand by his reason; of a society comparably fixed and "rational," in which all things had their immutable place, their only obligation being to know it and to keep it. This view prevailed in the poetry that reflected the sober side of life, the world of affairs and of manners. That it occasionally resulted in such triumphs of social and ethical discursiveness as the "Epistle to Doctor Arbuthnot" and "The Vanity of Human Wishes" (although this, of course, is not an "original" poem, and Johnson hardly a deist) is to the credit of the poets in question, not of the myth.

In the past the myth at its most fertile had provided a basis for comedy. Because its ideal of society was as rigid as its picture of the universe, it had allowed enormous ground for all manner of comic divagation. And if the comedy of the eighteenth century was inferior to that produced in the second half of the preceding century, that is because the myth was already being corrupted by the agent most destructive to comedy—sentimentalism. The harder the universe became, the softer the heart. The stricter the conventions, the more outrageous the rebellious taste. When the glitter of the French drawing-room became too bright for comfort, it was possible to substitute the gloom of a "Gothic" hall, and even in gardens that had imitated Versailles one could find space for a "grot" or a horrid ruin, and on that labor market one could easily afford to employ a hermit. The manners, like the poetry, of the century struggled continually to overcome the strictures of the myth. No less so religion; for the deeper the incursions that deism made into theology, or the more comfortable the parson became on a tavern settle, the more vigorous became the efforts of the revivalists, and the blacker the mood of the orthodox like Swift and Johnson. The century, like its greatest genius and many a lesser, died like a certain tree, "at top."

And the fault was in the myth. "Then tell me," Blake asked, "what is the material world, and is it dead?" What indeed had the picture of the universe presented by the mechanical philosophy to offer a poet who *was* serious, as no poet had been after the death of Milton? For Blake was a poet who constantly felt the imperative and undeniable energy of life, and he had—in the perhaps inadequate modern application of Yeats; for those convenient absolutes, good and evil, had already gone—the tragic sense and was therefore truly joyous. Joy is not the icy optimism of the *Essay on Man,* that highly enameled structure which in the opening lines of its second part cracks widely enough to admit all the shocking anomalies of the age—the melancholy of Samuel Johnson, the despair of William Cowper, and the madness of Christopher Smart being the least of them. *"Vous criez 'Tout est bien' d'une voix lamentable."* Nor are the alternatives to Pope—Johnson, Cowper, Smart—more useful to a poetry of joy than Pope himself. Blake needed to construct a picture of the world, a myth, that was in some sense the counterpart of his experience of life; and the Newtonian order, in its mathematical denial of that dynamic expansiveness and fluidity which energy connotes, was almost literally "death." When we talk of Blake and the nothingness of matter, we must always remember that it was most often *that* "material universe" which he had in mind. He addressed this epigram "To God":

> If you have form'd a Circle to go into,
> Go into it yourself & see how you would do.

Blake's experience—his temperament—demanded a universe that was above all "open," a universe that was not indifferent to man but an extension of man, a universe in which all things were in organic and active relationship with all others, and which was constantly interpenetrated by these relationships.* He could express his need in terms as hyperbolic as these:

> A Robin Red breast in a Cage
> Puts all Heaven in a Rage.

But it was nevertheless a peculiarly modern view; it suggests Bergson's vitalism, Einstein's relativity, Whitehead's "events," Freud's fluid levels of consciousness, and I. A. Richards's "mental balances." The tradition in which Pope found his ideas assumed the "rational" Newtonian universe, and deduced from that what seemed to be the inevitable conclusions for man and society. But Blake, who jeered,

> To be, or not to be
> Of great capacity,
>   Like Sir Isaac Newton,

and always argued that "Where man is not, nature is barren," began with his picture of man and from that deduced a comparable society and a comparable cosmos. There is at least this to be said for his innocence, or his arrogance: The static universe of the eighteenth century did not fit the facts of scientific experience for very long after it had failed the facts of poetic experience.†

* "Plato was the first man who perceived that this idea could be made to provide the philosopher with a vehicle of expression more powerful than any other. If a man will once plant himself firmly on the proposition that *he is* the universe, that every emotion or expression of his mind is correlated in some way to phenomena in the external world, and that he shall say how correlated, he is in a position where the power of speech is at a maximum. His figures of speech, his tropes, his witticisms, take rank with the law of gravity and the precession of the equinoxes. Philosophical exaltation of the individual cannot go beyond this point. It is the climax."—John Jay Chapman, *Emerson and Other Essays*, Scribner, 1898, pp. 12-13.

† It is of some interest to speculate whether Blake's enormous disrespect for the pretensions of the contemporary world picture was merely a temperamental difference—which, in large part at least, it certainly was—or whether it was also based on some understanding of the contradictions within the theory on which that picture rested. The speculation is suggested by a remark of J. H. Randall: ". . . if we start with Locke's assumptions, we are bound to end up with Kant, that whatever certainty our science may have, it does not give us any light upon the basic structure of the world; in

IV

BUT ALL THE TIME, out of these conflicting elements in the century, a new myth was in the making—was, one might almost say, being rescued from the ruins of religion. And this is as good an example as one can find of the interdependence of myth and history. For if on the one hand the myth of rationalism was construed to mean that society, like the universe, was static, and that men, like stars, were fixed by immutable law in the position to which they were born, on the other hand it could be argued that men could employ their reason not toward some passive understanding merely, but toward a new control of the frame and of themselves. Reason could be employed for revolutionary as well as for traditional purposes. Either way, it was useful to keep God—the old God—out of the universe; for divine interference is always confusing to that rational faculty on the superiority of which both arguments founded themselves. Thus that very deism which in Pope argued against man's progress could also, as in Paine, be used to argue for it; and into this second tendency flowed most of the rich protest against authority of the Nonconformist tradition.

The new myth, therefore, finds its modern beginnings as far back as Bacon's denial of authority ("*Bacon* has broke that Scarcrow Deitie") and the beginnings of scientific investigation; in

other words, that the mind of man cannot know reality as it exists, if indeed there be any such world at all apart from man's mind."—*The Making of the Modern Mind,* rev. ed., Houghton Mifflin, 1940, p. 270. Did Blake, in short, recognize that the distinction was between different pictures, literally—the scientist's, his own, etc., and that there was no reason to assume, even by the enemy's metaphysic, that the more respectable was the more "real"? And could he not have claimed that his picture was at any rate the more complete, since it was able to take the other into account? This brings us once more to the question whether his exception was not taken, primarily, to the limitations of the rationalistic view rather than to the materials that composed that view. "All that we saw," said Blake to an angel who had presented him with an unattractive view, "was owing to your metaphysics." —*Poetry and Prose,* p. 200.

Bacon's precedent applied to religion, with its insistence on the right to individual worship of seventeenth-century Protestantism. And this protest was summarized once and for all in that era by the metaphysical speculations of Locke and the argument of the tabula rasa. The myth is of man's native goodness, a vision of the liberated individual progressing into dignity when released from the most crushing forms of authority, whether economic, political, or theological. It is the concept of regeneration not in the next world, but in this—the regeneration of the social man. This is the chiliastic hope of seventeenth-century Protestantism given specifically political form, the millennium conceived anew in terms not of graves burst open but of institutions broken down. It is perfectibility. If there is no merely logical incongruity present in this concept, a sharply logical incongruity exists between perfectibility and an utterly antithetical idea with which it co-operated, namely, primitivism. But it disturbed no one. It is precisely this co-operation between these logical opposites, primitivism and progress, that marks the religious antecedents of the new myth. For what are these concepts but political terms for the older conceptions of Eden and the millennium, of paradise lost and paradise regained?

With the breakdown and bankruptcy of Christianity in the eighteenth century, the dissenting myth, combined with science, passes over to politics completely, and ever since it has been politics that, in terms of the liberal idea of progress and more recent, radical revisions of that idea, has performed the ethical functions of religion. The French Revolution, precisely because it was antiecclesiastical, was a revolution determined by values that politics had seized from a failing Christianity. The transmutation, however, meant a certain immediate loss in the poetic value of the myth and only if it was presented in reorganized terms of the old Christian imagery, as in Blake, or in a reorganized version of the older pagan imagery, as in Shelley, would it readily yield itself to poetic purposes. Nor should the ultimate failure of the myth in the life of the nineteenth century prevent us from recognizing its character at the end of the eighteenth.

For in the nineteenth century the myth was of course distracted. Here again, history and myth collide; for the distraction of the myth came about, in the first instance, by the necessities of a new and misapprehended and utterly uncontrolled industrialism, and in the second, by the necessities of an overweening imperialism. Under the blight of these forces, the idea of intrinsic human worth could only wither. And only when these uncontrolled forces resulted in the explosion of World War I did many men seriously begin to question the value of the distractions in the myth, and even now we are still only learning. These distractions had been at least obliquely sanctioned by some of the best minds of the nineteenth century, such as Mill's. To Blake, for example, the motive was liberty—freedom from all the repressive strictures of the past and the present. For this, the necessary condition was equality; but the end was always, and insistently, fraternity.

The impulse to individualism had as its goal not some ideal of aggressive competition, but the vision—the word is used advisedly—of harmony. And in general the eighteenth-century revolutionary myth may be described in these terms; they will not, of course, do for the nineteenth century. Then that individualism which was only the first tenet of revolutionary doctrine was utilized for economic purposes alone—and bad ones. It was isolated from those psychological and social purposes which it originally involved but which were either lost sight of, or—by the large middle-class element involved in the struggle—ignored. These developments were not intended by Locke or his successors, Voltaire, Rousseau, Holbach, Helvétius, Condorcet, and in England, Paine, Priestley, Godwin, and the host of pamphleteers who surrounded them. Yet they were foreseen by William Blake, who in his curious way and for his somewhat special reasons was immediately in this tradition, and whose aim it was to find a proper figurative embodiment for it, and so to correct what seemed to him its excesses. In its baldest terms the liberal myth of progress has long since been discredited, but our best hopes today attach to those portions of it which endure. Blake's modernity is nowhere clearer than in his manipulation of this material.

That Blake, for reasons of temperament, had certain qualifications as mythmaker seems indubitable. His pride, in the first place, was essential: "Genius has no Error." In the second place, his imagination was habitually animistic, yet, if only because of his horror of abstract systems, he never fell into the trap of pantheism, which would have reduced the mythopoeic faculty to the dogmatic. Again, metaphor is the indispensable vehicle of myth, and Blake, through that gift of vision which he so assiduously cultivated, saw things habitually in their metaphorical guises, and often, indeed, refused to distinguish between their literal values and these others precisely because his intention, his deliberate intention, was myth. Here the concept of a mask is essential. Blake's work contains evidences that he was quite aware, when he wished to be, of the distinction between the literal and the metaphorical; and that he felt it essential to his purposes as a poet to practice a kind of self-deception that would allow his mind to function in the primitive fashion.

The primitive intelligence produces and consents to articulated myth with an ease utterly alien to the cultivated mind; for it does not deal with abstractions but with images, and it makes no distinction between images and their symbolical (that is, their ideal) content. The primitive intelligence, too, enjoys a subject-object wholeness that intellectual discrimination splits into subjective and objective. Blake refused to make this distinction radically, holding, in advance of philosophy, that inner and outer were one. Jung, writing of science and gnosticism, has said: "In my picture of the world there is a vast outer realm and an equally vast inner realm; between these two stands man, facing now one and now the other, and, according to his mood or disposition, taking the one for the absolute truth by denying or sacrificing the other." Blake, standing between these realms, pulled them together, as they are together for the primitive. It is from this act alone that sound myth can proceed.

He was, of course, imposing upon himself a tremendously difficult task, for while he encouraged in himself a primitive habit of mind, he could hardly reproduce in the eighteenth century the conditions of a primitive life. And, one might add, unlike many of his contemporaries and such later primitives as D. H. Lawrence, he never showed the naïve inclination to do so; his lines

Tho' born on the cheating banks of Thames,
Tho' his waters bathed my infant limbs,
The Ohio shall wash his stains from me:
I was born a slave, but I go to be free . . .

carry no literal, pantisocratic significance; they are wholly symbolical. The myths of the primitive are rudimentary because his life is simple; but Blake's myth—if it was to serve its purpose—had to be relatively complex because the life of the late eighteenth century and of the nineteenth was enormously so. And he who hated systems was finally caught in a system of his own that entailed endless elaboration if it was to be useful at all. It is this, perhaps, which has discouraged prophets in the modern world; their "parables and allegories" are no longer able to work in the simple fashion characteristic of parables and allegories.

Nevertheless, the role of prophet presented Blake with the easiest terms in which to conceive his problem; and the prophet he opposed to the philosopher. "There are always these two classes of learned sages, the poetical and the philosophical." Wordsworth had found them equal, the bard and the sage, "twin labourers"; but not Blake. For him the prophet is that visionary poet who, through his enlarged senses, perceives the "eternal principles or characters of human life," the living basis of belief, myth. But the philosopher is the priest, who, through his closed senses and his reason, abstracts and externalizes those "eternal principles" and reduces them to dogma. The difference is between an agent that frees man and serves him, and an agent that restricts him and makes him serve. This is the great and abiding distinction in Blake: myth versus dogma. "Let the Philosopher always be the servant and scholar of inspiration and all will be happy." The distinction and the recommendation suggest at once Blake's primary revision of that contemporary myth for which he was trying to find the proper metaphors: his attitude toward reason.

To transcend the "universe" that dominated but did not satisfy the eighteenth century, to gain his own "universe," Blake felt it essential to reject that narrow rationalism which was the corollary of eighteenth-century science—felt it necessary to remove this from its central position in the myth and substitute his own ideal of intuitionalism:

> And 'tis most wicked in a Christian Nation
> For any Man to pretend to Inspiration.

Not only was contemporary rationalism inimical to Blake's own method of perception and to the prophetic faculty, and congenial instead to dogma and to the "dogmatic fallacy," but in Blake's conception it was also wholly inimical to the very end that the myth itself sanctioned—private and public harmony, a social regeneration. The really complex fact about Blake begins to appear. If on the one hand he encouraged certain facets of his temperament in order to write the kind of poetry he thought essential, on the other hand, he also formed his ideas in such a fashion that they would meet the needs of his temperament. This was a simultaneous collaboration, a nearly equal one that continued and progressed all his life. He wrote prophecy in order, as he thought, to guide his age or the next; but the ideas he proposed as guides were in themselves partially formed by the nature of prophecy. In no item of his creed is this clearer than in his attitude toward reason. That his antirationalism did not lead him into either of the extremes of anti-intellectualism attests to his greatness. These extremes are an unenlightened naturalism and total mysticism. Blake would no more have been capable of writing, with D. H. Lawrence,

> Yet, O my young man, there is a vivifier.
> There is that which makes us eager.
> While we are eager, we think nothing of it.
> Sum ergo non cogito.
> But when our eagerness leaves us, we are
> godless and full of thought,

than he would have been capable of plunging, with mystics like the pseudo-Dionysius or John of the Cross, into that "darkness of unknowing" which is the rejection of all ideas.

"The Woman Taken in Adultery"
By courtesy of the Museum of Fine Arts, Boston

"Every Harlot was a Virgin once."

V

THAT HE WAS NOT in the tradition of mysticism some few critics of Blake have indicated, but only one, Professor Helen White, has demonstrated.* No critic, however, has pursued the implications in Blake's work if it is indeed not mystical, and no critic has really stated the simple and significant fact that differentiates Blake once and forever from traditional mysticism. This is that his intuitions do not have a religious but an ethical content, do not deal with man's relationship to God but with man's relationship to his total being and to other men. Blake's emphasis was psychological when it was not social, and it was never directly theological. The fact that Blake may have conceived of himself as a mystic is of no particular importance. Delusion, no less than illusion, has been the source of poetry before. But it was a delusion that was peripheral and self-induced, a fiction that he proposed for himself in order that he might counter the intolerable condition of life in his time with a larger fiction for it.† In submitting to his delusion, in creating his fiction, Blake may have mistaken the accidents of mysticism (the gift

* It is perhaps only fair to the reader to point out now that Miss White seemed eager to separate the mystics from the dubious company of Blake, whereas I, as must be clear, am eager to separate Blake from the dubious company of the mystics.

† "Delusion," wrote Dr. Charles Macfie Campbell, "is no strange and mysterious element, it is no foreign parasite battening on the mind, it is not the meaningless expression of disturbed physiological processes; delusion is an attempt of the personality to deal with special difficulties, in which attempt the mind not infrequently tends to revert to primitive modes of adaptation, which are at variance with the actual level of thought of the period and group in which the individual finds himself. . . . Delusion, like fever, is to be looked on as part of nature's attempt at cure, an endeavor to neutralize some disturbing factor, to compensate for some handicap, to reconstruct a working contact with the group, which will still satisfy special needs. To those with no such special needs the delusion is apt to appear superfluous, repellent, grotesque."—*Delusion and Belief*, Harvard University Press, 1926, pp. 8-9.

of "second sight," or vision, and his consequent conviction that he was writing under extrahuman compulsions) as the distinguishing marks of mysticism, which in history they have never been; but even of this we cannot be certain.

What we can be certain of is that Blake's mind, like any mind, worked in at least three ways: it opposed some ideas, it accepted others, and it transformed still others. Unlike most of us, however, Blake rejected none. Even for those ideas of his time which he opposed with such dearly bought earnestness, Blake felt it essential to find a place in his myth. If he stated the myth amply enough, it would itself provide the corrective for them. Thus into it came that whole familiar catena of the century—a rationalist philosophy glazed over by a frigid skepticism, a barren mechanical-materialistic science, sensationalism in psychology, deism in religion, and neoclassicism in art.

Yet to articulate this myth, Blake had not only to break through the traditional vocabulary of poetry and devise a vocabulary of his own, but also to find the metaphorical terms for it that were not ready-made in traditional English thought and had not been employed in English poetry. Professor Tillyard has said that mythology and rhetoric are the two essentials for a poet; Blake had largely to invent both of them. Both, insofar as they were borrowed, he found in the Bible, in Milton, and in certain Protestant mystics low in the scale like Boehme, or in pseudo-mystics like Swedenborg, or in nonmystics like Paracelsus. Blake's earliest volume of verse shows no obligation to the last three, nor any mystical insights of his own, but borrows heavily instead from the traditional English poets for its form, and from conventional eighteenth-century thought for its attitudes. This fact may indicate either that Blake was still in a condition of nonillumination, or that his "mysticism," as I believe, was self-cultivated and external.

Or shall we say that Blake, like so many eighteenth-century poets, was mad, and rest complacently there, even admitting with Wordsworth that his madness is more interesting than the sanity of Byron or Scott? The question no longer deserves to be asked. Yet to those persons who still ask it with sincerity, to those readers of Blake who continue to be more baffled by him than they need be, something must be said. The failure to distinguish between fact and fancy is assuredly a mark of madness, and this is the point of arguing for what we may call the *mask* of madness. Blake himself argued as much: "Cowper came to me and said: '. . . You retain health and yet are as mad as any of us all—over us all—mad as a refuge from unbelief—from Bacon, Newton, and Locke.' " "Mad as a refuge"—could any remark be more sane or more revelatory? If Blake's mask was the refuge from unbelief, his myth was to be the means of circumventing unbelief.

Certainly his mind was not deranged; yet finally his sensibilities were. They were deranged in a curious way by the violence of his own unchallenged response to the leading ideas of his time. The difference between the compressed and lovely lucidity of an early poem like "Ah! Sun-flower" and the prolix and endless involutions of the later work reveals the extent of this derangement.

It is difficult to mark the points at which Blake accepts the mask as the end and forgets that it is a means only; yet this happens. To an outcast in the world of the early nineteenth century, the mask and the myth had great attractions in themselves. The figures of the myth attained the power of incantation for Blake, a hypnotic power, a power almost of ritual, over him. There are many points at which he takes the embroidery of the coat for the coat itself, the symbol for fact, the metaphor for history. Neither the mind that conceived the later ideas nor the later ideas are different, but the way of conceiving them—or of stating them—has changed. The problem is to distinguish, even when Blake sometimes fails to, between mysticism and that system of metaphor, Blake's myth for moderns, which he derived in part from a sort of mysticism.

CHAPTER THREE

Mysticism

I

MYSTICISM IS ACTIVE, only secondarily speculative. It is a technique, and its attempts to formulate even casual reports of what it believes it has discovered are incidental to the act of discovery. As a technique for a particular way of life, it inevitably suggests certain metaphysical conclusions; but these are effects in philosophy, not the causes of mysticism. Thus the mystic's basic impulse, to establish relation with a supernatural reality that is not accessible to reason or to sense but to what the mystic calls "love," implies at least a rudimentary theory of knowledge. The fact that "love" works not in any diffusive way but through a strictly concentrated discipline that is intended to release the mystic from all natural claims implies a sharp dualism. The fact that this discipline falls into stages through which the agent passes on the way toward his desired end points to an ultimate optimism. And finally, the fact that the goal of the mystic is not knowledge of that supernatural reality which he first assumes, but union with it, indicates that his whole paradoxical endeavor is to mitigate that dualism which he first establishes, that he struggles to come at last to some form of monism. These speculative results have no basic interest for most mystics, whose concern is the practical achievement of a goal, not the inferences that philosophy may make from it if it chooses. Yet the two together, the psychological characteristics of mysticism and these four philosophical concomitants, can be utilized to make the necessary distinctions if we bear in mind that one group takes priority over the other. These characteristics, with their ramifications, comprise the pattern of life and thought that may fairly be called mysticism; but outside the central pattern, there are many "mysticisms"—patterns of life and thought that share *in part* the characteristics of the central pattern. Defenders of orthodoxies, such as Dean Inge and Dom Cuthbert Butler, argue for the "true" and the "false" mysticism, depending on the special dogma with which their interests are allied. This habit is less useful than arguing for total mysticism and the countless variations of partial mysticism, or "mystihood." "The art of mysticism," Santayana has written, "is to be mystical in spots." On the practical side, William Blake was hardly even "mystical in spots." On the speculative side, the documents that chiefly influenced him were only "mystical in spots"—those of Swedenborg and Boehme; and that influence was hardly ever conceptual, but merely metaphorical, even when Blake would have denied the "mereness."

II

THE INTENTION of the mystic is to associate himself in the fullest way possible with supernatural reality by means of "love," and with no purpose in mind but the end in itself. Immediately a number of distinctions appear. Most "obstinate questionings of sense and outward things," intuitions of spirit "deeply interfused," do not comprise mysticism, nor even, necessarily, the mystical impulse. No more do most protests against the finality of the conclusions of reason and science. All religion and poetry exist if not inevitably to protest against reason and science, at least to supplement them; * and mysticism is a very special devel-

* Sir Francis Galton, in one of his statistical "surveys of human faculties," concluded that scientists have the weakest capacity of visualization among all classes of men. See Herbert Read, *Education through Art,* Ryerson Press, 1943, p. 46n. Blake would have been interested in this fact, and would have used it in his attack on the claims of science. It underlines the clash of

opment of the religious impulse (a "disease" to Paul Elmer More) and is no part of poetry at all. Wordsworth is no more mystical than D. H. Lawrence; both, with the mystics, protested against the strictures of rationalism, but the one did not intend, with the mystics, to achieve union with supernatural reality, and the other placed his reality entirely in the natural sphere. On the other hand, no man whose spiritual pursuit founds itself on the efficacy of reason, and no man who proposes for his end the increase of knowledge or of power, is properly termed a mystic. A philosopher like Spinoza and scholars like the Cambridge Platonists must be excluded for the first reason, and students of the occult and of magic for the second. Here again the analogy with Yeats is irresistible.

Both Blake and Yeats were repelled by the scientific picture of the universe. Blake saw God at the window at the age of four, and in one of his last letters wrote, "Sr. Francis Bacon is a Liar." Yeats was told that as a child he saw a supernatural bird, and late in life he wrote: "The mischief began at the end of the seventeenth century when man became passive before a mechanized nature; that lasted to our own day with the exception of a brief period between Smart's *Song to David* and the death of Byron, wherein imprisoned man beat upon the door." Both poets demanded a nature expansive enough for them to see God and supernatural birds with comfort. Nor is this necessarily to convict them, as the strictest rationalists would, of choosing to confuse fancy and knowledge, hence of madness. It is only saying that both felt more keenly than most men the disturbing contradiction that had been developing ever since the Renaissance —the breach between the scientific and the ethical view, in Whitehead's words, "between the materialistic mechanism of science and the moral intuitions, which are presupposed in the concrete affairs of life." It is a contradiction that only now is being alleviated, perhaps at the total expense of morals.

The poetry of the eighteenth century had relaxed into that easy discipline which has become the characteristic business of

temperament that is the motive of his criticism, and it suggests what is the most important reason why scientific fact, until we are a race of robots, cannot begin to satisfy the whole need of the human intellect.

intellect: the measuring and the mastering, not the understanding, of the world. Both Blake and Yeats, fearful of the trivial—Blake after a short exercise of it, Yeats after a long—were convinced that abstractions could not illuminate the daily experience of life and were destructive to art; and both refused to allow experience to be confined to the senses. Both therefore turned to magic, Blake to reading in the alchemists and the hermetics, Yeats to reading alchemy and practicing spiritualism extensively. Each felt that his pursuit would help to meet what seemed to be an instinctive need, which Yeats described as "an ungovernable yearning" in himself, and Blake, as "The Thing I have most at Heart—more than life."

Magic has curious and elaborate associations. In its simplest, most primitive forms, it assumes the reality of mysterious forces in nature that defy logic but which man, through traditional ritual, may control. In its more sophisticated forms, when it combines itself with both mysticism and science, it assumes the reality of supersensible universes that individuals may apprehend through a disciplined will, or experiment, or both. This spiritual plane penetrates and supports the world of sense. All things in nature are thus intimately and organically related by a vitalistic sympathy; indeed, all the multitudinous forms of nature contain within themselves the representation of the whole of nature. A systematic analogy and balance exists between the sensible and the supersensible spheres, the external forms of things half revealing, half concealing, the spiritual forces that sustain them. Thus emerge not only the doctrine of microcosm and macrocosm, but the doctrine of allegory in all its various forms. One such form is the study of analogy on which alchemy and occultism are based. The symbolism of medieval theology and the doctrine of signatures of medieval science are others. Still other forms are the systems of correspondence of Swedenborg and that of Boehme, who construed his ideas explicitly in terms of the alchemical vocabulary and point of view. All these efforts are related to magic in two ways. They are based on the premise that life is single and purposeful, a universalism more intimate than the Platonic unification by a remote intellect, more attractive than the later, Newtonian unification by matter;* and they all assume that the secrets of this universalism form a body of arcane wisdom available to initiates and adepts. Thus they also have at least a partial bearing on mysticism, which they have often influenced and have nearly always corrupted. It is useful to remember that in the early Christian centuries alchemy was a monopoly of the priests; that it is argued that the so-called spiritual alchemists, like Boehme after them, did not intend the transmutation of metals at all but the transmutation of man's material consciousness to spiritual consciousness, his lower to a higher self. And it is significant that Yeats once proposed to write a book in the style of Sir Thomas Browne that would construe the alchemic quest as the transmutation of life into art, which is simply the substitution of aesthetic for religious terms, and reveals the same impulse to perfect nature. The central tenet of alchemy—that all things possess a hidden quality opposite to their particular apparent quality, which fire can reveal—has a strong apocalyptic flavor.

The concept of regeneration, whether in the specific medical application of Paracelsus, or in the general, philosophical application of Cornelius Agrippa, lies at the heart of alchemy. It is this concept that was useful to the countless enthusiasts, mainly Protestant, in the sixteenth and seventeenth centuries who attempted to adapt the occult studies to Plotinian mysticism by simply abandoning their theurgic claims. But the kind of pursuit that resulted, usually called nature mysticism, is not, in the present definition, mysticism. The aim of magic, even if it operates through a knowledge of the spiritual world, is the increase of natural knowledge and the control of natural forces, and these interests mysticism initially impugns. To conjoin natural and spiritual ends, after the fashion of magic and its religious derivatives, is the exact antithesis of the mystical endeavor, which separates them sharply. Furthermore, the impulse and the agent of magic and its allied interests is not "love," but a restless and insistent intellectuality that, no less than "love," can sometimes be fantastically misled.

* I owe this distinction to Howard H. Brinton, *The Mystic Will*, Macmillan, 1930, p. 82.

The difference between science since the seventeenth century and the pseudo-science that preceded it is that modern method leaves no room for mystery. The attempt by pseudo-science to control nature by formula suggests the infinitely various and comprehensive universe of ancient times. The discovery by science that our control does not extend beyond our understanding of the ways in which nature controls us suggests the parsimonious universe of modern positivism. Blake and Yeats both attempted to reverse this process. Unwilling to submit their individuality to nature as science had discovered it, they turned to those older methods that science had discarded. And both found a release from the strictures of science in this fashion. Yeats's release, like D. H. Lawrence's, was personal and negative (if a body of fine poetry may be called negative), but Blake went beyond mere repulsion and offered a serious criticism of the science of his time.

I. A. Richards has said that "the imaginative use" of fictions "is not a way of hoodwinking ourselves. It is not a process of pretending to ourselves that things are not as they are. It is perfectly compatible with the fullest and grimmest recognition of the exact state of affairs on all occasions. It is no make-believe. But so awkwardly have our references and our attitudes become entangled that such pathetic spectacles as Mr. Yeats trying desperately to believe in fairies or Mr. Lawrence impugning the validity of solar physics, are all too common. To be forced by desire into any unwarrantable belief is a calamity. The state which ensues is often extraordinarily damaging to the mind. But this common misuse of fictions should not blind us to their immense services provided we do not take them for what they are not, degrading the chief means by which our attitudes to actual life may be adjusted into the material of a long-drawn delirium."

Blake may profitably be contrasted with Yeats and Lawrence in this matter, for he made no attempt to deny the validity of science as such, but merely insisted, although with increasing shrillness, that the facts of science existed in a very small realm within the larger realm of "eternal" truths; and his mythology, unlike theirs, encompassed scientific fact within what he regarded as the major facts. What he claimed was that the importance of scientific fact was relatively small and ultimately nil, which is a very different claim from that set forth by Lawrence. It is possible that in assailing rather than rejecting the mechanical materialism of the eighteenth century, Blake came in his poetic terms near to something like the "organic mechanism" of modern physics. That is, that he attempted to distinguish between *kinds* of matter, the living and the dead, that he was even saying that it is not matter at all which is fundamental, but energy and organism, individuality in its multitudinous differentiation.

Many ordinary men and a few poets still find an effective antidote to science in religion. Blake and Yeats, whose antidote was to be aesthetic, professed no doctrinal interest whatever in any dogma. Except for Blake's brief association with Swedenborgianism, he was allied with no sect. Likewise, although their exploration of antiscientific doctrines, ancient and modern, was unflagging, their use of these was not doctrinal either, but agential. Blake's chief source of influence lay in those quasi-mystics, modern and Protestant, who had taken over the vocabulary and the point of view of alchemy and occultism. Yeats's knowledge of speculative mysticism was both much more exhaustive and more exact than that of Blake, who with utter indiscrimination lumped Fénelon, Saint Teresa, and Madame Guyon with Whitefield, Wesley, and Hervey, the author of *Meditations among the Tombs*. Nevertheless Yeats found his chief influence not among the mystics but in the disreputable remnants of occultism in this age: theosophy and spiritualism. Yet neither poet, as far as one can tell, ever distinguished between mystics proper and those "helpless victims" of mystery whom the mystics deplore. What both needed was the metaphorical equipment by means of which to picture a universe that transcended modern mechanistic views, and conceptual sanctions for habits of mind that were opposed to the habit of positivism.

Blake, as a visionary, was constantly experiencing such a universe and such habits of mind, and his need was correspondingly less acute than Yeats's. His search for support was less systematic, and his application, even though much more extensive, predominantly verbal and symbolical. But Yeats, who in spite of his supernatural bird and his spirits was not a visionary, needed the ideas themselves, and his application was often literal, just as his faith in spiritualism, for example, seems to have been real enough. Yet when he proposed to abandon his poetry in order to devote himself solely to systematizing the wisdom of the spirits, Yeats had an explicit reply from them, who knew their own value: " 'No,' was the answer, 'we have come to give you metaphors for poetry.' " And even though, as Yeats himself sometimes felt, his poetry tends now and again to be "all metaphor," he too is explicit enough when he says of the figures in his system: "I regard them as stylistic arrangements of experience comparable to the cubes in the drawing of Wyndham Lewis and to the ovoids in the sculpture of Brancusi. They have helped me to hold in a single thought reality and justice."

It has already been suggested that when he seems most "mystical," Blake was really mistaking, as many of his critics have mistaken ever since, the embroidery on the coat for the coat itself. And if all this implies a mechanical understanding of the origins and the functions of metaphor, that is perhaps a defect in the principles on which both Blake and Yeats based their poetry, and nearly two centuries, their rhetoric. They may be contrasted in this with the English poets of the early seventeenth century and the French poets of the late nineteenth, whose conception of metaphor was truly organic. Certainly the mechanical element in the conceptions of both men is an effect of their particular historical dilemma, the necessity to articulate an adequate myth. But this dilemma makes Blake no more truly mystical than it makes Yeats. The antirationalism that their studies supported—

> I would be—for no knowledge is worth a straw—
> Ignorant and wanton as the dawn—

is a kind of aesthetic "ignorance," a freeing of the imagination from constrictive dogma and stultifying abstraction and from the narrow cell of logic, possibly comparable, but only comparable, to the mystic's "ignorance," which is a freeing of his mind and heart from natural claims. But Blake's assertion, like many in Yeats, that "the whole creation will . . . appear infinite and holy . . . by an improvement of sensual enjoyment" is naturalistic. Nor do mystics search out the curiosities of thought for metaphors and ideas; they are possessed instead by the determination to rid their minds of such ideas and finally even of such images as they already possess.

All this is not intended to identify the poetical achievement of Blake and Yeats. If Blake emerges from his spiritual researches with the more impressive content, Yeats emerges from his with a more satisfactory form. The problems of aesthetic restraint are of particular moment to poets who are intent on intellectual release; and Yeats, who was a much more self-conscious man than Blake, gave full recognition to his special disciplinary needs:

> Hands, do what you're bid:
> Bring the balloon of the mind
> That bellies and drags in the wind
> Into its narrow shed.

Blake, who did recognize the need in the practical sense, recognized it not at all in the aesthetic sense: ". . . in vain! the faster I bind, the better is the Ballast, for I, so far from being bound down, take the world with me in my flights, & often it seems lighter than a ball of wool rolled by the wind." What begins in Blake as intellectual release ends as poetical anarchy. Of Yeats—and this is his most remarkable achievement—one may claim the opposite.

Blake's independence from religious tradition, his intense refusal to submit to doctrine of any sort, should have warned us long ago of the dubious quality of his mysticism. "I must Create a System or be enslav'd by another Man's" is by no means the impulse of the mystic. Mysticism may seem to be the extreme of the Protestant impulse and the main agent of heterodoxy, yet most responsible writers on this subject agree that mysticism actually springs from and exists most comfortably within the frame of a fixed tradition. It is no paradox that a thorough skeptic, such as Hume or Gibbon, and a total mystic, such as John of the Cross, arrive at the same end in practice: a reinforcement of orthodoxy. Both are, in different ways—one by questioning the capacities of human reason, the other by questioning the value of it—"above" established institutions and thus, in the end, for them.* The mystic and the revolutionary are opposed in principle; for the revolutionary—Blake, for example—wishes to alter institutions in order to produce a better human situation; the mystic, whose interest is of another order, assumes that the human situation is good enough for what it is supposed to be. The typical attitude of the mystic is exemplified in the *Theologia Germanica:* ". . . they know very well that order and fitness are better than disorder, and therefore they choose to walk orderly, yet know at the same time that their salvation hangeth not thereon." Some mystics have been veritable Chesterfields in their abhorrence of any display of eccentricity; Gertrude More said that "singularity is a vice which Thou extremely hatest," and most mystics share this feeling.

With a few obvious and great exceptions, it can be shown that the historical function of mysticism is not the founding of religions but the renewal of dogma. The endeavor of the mystic when it is critical at all—and it need not be explicitly so—is to refresh the tradition, not to shatter it. One can use as evidence such diverse examples as the authors of the *Upanishads* and Saint Paul. William James effectively pointed out that Protestantism is without mysticism as a "methodical elevation of the soul towards God." The weakness of his definition lies in his failure to point out that while the mystical temper may remain without the "methodical elevation," mysticism itself vanishes. Orthodoxy supplies the method, and ultimately the method is the thing.

Protestantism, in spite of early efforts at closed systems, is without any complete theology, hence without a complete sense of order. Its mysticism, therefore, tends to be diffuse, without system, and even though sometimes ethically useful, fanatical. Because it has no rigid dogma, like Catholicism, or a traditional philosophical point of view, like the religions of the Orient, it can come to include a good deal more than is properly mystical. In the end it undermines itself and is not mysticism at all. It can exhaust itself in eccentricity, as many a modern sect will show.

* Voltaire, who "could not utter skeptical opinions without becoming, however unintentionally, the accomplice of the revolutionary party," seems to be an exception.—Leslie Stephen, *op. cit.*, Vol. I, p. 375.

It can develop the practical, ethical element in the fashion of the Quakers, or the political in the fashion of the "Levellers" or the "Diggers," and reduce the essential endeavor of union to mildly verbal, sporadic illumination—"inner light." Or it can elaborate enormously curious philosophical systems in the manner of Jakob Boehme or Thomas Vaughan and the other hermetics. The mood of mysticism is everywhere in the history of Protestantism, but it is nearly impossible to find a mystic.

Mystics, in the purest form, assert the validity and the accessibility of the supernatural and deny even relative validity to the natural. Plotinus declined to sit for his portrait, saying: "Is it not enough to carry about this image in which nature has enslaved us? Do you really think I must also consent to leave, as a desirable spectacle to posterity, an image of the image?" The unreality of nature is the first assumption of Oriental and Hellenistic mysticism—the fullest forms; their absolute is utterly transcendent, their effort the "passing of solitary to solitary." In Catholic mysticism, this sharp dualism begins to shade off, and transcendence, for obvious theological reasons, begins to be complemented if not profoundly qualified by immanence, a doctrine that grants some validity to nature.

The final mystical effort, as such, is still to achieve union with an uncreated absolute, even though the mystic makes characteristic returns to the world and, to some extent, to the claims of nature. But the very organization of Catholicism emphasizes the two realms by separating them, marking off some persons for the contemplative denial of the world, others for the active cultivation of it. The Catholic mystic, whether or not he happens to be a monk or a priest, inevitably groups himself with the favored few, the Marys, whose effort the Lord himself found more worthy than that of the humbler Marthas. Possibly the most moving moment in *The Divine Comedy* comes at the point where Dante, crossing this divide, must abandon the humane and civilized companionship of Virgil for that of the excellent Beatrice.

Catholic practice, with its characteristic shrewdness, has always attempted to maintain a balance between these two even while favoring one, as its dogma has attempted to maintain the balance between the doctrines of transcendence and immanence. Protestantism hoped to rescue the ethical content of Christianity from a highly rationalistic theology, to extend to all persons the privilege of that purity which shall see God, but in spite of Calvin and the Puritans, it could sustain no complete theology. Gradually, therefore, it tended to emphasize more and more the doctrine of immanence. And as the history of the sixteenth and the seventeenth centuries in Germany and England and Holland demonstrates, mysticism, while it seemed to flourish, actually began to flounder. It absorbed so much from the nonmystical realm—for instance, the doctrines and symbols of alchemy and magic *—and so little from the genuinely mystical that it presently ceased altogether. It is this development, together with that of scientific antiauthoritarianism, which finally resulted in those political revolutions on which modern culture founds itself.† Once freed from religious dogma, the least political of impulses gradually becomes the specific agent of political upheaval. In the history of these occurrences, Blake occupies not the first but the final position.

Boehme's system is a good illustration of mysticism that is well on the road to corruption and extinction. His devoted editor, William Law, reveals the defect at once in his Introduction to the works by grouping together *"magical, mystical, chemic* Philosophers," and by claiming for Boehme that "he has discovered . . . such Principles, as reach into the deepest Mysteries of Nature, and lead to the attaining of the highest powerful natural Wisdom, such as was among the Philosophers *Hermes Trismegistus, Zoroaster, Pythagoras, Plato,* and other deep Men, both ancient and modern, conversant in the Mysteries of Nature." Law's description is perfectly just. Boehme wrote:

* It is relevant to quote here a remark recently made by Horace Gregory on spiritualism, which he calls "that furthest, that last extreme of the Protestant attitude which develops from each man being his own priest and confessor to the logical conclusion . . . of being his own medium, echoing the voices of spirits from the dead."—*The Shield of Achilles,* Harcourt, Brace, 1944, p. 249.

† "In the seventeenth century any kind of political radicalism was far more likely to begin in religious non-conformity."—George H. Sabine, Introduction to *The Works of Gerrard Winstanley,* Cornell University Press, 1941, p. 11.

". . . thou rulest over all Creatures, being re-united with thine Original, in that very Ground or Source, out of which they were and are Created; and henceforth nothing on Earth *can hurt thee.* For thou art like all Things; and nothing is *unlike* thee." This is an exact statement of the hermetical ambition, the aggressive will to spiritual power.

But, declares the total mystic, "the human will is subdued . . . truly stript of itself and all things," and Boehme, in the precise degree to which he emphasizes "the highest powerful natural Wisdom" as the end, enfeebles the mystics' pretensions to seizing upon the supersensible through love alone, and for love alone. "My writing," he said in another place, "is only to the End, that Man might learn to know what he is, what he was in the Beginning"; and again, of the absolute itself, ". . . there must be a contrary will; for a transparent and quiet will is as nothing, and generateth nothing . . . for Nothing is nothing but a *stillness* without any stirring, where there is neither darkness nor light, neither life nor death." Now it is exactly a "stillness without any stirring" that the Buddhist and the neo-Platonist and some Catholics are after, the passively experienced Alone, the undifferentiated absolute, the uncreated God. But not Boehme, and not most Protestant mystics. Their search, like that of the hermetics, is predominantly in nature itself, and they have an announced interest in anatomizing man. Mystery is all around and in them, inextricable from their condition as ordinary human beings rather than remote from and above them, attainable only through renunciation of the human and the humane.

A characteristic symbol of Oriental, neo-Platonic, and Catholic mysticism is the two eyes, the eye of sense and the eye of spirit. The eye of spirit observes insofar as the eye of sense is closed.

> Be shelled, eyes, with double dark
> And find the uncreated light.

In Protestant mystics this is a less characteristic image. For "if God reveals himself to man," said Boehme, "then is he in *two* Kingdoms and seeth with *twofold Eyes.*" And this is also the point of view of Blake, whose concept of vision depends not only on the operation of two kinds of eyes but likewise on the multiple function of the real eye, on "the improvement of sensual enjoyment." The mystical impulse in Protestantism tends to destroy itself by perpetually throwing the emphasis on the immanental rather than on the transcendental, and consequently on the aesthetic rather than on the ascetic; and to express itself in terms of images rather than of ideas, of sensuous observation rather than of conceptual forms.

The seventeenth century in England is the great theater of the transformation, and when in the eighteenth William Law said that "there is nothing that is supernatural, however mysterious, in the whole system of our redemption; every part of it has its ground in the workings and powers of nature and all our redemption is only nature set right, or made to be that which it ought to be," he adequately exemplified that force which inverted the metaphysical superstructure of mysticism and turned mysticism into something else, something moral and political.* The thoroughness of the immanental here drives out the transcendental altogether. Redemption is placed entirely in nature, and regeneration is a problem in reorganization. It lays the groundwork for the even more characteristic development of later Protestantism, the shift in interest from the idea of God made man to that of man's godliness: incarnation versus deification. This is the intention of mysticism proper in the very private sense that deification is the monopoly of mystics. In Protestantism it becomes the property of all, a development that contains tremendous philosophical and political portents and portents wholly disastrous for theology. "Be frank about our heathen foe," W. H. Auden warns us today, in the mood of the new piety,

* This is the tradition in which both Blake and Yeats worked. "J.B.Y. would tell Willie that in him there was no trace of religion: 'You can only pretend it—your interest is in mundane things, and Heaven to you is this world made better, whether beyond the stars or not.' "—Joseph Hone, *W. B. Yeats,* Macmillan, 1943, p. 49. Of Blake, a Swedenborgian complained that he "naturalized the spiritual, instead of spiritualizing the natural," which may be even a step further from mysticism than that which Yeats took.—J. J. Garth Wilkinson, Preface to *Songs of Innocence and Experience,* London, 1839, p. xvi.

William Blake

For Rome will be a goner
If you soft-pedal the loud beast.

In Blake deification is a ubiquitous attitude. "All deities reside in the human breast" is a bluntly beautiful way of stating it; a more cryptic statement is this: "The desire of Man being Infinite, the possession is Infinite & himself Infinite . . . God becomes as we are, that we may be as he is." Blake's Christ is not the Word become Flesh, but the Flesh become the Word. He is not the gentle divinity of orthodoxy, but the rebel angel, identified in his most active moods with the figure of Revolution itself, which Blake called Orc, a significant anagram of the Latin word for heart. His Christ comes not to fulfill the law but explicitly to destroy it. The adjurations of the Sermon on the Mount find no support in Blake's work:

He has observ'd the Golden Rule
Till he's become the Golden Fool.

His Jesus is the symbol not of God's grace but of man's eternal gift for renewal. "The worship of God is: Honouring his gifts in other men, each according to his genius, and loving the greatest men best: those who envy or calumniate great men hate God; for there is no other God . . . if Jesus Christ is the greatest man, you ought to love him in the greatest degree." Compare this with John Tauler's remark about the Disciples, that "their Heavenly Father drew them up above all the corporeal ideas that they had of the humanity of Christ, making their minds as bare of those and all other images, as they were when first created." Or compare it with Saint Paul's, "Even though we have known Christ after the flesh, yet now we know him so no more." Or observe the exactly orthodox position as it was stated by Father Hopkins in "To What Serves Mortal Beauty?"

To man, that needs would worship block or barren stone,
Our law says: Love what are love's worthiest, were all known;
World's loveliest–men's selves. Self flashes off frame and face.
What do then? how meet beauty? Merely meet it; own,
Home at heart, heaven's sweet gift.

This is the familiar first half of the orthodox formula; the conclusion, the adjuration, contains the favored second half:

> —then leave, let that alone.
> Yea, wish that though, wish all, God's better beauty, grace.

The paradox of this dogma is given distinct poignancy, of course, by the poet's own latent conflict between a pagan homosexuality and monkish asceticism; but it is no less orthodox for that.

The balance of Catholic dogma between immanence and transcendence, deification and incarnation, which for the mystics of the Church has been so precarious and which many managed to maintain only verbally, Protestantism in its more extreme forms deliberately destroys. The mystic, shutting himself off from the creatures, finds a "better beauty" in the mere potentiality of creatures in a transcendent God with which he joins himself. The Protestant tends to say (and Blake frequently exclaims) that there is no God except in the creatures, no better beauty than men's selves. The traditional conflict between the supernatural and the natural, between God's goodness and man's necessary corruption, is transformed. It becomes the conflict between man's goodness and his needless corruption of himself. The object of religious endeavor ceases to be union with the supernatural and becomes instead a wider understanding of the natural, "a regress of visions, of the rectified mind and the freed heart." Life attains a more and more secular condition, and mysticism is superseded by politics.

III

OUR EFFORT has mainly been to distinguish mysticism from a number of "mysticisms" that had some impact on Blake. The crucial distinctions between Blake and mysticism proper are more easily made.

The mystic's assumption of the existence and the availability of supernatural reality is developed by means of a sharp tension between this reality and nature. "Love" invariably expresses itself in a double discipline, one physical, the other mental—mortification and purification, asceticism and contemplation—and the practice of the first would seem to be the essential condition to the successful practice of the second.

The mystic's curious dualism is most clearly expressed in the conclusion to the Buddhist formula of the Four Noble Truths. The way to the Escape from Sorrow is the practice of the mystical discipline, the harsh terms by which the mystic hopes to deny the authority of the creation and its fantasies, the equation of sorrow. These negative terms for denial he often states positively: the necessity to abandon the impulse to happiness. "Thy Saviour sentenc'd joy," cried Herbert. These, sorrow and joy, are the two sides of the coin that is the natural life, and the mystical act is not to erase one side of the coin, but to throw the coin away. Blake had no such intention; like the alchemists, he wished instead to improve the metal. He said that "a Man may be happy in This World," and he derided those who "say that Happiness is not Good for Mortals." Whitehead, in an eloquent comment on the influence of Platonism on Christianity, helps to define this quality in Blake: "In the hands of theologians both in the Middle Ages and in the first period of its supersession, the Platonic-Christian tradition leant heavily towards its mystical religious side. It abandoned this world to the Evil Prince thereof, and concentrated thought upon another world and a better life. Plato himself explicitly considers this solution at the end of his dialogue, the *Republic*. But he there gives it another twist to that adopted by later theologians. He conceives the perfect Republic in Heaven as an immediate present possession in the consciousness of the wise in the temporal world. Thus for Plato, at least in his mood when he concluded this dialogue, the joy of heaven is realizable on earth: the wise are happy. Theoretically, this doctrine also tinged mediaeval Christianity. But in practice there has always been the temptation to abandon the immediate experience of this world as a lost cause. The shadows pass—says mystical Religion. But they also recur, and recur—whispers the Experience of Mankind. Be tranquil, they will end—rejoins Religion. The mystical religion which most whole-heartedly adopts this attitude is Buddhism. In it despair of this world is conjoined with a program for the world's abolition by a mystic tranquillity. Christianity has wavered between Buddhistic renunciation, and its own impracticable ideals culminating in a crude Millennium within the temporal flux. The difference between the two consists in the difference between a program for reform and a program for abolition. I hazard the prophecy that that religion will conquer which can render clear to popular understanding some eternal greatness incarnate in the passage of temporal fact."

This conflict is evident in Blake, especially in his later work, as it is in the larger frame of Christianity. But in general Blake's demand was not a retreat from natural pleasures but an augmentation of them; not some premature slipping of "the coil of sense" but the "improvement of sensual enjoyment"; not that process of "hushing" which Augustine commended, "the silencing of the faculties," but the awakening and the ordering of them.

The mystic's discipline entails a striking psychological paradox, for it conjoins an apparent humility with a profoundly subtle egotism. His "soul" must be "naughted of all things," which is to say that his course is a systematic denial of his rights as a personality; but his aim is utterly concentrated on the single remnant of his personality that he spares. No humiliation of spirit or body is so bitter that he will not eagerly submit to it in struggling toward his God; yet his concern in that struggle is entirely with his own state of mind, or being. The most superficial reading of Blake thrusts on one's attention his downright admiration for honest pride and his continual abjuration of religious humility.

> Was Jesus Humble? or did he
> Give any Proofs of Humility?

"Pride may Love" was his answer to Lavater's comments on the indispensable connection between love and humility. Compare the voice of the God of Saint Catherine of Siena (". . . by humbling thyself . . . thou wilt know me") with the voice of the God of Blake:

> If thou humblest thyself, thou humblest me. . . .
> Thou art a Man, God is no more,
> Thine own Humanity learn to Adore.

The mystic makes no distinction between humility and self-humiliation; Blake makes this distinction sharply. With any form of ascetic self-humiliation he had no patience; but "True humility"—the "desire of being unnoticed, unobserved in your acts of virtue"—he respected more than most of us.

The mystic's disinclination to separate humility and self-humilation supports his brand of egotism. And here we must not only separate Blake from mystics, but Blake's poetry from religious poetry in general. Consider these lines from Traherne's little poem "Innocence":

> But that which most I Wonder at, which most
> I did esteem my Bliss, which most I Boast,
> And ever shall Enjoy, is that within
>   I felt no Stain, nor Spot of Sin.

The ubiquitous first person singular is characteristic of most devotional verse and of all mystical outpourings, but it is not characteristic of Blake, whose poetry is never concentrated in this direct fashion upon his own consciousness. Lavater wrote: "Who are the saints of humanity? those whom perpetual habits of goodness and of grandeur have made nearly unconscious that what they do is good or grand—heroes with infantine simplicity"; and Blake added, "This is heavenly." Blake's innocence is this state of un-self-consciousness, a condition in which purity and its opposite have made no impression on mind, or in which mind has transcended the impression. In the whole range of Blake's writing little is explicitly autobiographical, and none is the kind of autobiography to be found in a poet like Traherne.

Terms like "ethical strenuousness" and moral "self-scrutiny" are frequently applied to the mystical discipline, and it is true that the mystic hopes to reject "all that is ignoble and self-seeking." Yet it is also true that because his God is an unusually greedy one, demanding "infinite love and infinite grief," the mystic's effort exists at the expense of all other obligations. The improvement of one's soul under such circumstances is the ultimate and the most exclusive form of self-seeking. The problem is always the same, and is always exclusively so: "Wretched man that *I* am! who shall deliver *me* out of the body of this death?" It is not surprising that in simple and unsteady characters, or in very logical ones, this egoism frequently passes into a murderous brutality. Angela of Foligno congratulated herself on the succession of deaths in her family—mother, husband, children—because they were "a great hindrance unto me in following the way of God," and "because I had . . . prayed God that he would rid me of them, I had great consolation of their deaths." Plotinus's teachings on love of family and country are well known, and his placid acceptance of the most monstrous forms of tyranny and injustice no less so. These are hardly a portion of his inheritance from Plato. "Bad men," he said, "rule by the feebleness of the ruled; and this is just; the triumph of weaklings would not be just." To view public catastrophe as mere spectacle does not indicate a very enlightened form of moral self-scrutiny or an adequately strenuous ethics. Actually, this is the extreme moral irresponsibility of Hegel's "beautiful soul"—". . . from the moment your citizenship of the world becomes irksome you are not bound to it."

The mystic, in his combination of self-humiliation—even when this is moderate, as in Plotinus—and self-contemplation—even when this is most exalted under the term of "love"—is the type of the antihumanist. His progress consists in the systematic denial of nearly everything that makes us men, and this fact is not changed by the argument that his denial enables him to discover a more important order of experience. Such assertions we are in no position to argue; but we may insist that the order of experience that we know and respect, the mystic gladly abandons. His renunciation makes him an interesting and possibly a significant psychological and theological phenomena; but it hardly makes him an ethical agent.

Catholic theology does not try to make him one. It rests his case on the assumption that the mystic denial enriches the total spiritual community. Enthusiasts, however, insist on the mystics' ethical function. But the "returns to the world," where they work with renewed vigor and zeal and purpose, of Paul, Teresa, and the two Catherines, or even the magnificent courage of Bernard of Clairvaux, do not mean that mysticism itself is ethically purposeful. A vigorous conviction of any sort, no matter how fine or how foolhardy, tends to result in a zealous application to affairs; in this world conquerors, fanatical reformers, certain poets, and some mystics are alike. But the mystic, *as* mystic, is not concerned with the world or with returning to it. At most, the return to the world distinguishes one kind of mystical temper from another —the Oriental from the Catholic, for example; but it neither defines nor tests the quality of the mysticism of either.*

Of Blake it need only be said now that he did not deny the world either for the sake of philosophy or for his own sake. "Solomon says, 'Vanity of Vanities, all is Vanity,' & What can be Foolisher than this?" He may, in a broad sense, be regarded as a humanist. He wrote not of his condition, but generally, and often axiomatically; and the axiom represents an order of public wisdom with which the mystic may have no legitimate concern. One may, however, call Blake a humanist in a more exact sense than this—in the sense of T. E. Hulme when he opposed the humanist to the religious view. The first regards man as good and capable of progress; the second regards him as evil and capable of mere aspiration to perfection. It is unquestionable that out of the deep chaos of our time the religious view, among some of the most exquisite and discriminating minds of this and the previous generation, has come to enjoy considerable fashion, and that the humanist view, which one might better call the liberal, has in many quarters been discredited. But to predict, in the manner of Hulme, the collapse of the humanist ideal is also to predict the end of democratic society, the civilization toward which we aspire, and all the best ambitions in modern history. The fruitful course is to demand, in the manner of Reinhold Niebuhr, that liberalism be freed not only of its eco-

* "Gandhi's identification of 'soul-force' with non-egoistic motives and 'body-force' with egoistic ones, is almost completely mistaken. The type of power used by the will to effect its purposes does not determine the quality of the purpose or motive."—Reinhold Niebuhr, *The Nature and Destiny of Man: Human Destiny,* Scribner, 1943, p. 261n.

nomic abuses, but also of its intellectual abuses, those naïve expectations which history cannot fulfill. In the period of the Enlightenment, these expectations were at their most sanguine, and Blake is one of the few men of that time who at once remained within the tradition and attempted to enrich it with sobriety.

The psychological characteristics of asceticism are of more consequence to the present discussion than the actual practice of these rigors. It is a testimony either to human endurance or to human ingenuity that Catherine of Siena lived for years without any food except the consecrated host, but it is of no importance to the understanding of Blake. He loathed asceticism—

> Abstinence sows sand all over
> The ruddy limbs & flaming hair,
> But Desire Gratified
> Plants fruits of life & beauty there—

and again:

> The harvest shall flourish in wintry weather
> When two virginities meet together.

Blake never decreed an ascetic denial of nature, but usually, as in these lines, demanded a nature that had been renewed by gratified and harmonized impulse. His was the social (or poetic) intention to assimilate all the diverse materials of experience, not the religious (or philosophical) intention to suppress those which are refractory. "Chastity & Abstinence," Blake said, were the "Gods of the Heathen." Abstinence is to him the explicit denial of assimilation, of growth and of process in nature at large and, specifically, in mind and spirit: ". . . Enjoyment & not Abstinence is the food of Intellect," and "The road of excess leads to the palace of wisdom." Blake's Jesus was born of "adulterous bed" and was apparently educated in a naturalistic doctrine:

> Was Jesus Chaste? or did he
> Give any Lessons of Chastity?

The sophisticated pieties of Saint Francis, the morbid self-humiliations of Catherine of Siena or of Madame Guyon, would have revolted Blake. No less Blake, of course, with his motto, "The moment of desire! The moment of desire! . . . I cry: Love! Love! Love!" would have revolted them.

For when Blake used the word "love," he did not mean what the mystics intend by the term. To Blake, love means all the powers of human sympathy, among which the physical are not the least; to the mystic, love means the rejection of human sympathies for the sake of a complete submission of will and heart to the object of reality. The result:

> The Pilgrim with his crook & hat
> Sees your happiness compleat.

The mystic's contemplation is prayer carried to its ultimate both in devotion and in concentration, an expression of love made possible by a supreme effort of will. As mortification is a discipline that gradually dispenses with the familiar needs of the body, so contemplation is a discipline that gradually dispenses with the familiar needs of the mind: ". . . in the school of the Spirit man learns wisdom through humility, knowledge by forgetting, how to speak by silence, how to live by dying."

The effort of contemplation is that "silencing of the faculties" by which all interests but the single interest of God are removed. One may put this another way: By driving all the familiar interests from the mind, room is made for God. Contemplation, in its early form, is the attempt to pour all energies into the single act of religious meditation; in its final form, meditation itself is transcended. For as the "silencing of the faculties" continues, memory, imagination, and reason are all included. The final contemplative effort of the Catholic mystic who goes the whole way, as with mystics in earlier traditions, is to transcend the merely human proclivity of conceiving things in terms of forms, with the aid of the senses and the imagination. Contemplation at last is an effort to dispense not only with any visions that appear to some mystics in the ecstatic trance, but also with any image or idea of God in the mind itself. Saint John of the Cross, whose *Ascent of Mount Carmel* is one of the most systematic accounts of the silencing of the faculties, writes as follows: "We picture to ourselves Christ on the cross, or bound to the pillar, or God sitting on His throne in great majesty. So also we imagine glory as a most beautiful light, and represent before ourselves any other object, human or divine, of which the faculty of imagination is capable. All these imaginations and apprehensions are to be emptied out of the soul, which must remain in darkness." Words and language, image and analogy—all these vanish at last in that final condition of mystical receptivity, "the darkness of unknowing."

Sensory perceptions such as voices *heard* and visions *seen* are rudimentary manifestations in mysticism, and are among the first to be discouraged. The fact is that in some ages, as in the pre-Dionysian centuries in Catholicism, for example, visions did not accompany mysticism at all. In the later centuries, when they became commonplaces (chiefly characteristic even then of women, Dom Butler reports rather too monkishly), they were discounted almost unanimously among mystics as of no importance, and among many, indeed, as dangerous and deceptive. In the insistence that the God whom the mystic finally attains is without an image, such diverse figures as Eckhart, Teresa, Ruysbroeck, John of the Cross, and the pseudo-Dionysius agree. Visions are an accident in, not a condition of, mysticism.

But Blake, as everyone knows, insisted that vision was the central fact of his experience. The denial of vision was the denial of art, and the denial of art was the denial of Jesus. Blake's anthropomorphism would have prevented him from any abjuration of form, which he argued was the only possible mode of perception; and it is, indeed, on this tenet—the complete and precise articulation of form—that his aesthetics and his religion rest. "Man can have no idea of any thing greater than Man, as a cup cannot contain more than its capaciousness."

Other differences are perhaps less obvious. The concentration of will on a single object is the very antithesis of the poetic impulse, which is rather the diffusion of imagination over all objects. A discipline that attempts to divorce consciousness from experience, intuition from intelligence or understanding, can hardly result in poetry. Contemplation is the endeavor to depersonalize the self, to drive from being the element of "I." Poetry, like a proper politics, is the endeavor to impersonalize the self, to broaden and at the same time refine the element of "I."

As the value of vision is the central fact in Blake's religion and aesthetics, so the sanctity of personality, individuality, is the central fact of his philosophy. The mystic silences the faculties and expels personality. Blake exalts personality and demands that it reintegrate its faculties. Sometimes Blake's language seems to be identical with that of the mystics; but his meaning is usually opposite. Consider the Buddhist doctrine of self, for example: "Self is death and truth is life. The cleaving to self is a perpetual dying, while moving in the truth is partaking of Nirvana which is life everlasting." The language is similar, but the difference is radical. The Buddhist abolishes self, Blake reorganizes it. The mystical death of self is achieved when the last claim of personality has been annihilated; the annihilation of selfhood in Blake is achieved when the last claim of personality has been harmoniously fulfilled. In the Preludium to *America,* Vala, nature, is in the throes of rape, and she refers to the death of self. Like the mystic, she finds that this death brings her into a new life; but it is a life that has been achieved not because she has successfully denied her impulses, but because for the first time she has wholly recognized them.

Both terms of the mystical discipline were unknown to Blake, and he explicitly proposed opposite terms.

IV

IN THE FIRST of those stages by which the mystic proceeds he is frequently overwhelmed not by a sense of the transcendental at all, but by a new perception of nature, inhabited by God. This is characteristic of the pietistic mood, and of simple souls like Richard Rolle; it is also characteristic of a certain order of poets who take the first step on this perilous way but proceed no further: Wordsworth, Vaughan, Shelley, Whitman, possibly Blake. But as the mystic advances, this illumination gives way before a more powerful intuition. The final position is formulated as clearly as possible by the author of the *Theologia Germanica:* "For in what measure we put off the creature, in the same measure are we able to put on the Creator; neither more nor less"; and quite as firmly by Ruysbroeck: ". . . he shall with great zeal seek to rest in God, above all creatures and above all God's gifts, above all the works of virtue and above all feelings that God may infuse into soul and body." Occasionally, as with Francis of Assisi, a love of creatures seems to accompany the love of the creator with perfect ease. Yet Francis's denial of distinctions between the human and the brute condition does not improve the second, but degrades the first. It is a sophisticated form of soul "naughting," of contemplation in action.

Is is true, of course, that mysticism finds many Biblical sanctions for this choice. "The pure in heart" who "shall see God" is construed to mean the ascetic. "If any man cometh unto me, and hateth not his own father, and mother, and wife, and children, and brethren, and sisters, yea, and his own life also, he cannot be my disciple." But the Bible contains both ethical beauties and barbarisms, and the function of civilization is to rescue, in the traditions it inherits, the former from the latter. This assuredly was one of the aims that Blake in his revisions of orthodoxy set for himself. It is not the aim of the mystic, although many other precepts argue for it. The choice of Mary is more worthy than the choice of Martha, the Lord decreed. Rachel, who was barren, found favor from a lesser lord when Leah, who was fecund, did not; and Dante gives her place with Beatrice in the third circle of the Rose:

> . . . never does my sister Rachel rise
> Up from her mirror where she sits all day . . .
> Her, seeing, and me, doing satisfies.

But the Lord also decreed that we are to love God *and* our neighbor, and he prayed that his Father's "will be done *on earth* as it is in heaven." When this double obligation is separated—heaven and earth, innocence and experience, soul and body, grace and virtue, love and intellect—the conflict between the moral and the religious judgment becomes impossibly acute; action that the first finds reprehensible, the second finds heroic. The only possible resolution of the conflict lies in a crucial shift of terms: the object of devotion must be changed. This shift in terms we find in the main religious tradition of the seventeenth and eighteenth centuries, and we find it in Blake. There is a striking, if unconscious, ambiguity in the first part of this famous distich:

> Thou art a Man, God is no more,
> Thine own Humanity learn to Adore.

When man recognizes his full stature and power, God ceases to be necessary, vanishes, "is no more," It is, however, the very reverse of this that we find among mystics. Teresa is nearly unique (and adorable because of it) in arguing that to be at all certain of our love of God, we must test it by our love of his creatures. In general, mysticism achieves its total expression by a series of steps which, progressively denying this life, attains to that other.

This series, this pattern, it is impossible to find in Blake. The stages of progress, however they are numbered, represent alternations of a joyful achievement of reality and an agonized loss of it. Fundamentally, the pattern is tripodal: the first illumination, a period of purification, and final union. Miss Underhill, with the authority of many mystics, divided the way into five stages. The first of these she called Conversion, which may be gradual but is usually instantaneous, like Paul's. Purification is the attempt through the early operation of the dual discipline to maintain the first condition, and a second illumination follows. In this stage, as in the first, visions and voices are frequent, and the intuition is often of the immanental God. The doctrine of correspondence in its less systematic forms is a common method for the exposition of this perception, but exactly here, where the concept of divinity cloaked in matter is organized, the mystic most frequently feels his craving for divinity of another order. Ruysbroeck said, "Here there begins an eternal hunger, which shall never more be satisfied; it is an inward craving and hankering of the loving power and the created spirit after an uncreated Good." That "Dark Night of the Soul" which follows, the fourth stage, is the agonized attempt to silence the faculties and plunge into the darkness of unknowing. When this is achieved, the final and complete union of the mystic with his reality takes place. These five stages Mr. Damon and other writers believe they find in Blake.

The mystical progress is an increasingly rigorous system of exclusions. The mystic works from the outside to the inside. He begins in the world, has his overpowering intuition of a higher, spiritual experience, and systematically rejects the world until he has isolated spirit from it. But Blake, with poets in general, works from the inside to the outside. The first impulse is an imaginative, a private, perception of life, and in an attempt to make the first perception meaningful the poet proceeds, by diffusion rather than by system, to assimilate as much of experience, "of all worlds" as he is capable of. In "The Two Kinds of Asceticism," Yeats makes this basic psychological distinction: "The imaginative writer differs from the saint in that he identifies himself—to the neglect of his own soul, alas!—with the soul of the world, and frees himself from all that is impermanent in that soul, an ascetic not of women and wine, but of the newspapers. Those things that are permanent in the soul of the world, the great passions that trouble all and have but a brief recurring life of flower and seed in any man, are indeed renounced by the saint who seeks not an eternal art, but his own eternity." The poet's perception is tested by its ability to penetrate a various and multitudinous experience; the mystic's perception is developed only if he deserts variety and multitude and devotes his energy to a single experience. The distinction holds even if one admits the same categories, inclusion and exclusion, into poetry itself. Mr. Richards, for example, profitably contrasts "Rose Aylmer" (order through exclusion) with the "Ode to a Nightingale" (order through inclusion); and F. O. Matthiessen contrasts writers like Melville, whose view of art was of a process of assimilation, with writers like Emerson, whose view was of a process of refinement. These are important but relative differences within the framework of art itself, whereas the same differences exist radically between poetry and mysticism.

To be more concrete: The lesson of the mystic's conversion is that sense and reason had nothing to do with it, and in struggling to attain illumination again, he of course dispenses with sense and reason in order to encourage that other mode of perception which he previously enjoyed. He becomes, in all candor, an antinaturalist, an antirationalist, finally, an anti-intellectualist. Blake was neither the first nor the last of these, and even a partial reading of his work will indicate that, in any general sense, he was not the second. Reason is unquestionably the villain of his long poems, but like the villain of any melodrama, Reason, once brought to his knees, is a ready subject of reform. Blake does not object to reason, but to its authority. Like Boehme, he did not argue that reason was the agent of untruth, but rather of partial truth; both insisted on the Kantian distinction between *Vernunft* and *Verstand,* reason and understanding. When Blake seems most antirationalistic, when he says things like Emily Dickinson's

> Much madness is divinest sense
> To a discerning eye,

he is only saying that to the "sanity" of the eighteenth century a harmony of impulses would be "madness." "It is very true, what you have said for these thirty two Years. I am Mad or Else you are so; both of us cannot be in our right senses." Blake's agent of truth, his notion of intuition, is the harmony of all modes of perception. As he did not condemn the reason, as such, so he did not condemn the senses, but reason isolated and the senses closed. No mode of perception could be an exclusive agent of knowledge; and whenever any mode set itself up as such, it dislocated and disrupted and impoverished not only itself but all the other modes, and with them, the personality, and the society.

Conversion leads the mystic to a particular conclusion and method: "Unto this Darkness which is beyond Light we pray that we may come, and may attain unto vision through the loss of sight and knowledge, and that in ceasing thus to see or to know we may learn to know that which is beyond all perception and understanding (for this emptying of our faculties is true sight and knowledge)." This method, with astonishing precision, Blake exactly reversed. His method, like his argument, was based not on mystical exclusions, but on poetic assimilation.

"The Spiritual Form of Nelson Guiding Leviathan"
By courtesy of the trustees of the Tate Gallery

"What do these knaves mean by virtue? Do they mean war and its horrors, and its heroic villains?"

Evidences of conversion, or of any of the stages in the mystical progress, are absent in Blake's biography. With all intelligent men, Blake experienced dark moods of despair and loneliness; and with all men who have a constant love and a happy faith and creativity besides, he experienced long periods of singular joy. That is not to say that he knew those alternations of extreme agony and piercing joy which are the lot of the Christian mystic. Such occasional notebook jottings as "Tuesday, Janry. 20, 1807, between Two & Seven in the Evening–Despair" and "23 May, 1810, found the Word Golden" are at once too sporadic and too restrained to indicate other than normal moods.

Blake, who gave himself over to inspiration with unusual abandon, found himself frequently at the cruel mercy of this whimsical agent. When his creativity failed, he had no explanation but the loss of vision. Yet when we read in a letter to Hayley in 1804 that "Suddenly . . . I was again enlightened with the light I enjoyed in my youth, and which has for exactly twenty years been closed from me as by a door and by window-shutters," he is posturing, for those twenty years include every mature piece of work except his last two long poems; in 1784 only the *Poetical Sketches* had been completed. When a few months later Blake wrote Hayley again to say, "I have indeed fought thro' a Hell of terrors and horrors (which none could know but myself) in a divided existence; now no longer divided nor at war with myself, I shall travel on in the strength of the Lord God, as Poor Pilgrim says," one may suspect that Blake is referring, with his familiar overstatement, to the struggle against the influence of Hayley himself. The only sterile period in his life (and that by no means wholly so) was the period he spent with his patron, when, to a certain extent, he tried to make vision amenable to commerce. An artist of Blake's temperamental bias could not possibly know a more sharply "divided existence" than that.

The absence of evidence in Blake's biography for some pattern resembling the mystical progress has led critics to seek for the evidence in his work. The fallacy of making a necessary identification between periods of creative activity and periods of mystical fulfillment has been no deterrent. Yet, quite apart from the content of the work, if Blake had made more than a partial progress, he would not have produced poetry that always depended on vision and asserted with increasing fervor the reality of vision. The content of the poetry, and more particularly the fashion in which the content foliates, would seem to indicate that he hardly took even the first of those five steps which represent the mystic way. Without anticipating a full discussion of Blake's poetic development, we must examine the assertion that he took them all.

The *Poetical Sketches,* it has been said, were written in Blake's early, unilluminated condition. It can be shown that these early songs contain the seeds of both the *Songs of Innocence* and the *Songs of Experience (*which are supposed to represent the first two stages, conversion and purgation); that they reveal Blake's native sensibility, the mode of perception and statement that his later poems were to exploit more self-consciously; that they contain many of his characteristic ideas and images in an undeveloped stage; that, indeed, the later lyrics, implemented by Blake's reading and a mature experience of life, *unfold* from these poems. The characteristic fact of mystical conversion is its sharp break with previous experience, not its effort to develop the promising materials within it. Conversion is a violent displacement of experience. Consider the inarticulate instance of the *Mémoriale* of Pascal, among the most suavely articulate of men:

> *Feu.*
> *Dieu d'Abraham, Dieu d'Isaac, Dieu de Jacob,*
> *Non des philosophes et des savants.*
> *Certitude. Certitude. Sentiment. Joie. Paix.*

After such a moment, everything in the past must seem absurdly trivial.

The *Songs of Innocence* and *The Book of Thel,* which isolate and cultivate the pastoral elements in the *Poetical Sketches,* picture man and nature in a condition of pristine harmony; but they have nothing to do with sanctity or even with piety. Furthermore, on these azure horizons distant mutterings forecast a landscape less serene. The *certitude, sentiment, joie, paix,* are not without a suggestion of an alternate condition. There is evidence, in short, that while he wrote the *Songs of Innocence,* Blake contemplated the *Songs of Experience.* In his first conversion, a mystic does not show this realism.

The *Songs of Experience,* with *Tiriel,* isolate and state dramatically the humanitarian strain in the *Poetical Sketches.* These are to represent the stage of purgation. What, one asks, do they purge? "Experience" is the "World of Loneness," "the terrible desart of London," "City of Assassinations." It was a state in the world, the disruptive tyranny of eighteenth-century life: monarchy and priestcraft, education, monopolies, child labor, marriage, the industrial blight, the triumph of dogma. It was in no sense Blake's own unpurged state of sin, of sensuosity and pride. Later, in a miniature autobiography, Blake described this period as one in which "a mighty & awful change threatened the Earth" in the two revolutions. He is looking to historical events to establish a new order of life in the world. The mystic, at this point, has no interest whatever in the world; he is intent on getting the evil out of himself.

The Marriage of Heaven and Hell is taken as the signal of Blake's second illumination, and the Prophetic Books written at Lambeth in the next two years as the gradual waning of the light. But to separate the work between 1788 and 1793 from *The Marriage,* and all this from the Lambeth books, is to defeat Blake's aim. *The Marriage* is not only the synthesis of those two contrary states, innocence and experience, but it is also and quite as importantly the clue to the meaning of the series of poems that follow immediately upon it, poems in which Blake's mythology finds its formulation. To decline the dialectical view for the mystical here is to ignore Blake's essential purpose.

Sometimes Blake is so firm about his purpose that the reader is unable to ignore it. One of his most obscure short poems, "The Mental Traveller," which has been the subject of more than the usual variety of interpretation, has sometimes been taken as a brief and explicit representation of the mystic's five steps. At no point in Blake is it more difficult to sustain this view of him. To take it here is to make the mystic way a dialectical process, with cyclic alternations of thesis and antithesis, of stagnation and renewal, disorder and order, regression and regeneration. This is a simultaneous distortion both of mysticism and of Blake. For the way of mysticism (and of sanctity in general) is a straight road, the determined concentration on a single experience and on a single end; but, said Blake, "the crooked roads without Improvement are roads of Genius." No text, as John of the Cross was well aware, more aptly characterizes the mystic way than Matthew 7:14–"For narrow is the gate, and straitened the way, that leadeth unto life, and few are they that find it." Blake's crooked road, which prefigures Yeats's "path of the serpent," proposes not concentrated singleness, but diffused multiplicity. In general terms, it rejects theses of education and taste and approves the conception of original genius; and it rejects a strictly organized or a narrowly exclusive view of experience by committing poetry to a broad comprehension of it. In the most particular terms, it suggests the dialectical method that Blake's poetry espouses. Its ethical counterpart is contained in such a remark as "Damn braces. Bless relaxes," which reinforces at every point the distinction between Blake's way and the way of the mystic. "There is an old saying that God is a circle whose centre is every where. If that is true, the saint goes to the centre, the poet and artist to the ring where everything comes round again."

The interpretation of Blake as a mystic, especially in these poems written between 1788 and 1795, encounters another difficulty. For these poems have a concrete historical reference, and their argument is that every condition of life, like every man, is capable of a fruitful ordering of itself. To argue that this ordering is the mystical act is to subject history to an impossible interpretation, and is, further, to make every man in some sense a traveler on the mystic way. This is not the point of view of mysticism, which is without such ambitions.

The Lambeth books are Blake's first complete attempt to state, by means of an explicit myth, the simultaneity of cosmic, historical, and psychological events. Here as elsewhere in Blake, the psychological level is the core of meaning, the real "content." The historical level is the objective externalization of the first; and the cosmic is the metaphorical enlargement of both. What has been described as the "increasing pessimism" of these books and taken to mean Blake's gradual descent into the fourth of the mystical stages, the Dark Night of the Soul, is rather Blake's increasing emphasis on the psychological content and decreasing emphasis on the historical. But in Blake, since history and mind are always conjoined, it *is* a difference in emphasis, not in value. Blake's problem remains, and the mythical rather than the mystical method makes possible not their separation but their synthesis.

The Dark Night of the Soul, it is argued, shuts down completely during the so-called unproductive years between 1796 and 1804. Why these years are called unproductive it is hard to understand. For immediately upon the completion of the last of the Lambeth books, Blake set himself to work on his second longest poem, which, in a single frame, was to formulate everything he had said before in a series of different kinds of poems, long and short. Most of *The Four Zoas* was completed before he took up his residence with Hayley; during the three years at Felpham, under the burden of the hack employment afforded by his patron, he was apparently unable to complete it. The period unquestionably was the most miserable in his life; however, it was not the unregenerate state of his own soul that troubled him or kept him from the work he preferred. Immediately upon his release from Hayley's harrowing patronage, he wrote the last books of *The Four Zoas;* but this project had, after eight years, gone stale for him, and a number of exciting experiences and perceptions from the nearer Felpham years were demanding expression. Without completing his final revisions of *The Four Zoas,* therefore, Blake turned his attention to *Milton.* This poem is taken to signalize his achievement of the state of mystical union, and the remainder of his work—*Jerusalem,* and the illustrations to the Book of Job and Dante—his retention of it.

V

Union is the mystical goal, the last stage of the way, and it is also the final item in any definition of mysticism. Now at last the mystic and his object merge. The degrees of mergence that characterize the several traditions of mysticism need not detain us. Blake had no interest whatever in fusing his personality with a larger being, much less in losing it for the sake of knowing an uncreated absolute. His conception of the spiritual life, like all his conceptions, was active—"intellectual War," that "War & Hunting" which is the sport of gods, the conflict of ideas, the eternal dialectic of things.

This would have made repellent to him any conception of a passive samadhi or dhyana, or of the Plotinian rest in the super-essential solitary, or of the union of the Western mystic, which is also a state of "quiet." The condition is the same, whether with Richard of Saint-Victor we say of it that the mind is "ravished above itself," or with John of the Cross that, through the "holy oblivion" of the final night, the soul is completely transformed and "seems to be God Himself . . . and indeed is God by participation," or with a simpleton like Mechthild of Hackeborn, that the soul "swims in the Godhead like a fish in water"! All these represent conditions of metaphysical peace; but as Blake's spiritual life is philosophically active, so it is imaginatively active. When the mystic attains union at last, imaginative activity, like intellectual activity, like sensuous and volitional activity, has ceased. When Blake attains what has been called his "union" (his most violent state of vision), all these are most fiercely active. They are, indeed, so active, so fierce, that the poetry in which he attempts to embody them very frequently disrupts, explodes brilliantly, only to belabor the head of the reader with a heavy shower of fascinating if highly irregular fragments.

Both the mystic and Blake, it is true, strive to attain a condition of unity, of order; but again, order is of two kinds, exclusive and inclusive. The exclusive order of the mystic is exemplified by the Buddhist text: Sorrow, the Cause of Sorrow, the Escape from Sorrow. But the reason that the myth of "the fall" is so useful to and so ubiquitous in Blake is that he aimed at an inclusive order, which may be formulated in opposite terms as harmony, the loss of harmony, and the reachievement of harmony. Beside Lavater's remark, "Sin and destruction of order are the same," Blake wrote, "A golden sentence," and all his variation on the Miltonic theme was to dramatize this text.

Here are all the conflicting materials of life—how bring them to love each other? Blake's answer to this question is the very opposite to Saint John's of the mystical act of reciprocity in divine love. This state of co-operative union is brought about only by a process of isolation; but in Blake it is exactly isolation of any of the human materials that makes a co-operative unity impossible. Of reason he wrote in one of the Prophetic Books:

> . . . Urizen laid in a stony sleep,
> Unorganiz'd. rent from Eternity.
> The Eternals said: "What is this? Death.
> Urizen is a clod of clay."

Separated from the organic functioning of the whole of being, reason (or any other faculty) degrades itself and can only create (that is, perceive) a degraded universe, the miserable universe, for example, of eighteenth-century science, which is the work of Urizen. Blake conceived the problem as one of organization rather than isolation. "Unorganiz'd Innocence: An Impossibility." Therefore his poems are not visions of some transcendent harmony, of mystical union; they are mythological statements of an utterly different vision: the widening (after the narrowing) of human perceptions; the improvement (after the declension) of "sensuous enjoyment"; the achievement (after the destruction) of psychological and social order. Mystical union can come about only after it declares that none of these is worth having. Blake's vision can flourish only after these are achieved.

All mystics and all writers about mysticism seem to agree on the fundamental qualities of the unitive state. It is noetic, and it is ineffable. Of this we have already said, indirectly at any rate, a good deal. Mysticism in its highest moments is without images or symbols, is entirely nonsensory, just as it is without ideas that relate to nature. Any real system of correspondence, such as Swedenborg's, for example, is wholly unsatisfactory to the mystic; for this system declares the reality of symbols, hence of natural things, and such a system degrades the absolute of mysticism by thrusting it into the foolish role of the main actor in a universe conceived as a vast charade. In talking about his experience, the mystic is naturally compelled to use language and analogy; but unlike Swedenborg, he always insists that both are inadequate to his purposes, that they cannot express what he knows.

This is that tormenting paradox of noesis and ineffability which makes most mystical documents, with the exasperating refrain of "Not that! Not that!" so unreadable. This paradox also draws the line between genuine mystics and those creators of sectarian theologies and curious systems who are sometimes taken to be mystics. Whatever other privileges the mystic may be granted, the gift of tongues is not among them, and although his solitary flight often cuts through the overgrowth of ritual and of dogma, he is usually content to let his knowledge adjust itself to the dogma he knew before. He can tell us that he has crossed the borders of natural experience, but he cannot tell us what he learned there. It is possible that his knowledge consists of this affirmation alone, that natural borders are not final, and that the favors he has been granted are contained in an invigorated faith that fits him for apostolicity.

Blake, clearly, had no conception whatever of ineffable experiences, and no struggle whatever to express the experiences he had. Metaphor he found perfectly congenial to his purposes, and language perfectly amenable to vision:

> I write in South Molton Street what I both see and hear
> In regions of Humanity, in London's opening streets.

It is, in fact, language itself that gives form to human experience, which rescues it from primordial chaos and from the brute creation:

> I call them by their English names: English, the rough basement.
> Los built the stubborn structure of the Language, acting against
> Albion's melancholy, who must else have been a Dumb despair.

Here again Blake anticipates modern philosophy. "In language," Suzanne Langer writes, "we have the free, accomplished use of symbolism, the record of articulate conceptual thinking; without language there seems to be nothing like explicit thinking whatever." And this is only one of the many ways in which Blake anticipates Shelley, who wrote:

> Language is a perpetual Orphic song,
> Which rules with Daedal harmony a throng
> Of thoughts and forms, which else senseless and shapeless were.

The reiterated text of Blake's aesthetic doctrine is that articulateness is all. That which is without form is nothing. He could not have calculated a more antimystical theme.

The difficulty into which some of Blake's critics have fallen at this point is that they have failed to distinguish between the mystic and the gnostic. The mystic, however ineffectively, struggles to communicate his experience, and by his own admission fails. The gnostic, who conceives of his experience as occult, attempts to obscure it, and only the determined can discover it. A vast difference exists between the situation of Saint Paul, for example, who "was caught up into paradise and heard unspeakable words," and the decision of Blake, about whom his friend Linnell said, "to many he spoke so that 'hearing they might *not* hear.' " The mystic is unable to reveal his experience; the gnostic is unwilling.

Blake, partly because when he spoke clearly the world would not listen, assumed the gnostic mask and spoke obscurely. As his work approaches its end, his obscurity increases not at all because he is becoming more mystical, but because he is becoming more perverse. Blake's failure to find an audience had at least two enormously important results. First, he tended to throw his emphasis more and more on "other-world" concerns, to relinquish this world and its affairs, to choose "spiritual bread" because real bread was lacking. Second, he was driven further and further into his myth, impelled to accept as the content what had at first been merely the frame, "the Persons & Machinery," to despise more and more mere communication, since in the absence of real communicants he could address himself only to "spiritual" communicants. This development is best exemplified in some of his late illustrations to the poems, where he deliberately indulges in "mirror" engraving, as if there were some advantage to his meaning in making the reader puzzle out these aphorisms, the letters of which have been turned round. This, no doubt, is a serious lapse in Blake's judgment, for it is a rather childish effort to rationalize and make willful an obscurity that often enough was essential to his mode of perception and which he believed he had no way of controlling. When he mixes obscurity with obfuscation, he comes near to discrediting his visions, and to the unsympathetic, he lays his entire work open to the charge of deliberate mystification.

But mysticism, in spite of our current loose use of the term, has nothing to do with mystification.

VI

THE FIRST of the philosophical characteristics of mysticism is epistemological. The basic philosophical assumption of total mysticism is that through the suspension of all familiar modes of cognition, the mystic is able to identify himself completely with the object of knowledge; that knowledge is most complete when the distinction between knower and known is obliterated, a phenomenon that may be achieved when the knower gives complete place to the known. But in Blake the "known" is no more than the sum of our capacities for knowing, and the more harmonious our capacities, the more whole and complete is the known. "As the Eye, Such the Object," and "they became what they beheld" are two ways of stating this view. This is a subjectivism no less complete than the mystic's, but it is attained by an exactly opposite method. The mystic demands an emptying of self to receive his knowledge, Blake, fulfillment of self. And yet in Blake this is not merely subjectivism. It is also a means of allowing for new experience, for renewal and process, for new adjustments of old elements within the familiar framework of experience. On this view Blake insisted no less than on the other: "What is now proved was once only imagin'd" and "Reason, or the ratio of all we have already known, is not the same that it shall be when we know more." These are only ways of saying, with Whitehead, for example, that "A self-satisfied rationalism is in effect a form of anti-rationalism. It means an arbitrary halt at a particular set of abstractions." It was Blake's very faith in the capacities of the human mind that made him reject the view of mind (and its products) that the eighteenth century clung to—"I always thought that the Human Mind was the most Prolific of All Things & Inexhaustible." Blake's opposition to skepticism is no more thorough than his opposition to mysticism.

The second of the philosophical characteristics of mysticism is the dualism by which it operates. This begins as the familiar dualism of all religion and of most philosophy: the natural order, which is available to reason and to sense, and a supernatural order, which is available to spirit. Its ethical counterpart is the conflict between body and soul. The mystical progress is incapable of beginning without an explicit avowal of this dichotomy, but the mystical impulse differs from the normal religious impulse in that from the first it makes the separation more sharply and feels about it more intensely, and then devotes itself exclusively to the second term.

The problem of duality in Blake is a pitfall. There are certainly many places in his poems that seem to assert, with all the fervor of the mystics, the reality of the supernatural order and the unreality of the natural. But he was not called an "interior naturalist" without reason, and there are many more places where the two are not separated at all, but are made either identical or contiguous. This is that basic conflict in Blake's personality represented by the two orders of his vision, and it must not be minimized. Nevertheless, in spite of the apparent resemblance of the first of these attitudes to the mystical dualism, there is still a profound difference—that in Blake one cannot discover the ethical concomitants. Even when he separates reality into a lower and a higher order, he does not permit the separation of the human faculties into corresponding categories. "Be assured, My dear Friend," he said, "that there is not one touch in those Drawings & Pictures but what came from *my Head & my Heart in Unison.*" The means, which would interest a modern psychologist, is the opposite of repression or purgation. Blake made even his "spectrous fiends" work for him. "I was a slave bound in a mill among beasts and devils; these beasts and these devils are now, together with myself, become children of light and liberty, and my feet and my wife's feet are free from fetters . . . he is become my servant who domineered over me, he is even as a brother who was my enemy."

The struggle between spiritual and sensual impulses, as between the rational and the imaginative faculties, is the way to lose truth, not the way to find it; for "Man has no Body distinct from his Soul . . . that call'd Body is a portion of Soul discern'd by the five Senses, the chief inlets of Soul in this age"; and if these "were cleansed every thing would appear to man as it is, infinite."

In this way, the two views of reality are constantly colliding and coalescing, for it is metaphysically impossible to maintain a dichotomy in the universe if one is unwilling to maintain it in the individual. The dilemma is capable of resolution only if one is able to modify the degree of duality and establish a dialectical view. This Blake attempted, and in doing so he broke away decisively from the point of view of mysticism.

The third of the philosophical qualities of mysticism is its optimism. The mystic, as Charles Bennett claimed, believes that he has discovered the best and that he is capable of attaining it. In his resolution to attain it he confidently opposes himself to the worst elements in human experience. It is, in fact, precisely his struggle with the worst that enables him to attain the best; for mortification is the means: ". . . men may," wrote Meredith, "by power of grip squeeze raptures out of pain."

Nevertheless, the mystic's struggle cannot be formulated in the terms of good and evil that are the privilege of a more restrained religious impulse. The mystic's intention is private, and in the curious sense that he not only sets his goal for himself alone, but also himself induces his suffering. "Essential oils," said Emily Dickinson,

> . . . are wrung;
> The attar from the rose
> Is not expressed by suns alone,
> It is the gift of screws.

And Dostoevsky, "I feel certain that man never wholly rejects adversity (in the sense of chaos and disruption of his schemes); for adversity is the mainspring of self-realization." Precisely—adversity, the genuine suffering. Good and evil, to mean anything, must represent the terrors and the triumphs that the human will endures and attains in the normal texture of life; not the degradation of flesh and mind that the mystic creates in order that he may have something to triumph over. This is not to deny the remarkable effort of will that mysticism dramatizes, nor the ecstatic faith which is the reward of its expedition. Yet the optimism of the mystic, like all his qualities, is of a very special, a quite narrow, variety. He assures us that the human spirit is capable of tremendous suffering in its progress toward a tremendous good; but he conducts his experiment under laboratory conditions from which all the situations that ordinarily baffle the human spirit, abundant enough in a sublunary realm, have been removed. "The lie," as Emerson said brilliantly of Jones Very's piety, "the lie is in the detachment."

The optimism of Blake, as should be clear, is again of a totally different order. His recognition of evil is general, not particular, and his program is general. He sees a universal want of harmony, but he believes in the possibility of universal order. His method is not by purgation, but by affirmation, which means that order is not achieved by denying elements in human nature, but by asserting their totality and its integrity. He opposed both the conservative and the revolutionary branches of philosophical optimism in his time by arguing that the eighteenth century was the worst of all possible worlds, and that it would not be improved in the least by continuing the claim of authority for a single human faculty, the reason. And he opposed the extreme religious optimism of the mystic by showing in his poems that the claim of authority for any other single human faculty, even the spirit, had results no less disastrous. Blake admitted only one authority, the authority of the whole man. The paradox, as in political theory later, is that when man integrates himself and works as a whole, authority vanishes; ". . . henceforth," said Blake in the tones of that extreme Protestantism which slides into explicit political avowals, "henceforth every man may converse with God & be a King & Priest in his own house." To say that he believed such a condition possible indicates the breadth of his optimism. It was not without its depth as well.

The final philosophical distinction of mysticism is its special understanding of the dualism that is its essential condition. The mystic creates his dualism in order that he may disregard one of its terms and devote himself to the other, which is a way of mitigating it. Furthermore, as Paul Elmer More pointed out, in its extreme forms mysticism tends to absolve its dualism altogether by making, finally, no distinction between knower and known, between the depersonalized agent and the undifferentiated object. The ethical implications of these two pursuits have already been touched upon. The mystic creates a conflict between the world and himself in order that he may abolish the world; and it is just that we remind ourselves again of a more fruitful ethical dualism that enjoins us to respect both terms and the claims of each. It is this element in Platonic thought which keeps it firmly on this side of mysticism; and when neo-Platonism slips into mysticism, it does so by closing its ears to what is perhaps the master's most august charge. Blake made a not dissimilar charge: ". . . it is a part of our duty to God & man to take due care of his Gifts; & tho' we ought not [to] think *more* highly of ourselves, yet we ought to think *As* highly of ourselves as immortals ought to think."

Yet his dualism differs from both these. He does not admit, most of the time, a radical dualism at all, but rather contrary conditions of energy. Evil is not the opposite of good, but misdirected energy; the supernatural is not the opposite of the natural, but both misunderstood; body is not the opposite of soul, but as much of soul as a half-closed eye can see. There is a dichotomy here, of course, but so adjusted that it is constantly capable of being transcended. This process is the dialectic in terms of which Blake conceives life: "Without Contraries is no progression."

CHAPTER FOUR

The Source and Use of Metaphor

I

THAT POETRY is inadequate to the full mystical experience, and that the mystical experience is inadequate to a full poetry, are perhaps obvious propositions. Expression is at best an unsatisfactory by-product of mysticism, but poetry is expression itself. Poetical insights may be about some phase of mysticism, as they may be about anything else; however, they are not, in any final sense, mystical, but poetical, and to confuse the two is to misunderstand both. Persons who are enthusiastic about mysticism rather than persons who are more than merely enthusiastic about poetry tend to identify the two. Miss Underhill's definition of art as "the link between appearance and reality" not only implies that poets are unsuccessful mystics but also imposes upon poetry an unsupportably narrow construction. Henri Bremond, admitting that the poet cannot at the same time be a mystic, yet asserted that he is a *mystique manqué*. Both base their remarks on a nineteenth-century conception of poetry that is not broad enough to explain the poetry of the nineteenth century, let alone the poetry of other times and moods.

Other times have given a no less official consent to similar definitions of poetry, but in the nineteenth century a more thorough coalescence of this theory, in a watered condition, and of the actual moods of poetry took place than in any previous time. Yet even then, in spite of the prevailing transcendentalism, the notion that poetry is dedicated exclusively to ends known as "Spirit" and "Beauty" by no means expelled a sound secularity in much practice. There is more than one Wordsworth, more than one Tennyson. And with Wordsworth comes Byron, with Shelley, Keats. If we have Tennyson, we also have Arnold and Landor; if the early Yeats, also the later, and all of Hardy. To insist that the purpose of poetry is to discover transcendental truths is to ignore whole periods and most of the great human moments in literature, including necessarily nearly all poetic drama. It is to prefer the "Hymn to Intellectual Beauty" to the "Ode to Autumn," Tennyson's "Higher Pantheism" to his "Tithonus." It is to say that Richard Rolle is a truer poet than Geoffrey Chaucer; that Traherne's thin pipings of purity are more "poetical" than Donne's robust struggles with his God; that Dryden and Pope are not poets at all. It is a view of poetry that had a serious vogue in the last century, and which endures even now.

The confusion of the poet's perception of the "reality" of universal human experience with his occasional interest in transcendental "reality" is of some importance. Instead of saying that religion is one of the many functions of human experience on which poetry may draw, it says that the poetic function is religious. And if mysticism is taken to be the highest expression of the religious impulse, and connections are made between mysticism and poetry, the confusion becomes impossible. For then it is suggested that language and image, which are shackles to the mystic, are also shackles to the poet; and this is not true of poets who are writing about mysticism, or even of poets who, in nonpoetical moods, are mystics.

It is folly to designate as mystical a poem like *The Divine Comedy,* which employs as its framework a mystical theology; or to think of Dante, who at the end of the *Paradiso* said that his "wings were not for such a flight," as a mystic because his poetry talks about mysticism. And even when a mystic writes poetry, he is employing other faculties as a poet from those which he employs as a mystic. As a mystic, he must allow will to supersede, indeed to extirpate, imagination; as a poet, he must come down from his heights and cultivate imagination again. The lyrics of Saint John of the Cross are interesting as poems not because they describe the state of mystical union, which they do not, but because they attempt to describe it in excited language and in images that, like those of much other poetry, are erotic:

> Upon my flowery heart,
> Wholly for him, and save himself for none,
> There did I give sweet rest
> To my beloved one;
> The fanning of the cedars breathed thereon.

One might even say that the merit of these poems exists in their paradoxical application of sexual passion to piety. The function of paradox is to conjoin contradictory terms and in doing so to enrich the content of each; and in these lyrics, piety is given body and passion, sanctity. It is the peculiar merit and hazard of poetry that its tools (all the resources of rhetoric) constantly force it beyond its intention. A metaphor is employed to illuminate one poetic object by substituting another, but the effect is frequently to illuminate both, or to broaden the realm of the first by bringing it into the realm of the second, where, in a more exact discourse, it has no right to be. Poetry has been defined in part as the constant manipulation of such perspectives.

Thus poetry that is concerned with mysticism does not present us with the mystical experience as it is—and, by the character of that particular experience, could not attempt to—but is constantly rebodying it and bringing it back into the realms of nature. In the truly mystical fashion Richard Crashaw prayed, "Leave nothing of my Self in me." Yet he presents us with an experience that, to contemporary taste at least, is *too* lavish in its dependence on the red and blue and gold magnificence of Counter-Reformation ritual, too feverishly erotic in its address to the Virgin and Teresa. Consider that later poet, Francis Thompson, the defect of whose poem "The Hound of Heaven" is again the hysterical riotousness of his imagery, so that the experience which his poem is intended to present is utterly debased. It is to be expected of poets who have made commitments to mysticism that, having repudiated imagery in their first function, they are unable to control it in their second.

Inversely, having put an excessive value on vision as a man, Blake is finally dominated, perhaps defeated, by imagery as a poet.

An emotional quality more nearly descriptive of the mystical experience than that of Thompson's poem is to be found in George Herbert. Yet a poem like "The Collar," for example, deals with the conflict between the world and God that characterizes a normal religious impulse and an early stage rather than the goal of mysticism. Other poems by Herbert do not attempt to go even as far as this in the direction of mysticism. "The Pulley," for example, is a dramatic statement of the psychological basis of mysticism ("weariness"), but no more. In Donne it is exactly the rich secularity that makes his devotional verse the most vigorous in our language. In Vaughan, it is the enrichment of our experience of the natural universe above which mysticism itself arises early. The thin quality of Traherne's verse, in contradistinction to that of these others, results from the fact that his poetry, unlike theirs, is relatively free of secular associations. Poetry about mysticism, like poetry about anything else, depends for its vigor on the breadth of experience with which it can, through its play of image, associate itself. But the broader these associations, the farther it removes itself from mysticism, or from a statement descriptive of mysticism. It cannot be argued that no poet has been a *mystique manqué;* but no poet writes in the capacity of a mystic.

The mystic's thorough intoxication with God is of no great use to art. Yet Blake himself used almost exactly this figure: "I am really drunk with intellectual vision." Nor would one wish to exempt him from the charge of self-indulgence of his own sort. The difference is that Blake's drunkenness apparently represents the inability to resist a delirium of symbols, which is not the mystical intoxication; and this difference is the crucial fact in distinguishing Blake's poetry from other religious poetry.

It is difficult to think of any religious poet with whom Blake can be profitably compared. On the one hand, he lacks the Dantesque and the Miltonic objectivity, and the systematic long forms into which their objective devotion to remote religious ends molds itself. On the other hand, he is without that homeliness, the casual intimacy that a more subjective devotion affords, and which finds its characteristic expression in the lyric. One cannot find in Blake any tone resembling the typical religious note of poets like Rilke (*"Du, nachbahr Gott"*) or Hopkins ("He of all can handle a rope best") or Vaughan ("Sometimes I sit with thee, and tarry") or Herbert ("Having been tenant long to a rich Lord"); nothing like the audacity of Emily Dickinson's "And the astonished Wrestler Found he had worsted God"; nothing resembling the pious note of Traherne, and nothing resembling the note of alternate anger and abjectness that is characteristic of Donne. This is to say that Blake had neither that intellectual religious passion which systematic theological conviction brings into poetry, nor that intensely personal passion which is the contribution of the pietistic and the mystical moods.*

Blake is a religious poet in the quantity rather than in the quality of his aspiration, a religious poet who is without either a theology or a proper God; for the first he substituted a mythology, for the second, the image of Man. In Dante and Milton an established mythology is the means of stating the theology poetically, that is, dramatically, concretely. In Blake, an invented mythology is the means of abstracting and *then,* if possible, of dramatizing the problems, the "eternal principles or characters of human life." Dante and Milton supported the abstractions of philosophy by giving them concrete expression in their poetry. Blake employed abstractions in his poetry in order to overcome them in his philosophy.

Blake's "intellectual vision" is not to be understood either as direct communication with God as this is represented in devotional lyrics, or as the allegorical perceptions of Milton and Dante. Blake's vision is the perception of symbols for his myth, and the poems that were based on this perception he was careful to distinguish from allegory by the clumsy expression "Allegory

* Ralph Bates has suggested Southwell's "Burning Babe" as an exception. The stark hallucinatory quality of the first stanza is quite Blakean, but I do not think that the metaphysical paradox and the pietistic conclusion of the second stanza are. The opening lines of "A Prophecy" in *Europe* are of course reminiscent of Milton's "Nativity Ode," which they deliberately imitate, but Blake is unable or unwilling to sustain the imitation beyond three lines.

addressed to the Intellectual powers." The visionary poet is the man who by the breadth and penetration of his perceptions, his "Copiousness of glance," discovers the materials which compose these allegories "addressed to the Intellectual powers." Blake defended his view of original genius so fervently for precisely this reason. The original genius is the visionary who, unhampered by education and tradition and taste, retains the prophetic or mythmaking faculty, which discovers the "eternal attributes or characters of human life," and which does not restrict itself to the mere recalling and rearranging of experience limited to nature at a given time and place, much less to the mere description of social convention.

Eve, in the playlet *The Ghost of Abel,* asks:

> . . . were it not better to believe Vision
> With all our might & strength, tho' we are fallen & lost?

When human life is most degraded, human faculties most inharmonious, human sight most dim, exactly then we must cling to vision, by which we perceive (and therefore attain once more) harmony and the qualities that pertain to it.

II

THESE QUALITIES, which are ideal, can be expressed only in mythical terms, and these are the terms on which Blake attempted to construct his art and by which he understood the art of other men. He describes his pictures of Nelson and Pitt as "compositions of a mythological cast," whereby English heroes are presented not in their historical guise, but in their ideal grandeur or essential depravity—"spiritual forms" involved with "spiritual" forces—Leviathan and Behemoth. These works, Blake said, were imitations of "wonderful originals seen in my visions . . . some of them one hundred feet in height . . . all containing mythological and recondite meaning, where more is meant than meets the eye." "The Vision of the Last Judgment" he described in much the same way: "My Picture is a History of Art

& Science, the Foundation of Society, Which is Humanity itself." Blake's rejoinder to protests that spirits and spiritual forms could not be properly represented with the degree of articulation that was his habit, indicates how literally he conceived himself to be developing a mythology: ". . . the Venus, the Minerva, the Jupiter, the Apollo, which they [connoisseurs and artists] admire in Greek statues, are all of them representations of spiritual existences, of Gods immortal . . . and yet they are embodied and organized in solid marble. . . . The Prophets describe what they saw in Vision as real and existing men . . . the Apostles the same; the clearer the organ the more distinct the object. A Spirit and a Vision are not, as the modern philosophy supposes, a cloudy vapour, or a nothing." And then the magnificently equivocal statement: "Spirits are organized men."

Vision is not a delusive power to observe phantasms, but the ability to visualize psychological facts. These facts Blake called "states," the multiple conditions of mind to which human life is immemorially susceptible: "these States Exist now. Man Passes on, but States remain for Ever; he passes thro' them like a traveller who may as well suppose that the places he has passed thro' exist no more, as a Man may suppose that the States he has pass'd thro' Exist no more. Every thing is Eternal." The difference between myth and allegory is that myth is a direct representation of experience, allegory an abstraction from it, and that myth observes things in their vital shapes, allegory in their diagrammatic and their dogmatic guises. "Fable or Allegory are a totally distinct & inferior kind of Poetry. Vision or Imagination is a Representation of what Eternally Exists, Really & Unchangeably. Fable or Allegory is Form'd by the daughters of Memory. . . . Note here that Fable or Allegory is seldom without some Vision. Pilgrim's Progress is full of it . . . the Greek Fables originated in Spiritual Mystery & Real Visions, which are lost & clouded in Fable & Allegory, while the Hebrew Bible & the Greek Gospel are Genuine." Blake seems to mean that allegory is a late development in which the mercurial truth of myth has been fixed, externalized, and dogmatized, and to that extent, falsified. The poetic perceptions that suit the conditions of all life are channeled into moral and religious perceptions that suit only separate sections of life ". . . a system was formed, which some took advantage of, & enslav'd the vulgar by attempting to . . . abstract the mental deities from their objects: thus began Priesthood; Choosing forms of worship from poetic tales." Psychological facts are forced into theological beds; myth constricts into dogma.

This process Blake described in his own myth of "the Antediluvians who are our Energies." "The Giants who formed this world into its sensual existence, and now seem to live in it in chains, are in truth the causes of its life & the sources of all activity; but the chains are the cunning of weak and tame minds which have power to resist energy; according to the proverb, the weak in courage is strong in cunning." This passage, one of the most central in Blake's text, explains his need of a mythology and offers the clue to the mythology he constructed; for he needed myth to state in adequately inclusive terms the dilemma of man's energies enchained, and he developed a myth that dramatized the means by which those energies may be freed.

Since the antediluvian energies, even in their weakened condition, are the bases of our "life & the sources of all activity," Blake, by a slight twist in his logic, could view all recorded history and literature as mythical in essence, and all true poetry as visionary. In Blake's interpretation, Chaucer, least visionary of poets—and, curiously, he said more in print about Chaucer than about any other poet—is as visionary as any, and performs with the best of the others the function of mythology: ". . . Chaucer makes every one of his characters perfect in his kind; every one is an Antique Statue; the image of a class, and not of an imperfect individual." Blake, who is conventionally considered to be the complete rebel against neoclassicism, comes close here to expressing the traditional view of decorum and imitation in the mythological construction he is trying to make. "The Franklin is one who keeps open table, who is the genius of eating and drinking, the Bacchus; as the Doctor of Physic is the Esculapius, the Host is the Silenus, the Squire is the Apollo, the Miller is the Hercules, &c. Chaucer's characters are a description of the eternal Principles that exist in all ages."

Because the import of history, like that of literature, is

mythological, Blake found it necessary to quarrel with historians in the eighteenth century. "The reasoning historian, turner and twister of causes and consequences, such as Hume, Gibbon, and Voltaire, cannot with all their artifice turn or twist one fact or disarrange self evident action and reality. Reasons and opinions concerning acts are not history. Acts themselves alone are history, and these are neither the exclusive property of Hume, Gibbon, nor Voltaire. . . . Tell me the Acts, O historian, and leave me to reason upon them as I please; away with your reasoning and your rubbish! All that is not action is not worth reading. Tell me the What; I do not want you to tell me the Why, and the How; I can find that out myself, as well as you can, and I will not be fooled by you into opinions, that you please to impose, to disbelieve what you think improbable or impossible. His opinions, who does not see spiritual agency, is not worth any man's reading; he who rejects a fact because it is improbable, must reject all History and retain doubts only." The last sentence explains Blake's ire. He demands the freedom to interpret history mythologically.

This he did, and from the point of view of the "reasoning historian" his effort was fantastic. An admirable example of his method is the picture "The Ancient Britons." "In the last Battle of King Arthur, only Three Britons escaped; these were the Strongest Man, the Beautifullest Man, and the Ugliest Man; these three marched through the field unsubdued, as Gods, and the Sun of Britain set, but shall arise again with tenfold splendor when Arthur shall awake from sleep, and resume his dominion over earth and ocean." This subject interested Blake because it stated, in particular metaphors, the favorite item in his own mythology, his central myth: paradise lost and paradise regained. As Milton might have shown had he pursued the subject, according to his plan, Arthur is an admirable symbol for the loss of harmony and the promise of regeneration. That this is Blake's reading of the passing of Arthur is evident from his interpretation of the last three men. They are "the human sublime," "the human pathetic," and "the human reason." More important, "They were originally one man . . . he was self-divided, and his real humanity slain." Blake is speaking again of those

"Antediluvians who are our Energies. . . . The Giants who . . . now seem to live . . . in chains." The three men are the separate parts, the unharmonious faculties, of the fallen Arthur himself. When we read further that "The stories of Arthur are the acts of Albion, applied to a Prince of the fifth century," and remember that in Blake's long poems Albion is the original giant fallen from pristine harmony, we see how Blake is attempting to read psychological truths into historical situations. These are the particular "truths" which, in elaborated metaphorical terms, are the core of his own mythology. "Mr. B. has done as all the ancients did . . . given the historical fact in its poetical vigour so as it always happens." To Blake history, if properly written, was not essentially different from poetry and painting, "all containing mythological and recondite meaning, where more is meant than meets the eye." The quarrel with Hume and Gibbon was necessary.

Having reduced history to myth, Blake had no great inclination to argue for the historicity of the Bible. This book he considered one long poetic vision, the most magnificent mythology of all, but essentially no different from "The antiquities of every Nation under Heaven." When Paine questioned the authorship of various Old Testament books, and Bishop Watson railed, Blake was calm enough: "it ceases to be history & becomes a Poem of probable impossibilities, fabricated for pleasure, as moderns say, but I say by Inspiration." In his view, what could be better? He had no interest whatever in the surface meanings of the Bible. "I do not believe there is such a thing litterally, but hell is the being shut up in the possession of corporeal desires which shortly weary the man, *for* ALL LIFE IS HOLY," he declared. No less bluntly he wrote: "It ought to be understood that the Persons, Moses & Abraham, are not here meant, but the States Signified by those Names . . . these various States I have seen in my Imagination." And again: "Two persons, one in Purple, the other in Scarlet, are descending down the steps into the Pit; these are Caiaphas & Pilate–Two States where all those reside who Calumniate & Murder under Pretence of Holiness & Justice." Of another picture he said: "I have given, in the background, a building, which may be supposed the ruin of a

Part of Nimrod's tower, which I conjecture to have spread over many Countries; for he ought to be reckon'd of the Giant brood." That is Blake's way of saying that the dilemma of Babel —man's unintelligibility to man?—is a portion of universal human experience, for which the broken tower itself is an adequate symbol in the mythological corpus. Blake's reading of the Bible was like his reading of everything else; he was interested not in historical or in theological but in psychological facts, and these facts, in the metaphorical embodiment that vision perceives, compose mythological statement.

In some such way he conceived his own poems, certainly his long poems. In his discussion of the painting of "The Ancient Britons" he said: "How he became divided is a subject of great sublimity and pathos. The Artist has written it under inspiration, and will, if God please, publish it; it is voluminous, and contains the ancient history of Britain, and the world of Satan and of Adam." The reference is to his last long poem, *Jerusalem*. Of *The Four Zoas* he said: "I have in these three years composed an immense number of verses on One Grand Theme, Similar to Homer's Iliad or Milton's Paradise Lost, the Persons & Machinery intirely new to the Inhabitants of Earth (some of the Persons Excepted)." He conceived of his long poems as traditional epics, in terms of a mythological framework. To this framework, his vision was indispensable, but no more indispensable, perhaps, than his reading.

As Swedenborg read the Bible for its theological "correspondences," which did not interest Blake in the least, so Blake read it for its psychological "correspondences." These, embodied in fresh figures, supplied him with the bulk of his frame. Milton's explicit treatment of the central Biblical theme—the fall and the promise—was hardly less useful than the Bible itself. But Blake, most undiscriminating of eclectics, leapt beyond such orthodox sources. Everything was grist to his metaphorical mill, and the more curious the document, the more useful it seemed to his recondite purposes. An excellent example of the precision with which Blake translated the literal into the metaphorical is his use of the theory of Anglo-Israelism, propounded over thirty years by the fanatic Richard Brothers. The theory, as Mr. Damon explains it, is of the origins of the British people in the ten tribes of Israel, and it enjoyed then, as it apparently does again now, a considerable vogue. To Blake it was an unusually useful concept for his central idea of the universality of human experience, for relating national with Biblical affairs, for further elaborating his metaphor of the disintegration of life, and for underscoring his democratic notion that the individual, like society, is capable of a peaceful equality.

Blake's use of his most eccentric sources usually involved such a transposition of a literal intention into a metaphorical tool. When he plunged into the theological jungles of Swedenborg and Boehme, the most "mystical" writers he knew, it was to plunder them for figures, not for concepts.

III

EMANUEL SWEDENBORG DECLARED in 1758 that the year before —the year, it happened, in which William Blake was born—had witnessed the Last Judgment: the spiritual accounts audited, the heavens and hells ordered at last, the "equilibrium between good and evil . . . restored." The coincidence must always have given Swedenborg a certain charm for Blake.

With elementary New Church doctrine such as the principle of the last judgment Blake was acquainted early, for his father was at least sympathetic to Swedenborg's teachings, and his brother Robert was actively associated with a Community. About 1783, when the first meetings of the New Church were being held in London, Blake met John Flaxman, an ardent Swedenborgian. Their friendship was not always smooth, but it was long and intense. As a Swedenborgian, Flaxman probably came nearer to understanding Blake's personality and work than any other contemporary, and Blake's letters to him show that they shared the same special language. In 1787, when the first London Community was formed in Great Eastcheap, Blake read and annotated the *Aphorisms* of Lavater, whose ethics were deeply influenced by both Swedenborg and Boehme. In 1789 the names of Catherine and William Blake appear in the minute book of the Great Eastcheap group. This was the year in which Blake engraved the *Songs of Innocence,* and a Swedenborgian asserts on respectable evidence that one of the songs was composed in the New Jerusalem Church. In the same year a scandal rocked the Community. Blake was surely interested, and he may well have entered the controversy: ". . . a very sorrowful occurrence befell the infant New Church," the record laments, "whereby the floodgates of immorality were in danger of being thrown open, to her inevitable destruction. The Church held many solemn meetings on the occasion, which ended in her withdrawing herself from six of her members. . . . It was a perverted view of Swedenborg's doctrine of concubinage in his work on Conjugial Love, then just published; whereby some held that if a husband and wife did not agree, they might separate, and the man take a concubine; I forget whether or not the wife was to have the same privilege." In these years Blake was beginning the *Songs of Experience,* which sing bitterly of monogamy, of "the Marriage hearse" and "the cage." Now those long-surviving legends about Blake's desire to establish a community of wives and to introduce into his house a concubine, sometimes thought to have been Mary Wollstonecraft, take on sudden body.

In 1788-90 Blake was reading Swedenborg with some attention, as we know from his annotations to *Divine Love and Wisdom* and *Divine Providence.* His jottings indicate the nature of his interest in the teachings and in the activities of the society; a number suggest a New Church controversy in which he shared, and Swedenborg's text seems to support Blake's position in the argument. Then presently Blake ceased to participate in the New Church.

Yet Swedenborg remained one of the steadfast influences on his work. His name continues to appear in his poetry, and late in life Blake talked of Swedenborg repeatedly to Crabb Robinson. In the *Descriptive Catalogue* of 1809 he describes a picture based on *The True Christian Religion.* "The works of this visionary are well worthy the attention of Painters and Poets; they are foundations for grand things," he said. *The Marriage of Heaven and Hell* derives its title from Swedenborg's *Heaven and Hell,* and borrows his favorite device of visionary anecdotes. Negatively, much of its content is indebted to Swedenborg, for it sporadically refutes his teachings. Even here, however, Blake proclaims Swedenborg the angel of the millennium, not, we may be sure, because Swedenborg was a theologian, but because he valued vision. In Blake's last long poem, Swedenborg was still the starting-point, the metaphorical foundation, for this "grand thing." The New Jerusalem is Swedenborg's term for the millennial life, and because this involved ideas of order, it was useful to Blake, in whose work Jerusalem is the symbol of freedom. One finds everywhere some fragment of Blake's debt. It was of two kinds. It provided him with those sanctions for his visionary method for which he was always searching, and it supplied him with a large portion of the symbolical apparatus in which he embodied his vision.

Swedenborg's temperament was arid, scientific, and, despite his visions, nonintuitional. Nevertheless there is such a marked similarity in the understanding of the two of "vision," and in its kinds of content, that it seems possible that Blake's "second sight" and the expression of what he saw by it were in some way formed by the older man's.

Swedenborg, like Blake, seemed to be subject to at least two orders of vision: the sort that observed spiritual causes in natural objects, or correspondence, and the conversational variety, the genuinely hallucinatory, in which he held colloquies with willing spirits. This similarity results not only in the same general attitude toward the closed senses and the limited reason, but also in a similar analysis of the physical and psychological circumstances of vision. Swedenborg wrote: "Man is brought into a certain state that is midway between sleep and waking, and when in that state he seems to himself to be wide awake; all the senses are as perfectly awake as in the completest bodily wakefulness, not only the sight and the hearing, but what is wonderful, the sense of touch also, which is then more exquisite than is ever possible when the body is awake. In this state, spirits and angels have been seen to the very life, and have been heard, and what is wonderful have been touched, with almost nothing of the body intervening. This is the state that is called being withdrawn from the body, and not knowing whether one is in the body or out of it." The striking item here is the emphasis on touch ("what is wonderful"), since in Blake touch is among the most precious of the senses and the fructifier of the others, including, as it does for him, the act of sex. Mr. Damon, independently of the passage in Swedenborg, explains in much the same way the reason that most of Blake's writing and all his visionary painting were done at night, sometimes, as he claimed, automatically. Blake described what seems to be exactly the same condition.

As when a man dreams he reflects not that his body sleeps,
Else he would wake, so seem'd he entering his Shadow: but
With him the Spirits of the Seven Angels of the Presence
Entering, they gave him still perceptions of his Sleeping Body
Which now arose and walk'd with them in Eden, as an Eighth
Image Divine tho' darken'd and tho' walking as one walks
In sleep, and the Seven comforted and supported him.

The gift of vision convinced both writers that they, like ancient prophets, were the vessels into which the divine wisdom flowed, and that in modern times they were designated to revive that ancient habit. Blake's assertions of heavenly dictation are always reminiscent of Swedenborg. The structure of Swedenborg's theological works "attests" to divine command, for to his general statements of principles he always appends one or two or a half-dozen of those "Memorable Relations" in which he recounts his experiences with angels and other spiritual creatures who instructed him in the preceding theological truths. Blake, humorously following him, included in *The Marriage* illustrative "Memorable Fancies," the tone in which he reports his visions exceeding the casualness even of the master's. The differing implications of "Relations" and "Fancies" are notable, and there is the further difference that Blake's angels behave interestingly and unpredictably, and are concerned with matters of general rather than sectarian interest, whereas Swedenborg's are the merest projections of the pedantic theologian himself. It was Swedenborg's device, not his content, that interested Blake.

Angelic dictation included for both writers a good deal of miscellaneous information, the basic item being the doctrine of correspondence. Swedenborg explains: "The whole natural world corresponds to the spiritual world, and not merely the natural world in general, but also every particular of it." The discovery of correspondence, said Blake, was a function of the imagination, an act of vision of one kind. "This world of Imagination is the world of Eternity. . . . There Exist in that Eternal World the Permanent Realities of Every Thing which we see reflected in this Vegetable Glass of Nature."

This cannot be read as an acknowledgment of Blake's debt to Platonic idealism; for in his system the "Permanent Realities" are not the inaccessible archetypes of things themselves, but the enduring qualities of human nature. Blake was the most thorough of anthropocentrists: heaven and hell and "all deities" are within man; heaven consists of his capacities fulfilled, hell of his capacities denied, and God, created in man's image, is the sum of all his potentialities. How Swedenborg's theory of correspondences served Blake's anthropocentric interest is made clear by a passage on the animals: "The animals of the earth in general correspond to affections, the tame and useful ones to the good affections, the savage and useless ones to evil affections: oxen and bullocks specifically correspond to the affections of the natural mind; sheep and lambs to the affections of the spiritual mind; but winged animals, according to their species, correspond to the intellectual things of each mind." Blake had no interest in a tight system of analogies such as this, yet he had his lamb and tiger and eagle, his horse and wolf. "Did he who made the Lamb make thee?" is a question addressed not only to the tiger in the jungle but also to the tigerish elements in the nature of man, a jungle too.

The system of correspondence was useful to Blake because it enabled him to write a richly or at least an intricately symbolic poetry, dense with layers of meaning; because it allowed him to include within single images the individual, society, and the universe, one lapsing into the other without fixed boundaries anywhere. For this reason he followed Swedenborg in making the ancient concept of macrocosm and microcosm the central aspect of the doctrine; but it was central to Blake for a reason different from Swedenborg's. It was the metaphorical tool that enabled him to counter the prevailing mechanical view of man and the universe with his own organic view. The best example of the instrumental value of the Swedenborgian concept is Blake's poem "Auguries of Innocence."

The organization of this poem has teased many critics, and it is consistently regarded as uncertain and lopsided. Yet although the poem is unfinished, its general outlines are not uncertain. It begins with the famous statement of the macro-microcosm, which has always been regarded as literally intended:

> To see a World in a Grain of Sand
> And a Heaven in a Wild Flower,
> Hold Infinity in the palm of your hand
> And Eternity in an hour.

Then, subjecting this concept to a very special interpretation, the poem proceeds in a much less general vein. Immediately it is diverted into a series of apparently pious distichs about cruelty to animals, and especially about animals in captivity:

> A Robin Red breast in a Cage
> Puts all Heaven in a Rage.
> A dove house fill'd with doves & Pigeons
> Shudders Hell thro' all its regions.

Interspersed with these comments are others on the skeptical attitude of science, and on the alternations of "Joy & Woe" in human life, with the assurance:

> Under every grief & Pine
> Runs a joy with silken twine.

Nor is Blake only saying with Pope—although he is saying this too—that all partial evil is universal good, but rather, with the hermetics, that if one can really see, everything is double—dead and alive, temporary and eternal, material and spiritual, mechanical and dynamic.

Once again the emphasis shifts, and the distichs concern themselves increasingly now not with animals but with men, and especially with the cruelty of bondage and of authority:

The Babe that weeps the Rod beneath
Writes Revenge in realms of death.
The Beggar's Rags, fluttering in Air,
Does to Rags the Heavens tear.

Once more, these are varied with comments on skepticism, and the poem is brought to a close with a restatement of the "Joy & Woe" theme:

Some are Born to sweet delight.
Some are Born to endless Night. . . .
God Appears & God is Light
To those poor Souls who dwell in Night,
But does a Human Form Display
To those who Dwell in Realms of day.

These final lines establish the relationship to the whole of the apparently unrelated remarks both on science and on "Joy & Woe," for the scientist, who questions what cannot be proved, who sees *with* the eye, is the wretched man in a mechanical universe of dead matter, and his God, at best, is a phenomenon scientifically explicable but as remote from man himself as "Light." One recalls "Newton's Particles of light" in "Mock on, Mock on, Voltaire, Rousseau," and the passage may well be an ironic comment on Newton's concern with optics. For the visionary "need not first put an *Academy* upon" his nose, "nor use any such Spectacles"; he acts by intuition and on faith, he sees "Thro' the Eye," he is the happy man able to perceive an organic or "spiritualized" universe, and the necessary interdependence of all things in it. His God is man himself, and every transgression against man necessarily rends the whole. One may say this in another way. All offenses against life, in whatever form, are ultimately directed against the offender.

Each outcry of the hunted Hare
A fibre from the Brain does tear.

But the brain is the hunter's, not the hare's.

In some such complex way, Swedenborg's macro-microcosm was of use to Blake. He had no interest in simply taking over a static theological system of analogies. He was intent on stating the organic nature of human no less than of universal experience, and the relation of each to the other. In the eighteenth century this meant that he had to oppose the visionary to the physicist.

A simpler example of his symbolical use of Swedenborgian fact is the double sun—the celestial sun that radiates God's "heat and light" (love and wisdom) and the natural sun, a reflection of the other, and dead except that its "heat and light" nourish the vegetable world. In Swedenborg's cosmography these two suns are real: ". . . without two Suns, the one living and the other dead, there can be no Creation." To this Blake replied, "False philosophy according to the letter, but true according to the spirit." Swedenborg defies scientific fact, but speaks metaphorical truth. The element of metaphor is supplied by Blake. He did not deny the literal truth of science. Swedenborg wrote: "The reason why a dead Sun was created is to the End that in the Ultimate all Things may be fixed. . . . The terraqueous Globe . . . is as it were the Basis and Firmament." Blake wrote: "They exist literally about the sun & not about the earth." On the word "literally" a good deal depends if the next of these annotations is to be properly understood. For when Swedenborg wrote, ". . . all Things were created from the Lord by the living Sun, *and nothing by the dead Sun,*" Blake underscored the last six words and added, "The dead sun is only a phantasy of evil Man." And we are again in the realm of the "Auguries of Innocence." The actuality of the "dead sun" and the figurativeness of the "living sun" Blake has already insisted upon. Yet in the end all depends on the perception of the figurative, and the "evil Man" is that half-blind creature who sees *with* the eye, and the good man, like the happy man, is the visionary able to transcend mechanical explanations. The real sun as ordinarily perceived "is Satan," the dead matter of Newtonian physics; and the "Spiritual Sun," which Blake told Robinson he beheld on Primrose Hill, and presumably could see anywhere, is the same sun illuminated, nature transfigured by vision.

"All that we saw was owing to your metaphysics," said Blake to an angel guide with poor vision, which is to utter the Coleridgean cry. No more than Coleridge could Blake derive comfort from "that cold world allow'd To the poor loveless ever-anxious crowd," and he was anticipating Coleridge when he wrote of Catherine and himself:

> We eat little, we drink less;
> This Earth breeds not our happiness.
> Another Sun feeds our life's streams,
> We are not warmed with thy beams.

Discarding all of Swedenborg's theology and nearly all of his cabalistic claptrap, Blake yet preserved the manner of speaking, the metaphor, and was thus enabled to present his way of seeing concretely, that is, in the language of poetry.

The habit of using the Swedenborgian device without regard to its content appears in another important corollary to the doctrine of correspondence, the mystagogical interpretation of the Bible. The Swedenborgian view is that this book has in it literal truth dealing with history and externals, but that its essential truth, which is "spiritual" (meaning theological, cosmogonal, and cosmographical) is hidden in the symbolical language. Only by a knowledge of correspondences does this truth, the Word, become apparent. On the basis of this principle, Swedenborg wrote the *Arcana Coelestia* and two other of his enormous explications.

The first result of the principle was the assumption that throughout, the Bible was the direct dictation of God. Blake was willing enough to accept this doctrine, but he subjected it, like everything else, to his particular aesthetic purposes: ". . . astonishing indeed," he wrote of the New Testament, "is the English Translation, it is almost word for word, & if the Hebrew Bible is as well translated, which I do not doubt it is, we need not doubt of its having been translated as well as written by the Holy Ghost." Blake's "Holy Ghost" is nothing more than true poetic genius itself, and the translators of the New Testament, as well as its authors, are true poets. Blake's mode of writing, like Swedenborg's, found its sanction in this principle.

Blake planned, apparently, to write a poem after the fashion of the *Arcana Coelestia,* and actually began the work. Robinson saw "his Version . . . of Genesis, 'As understood by a Christian Visionary.'" Blake mentions another similar lost work, his *Bible of Hell,* which he said the "world shall have whether they will or no." One of his last works, *The Ghost of Abel,* was intended as a reinterpretation of the implicit spiritual meanings of the Cain-Abel story, a portion of Genesis to which both Swedenborg and Boehme gave particular attention. Blake's graphic masterpiece, the Book of Job, like many of his illustrations, is nothing more nor less than the theory of correspondences worked out by drawings. So are all the long poems and some of the shorter; for they may, from one point of view, be considered as Swedenborgian revelations of the inner meanings of Scriptural story. But the difference is striking; Blake and Swedenborg have an utterly opposed conception of what is hidden. For Swedenborg, the Bible revealed a new sectarian dogma; for Blake, it assisted in the development of a poetic myth. Where one found evidences for what are now theological curiosities, the other found symbols for psychological insights that have grown rather than diminished in value.

The most curious and the most complex of Swedenborg's doctrines is the dogma of heavenly cartography, which assumes a relationship between man's body and the form of heaven. Heaven, indeed, is in the form of man's body, and every part of man's body corresponds to some part of the Grand Man. The place of separate spirits in the whole is determined by correspondence, since "Every one who becomes an angel carries his own heaven within himself, because he carries in himself the love of his own heaven; for a man by creation is the smallest effigy, image, and type of the great heaven, and thence the human form is derived; therefore every one after death comes into that society of heaven of whose general form he is an individual effigy." And ". . . the angelic societies, of which heaven consists, are arranged therefore as the members, organs, and viscera are in man, that is, some are in the head, some in the breast, some in the arms, and some in each of their particulars." Also, ". . . the head signifies intelligence and wisdom; the breast charity; the loins marriage; the arms and hands power of truth; the feet what is natural; the eyes understanding; the nostrils perception;

the ears obedience, the kidneys the scrutiny of truth, and so on."

Swedenborg's Grand Man became one of Blake's controlling symbols, but what in Swedenborg is the shape of the literal heaven is in Blake the symbol of universal humanity. As in Swedenborg heaven is the place of life after it has been ordered, so in Blake an ordered life, whenever and wherever it occurs, is heaven. Lavater had said, "Beauty we call the MOST VARIED ONE, the MOST UNITED VARIETY. Could there be a man who should harmoniously unite each variety of knowledge and of powers—were he not the most beautiful? were he not your *god?*" And Blake had answered, "This is our Lord." The Grand Man, for Blake, was a symbol for both God and humanity. The human body, with its complex articulation, its harmony of multiple functions, is a probable metaphor for order. Blake, without implicating himself in the complexities of Swedenborg's system, yet found that it suggested useful figures, and—particularly in the later poems—he used the parts of the body in this fashion.

Within the whole form of heaven, according to Swedenborg's cosmic map, exist innumerable heavens, and, correspondingly, innumerable hells combine into another grand form, Satan. The plurality of the heavens and hells results from the dogma that in his lifetime every man determines his own heaven or hell through his leading love. Blake, interpreting this idea more mundanely than Swedenborg, frequently employs it:

> . . . in your own Bosom you bear your Heaven
> And Earth & all you behold; tho' it appears Without, it is
>   Within,
> In your Imagination.

Lavater's statement that our gods are our motives Blake found amplified in Swedenborg, and to express this idea of "man's leading propensity" as "his leading Virtue," he accepted as symbol Swedenborg's plurality of heavens and hells. Blake's heavens are twenty-seven in number, to correspond with the twenty-seven churches, and while he does not seem to insist that the individual soul must take a particular place in the grand body according to his life on earth, he nevertheless recognized a variety of ethical "heavens" and a multitude of psychological "hells."

It is in the nature of the heavens and the hells that one discovers the difference again. The Swedenborgian heavens are as dreary as seminaries occupied by unusually loquacious and disputatious candidates. His hells, which seem to be the only portion of experience able to arouse something like a true imaginative effort in him, are sections of sewers, clogged with the stinking fragments of the eternally damned. The fixed alternative of monotonous colloquy and odorous agony could not satisfy Blake, and in *Milton* he condemned Swedenborg for

> Shewing the Transgressors in Hell, the proud Warriors in Heaven,
> Heaven as a Punisher, & Hell as One under Punishment.

The plurality of the heavens and hells supplied the poet intent on the idea of individualism with a useful symbol for ethical variations; but Swedenborg's actual vision of these places was wholly unsatisfactory to the poet for whom vision itself denied the possibility of penalty:

> & Throughout all Eternity
> I forgive you, you forgive me.

Metaphor emerging from literally intended sources is plain again in the landscape of heaven. Swedenborg's celestial world contains all the ideal forms of earthly objects—houses, trees, libraries, even dinners—everything, Plato reduced to the visionary absurd. Blake speaks now and then of the "houses" of heaven, which are ethical states, and his description of his "Last Judgment" deals with the properties of heaven; but he employs these objects as symbols that a graphic art and a mythological poetry necessitated. Again, in the points of the compass as these signify meanings to the two men the same difference exists. To Swedenborg, north, south, east, and west are real cosmic representations of possible leanings of the soul, and the angels are disposed accordingly, and actually. To Blake, the compass points, like all things in his poems, are representations of human proclivities. Swedenborg's quaint geography of heaven serves Blake as an instrument by which he anatomizes the nature of man and draws in concrete terms the vision of man's potentiality for order.

The most important consequence of the Grand Man theory is the emphasis it allowed Blake to put on the divinity of humanity, an idea first clearly stated in "The Divine Image," that poem which, it is said, was written in the New Jerusalem Church. Swedenborg insisted upon the importance of an abstraction he called the Human, and thereby, on the unity of God in Jesus Christ, who is the complete embodiment of the Human. This Human is all the virtues of man taken collectively, separated from all the evils that are part of the lesser *h*uman; but it is still the essence of being in the natural life, and the whole of being in the supernatural. Blake does not capitalize his "human" in "The Divine Image," any more than he abstracts good from evil to create his heavens and his hells; *"for* ALL LIFE IS HOLY." He again connects "the human form divine," just as he does correspondence, the Bible, vision, and so on, with the poets' property, imagination. Poetic genius is at once the Holy Ghost and the means of perceiving the "human form divine." The difference between Swedenborg and Blake is that Swedenborg's "Human" relates man to God, whereas Blake's "human" relates God to man, and especially to artists. The "Human" is a concept by which Swedenborg separates man's good from his bad; the "human form divine" is the symbol by means of which Blake prohibits any such separation.

A central doctrine in Swedenborg is the unity of God and the divinity of Christ: Jehovah and Jesus are identical. Blake likewise asserted the singleness and the divinity of Jesus, but he did so by denying the reality of Jehovah and, in a sense, the divinity of Jesus. Robinson remembered this: ". . . on my asking in which light he viewed the great question concerning the Divinity of Jesus Christ, He said—*He is the only God*—but then he added—'And so am I & so are you.'"

Swedenborg's conception of Christ's function, in spite of strong millennial overtones, limits itself to something like the traditional view. Blake's view, which accepts this much, adds more; the millennium presents itself each moment to every man in his daily life, and Christ is the symbol of the possibility of illumination and harmony in every man. This distinction is clarified by what the two have to say of the important virtues, on the names of which they agreed, those saving graces which we ordinarily associate with the character of Jesus. To Blake, "The Spirit of Jesus is continual forgiveness of Sin," and "holiness" and "righteousness" are both irrelevant, indeed damaging, to the Christian character. Forgiveness is all, and forgiveness is identical with imagination. This goes far beyond the Swedenborgian ethics, yet Swedenborg helped Blake to his position.

They begin together. Swedenborg insisted that faith is intuitional, and Blake illustrated one of Swedenborg's texts that dealt with the attempt of the learned to achieve faith by demonstration and argument. Swedenborg said that it is not allowable "to inquire into the mysteries of faith by means of the things of the sense and of the memory, for in this case the celestial of faith is destroyed." The "celestial of faith" is Divine Love, which animates all things, and of which light is the visible correspondence: ". . . if the love of God diminished, the sun would grow cold, and if the knowledge of God ceased, all the stars would lose their light," Paul Berger summarized in order to point out the similarity in diction to Blake's

> If the Sun & Moon should doubt,
> They'd immediately Go out.

But the similarity is superficial. Swedenborg's cosmography supplied Blake with a symbol by means of which he could assail the contemporary habit of skepticism, and manipulate, sometimes magnificently, the formula of *Cogito ergo sum* for nonrationalist purposes. It became *Credo ergo sum.*

The end of love, says Swedenborg, is faith, for one is the affection of good and inevitably directs itself to the other, which is the affection of truth. This is congenial to Blake. In neither of them is love static, but Blake's concept of active love goes far beyond Swedenborg's. Both insisted on "charity," and both rigorously condemned an ascetic life because it deliberately cast out active love, which includes both "charity" or "good to the neighbor," and sex love. "The Whole of Charity and Faith is in Works," said Swedenborg, and on this remark Blake wrote in the margin: "The Whole of the New Church is in the Active Life & not in Ceremonies at all." Active love is the only real expression of faith to Swedenborg, but his definition of charity is haunted by a curious utilitarianism. In Blake there is no such notion of "use to society, and use is good." Love, charity, and faith were to him acts and moods that cast off the selfish interests of the individual and integrated his humanity. Swedenborg's ethics supplied the vocabulary, but by no means the core of meaning, which in Blake is at this point profoundly political.

Sometimes the consequence is that Blake cannot accept even the way of speaking. Both men denounced asceticism and exalted sexual love, and Swedenborg gave an entire volume to the subject. *Conjugial Love and Its Chaste Delights* begins with the proposition that the male and the female are eternal principles in all life. The two are forever separate and contrary, although they struggle forever toward "conjunction." Therefore, heaven is inhabited by both male and female spirits, and in heaven marriages exist as they do on earth, except that there is no reproduction and that all misalliances are corrected. On earth, however, it is possible to have both "true" and "false" marriages, and the love in "true" marriages is as near to heavenly delights as anything of earth can be. The sexual act itself is the natural correspondent of the celestial impulse toward union and order, and for this reason is pure. The pure has its inverse, the impure.

Blake found it impossible to concur in Swedenborg's placid theory of heavenly monogamy. He insisted that eternity was complete harmony, and that therefore angels and spirits were androgynous, with no separate principles of male and female, but only the one of Man. The female will was a creation that occurred in the fall, one of the multitude of disharmonies to which humanity is subject. He found Swedenborg's "sexual religion . . . dangerous" because he believed that "Humanity knows not of Sex," and that "In Eternity Woman is the Emanation of Man; she has No Will of her own. There is no such thing in Eternity as a Female Will, & Queens." Absolute unity makes heaven what it is. He could not borrow, even as metaphor, one that allowed duality to remain. Like Swedenborg, he believed that sex impulses are the manifestation in individuals of the cosmic impulse to order, and that the sex act itself is the earthly equivalent of that union. Therefore, like Swedenborg, he too exalted sexual love. But taking a somewhat more impassioned view of the psychological union that is love, in his mythological construction he did not hesitate to do away entirely with the principle of separation. If one denies the mythological interpretation, one must, of course, convict Blake of gibberish, and not of passion at all, but of malaise.

In their understanding of the function of love, the two men are alike. True love is selfless, both argued, Blake thus elliptically:

> Love seeketh not Itself to please,
> Nor for itself hath any care,
> But for another gives its ease,
> And builds a Heaven in Hell's despair.

Blake and Swedenborg do not meet on many points in their respective doctrines of evil, for Blake takes the antinomian position, Swedenborg the legalistic, and the only concept that unites them here is that which Blake called "Selfhood," Swedenborg, the "proprium," or "ownhood." Blake lumped all evil under the term, because he conceived it to be the essentially nonimaginative state, the mind turned inward upon self rather than outward upon others. Swedenborg, substituting a knowledge of correspondence for imagination, only seems to approximate Blake's point of view: ". . . where self and the world are the ends, the mind, in reading the Word, abides in self and in the world, and hence their thoughts are constantly derived from their own *proprium* or selfhood, and the *proprium* of man is in utter darkness respecting all things that relate to heaven and the church; so that in such a state it is impossible for a man to be under the Lord's guidance, and to be elevated by him into the light of heaven." Selfhood was by no means the whole of evil to Swedenborg, as it was to Blake, who wrote of "the Spectre . . . the Great Selfhood, Satan, Worship'd as God by the Mighty Ones of the Earth," and made of the destruction of this selfhood man's greatest imaginative experience and therefore the act of his salvation.

In their definition of atheism, as in the definition of love, analogies exist again. Swedenborg called those men who "have not the will, and consequently not the capacity, to receive any good from any other source than from their *proprium* or selfhood" "atheistical naturalists," and Blake concurred. As "selfhood" was an unenlightened *moral* condition, so "atheism" was the concomitant condition of *intellectual* (one is tempted to say *visual*) unenlightenment. The imaginative man overcomes selfhood, the visionary, atheism; in theological terms, this is the conflict between the spiritual and the natural man. Thus Blake told Robinson that "everything is Atheism which assumes the reality of the Natural & Unspiritual world." Swedenborg wrote: "Hence it may appear, that Man from a *merely natural* Idea cannot comprehend that the Divine is every where, and yet not in Space; and yet that Angels and Spirits clearly comprehend this; consequently *that Man also may,* if so be he will admit something of spiritual Light into his Thought; the Reason why Man may comprehend it is because his Body doth not think, but his Spirit, therefore not his natural but his spiritual Part." The italics are Blake's, and his comment was: "Observe the distinction here between Natural & Spiritual as seen by Man. Man may comprehend, but not the natural or external man." The emphasis on "merely natural" implies that counter-condition of enlightened naturalism by which he often opposed the materialism of contemporary philosophy. In Blake, the distinction is not quite between the sensual and the spiritual man, but between the man with closed and the man with expanded senses. When Blake defined "Newton's sleep" as "seeing with the eye," it was neither to the eye nor to the object that he objected, but to the way in which the eye was used and to the aspect of the object which that way isolated.

> Let the Human Organs be kept in their perfect integrity,
> At will Contracting into Worms or Expanding into Gods.

These are the reasonably certain points of Swedenborg's influence on Blake, but there is of course a great deal more in

Swedenborg that did not touch him at all. He must have skipped through hundreds of pages; the purely theological discussion could only have irritated him, and such central concepts as Swedenborg's cosmogony are the very reverse of Blake's. Even when he borrowed from him, Blake was severely critical. He attacked him for repeating "all the old falsehoods" and for adding little that was new, called his works a mere index to those of his predecessors, Boehme and Paracelsus. He criticized him for emphasizing the passive virtues, the petty moralities of this world, for his spiritual predestinarianism, and for his rationalism. A "divine teacher" he was, but for all that, "the Sampson shorn by the Churches." Swedenborg's own system, written to revolutionize religious belief and to cast out dogma, became dogma almost at once, and froze up again into the externals of a mere church. By this dogma Blake would not be enslaved.

His criticism of Swedenborg reinforces the present argument. He saw very soon that the announcement of the year 1757 as the beginning of the new dispensation meant no more than the beginning of a new sect. But if 1757 was the year in which Swedenborg was granted his revelation, it was also the year in which the world was given "a Mental Prince," William Blake. Without accepting the Swedenborgian dogma, he took enough of its paraphernalia and had enough confidence in himself to write that "the time is arriv'd when Men shall again converse in Heaven & walk with Angels" and that "The Kingdoms of this World are now become the Kingdoms of God & His Christ, & we shall reign with him for ever & ever."

Swedenborg's revelation of the New Jerusalem became only the dogma of the New Jerusalem Church; in Blake, Jerusalem is that condition of freedom which man enjoys when revelation withstands the claims of dogma. Swedenborg's last judgment is a theological curiosity in which the heavens and the hells are ordered and spirits take their proper places in the cosmic harmony. Blake's "last judgments" (and the plural is imperative) are those persistent and triumphant moments in human experience when men transcend the selfish interests that isolate them from and pit them against one another, when the psychological and moral myopia to which all men are inclined to submit is overcome, and the individual, because he *perceives* the possibility of a co-operative order within and without himself, achieves it, and finds that within and without are the same.

O search & see: turn your eyes upward: open, O thou World
Of Love & Harmony in Man: expand thy ever lovely Gates!

A better New Churchman than Blake is disconcerted by the use to which he put Swedenborg, for while maintaining the way of speaking, the metaphorical equipment, he yet shifted the whole ground. Blake's first editor, J. J. Garth Wilkinson, who was a Swedenborgian, discerned the difference when he criticized Blake because he "naturalized the spiritual, instead of spiritualizing the natural."

Examples of critical insight are rare in the remarks of Crabb Robinson, yet when he observed that Blake "is not so much a disciple of Jacob Böhmen & Swedenborg as a fellow visionary," he offered a valuable clue to criticism. Blake distinguished between dogma and myth, between functions that enslave man and functions that serve him. The striking fact about his use of Swedenborg is that he derived one from the other, the materials for his myth from the dogma that he rejected. "Swedenborg had been a sort of second Bible to him from childhood, and the influence even of his 'systematic reasoning' remained with him as at least a sort of groundwork, or despised model." We may extend this remark of Arthur Symons's to mean that while Blake would not be enslaved by the system, he did, in the strictest rhetorical sense, make it serve his poetry.

IV

Boehme's influence, almost certainly coming later than Swedenborg's, was of a "most accidental or partial kind." Yet it came from a source more attractive to Blake, and therefore, in some of its details, more acceptable, or even already part of his equipment. Much that he encountered here was identical with much that he had already encountered in Swedenborg, although some of it was stated in terms more nearly his own. And of the five or six concepts that were new, two, to be sure, became basic elements in Blake's thought, but the remainder he subjected to the same transformation.

Boehme's personality and mind were much more congenial to Blake than Swedenborg's, for Boehme, far from being a distinguished public servant, let alone an engineer and a naturalist, was an uneducated and humble craftsman whose learning, like much of Blake's own, consisted of the tag ends of out-of-the-way tradition, and who, again like Blake, built his curious unsymmetrical *gothique* as best he could from the materials at hand. Unlike Swedenborg and like Blake, the shoemaker was a genuine visionary, whose best-known illumination came to him as he stared at a polished pewter dish that held the reflection of the sun, and who, in general, gloried in a sense of nature illuminated. In his writing a crude but genuinely imaginative insight functioned, especially when it contemplated the delights of paradise or when it explored the complex drama of the cosmic will and the dialectical agonies of creation. Most important is the fact that Boehme's influence was deeply imbedded in that tradition of dissent that was Blake's own inheritance, and that many of Boehme's ideas were already Blake's.*

Like many other seventeenth-century pietists among the sects, Boehme gave the world, even political society, a major role in the drama of damnation and salvation, and he expressed social attitudes that by the eighteenth century had become the commonplaces of radical humanitarianism. He saw the connection between state religion and political tyranny, and like Blake after him attacked the familiar duo, priests and kings. He saw the connection between tyranny and warfare, and like Blake attacked war. He deplored the dry casuistry of a learned, rationalistic clergy and like Blake insisted on the primacy of feeling and the privacy of regeneration, on the barriers of

* It is sometimes difficult, for example, to distinguish between Boehme's influence on Blake and Milton's, for Milton was himself influenced by Boehme, whose ideas were widely current in seventeenth-century England. See Margaret Lewis Bailey, *Milton and Jakob Boehme,* Oxford University Press, 1914.

dogma and ritual. All this and all that it implies Blake used in his early work and would have developed in his later without the aid of Boehme.

Much more Blake had already seized upon in Swedenborg and used in the fashion we have noted. The distinction between the closed and the open senses, between Boehme's *Verstand* and *Vernunft,* was not new to Blake, nor the relation of vision and heavenly command. No more was the doctrine of correspondence as Boehme developed it in the *Signatura Rerum,* nor its concomitant, the theory of microcosm and macrocosm. In Boehme's *Mysterium Magnum* Blake found again the Swedenborgian device of Biblical interpretation, which sanctioned his own composition of spiritual allegories. And here again Blake encountered the doctrine of the selfhood: "Whatsoever *strives* and contends in this World about Selfhood, Self-interest, temporal Honour, its own *Profit,* for its own Advancement, the same is bred and born of the Serpent's *Ens,* be it either Rich or Poor, in Superior or Inferior, no Order, Rank, or *Condition* whatsoever excepted." But again, in Boehme the renunciation of self, the achievement of "the resigned Ground of a Soul, to which nothing cleaveth," implies the mystical discipline, although modified, whereas Blake forced the annihilation of self (and of the serpent) to mean the triumph of imagination in the brotherhood of men and of man's parts. And in Boehme as in Swedenborg, the selfhood is only one portion of evil, which is a large and positive element, not, as in Blake, a negative condition that results alone from an improper view of things, one might almost say an inadequate aesthetics.

Still other concepts in Boehme are near to some in Swedenborg but in expression or in actual content are even nearer to Blake himself. Boehme too insisted on the divinity of Christ, but like Blake he opposed Christ to a wrathful Lord. The difference is that Blake's Jehovah, his Accuser, the "God of This World," or his Urizen, do not represent eternal actualities but creations of unorganized man, the faculty of law and the spirit of lawgiving that unregenerate man, in the failure of love, sets up to rule within himself, and the image of which he mistakenly establishes outside himself as his God. Of the Christlike virtues that compose divinity, emphasized by both Blake and Swedenborg but opposed by Blake to the Jehovian impulse to judge and punish, Boehme said little. He dwelt rather on such negative virtues as meekness and humility, which Blake scorned and wished to write out of the character of Jesus. Of sexual love Boehme said nothing at all, and for somewhat other reasons than Blake, who said so much on this subject, Boehme's angels, unlike Swedenborg's, are androgynous.

In Boehme, too, Blake found—but with a difference that for him must have seemed major—the Swedenborgian doctrine of the "leading love"—". . . that Image which thou hast borne here in thy Mind, with that thou shalt appear; for there can no other Image go forth out of thy Body at the Breaking or Deceasing of it; but even that which thou hast borne here, that shall appear in Eternity." The difference is in Boehme's use of the word "image" instead of a word more explicitly suggestive of a merely moral condition.

Imagination plays a major role in Boehme's system of salvation, for he uses the word to mean the variety of ways in which man is able to regard his life and the life of the universe. It can be either good or bad, and can lead either to heaven or to hell. "If we put our Imagination into the *Light* of God, and go with earnest sincerity into that, then we *come* into it, and are also with earnestness drawn into it." But there is also "a beastial Nature and Condition of the imaginary Life." Blake would never have used the sacred word "imagination" to represent a base condition, but he did think of it as the only genuine ethical agent man knows, and this unusual conception of the term he may very well have found in Boehme. Boehme's conception, at any rate, points to the use to which Blake put the doctrine of the "leading love" in his poetry, where it supports his exalted view of vision and his subjective interpretation of nature and events.

Boehme's most important contribution to Blake is the metaphysical basis of his cosmogony. This apparently supplied Blake with a concept that was no less than vital to his work, and with any number of symbols by means of which he could dramatize it. Blake may have seized upon the concept himself in a moment of brilliant intuition; or he may, like Boehme, have pieced it together from his own reading in the alchemists, and developed it. The concept is Boehme's extraordinary pre-Hegelian dialectic. His was not a trained intelligence, and it could build only a strangely crude and creaking metaphysical apparatus. Yet it seems clear that Blake derived his own principle of contraries from him. Boehme's whole concept of creation and of life depends upon the operation of contrary wills: ". . . if there were no *contrary Will,* then there would be no Motion." As this remark prefigures Blake's "Without Contraries is no progression," so Boehme's elaboration suggests the source of the titanic conflicts in which those symbolical "immortals" in the Prophetic Books endlessly engage. Boehme's writings are constantly returning to statements such as this: "For the Eternal Nature has produced nothing in its Desire, except a Likeness out of itself; and if there were not an everlasting Mixing, there would be an eternal Peace in Nature, but so Nature would not be revealed and made manifest, in the Combat it becomes manifest; so that each Thing elevates itself, and would get out of the Combat into the still Rest, and so it runs to and fro, and thereby only awakens and stirs up the Combat." And this: ". . . there are two Wills in one Being, and they cause *two principles* . . . and in the first Will, Nature could not be manifest, the second will it is that maketh Nature manifest, for the second will is the virtue in the strength, and the one would be *nothing* without the other." Probably in such statements lies the abstraction that suggested Blake's complicated metaphorical dramas; yet the difference is the entire difference between the abstract and the dramatic, the metaphysical and the metaphorical.

In Boehme, creation begins when the will of God acts upon itself; in Blake too, the eternal will is the original fact:

> Earth was not: nor globes of attraction;
> The will of the Immortal expanded
> Or contracted his all flexible senses;
> Death was not, but eternal life sprung.

Already, however, a portion of the eternal will has asserted and therefore separated itself. This is Urizen, whose determination is to deny the dialectic of expansion and contraction of life:

> I have sought for a joy without pain,
> For a solid without fluctuation.

To achieve this vast error he has plunged into "the indefinite Where nothing lives," the "petrific, abominable chaos." This region of nothingness is Boehme's eternal "Abyss" where the struggle between wills takes place and the enormous process of creation begins to unfold. In Blake it is always Los who pits himself against the will of Urizen, gives him a body, creates a universe and a world, and thus puts limits on error against which error rages but by means of which it is at last redeemed.

Creation in Boehme proceeds by the operation of seven interdependent "forms." The first is attraction, or contraction, and is opposed to the second, expansion, and from their conflict arises the third, motion, which apparently corresponds to matter as it is presented to the senses. Then a crucial clash occurs with spirit, and the redemption of matter and plurality proceeds through the fourth form, fire; the fifth, light; the sixth, sound; and the seventh, body, which is the complete self-realization of the will and a condition that Boehme calls "eternal nature." Blake did not take over these seven forms in any complete way, but attraction and expansion became the basis of his cosmogony, and a certain correspondence with Boehme's account may be found in Blake's "Seven Eyes of God," the first of which is Lucifer and the last of which is Jesus, and who, collectively, are in charge of fallen man's redemption. So, too, Boehme's seven forms may have suggested Blake's seven ages of creation, during which Urizen is given body and a universe, and is at last brought back into unity.

Yet the real contribution of Boehme's seven forms is a particular emotional quality, the tremendous agony that is the condition of their operation. Boehme's language beats haplessly against itself as it aches to express this agony in his curious vocabulary of *Blitz* and *Angst* and *Shrack;* these are cognates of the "fierce anguish" of Blake's creation, his "Pangs of Eternal birth," the "universal shrieks" running "thro' the Abysses," his thunders and his quakes, his groans and crashes, and all his clanking terrors. The seven abstractions themselves Blake seems to have transferred to the bodies of his four contrary Zoas and their divisive parts. And although Blake amplifies their symbolical conflicts with imagery of factory and forge, physics, architecture, and art, Boehme's metaphysic of God's realization of himself is the abstract ground, perhaps the clue, out of which Blake develops the chief apparatus of his myth.

In Boehme, finally, Blake found a number of particular figures that he managed to incorporate in his poems. Of these the most important is the fall of Lucifer and of Adam after him, and the creation of Eve and a quarrelsome race. This material, which he already knew in the Miltonic interpretation, was amplified for him in Boehme's treatment, where the fall always appears as the assertion of an egoistic will that brings about a condition of blind selfishness. In this interpretation Blake merely increased the ethical, and added aesthetic and political overtones. Less singular, perhaps, is Boehme's use of childhood as a proper symbol for harmony; he repeatedly compares the innocent play of children with the "play" of God, which is his image of the final goal. Blake's immortals "play," too:

. . . All were forth at sport beneath the solemn moon
Walking the stars of Urizen with their immortal songs,
That nature felt thro' all her pores the enormous revelry . . .

Certain portions of Boehme's alchemical vocabulary Blake found useful to express ideas of hidden and apparent values, and the use of the serpent as the symbol of unenlightened materialism he may also have found in Boehme. Of such specific figures there may be more, but of concepts, beyond the very important ones of the dialectical progress and of the imagination as a moral agent, there seem to be none. In general, Boehme, like Swedenborg, supplied Blake with symbols that he suited to his own purposes, and with sanctions rather than with ideas. Their service to him, finally, was not unlike the service of Law and Fox and Boehme to Coleridge: they "acted in no slight degree to prevent my mind from being imprisoned within the outline of any single dogmatic system. They contributed to keep alive the heart in the head; gave me an indistinct, yet stirring and working presentiment, that all the products of the mere reflective faculty partook of death."

"Bring forth the New Jerusalem; *It is Day:* why should we sleep in the Day?" cried Boehme. Blake, with the same Protestant enthusiasm, cried the same words many times. But they were the same words with a difference:

The morning comes, the night decays, the watchmen leave their stations. . . .
Let the slave grinding at the mill run out into the field,
Let him look up into the heavens & laugh in the bright air;
Let the inchained soul, shut up in darkness and in sighing,
Whose face has never seen a smile in thirty weary years,
Rise and look out; his chains are loose, his dungeon doors are open;
And let his wife and children return from the oppressor's scourge.

An analysis of the religious ideas contained within Blake's elaborate metaphorical structure shows that they are not very complex or, even though they anticipate certain nineteenth-century ideas, very original. His originality consists in ideas that pertain specifically to politics and to psychology, in his address, that is, to "the slave . . . at the mill" and to "the inchained soul, shut up in . . . sighing."

V

In examining Blake's religious attitudes, let us begin with the set of ideas nearest him in time and apparently remotest from him in spirit—that deism or natural religion which he professed to despise.* For there was more to the complex of natural religion than the acceptance of the reason as the religious faculty; more

* The most famous short discussion of deism is A. O. Lovejoy's "Parallel of Deism and Classicism," *Modern Philology,* Vol. XXIX (February 1932), pp. 281-99. My indebtedness to that essay is patent.

than a particular concept of deity and of a harmoniously "rational" universe; more than the theory that religion consists of a few generally acceptable items of morality. The structure of deism rested on the assumption of uniformitarianism, on the theory that all men share an identical reason, and that since they do, all eccentricity is error. It followed that there can be only one "right" religion, a religion that appeals to the reason of all men everywhere, a cosmopolitanism so broad that no sect, no nation, no continent, no planet even, could be allowed to claim a superior revelation or a pre-eminent historical function. The implication was of a kind of universal intellectual democracy, although in the least fortunate sense of that term; namely, that the truth could consist of nothing more than that which was acceptable to the lowest common human denominator.

But if this point of view meant the denial of religious genius, it also had the more fortunate result of insisting, with a large body of pietist thinking in the previous century, that elaborations of dogma and distinctions of sects were accidents, indeed errors, and that true religion must be reduced to essential doctrines. If at one extreme this kind of simplification meant an attitude of religious indifference, at the other extreme it meant the assertion of religious tolerance, of the rights and responsibilities of the laity, and of the secondary character of religious institutions. The forests of dogma were, indeed, the fault of institutions, of groups and orders and societies that had moved far away from the basic truth, and the implication was always that at one time a state of nature had prevailed (or could be discovered in the present under layers of historical incrustation) in which the truths stood out fair and clear, free of the mistaken overgrowths of history. To achieve or reachieve this condition, all that was necessary was to practice a universal, a mysterious and ill-defined, laissez faire in all things.

All of this, with whatever radical difference in vocabulary, is to be found in Blake. He could not endure the terms of deism, nor its tone, but he retained much of its content and even a portion of its logic. He had his own uniformitarianism, even though it was of a variety that, not at all paradoxically, allowed him to exalt rather than deplore eccentricity. Whether one makes reason the universal human quality or the capacity of receiving revelation, the result is the same—in Blake's phrase as in the deist's, "All Religions Are One." His was a cosmopolitanism quite as uncompromising as that of the most extreme deism: "The antiquities of every Nation under Heaven, is no less sacred than that of the Jews," he said, and, agreeing with Paine, "That the Jews assumed a right Exclusively to the benefits of God will be a lasting witness against them & the same will it be against Christians."

The implicit equalitarianism of deism is always explicit in Blake, and a good deal less ambiguous: ". . . he eagerly assented to a remark I made," said Robinson, "that All men have all faculties to a greater or less degree," and to Robinson he made it clear that among the faculties men share or could share was the visionary imagination. Blake occasionally carried this idea to an extreme which, if not as dull as that of the deists, is yet one of its less interesting possibilities: "The Beauty of the Bible is that the most Ignorant & Simple Minds Understand it Best." And he went quite as far as they, of course, in deploring the elaborations of dogma and the distinctions of sects, and in this his biography speaks as clearly as his writing. The simplification of doctrine in Blake is no less extreme, and if he did not reduce the essentials of religion to a few moral platitudes, like the deists, he did reduce them to a single item that is, in essence, ethical: the forgiveness of sins. This in itself indicates how central in Blake is the idea of tolerance, albeit a tolerance much less negative in kind than that which deism found attractive. And so, too, his insistence on the rights of the laity and his attack on institutional authority were as sharp and as excessive as the insistence in these matters of the shrillest of all deists, Thomas Paine.

Blake, frequently attacking naturalism with uncommon violence, yet had his own concept of "a state of nature," and, contradictory as it may seem to his view as a whole, primitivism, that ignis fatuus, always glimmers, although sometimes only fitfully, throughout his work. Contradiction is of his essence, perhaps; while he upbraided the deists on most occasions and wrote two "Tractates" under the title *There Is No Natural*

Religion, he could also say, with true deistical equanimity—for here even the vocabulary is identical—"Truth is Nature" and "Natural Religion is the voice of God."

The difficulty arose for Blake not only because of his own unsettled attitudes toward "nature" and "matter," but also, as it did for many another man in the eighteenth century, because he was never quite certain where he wished to locate his "natural" state. At one time or another, and often simultaneously, he accepted each of the three possibilities.

The first is the irreproachable primitivism of the second chapter of Genesis, irreproachable because it is fabulous and because, admitting no easy compromise with history or with the present, it is the only possible ground of a genuine theology. "The Bible tells me that the plan of Providence was Subverted at the Fall of Adam & that it was not restored till Christ." When Blake takes this view, radical evil is imputed to nature, and there is no remedy within nature. At such points, his castigation of the world is nearly Calvinistic in its vehemence, and the restoration of the providential plan through Christ is construed in the most final eschatological sense, beyond nature, beyond life. But of the three possibilities this view is least characteristic of Blake and is least frequently expressed.

Nearly all the strands of his temperament and nearly all the ideas he had inherited forced him into the typical Protestant compromise, the second possibility. Evil is not radical but negative, and the ideal state is a psychological condition that exists in the present and within nature, under the errors of institutions, under man's own mistaken concept that evil is real. Not only Adam but every man "falls" when he makes this mistake, and every man achieves the original harmony the minute that, seeing Christ clearly, he corrects the mistake. This is, of course, the very theme of Blake's long poems. The theme ramifies, quite naturally, into typical Rousseauistic attitudes, even though—and here is the inevitable contradiction again—Blake had no good word to speak for Rousseau, who, like Wordsworth, was an "atheist." But if "There is no such Thing as Natural Piety," what are we intended to make of the *Songs of Innocence,* of Blake's persistent view of childhood, and of that pastoral brightness which, not only in the *Songs of Experience,* but everywhere, he contrasted with the blighting gloom of cities? "Alas, in cities where's the man whose face is not a mask unto his heart?" he lamented in a juvenile work, and both mood and contrast persisted to the very end of his life. Nor did he exclude from the realm of innocence that other member of the eighteenth-century pair, the savage: ". . . the Innocent civilized Heathen & the Uncivilized Savage, who, having not the Law, do by Nature the things contain'd in the Law." This is deism unadulterated, and the mood is pervasive: ". . . the Ancient Britons . . . (say historians) were naked civilized men, learned, studious, abstruse in thought and contemplation; naked, simple, plain in their acts and manners; wiser than after-ages. They were overwhelmed by brutal arms."

The third possibility exists between the first and the second: it locates the state of nature not in prehistory, nor, though buried, in the present, but somewhere in the ancient and actual past. To the fruitless but perennially attractive idea of a Golden Age Blake was inevitably led by his view of art. His poem *Tiriel,* describing poetry and painting in their degraded eighteenth-century condition, as he thought, looks back to a time when man exercised his faculties freely, and his productions were many and beautiful. Then vision flourished, for although "Influx from above" is "unusual in our time," it was "common in ancient."

Blake's ideas of the limits of ancient times were perhaps no more precise than those of most of his contemporaries. Whether, according to the odd speculations of the Celtomaniacs, the Golden Age should properly be associated with the lost Atlantis and with the fifth of its scattered peoples, the Semites, who founded Jerusalem on "Albion's Ancient Druid Rocky Shore"; or, contrary as this may be to Blake's usual evaluation, with early Grecian times; or, like the most general Rousseauism, with a simple primitive life in any time at all, ancient or modern—this Blake never seemed to decide. "Read the Edda of Iceland, the Songs of Fingal, the accounts of North American Savages (as they are call'd). Likewise read Homer's Iliad. He was certainly a Savage in the Bishop's sense. He knew nothing of God in the Bishop's sense of the word & yet he was no fool." Vague (and mistaken) as some parts of this assertion may be, it expresses the great commonplace of eighteenth-century primitivism, and it is inextricably bound up with that more special commonplace of deism, which Blake also stated: "All had originally one language, and one religion: this was the religion of Jesus, the everlasting Gospel. Antiquity preaches the Gospel of Jesus."

This assumption often led Blake, as it did the deists, to assume a wholly negative view of history in which all the works of civilization are seen as merely obstructing more and more the grand light of primitive times. "That mankind," said Blake, "are in a less distinguished Situation with regard to mind than they were in the time of Homer, Socrates, Phidias, Glycon, Aristotle, etc., let all their works witness." But the attack on institutions caught Blake in the identical conflict that plagued the thinking of a deist like Thomas Paine—the clash between primitivism and progress. It is not surprising. There are a number of matters which Blake, like his religious tradition and like the century that nourished him, could never quite settle.

The conflicts in Blake's thinking are more extensive and more acute than those within deism itself in the degree to which, while accepting so much of the wrappings of deism, he yet clashed with it on central matters. The major historical fact about deism is probably its tone, which is one of utter complacency; and Blake is perhaps the least complacent of poets. For like Hopkins and Milton in the description of Charles Williams, he had a "simultaneous consciousness of a controlled universe, and yet of division, conflict, and crises within that universe," and it is precisely this "consciousness" in the character of traditional Christianity that deism attempted to overcome. It made its attempt by three assumptions, with each of which Blake disagreed: the nature of the religious faculty (the reason), the nature of the deity (the clockmaker god), and the nature of the universe (the harmoniously "rational" cosmos). These were necessary terms if, in the aspirations of deism, religion was to be reconciled with contemporary science, and deism has at least this dubious eminence, that it was the first attempt in modern times to identify belief and knowledge. Blake, perhaps more insistently than any other modern man, strove to separate them. The excess of each effort was probably its weakness; for it is as difficult to equate attitude with fact as it is perverse to flout, even though half-heartedly, fact by attitude. But for the very reason that the discrepancy in these three items, and in their motive, is so sharp and so deep, the remainder of Blake's religious attitudes can be defined in their terms.

To the reason as the faculty of religious truth, Blake opposed a faculty for which he produced a multitude of names: vision, imagination, poetic genius, "the Spirit of Prophecy," energy, desire, enthusiasm, and so on; for Blake was Pauline in at least this sense, that he was certain that "The world through its wisdom knew not God." All his terms represent his special interpretation of the evangelical concept of "faith," and in his insistence on the centrality of faith and the inadequacy of reason as such, Blake's subjectivism approximates that of Methodism. But Blake was not a Methodist, and it is a mistake to attempt a more complete identification. For the religion of Wesley as it was first preached was a profoundly conservative doctrine. It reasserted the importance of faith because natural religion, in eliding the idea of original sin, exalted the idea of the adequacy of the human being and of the sufficiency of his reason; and in its reaction, Wesleyan doctrine withdrew itself from any attitudes (and thereby took the Tory attitude) toward institutions and political society. This was hardly the motive of Blake. For his antecedents one may look more safely to the subjectivism of William Law, and, in turn, to his antecedents, Boehme and the seventeenth-century pietists, and, for certain ramifications, to the poet Milton.

Blake's subjectivism, his opposition of faith to reason, of feeling, which is internal, to the passive observation of a body of dogma, which is external, has many connections with earlier Protestantism. Blake was like one of those "Seekers" of the seventeenth century who, achieving his own revelation, required no other and passed beyond the need of any institutional authority. His "vision" was an artist's term for the layman's "inner light," and it carried with it, besides its particular aesthetic content, the full burden of religious conviction. In the extreme subjectivism of his "illumination" and in certain of its consequences, Blake most resembles, among sectarians, the members of the curious group called Familists, which, although founded in Holland in the sixteenth century under the name of The Family of Love, persisted as a society in England until some time in the first decades of the eighteenth century. The Familists' faith in their "inner light" was so intense that they adopted a completely antinomian position. Regeneration corrects the fault of Adam, and God and man become one; to this achievement, religious law can contribute nothing; the Bible is allegorical, and good and evil angels are merely states of mind. All these beliefs are to be found in Blake.

Yet if Blake, in his insistence on the centrality of the individual intuition, looks back to the seventeenth century, he also looks forward to the nineteenth; for the emphasis on religion as feeling and as experience is the whole basis of later liberal theology, and this is only the first of a series of ways in which Blake anticipates such theologians as Schleiermacher and even such philosophers as Schelling, who like Blake identified the religious and the aesthetic sense. Deism, resting its case on reason, had reduced religion to morality, as in the famous definition of Voltaire: *"J'entends, par religion naturelle, les principes de morale communs au genre-humain."* But Blake, who said that "If Morality was Christianity, Socrates was The Savior," argued like Schleiermacher that religious intuition lifted the believer into a higher sphere, provided him with an enriched perception of the wholeness of experience, and substituted for the Newtonian harmony of deism an aesthetic experience of harmony that is potential in the world and upon which the visionary, or the true believer, can seize.

Rejecting the utilitarian morality of rationalism, Blake, like Schleiermacher, asserted a more plausible ethics; for both insisted that genuine religious experience involved a truly imaginative moral act, in which the selfish isolation of individual needs is transcended in the sense of a larger unity and a nobler universe. They sought an "*expanded* benevolence" in place of the narrow benevolence of a Tindal or a Paley. All this points back to Boehme, to his old distinction between *Verstand* and

Vernunft, and these very terms, of course, became the tool by which the flat rationalism of the Enlightenment, in England as well as in Germany, was pried apart. One should not, however, overlook the fact that Blake, like later liberal theologians and unlike any genuine mystics, emphasized in his doctrine of intuition its object, which was man in a world.

This, as much as anything else, underlay his ideas on the nature of deity, and its correlate, his doctrine of evil. For the sources of Blake's denial of Jehovah and his interpretation of the character of Christ, we may go back in history as far as the Oriental gnostics and the earliest Christian heretics, whom Blake probably read about in Mosheim's popular *Ecclesiastical History,* or we may come as near to him as Thomas Paine. Blake was neither a Manichaean nor a Marcionite, but in reading about either he could find shades of belief in which the sharp dualism between two eternal principles of good and evil to which these subscribed dropped off into the kind of quasi-dualism that Blake himself developed. Mosheim wrote, for example: "Others maintained, that the being, which presided over matter, was not an eternal principle, but a subordinate intelligence, one of those whom the Supreme God produced from himself," and "They also foretold the approaching defeat of the *evil principle,* to whom they attributed the creation of this globe, and declared, in the most pompous terms, the destruction of his associates, and the ruin of his empire."

These quotations suggest Blake's idea of the "God of This World," that Urizen to whom man mistakenly gives authority, and who must himself be redeemed (not destroyed) by the spirit of Jesus. Blake, too, renounced "the worship of the God of the Jews, who is the Prince of Darkness" for the sake of Christ, but unlike the Manichaeans, he did not give Jehovah real powers. For this point of view, he might have found support in Mosheim's description of the Valentinians, who believed that Jesus is the first and ultimate deity and that only "by the assistance of Jesus" is "the *demiurge,* the lord and creator of all things," produced. And even for his curiously naturalistic view of Jesus there was precedent here: "For though they believed the celestial mission of Christ, and his participation of a divine nature, yet they regarded him as a man born of Joseph and Mary, according to the ordinary course of nature." Blake went even further than these Ebionites:

> Was Jesus Chaste? or did he
> Give any Lessons of Chastity?
> The morning blush'd fiery red:
> Mary was found in Adulterous bed;
> Earth groan'd beneath, & Heaven above
> Trembled at discovery of Love.

Once more Blake thrusts ahead into the realm of modern liberal theology. It is the insistence of liberalism on the humanity of Jesus and the divinity of man that enables it, however mistakenly from the point of view of a more adequate theology, to substitute for the traditional paradox of the incarnation the easier idea of grace as the individual's awareness of his own sanctity.

How much the deistical view of the New Testament in relation to the Old has to do with this transformation it would be hard to say. The deists, optimistically proclaiming the sufficiency of human reason as a moral and religious instrument, argued that the religion of the Old Testament, founded on the concept of human error and the consequent necessity of law and of a legal God, was unnatural, that the religion of Jesus was the true religion, or, as Blake said, the religion of antiquity. Quite like Blake, Paine pointed out that the tyrant Jehovah was an idealization of tyrant priests and kings but hardly Christian, and pursued, with unnecessary vehemence, the inconsistencies in Old Testament history. Shelley, in *Queen Mab,* argued on the same theme: Jehovah is a construction of the degraded human mind, a mythological extension of man's own failings of pride and ignorance, and a sanction for his most wretchedly selfish political and social acts. Paine and Shelley were expressing a commonplace of the Enlightenment, a commonplace that is come upon quite as readily in Voltaire or Volney or Lessing. Lessing, for example, argued that the function of Christ was to return religion tc its natural purity. And how near Blake was to all this! He said: "Why did Christ come? Was it not to abolish the Jewish Imposture?"

Yet there is a sharp difference between Blake's concept of God and that of the deists, for if the God of natural religion is not a judge who lacks a sense of justice, he is an archetype of Newton—"the great mechanic of the creation; the first philosopher and original teacher of all science." This is a deity no more satisfactory to Blake, yet proving, perhaps, his argument that "Man can have no idea of any thing greater than Man, as a cup cannot contain more than its capaciousness." The difficulty was that, in the eighteenth century, "man has closed himself up, till he sees all things thro' narrow chinks of his cavern." The whole narrative principle of Blake's prophecies is that when Albion, the universal man, falls, then God is falling too, which is saying that our gods are fashioned to express our own condition. If we are plagued by a sense of sin, our God is a judge; if we inflate our reason, our God is a rationalist. In Blake's mind, the weakness of both the God of judgment and the Newtonian God was that both were held apart from man in abstract heavens, the one bound by his moral law, the other by the laws of physics. To law, for gods and men, Blake opposed love.

"Listen! Every Religion that Preaches Vengeance for Sin is the Religion of the Enemy & Avenger and not of the Forgiver of Sin, and their God is Satan, Named by the Divine Name." "Love Is Life," Blake said, and therefore all religions are indeed one, but they cannot be religions of law. "Ye are united, O ye Inhabitants of Earth, in One Religion, The Religion of Jesus, the most Ancient, the Eternal & the Everlasting Gospel." A God of law is a God of will, and "There can be no Good Will. Will is always Evil." To posit such a God is to sanction man's own worst qualities: his will, his lust for power, his tyrannies, his atomistic isolations, his ego, all the schisms of his spirit. But to posit a God of love is to sanction man's best qualities: sympathy, forgiveness, brotherhood, imagination. This is the voice of the nineteenth century again, of Tolstoy and Ritschl and Mazzini. "All Penal Laws court Transgression & therefore are cruelty & Murder. The laws of the Jews were (both ceremonial & real) the basest & most oppressive of human codes, & being like all other codes given under pretence of divine command were what Christ pronounced them, The Abomination that maketh desolate, *i.e.* State Religion, which is the source of all Cruelty."

Blake's Jesus was an antinomian and his function was to break laws, including every item of the decalogue. Blake's basic assumption was at least as old as Protestantism, and the extreme to which he pushed it had been arrived at by at least some of the sects in the Commonwealth more than a hundred years before him. Milton argued that the coming of Christ annulled the entire body of Mosaic law, and he did not hesitate to make radical inferences concerning civil as well as church government from his premise. Yet Milton's doctrine of Christian liberty remains safely legal, for he does not wantonly make his Jesus a God of love alone, but of reason, too, of an inner law that, replacing the old external law, serves quite as well as guide and check. But Blake wrote:

> Jesus was sitting in Moses' Chair,
> They brought the trembling Woman There. . . .
> "Good & Evil are no more!
> "Sinai's trumpets, cease to roar!
> "Cease, finger of God, to write!"

Here Milton's inner law has vanished with Moses' outer, and to make his difference from Milton perfectly explicit, as well as to correct Milton's error and save him further suffering in eternity, Blake wrote the long poem that has the older poet's name as its title.

The error was not difficult to correct, for in most matters in this connection Blake found an agreeable precedent among the Puritans and related groups, and he needed only to shift some of their terms to arrive at his own position. The trust in the individual and the distrust of the state and of state religion were everywhere. Among Puritans, as among the Quakers and others, there was the distrust of force and the faith in free discussion for which Blake had his images of mental strife and the sword of love, the intellectual sport of pacifist gods. Among

Levellers and Diggers there was deep faith in human equality, not only in the eyes of God but here and now in the brotherhood of Jesus. And among the Diggers there was even that utopian socialism which prefigures Morris's, and which Blake expressed with his characteristic aesthetic turn: "The Whole Business of Man Is The Arts, & All Things Common." Yet the shift in terms, while easy (for the Enlightenment had intervened), was crucial, and in separating Blake from seventeenth-century Protestantism it brings him again much nearer to certain elements in the nineteenth. Surely he was the very first of "those writers" urged upon our attention by Melville "who breathe that unshackled, democratic spirit of Christianity in all things, which now takes the practical lead in this world."

Blake's doctrine of evil and his ethical view in general proceed directly from his view of Jesus, and perhaps no more need be said about them here than to locate them as far as possible in their historical framework. The belief that sin consists in defects of love alone goes back at least as far as Dante, but for the particular negative emphasis on the notion of "defect" and for the particular optimism implied by later use of the concept "love," we must come up, once more, to the mood of Protestantism in the Commonwealth. The faith of the Quakers and other sects in the divinity of man; in the notion that the "fall" does not imply radical evil but the obstruction of natural goodness by pride or selfishness—a psychological condition capable of cure; and the faith in the inevitability of the cure—that the reason or the love of God *must* prevail, the "light" *must* shine, that men *must* return to a perfected condition because the alternative is the impossible, the defeat of God—all this Nonconformist doctrine is in the background of Blake's ideas.

Yet a Quaker or a Leveller, with another emphasis, could still have said with George Herbert,

> The world an ancient murderer is;
> Thousands of souls it hath and doth destroy
> With her enchanting voice.

But Blake could almost never have said it. For the eighteenth century had come between, and with it a secularized ethics that did not leave Blake untouched. It is not an accident that the word "harmony" is as common in Blake as it is in Shaftesbury, or the word "order" as it is in any Newtonian. And while the two parties intended different kinds of harmony and order, they shared this much, that the words could not have been applied to man or nature by either party if both had not first abandoned all ideas of original sin. Shaftesbury, in his universal harmony, emphasized the role of nature, which was in itself divine. Blake emphasized the part of man, who was divine. Blake, as we have repeatedly seen, is divided in his attitudes toward nature, yet the characteristic ending of his prophecies is a regenerate man beholding a harmonized nature: "How is it that all things are chang'd, even as in ancient times?" Then all things, even dumbest matter, "even Tree, Metal, Earth & Stone," are seen to be animated by spirit, and it would be hard to say that Blake's theism is utterly different from Shaftesbury's.

Both Blake and Shaftesbury rested their case for ethics on the concept of "sympathy." But Blake gave the meaning of the word the significant additions of the old Christian notion of selflessness and of the modern metaphysical notion of "perception." Shaftesbury's "sympathy" resulted in a sentimental and utilitarian ethics; Blake's, in an imaginative ethics. The standard eighteenth-century faith in a tattered concept of benevolence as self-interest, which Blake despised, he also attempted to renew; and he achieved an ethics that, looking back to the century of Locke, yet looks forward too, to the most revolutionary elements in the century of Hegel. Its pivot is the idea of "Universal Love" that we associate with Shaftesbury:

Turning from Universal Love, petrific as he went,
His cold against the warmth of Eden rag'd with loud
Thunders of deadly war (the fever of the human soul)
Fires and clouds of rolling smoke! but mild, the Saviour follow'd
    him,
Displaying the Eternal Vision, the Divine Similitude,
In loves and tears of brothers, sisters, sons, fathers and friends,
Which if Man ceases to behold, he ceases to exist.

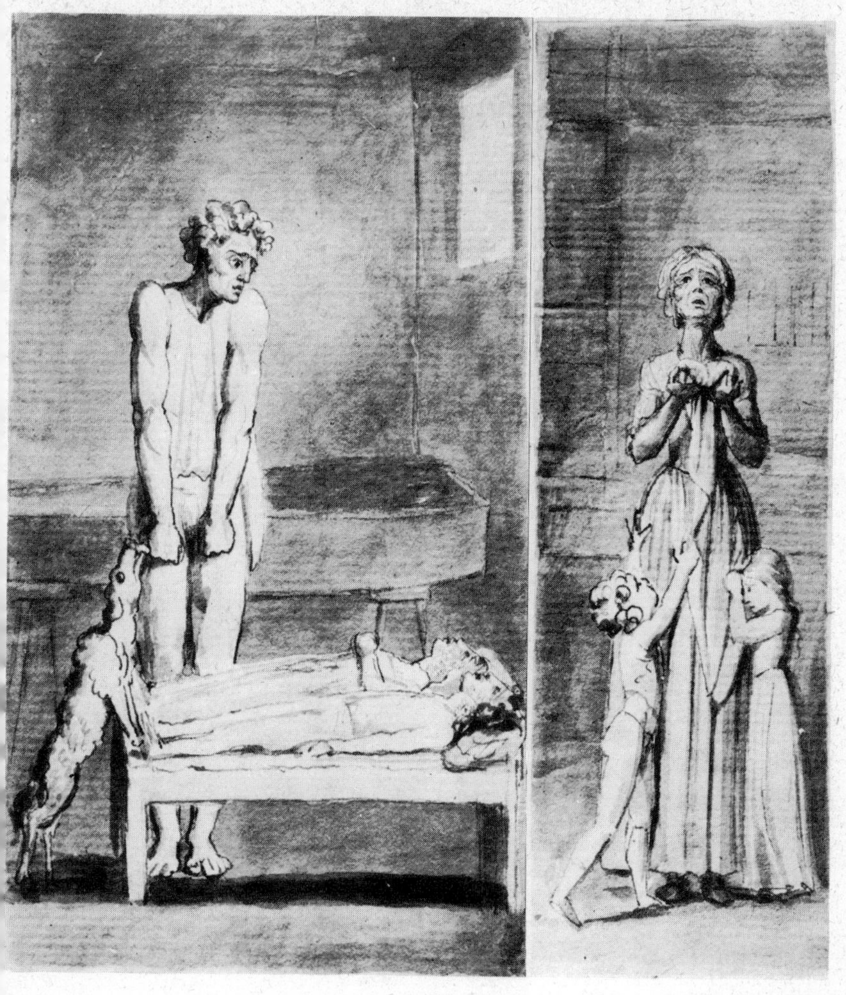

Two illustrations from Mary Wollstonecraft's
Original Stories from Real Life
By courtesy of the Rosenwald Collection in the Library of Congress

"What is the price of Experience? do men buy it for a song?
Or wisdom for a dance in the street? No, it is bought with the price
Of all that a man hath . . ."

This is Shaftesbury reconverted to Christianity, but in its later terms of ethical theism, not of orthodoxy. When Albrecht Ritschl, in the second half of the nineteenth century, declared that God is love, he meant the love of man for men. Its effect was in active sympathy and service, in "loves and tears of brothers, sisters, sons, fathers and friends." Thy kingdom come, in short, on earth. It was a prospect that Blake could not resist.

Blake's view of the universe varies with the variations of his moods from the joyous to the splenetic. The utter rejection of nature appears mainly in epistolary outbursts and in the fragmentary jottings of his last years. Then the universe is so much dross, the illusory creation of Satan. The affirmation of nature appears in his earlier works, both whole and fragmentary, and in all his long poems, which are not the productions of a moment's mood of dismay but of a studied effort to state his view as, most soberly, he held it. Then the universe in its grossest and most mechanical forms is regarded as the limited point of view of the rationalist and the scientist, and this is "meer Nature or Hell." Or alternately, it is considered in its illuminated or spiritualized forms, as the enlightened point of view—and the reality—of the visionary, the whole man, and this is "Universal Nature." On these occasions he anticipates the Yeatsian view,

That this pragmatical, preposterous pig of a world, its farrow
    that so solid seem,
Must vanish on the instant if the mind but change its
    theme . . .
Everything that is not God consumed with intellectual fire.

In both his splenetic and his affirmative moods, Blake adheres to a doctrine of divine immanence, but on the occasions of the first, divinity inhabits man alone, and on the occasions of the second, it inhabits man and nature both. On the occasions of the second, then, Blake gropes toward something like the aesthetic naturalism of the nineteenth century; and because it almost always follows on the faith in "an immanent *logos* principle," the doctrine of progress, at the very least in its evangelical form, is the object of Blake's constant flirtation.

Blake's inconsistencies are the usual conflicts within Protestantism itself. Once the idea of the perfectibility of the individual soul in this life established itself, the notion of a perfected society was difficult to suppress. Milton presents a moderate example. With his conviction that the individual Christian was capable of improvement through the free exercise of his reason came the idea that Church and civil government were capable of improvement through the free exercise of the reason of the community. Winstanley presents an extravagant example. His faith in the immanent divinity of every man led him to expect and to urge his followers to achieve the New Jerusalem in this world, as a social and an economic fact. Even Wesley's doctrine of the perfectibility of the individual soul, in spite of the sharp line he himself drew between institutions and grace, was subject to a certain ambiguity, as is evident in Cowper's humanitarianism, for example, or in the actual practice of extensive humanitarian acts among the working classes that was the habit of the Methodists. The divinity of man and his capacity for a regenerate perfection was a permanent part of Blake's thinking: ". . . to think of holiness distinct from man is impossible," he said, and ". . . knaveries are not human nature; knaveries are knaveries."

Another and less obvious strand that ties Blake to his time is the kind of theism we have already mentioned as characteristic of Shaftesbury. The notion that God inhabits every portion of the universe implies the peculiar rightness of every item in the universe, and suggests that evil is apparent only. The Popian theory that the seeming imperfections in the universal harmony are really the limitations of the observer is not entirely unlike Blake's insistence on the importance of vision to truth. The idea of the peculiar merit and excellence of every portion of the creation, as old as Plato and very popular in the eighteenth century through the wide familiarity enjoyed by the notion of The Great Chain of Being, likewise has its echo in Blake. Pope exalted the individual identity in these terms:

> What if the foot, ordain'd the dust to tread,
> Or hand to toil, aspired to be the head?

What if the head, the eye, or ear repin'd
To serve mere engines to the ruling mind?
Just as absurd for any part to claim
To be another in the gen'ral frame.

And in these:

Why has not man a microscopic eye?
For this plain reason, man is not a fly.

Blake exalted the individual identity in these terms: "Deduct from a rose its redness, from a lilly its whiteness, from a diamond its hardness, from a spunge its softness, from an oak its heighth, from a daisy its lowness, & . . . we shall return to Chaos"; and in these: "The roaring of lions, the howling of wolves, the raging of the stormy sea, and the destructive sword, are portions of eternity, too great for the eye of man."

That Pope and Blake, beginning with opposite motives, drew opposite conclusions is, for the moment, beside the point; they agreed on the central issue, that a divine principle of order exists in the universe. This is the meaning of Blake's aphorism "Eternity is in love with the productions of time." Likewise, "Time is the mercy of Eternity," which is to say that divinity, inhabiting nature and the present, makes possible our salvation. "God is in the lowest effects as well as in the highest causes; for he is become a worm that he may nourish the weak. For let it be remember'd that creation is God descending according to the weakness of man, for our Lord is the word of God & every thing on earth is the word of God & in its essence is God." Those apocalyptic visions with which Blake ends his long poems are the climax of dialectical struggles between human weakness and human divinity, and in the climax both are rescued, and both are renewed in a higher innocence.

In motive and in conclusion, Blake is more like certain thinkers he had not read at all than he is like Pope. He is less Hegelian than his predecessor Boehme, for instance, only to the extent that he did not systematize his ideas in abstract terms. But the dialectic is there in a rudimentary form, and with it the theory of immanence, the doctrine that the world is the scene of salvation, and even, shadowy as it sometimes is, the idea of God's realization of himself in the spiritual progress of man.

Surely there are parallels with Herder here, and with Schleiermacher. Because of his faith in immanence, Blake likewise frequently wiped out the old spatial and temporal distinctions between heaven and earth, since God is in man here and now, and he abolished hell entirely. A final comparison of some value is with the ideas of Mazzini, with his identification of politics and religion, his revolutionary faith in man's capacity for social and spiritual progress, and yet with the ultimate check on his optimism that the final progress lies beyond historical developments.

For this check is in Blake, too, and it plays an increasingly important role in his poetry. Some of the contradictions we have observed may indeed have arisen from his inability to arrive at it earlier. Paradox was by no means an unfamiliar tool of logic to Blake, yet he was never quite able to seize upon the paradox of the incarnation, for example, and hold to it firmly. If he had, he would have spared himself many of the pendulumnar inconsistencies to which he was subject. Another paradox, however, he seems to have grasped, at least faintly, in the end. It is the paradox of which Reinhold Niebuhr writes so much: "There is no escape from the paradoxical relation of history to the Kingdom of God. History moves towards the realization of the Kingdom but yet the judgment of God is upon every new realization." Even at the end of his life, Blake would not have written in terms of judgment, but he had analogous terms. No development was final for him; innocence always suggests experience, and every progression toward good involves a new potentiality of error. The soul perfects itself, but it does not fall into "a stillness" when it has, and the possibilities of the eruption of will remain, and with them those of spiritual dread.

Yet, beyond this slight connection it will not do to attempt to force Blake into the framework of serious theology today. He came out of an atmosphere of Nonconformist doctrine; he developed its antinomian implications; and he anticipated almost point for point the liberal theology of the nineteenth century. There was little in his religious ideas that was genuinely striking except his identification of revelation and art, or prophets and poets. This brings us back to the point at which we began. Blake was not a theologian; his theology, like everything else about him, was developed almost entirely in order that he might pursue his art and hold to his faith in himself as the kind of artist he was.

Today, to the deep sense of failure and discontent of this decade, when the only theology that makes any appeal is the drastic "theology of crisis," when the Kierkegaardian and the Barthian view is in the ascendant and among poets Mr. Eliot still speaks with the greatest authority, these ideas of Blake's, as we have summarized them, are bound to seem old-fashioned and inadequate. But where, then, does the undeniable impact of his work lie, and the mystery? Why, precisely now, and for the first time, has his work really sunk deep into the consciousness of many poets, as forty years ago it had sunk into the consciousness of only a few, say Yeats and A.E.? * Why now, in this decade, has his work for the first time gained general acceptance among critics as a legitimate poetic product, gained even a considerable primacy among them? No one today would be willing to denounce him, yet thirty years ago, even twenty, when religious ideas such as his own were most widely popular, he was still, as in the work of Sturge Moore, the subject of diatribe.

The impact and the mystery lie somewhere else. They are not

* A recent example of the indebtedness of modern poetry to Blake is Stephen Spender's poem, "Rejoice in the Abyss," *Partisan Review,* Vol. XI (Summer 1944), pp. 283-84. Here Blake may be seen in the poet's mind not only in the familiar manner of influence (echoed phrases, the form of the imagery, the nature of some of the rhythms) but also as a figure in himself, of symbolic "ancestral" value. The same kind of debt and much more pervasive is acknowledged by W. H. Auden in the notes to "New Year's Letter" *(Collected Poems,* Random House, 1945), the very poem in which Auden is in the process of detaching himself from many of Blake's most characteristic ideas. Or one might consider the paradox of a poet like Mark Van Doren, who even in such a volume as *The Seven Sleepers* (Holt, 1944), which takes as its theme the praise of authority, yet makes his bow to Blake. See, for example, "Is Now," p. 51. A useful summary of Blake's influence on modern poets in general is Kerker Quinn's "Blake and the New Age," *Virginia Quarterly Review,* Vol. XIII (Spring 1937), pp. 271-85.

in the expression alone, as A. E. Housman perversely thought.* They lie in the expression of certain psychological and political insights, which together comprise what we may take to mean in Coleridge's fascinating phrase "the permanent politics of human nature." We must not lose sight of the fact that these ideas are themselves deeply rooted in Blake's religious beliefs, but the very fact that his religious beliefs are so watered by liberalism gives his psychological and his political ideas a kind of independence and a value of their own. This is only to say that when theology decays, other ideas once associated with it gain autonomy and potency of their own. In a sense, these ideas in Blake's work are even separate, for they sometimes seem to stand in judgment on the religious ideas and to express their discontent:

> Now as at all times I can see in the mind's eye,
> In their stiff, painted clothes, the pale unsatisfied ones
> Appear and disappear in the blue depth of the sky
> With all their ancient faces like rain-beaten stones,
> And all their helms of silver hovering side by side,
> And all their eyes still fixed, hoping to find once more,
> Being by Calvary's turbulence unsatisfied,
> The uncontrollable mystery on the bestial floor.

* "For me the most poetical of all poets is Blake. I find his lyrical note as beautiful as Shakespeare's, and more beautiful than anyone else's; and I call him more poetical than Shakespeare, even though Shakespeare has so much more poetry, because poetry in him preponderates more than in Shakespeare over everything else, and instead of being confounded in a great river can be drunk pure from a slender channel of its own. Shakespeare is richer in thought and his meaning has power of itself to move us, even if the poetry were not there; Blake's meaning is often unimportant or virtually non-existent, so that we can listen with all our hearing to his celestial tune." —*The Name and Nature of Poetry,* Macmillan, 1933, p.39.

PART TWO

Politics and Psychology

☼

"Blake: Never did a braver or a better man carry the sword of justice."

—Walter Savage Landor, *Notebook*

CHAPTER FIVE

Blake at the Turn of a Century

I

WE TURN NOW to the impact on Blake of "the specious Liberal stuff that," according to Hopkins, "crazed Shelley, and, indeed, in their youth, Wordsworth and Coleridge." Far from crazing Blake, it was this stuff that helped him keep his hands in the world and his eyes upon it. Even in his youth he did not accept the stuff whole, but abruptly winnowed it of its absurdities; and in his age he was not faced with the rejections of his contemporaries. In Shelley the Godwinian absurdities remain, for Shelley mainly made mixtures, not transmutations. In Blake, where the texture is richer and the heat burns, Godwinism becomes wisdom, revolutionary doctrine that continues to speak with relevance.

That the content of Blake's poetry is primarily social and that his criticism of society is radical, commentary on Blake does not readily concede even now. Not many years ago Stephen Spender wrote: "The error of poetry was surely the romantic movement. . . . If Blake had not been so unique a figure, if he had been a greater poet and perhaps less of a genius, he might have been the leader of a reaction from the late eighteenth century, which would have been a 'criticism of life'—that is, of the Industrial Revolution.

> But most through midnight streets I hear
> How the youthful harlot's curse

Blasts the new-born infant's tear,
And blights with plagues the marriage hearse,

is poetry that is a function of life, as distinct from poetry that is an escape into dreams." Mr. Spender meant that in Blake, as in his contemporaries, in spite of the flickering promise of genuine perception into the actual, the "escape into dreams" triumphed over the "criticism of life."

This is the conventional view of Blake's development, but it is a view that declines to read closely. If a radical is a thinker who challenges and repudiates the assumptions of the dominant class in his society on the basis of revolutionary assumptions of his own, and if a radical poet is one whose utterance, in image and structure as well as in matter, is informed by the challenge and the repudiation—then Blake was and always remained a radical poet. The radical content of his poetry came out of well-known revolutionary discussion concentrated in the thought of that "remarkable coterie" associated with the London printer Joseph Johnson at the end of the eighteenth century. Yet the influence on Blake of republicans like Price and Paine and Priestley, of anarchists like Holcroft and Godwin, of the feminist Mary Wollstonecraft, of industrial and social developments toward which these persons held attitudes, is a focus for Blake rather than a "source," an atmosphere of opinion in which he found a direction rather than a set of fixed ideas. They provided a point at which his own revolutionary concepts were freed and from which they more or less evolved.

Blake was a libertarian from the beginning, and like other poets, he chose his sources not that they might form his thought but because they were congenial to the inclinations of his thought. As he turned to Milton because Milton combined attitudes of political and religious liberty; as he turned to the Book of Revelation because it supplied him with imagery suitable to millenarian hankerings; as he turned to the forgeries of Macpherson because he thought primitive poets grandly enjoyed freedom from taste—so he turned, inevitably, to the revolutionary theorists of his own generation for a valuable exposition of insights that he had not yet verbalized.

Blake criticism has not always denied the influence of these theorists, but it has decreed a sharp separation—dating the year, of course, as 1792, and the month as September—between Blake the heedless young radical and Blake the sagely retreating mystic. His biography and his casual utterances show that this separation is not real, that he maintained his connections with other radicals while they were available, and sustained his interest in their ideas after they were not. These ideas can be conveniently summarized in categories that involve Blake's attitude toward four social facts—industrialism, organized religion, political society, and the relation of the sexes. Then, remembering always that although we are discussing a group of prose writers, we are considering their influence on a poet, and an unusual one, Blake's poetic product can be surveyed.

What is stated as politics becomes poetry. For most eighteenth-century poets, men who found botany, psychology, commerce, gardening, and the wool trade agreeable subjects, this would have meant no more than versifying political sentiments; but Blake was not so much a poet of the eighteenth century as that. The experience of Wordsworth is instructive. It was not from his reading or from conversations that he became for a time a revolutionary poet, but from looking into the face of a peasant who, leading a starved cow, presented to his imagination the whole face of suffering France. Yet that imagination had been plowed by ideas, and to the extent that it had been, its poetry became political.

The fact that ideas as used in poetry are subject to the imagination sometimes makes them difficult to recognize, and with a poet like Blake, who seized at ideas from so many diverse directions * and who was almost always so different in one way or another from their source, the opportunity of overlooking his

* An entertaining example of Blake's eclecticism is this: His Platonism, insofar as he contains any, was derived from the popularizer Thomas Taylor; yet it was Taylor who, in *A Vindication of the Rights of Brutes,* attacked with the greatest malice and scurrility radicals like Paine and Mary Wollstonecraft, through whom Blake developed his political feeling. This will also serve as another representation of the clash of idealism and materialism in his work.

debt is great. Face Blake with Godwin in fancy—one could hardly produce a temperamental clash more harsh. And of course Blake's sharp opposition to some of the most basic assumptions of current revolutionary dogma makes this debt particularly obscure. Yet ideas mesh and are pushed into movement not so much through gentle elisions as through partial antagonisms, and this is the relation between revolutionary theory and Blake's intellectual development. He sharpened his borrowings by his rejections; and by his very rejection of certain elements in that theory he refreshed it, and at precisely the point in history when it seemed to be expiring.

Blake's intellectual and poetic stature was greater than Shelley's precisely to the extent that he attempted a restatement of the assumptions of revolutionary doctrine. Whitehead has said: "The literary exposition of freedom deals mainly with the frills. The Greek myth was more to the point. Prometheus did not bring to mankind freedom of the press. He procured fire." One would despair of reading a poem on the freedom of the press, to be sure, and Prometheus brought mankind more than fire. Yet Shelley's Prometheus brought less than either, the unconverted theory, and even those poems of his over which we murmur names of real events like Peterloo are nearly as abstract as the doctrine of his mentors. The rejection of the doctrine of necessity was not enough; for poetry, a *recasting* was the required act. In two important ways Blake avoided the defect of Shelley. He fought against the abstraction of revolutionary theory by criticizing, and not abstractly, that element in the theory itself; and he countered it further by building the most intimate portion of his poetry, its imagery, not on the frills of freedom but on the facts of contemporary life.

In his extremely personal way Blake measures up to the very definition of poetry by which Mr. Spender finds him wanting. "The task of the poet of the future," the latter said, "is to win back the ground that has been lost by the romantic movement: that is to say he has to apply himself minutely to observe the life of people round him, and he has also to understand and to feel in himself the development of recent history. Poetry is at once a description of the conditions of living and an affirmation of the permanent in life, of real values. . . . I do not mean that poets must write exclusively, or even of necessity at all, of machines and towns. . . . What is required of the poet is not up-to-dateness but an awareness of the extent to which the external conditions of today, towns, machinery, etc., have, like an acid, eaten into conscious and subconscious humanity."

Blake's poetry is of an elaborately concentric order. He is the most difficult of English poets because he was the most ambitious. He wished, in a system of ever-widening metaphorical amplification, to explain his story, the story of his England, the history of the world, prehistory, and the nature of all eternity. Almost unanimously, critics have attended to the eternal elements, to what they have called the "mysticism," or at least to the religion, or simply to an exposition of the system itself. Or they have elucidated in very general terms what Spender calls the "real values" at the expense of "the conditions of living," and in separating the two, they have altered the meaning of the first. In Blake's scheme, "eternity" is the cause, but man, and most specifically man in Blake's day, is the tragic or the triumphant effect, and "eternity" itself is a solid, even a somewhat lumpish, affair. "All things Begin & End," in his narratives, "in Albion's Ancient Druid Rocky Shore," and Ephesians 6:12 serves as the epigraph to one of his longest and perhaps his central poem: "For our contention is not with the blood and the flesh, but with dominion, with authority, with the blind world-rulers of this life, with the spirit of evil in things heavenly."

This was Shelley's implicit epigraph, but the two dramatized it differently. Several of Blake's poems, like some of Shelley's, take historical events as their subject matter, but in Shelley the "conditions of living" vanish in moonlight and high sound; in Blake, even as the poetry grows more bewildering, the "conditions of living" more and more insistently force themselves into the imagery, the fabric of the poems. In Shelley, the Rights of Man remains the defective historical generalization that it was in eighteenth-century liberal theory. In Blake, it is converted into its psychological actuality, which, as a political axiom, remains undisputed even though varieties of interest have interpreted it in varieties of ways. The slogan The Rights of Man Blake avoided, as he avoided most slogans.* But the abiding theme of all his poems is the integrity of the individual, and the imperative right of the personality to expression and fulfillment.

When Blake said, "I in Six Thousand Years walk up and down," he was laying claim to a vaster knowledge of the developments of history than any man can support, and he was placing on poetry a greater burden than it can endure apart from religious ritual. He did so because he was convinced that his function, in spite of his inadequate theology, was religious, that under the multiple and shifting historical tides he perceived the enduring psychological facts. These, as he envisaged them, he could not have perceived except at the end of his century, in a generation of political upheaval and in the time of a terrorized reaction, and even then, he could not conceivably have expressed them if his eyes had indeed been only on the elusive "real values" and never on the mere, brutal, corrosive, outrageous fact. Walking up and down in six thousand years meant that Blake, like Shelley, was

> . . . as a nerve o'er which do creep
> The else unfelt oppressions of this earth;

but much more, too.

II

Psychology might be able to discover the roots of Blake's antiauthoritarianism in his relations with his father. The evidence in Blake's work for such a case is almost classic. Yet on the biographical surface there is no violence. In that household, where the

* Only once did he use a phrase even close to it, and that was in a wholly personal reference: ". . . I was set at liberty to remonstrate against former conduct & to demand Justice & Truth; which I have done in so effectual a manner that my antagonist is silenc'd completely, & I have compell'd what should have been of freedom—My Just Right as an Artist & as a Man; & if any attempt should be made to refuse me this, I am inflexible."—*Poetry and Prose,* p. 1077.

atmosphere of dissent inevitably bred attitudes of tolerance and the Swedenborgian and Moravian interests of the father made his child less baffling to him than he would otherwise have been—in that household Blake's ideas would seem to have been a normal development rather than the product of neurotic inversions. Once, when the father threatened to thrash the boy because he reported seeing a tree full of angels, the mother intervened; and it was she rather than the father who whipped him when, at eight, he told them about an encounter with Ezekiel.

A visionary child could be something of a trial about the house, certainly; yet the fact is that, considering their station in life and the pressures toward the ordinary that it imposed upon them, the elder Blakes showed extraordinary sympathy toward the temperamental needs of their child. He was not sent to school because the father observed that whippings shocked him deeply—this from a London hosier of no more than moderate means who had four other children to support and get out into the world. As the apprentice to an engraver, Blake was allowed to develop his talent for drawing. The lawgiver whom Blake assailed seems to have been drawn in the image of another father than his own. Until his marriage, while writing and painting—and that is a test—Blake lived, presumably by preference, in his father's house, and throughout his life he seemed to entertain feelings either kindly or indifferent, but never antagonistic, toward his parent, who was himself a kindly man.

When did the violence begin, and its object grow clear, and the characteristic imagery take shape? It may be of no real significance to his biography that in 1780, when Blake was twenty-three, he was caught in the rush of a rioting mob in the streets of London and swept along "in the very front rank" to "witness the storm and burning of the fortress-like prison," Newgate. Yet who can say how deeply the event burned itself into his consciousness, or what eternal significance to souls he saw even then in the spectacle of three hundred prisoners of law and darkness freed suddenly, against the background of fire, to the open air? Whether, as one biographer insists, Blake "rioted with the rest," is a matter of conjecture; but there is no conjecture in the assertion that here was an experience that combined, in a curiously Blakean way, the revolutionary idea with the revolutionary image.

In about the same year a quieter event took place that was to prove of enduring significance; for with his introduction to Joseph Johnson, bookseller and publisher, famous a decade later for his espousal of the Revolutionary cause, and finally imprisoned for his interest in it, Blake began his experience of the abstract revolutionary theories of his generation. Johnson was among the first to give Blake employment as an engraver, and it was as an engraver that Blake was to derive his chief support, minute as it sometimes was, for the rest of his life. In 1784 he was given similar employment by Thomas Holcroft, editor of *The Wit's Magazine* for the first four months of its existence. Within a few years Holcroft was to outline in his novels the system of anarchy later organized and completed in Godwin's *Political Justice,* and because of his interest in the Revolution and his connection with the London Corresponding Society, was to be indicted for high treason, and–along with Horne Tooke, John Thelwall, and Thomas Hardy–imprisoned. That Blake should have been engraving for *The Wit's Magazine* in the very months of Holcroft's editorship and for only one month beyond it suggests a particular connection or sympathy between the two, and it demonstrates his very early entrance into that group, of which Holcroft formed a significant part, which a common interest in revolution was to bring together two or three years later, and which the frenzy of the Reaction was to split asunder.

According to Gilchrist and others, in these years Blake was a favorite of the bluestocking Mrs. Henry Mathew, whose husband, together with Flaxman, was responsible for the printing of the *Poetical Sketches* and has usually been thought to be the author of its patronizing little preface. With his illiterate young wife Blake attended the strident gatherings of pretentious people that Mrs. Mathew superintended in her Gothic drawing-room, and one witness said much later that he sang his songs there to his own tunes. His prose satire, *An Island in the Moon,* written in about 1787, lends some support to this assertion, for its characters sporadically break into songs, some comic, some scatological, some mere gibberish, until the end, when Quid, who is

Blake himself, in one of the great, unexpected moments of literary history, triumphantly sings the first notes of the *Songs of Innocence*. Except for these final songs, *An Island in the Moon* has small literary value, but it has real biographical value, for it gives us the less obvious reasons for and the approximate date of Blake's repudiation of the smart Bohemian society the Mathews represented. His reasons were no doubt partly personal, as always (the women scorning Catherine, and the Mathews at last patronizing Blake), but they were also intellectual: his impatience with the affectations of learning ("Fissie Follogy, Pistinology, Aridology, Arography, Transmography, Phizography, Hogamy, Hatomy"), and with the pretensions of experimental science, which had its fashionable amateurs. Science Blake already regarded as accompanied by a curse, whether it is the figurative "Pestilence" that comes from the broken bottles of Dr. Priestley's "Flogiston," which "will spread a plague all thro' the Island," or the brutal learning in the low song to Surgery:

"For now I have procur'd these imps
"I'll try experiments."
With that he tied poor scurvy down
& stopt up all its vents.

And when the child began to swell,
He shouted out aloud,
"I've found the dropsy out, & soon
"Shall do the world more good."

He took up fever by the neck
And cut out all its spots,
And thro' the holes which he had made
He first discover'd guts.

The satire against Priestley is interesting, for it suggests not only a certain overlapping between the Mathew and the Johnson circles, but also, since Blake does not attack Priestley's politics, the direction in which his mind was moving. Indeed, most of the radical social attitudes, buried though they are in the swamps of *An Island,* may be found there if one looks: the theory of natural goodness and the role of environment, satirically expressed ("I think that any natural fool would make a clever fellow, if he was properly brought up"); the value placed on women ("I think the Ladies' discourses . . . are some of them more improving than any book. That is the way I have got some of my knowledge"); * and the criticism of marriage ("Matrimony's Golden cage"); the concern with poverty ("The hungry poor enter'd the hall"); the attack on clerical authority ("a person may be as good at home"); on war ("A crowned king, On a white horse sitting"); and on law ("a shameful thing that acts of parliament should be in a free state"). Some of these ideas Blake had already expressed in the *Poetical Sketches* in the same "buried" way; but they were ideas that did not lend themselves to serious amplification at the conversaziones of Mrs. Mathew. And when Quid, at the end of *An Island in the Moon,* angrily declares, "I'll hollow and stamp, & frighten all the People there, & show them what truth is," he already knew that for "hollowing" and stamping and frighting, he would find the proper material among other people, at another place.

At the house of Joseph Johnson they assembled, this "remarkable coterie of advanced thinkers," including in their number not only the anarchists Holcroft and Godwin, but the advanced republicans Priestley and Paine and Mary Wollstonecraft, and, among others, that Dr. Richard Price whose famous *Discourse* of 1789 drew up the lines between republicans and conservatives, and launched the acrid controversy between them that Edmund Burke was happy to take up. Here too came Henry Fuseli, the Swiss painter who many years later jested with cause that Blake was "damned good to steal from," but who was nevertheless as genuine a friend as Blake ever found and for whose friendship Blake held a high regard:

* This is the first of a number of passages in Blake that suggest Yeats's endearing quatrain:

> Though pedantry denies,
> It's plain the Bible means
> That Solomon grew wise
> While talking with his queens.
> —"On Woman"—*Collected Poems,* p. 167.

The only Man that e'er I knew
Who did not make me almost spew
Was Fuseli: he was both Turk & Jew—
And so, dear Christian Friends, how do you do?

Here, in 1790, Fuseli and Mary Wollstonecraft met, "her clothes . . . scarcely decent," for she was attracted by the "notions of privation which some of the revolutionists in France were now endeavoring to inculcate." Fuseli "found in her (what he most disliked in women) a philosophical sloven, her usual dress being a habit of coarse cloth . . . black worsted stockings, and a beaver hat, with her hair hanging lank about her shoulders." Blake observed with sympathy her futile pursuit of Fuseli, happily married and quite unattracted to her even when she changed her garb for his pleasure and put up her hair. His wife showed small patience with Mary's proposal that she enter the Fuseli household as a concubine of the soul, and after two years and a harsh rebuff, Mary removed herself to France.

The affair is of interest only because for years now Blake biography has kept alive a story that Blake himself proposed to bring a mistress into his household. That Mary Wollstonecraft's unhappy plight impressed him is evident from the poem called "Mary," written about 1803, and there is a certain pathos in Blake's discovery, by that time, that the lament he ascribes to Mary—"O, why was I born with a different Face?"—could by that time be applied with equal appropriateness to himself. All of this brings to mind Blake's remark to Henry Crabb Robinson, years later, recorded so discreetly: "He says that from the Bible he has learned that Eine Gemeinshaft der Frauen statt finden sollte." This was an idea that Blake's mind could never quite resist. He may have encountered it earlier in Swedenborgian discussion; he became involved in it at Johnson's; and Joseph Wicksteed's persuasive case—on the evidence of the *Songs*—for some disturbance in the Blakes' marriage in these years suggests that the involvement may have been deep and intimate. Mary Wollstonecraft's ideas were felt by others; they were incorporated in a number of novels written by members of the Johnson set and in the system worked out by the cold man she was to marry.*

Blake found himself in the midst of a group of excited second-rate minds; and the pitch of excitement may well have concealed the quality of mind. With a kind of magnificent slovenliness, the group threw itself into literary-political activity, and Blake himself was stimulated to his most intense creative efforts. In 1790, Mary Wollstonecraft published her answer to Burke, *A Vindication of the Rights of Men,* and Blake supplied for Johnson the engravings to two other books by her. In 1791, Johnson began the publication of Blake's poem *The French Revolution,* but dropped it; in the same year he began the publication of the first part of Paine's *The Rights of Man,* and dropped that. Johnson was among the first to feel the thickening atmosphere of repression. Such groups as the Association for Protecting Liberty and Property against Republicans and Levellers, which feared the Revolution as a socialistic effort and reiterated the assumption of all good Englishmen that liberty and property were the same, were already making their influence felt. In 1792, when Paine's new publisher, Jordan, brought out the second part of *The Rights of Man,* author and printer were both indicted. England belonged to Pitt.

* They were felt, too, by a man who was not, so far as is known, associated with Johnson, but who was later to become Blake's friend and patron. This was George Cumberland, who seems to have handed a novel of his to a number of friends, and it is possible that Blake, involved as he was in this relationship, was among them. The comments on this work of two persons who were associated with Blake—Thomas Taylor, the lecturing Platonist, and R. H. Cromek, Blake's villainous publisher—are extant. Cromek merely said, "Touching your printed Book, I can do nothing about it. It is generally thought that the descriptions are too *luxuriant.* I shall be at Bristol about Decr. and will bring it with me." Taylor, who abominated Mary Wollstonecraft, wrote more expansively: "With respect to your novel, since you desire me to give you my opinion freely of its merit, I must own that I think it more entertaining than instructive, more ingenious than moral. I will not, indeed I cannot suppose that you would undertake to defend lasciviousness publickly; and yet to me it appears that it is as much patronized by the conduct of your Sophisms, as by the works of Mrs. Woolstoncraft." These letters were quoted from the Cumberland Papers by Arthur Symons in an article called "Some Notes on Blake," *Saturday Review,* Vol. CII (August 25, 1906), pp. 231-32.

In 1792, Mary Wollstonecraft published *A Vindication of the Rights of Woman,* and left England for France. In the same year, Holcroft published his seven-volume revolutionary novel *Anna St. Ives;* Robert Bage in *Man As He Is* and Charlotte Smith in *Desmond* each employed the novel as a turgid means of defending the Revolution and the rights of man; and there were others, Mrs. Inchbald and the nearly unknown Mary Hays, who were writing more quietly but to the same purpose. Discussion was passionate and fierce, and the prose that came of it was flamboyant and shabby. Of them all, only Blake was writing greatly; and it is exactly in this year, when he was composing *Songs of Experience,* that he achieved his most intense and most indignant expression.

He was not content to write. "Thought is act," he said, and with greater boldness than any of his friends displayed, he wore the white cockade and the *bonnet rouge* in the streets of London. Then suddenly, in this gray assemblage of honest zealots, his figure really emerges, leaps out clear, as it were, and is somehow wonderful. It was an evening at Johnson's, September 13. Paine was talking. His trial had been appointed for December. He was trying to give his listeners "an idea of the inflammatory eloquence he had poured forth at a public meeting of the previous night," when he had addressed a new political association, The Friends of Liberty. Later, when he started to leave, Blake stood up with him. He "laid his hands on the orator's shoulder, saying, 'You must not go home, or you are a dead man!' and hurried him off on his way to France. . . . By the time Paine was at Dover, the officers were in his house . . . and some twenty minutes after the Custom House officials at Dover had turned over his slender baggage . . . and . . . he had set sail for Calais, an order was received from the Home Office to detain him. England never saw Tom Paine again." Throughout the country his effigy was burned; in December the official exile was pronounced.

This was not vision. Blake walked up and down London in the year 1792, and he could read the times. His reading impressed him; six years later he seems to be remembering the incident when he says of Paine that "God has preserved him."

And perhaps what he read in his times frightened him, for nine months later, after England and France were at war, he wrote, "I say I shan't live five years, And if I live one it will be a Wonder." He was in excellent health. He was writing intensively; but his writing had begun its strategic retreat.

After the September Massacres of 1792 and the declaration of war in February of 1793, for most radicals retreat became a rout. Holcroft produced another novel much like *Anna St. Ives* in doctrine. Mary Wollstonecraft, two years later, brought out her unflinching defense, *An Historical and Moral View . . . of the French Revolution,* and then returned to England to marry Godwin. In 1793 Godwin published *Political Justice,* which contains, under a stringent subjection to the interpretation of anarchism, the substance of Continental philosophical radicalism and of nearly everything his pamphleteering friends had written. But Pitt did not fear a book that cost two guineas, nor one that put its faith not in revolution but in free and rational discussion. For free and rational discussion Pitt had bright new weapons in the law. In 1794, when Godwin published his novel *Caleb Williams,* the political content is no longer boldly stated, but obscurely figured in the symbols of melodrama.

What happened to Blake in this time, when recantation became a commonplace, is not so simple as most of his critics have described it, nor is it yet so obscure that it cannot be described at all. First, Blake had never held the particular faith of his friends in the Revolution, and therefore he was not faced with their dilemma when the Revolution disappointed them. Next, he was genuinely frightened by the Reaction, and therefore he made a strategic retreat in his work; but he did not cease to think of himself as a "Liberty Boy" and he did not change his convictions. Finally, there is the crucial fact that history had changed, and that in the remainder of Blake's lifetime the alternatives it presented left little room for his choice.

Revolutionary theory regarded man generically and looked forward to a perfected species. Blake, in spite of such characteristic generalizations as "the human form divine," regarded men individually, and he did not assume that social amelioration meant an automatically regenerate individual. Revolutionary theory, with its curious atomism, regarded all men as reasonable creatures capable of building a system on abstract principles. Blake, regarding all men as creatures of energy, thought of them as capable of infinite variety and infinite complexity, and not capable either of acting or of being satisfied by reason alone. Revolutionary theory decayed in the face of events, and for many men that meant a loss of faith in man and in liberty, as it has again in our time. For Blake, with his deeper estimate of men, the question of faith did not arise at all.

The question was of circumspection and of keeping hid, and it is now that Blake begins to show slight traces of the man who believes that he is persecuted and pursued. This was a habit of mind that remained with him, and which in his last long poems became a considerable infection. It arose from opposite sources—in part, certainly, from the complete indifference that the world displayed toward his work; but in part, just as certainly, from his belief that there were men in power who were all too interested. Nor was this belief wholly mistaken. Blake was not the only poet in these times who felt himself under official surveillance; readers of Medwin's *Life* will recall Shelley's fears when he had returned from Ireland, and for "many years afterwards" in Italy. For the first time, a network of spies and secret agents was operating for the Crown; habeas corpus was suspended in 1794; Lord Eldon, of infamous memory and long office, had become Attorney General. Nor was the history of Blake's friends reassuring. In 1791, Priestley's house had been burned to the ground by a mob probably incited by government agents; in 1794, after three years of uneasiness, he fled to America, and died there. In 1794, Holcroft, with the leaders of the London Corresponding Society, was arrested and tried, and although these men were released, they underwent a treatment at the hands of the populace and of the police that only the most hysterical political atmosphere could engender and condone. At the head of his annotations to the Bishop of Llandaff's *Apology for the Bible,* an attack on Paine's *The Age of Reason,* Blake wrote: "To defend the Bible in this year 1798 would cost a man his life. . . . I have been commanded from Hell not to print this, as it is what our Enemies wish." This was strong language but it was not without its wisdom of the times. In 1798, Joseph Johnson was imprisoned; he had sold a "seditious" pamphlet, and the pamphlet was a *Reply to Some Parts of the Bishop of Llandaff's Address to the People of Great Britain* by Gilbert Wakefield. Wakefield was a respectable dissenting divine, of known character and with small influence, a devout adherent to constitutional principles if not to the Tory administration of them; but for his pamphlet, which the jury did not trouble to read, he was charged with "being a *seditious, malicious,* and *ill-disposed* person," and was imprisoned for two years! William Blake would have been handled no less severely.

That Blake still regarded himself in 1798 as absolutely of "the Devil's party" his notes on Watson's *Apology* make perfectly clear. Watson was, of course, the kind of man whom Blake most despised; better a criminal than such a soft and treacly moral villain as he. Of a predominantly Whiggish color, he had been the friend of dissenters, had opposed the Test and Corporation Acts, had supported the American Revolution, had denounced the slave trade, had sympathized with the first efforts of the French Revolution, and had begged for an early end to the war against France. One could not ask for a worthier set of principles. Yet Watson was of that most unattractive species, the liberal without stamina, who is the man without friends. When recantation was in order, he recanted; but even that he could not bring himself to do very thoroughly. The easy tool of power, in 1793 he preached piously—to Wordsworth's distress—of "The Wisdom and Goodness of God in having made both Rich and Poor." ". . . the common people were, in every village, talking about liberty and equality without understanding the terms. I thought it not improper to endeavor to abate this revolutionary ferment, by informing the understandings of those who excited it."

When Wakefield, whose learning Watson praised and with whose irreproachable character he was perfectly familiar, asked him at the time of his trial for a statement "with respect to the sincerity and conscientiousness of" his "conduct in general"—and such a statement from Watson would no doubt have saved Wakefield—Watson, without admitting malice or even pique, but in the very guise of moral scrupulousness, replied: "I cannot think that it will be in my power, how much soever it will be in my inclination, to serve you on your trial, since, to the best of my knowledge, I never either saw or spoke to you in my life." Watson's principles were worthy enough, but his character was noxious; this character Blake read accurately in his annotations when he assailed the Bishop's "glittering Dissimulation." To Watson's hypocrisy, Blake groaned in dismay, "The Beast & the Whore rule without control." This is a depressed view. It does not reflect the resilient optimism of the young radical. It comes years after Priestley had been able to say "whatever was the beginning of this world, the end will be glorious and *paradisaical,* beyond what our imaginations can now conceive." But it comes only seven years after the time of which Wordsworth could say:

> Bliss was it in that dawn to be alive,
> But to be young was very Heaven,

and only five years after Blake himself declared, "AND NOW THE LION & WOLF SHALL CEASE." Blake was no longer young; he was forty-one. History had moved, and he, like everyone, had changed; but he had not, like Wordsworth and many another, swung round completely. He was depressed, but he was also outraged. Watson was the kind of man most calculated to call forth Blake's fury. He was, indeed, the very type of Blake's miserable "angels" in *The Marriage of Heaven and Hell:*

> Now the sneaking serpent walks
> In mild humility,
> And the just man rages in the wilds
> Where lions roam.

The lines were prophetic of Blake's career as an artist and a poet. Thrust out, his rage grew, and sometimes it grew inarticulate; but its object, from beginning to end, was the same—entrenched authority, "the blind world-rulers of this life."

This object was also Paine's object, and although Blake was always able to see the object in many more and in many more subtle forms than Paine, he chose to defend Paine's forthright deism against the Bishop's dishonest Christianity. The Bishop is a "State Trickster," but "the Holy Ghost . . . in Paine strives with Christendom"—that is, with corrupted Christianity, or state religion—"as in Christ he strove with the Jews." Watson "would be as good an inquisitor as any other Priest," and like any other, is the tool of tyranny. The "English Crusade against France"—and that was no longer a war against the Revolution, but the war now against Bonaparte!—must be attributed "to State Religion." "Blush for shame," Blake cries. He agrees with Paine that "Kings & Priests have done him harm from his birth." He criticizes law on Godwin's grounds: "All Penal Laws court Transgression & therefore are cruelty & Murder"; and "State Religion," which pronounces legal codes "under pretence of divine command," he names as "the source of all Cruelty." The Bishop's theory that economic inequalities are sanctioned by divinity Blake calls "blasphemous," and replies: "God made Man happy & Rich, but the Subtil made the innocent, Poor."

This is a comment of central importance, and its background in the revolutionary faith not only in natural rights, but in natural goodness, may be found in an earlier comment in Blake's notes to Lavater: "It does not signify what the laws of Kings & Priests have call'd Vice; we who are philosophers ought not to call the Staminal Virtues of Humanity by the same name that we call the omissions of intellect springing from poverty." To declare that evil is negative, "the omissions of intellect springing from poverty," is to adapt Locke's tabula rasa to revolutionary ends in exactly the manner of eighteenth-century republicanism.

The same kind of republican sentiments are to be found in the notes to Bacon's *Essays,* also written about 1798. "A tyrant is the worst disease, and the cause of all others. Everybody hates a king!" Such a comment suggests the mood of 1792, not of 1798; and so the attack on war suggests not 1798, but 1793, when the French war began, and a poem like "London," the "hapless Soldier's sigh" running "in blood down Palace walls." "What do these knaves mean by virtue?" Blake demands. "Do they mean war and its horrors, and its heroic villains?" Was it a "heroic villain" who, dying at Trafalgar in 1805, said, like a character in a history play, "Kiss me, Hardy"? Blake would have thought so. For to him war was always the affair of tyranny and an assault on intellect. "Bacon calls intellectual arts unmanly: and so they are for kings and wars, and shall in the end annihilate them." The war against Bonaparte was no exception: "The increase of a State, as of a man, is from internal improvement or intellectual acquirement. Man is not improved by the hurt of another. States are not improved at the expense of foreigners."

In finding that there was very little to chose between Pitt's struggle to maintain his government and British privilege, and Bonaparte's struggle to win an empire, Blake was surely extraordinary. His references to the French war in these later years are always indignant, and those to the Revolution, nostalgic in their sympathy. In a letter to Flaxman in 1800, he tells of the major part the American and the French revolutions played in his spiritual biography, and of the distress of his well-intentioned friends and of the danger to himself that his continued faith in these events brought on:

And My Angels have told me that seeing such visions I could not subsist on the Earth,
But by my conjunction with Flaxman, who knows to forgive Nervous Fear.

In 1801, just before the brief truce of Amiens, he reveals in another letter to Flaxman the tremendous value he placed on peace: "Peace opens the way. . . . The Kingdoms of this World are now become the Kingdoms of God & His Christ, & we shall reign with him for ever & ever. The Reign of Literature & the Arts commences. . . . Now I hope to see the Great Works of Art, as they are so near to Felpham: Paris being scarce further off than London. But I hope that France & England will henceforth be as One Country and their Arts One, & that you will ere long be erecting Monuments In Paris—Emblems of Peace." The war began again, and Blake never left England. In 1808, when he came across a couplet from Pope—

They led their wild desires to woods and caves,
And thought that all but savages were slaves—

applied to "the ferocious and enslaved Republick of France," Blake parodied:

> When France got free, Europe, 'twixt Fools & Knaves,
> Were Savage first to France, & after—Slaves—

slaves to their own frights and fears, to political terrorism and social regressions, to the "arts of war" that despise and destroy the "intellectual arts" synonymous with freedom. In 1811, when the war was still dragging on, Blake once more makes this point:

> "Now Art has lost its mental Charms
> France shall subdue the World in Arms."
> So spoke an Angel at my birth,
> Then said, "Descend thou upon Earth.
> Renew the Arts on Britain's Shore,
> And France shall fall down & adore.
> With works of Art their Armies meet,
> And War shall sink beneath thy feet.
> But if thy Nation Arts refuse,
> And if they scorn the immortal Muse,
> France shall the arts of Peace restore,
> And save thee from the Ungrateful shore."

If there is a preference here, it is for France, not England; but its claim is for peace over nations. In 1827, the year of his death, in a defense of what he calls "Republican art," Blake ("very weak and an old man, feeble and tottering, but not in spirit and life, not in the real man, the imagination") still declares his allegiance to youthful principles. He wrote: ". . . since the French Revolution Englishmen are all intermeasurable by one another: certainly a happy state of agreement, in which I for one do not agree. God keep you and me from the divinity of yes and no too—the yea, nay, creeping Jesus." *

* In a very odd reading Yeats interpreted this remark as an attack on the French Revolution, and took Blake to mean that "since the rule of reason" inaugurated by the *philosophes,* all Englishmen are intermeasurable, etc. (See "William Blake and His Illustrations to *The Divine Comedy;" Ideas of Good and Evil,* London, 1903, p. 155.) Blake's comment recognizes the defeat of the Revolution, to be sure, or at least of those elements in the

He had written: ". . . by my conjunction with Flaxman, who knows to forgive Nervous Fear." Flaxman was among those who in 1800 were instrumental in removing Blake from London, where he had been having an increasingly difficult time, to Felpham and the patronage of Hayley. Another was Thomas Butts, a kindly man who kept the Blakes going in their bleakest years by generous commissions. Flaxman and Butts were both among Blake's "Angels," the right-thinking souls who had his best interests at heart but, in his opinion, had no conception whatever of his real needs. Blake addressed them as "Archangel" and "Friend of my Angels" with genuine gratitude yet preserved the private irony.

That their good intentions in moving him out of town had something to do with the company he was keeping, and with the "enthusiastic" ideas he held, is made clear in a letter from Butts: ". . . you cannot but recollect the difficulties that have unceasingly arisen to prevent my discerning clearly whether your Angels are black, white, or grey, and that on the whole I have rather inclined to the former opinion and considered you more immediately under the protection of the black-guard. . . . Whether you will be a better Painter or a better Poet from your change of ways & means I know not, but this I predict, that you will be a better Man—excuse me, as you have been accustomed from friendship to do, but certain opinions imbibed from reading, nourish'd by indulgence, and rivetted by a confined Conversation, and which have been equally prejudicial to your Interest & Happiness, will now, I trust, disperse as a Day-break Vapour, and you will henceforth become a Member of that Community of which you are at present, in the opinion of the Archbishop of Canterbury, but a Sign to mark the residence of dim incredulity, haggard suspicion, & bloated philosophy—whatever can be effected by sterling sense, by opinions which harmonize society and beautify creation, will in future

Revolution by which he put store, but so far from repudiating the Revolution, it states Blake's continuing allegiance to it and assails the elements that triumphed over it, not in France, but in England—the pious embrace of institutional authority and the official refutation of the doctrine of individual liberty.

be exemplified in you, & the time I trust is not distant." To this Blake replied: ". . . thank you for your reprehension of follies by me foster'd. Your prediction will, I hope, be fulfilled in me, & in future I am the determined advocate of Religion & Humility, the two bands of Society." What guile there is in this jargon! ". . . thank you for your reprehension of follies by me foster'd"! Blake apparently thought that "angels" (who lied to themselves) deserved lies.

For there is no reason to think that he now tried to become the friend of "Religion & Humility." In the country life of Felpham, under the aegis of Hayley, who was another Richard Watson but of poetry rather than of theology, Blake had no such company as he kept in the city, and he lived for three years, with increasing resentment and discomfort, a life of quiet retirement. Yet the end of the sojourn was nothing less than explosive in its excitement, for in 1803 he was arrested and tried for high treason at the accusation of a drunken soldier whom he had expelled from his garden. The soldier, named Schofield, and a comrade he found to support him, swore that Blake had "uttered seditious and treasonable expressions, such as 'D–n the king, d–n all his subjects, d–n his soldiers, they are all slaves; when Bonaparte comes, it will be cut-throat for cut-throat, and the weakest must go to the wall; I will help him; etc. etc.' " All these charges Blake denied (although it does not seem wholly unlikely that, in his fury and under the stress of the moment, his circumspection dropped and he shouted something of the sort), and he was acquitted; but his acquittal did not allay his own suspicions, for afterward he "used to declare"–according to Gilchrist–that "the Government, or some high person knowing him to have been of the Paine set, 'sent the soldier to entrap him.' "

Back in London again, Blake resumed his old connections, or at least those of them which it was possible to resume. Price and Mary Wollstonecraft were dead; Priestley and Paine were in exile. Of those who remained, Fuseli had been made respectable by the Royal Academy; Godwin had qualified his position and married an impossible shrew, Lamb's "Bitch," who drove his friends from his house. Holcroft, another writer who now felt himself persecuted for his opinions, was struggling with every kind of hack employment simply to survive. Johnson, who like Holcroft died in 1809, had apparently lost his interest in Blake. Yet with this remnant of four Blake seems to have maintained some connection. A number of letters to Hayley show that he still saw Johnson, although on Hayley's business now rather than on his own. Fuseli continued to befriend him, and in 1805 wrote an advertisement for the illustrations to Blair's *The Grave*. Holcroft, at a time when he could not support his family, found money enough to subscribe to that work.

Godwin never appears by name in the records of Blake's life, yet it is generally agreed that he appeared in the life itself. An anecdote of these later years is particularly suggestive. This was Blake's loan of £40 to "a certain free-thinking speculator, the author of many elaborate philosophical treatises," who "said that his children had not a dinner." (We are emphasizing here the identity of the "speculator," not Blake's humanitarian impulses, which are well enough known—how he rescued a hobbled boy from his employer, defended an imprisoned astrologer whom he had never heard of before, housed and tended until his death an "interesting and eager, but sickly" young art student, a stranger, and so on.) One cannot insist that the impoverished "author of many elaborate philosophical treatises" was Godwin, but no one then living in London fits the description more exactly. Godwin's requests for money not only from Shelley but from any willing acquaintance were nearly daily affairs; and if one remembers that the second Mrs. Godwin, who brought the philosopher as dowry two children to add to Mary's two, and then added still another, was a "brisk, buxom, good-looking," and generally showy woman, the resolution of the anecdote is tantalizing. For when Blake called on the man "on the following Sunday," he found "that his wife, who was a dressy and what is called a pretty woman, had squandered some large portion of the money upon her worthless sides." *

* In 1809, the two men seem to come together again. In that year Godwin published his least political and perhaps his most interesting work, a very small book called *An Essay on Sepulchres*. A copy now in existence bears on its inside cover the name of John Linnell, the young artist who was later

In 1809, Blake and Paine seem to meet again. In this year Blake exhibited a recently finished picture called "The Spiritual Form of Pitt Guiding Behemoth." Here Pitt, a deceptively handsome and heroic figure, like a magician with curiously gentle hands, blesses the monster of worldly power in whose great jaws are "struggling men, some of whom stretch imploring hands to another spiritual form, who reaches down from a crescent moon in the sky, as if to rescue them. This face and form," says Paine's biographer, "appear to me certainly meant for Paine."

The suggestion is again tantalizing; and it is given some substantiality by a companion picture exhibited in the same year, "The Spiritual Form of Nelson Guiding Leviathan." Here the deception is even more complete, for the leviathan is not only the symbol of the sea, with which Nelson would quite properly be coupled, but also of the tyrannical state. Again, the central figure is heroic, and of a golden tint, but the toils of the monster, the "heroic villain's" instrument, are wrapped about struggling, shrieking, and exhausted men, and the hero himself stands on a pediment composed of a coil of the beast and the collapsed body of a Negro. This, after the hero's own figure, is the most prominent object in the picture, and both in position and in color is in sharpest contrast to the hero.

Blake's paintings were almost always symbolical, but they were seldom symbolical in quite this way, which is the way of most of his later poetry—a way designed to conceal and deceive, and a way designed by an artist who, for the moment at least, is almost completely engrossed by the psychology of the hunted man. Blake's language in his description of these pictures in the *Catalogue* is exactly as equivocal as the pictures themselves, and the equivocation is now so shrewd that probably he alone perceived the irony. Perhaps that is why, in the same *Catalogue,* he

to be Blake's friend and ardent disciple, and throughout the copy are marginal pencil drawings of spiritual beings that may very well be Blake's; at the least, they are Fuseli's or some other imitator's. Whether the book was originally Blake's and later given to Linnell, we do not know, or whether it was after 1818, when Linnell first came to know Blake, that the drawings were made. At any rate, in his twenties Linnell was himself acquainted with Godwin and Shelley, and this is the one point in Blake's life at which a meeting with Shelley seems likely.

"Binding of the Dragon"
By courtesy of the Fogg Museum of Art, Harvard University

"Striving with Systems to deliver Individuals from those Systems."

said, and could believe, "The Times require that every one should speak out boldly; England expects that every man should do his duty, in Arts, as well as in Arms or in the Senate." He was speaking out boldly enough for anyone who cared to hear him; but his boldness by this time was of such an involuted variety that no one troubled to listen any longer.

Taste, too, provides a considerable barrier. Persons trained to the monstrous comedy of Hogarth could not be expected to read satirical intentions in hands as pliant as a sorceress's, in a golden body, in an angelic form. Or if they had, would they have thought that duty done "in Arms or in the Senate" was a slur at Nelson and at Pitt? Or would they have thought, for all Blake's obviousness, that having obscurely satirized these "heroes" in his two pictures, he was also parodying the charge of the great "heroic villain" to his men before his last battle—"England expects that every man will do his duty"—and, having foolishly made a target of himself by parading in his decorations, his dying remark below decks—"Now I am satisfied. Thank God I have done my duty"—which he repeated over and over?

Boldness of the more ordinary variety one still finds in Blake's annotations, which were not intended for even a narrowed public eye. In 1808, the year before the bitterly disappointing exhibition in which the "heroes" were displayed, Blake makes it quite clear in his notes on Sir Joshua Reynolds's *Discourses* that after fifteen years he has not lost track of Paine's values. "This Whole Book," he declares, "was Written to Serve Political Purposes"—this in response to a comment by Reynolds's editor, in a fulsome dedication to the King, on "the wealth and prosperity of England," and an attack on the French. Reynolds, "this President of Fools," is, like Watson, a state trickster, one obliged to corruption by the nature of his support, one committed to "A Pretence of Art, To destroy Art." The concern of these notes is necessarily with art, but in what is perhaps the most significant shift of emphasis in Blake's career, their specific concern is with the relation of art and commerce, or rewards.

The problem had always chafed; now it had become such an irritant as to emerge an explicit and a central concern. Blake's attack is upon "The Rich Men of England," who form an

Academy to sanction the mediocre and to outlaw the excellent, for excellence destroys tyrannies. At Reynolds's phrase "royal liberality," Blake sneered, and stormed: "Liberality! we want not Liberality. We want a Fair Price & Proportionate Value & a General Demand for Art." What Blake was asking for was a democratization of art and letters—for art, he believed, was the only true commonwealth—as in the past he had asked for a democratization of society. To this end, "royal liberality" or any other system of patronage was an obstruction:

"O dear Mother outline, of knowledge most sage,
What's the First Part of Painting?" she said: "Patronage."
"And what is the second?" to please & Engage,
She frown'd like a Fury & said: "Patronage."
"And what is the Third?" she put off Old Age,
And smil'd like a Syren & said: "Patronage."

In art as in society, institutionalized authority is a way not of elevating but of standardizing and therefore of debasing taste. The artist becomes a "Hired Knave," whose "Eye is on the Many, or, rather, the Money." Only the mediocre is honored, and the exceptional, thrust out, as Blake was from the exhibitions at the Academy.

The year 1809 seems to be a much more crucial year in Blake's life than 1792 or 1793. He was now fifty-two years old, and his life was a mounting record of failures. The defection of friends who had succeeded in the world, the obscure but haunting sense of political persecution, the miserable fiasco of Hayley's patronage, the chicanery of publishers into whose meshes Blake fell, his betrayal at the hands of fellow artists, and finally the enormous failure of his private exhibition in 1809—one by one, these things forced him into the recognition of what he was: an artist without an audience, a citizen outside his society. The exhibition of 1809 was, as it were, Blake's last attempt to give society a chance. Society did not trouble to take it.

His remarks of 1808 on art and money are the clue to his later social attitudes as they began to find expression after the exhibition. They underline his attack on commerce and industry; they point toward his intensified criticism of economic inequality, of the war between classes, the rich on the poor, the "Subtil" on the "innocent." They point toward his occasional expressed "rejection" of politics and of merely political ideas. And in a sense they explain the direction of his final development, the increasing subjectivity of his last long poems, *Milton* and *Jerusalem,* their greater emphasis on the centrality of individual regeneration, and Blake's increasing despair of the efficacy of institutions. This development, however, is itself the amplification of a political idea, that of anarchy, an idea that emerged from the context of revolutionary doctrine. It is a political development almost exactly opposite to that of Coleridge, for example—or of Wordsworth, or of Southey. For while Coleridge in his political writings increasingly emphasized the importance of institutions to the moral life of man, Blake more and more emphasized their irrelevance.

Blake's despair of politics was not a sustained mood, even in his years of greatest neglect. In his poems it is difficult to find it expressed at all, and in his more casual writings and conversations, into which he poured his disappointments and his fury wholeheartedly, it appears only sporadically and in conflict with other statements. In the *Public Address* of 1810, for instance, he emphasizes again, as he did in the notes to Reynolds, the importance of a healthy political life to a healthy art: "The wretched State of the Arts in this Country & in Europe, originating in the wretched State of Political Science, which is the Science of Sciences, Demands a firm & determinate conduct on the part of Artists to Resist the Contemptible Counter Arts Establish'd by such contemptible Politicians as Louis XIV." Surely the comment that immediately precedes is a contradiction: "I am really sorry to see my Countrymen trouble themselves about Politics. If Men were Wise, the Most arbitrary Princes could not hurt them. If they are not wise, the Freest Government is compell'd to be a Tyranny. Princes appear to me to be Fools. Houses of Commons & Houses of Lords appear to me to be fools; they seem to me to be something Else besides Human Life."

Two other such remarks are recorded. One, of 1825, was put down from Blake's conversation by Crabb Robinson: "Now he had just before . . . been speaking of the errors of Jesus Christ.

He was wrong in suffering himself to be crucified. He should not have attacked the govt. He had no business with such matters." The other, in the prospectus notes to the "Vision of the Last Judgment," reads: "Many Persons, such as Paine & Voltaire, with some of the Ancient Greeks, say: 'we will not converse concerning Good & Evil; we will live in Paradise & Liberty.' You may do so in Spirit, but not in the Mortal Body as you pretend, till after the Last Judgment. . . . You cannot have Liberty in this World without what you call Moral Virtue, & you cannot have Moral Virtue without the Slavery of that half of the Human Race who hate what you call Moral Virtue."

These three comments, very difficult to fit into the picture of Blake's work as a whole, suggest that he lapsed at last into the Lutheran dogma that separates the "spiritual" or "inner" and the "worldly" or "outer" kingdoms; and that, having made the separation, he necessarily chose the first alone. Yet in fact this interpretation cannot be allowed. One can also say, and with more support from the text, that these comments indicate that Blake had become aware of the historical but not in the least of the absolute truth of Coleridge's dictum on government and property: "The chief object for which men first formed themselves into a state was not the protection of their lives, but of their property. . . . To property, therefore, and to its inequalities all human laws directly or indirectly relate . . ." ". . . that government is good in which property is secure and circulates; that government the best, which, in the exactest ratio, makes each man's power proportionate to his property. . . . Artificial power must here be balanced against physical power; and when the physical strength of a nation is in the poor, the government must be in the hands of the rich." Coleridge's incisive political cynicism was characteristic of his generation in British life, and Blake's later attitudes toward money, toward commerce, toward industry, toward every social conflict, have meaning in relation to this cynicism. One might almost say that in his last twenty years Blake enjoyed an intuition which anticipates Marx; that in these years, at the very point when he struggled to escape the remnants of his materialism, he also saw that it is futile to attack government, which is an effect, rather than its determinants. He turned his attention to the determinants.

In 1810, he denied salvation to "All Those who, having no Passions of their own because No Intellect, Have spent their lives in Curbing & Governing other People's by the Various arts of Poverty & Cruelty of all kinds." Any attempt to justify poverty, with "the Various arts" of which Blake had a daily, cruel experience—whether it was Watson's argument from divine design, or the familiar one that deprivation encourages art—Blake excoriated. "Poverty is the Fool's Rod, which at last is turn'd on his own back. . . . Some People & not a few Artists have asserted that the Painter of this Picture would not have done so well if he had been properly Encourag'd. Let those who think so, reflect on the State of Nations under Poverty & their incapability of Art; tho' Art is Above Either, the Argument is better for Affluence than Poverty; & tho' he would not have been a greater Artist, yet he would have produc'd Greater works of Art in proportion to his means."

The arts of cruelty had made themselves felt in Blake's life in another way, in those industrial developments which throughout his lifetime were among the major causes of a quaking British economy, when panics, inflation, and rioting were commonplaces, and which, more specifically, were to threaten the livelihood of engravers just as surely as they were to threaten those of small farmers, metalworkers, weavers, hosiers, and all the rest. Blake was the child of the Industrial Revolution as well as of the French Revolution; and the mechanical in everyday life underlies and is used to express his protest against the mechanical in ideas—in ethics, in psychology, in philosophy, and in religion. "A Machine is not a Man nor a Work of Art; it is destructive of Humanity & of Art; the word Machination."

The record of Blake's last years is, like the life, sparse. From the ten years between 1809 and 1818, only one letter survives, a note of a few lines to Josiah Wedgwood on a matter of business. His obscurity now was almost total. In 1817 a sympathetic critic wrote: ". . . so entire is the uncertainty, in which he is involved, that after many inquiries, I meet with some in doubt whether he is still in existence. But I have accidentally learned from a Lady, since I commenced these remarks, that he is, certainly, now a resident in London." (One thinks of Shelley's first letter to Godwin, in 1812: ". . . you will not be surprised at the inconceivable emotions. . . . I had enrolled your name in the list of the honorable dead.") The triumph of the world, in its machination, was almost complete. Blake's temptation and his final tendency were to flee from it silently, "Leaving the delusive Goddess Nature & her Laws, to get into Freedom from all Law of the Members, into The Mind."

Yet in that very flight Jacobinical ideas and interests persisted. In 1810 he considered "the word Machination," the plot of power to destroy individual merit, and argued: "Each Identity is Eternal," which is the metaphysical extension of Godwin's logic on which Blake had insisted for more than twenty years. In 1813, he made a relief etching entitled "The Chaining of Orc." In the poetic myth that Blake formulated twenty years before, Orc is Revolution. In 1813, too, he reissued several copies of his early political poem *America,* and several of *Europe,* both integral to the revolutionary Lambeth series. In 1820, in the annotations to Berkeley, he speaks again in the voice of *The Marriage of Heaven and Hell* when he opposes "Imagination & Visions" to "Moral Virtues," sympathy to judgment; for the "Moral Virtues . . . the baseness of . . . all Warriors . . . are continual Accusers of Sin & promote Eternal Wars & Dominency over others."

He is concerned as much as ever with the roots of tyranny, and while his vocabulary of "Visions" and "Virtues" differs from and has vastly extended the political jargon of 1790 and its attack on tyranny, the concepts, even that of natural goodness, linger. "I have never known a very bad man," he told Robinson, "who had not somethg. very good abt. him." Thirty years after Godwin rejected his doctrine of the "domestic affections" and perfect disinterestedness, Blake clings to it: "When I asked whether if he had been a father he would not have grieved if his child had become vicious or a great criminal, He ansd. 'I must not regard when I am endeavouring to think rightly my own any more than other people's weaknesses.' "

The aspiration was always the same, even when its terms

changed, even in despair: that everyone be "King & Priest in his own House. God send it so on Earth." Such remarks bear out Gilchrist's statement that "Down to his latest days Blake always avowed himself a 'Liberty Boy,' a faithful 'Son of Liberty'; and would jokingly urge in self-defence that the shape of his forehead made him a republican. 'I can't help being one,' he would assure Tory friends, 'any more than you can help being a Tory: your forehead is larger above; mine, on the contrary, over the eyes.' " There was a kind of lightness that he never lost.

His last letters are full of it; and his last days were a little less bleak. He had found a new group of friends, a small circle of young artists who adored him and some of whom emulated his style—first Linnell and his wife, then Palmer, Calvert, Richmond, and Finch, who somewhat solemnly formed themselves into a kind of brotherhood and called themselves "The Ancients." To Blake, who was their master, they gave entire reverence. He was nearly seventy years old and for the first time he found himself—except for Catherine, his wife—taken with complete seriousness. But resurrection seldom occurs in life, and such reverence, coming late, has its irony.

It comes too late to temper "intellectual peculiarity" or to soften anger. Blake's bitterest meditations, even when he can write humorously of the ailment that is killing him, appear among the last words he wrote, his annotations to Thornton's *New Translation of the Lord's Prayer*. Here all the old radical strands are pulled together. Thornton, with his "Tory Translation," is another hireling of tyrants. He perverts Christianity in the name of a tyrant God modeled after tyrant kings: "Our Father Augustus Ceasar, who art in these thy Substantial Astronomical Telescopic Heavens . . . Thy Kingship come upon Earth first & then in Heaven. . . . For thine is the Kingship, [or] Allegoric Godship, & the Power, or War, & the Glory, or Law, Ages after Ages in thy descendants; for God is only an Allegory of Kings & nothing Else. Amen."

War is waged and murder committed in the name of this God, "just such a Tyrant as Augustus Ceasar," and law is made to defend his false image. "Lawful Bread, Bought with Lawful Money, & a Lawful Heaven, seen thro' a Lawful Telescope, by means of Lawful Window Light! The Holy Ghost, & whatever cannot be Taxed, is Unlawful & Witchcraft." By law the tyrant establishes his tax, by his taxes he collects money, through money he exploits his subjects, reduces them to poverty and powerlessness, and so, through money, doubly establishes his tyranny: ". . . when the physical strength of a nation is in the poor, the government must be in the hands of the rich," said Coleridge.

Blake saw this "balance" in operation and had felt its "machination," and at the end of his life he repeatedly denounced it. On his engraving of the Laocoön made seven years before his death, one reads: "The True Christian Charity not dependent on Money (the life's blood of Poor Families), that is, on Caesar or Empire or Natural Religion: Money, which is The Great Satan or Reason, the Root of Good & Evil In The Accusation of Sin. Good & Evil are Riches & Poverty, a Tree of Misery. . . . Where any view of Money exists, Art cannot be carried on, but War only." Money, not only as economic power, but, after that, as power able to destroy spirit and intellect in the oppressed—this was Blake's final equation of tyranny; and in his last year, the year of Canning's new Corn Laws, in the very voice of the bread rioters, Blake was not above demanding the "corporeal" item: "Give us the Bread that is our due & Right, by taking away Money, or a Price, or Tax upon what is Common to all in thy Kingdom." He had said the same thing before, more beautifully, more cryptically: "The Whole Business of Man Is The Arts, & All Things Common."

"Each Identity is Eternal" and "All Things Common"—the intellectual struggle to which Blake gave his life was to bring these two together. In French Revolutionary doctrine, their names were Liberty and Fraternity, but the French Revolution failed to unite them. In Blake's lifetime and (with the possible exception of such ambiguous social experiments as Robert Owen's), at least until the formulations of Marx, liberty alone found defenders. Isolated from its triad, it developed on the one hand into the dreary shopkeeper's philosophy of Bentham, and on the other into the aggressive power philosophy of Carlyle, where liberty was the monopoly of the exceptional, and most men were intended to lapse gratefully into the slavery they deserved.

Blake's correction of eighteenth-century liberalism, from which he certainly derived, prevented his falling into some poetic approximation either of the drab Benthamite liberalism, with its uninspired approval of the bourgeoisie, or of the glittering negations of Carlyle and Nietzsche, with their exaltation of the most frightening aristocracy of all. For Blake, exalting neither man's reason nor, in the usual sense, his virtue, yet *loved* men, individual men. To Bentham the mass of individuals were colorless atoms; to Carlyle and Nietzsche they were scum in a quagmire. Blake's concern was with the individual man within the mass of individual men.

Individualism was his main value, as it was the main value of all liberals of whatever color in the first half of the nineteenth century; but he detected the ambiguities and the contrasts that inhabit this term, and he struggled in his poetry to express them, and to assert one set of meanings against another. His long poems are dramatic parables about the conflicts between these forms of individualism. Urizen, the mistaken spirit, represents individualism, after all, as much as does Orc, or Los, or any good spirit. When is the impulse mistaken, and when is it good? It is mistaken when, like Urizen, it separates itself from its members to exalt itself, when it is in competition with its members, when it destroys order. It is good when, like Orc or Los, it attempts to force or weld the original whole together again and establish a harmony of parts. Individualism is evil when it is a will to power, good when it is a will to order. The quarrel is between competition, a reckless laissez faire, and co-operation. The way to achieve the good is through the only social virtue that Blake recognized, love, or forgiveness, or brotherhood, which as often as not he called imagination.

"Each Identity is Eternal" and "All Things Common." This is to ask for complete individuality within the widest universality. The paradox here between individualism and harmony is the great paradox of democracy itself: the right of the personality to develop, and the evil of any personality's "developing" at the expense of any other. The second "developing" is crucial, and it resolves the paradox; for preventing another means reducing, not expanding, the self and thereafter the society. This concept

Blake labored ceaselessly, in every way, to express; in the lyric imagery of nature—

> Each outcry of the hunted Hare
> A fibre from the Brain does tear.
> A Skylark wounded in the wing,
> A Cherubim does cease to sing—

and in moralistic verse—

> The iron hand crush'd the Tyrant's head
> And became a Tyrant in his stead—

and in straightforward prose: "All Those who, having no Passions of their own because No Intellect, Have spent their lives in Curbing & Governing other People's by the Various arts"; "Poverty is the Fool's Rod, which at last is turn'd on his own back"; and ". . . the omission of act in self & the hindering of act in another; This is Vice, but all Act is Virtue. To hinder another is not an act; it is the contrary; it is a restraint on action both in ourselves & in the person hinder'd, for he who hinders another omits his own duty at the same time. Murder is Hindering Another. Theft is Hindering Another. Backbiting, Undermining, Circumventing, & whatever is Negative is Vice."

But the difficulty of stating a perception that had not yet been formulated in history was great— ". . . he who hinders another omits his own duty" and "Poverty is the Fool's Rod, which at last is turn'd on his own back"—these were as close as Blake could come to it in simple prose. Chiefly, he had to rely on his mythical representations, in which the unity of opposites could be embodied, and this paradox resolved. The figure of Albion, who "falls" into sleep and sickness when a part (which now degenerates, too) rebels, and awakens to a glorious day when the part is reassimilated (and finds itself well again)—this figure may be taken as the symbol of a great composite democratic individual, the archetype for a society whose members live co-operatively, and for the individual whose self-expression is then complete and who is then in perfect health. Blake's treatment of the sexes represents a parallel unity of opposites. They are separate, with separate impulses, and only when the impulses of each are given free expression *in love* is the separateness broken down. The androgynous figure of Blake's eternity is the symbol of this attainment.

Blake could sometimes only perilously maintain his concept of variety in unity ("the MOST UNITED VARIETY"). Often enough he rejects his ideal of individuality within the whole for that other individualism which pits the single *against* the whole, man *against* the universe, and the poet *against* society; when he seems to say that his concern, like that of the mystics, is the development of his individuality alone, the achievement of his own spiritual life, of a private salvation–all of which is laissez faire, too. But these occasions are found in his discouraged, fragmentary utterances, not in his poems. He wrote no palinodes. In his poetry he repeatedly sought to state what we recognize now as the greatest modern social paradox. He did not think this paradox through as a political or an economic problem, but he struggled with it valiantly and constantly as a psychological problem, and he knew how current politics and economics taxed it. He was the first to know. When others fought for liberty alone, he insisted on equality and fraternity also; and he saw that you cannot gain the first if you sacrifice the second or the third. Toward the adjustment of these three our civilization still strives.

It has been suggested that Shelley's concept of Intellectual Beauty is a representation of his own desire for sympathy from the world, and it is quite possible that Blake's increasing emphasis on the doctrine of "Universal Love" is a representation of his desire for sympathy from a world that had shown him none. This is the other part of his bitter rejections. "I am hid," he said with simple desolation in 1808. So he was, and so he remained–"hid" even in the midst of friends, when he had them. The young men at the end of his life were eager enthusiasts and they brought him some light, surely; but they came too late. Blake had gone beyond the need of their gifts. His poetry stopped in 1818 or 1820 and, an old man who had suffered what must have seemed to be all the plagues of the world, he turned to his pictures of the tribulations of Job, another worthy ancient. He wrote an old man's gentle letters to his young disciples, and spoke humorously of his ailments: "a young Lark without feathers" . . . "I am still incapable of riding in the Stage, & shall be, I fear, for some time, being only bones & sinews, All strings & bobbins like a Weaver's Loom." Death was near, and the bitter image of the machine lingered appropriately.

Yet he died happily, singing impromptu hymns, observers said, as he came at last within sight of justice. This is an ending like those final paeans in his Prophecies.

III

THE TRACEABLE THREAD of radicalism in Blake's life, in events and in ideas familiarly expressed, has a parallel thread and direction, both clearer, in his poetry. One makes easier the following of the other. It has been pointed out that there is no very definite date for his introduction into the Johnson circle. In his writing, however, the year in which he first expressed the influence of that group is evident—it is 1788. Until then, in both his verse and his prose, he had mixed ideas and types in a fashion that suggests that his self-consciousness, his awareness of his beliefs and the sense of his poetic purpose, was as yet undeveloped. After he felt the impact of the radical discussion of existing conditions and of its future expectations, the confusion is cleared and the poet strikes out in a line.

The conventional eighteenth-century vocabulary of this discussion and some striking items in its content, Blake instinctively rejected, firmly and at once. These rejections he recorded in the axiomatic prose of his *All Religions* and *No Natural Religion* and in the annotations to Lavater, all written in 1788, and in *Tiriel,* of 1789; but these state also his revolutionary affirmations in their first form. At the same time he was writing the *Songs of Innocence* and *The Book of Thel,* the purest idyls in English verse and his approximation, in verse and according to his temperament, of the revolutionary hope, those "glorious and paradisaical" expectations toward which events in the Europe of 1788 seemed, for overwrought minds, to be pointing. The mixed mood of primitivistic nostalgia and progressivistic faith, which disturbs logicians, is a quality that Blake shares with all French Revolutionary theorists. The two enduring strands in Blake's poetry are the criticism of social fact and the vision of pastoral perfection. For Experience and Innocence it is easy enough to find the analogous terms in the vocabulary of the prosaic radicals who were Blake's contemporaries.

Before he encountered the ideas of these people, Blake had written only the *Poetical Sketches,* the burlesque *An Island in the Moon,* and three short pastoral poems written into a copy of *Poetical Sketches.* No development in his ideas is apparent between 1783 and 1787; an abrupt development is apparent in the next year.

The *Poetical Sketches* and the burlesque contain the two elements; but the depths of both are unperceived, their values still unexplored.

"Blow, boisterous wind, stern winter frown," sings the old shepherd in one of the pastoral poems of 1787,

> Innocence is a winter's gown;
> So clad, we'll abide life's pelting storm
> That makes our limbs quake, if our hearts be warm.

Innocence here is invulnerable to the assaults of Experience and gains nothing from them; this is not Blake's later point of view, in which Innocence is penetrated by Experience and both are transformed into a richer Innocence. It is as if Blake, through the conventionalities of the pastoral, has stumbled upon but not yet discovered the meanings of the terms that were to direct his verse and embody his revolutionary contrast.

Toward this contrast much of the imagery of the *Poetical Sketches* strains, but without conspicuous achievement. One may compare, for example, the conventional song "I love the jocund dance" with "The Ecchoing Green," its developed form in *Songs of Innocence,* where the identical images have taken on the value of symbols, and the poem is no longer a mere song, but a parable of the progress of human life through innocence and experience, and possibly of the theme of satisfied desire.

The permanent associations of certain ideas and images has

already been established, but the association has not been explored. The rich are like greedy wolves, and the poor are the pastoral innocents ("The Nobles . . . tear the poor man's lamb"). Agriculture, trade, and industry are as yet indiscriminately contrasted with warfare:

> The husbandman does leave his plow,
> To wade thro' fields of gore;
> The merchant binds his brows in steel,
> And leaves the trading shore;
>
> The shepherd leaves his mellow pipe,
> And sounds the trumpet shrill;
> The workman throws his hammer down
> To heave the bloody bill.

The "trading shore" is not yet the subject of abuse, nor has the workman yet been caught in the mill. The imagery expresses a yearning, but hardly consciously, for fulfillment (". . . scatter thy pearls Upon our love-sick land that mourns for thee"); for social harmony:

> Cities shall sing, and vales in rich array
> Shall laugh, whose fruitful laps bend down with fulness;

for psychological integration:

> . . . if the heart is sick, the head
> Must be aggriev'd; if but one member suffer,
> The heart doth fail;

and, in an echo of Rousseau, for intellectual liberty:

> The enemy fight in chains, invisible chains, but heavy;
> Their minds are fetter'd; then how can they be free?

All these are the fugitive rather than the primary facts of the *Poetical Sketches.* We detect them only because we already know what they are to become.

So too with the expressed social criticism, which is, if not submerged like the irony in the love poems, confused and contradictory, like the sentiments in the war poems. In the love poems Blake seems to be reviving the conventional attitudes of Petrarchism. At the same time we detect faint imagery suggestive of the stern and original concept of "the Marriage hearse:"

> He caught me in his silken net,
> And shut me in his golden cage.
>
> He loves to sit and hear me sing,
> Then, laughing, sports and plays with me;
> Then stretches out my golden wing,
> And mocks my loss of liberty.

The flippant Elizabethan note does not quite obscure the sound of what is later to be grave, and of what is to be impressively Blake's own; nor does it do so in the even more imitative song that follows:

> My silks and fine array,
> My smiles and languish'd air,
> By love are driv'n away;
> And mournful lean Despair
> Brings me yew to deck my grave:
> Such end true lovers have.

This is characteristic Petrarchan hyperbole; yet it is worth remembering that Blake's later "lovers," the mythological "Spectre" and "Emanation," wither and agonize and threaten to die when they separate, quite as the Petrarchan lovers did. The connection, not yet made by Blake, is borne in upon his reader by the third song in this series, which begins:

> Love and harmony combine,
> And around our souls intwine,
> While thy branches mix with mine,
> And our roots together join.

The imagery has become sexual and later it was to be consciously and consistently so. More than this, in the conjunction of love and harmony, the image is of unity, which in the later poems is the equation of happy love on the personal as well as on the social level, just as separation or disunity is the equation of unhappy love and social chaos. One more unconscious association in these lines is worth observing—the identification of love and art (harmony), which later will be made explicit in terms of brotherhood and imagination.

Less fugitive, and clearly contradictory, are the expressed humanitarian attitudes. In "Gwin, King of Norway" there is a firm protest against war and against the oppression of the poor. There is a picture of revolt against tyranny; and the responsibility for the bloody state is put on the kings and nobles who have tyrannized it:

The Nobles of the land did feed
  Upon the hungry Poor;
They tear the poor man's lamb, and drive
  The needy from their door!

"The land is desolate; our wives
  And children cry for bread;
Arise, and pull the tyrant down!
  Let Gwin be humbled!"

. . . . .

The god of war is drunk with blood;
  The earth doth faint and fail;
The stench of blood makes sick the heav'ns;
  Ghosts glut the throat of hell!

O what have Kings to answer for,
  Before that awful thone!
When thousand deaths for vengeance cry,
  And ghosts accusing groan!

This is not impressive verse but its object is clear, and characteristic. On the other hand, in "Blind Man's Buff" Blake defends the concept of law and quite as clearly, however frivolous the context, the notion of social contract, later alien to his ideas:

. . . long a-gone,
When men were first a nation grown,
Lawless they liv'd—till wantonness

And liberty began t'increase,
And one man lay in another's way;
Then laws were made to keep fair play.

In the abortive drama *King Edward the Third,* the king, no less, speaks up for liberty; and precisely because it is that roast-beef liberty which the later Blake could not endure, the passage is notable. Here, too, we find nationalist sentiments worthy of a minor Elizabethan:

. . . sovereigns
Of the sea; our right, that Heaven gave
To England, when at the birth of nature
She was seated in the deep, the Ocean ceas'd
His mighty roar; and, fawning, play'd around
Her snowy feet, and own'd his lawful Queen.

We find also pious sentiments on English commerce and on that selfish eighteenth-century ethics of "benevolence" which, ten years after these poems were printed, Blake was to describe as "nets & gins & traps." Throughout the play runs a notable conflict between patriotic and republican sentiments. Blake did not intend this as the essential conflict of patriotic drama; indeed, the play fails and was probably abandoned because there is no dramatic conflict. These characters are not meant to be understood as voicing the treacherous ambiguities of "heroic villains," although that surely is how Blake would have considered them later.

King Edward the Third, an extended defense of war and national interests, is followed in a "Prologue" to another intended drama by a curse for the tyrant whose ambition underlies war:

O for a voice like thunder, and a tongue
To drown the throat of war!—When the senses
Are shaken, and the soul is driven to madness,
Who can stand? When the souls of the oppressed
Fight in the troubled air that rages, who can stand? . . .

O who can stand? O who hath caused this?
O who can answer at the throne of God?

The Kings and Nobles of the Land have done it!
Hear it not, Heaven, thy Ministers have done it!

Yet a few pages later, in "A War Song to Englishmen," the defense of war is one of the most blatant ever written:

Had I three lives, I'd die in such a cause,
And rise, with ghosts, over the well-fought field. . . .
Soldiers, prepare! Our cause is Heaven's cause.

The main tendency of mind in this juvenile welter is nevertheless clear, and it emerges in the final piece of excessive prose called "Samson." "The sword was bright, while the plow-share rusted, till hope grew feeble, and was ready to give place to doubting. . . . 'Oppression stretches his rod over our land, our country is plowed with swords, and reaped in blood! The echoes of slaughter reach from hill to hill! Instead of peaceful pipe, the shepherd bears a sword; the ox goad is turned into a spear! O when shall our Deliverer come?' "

Here the humanitarian note dominates. Here, too, Experience has been thrust upon the innocent, and they cry to be delivered. But to advance the dialectic of "The Two Contrary States," Blake needed first to find for himself a clear direction that would free him of much of his imitativeness and of his sentimentality, which would make conscious his impulses, which would help him to straighten out and then explore the natural inclination of his ideas and of his genius. This direction he found in the next few years in the extremes of English liberal thought then current, and we must pause to define as briefly as can be its main outlines as these presented themselves to Blake's poetic intelligence.*

* In summarizing the ideas of the people in this group, I have not confined myself to as much of their writing as was produced during the exact years of Blake's meetings with them, but have assumed that works produced both earlier and later express their more or less constant preoccupations. Nor have I felt obliged to include in my summary the entire body of their writings, but only as much of it as is pertinent to Blake's own intellectual development. I am not attempting to trace sources, but to establish, as clearly as possible, an atmosphere of ideas into which Blake moved. It is not really to the point to insist that Blake and Godwin knew each other, for

What, then, at his youngest, was Blake, and what, at its rawest, was his "poetic intelligence"? He seems to have been equally attracted to the music of poetry and to the poetry of social statement but, with a few exceptions, his earliest poems show no large talent for combining the two. On those rare occasions when they do combine, they do so in the intuitive play of his capacity for visualization, but never as a result of conscious poetic purpose. In general, he was led into pastoral reverie by the attraction to verbal music, and into a bald didacticism by the attraction to social criticism. What Blake needed, besides that larger experience of life which discourages imitation, was an experience of mind which would present life more intensely and more coherently to his vision. This experience it was his fortune, or his fate, to find.

example, or even that Blake had read *Political Justice;* it would be impossible to prove that he had except from internal evidence. I have therefore made no effort to point out line parallels between Blake's text and that of the radical theorists. Other writers, however, have indicated several lines in Blake which seem to be either echoes of Godwin or definite confutations. See, for example, Thomas Wright, *The Life of William Blake,* Olney, 1929, Vol. II, pp. 34 and 94; see, too, Ford K. Brown, *The Life of William Godwin,* London, 1926, pp. 45-46. One might regard the passage in Blake's letter to Hayley of January 14, 1804, beginning with the apostrophe "O foolish Philosophy!" as a refutation of Godwin's "no gratitude" concept (*Poetry and Prose,* p. 1089). There are numerous other pieces of such evidence. But they are not much to the point.

CHAPTER SIX

Expectations "Glorious and Paradisaical"

I

AT THE END of the eighteenth century, republican extremists entertained millennial expectations that partook of fantasy, and in that realm most of their expectations remain. Yet it is not so remarkable that no more happened in the social structure of European life in the last decade of the century as it is that so much did.

Their fault, among others, was a too exclusive political concern, with the consequence that they did not perceive as clearly as they might have the extent of actual economic change, or, except very casually, the relationship between economics and politics. Price wrote on insurance, finance, and population. The second part of Paine's *The Rights of Man,* widely read by industrial workers, dealt with state finance and taxation, and Paine stated on a number of occasions the connection between political and general social change: "A revolution in the state of civilization is the necessary companion of revolutions in the system of government. If a revolution in any country be from bad to good, or from good to bad, the state of what is called civilization in that country, must be made conformable thereto, to give that revolution effect." Like Price, Godwin wrote an extended essay on the problems of population in answer to Malthus, and he at least was specifically concerned in a number of his works with industrialization and the state of the industrial poor. His interest, however, was occasional and incidental, and the Industrial Revolution found no theoretician in this group. Such a man was not to emerge for some years, certainly not before Robert Owen. Yet the people in this group, and especially the poet Blake, made the observation that later became the foundation of Owen's efforts: "I early noticed the great attention given to the dead machinery, and the neglect and disregard of the living machinery."

The dates of Blake's life (1757-1827) correspond as exactly as any can with the change from what Marx called "the age of manufacture" to "the factory age." This change was hastened if not made possible by two causes that were also, in part, results. The first was a tremendous expansion of commerce and an extension of trade that destroyed the barriers of the village market and opened up a continent and more to the products of British industry. The second was the decay of a venerable system of agriculture that in uprooting the yeomanry tended to concentrate the population of England in towns, and placed at the disposal of developing industry the energies of an entire army of laborers. But machinery itself was the revolutionary element.

Technical innovation had been proceeding slowly for several centuries, at first in the coal, then in the textile, and at last in the iron industries. Experiments with various types of motive power were climaxed by the construction of the first steam engine in 1775. Immediately mechanical invention leapt ahead at a tremendous rate. Almost as immediately the concentration of capital began, and factories usurped and transformed the English scene. One must remind oneself of the considerable impression that this change, as a physical fact alone, would make on the minds of men born before such sights were common. The sensibilities of a poet would almost necessarily be appalled. A contemporary French traveler has left a record of his impression of an English factory of these years in terms that are curiously suggestive of some of Blake's industrial images: "Amongst these warlike machines, these terrible death-dealing instruments, huge cranes, every kind of windlass, lever and tackle for moving heavy loads, were fixed in suitable places. Their creaking, the piercing noise of the pulleys, the continuous sound of hammering, the ceaseless energy of the men keeping all this machinery in motion, presented a sight as interesting as it was new. . . . There is such a succession of these workshops that the outer air is quite hot; the night is so filled with fire and light that when from a distance we see, here a glowing mass of coal, there darting flames leaping from the blast furnaces, when we hear the heavy hammers striking the echoing anvils and the shrill whistling of the air pumps, we do not know whether we are looking at a volcano in eruption or have been miraculously transported to Vulcan's cave, where he and his cyclops are manufacturing lightning."

The factory system had immediate social consequences of vast importance. The first was the further concentration of population in industrial centers, England's great ugly black towns. The second was the almost immediate inception of periodic economic crises in which industry throws out of work large portions of the class it creates and depends upon. This clearly involves a third consequence, the revision of class lines and the intensification of class antagonisms. The urgency of these matters is most clearly reflected in the rounded brutalities of Malthus's *Essay on Population.*

From the agricultural freeholders came not only a large proportion of labor but almost all the factory owners. By the end of the century the separation of these interests was complete. From the beginning of the change, the laborers had recognized the menace of technological developments to their interest and had promptly seized upon their one defense, the destruction of machines. The Spitalfields Riots of 1763 were only one of the many riots in which tools were destroyed and factories burned. Byron's theatrical opposition to a bill against loom-breaking took place as late as 1812.

Ironically, the very repugnance of English laborers to the factory system was almost entirely to the advantage of the owners, for it enabled them to employ without scruple women and children, docile to brutality, and cheaper. Children of no more than five or six were literally sold into bondage if they happened to be parish charges, and the number of parish charges had mounted steadily throughout the century. They worked for as long as eighteen hours a day in factories without any kind of regulation. In the 1780's, under the pressure of various problems created by the Industrial Revolution, but especially that of education, evangelical Sunday schools began to flourish in the factory areas. They were to provide Blake with his greatest piece of formal irony.

Political consequences were inevitable in these conditions. With the sharpening antagonism between classes finding expression in frequent riots, and with the near example of the French Revolution before them, many Englishmen feared a workers' revolution at home. Repressive legislation followed, and a good deal of systematized Tory piety of the sort preached by Richard Watson. Until 1834 the incessant tampering with the wretched Poor Laws continued to be an advantage to the industrial employer and a serious handicap to the unemployed worker who genuinely wanted employment. Then there were the laws against the destruction of machines, and the strict regulations against all "combinations" of workers. In 1835 relatively enlightened men like Wordsworth were still horrified by the notion of "unjust combinations," and he, for example, tried to devise means by which the worker "would be less tempted to join" them. Not until 1802, in Peel's bill for factory inspection and the improvement of the conditions of child labor, was a law passed that was even remotely to the interest of the worker. This law, ignored by many and inadequate when observed, became finally the precedent for progressive legislation that Peel himself would have opposed. But that was not until 1832. Blake, by that time, had been dead for five years.

Godwin and Paine grasped the essential facts in this development. The first result of mechanical innovation, the division of labor and the consequent meaninglessness of work, was seized upon in *Political Justice* ("It has been found that ten persons can make two hundred and forty times as many pins in a day as one person") and in the novel *Fleetwood,* which describes at length the operation of a silk manufactory in Lyon. Godwin insisted that individual talent was the only intelligent basis of labor division: ". . . every human creature, idiots and extraordinary cases excepted, is endowed with talents, which, if rightly directed, would shew him to be apt, adroit, intelligent and acute, in the walk for which his organization especially fitted him." Further, Godwin repeatedly insisted on the disastrous moral effects of the industrial system as it had developed; long hours and low wages gave the laborer neither the opportunity nor the means to leisure, and without such relief, the monotony of his work destroyed both his mind and his body. Mary Wollstonecraft, fearful that the Revolution might merely replace an aristocracy of rank with an aristocracy of industrial wealth, argued similarly before Godwin did. Godwin's handling of the factory scenes in *Fleetwood* is melodramatic, but his description, deprived of its sentiments, corresponds with the facts. The result of machinery, he said, is that the worker himself becomes a machine: "A mechanic becomes a sort of machine; his limbs and articulations are converted, as it were, into wood and wires. Tamed, lowered, torpified into this character, he may be said perhaps to be content."

The great defect of modern machinery as it was at first employed was exactly what Godwin saw, what Lewis Mumford has since described as "a sterilization of the self, an elimination, as far as possible, of the human bias and preference." This is the irony in a remark such as that of even the well-intentioned Owen: "the living machinery." It is the image that is significant, the unconscious but rhetorically convenient imposition of the mechanical upon the living value, and the disappearance, in a figure suggesting "bones & sinews, All strings & bobbins," of "the human form divine." Mr. Mumford has made another suggestion that is valuable to the understanding of Blake's habitual associations: "Perhaps the most positive influence in the development of the machine has been that of the soldier," not only because the spread of soldierly habits throughout the population in the seventeenth century was a psychological preparation for the performance of other kinds of mechanical duties, but because the social and moral effects of barracks and factory discipline are almost identical. In Blake's poetry, war and industry are never far apart and are often identified; the connections, one begins to see, are multiple.

The intention and the method of the artist stand directly opposed to those of the modern soldier and the mechanic. Art is the anomaly it is in an industrial society because it is the only item that is still produced more or less singly, a picture or a poem remaining one man's work in an economic order that more and more depends upon the division of labor. The organic connection between life and art is strained and often broken. Art becomes a toy of the bourgeoisie, and the artist—except for the draftsman, the architect, and possibly the muralist—is isolated from the main stream of his society. This is a distinctly modern phenomenon, and Blake is perhaps at the head of that long series of artists who have struggled with a problem that does not yet seem to have admitted a solution. For Blake the problem was particularly acute. He was not only an artist but, like Morris later, an artist with a strong impulse to handicraft. His protest against the machine ("A Machine is not a Man, nor a Work of Art") and against the spread of commercial values ("Commerce Cannot endure Individual Merit") was therefore particularly sharp, and he was forced into his curiously medieval manner of production because it alone could save his talents.

This impulse remained alive among artists throughout the nineteenth century, as one after another attempted to substitute for current social attitudes an attitude based on aesthetic, or individual, values rather than on the mass values produced by the machine. Blake was the first of these, and Shelley perhaps the second. Social abuses, Shelley said, arose from the absence of "the poetical faculty" in the "cultivation of those sciences which have enlarged the limits of the empire of man over the external world. . . . To what but a cultivation of the mechanical arts in a degree disproportioned to the presence of the creative faculty, which is the basis of all knowledge, is to be attributed the abuse of all invention for abridging the combining labour, to the exasperation of the inequality of mankind?" This is not a lucid sentence, but it expresses a point of view that underlies Blake's vast claims for the faculty of the imagination, and which was to haunt the most enlightened men for a hundred and fifty years. There is much that is foolish and much that is repugnant in the philosophy of Godwin, but his perception that individual values were destroyed by the principle of labor division as it had developed in his generation was neither.

Godwin made a more difficult perception than this. Observing the realignment of class interests that developing industry had brought about, he opposed capital wealth to labor, and described capital wealth as an effective tool in maintaining a perpetual war: "The superiority of the rich, being thus unmercifully exercised, must inevitably expose them to reprisals; and the poor man will be induced to regard the state of society as a state of war, an unjust combination, not for protecting every man in his rights and securing to him the means of existence, but for engrossing all its advantages to a few favoured individuals, and reserving for the portion of the rest want, dependence and misery." Paine expressed much the same idea somewhat more simply when he said: "The peer and the beggar are often of the same family. One extreme produced the other: to make one rich many must be made poor; neither can the system be supported by other means." It is a remark that finds its psychological equivalent in Blake's quatrain:

Pity would be no more
If we did not make somebody Poor;
And Mercy no more could be
If all were as happy as we.

A point of view toward money somewhat different but likewise approximated by Blake is Paine's: "Though I care as little about riches, as any man, I am a friend of riches because they are capable of good." Intending as he did a juster distribution rather than the actual concentration of wealth, Paine's point, that good can come of wealth but not of poverty, is much the same as Blake's when he said that "the Argument is better for Affluence than for poverty." Under less intense economic pressure he would have produced greater works of art.

Godwin and Paine touched on nearly all the obvious contemporary political and economic abuses. Godwin was aware that contemporary legislation was almost always on the side of the owners: "The rich are encouraged to associate for the execution of the most partial and oppressive positive laws. Monopolies and patents are lavishly dispensed to such as are able to purchase them. While the most vigilant policy is employed to prevent combinations of the poor to fix the price of labour [at its minimum level, that is, for it was fixed at its maximum], and they are deprived of the benefit of that prudence and judgment which would select the scene of their industry." Paine said that a charter did not give rights to one man but took them away from many. He argued in the same way in his attack on "the poor laws, those instruments of civil torture," and in his insistence that employment was the least obligation of society to its members, including "the casual poor."

Godwin and Paine looked to political change for the relief of economic distress. Neither planned to abandon machinery in the utopia. Like Paine's money, it could produce good, even though its first developments had produced evil only. Godwin wrote: "When we look at the complicated machines of human contrivance, various sorts of mills, of weaving engines, of steam engines, are we not astonished at the compendium of labour they produce? Who shall say where this species of improvement must stop? At present such inventions alarm the labouring part of the community; and they may be productive of temporary distress, though they conduct in the sequel to the most important interests of the multitude. But in a state of equal labour their utility will be liable to no dispute. . . . The conclusion of the progress which has here been sketched, is something like a final close to the necessity of manual labour. . . . Matter, or to speak more accurately, the certain and unintermitting laws of the universe, will be the Helots of the period we are contemplating."

The machine was a congenial image to Godwin's mind, and in this he was a more modern man than Blake, who, like the loom-breakers, saw it as a threat to life. The associations within images supply the clue to the difference of temper. "The way of life congenial to the terms of the myth of rationality," Robert Penn Warren has said, "is called industrialism." Lewis Mumford argues that the picture of a mechanical universe was essential to the Industrial Revolution; it furnished the necessary philosophical sanction for the machine.

No intuition in Blake's poetry is historically so brilliant as that which is revealed by his habitual associations with the imagery of the machine. His protest against the inhumanity of machinery is an extension of his protest against the inhumanity of the contemporary mechanical philosophy, or vice versa. Man in a factory was a slave in precisely the sense that man was a slave in the Newtonian universe. The tyranny of Urizen, the rationalist, is symbolized by creatures caught within wheels, by slaves grinding at the mill. War, which after Blake's time was to become the greatest industrial operation of all, was inhuman in exactly the same way, and he made the association in his verse. His objections to Sir Joshua Reynolds and his attack on the neoclassic dogma were a portion of the attack on Bacon, Newton, and Locke, and the imagery of industrial slavery was again appropriate. "Bring out number, weight & measure in a year of dearth" is a proverb that points in many directions; but for Blake all these directions pointed back to a single fact: the substitution of mechanical for living values.

II

Less lively minds employed the imagery of the machine without Blake's denunciations. Godwin abandoned the old and more vital symbols for the state and spoke of "the *machine* of human society." Paine thought of Christianity as a machine that had been badly designed and could not operate efficiently: "The Christian religion of Gods within Gods, like wheels within wheels, is like a complicated machine that never goes right, and every projector in the art of Christianity is trying to mend it."

Paine's être suprème, however, far from being inefficient, was the archetype of the technological genius: "The Almighty is the great mechanic of the creation, the first philosopher, and original teacher of all science. . . . Had we, at this day, no knowledge of machinery, and were it possible that man could have a view . . . of the structure of the machinery of the universe, he would soon conceive the idea of constructing some at least of the mechanical works we now have. . . . Or could a model of the universe . . . be presented before him and put in motion, his mind would arrive at the same idea. Such an object and such a subject would, whilst it improved him in knowledge useful to himself as a man and a member of society, as well as entertaining, afford far better matter for impressing him with a knowledge of, and a belief in the Creator, and of the reverence and gratitude that man owes to him."

The implications of Newtonianism, of the image of God as the ideal machinist, were important in the rapid spread of scientific deism in the latter part of the seventeenth century and the early part of the eighteenth. And it would be interesting if a similar relationship could be demonstrated between the actual images of real machinery impressed on the popular consciousness by the mechanization of English industry and the recrudescence at the end of the eighteenth century of the deistic, or mechanistic, view of God. Burke was right when in 1790 he demanded: "Who, born within the last forty years, has read one word of Collins, and Toland, and Tindal, and Chubb, and Morgan, and that whole race who called themselves Freethinkers? Who now reads Bolingbroke? Who ever read him through?" But he was also wrong. For thousands of people, and mainly workers, were reading or were about to read Thomas Paine, who gave them Collins and Toland and Bolingbroke and "that whole race" in a much more accessible form, popularized and slangy, and without the barrier of philosophical system to stand between his fierce rationalizations and the grasp of the most ordinary mind.

The old theology, defended throughout the century with such lazy intellect, could not withstand the rough brutality of this assault. The fact that Paine's audience was made up in large part of industrial workers is suggestive in a number of ways, and not the least of these ways is that they had become intimately involved with machinery. Some such relationship seems to have existed in Paine's mind, at any rate, and even more precisely in Blake's. For when the image of the "mill" first appears in his writing, it is in his attack on deism, *There Is No Natural Religion,* and it is the symbol not of the factory itself but of the method of logic, of rationalism, and of scientific theology. Later it becomes more expressive of industry itself, and of other elements; but it came from industry in the first place, from the novel sight of men at machines. Blake cannot be taken with entire seriousness when he sometimes denies the basic role of simple sensation in poetry.

Blake wanted this machine, as symbol or fact, demolished, for he despised its barrenness, its cold diagrammatic quality, its deficiency as myth in rich and vital figures. Paine's imagination was satisfied by the machine, both as symbol and as fact, and he did much to popularize it. And for Paine it must be said that, unlike his predecessors of a hundred years before, whose deism had been addressed to cultivated minds and had acted as a regressive social force, Paine's was flung out to the uneducated in support of a revolutionary politics. It is this connection which involves Blake, the visionary enthusiast, with the cerebral calculations of natural theology.

The late revival of this point of view was important to Blake because in one degree or another it was the view of all the more impressive figures in the "Paine set." All of them, Blake included, were dissenters if they were not atheists, which meant that all of them held a general disrespect for Establishment. Priestley, the mildest republican in the group, was unwilling to relinquish revealed religion; but in spite of the fact that he wrote an answer to *The Age of Reason,* he defended his own Unitarianism largely in terms of natural theology. Price, Godwin, and Mary Wollstonecraft were less moderate than he, and Paine, together with his friend Joel Barlow, was without any moderation. For all of them, religious ideas underlay their politics, the clearest example being Paine's transliteration of Quakerism into revolutionary republicanism. Godwin, through the force of science and the mechanical philosophy, transformed the strictures of Calvinism into the idea of social necessity. Blake, through a reaction from science, changed the dissenting attitude into an aggressive defense of free will. These two extremes were adaptable to the conclusions of anarchy with equal ease.

The deistic discussion was important to Blake because, springing as it did from the general philosophy that lay at the root of the French Revolution as well as from the actual events of the Revolution in its conflict with the Church, it brought with it a general criticism of established Christian doctrine and discipline, and, ordinarily, a strong disrespect for Church and clergy that gave a radical political bias to even moderate dissenting opinion. Blake's little songs are sometimes treated as though they embodied, in pietistic vein, the traditional Christian view; actually, they are founded on the observation of Rousseau, that man is born free and somehow slips into chains. This political bias Blake, who repudiated the theology of deism, nevertheless took from it, and a large part of his poetry, like a large part of the prose of Paine and Priestley, may be read as a conventional eighteenth-century attempt to strip Christianity of what were called its "corruptions." Given the way in which Blake's mind seized upon ideas, it is not at all curious that, sharing in so many ways the spirit of those enthusiastic groups which were antagonistic to the deists, he yet drew from the deists for as much of his attack on religious discipline and conformity as was convenient.

The scope of this criticism was not large, nor were its motives ever remote from its particular political view. A sermon of 1791, before Blake had devised his revolutionary Jesus or even his figure of Orc, begins: "Jesus Christ was a Revolutionist; and the Revolution he came to effect was foretold in these words, 'He hath sent me to proclaim liberty to the captives, and the opening of the prison to them that are bound.'" This remark states the historical grounds on which the Church was attacked.

Priestley, more than any of these men, tried to construct a body of criticism on a definition of primitive Christianity and the character of Jesus, and devoted a number of his longest works to the subject. Paine and Price more or less followed his lead, but they were not as interested as he in demonstrating the case. Priestley's answer to Burke, unlike Paine's answer or Price's challenge, was a defense of religious rather than of political liberty, and even in works that were mainly interested in showing the decay of Christian doctrine since primitive times, Priestley extended the point to include church government. "As to the abuses in the *government of the church,* they are as easily accounted for as abuses in civil government; worldly-minded men being always ready to lay hold of every opportunity of increasing their power; and in the dark ages too many circumstances concurred to give the Christian clergy peculiar advantages over the laity in this respect." The corruptions were inevitable once Christianity lost sight of the ideal of Christ: "It is nothing but the *alliance* of the kingdom of Christ with the kingdoms of this world (an alliance which our Lord himself expressly disclaimed) that supports the grossest corruptions of Christianity." Paine used the identical argument against church power: ". . . the church has set up a system of religion very contradictory to the character of the person whose name it bears. It has set up a religion of pomp and of revenue in pretended imitation of a person whose life was humility and poverty."

It was Paine, in fact, rather than Priestley, who stated most incisively the primitive ideal as it had come to be understood: "The intellectual part of religion is a private affair between every man and his Maker, and in which no third party has any right to interfere. The practical part consists in our doing good to each other. But since religion has been made into a trade, the practical part has been made to consist of ceremonies performed by men called priests; and the people have been amused with ceremonial show, processions, and bells. By devices of this kind true religion has been banished; and such means have been found out to extract money even from the pockets of the poor, instead of contributing to their relief." The opposition between an Establishment and the true spirit of Christianity was defined most simply, perhaps, by Joel Barlow when in speaking of "church" and "religion" he said: "I consider no connection as existing between these two subjects." Unless religion is to be a means of "darkening the consciences of men, in order to oppress them," it must be "a personal and not a corporate concern."

Political control and interest corrupted the purpose of Christ's example and message. According to Paine, the corruption was possible only because government, to maintain itself, forbids free inquiry and discussion, and thus pits religion, with itself, against truth. Godwin pointed out that a national Church was vicious in exactly the way a system of national education was vicious—both control free inquiry. One begins to see freshly the extent and the kind of reaction in Coleridge's political thinking, which developed an exactly opposite point of view about both these institutions. Unlike Paine, the quondam Quaker, Godwin looks beyond his generation to the positive atheism of Marxism: "Religion is in reality in all its parts an accommodation to the prejudices and weaknesses of mankind. Its authors communicated to the world as much truth, as they calculated that the world would be willing to receive. But it is time that we should lay aside the instruction intended only for children in understanding, and contemplate the nature and principles of things." Against such extremist tendency, ideas like Coleridge's were the bulwark.

Paine and Blake did not follow Godwin to his extreme. Paine, after all, retained some dim notions of immortality, and his objection to Christianity was, like Blake's, chiefly to its institutionalized forms. These, no matter in what religion they developed, represented the interference of government: "All national institutions of churches, whether Jewish, Christian or Turkish, appear to me no other than human inventions set up to terrify and enslave mankind, and monopolize power and profit." Church hierarchy, assuming that some men are closer to God than others is based on the idea of human inequality, a lie maintained by priests with the connivance of government. Like all lies, it finally harms the priests as much as the worshiper who is kept in ignorance.

Godwin drew a character of the Priest in several places, and in one called him "a mere abortion and blot upon the face of the earth," because he must represent "study rendered abortive, artificial manners, infantine prejudices, and a sort of arrogant infallibility." To Paine, the clergyman was a hireling, the mainstay of a decayed despotism that makes "the object of the church . . . power and revenue, and terror the means of it." The point of view was not without its support in contemporary events. "Church and King!" was the cry of rioting mobs under the direction of government agents. This shibboleth rang in Priestley's ears as his house burned, and in Paine's across the Channel as innumerable times his effigy went up in fire.

"I saw the exceeding probability," Paine wrote, "that a revolution in the system of government would be followed by a revolution in the system of religion." Priestley held the same expectation: ". . . perhaps we must wait for the fall of the civil powers before this most unnatural alliance be broken. Calamitous, no doubt, will that time be. But what convulsion in the political world ought to be a subject of lamentation, if it be attended with so desirable an event?" On this ground alone, the French Revolution justified itself to a moderate man like Richard Price. Once it succeeded, "the proper office of the civil magistrate" would be "to *maintain peace;* not to support *truth.*—To defend the *properties* of men, not to take care of their *souls.*—And to protect *equally* all honest citizens of all persuasions, not to set up one religious sect above another." Once it succeeded, Priestley could make his quite modest recommendation with impunity: "Respect a Parliamentary king, and cheerfully pay all parliamentary taxes; but have nothing to do with a parliamentary religion, or a parliamentary God." Then Paine could practice quietly (if quiet was possible for him) as he preached noisily his maxim "My own mind is my own church."

It was obvious and blundering invective, to be sure, but it found its way into an intelligence that was neither: ". . . get into Freedom . . . into The Mind, in which every one is King & Priest in his own House."

III

After the goddess Reason had been given official status in France, English revolutionaries doubled their efforts in her behalf. It is curious, on the surface at least, that the most comprehensive apotheosis of reason in English did not approve of the methods of the French Revolution. Yet this is characteristic of William Godwin, who made of logic a kind of icy reverie. This is the essential difference between Holcroft's and Godwin's ideas and the ideas of Price, Paine, Priestley, Barlow, Mary Wollstonecraft, and the rest; yet their essential similarities make a discussion of Godwin without reference to these others impossible. Godwin's practical-minded, pamphleteering friends did not escape the reach of his greedy eclecticism. He took their ideas as he took those of their philosophical predecessors on the

Continent, and while he did not correct their logic, he at any rate extended it. In his faith in the human reason he was at one with them; and one may say for his logic that if man were indeed the rational creature that they all assumed him to be, revolutionary force would hardly be a tenable conclusion.

They all began with Locke by sweeping aside the notion of innate ideas, and they all arrived at their equalitarianism by assuming that every man is born with a rational faculty capable of development, and that every man's happiness depends upon the cultivation of this faculty. Its function is the discovery on the one hand of natural rights, or on the other, of virtue, or justice, or immutable truth. "We are all of us endowed with reason, able to compare, to judge and to infer," declared Godwin. Individuals vary in talents, but every individual has *a* talent that should be allowed exercise and development. That individuals vary as widely in the ability "to compare, to judge and to infer," Godwin did not admit. His intention was to establish the moral equality of man, and therefore he insisted that reason is the common endowment and the seat of all actions. If man's actions are concurrent with the dictates of his reason, whether it has been corrupted or kept pure, then man is a creature not of free will but of necessity; as the universe must act in accord with the laws of nature, so man must act in accord with the laws of mind. There are pits of intellectual confusion here that did not trouble Godwin, or Priestley, who was also a necessitarian; these pits, at least, do not yawn so widely in the works of Price and Paine and Blake, who were not.

If men by their single natal endowment are made morally equal, their errors are merely the negative expression of what is naturally good. Character is determined by environment: "From these reasonings it sufficiently appears, that the moral qualities of men are the product of the impressions made upon them, and that there is no instance of an original propensity to evil. Our virtues and vices may be traced to the incidents which make the history of our lives, and if these incidents could be divested of every improper tendency, vice would be extirpated from the world." Benevolence, disinterested generosity, and sympathy—the mainstay of revolutionary thought as it was of all the sentimental humanitarianism of the age—are natural to man. Once the environment allows these to express themselves, man, perfectible, moves on into perfection. Whatever the incursions made into revolutionary doctrine by primitivism, all these radicals were agreed on the theory of perfectibility. They would not hold it for their "consolation and luxury, fondly to imagine that the throne of ignorance and vice is placed on so firm a basis that it can never be removed." They cried as in one voice: "Man is perfectible; we must by reason destroy the myth of original sin."

The conflicts within this thought are largely extensions from the religious thinking that underlay it, but they came to the surface because "sin" was omitted from its calculations. Thus primitivism and progressivism become mixed notions, whereas formerly "sin" had put the first in a past that lay beyond nostalgia and the second in a future that lay beyond life. For the same reason, "natural right" and "ultimate justice" were confused—what man was born with before sin, and what he might expect after his release from it. Thus too came the confusion between the idea of a slow progress toward good, which corresponds to the idea of the soul's painful salvation from sin to grace, and the idea of a revolutionary regeneration, which corresponds to the idea either of the apocalyptic seizure, or, in the individual, that of the breaking through of inner light. All these confusions are apparent in Godwin and his fellows. They are also apparent in Blake, who was more deeply religious than they, and only somewhat less political.

Godwin's theory of the nature of the universe follows upon his theory of the nature of man. The universe is a system of cause and effect "palpable to the mind." Such a system implies the existence of an absolute code of moral principles; virtue, or benevolence, the principle that discovers justice (justice being the undisturbed and naturally ordained harmony between the parts of the system) is integral in the universe. This justice, or harmony, every man is duty-bound, by the nature of things and his place in the whole, to discover. Private judgment can and will direct man to his moral duty in every circumstance if reason is employed, for reason unperverted involves a necessary calculation as to which path of action is most useful to the whole.

Godwin, following Rousseau, assumes the existence of a natural order that man can infer and adapt to his own order. If he has erred, and committed himself to an artificial order, he must correct his error by abolishing the artificial elements, political and social institutions that nature cannot sanction. Rousseau, through a certain legerdemain, limited the extent of the abolition; Godwin did not. The reason that Godwin found it unnecessary to set these limits is that, for all his discussion of "private judgment" and all his insistence on the importance of individual expression, he thought of society not as an array of richly diversified personalities but as an aggregate of interchangeable atoms, with an identical reason and harmonious interests. A. D. Lindsay has brilliantly analyzed the consequences of such a theory in laissez faire, as well as in the conflict, deeply rooted in liberal thinking and quite apparent today, between the view "that men's interests were naturally harmonious and that men's interests had to be artificially harmonized. The first view is a defense of anarchy. . . . The second view implies government, but a government which is disinterested."

In general, Godwin held the first view and Paine the second. If as Godwin said man has a single prescribed *duty* in the world—the discovery of justice—he needs no further equipment to attain happiness. The doctrine of *rights* is therefore unnecessary and fallacious. It was a conclusion of considerable importance to Godwin's position; for "rights" involve institutions to protect them, while "duties" involve nothing beyond themselves.

Godwin's anarchy came with perfect logic out of the assumptions he was developing, and the failure in logical completeness lies at the beginning, with Locke, as Leslie Stephen showed, rather than at the end, with Godwin. If, as Locke argued in the *Treatise on Government,* "a child is born a subject to no country or government," and "if no man can be lawfully governed except by his own individual consent," then all government indeed becomes "a mere rope of sand." In the ascendancy of the Whigs that followed upon Locke, it was a Whig, Edmund Burke, who detected the dynamite in Locke's theory and who attempted to remove the fuse. In *A Vindication of Natural Society,* his first work, published in 1756, Burke parodied the ideas of Locke's Tory follower Bolingbroke, whose principles, which anticipated Rousseau, Burke regarded as anarchical.

Rousseau himself, making almost all the assumptions later made by Godwin, checked his argument with the doctrine of the general will, which in turn allowed his followers, such as Paine, to devote themselves to the idea of republican government: "Willingly or unwillingly, all citizens will be under the Law." Godwin, with his concept of duties and of the accuracy of private judgment, was able to sweep away the notion of the general will, and abolish government entirely. His failure was not the unimportant one of logic. It was the vastly more important one of observation and imagination, and it is interesting to observe what happens to this logical apparatus when it is presented to the imagination of a zealot.

In Godwin's system, no one shall be "under the law," for the doctrine of legislation disappears with the principle of government. The laws of truth exist in the nature of things. They cannot be made, because they already are. "Just" government is therefore an impossibility. Under present unjust governments, man, capable of moral improvement, has as his first duty the determination of the sources of his improvement. He must examine and consequently reject all existing civil institutions and their accepted bases for "common deliberation" and "perfect sincerity." This is far from Robespierre's argument that "To obey the Committee . . . is to obey one's better self, to be really free," and that the new government of France was "the despotism of liberty against tyranny."

Godwin scrutinizes political institutions and finds that, for one or more of three reasons, all are evil. Every form of government introduces social values incongruent with the principles of truth; no form of government can cope with all individual cases without resorting to injustice; and every form—monarchy, aristocracy, and democracy—comes "sooner or later . . . to seek some other purpose . . . and all forms of coercion are evil." To his republican friends, Godwin concedes only that democracy is less evil than the other forms; for monarchy and aristocracy corrupt not only their subjects but themselves. They imply established religious forms that involve the suppression of free inquiry and breed hypocrisy, to the destruction of "perfect sincerity." Furthermore, systems based on political oppression give rise to the vicious concept of charity. Mary Wollstonecraft agreed: "You know that I have always been an enemy to what is termed charity, because timid bigots endeavouring thus to cover their *sins,* do violence to justice, till, acting the demigod, they forget that they are men. And there are others who do not even think of laying up a treasure in heaven, whose benevolence is merely tyranny in disguise." Finally, monarchy and aristocracy have given and must give rise to unjust wars. All war of acquisition is unmitigated evil; only that war is justifiable which is waged in "the defense of our own liberty and of the liberty of others" if they "desire to possess it." But for Godwin "war in defense of our own liberty" does not include revolution. Indeed, he opposed even reform associations, because they often led to violence. With the possible exception of Paine, who seemed to make some compromise, and Blake, who advocated revolution in a number of works but whose ideal was one of "mental warfare," this is the most important difference between Godwin and his fellows. To Godwin, the dissemination of truth through "common deliberation" or unrestricted inquiry is the only way to the regeneration of the species.

Godwin's rejection of law follows upon that of political institutions, and leads him to argue that in the future age there can be no theatrical performances, because they involve the individual actor in the "formal repetition of other men's ideas," nor any concert music, for the concert musician is reduced to a "miserable state of mechanism." This notion was founded on a view of the sanctity of what Blake called the "identity." It is an idea that comes from the ancient notion of the "diversity" of the creation, an idea attached to the larger one of The Chain of Being. "Instead . . . of endeavoring, then," wrote Priestley, "by uniform and fixed systems of education, to keep mankind always the same, let us give free scope to every thing which may bid fair for introducing more variety among us. The various characters of the *Athenians* was certainly preferable to the uniform character of the *Spartans,* or to any uniform national character whatever. Is it not universally considered as an advantage to *England,* that it contains so great a variety of original characters? And is it not, on this account, preferred to *France, Spain,* or *Italy?* Uniformity is the characteristic of the brute creation. Amongst them every species of birds build their nests with the same materials, and in the same form; the genius and disposition of one individual is that of all; and it is only the education which men give them that raises any of them much above others. But it is the glory of human nature, that the operations of reason, though variable, and by no means infallible, are capable of infinite improvement."

Blake might almost have had Priestley's deficient ornithology in mind when he wrote

How do you know but ev'ry Bird that cuts the airy way,
Is an immense world of delight, clos'd by your senses five?

Godwin, without a poetic sense of "diversity" and in spite of his atomistic assumptions, argued on these grounds. Law lumps individuals together and treats them as if they were similar, when actually nothing is like anything else. "There is no maxim more clear than this, Every case is a rule to itself. . . . It should seem to be the business of justice, to distinguish the qualities of men, and not, which has hitherto been the practice, to confound them. . . ."

It is supreme injustice to enforce law by a system of punishment. Such a system implies that the punishment fits the crime, and, in Godwin's squirrel cage, that the criminal might have done otherwise than he did. With the abolition of law and penal codes, Godwin would abolish the promise, which, like the notion of rights, is irrelevant to duty.

The third subject of denunciation in Godwin's examination of social forms is property. Property, which destroys character, must be abolished in order that each man may have what he needs, not what, through greed and selfishness and crime, he can acquire. Here again Godwin differs from Paine, among whose "rights" was the right of property, in which there could be no strict equality: ". . . for to distribute it equally it would be necessary that all should have contributed in the same proportion, which can never be the case." Property, indeed, is at the root of Paine's difficulties, for, believing that that government is best which governs least, he preached laissez faire, but suspicious of power, he argued for a system of taxation and other forms of governmental action that would prevent the accumulation of fortunes. Godwin's more consistent utopia was without property rights of any sort.

His utopia was never very clearly defined. At the bottom of his theory lay the common sentiment of simplification. This is one of the few subjects on which Godwin quotes Paine: "Excess of government only tends to incite to and to create crimes which else had never existed." The degree of simplification varied, Godwin's theory being that law is unnecessary, and that when a law is needed to meet a particular case, it can easily be inferred from those laws implicit in the cosmos. If legislative bodies are abandoned, the idea of nationality will wither, and as the world slowly comes to be composed of smaller and smaller communities in which opinion, or individual inclination, rules, organization will disappear. The rule of society will have been reduced to its just form: simple need inevitably satisfied.

The radicals argued a social theory based on the concept of unraveling. It was their ambition to take man back to his natural condition, or away from his irrational to his rational state. This concept depended on a generic view. Burke, arguing on the basis of an institutional view, pictured man not as he intrinsically *was,* but as he actually had become, as the thing that his history had wound him up to be. Burke urged a nationalistic theory; the radical view, as Godwin implied it and as Paine expressed it, was international. Paine, like many men today, believed that the mold of society was breaking, and that no one could limit the grandiose possibilities the breach contained. At the end of the first part of *The Rights of Man* he envisaged an association of nations that would abolish national intrigue and war. Universal peace is another of those religious hopes which politics had seized upon, and which Blake, the religious political, demanded. Nations, like the morning stars, will sing together.

IV

On Paine's principle that "A revolution in the state of civilization is the necessary companion of revolutions in the system of government," Godwin extended the content of the word "political" to include all forms of social activity. It followed that in his discussion of property he should have included marriage, which he saw as a degrading system of economic slavery that resulted in the moral deterioration of women. Marriage is inimical to Godwin's individualism because, by binding two people together under legal strictures, the development of each is retarded. A much milder discussion of the position of women in society had come from Paine a number of years before, in his *Letter on the Female Sex,* and Condorcet had written on the subject before him. But for a treatment less extravagant than Godwin's and more forceful than either Paine's or Condorcet's, one looks to Mary Wollstonecraft.

A Vindication of the Rights of Woman is constructed on the familiar assumption of radical politics that men, sharing the gift of reason, are responsible moral beings and are morally equal. Woman is by nature no different, and society must recognize her rationality and abolish the economic and moral tyranny to which she has always been subjected. Man is the tyrant (like God and king) who finds it convenient to his domestic despotism to think woman inferior and weaker in will than himself. He has therefore formed her according to his wishes, and her education has been a training in folly. From her earliest years she has been instructed to believe that she must substitute physical for intellectual charm, yielding grace for a resolute will. She must play the coquette rather than the wife, act as slave and mistress rather than as companion, and bring to her relations with men a hypocritical modesty in place of a rational co-operation.

Mary Wollstonecraft, a kind of realist in a vividly sentimental age, assumed the impermanence of passionate love, yet she insisted that marriage, properly practiced, is "the cement of society," the foundation of social virtue.* The only rational attitude toward marriage is the recognition that when passion ceases, some quieter quality must be prepared to take its place. This was not, she believed, the view of her contemporaries. Deceiving themselves with the notion that love can be permanent, women enter marriage with the idea that they must hold love by female arts, and never discover that another relationship could follow if their understanding was conceded and properly trained.

Wives are "short-lived queens" until passion fails, when, unable "to attain the sober pleasures that arise from equality," they of necessity become slaves. In the meantime, unaffected by the fatuous coquetries of an aging woman or by her hypocritical arts of "modest" restraint intended to tease, the husband completes the vicious circle by seeking out the prostitute. "The shameless behaviour of the prostitutes, who infest the streets of this metropolis, raising alternate emotions of pity and disgust . . . trample on virgin bashfulness with a sort of bravado, and glorying in their shame, become more audaciously lewd than men, however depraved, to whom this sexual quality has not been gratuitously granted, ever appear to be."

The solution lies in granting women moral equality with men by denying "sexual qualities." "I wish to sum up what I have said in a few words, for I here throw down my gauntlet, and deny the existence of sexual virtues, not excepting modesty." Only "where love animates the behaviour" should a distinction in the moral and psychological equipment of the sexes be admitted. Otherwise, the essential human character is destroyed by an artificially elaborated sexual character: ". . . the sexual should not destroy the human character."

Education alone can bring woman out of the false role in which (paraphrasing Mrs. Piozzi's recommendation) all her "*arts* are employed to gain and keep the heart of man," into the more generous human role for which nature has equipped her. Then

* In *Mary: A Fiction* (1788) appeared an implicit criticism of the legal status of the married woman that was to be developed later in *A Vindication.* There, the heroine not only allows herself to fall in love with a man who is not her husband, but declines to live with her husband. She does not consider that her marriage vow prohibits adultery with honor.

there will be no need for these arts: "The woman who has dedicated a considerable portion of her time to pursuits purely intellectual, and whose affections have been exercised by humane plans of usefulness, must have more purity of mind . . . than the ignorant beings whose time and thoughts have been occupied by gay pleasures or schemes to conquer hearts. The regulation of the behaviour is not modesty, though those who study rules of decorum, are, in general, termed modest women. Make the heart clean, let it expand and feel for all that is human, instead of being narrowed by selfish passions; and let the mind frequently contemplate subjects that exercise the understanding, without heating the imagination, and artless modesty will give the finishing touches to the picture."

A fragment of a novel, published posthumously and called *The Wrongs of Woman; or, Maria,* is a miserable attempt to dramatize the ideas first presented in *A Vindication.* All the arguments reappear, but certain new arguments are made. The Author's Preface states the purpose as being "the desire of exhibiting the misery and oppression, peculiar to women, that arises out of the partial laws and customs of society." "Partial laws" has been added to "customs of society," and the emphasis in the attack is not so much on the training of women as it is on the fact that law can irrevocably bind a woman to a despot male. Maria, pleading for a divorce, cries out: "Marriage has bastilled me for life . . . fettered by the partial laws of society, this fair globe was to me an universal blank. . . . The marriage state is certainly that in which women, generally speaking, can be most useful; but I am far from thinking that a woman, once married, ought to consider the engagement as indissoluble . . . for a woman to live with a man, for whom she can cherish neither affection nor esteem, or even be of any use to him, excepting in the light of a housekeeper, is an abjectness of condition, the enduring of which no concurrence of circumstances can ever make a duty in the sight of God or just men."

Godwin asserted the necessity of abolishing marriage altogether as a legal institution. To tie two people together, "To oblige them to act and to live together," vitiates both of them. "Marriage is law, and the worst of all laws." As "an affair of property," marriage involves identical evils: "So long as I seek to engross one woman to myself, and to prohibit my neighbour from proving his superior desert and reaping the fruits of it, I am guilty of the most odious of monopolies. Over this imaginary prize men watch with perpetual jealousy." In Godwin's future society, love will be free and will grow away from the arts of the female and the jealousies of the male into a rational relationship suitable to the calculated arrangements of utopia. Action springs from the reason, and the "passions" are of no real account.

Yet apparently even Godwin, this robot of intellect, was capable of learning from his experience of love. "We did not marry . . . certainly nothing can be so ridiculous upon the face of it, or so contrary to the genuine march of sentiment, as to require the overflowing of the soul to wait upon a ceremony, and that at which, wherever delicacy and imagination exist, is of all things most sacredly private, to blow a trumpet before it, and to record the moment when it has arrived at its climax . . . the laws of etiquette ordinarily laid down in these cases are essentially absurd, and . . . the sentiments of the heart cannot submit to be directed by the rule and square."

". . . the genuine march of sentiment . . . the overflowing of the soul . . . the sentiments of the heart"! Godwin's stiff nod to the "passions" is interesting because it suggests the transformation that Blake, who was concerned with emotional freedom, worked upon this entire discussion. His attitude toward woman was not without its ambiguity, to be sure, for very often he seems to be combining the ideas of Mary Wollstonecraft with the idea of the Miltonic wife, which Mary used as an example of human wretchedness and suffocation. One hears Blake echo Rousseau's attitudes toward education, his famous dictum that "The only habit the child should be allowed to contract is that of having no habits." Yet Mary Wollstonecraft used Sophia as another example of the Turkish arrogance of the male toward the female. She was herself deeply concerned with education. She conducted a school and acted as a governess. In 1787 she published her *Thoughts on the Education of Daughters; with Reflections on Female Conduct,* in the next year, a translation of Salzmann's *Elements of Morality for Children,* and in *A Vindi-*

cation of the Rights of Woman she included a section called "Strictures on Education." She pleaded for equal education of the sexes within a system of national education. With this idea Blake would have shown no sympathy and probably no patience, for national education would have seemed to him, as it did to Godwin, an encroachment of institutionalism upon the individual.

The problem, however, is not so much to observe where Blake departed from particular ideas incorporated in this body of radical thinking as to define his transvaluations, to observe how he took the most basic assumptions of this thinking and, inverting them, gave vitality and a greater relevance to the particular abuses that the radicals had hoped to cure by their assumptions. Blake listened to these people and to their conclusions, and then he began anew for himself with a less simple account of human nature. And this was to be his perpetual concern: the infinite complexities of the many-mirrored self.

CHAPTER SEVEN

The Broken Mold: Toward Restatement*

I

"O WHEN shall our Deliverer come?" More important, who shall it be? Not, Blake decided, the abstract giantess Reason. This was a decision that involved him at once in simultaneously rejecting certain premises and accepting certain conclusions that had sprung from those premises. This process gave rise to the expression of apparently contradictory points of view, and Blake's work for a number of years is devoted to fashioning a restatement—that is, his own statement—of a revolutionary doctrine that would overcome the contradiction.

The process is first apparent in the last of those notes to Lavater's *Aphorisms,* of 1788, in a passage that is nothing less than crucial to the understanding of Blake's development. "There is a strong objection to Lavater's principles . . . & that is . . . He makes the vicious propensity not only a leading feature of the man, but the stamina on which all his virtues grow. But as I understand Vice it is a Negative. It does not signify what the laws of Kings & Priests have call'd Vice; we who are philoso-

* In this chapter and the next, the discussion does not observe strict chronology. These chapters treat the poems Blake wrote between 1788 and 1795, and instead of taking them in the exact order of their composition or publication, they take them up in two groups with intellectual or narrative unity. This treatment does not involve any very great dislocation of chronology, and is a considerable aid to exposition and economy.

phers ought not to call the Staminal Virtues of Humanity by the same name that we call the omissions of intellect springing from poverty. Every man's leading propensity ought to be call'd his leading Virtue & his good Angel. . . . Accident is the omission of act in self & the hindering of act in another; This is Vice, but all Act is Virtue . . . whatever is Negative is Vice. But the origin of this mistake in Lavater & his contemporaries is, They suppose that Woman's Love is Sin; in consequence all the Loves & Graces with them are Sins."

This is the point from which Blake's entire doctrine emerges. Nothing he had written before expressed this point of view, but everything he was to write in the future must be referred back to it: ". . . as I understand Vice it is a Negative. It does not signify what the laws of Kings & Priests have call'd Vice." Kings and priests are restraints on freedom. Their laws, our thou-shalt-nots, label action as good and evil; but the label itself creates the distinction and is therefore in itself the only real "vice." For all human energy is pure. Every individual has a genius, a "leading propensity," that directs his energy into "act," and unless it is restrained, it expresses itself with integrity; for it is the very man himself, who has no original "propensity" to evil. This is almost pure Godwinian doctrine, and the abrupt conclusion of the paragraph brings the whole even more intimately into that context: "They suppose that Woman's Love is Sin; in consequence all the Loves & Graces with them are Sins."

Yet the conventional couple of king and priest afforded no adequate explanation in itself. Kings and priests and their laws were restraints, to be sure, but they were not the source of restraints; they were the representation of some human fallacy that established and tolerated them.

> How small, of all that human hearts endure,
> That part which kings or laws can cause or cure,

declared Samuel Johnson in his famous addition to Goldsmith's *The Traveller*. What Blake set himself to show was that kings and laws are not merely external facts, but impulses perversely generated in human nature itself. It was the announced end of the Revolution to free the physical being of man from oppression and the mind from superstition and the folly of ignorance. Before the Revolution was well under way Blake discovered for himself the source of both social and mental restraint in that very reason by means of which the revolutionists hoped to escape restraints. Blake's correction of liberal thinking is analogous to Burke's correction of conservative thinking. Both turned away from abstract, mechanical conceptions of man and society and insisted that to be effective political ideas must find their roots in the complexities of psychological fact.

Blake states his discovery in the little tractates called *There Is No Natural Religion* (1788). In the First Series, he defines the Godwinian concept of reason; in its conclusion and in the Second Series, he refutes it.

FIRST SERIES

The *Argument.* Man has no notion of moral fitness but from Education. Naturally he is only a natural organ subject to Sense.

I. Man cannot naturally Perceive but through his natural or bodily organs.

II. Man by his reasoning power can only compare & judge of what he has already perceiv'd.

III. From a perception of only 3 senses or 3 elements none could deduce a fourth or fifth.

IV. None could have other than natural or organic thoughts if he had none but organic perceptions.

V. Man's desires are limited by his perceptions, none can desire what he has not perceiv'd.

VI. The desires & perceptions of man, untaught by any thing but organs of sense, must be limited to objects of sense.

Conclusion. If it were not for the Poetic or Prophetic character the Philosophic & Experimental would soon be at the ratio of all things, & stand still, unable to do other than repeat the same dull round over again.

SECOND SERIES

I. Man's perceptions are not bounded by organs of perception; he perceives more than sense (tho' ever so acute) can discover.

II. Reason, or the ratio of all we have already known, is not the same that it shall be when we know more.

III. [*This proposition has been lost.*]

IV. The bounded is loathed by its possessor. The same dull round, even of a universe, would soon become a mill with complicated wheels.

V. If the many become the same as the few when possess'd, More! More! is the cry of a mistaken soul; less than All cannot satisfy Man.

VI. If any could desire what he is incapable of possessing, despair must be his eternal lot.

VII. The desire of Man being Infinite, the possession is Infinite & himself Infinite.

Application. He who sees the Infinite in all things, sees God. He who sees the Ratio only, sees himself only.

Therefore God becomes as we are, that we may be as he is.

This is Blake's explicit reply to the Lockian-Hartleian propositions on which revolutionary thought was grounded. When Godwin wrote, "We are all of us endowed with reason, able to compare, to judge and to infer," Blake had already written, "Man by his reasoning power can only compare & judge of what he has already perceiv'd." Godwin's rationalism was the essential ingredient in his doctrine of necessity, that very doctrine which Shelley, with so much poetic pain, learned that he had to reject. Blake saw at once that a universe so conceived supplied no rationale for poetry, and to sensation he therefore opposed "the Poetic or Prophetic character" as the source of real knowledge.

In the Second Series, which carries on from this conclusion, Blake denies the finality of "all we have already known"; that is, the sum of knowledge granted us by the senses, or by experimental science, that small, bound body of certain physical fact which is the jealous possession of positivism. Whitehead has said: ". . . the true rationalism must always transcend itself. . . . A self-satisfied rationalism is in effect a form of anti-rationalism. It means an arbitrary halt at a particular set of abstractions. This was the case with science." Blake was trying to say exactly that: "The bounded is loathed by its possessor." Reason, as the eighteenth century used the term and as the revolutionists preserved it, meant the denial of man's capacity for liberty and self-expression; it imposed restraints, or laws, that reduce the mind to "a mill with complicated wheels," a dull round repeated over and over again, denying man "the Infinite" that he desires, or any further knowledge than an endless and mistaken self-contemplation can provide.

More successfully than in the *Tractates,* perhaps, Blake expressed this idea in his picture called "Newton," of which W. Graham Robertson, who long owned it, has given the most eloquent description: "His 'single vision' is intent upon solving some problem which needs no solution; his fair, haggard face, worn and lined with thought, is turned resolutely earthwards. Darkness is about him, vaguely blue below as though dim skies were mirrored in deep, shadowed waters, purple and dun above as with the gloom of overhanging cliffs. The great rock upon which he sits is covered with thick lichenous vegetation, and is as a symbol of his mind—choked with endless minutiae—abnormally developed like those strange night blossoms, half plant, half zoophite; pale flowers of thought that have never looked upon the spiritual Sun."

In a third tractate, *All Religions Are One,* Blake speculates further on the true source of knowledge: "That the Poetic Genius is the true Man, and that the body or outward form of Man is derived from the Poetic Genius. Likewise that the forms of all things are derived from their Genius, which by the Ancients was call'd an Angel & Spirit & Demon." This brings us back to the paragraph from the notes on Lavater, and the sentence "Every man's leading propensity ought to be call'd his leading Virtue & his good Angel." That "Infinite" which man desires, and which only his "genius" or unhampered individual energy can attain to, exists in everything, and everywhere; but from everything it receives a different expression, and its value lies in the difference. The source of diversity, which makes everything precisely what it is, is the source of character. Thus energy is the true humanity, which in turn is God.

For the basic idea here, the respect for the principle of individuation and its attendant holiness, Blake may have been indebted to Lavater himself, even before he was indebted to Godwinian ideas, and not so much to Lavater's *Aphorisms* as to his *Essays on Physiognomy,* which were translated by Holcroft and for another translation of which Blake provided a number of engravings in 1789. The motto on the title page of this book is "God created man after his own image," and there is a good deal on this theme in the text to promote the idea of man's dignity. The theme of the whole, as its title might not readily suggest, is the basic harmony and the specific variety of all human forms and characters, and in support of this theme Lavater frequently invokes the magnificently diverse array of the creation as a whole. "Every grain of sand is an immensity," he says, "every leaf a world, every insect an assemblage of incomprehensible effects, in which reflection is lost. Who is able to mark and reckon the intermediate *degrees* from the *insect* up to Man?"

Note "in which reflection is lost"—to the understanding of which, that is to say, reason is incompetent. It is oddly like Blake:

> How do you know but ev'ry Bird that cuts the airy way,
> Is an immense world of delight, clos'd by your senses five?

To perceive such a universe, to see a world in a grain of sand or heaven in a wild flower, reason is as useless as Newton's compasses. More than this, reason is destructive of such a universe. Reason analyzes, sets limits, and restrains; these are the functions of law. As law and anarchy are irreconcilable, so are reason and freedom. To the reason of the philosophical radicals, and the assertion that every man can "compare, judge and infer," Blake opposed energy and its limitless propensities toward the infinite. It is the basis of his equalitarianism, as it is of every view he held. It swings him directly back into radical thinking, for it enables him to assert in new terms the integrity of the individual man and his need to express unhampered his genius, his energy, his talent, which are all one. In the meantime, however, his fresh intuition operating on his queer old learning, Blake has made the considerable discovery of the demonic elements in human nature and performed the considerable historical service of shattering the then still powerful but hopelessly inadequate faculty psychology. We have entered, with Blake, the modern world, and for the first time, for better or for worse, we hear what is to become a basic conception in modern philosophy and art.

> Whatever stands in field or flood
> Bird, beast, fish or man,
> Mare or stallion, cock or hen,
> Stands in God's unchanging eye
> In all the vigour of its blood;
> In that faith I live or die.

II

HAVING ESTABLISHED these definitions, Blake turned again to poetry. *Tiriel,* written about 1789, presents dramatically, or at least allegorically, the rejection of reason that Blake had first recorded in the axiomatic prose of his little tractates. But these loose and mournful septenaries are more like the overwrought prose of "Samson" and "Then She Bore Pale Desire" than they are like Blake's early songs. His talent is hot on the track of his rationalizations, his own genius already struggling away from the authority of technique. Only on rare occasions thereafter was it to submit.

Tiriel (a poor anagram of "ritual"?) is the representative of outworn authority, or dogma, a kind of Lear reduced to his barest psychological essence, his authority gone, his abilities sterile, his recourse a curse on his children, who ignore his laws.

His inspiration is "fading in death," and he is blind. His creations loathe him and scorn his impotent judgment. He resorts to pity: "Look at my eyes, blind as the orbless scull among the stones!" but his plea is without effect, and he wanders away from his ruined palace. He comes at last to the place of Har and Heva, poetry and painting, who have declined under his rule. He finds them sitting under a flourishing oak, the tree of abounding error, guarded by Mnetha ("Greek" wisdom, Athena?), whose watch has reduced them to the triviality and the puerility—as Blake regarded it—of neoclassic poetry:

Playing with flowers & running after birds they spent the day,
And in the night like infants slept, delighted with infant dreams.

Tiriel's withered look frightens them, "For he is the king of rotten wood & of the bones of death," but when they see that he is harmless, they let him sit down and they feed him. Har, who is the poetic principle, although degraded, asks:

Thou art a very old old man, but I am older than thou.
How came thine hair to leave thy forehead? how came thy face
 so brown?

He is enunciating the fifth principle of *All Religions Are One*, and the principle, which claims the seniority of prophecy, abashes Tiriel, who denies his identity. Then he is invited to listen to "Har sing in the great cage"—the "bounded" couplet, and the conventional forms of eighteenth-century verse. But Tiriel wanders off again. He meets Ijim (image?), popular religion and superstition, through whom dogma retains power, who takes him back to his palace. Again Tiriel curses his sons, and now also his daughters, who are the five senses, the servants of reason. Only one of these he spares, Hela, who leads him from the desolation his curse has brought about. The scene is intended to suggest the suppression of heresies under a reigning dogma:

. . . all the sons & daughters of Tiriel,
Chain'd in thick darkness, utter'd cries of mourning all the
 night;
And in the morning, Lo! an hundred men in ghastly death!

The four daughters stretch'd on the marble pavement, silent all,
Fall'n by the pestilence!—the rest moped round in guilty fears;
And all the children in their beds were cut off in one night.
Thirty of Tiriel's sons remain'd, to wither in the palace,
Desolate, Loathed, Dumb, Astonish'd, waiting for black death.

Through Hela, who is touch, Blake's symbol for sex, Tiriel hopes to return to innocence, the freshness of his first insights before they hardened into authority:

"Now, Hela, I can go with pleasure & dwell with Har & Heva,
Now that the curse shall clean devour all those guilty sons."

This is his error, for while he knows that "the time of grace is past," he hopes still to achieve the pastoral pleasures through judgment and repression, not recognizing yet that the rule of repression has already degraded them, and that the only way they can be reachieved is through a sympathetic act of imagination. His trust in Hela, from whose grace he hopes to regain his earlier state of power, is equally mistaken; for more than any of his daughters, she resents the rule of law, and leads him back to Har and Heva only because she knows that the effects of the curse are most disastrous for her. When she defies him at last, he lets her feel his old power, and snakes spring from her head; sex, rebelling against conventional order, is reviled and made to seem loathsome. But Tiriel knows that his power is gone, and as he comes again to the place of Har and Heva, he recognizes his error:

"Why is one law given to the lion & the patient Ox?
Dost thou not see that men cannot be formed all alike?"

Then he understands, too, that both his power and his fate sprang from an original mistake that he has since imposed upon others:

". . . Such was Tiriel,
Compell'd to pray repugnant & to humble the immortal spirit
Till I am subtil as a serpent in a paradise,
Consuming all, both flowers & fruits, insects & warbling birds.
And now my paradise is fall'n & a dreary sandy plain

Returns my thirsty hissings in a curse on thee, O Har. . . ."
He ceast, outstretch'd at Har & Heva's feet in awful death.

Here for the first time Blake has put into a symbolical narrative his revolutionary statement. Reason, or dogma, uses as its tool the prohibiting law that ignores individuality. Reason exalts itself in the first place by humbling "the immortal spirit"—that is, infinite energy—and it maintains itself for as long as it can by restraining in judgment and stricture the energy of its subjects. At last, amid a general decay of life, including not only dogma itself but also the arts and sciences, reason is forced to see the error of its religion: law betrays the principle of life. One law cannot be given to the lion and the patient ox, for every "genius" has its own law. Recognizing this, reason expires, and the promise is of a freed energy.

Yeats was not quite accurate when he grouped Blake with Shelley and Wordsworth as poets who were not preoccupied with evil but were resolved to dwell upon good only, as poets for whom "human nature has lost its antagonist." Already the glittering optimism of philosophical radicalism had been qualified, and Blake presents man in his interior drama, faced with the only antagonist he has ever had—his own capacity for bewilderment and self-degradation.

III

". . . Flowers & fruits, insects & warbling birds." *Songs of Innocence* seizes these idyllic elements from the *Poetical Sketches*, isolates them from the conditions of humanitarian protest almost completely, and develops them for their sake alone, in a paradisaical scene where only the possibility of the "subtil serpent . . . consuming all" exists.* Yet exist it does, although very

* For a much more comprehensive account than mine of the meanings of the *Songs of Innocence* and the *Songs of Experience*, and especially for the recondite meanings, readers must consult Joseph Wicksteed, who considers the symbolism of the songs not only in the text, but in the entire illustrated page.

faintly indeed in the most purely pastoral poems. In the opening song, "Piping down the valleys wild," the child who laughs in the tree and asks the poet to sing a song of a lamb, weeps when he hears it, first simply, and then "with joy." Is it that the "child" knows all too well the first fate of the "lamb," although he knows, too, and can therefore mix joy with his weeping, what lies beyond it? The association of shepherd and lamb, Jesus and child, is clearer in the second song, "How sweet is the Shepherd's sweet lot," in the shepherd whose "tongue" is "filled with praise" of man, and most significantly in the fourth, "Little Lamb, who made thee?" where the connection is not at all submerged but is the point of the poem. The figure of Jesus, whether as lamb or child, carries primary overtones of tragedy, and these are absent from only three songs in the entire group—"Infant Joy," "Spring," and "Laughing Song," the last of which at least is more appropriate to the insouciant *Poetical Sketches.*

These elements should not be stressed, perhaps, since they are significant only in a later context. By and large, the impression left by the *Songs of Innocence* is of a vision of pastoral felicity in which the errors of Tiriel do not exist. Innocence, when one views it thus, is a condition of unimpaired consciousness that makes possible a perception of experience unhampered by schism, or by reason and its products; experience apprehended wholly, with all the faculties as they are given to us, and differing from the normal adult experience in that it is "pure," the *whole* experience. "Unorganiz'd Innocence: An Impossibility," Blake was to say a few years later, and the remark is useful to an understanding of the kind of psychology that he is trying to organize in the *Songs,* a psychology opposed to that of Locke and Hartley, in which mind was made relative to the sensuous experience of the individual, and made more and more relative as he developed more and more complexities of association. Without negating individuality, Blake is yet trying to give us a picture of an entire experience, absolutely perceived, without particularizing shutters. That this picture should be associated with a child's world raises a number of points.

Blake does not explicitly assume a primitive condition of innocence in society at large, but only in the individual life, and only in the life of the child. Yet the furnishings of that life have a real significance in the eighteenth century. Not only are the happy poems consistently rural, but they are more devoid of the ordinary habiliments of rural life than any other pastorals that have ever been written. This is such a complete picture of natural "simplicity" that the poems can hardly be considered of "nature" at all. That they were intended to be so is suggested by the fact that two of the three poems based on real social problems are of the city, and that the poems of social misery in the *Songs of Experience,* if they have an explicit setting, are all of the city, and a city great in wealth and commerce. The suggestion is that at the back of Blake's mind hovered that bugaboo of the century, "luxury." "Luxury," attacked by all manner of men, arose from an expanded commerce, and in allowing the people of a nation to depart too far from the simplicity of the natural state sapped them of their virtue. At the back of Blake's mind, and in the background of these poems, lie the assumptions, ultimately revolutionary, of Rousseau.

Do they point in any way to the revolutionary future? Again, the imagery itself is suggestive. External nature, as Blake presents it here, is kindly to man and generally it is co-operative within itself, as in the poem of the lost emmet, "A Dream."

> Pitying, I drop'd a tear;
> But I saw a glow-worm near,
> Who replied: "What wailing wight
> Calls the watchman of the night?
>
> I am set to light the ground,
> While the beetle goes his round;
> Follow now the beetle's hum;
> Little wanderer, hie thee home."

If, as in "Night," natural creatures do not live in harmony, they yearn to do so, and there is a promise of such a situation, even though it is reserved until "our immortal day." There are two poems of separation in this group, that of the emmet and its young, and that of the father and his lost boy. Separation is the equivalent of experience, as unity is of innocence; both poems end with the reachievement of unity. Another characteristic of these poems is the utter absence of ego, the degree of impersonality. They are poems of joy, but joy that suggests Yeats's distinction, "pleasure which is personal and joy which is impersonal," and the regenerate state as Blake himself later describes it, in which selfishness has given way to brotherhood.

One more point is useful to remember, and that is the distinction Blake had already made between "the innocence of a child" and "the errors of acquired folly." This is the primitivistic strand. The progressivistic is contained in the remark "Innocence dwells with Wisdom, but never with Ignorance." Whatever the felicity of the children in *Songs of Innocence,* they can hardly be described as wise. Something lies between—experience; and it hovers at the edge of all these poems. What is its quality, and what is its value?

In "The Blossom," while the sparrow sleeps the robin unaccountably sobs. When, in "The Ecchoing Green," the sun sets,

> . . . the little ones, weary,
> No more can be merry.

Somewhere on the outskirts of this pastoral area is a "lonely fen," and there the little boy is lost in the mists. Those "virtues of delight," mercy, pity, peace, and love, are opposed to human "distress," out of which men pray. And when the mother sits over the cradle of her sleeping, smiling child, she weeps, as Jesus wept, until she remembers that Jesus "Heaven & Earth to peace beguiles." (Yet the intended counterpart for this poem in Blake's manuscript book, where "infant smiles" became "infant wiles," which creep in the "little heart asleep" and which "Heaven & Earth *of* peace beguiles," Blake never printed. Nor was this because the grammatical difficulty was unsurmountable; rather because it was a too depraved view of human nature, which he could not publicly admit.)

Then there are the three poems founded on social situations—the song of the chimney sweeper, who weeps while he works and who dreams of resurrection; the children of the charity school in "Holy Thursday," singing in St. Paul's to "aged men, wise guardians of the poor"; and the little black boy, born into slavery, whose sufferings have made him wise. Through experience—or through a particularly degrading social experience—the little black boy has achieved another innocence, which "dwells with Wisdom."

This implication, which lurks mainly in evangelical guise in the *Songs of Innocence,* relates them closely to Blake's developing revolutionary doctrine. They are a more positive expression than *Tiriel* of his belief that evil and the misery it brings with it are a mere incrustation on life and the spirit, a negative. In most of these songs the restraints that create evil do not hamper energy or limitless joy, and man's sympathy with man is praised:

> Then every man, of every clime,
> That prays in his distress,
> Prays to the human form divine,
> Love, Mercy, Pity, Peace.
>
> And all must love the human form,
> In heathen, turk, or jew;
> Where Mercy, Love, & Pity dwell
> There God is dwelling too.

The serenity of this envisioned world Blake fashioned out of the conventional imagery of evangelicism, and it is sung in the voice of the Sunday school. It was only 1789; the thunder was not yet loud, as it is not yet loud in the poems. The irony of Blake's forms has yet to become apparent. So, too, has the overt recommendation of violence against restraint if, indeed, out of experience, we are "to inherit" the promised "New worlds." "Joys impregnate," he was yet to say, but "Sorrows bring forth."

IV

The Book of Thel, of the same year, is a brief allegory that, while it employs the Platonic concept of pre-existence for its metaphor of innocence, peers tremblingly, like the *Songs of Innocence,* into the pit of experience.

Thel's motto is famous:

> Does the Eagle know what is in the pit?
> Or wilt thou go ask the Mole?
> Can Wisdom be put in a silver rod?
> Or Love in a golden bowl?

It is a nice ambiguity. Thel (is her name to suggest Lethe?) is an unborn spirit unwilling to enter life, yet she knows, as her first two questions indicate, that if she is to learn the lessons of experience, she must mix with its inhabitants. It is the mole, the earth animal, whom she must consult, not the inhabitant of air, which has been her domain. Yet her third and fourth questions are rejections, and her answer to them, within the limits of the poem, is no. Her fright is of sexuality, and as she retreats she cannot believe that wisdom or love can be found in it. Blake lets her answer rest in the question, because his own answer is yes.

To the unborn spirit birth is like death, and while this is suggestive of Shelley's inversion, "Death is a veil which those who live call life," it is also, in the whole context of the poem, suggestive of a more mundane paradox, the Elizabethan connotations of sexual intercourse in the word "dying." From the pastoral delights of infinity, Thel wanders away, knowing that she must suffer this dying into life, must "fade away like morning beauty from her mortal day." She seeks out the simplest, most perishable forms of life—a flower, a cloud, a worm, a clod of clay—to inquire why this passage is necessary, why she should be born only "to be at death the food of worms." The lily tells her of its part in the co-operative life of nature, and sends her to the cloud, which describes its part, and then charges:

> ". . . if thou art the food of worms, O virgin of the skies,
> How great thy use, how great thy blessing! Every thing that lives
> Lives not alone for itself. Fear not, and I will call
> The weak worm from its lowly bed, and thou shalt hear its voice."

One need not press the sexual values in the imagery of the next passage. The worm appears, "helpless & naked, weeping, And none to answer, none to cherish" it, for Thel has not made her commitment. Then the "matron Clay," who houses the worm, intervenes:

"O beauty of the vales of Har! we live not for ourselves.
Thou seest me the meanest thing, and so I am indeed . . .
I ponder, and I cannot ponder; yet I live and love."

Momentarily Thel is comforted, and she accepts the invitation of the Clod of Clay to enter life:

Thel enter'd in & saw the secrets of the land unknown.
She saw the couches of the dead, & where the fibrous roots
Of every heart on earth infixes deep its restless twists:
A land of sorrows & of tears where never smile was seen.

She wanders from grave to grave, "list'ning to the voices of the ground," until she comes to her own grave plot and hears from a voice that is to be her own the price of experience. It is the imposition of restraint, through narrowed perceptions, upon infinite energy:

"Why cannot the Ear be closed to its own destruction?
Or the glist'ning Eye to the poison of a smile?
Why are Eyelids stor'd with arrows ready drawn,
Where a thousand fighting men in ambush lie?
Or an Eye of gifts & graces show'ring fruits & coined gold?
Why a Tongue impress'd with honey from every wind?
Why an Ear, a whirlpool fierce to draw creations in?
Why a Nostril wide inhaling terror, trembling & affright?
Why a tender curb upon the youthful burning boy?
Why a little curtain of flesh on the bed of our desire?"

The final questions are the most appalling, and with a shriek Thel flees back into the land of lethal bliss, still unready for the wisdom of the body.

Thel has been instructed in three lessons, all of which are implied in the final lyric of the *Songs of Innocence,* "On Another's Sorrow." The first is that every item in the creation has its particular character and function in the universal harmony; the second is that the operation of that function breaks down the self in acts of altruism. So stated, these are the recognizable elements of popular eighteenth-century ethics. It is the third item that is characteristically Blakean, and which represents his extension both of that ethics and of revolutionary dogma. Life entails suffering, the strainings of energy against bondage in the self and outside it, and especially the bondage of "sexual strife."

V

THE FORMS OF BONDAGE, especially the bondage of "sexual strife," are the chief ingredients of the *Songs of Experience.* They develop out of the second, the humanitarian, element of the *Poetical Sketches,* but they are expressed now with that intensity which is the particular mark of Blake's genius, and without contradiction.

The children of *Songs of Innocence* have become captives who cry for liberty, and, denied it, suffer a deterioration of natural virtue. The onslaughts of authority and the moral consequence begin at once, in infancy:

> Struggling in my father's hands,
> Striving against my swadling bands,
> Bound and weary I thought best
> To sulk upon my mother's breast.

The onslaughts of authority continue. "The Schoolboy" reminds us not only of Blake's resistance to education but of the Godwinian assault on it as the root of prejudice. Religion listens to the little lost boy's intuition that man is godly and that God is human, and burns him as a heretic, which is to say that in experience, dogma destroys intuition. The same child, perhaps, pleads in "The Little Vagabond" that the free pleasures of the alehouse are more desirable than the repressions of the Church, which decrees good and evil in its law. The protest in all these poems is against authority because it ignores individuality by restraining natural impulse. The impulse that is most emphatically in Blake's mind becomes evident in the yearnings for liberty of the young man and woman in "Ah! Sun-flower":

> . . . the Youth pined away with desire,
> And the pale Virgin shrouded in snow.

The bulk of the poems in *Songs of Experience* are directed against the conventional restraints imposed upon sexuality, and the fact that mistaken attitudes toward sexual love are made the root of all the errors in experience is not surprising when one remembers Blake's remark, possibly startling in the context of 1788, that "the origin of this mistake in Lavater & his contemporaries is, They suppose that Woman's Love is Sin; in consequence all the Loves & Graces with them are Sins." The infant who learns to "sulk" immediately is a creature not out of Lavater's psychology but out of Freud's.

The *Songs of Experience* begin with the poet's cry to the earth, the plea that she renew herself: "O Earth, O Earth, return!" And Earth answers:

> "Prison'd on wat'ry shore,
> Starry Jealousy does keep my den:
> Cold and hoar,
> Weeping o'er,
> I hear the father of the ancient men.
>
> Selfish father of men!
> Cruel, jealous, selfish fear!
> Can delight,
> Chain'd in night,
> The virgins of youth and morning bear?
>
> Does spring hide its joy
> When buds and blossoms grow?
> Does the sower
> Sow by night,
> Or the plowman in darkness plow?
>
> Break this heavy chain
> That does freeze my bones around.
> Selfish! vain!

Eternal bane!
That free Love with bondage bound."

Authority, bondage, jealousy—it is to become one of the most familiar couplings in Blake, and with it, a particular image that is worth observing:

Break this heavy chain
That does *freeze* my bones around.

The chain grows into the bone, becomes the bone, which is to say that restraint *becomes* the character. It is one of the innumerable changes that Blake rings on the theme of interdependence, the subject of "Auguries of Innocence." It is characteristic, too, that with this image comes that of repressed fruition, in the sower and the plowman.

In a song rejected from the final manuscript, Blake had written:

Love to faults is always blind,
Always is to joy inclin'd,
Lawless, wing'd, & unconfin'd,
And breaks all chains from every mind.

Deceit to secresy confin'd,
Lawful, cautious, & refin'd;
To every thing but interest blind,
And forges fetters for the mind.

The rejection was probably based on the awareness that this antithesis was too sharp and too simple. In these poems deceit is not the opposite of love, but a portion of it, its inversion. The real difference, that between free love and fettered love, Blake expressed much more adequately in "The Clod and the Pebble," where the familiar "Clay" of *Thel,* the pliable earth capable of fertility and growth, expresses one view—

"Love seeketh not Itself to please,
Nor for itself hath any care,
But for another gives its ease,
And builds a Heaven in Hell's despair"—

and the hard, rounded "Pebble of the brook," incapable of anything, sterile and without plasticity, "bound," sings:

"Love seeketh only Self to please,
To bind another to Its delight,
Joys in another's loss of ease,
And builds a Hell in Heaven's despite."

The agents that reduce joy to deceit and love to cunning are the familiar slaves of reason, of the "Selfish father of men"—theologians and philosophers, kings and judges and priests:

Remove away that black'ning church:
Remove away that marriage hearse:
Remove away that place of blood:
You'll quite remove the ancient curse.

Or again:

The King & the Priest must be tied in a tether
Before two virgins can meet together.

These, again, are rejected verses that achieved more exact expression in "The Garden of Love":

I went to the Garden of Love,
And saw what I never had seen:
A Chapel was built in the midst,
Where I used to play on the green.

And the gates of this Chapel were shut,
And "Thou shalt not" writ over the door;
So I turn'd to the Garden of Love
That so many sweet flowers bore;

And I saw it was filled with graves,
And tomb-stones where flowers should be;
And Priests in black gowns were walking their rounds,
And binding with briars my joys & desires.

It is impossible when reading this poem not to think of another of Blake's rejected poems, and since it has impressive elements in itself, to speculate on the reasons for its rejection.

I saw a chapel all of gold
That none did dare to enter in,
And many weeping stood without,
Weeping, mourning, worshipping.

I saw a serpent rise between
The white pillars of the door,
And he forc'd & forc'd & forc'd,
Down the golden hinges tore.

And along the pavement sweet,
Set with pearls & rubies bright,
All his slimy length he drew,
Till upon the altar white

Vomiting his poison out
On the bread & on the wine.
So I turn'd into a sty
And laid me down among the swine.

In tone and pattern this is a good *Song of Experience,* but something has gone awry in Blake's meaning. His fascination with ambiguous images has got out of hand, and the poem ends by saying something quite different from what most of his lyrics say. The chapel is probably the same as that of "The Garden of Love," and the "Weeping, mourning, worshipping" people without are the frustrated lovers who in "The Garden" are "graves" and "tomb-stones." Then the "serpent" reared up and "forc'd & forc'd & forc'd," and violated the church; but here Blake has turned round upon himself. For while it is true that thwarted sexuality takes unattractive forms, the thwarting originates with the restraining Church, not vice versa. If this was first thought of as a sequel to "The Garden of Love," and a development of the idea of the interdependence of energy and force, yet for some reason Blake did not use it. It is reasonable to suppose that he found the involutions of his meaning becoming a little too complex for a message that he wished to be direct and forthright. He did not wish to seem to say that the "serpent" was at fault when the fault was with the "priest."

For the same idea and without the extreme ambiguity, he

found a more satisfactory image than the "chapel all of gold" in "The Sick Rose," where that thwarted impulse which becomes poisonous deceit and jealousy is "The invisible worm That flies in the night' and eats out the heart of the rose.

That "Love, free love, cannot be bound" without suffering a tragic change is the steadiest proposition throughout these poems. When the initial spontaneity of impulse, or act, is hindered, it turns to calculation, and jealousy is born:

> A flower was offer'd to me,
> Such a flower as May never bore;
> But I said "I've a Pretty Rose-tree,"
> And I passed the sweet flower o'er.
>
> Then I went to my Pretty Rose-tree,
> To tend her by day and by night;
> But my Rose turn'd away with jealousy,
> And her thorns were my only delight.

Lavater had written, "As the shadow follows the body, so restless subtleness the female knave"; but Blake, who was thinking of the effect of the punishment of "thorns," crossed out "subtleness" and wrote "sullenness" over it. But "subtleness," too, has its part in Blake's text, as in an unpublished poem which also shows that he was not without humor in a matter that ordinarily compelled only his anger:

> I asked a thief to steal me a peach:
> He turned up his eyes.
> I ask'd a lithe lady to lie her down:
> Holy & meek she cries.
>
> As soon as I went an angel came:
> He wink'd at the thief
> And smil'd at the dame,
> And without one word spoke
> Had a peach from the tree,
> And 'twixt earnest & joke
> Enjoy'd the Lady.

The hypocritical "angel" triumphs over the sincere man of open impulse. Sincerity, Godwin's "perfect sincerity," is the great neglected virtue in all these poems. The depraved moral of "Never seek to tell thy love" recommends reservation:

> I told my love, I told my love,
> I told her all my heart,
> Trembling, cold, in ghastly fears—
> Ah, she doth depart.

The tragedy of other relationships, no less than that of love, is the absence of "perfect sincerity":

> I was angry with my friend:
> I told my wrath, my wrath did end.
> I was angry with my foe:
> I told it not, my wrath did grow.

Wrath grows into a tree of dissimulation that bears fruit that finally kills the foe. The tree itself is significant: it is the tree of judgment, of good and evil, of restraint, and it will appear again and again; it is authority, law, and it "grows . . . in the Human Brain." Its causes, hardly those intended by Genesis, have effects no less devastating. Blake does not believe that they need last so long:

> Children of the future Age
> Reading this indignant page,
> Know that in a former time
> Love! sweet Love! was thought a crime.

These lines suggest that later lyric which is often thought to be a reminiscence of Mary Wollstonecraft. The poem opens with a description of Mary's appearance at a ball where her charm and beauty win her instant friends and sympathy. But her doctrine is "sincerity," and she makes an inexcusable faux pas:

> Mary moves in soft beauty & conscious delight
> To augment with sweet smiles all the joys of the Night,
> Nor once blushes to own to the rest of the Fair
> That sweet Love & Beauty are worthy our care.

Next morning she is an outcast (". . . no Friend from henceforward thou, Mary, shalt see"):

Some said she was proud, some call'd her a whore,
And some, when she passed by, shut to the door;
A damp cold came o'er her, her blushes all fled;
Her lillies & roses are blighted & shed.

"O, why was I born with a different Face?
Why was I not born like this Envious Race?
Why did Heaven adorn me with bountiful hand,
And then set me down in an envious Land?"

Blake's sympathies are expressed in the concluding comment:

All Faces have Envy, sweet Mary, but thine;

And thine is a Face of sweet Love in despair,
And thine is a Face of mild sorrow & care,
And thine Is a Face of wild terror & fear
That shall never be quiet till laid on its bier.

Mary Wollstonecraft had written of her own situation, "I have . . . considered myself as a particle broken off from the grand mass of mankind;—I was alone."

All of man's energies are defaced when bound. Snakes sprang from Hela's head, and Har piped fatuously within a cage. Tiriel himself expired, and his sons and daughters. There are other miseries than "sexual strife" in *Songs of Experience:* pious humiliation and poverty, cruelty and hatred, kingship and warfare. Where now are those "virtues of delight," mercy, pity, peace, and love? They are here, but in another form, as the virtues of Satan, and it is here that Blake's political judgments stand most clearly opposed to his religious judgments:

Pity would be no more
If we did not make somebody Poor;
And Mercy no more could be
If all were as happy as we.

And mutual fear brings peace,
Till the selfish loves increase:

Then Cruelty knits a snare,
And spreads his baits with care.

The second quatrain is especially compelling, for it seems to be an attack on the depraved Hobbesian view of human nature, in which society arises from man's worst qualities rather than from his best. It is a view that lurks at the bottom of even the more enlightened theories of social contract, and it is a view that Blake, who has already indicated his concept of the state of nature, cannot approve. Because it is a "view," it is no less "real." It is, indeed, the reality of experience as Blake has pictured it. The conception of man as a selfish creature, and the resulting necessity of authority, which passes into the hands of the most selfish, ends in every tragic social paradox Blake pursues. Now the real status of those innocents—parish charges—who sing above the heads of "aged men, wise guardians of the poor," is revealed:

Is this a holy thing to see
In a rich and fruitful land,
Babes reduc'd to misery,
Fed with cold and usurous hand?

Is that trembling cry a song?
Can it be a song of joy?
And so many children poor?
It is a land of poverty!

And now finally, in this poem the genuine irony of Blake's *Songs* becomes clear. Imitations of the "good-Godly" songs of the newly founded Sunday schools, the *Songs of Innocence* appropriate the piety doled out to the underprivileged children of the factory and the mining districts, and then, in the same meters, the *Songs of Experience* shift from the ideal images of shepherds and lambs, flowers and fruits, and retain only those which the children of the poor really knew, the images of poverty, despair, and death:

A little black thing among the snow,
Crying " 'weep! 'weep!" in notes of woe!

"Where are thy father & mother? say?"
"They are both gone up to the church to pray.

Because I was happy upon the heath,
And smil'd among the winter's snow,
They clothed me in the clothes of death,
And taught me to sing the notes of woe.

And because I am happy & dance & sing,
They think they have done me no injury,
And are gone to praise God & his Priest & King,
Who make up a heaven of our misery."

Social criticism no less direct informs many of Blake's lyrics. In a poem written about 1793 and sometimes called "Fayette," the poet pictures the King and Queen of France as oppressing their subjects with war, famine, and pestilence in order to maintain their power; and he pities Fayette, who has sold his honesty in defending his monarchs instead of saving it by protesting their cruelty:

Fayette, Fayette, thou'rt bought & sold,
And sold is thy happy morrow;
Thou gavest the tears of Pity away
In exchange for the tears of sorrow.

Who will exchange his own fire side
For the steps of another's door?
Who will exchange his wheaten loaf
For the links of a dungeon floor?

O, who would smile on the wintry seas,
& Pity the stormy roar?
Or who will exchange his new born child
For the dog at the wintry door?

This again is imagery—the imagery of desolation—that will haunt Blake's later poems. It appears once more in the poem about the Grey Monk who accepts Fayette's alternative. He is persecuted for his sympathy with the mother who cries to him:

"I die, I die," the Mother said,
"My Children die for lack of Bread.
What more has the merciless Tyrant said?"

The monk knows the necessity of adequate means to adequate ends, and expresses it in eloquent verse:

"But vain the Sword & vain the Bow,
They never can work War's overthrow.
The Hermit's Prayer & the Widow's tear
Alone can free the World from fear.

For a Tear is an Intellectual Thing,
And a Sigh is the Sword of an Angel King,
And the bitter groan of the Martyr's woe
Is an Arrow from the Almightie's Bow.

The hand of Vengeance found the Bed
To which the Purple Tyrant fled;
The iron hand crush'd the Tyrant's head
And became a Tyrant in his stead."

In the "Auguries of Innocence," the couplets ring sharply with this protest:

The Strongest Poison ever known
Came from Caesar's Laurel Crown.
Nought can deform the Human Race
Like to the Armour's iron brace.
When Gold & Gems adorn the Plow
To peaceful Arts shall Envy Bow.

Nor does the protest against sexual convention and commercial values abate:

The Whore & Gambler, by the State
Licenc'd, build that Nation's Fate.
The Harlot's cry from Street to Street
Shall weave Old England's winding Sheet.
The Winner's Shout, the Loser's Curse,
Dance before dead England's Hearse.

William Blake

This is poetry with a dreadful power, yet it is not Blake's best. His most incisive attack, that which includes his whole catalogue of miseries and includes them most poetically, is in the terrible poem "London." In a rejected version of this poem, he had sung more naïvely, even blithely, and he had looked toward an escape:

> Why should I care for the men of thames,
> Or the cheating waves of charter'd streams,
> Or shrink at the little blasts of fear
> That the hireling blows into my ear?
>
> Tho' born on the cheating banks of Thames,
> Tho' his waters bathed my infant limbs,
> The Ohio shall wash his stains from me:
> I was born a slave, but I go to be free.

This was a little too near the mood of rural nostalgia in Samuel Johnson's un-Johnsonian poem of the same title, a poem that Blake may have had in mind as contrast. In another version he wrote of "each dirty street" and of "the dirty Thames," and while the filth of London was a European scandal, these details were inadequate to the basic social fact. Blake then combined his two versions and produced his famous third:

> I wander thro' each charter'd street,
> Near where the charter'd Thames does flow,
> And mark in every face I meet
> Marks of weakness, marks of woe.
>
> In every cry of every Man,
> In every Infant's cry of fear,
> In every voice, in every ban,
> The mind-forg'd manacles I hear.
>
> How the Chimney-sweeper's cry
> Every black'ning Church appalls;
> And the hapless Soldier's sigh
> Runs in blood down Palace walls.

But most thro' midnight streets I hear
How the youthful Harlot's curse
Blasts the new born Infant's tear,
And blights with plagues the Marriage hearse.

The lines echo with Paine on monopoly, Godwin on child labor, Mary Wollstonecraft on marriage; but these echoes fade before the total impact of Blake's own juxtapositions. The poem is as unrelieved as the misery it contemplates, and certainly no other work in English makes such a powerful indictment of authority and social tyranny. Blake seems to be saying to a placid world, "It is very true, what you have said. . . . I am Mad or Else you are so; both of us cannot be in our right senses."

Against this social scene, external nature—or such glimpses of it as we are permitted—is relatively serene. The fly, in the poem of that name, takes a dizzy delight in being precisely itself, and "beasts of prey"—lion, leopards, tigers—show a kindness to the lost little girl that the citizens of London are unable to show to one another:

And her bosom lick,
And upon her neck
From his eyes of flame
Ruby tears there came.

When her parents found her—"And saw their sleeping child Among tygers wild"—they chose as a home the wilderness, which seems more peaceful:

To this day they dwell
In a lonely dell;
Nor fear the wolvish howl
Nor the lions' growl.

The choice is metaphorical, suggesting that nature is not necessarily savage. The tree of good and evil is not rooted in the universe:

The Gods of the earth and sea
Sought thro' Nature to find this Tree;

But their search was all in vain:
There grows one in the Human Brain.

It is in the mind, and not intractably there. The article in the title "A Divine Image" is vastly important:

Cruelty has a Human Heart,
And Jealousy a Human Face;
Terror the Human Form Divine,
And Secrecy the Human Dress.

The Human Dress is forged Iron,
The Human Form a fiery Forge,
The Human Face a Furnace seal'd,
The Human Heart its hungry Gorge.

This is only *a* divine image, drawn after a particular god, the cruel judge and mechanist of Iron, Forge, and Furnace; it is opposed to *the* divine image of the earlier poems, drawn after Jesus, the God-Man, lover of sinners. In the cant of Blake's day, it is the difference between man as he is and man as he is not. The distinction promises everything.

Then who will restore lost pastoral delights, bring back the lamb? The answer is the tiger. "The Tyger" can be read in many ways—as the simple opposition of innocence and experience; as the paradox of the creation and of Christianity, the antithesis of spirit and matter, love and wrath, good and evil; as the expression of delight and awe before the magnitude and variety of the creation; even as an embodiment of the Popian proposition that all partial evil is universal good. It can be read in all these ways and give pleasure in each, yet in Blake's context it has a more particular and, for that context, a crucial meaning.

The juxtaposition of lamb and tiger points not merely to the opposition of innocence and experience, but to the resolution of the paradox they present. The innocent impulses of the lamb have been curbed by restraints, and the lamb has turned into something else, indeed into the tiger. Innocence is converted to experience. It does not rest there. Energy can be curbed but it cannot be destroyed, and when it reaches the limits of its endurance, it bursts forth in revolutionary wrath. The crucial quatrain is:

> When the stars threw down their spears,
> And water'd heaven with their tears,
> Did he smile his work to see?
> Did he who made the Lamb make thee?

"Starry Jealousy does keep my den," Earth complained in the second song. Why "starry"? The stars in Blake are the symbols of a dominant reason, the association being that of the mechanistic philosophy of science and eighteenth-century rationalism. And when the stars throw down their spears and weep, they are soldiers abandoning their arms in contrition and a readiness for peace. When reason capitulates before wrathful energy, is the creation satisfied? The tiger is necessary to the renewal of the lamb.

"The Tyger," more than any other single poem in *Songs of Experience,* looks forward to the revolutionary synthesis of *The Marriage of Heaven and Hell.* But there are others, and it is significant that in the first copies both the opening and the closing poems were poems not of despair but of millennial expectation, and that at least one poem in the body of the volume looks to "futurity," when "the desart wild" shall "Become a garden mild." In the first poem, "Introduction," the prophetic character, already identified with energy, summons the imprisoned earth:

> Hear the voice of the Bard!
> Who Present, Past, & Future, sees;
> Whose ears have heard
> The Holy Word
> That walk'd among the ancient trees,
>
> Calling the lapsed Soul,
> And weeping in the evening dew;
> That might controll
> The starry pole,
> And fallen, fallen light renew!

"O Earth, O Earth, return!
Arise from out the dewy grass;
Night is worn,
And the morn
Rises from the slumberous mass.

Turn away no more;
Why wilt thou turn away?
The starry floor,
The wat'ry shore,
Is giv'n thee till the break of day."

This is a challenge to unregenerate man to enjoy his whole powers in natural harmony. The last poem, "The Voice of the Ancient Bard," repeats the invitation. Again, poetry, the life of intuition and of satisfied impulse, which is the true source of knowledge, is set against the authority of reason and of law, the source of multiplied errors:

Youth of delight, come hither,
And see the opening morn,
Image of truth new born.
Doubt is fled, & clouds of reason,
Dark disputes & artful teazing.
Folly is an endless maze,
Tangled roots perplex her ways.
How many have fallen there!
They stumble all night over the bones of the dead,
And feel they know not what but care,
And wish to lead others, when they should be led.

The central lines are echoes of old Elizabethan verses, but the challenge of the whole is new.

It is newer, for example, than Shelley, who twenty years later was to make the same attacks that are made in these songs—on the Church, on the God of law, on priests and kings, on custom, on commerce and finance, on marriage—but who was still to make them in terms of that eighteenth-century rationalism from which he finally had to struggle free if intellectual beauty and an ideal of liberty were to be supported in his verse.

Blake's instantaneous rejection of it is perhaps the most amazing of his feats of intellect. Before he could properly use in his poetry the texts of revolutionary social criticism, he had to transform the Lockian psychology and its evaluation of life. The indignation of *Songs of Experience* is founded on the easy delight of the *Songs of Innocence*.

VI

THE "ARGUMENT" OF *The Marriage of Heaven and Hell* opens in angry clouds, the destructive wrath of revolution, for "the just man," energy, has been compelled from his own dangerous and flourishing pursuits into "barren climes" by reason, the hypocrite who "in mild humility" pretends to virtue in the power of moral law:

> Once meek, and in a perilous path,
> The just man kept his course along
> The vale of death.
> Roses are planted where thorns grow,
> And on the barren heath
> Sing the honey bees.
>
> Then the perilous path was planted,
> And a river and a spring
> On every cliff and tomb,
> And on the bleached bones
> Red clay brought forth;
>
> Till the villain left the paths of ease,
> To walk in perilous paths, and drive
> The just man into barren climes.
>
> Now the sneaking serpent walks
> In mild humility,
> And the just man rages in the wilds
> Where lions roam.

Revolutionary wrath roars, "shakes his fires in the burden'd air," and gathers force in the hovering black clouds as the voice of Blake speaks out to state the doctrine implicit in the scene.

Swedenborg was right. This is a millennial occasion, and at this point the opposition of the just man and the hypocrite is philosophically and politically correct. Blake enunciates the revolutionary principle of thesis and antithesis toward which the ideas no less than the arrangement of the lyrics had pointed —the conflict of contrary interests and the tension between them that is the condition of their development. He does this in such terms as were available to him, a mixture of theological and metaphysical abstractions: "Without Contraries is no progression. Attraction and Repulsion, Reason and Energy, Love and Hate, are necessary to Human existence. From these contraries spring what the religious call Good & Evil. Good is the passive that obeys Reason. Evil is the active springing from Energy. Good is Heaven. Evil is Hell." Blake has employed familiar abstractions, but again he has completely inverted their familiar values. Since passive good is "Heaven," "angels" are the agents of corrupting restraint, "devils," of abounding energy. And it is "The Voice of the Devil"—that is, of "the just man," of Blake, the tiger—which continues: "Man has no Body distinct from his Soul; for that call'd Body is a portion of Soul discern'd by the five Senses, the chief inlets of Soul in this age. Energy is the only life, and is from the Body; and Reason is the bound or outward circumference of Energy. Energy is Eternal Delight."

Blake, with his ill training, is striving to say something that men of the nineteenth century, like Emerson, or of our own, like Yeats—men educated after a formal subjective philosophy had been propounded—found simple enough. There is no basic difference between Blake's angular and energetic statement and Yeats's easy

> The body is not bruised to pleasure soul. . . .
> O chestnut tree, great rooted blossomer,
> Are you the leaf, the blossom or the bole?
> O body swayed to music, O brightening glance,
> How can we know the dancer from the dance?

Above: "War"
By courtesy of the Fogg Museum of Art, Harvard University

Top right: "Famine"
By courtesy of the Museum of Fine Arts, Boston

Bottom right: "Plague"
By courtesy of the Museum of Fine Arts, Boston

The Malthusian Triad
". . . there are enough
Born, even too many, & our Earth will be overrun
Without these arts."

Yeats resorts to metaphor by the poet's preference. Blake was forced from an angular prose into an even more angular metaphorical statement of his theme. In *The Marriage* he continues to strive with his prose: "Those who restrain desire, do so because theirs is weak enough to be restrained; and the restrainer or reason usurps its place & governs the unwilling." Reason and energy, body and soul, matter and spirit—these are the familiar duos. Blake is struggling toward a higher conception of reason (toward *"Vernunft"* from *"Verstand"*) that will transcend the antithesis.

When Tiriel, admitting his error, says that his fault lay in humbling "the infinite spirit," in restraining his energy and the energy of others by law, he is convicting the reason of eighteenth-century rationalism, which was derived from narrowed sensual perceptions and is opposed to another reason, derived from the expanded perceptions of "the Poetic or Prophetic character." The poet Milton was a sublimer Tiriel, and in *The Marriage,* Blake now, in one of his most famous passages, uses Milton as his example of the mistaken man, as he was to use him later again, although more complexly, in his long poem. Milton's evaluation of the opposition of Satan and Jehovah was false to his own instincts, and his opposition of Satan and Christ was a vulgar error that followed. A devil corrects him: Does a bird, as it "cuts the airy way," impose restraint on an unwilling energy? Presumably not. Then what controls its flight? ". . . the bound or outward circumference of Energy." False reason is that "ratio," the abstraction that attempts to give one law "to the lion & the patient Ox," the external restraint. But that other reason, which is the source of real knowledge, is not external, does not impose restraint, but is the limit which energy achieves in freely expressing itself. False reason is the judge of action, which imposes moral and legal forms, separates body and soul, and cuts man off from a total experience of the cosmos, including the flight of birds. True reason is the organic form, a part of energy, harmonious with it and necessary to it, and co-operative. Blake is trying to free himself from the dichotomies of the old faculty psychology and to describe what in our time is known as the psychology of integration.

Disintegration, in that psychology as in Blake's, threatens constantly, for true reason is easily externalized, readily "usurps its place & governs the unwilling." What happens has been seen. "He who desires but acts not, breeds pestilence," said Blake in the "Proverbs of Hell," perhaps the most astonishing portion of this astonishing document. He spoke here, as he does throughout, an axiom that we like to look upon as peculiar to the province of our contemporary wisdom. (W. H. Auden has said that "The whole of Freud's teaching may be found in *The Marriage of Heaven and Hell.*") This is one of Blake's most expert intuitions. It underlies his insistence on impulsive action as well as on his particular view of the emotional life, at once intense and relaxed:

> He who binds to himself a joy
> Does the winged life destroy;
> But he who kisses the joy as it flies
> Lives in eternity's sun rise.

This is also the reason why Blake associates all law and authority, all repressive acts, with the imagery of blight and sickness, impoverishment and famine, and frost. "As the caterpiller chooses the fairest leaves to lay her eggs on, so the priest lays his curse on the fairest joys." Blake's psychology and social criticism form a logically consistent whole that puts the vaunted logic of the rationalist utopians to shame. "Prisons are built with stones of Law, Brothels with bricks of Religion." It is an observation that Godwin would have applauded, one in fact that he often made in his words; but he would not have understood the assumption on which Blake had made it rest.

"Proverbs of Hell," which offer almost endless delights to contemplation, suggest a related motive for Blake's rejection of reason as the être suprème. The intention of these axioms is a desire to rout the respectable, those "angels" who are under attack throughout *The Marriage*. They read almost as if Blake, like many poets and artists some time after him, is pitting the artist and the impulses of art against the bourgeoisie and the pieties of trade and a meager intellectual orthodoxy. "Prudence is a rich, ugly old maid courted by Incapacity." "The hours of folly are measur'd by the clock; but of wisdom, no clock can measure." "Bring out number, weight & measure in a year of dearth." "The most sublime act is to set another before you." "The lust of the goat is the bounty of God." "The nakedness of woman is the work of God." ". . . the genitals Beauty. . . . Exuberance is Beauty." "Improvement makes strait roads; but the crooked roads without Improvement are roads of Genius."

In one way or another, each of these and most of the other proverbs are calculated to outrage the favorite precepts of the middle class, and it does not seem too far-fetched to wonder whether Blake, in denying that reason which all his proverbs oppose and which the French Revolution apotheosized, did not instinctively recognize its political defect, which we, with the advantage of history, can see so easily. Much later, Engels wrote: "We know today that this kingdom of reason was nothing more than the idealised kingdom of the bourgeoisie; that this eternal right found its realization in bourgeois justice; that this equality reduced itself to bourgeois equality before the law; that bourgeois property was proclaimed as one of the essential rights of man; and that the government of reason, the *Contrat Social* of Rousseau, came into being, and only could come into being, as a democratic bourgeois republic." Blake did not deplore the revolutionary impulse, but one could argue quite plausibly that his sympathies moved away from the French Revolution only insofar as he denied the finality of its achievement. He demanded a bigger democracy than that. From any point of view except that of the artist and of the poor man, this is indeed the very voice of the devil, and these are the proverbs of hell.

Blake's next section deals with the process by which authority comes to dominate religious energy or "genius," and externalizes deities as it has itself. This is followed by the famous illustrative colloquy of the prophets which demonstrates that poets and prophets are one. Both sections develop the aim of the whole, to show that good and evil are the creations of dogma, and that it is the function of energy, especially poetic energy, to suspend the duality. This operation is to be performed in nature, for "Eternity is in love with the productions of time," and performed with revolutionary zest: "Drive your cart and your plow over the bones of the dead." To this end Blake invokes "The ancient tradition that the world will be consumed in fire at the end of six thousand years."

Hell has assured him that the prediction is true, and he tells us that the consummation (which is not destruction, but purification) will come about through abolishing the distinction of body and soul, and, in guarded language, that this is to decree a new sexual dispensation. "For the cherub with his flaming sword is hereby commanded to leave his guard at tree of life; and when he does, the whole creation will be consumed and appear infinite and holy, whereas it now appears finite & corrupt. This will come to pass by an improvement of sensual enjoyment." Of the singleness of body and soul, Blake's printing method is an allegory: ". . . printing in the infernal method, by corrosives, which in Hell are salutary and medicinal, melting apparent surfaces away, and displaying the infinite which was hid. If the doors of perception were cleansed every thing would appear to man as it is, infinite. For man has closed himself up, till he sees all things thro' narrow chinks of his cavern."

The radicals declared: ". . . we must by reason destroy the myth of original sin," and ". . . we must, I am persuaded, give a greater scope to the enjoyments of the senses." Their meanings begin to appear quite moderate, yet they are included in Blake's excesses. And for his exaltation of energy it is not difficult to find equivalents in their more mundane discussion, all of which pointed, after all, to a more intelligent use of man's energies than existing social institutions allowed, and a greater fruition of energy in the individual life.

The remainder of *The Marriage* is largely concerned with a fuller account of energy. In his next "Memorable Fancy," Blake gives names to some of the energies; he shows them expanding that cavern through whose "narrow chinks" unregenerate man sees his experience; and he points out again that they are the true source of knowledge:

> In the first chamber was a Dragon-Man, clearing away the rubbish from a cave's mouth; within, a number of Dragons were hollowing the cave.

In the second chamber was a Viper folding round the rock & the cave, and others adorning it with gold, silver and precious stones.

In the third chamber was an Eagle with wings and feathers of air: he caused the inside of the cave to be infinite; around were numbers of Eagle-like men who built palaces in the immense cliffs.

In the fourth chamber were Lions of flaming fire, raging around & melting the metals into living fluids.

In the fifth chamber were Unnam'd forms, which cast the metals into the expanse.

There they were receiv'd by Men who occupied the sixth chamber, and took the forms of books & were arranged in libraries.

Man's narrowed perceptions narrow down his cave, but the expanded senses and a rich impulsive life cause "the inside of the cave to be infinite." At the end of this chain of activity are poets, able at last to work with the best human materials and promulgate wisdom, which has been defined in our time as Blake conceived it, as "The mode of coalescence of instinct with intelligence." Blake has put this down with reasonable clarity, but he is not satisfied and tries once more. "The Giants who formed this world into its sensual existence, and now seem to live in it in chains, are in truth the causes of its life & the sources of all activity; but the chains are the cunning of weak and tame minds which have power to resist energy; according to the proverb, the weak in courage is strong in cunning." Then follows the distinction between the two classes of men, the prolific and the devourer, and with that Blake is back again at his beginning, the discontent with the principle of law.

He is asking for an expansion of man's means to knowledge, and to that end it is necessary for him to assail what Mr. Richards has called "the separatist's illusions," that "difference between heart and head" which until it "be overcome . . . is the mark of our imperfection." The attack on eighteenth-century rationalism was essential not only because rationalism set up an unreasonable concept of reason as a function opposed to other human functions, but because the whole method of its philosophy and science was an extension of such an inorganic departmentalization of phenomena, whether in the external world or in psychology.

Blake's juvenile protest against surgery was symbolic of his mature protest against rationalism and eighteenth-century scientific method. Its "analysis" was a dead process; it killed the thing it examined by isolating it from its total context in order to examine it. Another revolution was in order. Whitehead, who defines "mankind" as "that factor *in* nature which exhibits in its most intense form the plasticity of nature," has argued that a number of Blake's contemporaries, in their objections to the mechanistic science of their time, were in the vanguard of a philosophical revolution. It was Wordsworth's desire to show how deeply man was implicated in nature, and through the psychology of Hartley he was able to work out a whole doctrine of the natural education of the sensibility and of the moral man. Coleridge extended Wordsworth's claims, and in the famous lines

> O Wordsworth, we receive but what we give,
> And in our life alone does nature live,

pushed the argument for the interdependence of phenomena as far as the well-known poets of this time, even Shelley in the frenzy of discovery that makes up *Queen Mab,* were to carry it.

Blake went further, and if we can see how this happened we can understand one important reason why he became the kind of poet he is. Hartley he left behind as still smacking too much of the old mechanical departmentalization of the faculties, and he created a symbolism in which the spirit of man was implicated not only in the life of external nature but in the life of the entire cosmos, and not only implicated, but creating it and wreaking havoc in it, and demanded then where was the *machine* of the universe, or that neat clock which, once it had been started, ran quite by itself. The point is that, for this purpose, he created a symbolism.

In one of the classic chapters of modern criticism Edmund

Wilson pointed out how "the metaphysics of the Symbolists" was related to the doctrine of relativity, how the theory of the uniqueness of "events" is identical with the concept of the symbol. What Blake discovered very early in his career was that he could not state his perceptions accurately without recourse to symbols, and the reason that his "system" of symbols can be only approximately defined is that he himself constantly eludes a system of fixed meanings for precisely the reason that he is trying to overcome such a concept. He believed in the uniqueness of all "events" quite as firmly as Professor Whitehead, so firmly indeed that even his admirers continue to feel dismay.

The simplest fact in this whole matter is Blake's repudiation of reason. A total man has something like a total experience; a single faculty has a segmented experience. A segment of an experience is not "true," and therefore the poetic genius, who is "the true man" (the total man), is to be trusted for "the true method of knowledge." "If the doors of perception were cleansed every thing would appear to man as it is, infinite." We know what closes them—the separation of reason from the whole and its imposition on the rest, the function of law.

". . . We receive but what we give." This might be the text of Blake's next "Memorable Fancy." Here an "angel" (a devourer, the passive good) offers to show Blake his eternal lot, and leads him through a stable, a church, a mill, to a cavern (through contemporary education, religion, logic, to the narrow view of the century) and they hang in trees looking down into a Blakean inferno. Then the angel climbs up into the mill again, and Blake at once finds himself "on a pleasant bank beside a river by moonlight, hearing a harper, who sung to the harp." When he finds the angel presently, and the angel demands to know how he escaped, Blake replies: "All that we saw was owing to your metaphysics." Then he offers to show the angel his eternal lot. What follows is Blake's Swiftian vision of modern man in the process of dehumanizing himself: "Soon we saw the stable and the church, & I took him to the altar and open'd the Bible, and lo! it was a deep pit, into which I descended, driving the Angel before me; soon we saw seven houses of brick; one we enter'd; in it were a number of monkeys, baboons, & all of that species, chain'd by the middle, grinning and snatching at one another, but withheld by the shortness of their chains: however, I saw that they sometimes grew numerous, and then the weak were caught by the strong, and with a grinning aspect, first coupled with, & then devour'd, by plucking off first one limb and then another, till the body was left a helpless trunk; this, after grinning & kissing it with seeming fondness, they devour'd too; and here & there I saw one savourily picking the flesh off his own tail; as the stench terribly annoy'd us both, we went into the mill, & I in my hand brought the skeleton of a body, which in the mill was Aristotle's Analytics. So the angel said: 'thy phantasy has imposed upon me, & thou oughtest to be ashamed.' I answer'd: 'we impose on one another.' "

The rest continues the attack on "angels," and in a demonstration that Jesus was a revolutionary who broke every one of the commandments that old Nobodaddy, or the false religion of Jehovah, attempted to impose, Blake puts him in "the Devil's party." "The Devil answer'd: 'bray a fool in a morter with wheat, yet shall not his folly be beaten out of him; if Jesus Christ is the greatest man, you ought to love him in the greatest degree; now hear how he has given his sanction to the law of ten commandments: did he not mock at the sabbath, and so mock the sabbath's God? murder those who were murder'd because of him? turn away the law from the woman taken in adultery? steal the labor of others to support him? bear false witness when he omitted making a defence before Pilate? covet when he pray'd for his disciples, and when he bid them shake off the dust of their feet against such as refused to lodge them? I tell you, no virtue can exist without breaking these ten commandments. Jesus was all virtue, and acted from impulse, not from rules.' " Then, converting the question of *Tiriel* to statement, *The Marriage* closes: "One Law for the Lion & Ox is Oppression."

Yet it is not complete. Blake's "Argument," of the just man driven into perilous paths by the hypocrite villain, the devourer pushing out the prolific, remains to be concluded. This conclusion comes in "A Song of Liberty," which follows *The Marriage* and completes it.

In the first of the *Songs of Experience,* Blake called to the earth: "O Earth! O Earth! Return!" but Earth could not. Now the renewal begins:

The Eternal Female groan'd! it was heard over all the Earth.
Albion's coast is sick, silent; the American meadows faint!
Shadows of Prophecy shiver along by the lakes and the rivers, and mutter across the Ocean: France, rend down thy dungeon!
Golden Spain, burst the barriers of old Rome!
Cast thy keys, O Rome, into the deep down falling, even to eternity down falling,
And weep.

All creation is sick, and the earth labors to free herself; then at last she seizes in her hands "the new born terror, howling"—the synthesis, Revolt. He faces "the starry king," the restrainer, reason, and is seized by the head and hurled out of reason's kingdom, into the West, into America:

The fire, the fire is falling!
Look up! Look up! O citizen of London, enlarge thy countenance! O Jew, leave counting gold! return to thy oil and wine. O African! black African! (Go winged thought, widen his forehead.)
The fiery limbs, the flaming hair, shot like the sinking sun into the western sea.

Having divorced himself from energy, reason falls, and he falls into the regions of Urthona, or spirit (one critic has suggested "Earth-Owner"), where, because he has created duality, he attempts to rule and "promulgates his ten commands." But "the son of fire" breaks out in destructive action in America, and,

Spurning the clouds written with curses, stamps the stony law to dust, loosing the eternal horses from the dens of night, crying: EMPIRE IS NO MORE! AND NOW THE LION & WOLF SHALL CEASE.

Thus we come again into the meadows of innocence, where the lion, who will lie with the lamb, no longer struggles with the wolf, who would also devour it. Man's cruelty to man has gone.

"A Song of Liberty" ends with a chorus that anticipates social liberation. Let the Church no longer lay a curse on man's impulses, nor government build repressive legal structures that departmentalize good and evil, nor passive sterility, theology and every form of dogma, "call that virginity that wishes but acts not! For every thing that lives is Holy."

It is the black year of 1793. These are vistas of idyl which suggest Marx's vision when, in the years of his greatest political impotency, he wrote, "The new world citizens will be unable to realize how small our world was."

The Marriage of Heaven and Hell, which is Blake's supreme effort at definition, is therefore the central document in his work. It finds new and more satisfactory terms for the pastoral and humanitarian strains that make up his earliest poems. It reinforces these with cosmic metaphor, and it roots them in a newly devised psychology. This is most simply described as a psychology of revolution, and not only because through it a revolutionary synthesis of contrary elements is made possible, but because, in a less metaphysically political sense, it directs itself against treacherous social forms. Two elements of almost equal strength have gone into the formation of this psychology—the persistent strains of evangelical idealism and of the harsher revolutionary optimism. For that cleansing of the universe which Blake decrees one finds a parallel in Cowper's Methodism:

> Nature, assuming a more lovely face,
> Borrowing a beauty from the works of grace,
> Shall be despis'd and overlook'd no more.

Yet because Blake has construed such an extremely different view of man from Cowper's, the renewal of the actual that he anticipates is at least as political as it is religious, and his angels and devils have political as well as theological rôles.

> I heard an Angel singing
> When the day was springing,
> "Mercy, Pity, Peace
> Is the world's release."

Thus he sung all day
Over the new mown hay,
Till the sun went down
And haycocks looked brown.

I heard a Devil curse
Over the heath & the furze,
"Mercy could be no more,
If there was nobody poor,

And pity no more could be,
If all were as happy as we."
At his curse the sun went down,
And the heavens gave a frown.

Down pour'd the heavy rain
Over the new reap'd grain,
And Miseries' increase
Is Mercy, Pity, Peace.

The angel preaches the conventional eighteenth-century ethics of benevolence and the moral sense; the devil sees the large ingredient of selfishness that this ethics cloaked; but piety is appalled at his expression, and for the moment the conventional view holds. The implications of this opposition are almost entirely political.

Yet a central achievement of *The Marriage* is its easy transcendence of mere political considerations. Political institutions, like all conventions, are accidents, and Blake's search is for the cause. They are, to be sure, as "A Song of Liberty" suggests, the first restraints to be abolished, but that is because they are the last effects in a long series. To abolish the effect and praise the cause—as in the avowals of the theorists—would gain men nothing, and therefore Blake decreed an equalitarianism founded not on one energy but on man's total energies. Before a democracy is possible among all men, individual men must achieve a democracy of their faculties. It is as simple and as difficult as that.

The picture of man with and without restraints raises the problem of evil and the extent to which Blake was capable of a tragic view. "There grows one," he said of the tree, "in the

Human Brain." His reaction to Godwinian discussion bears some resemblance to Hawthorne's reaction "when the activity of the Millerites had caused him to ponder how reforming zeal might bring to destruction all the age-old abuses and encumbrances of the world," and "he observed that 'there's one thing that these wiseacres have forgotten to throw into the fire,' without which all their efforts for perfectibility would still remain futile: 'What but the human heart itself?'" Yet it was a less complete reaction than that, one that made an immediate uprooting of the tree and cleansing of the heart possible, and therefore it did not lend itself to an intensely tragic view of life such as Hawthorne's.

In essence, the modifications that Blake worked on Milton were a denial of the Christian view of evil, and the assertion of what can best be described as a paganized version of Jesus, which deifies energy for its own sake. This is tragic only in the curious sense that Yeats made of it, and quite opposite to tragedy as we are accustomed to think of it. Yet there is more of the tragic in Blake than Yeats saw or could usually draw into his own poetry. The last lesson of experience is that wisdom comes from it, and that is to state the traditional view that suffering is essential to life. But Blake could never let it rest there, as the traditional view does, but continually looked forward to an act of transcendence. The very achievement of wisdom from experience is the revolutionary act and the discovery of innocence again. This expresses the least tragic Protestant interpretation of life and the political optimism that denies the reality of evil entirely. Between his perception of the tragic social fact and his desire for the joyous possibility, Blake's poetry works its constant orbit.

So far, his desire had not been able to express itself as more than desire. He had worked out a means to the possibility, but he had not yet found a means of dramatizing its achievement. Nor was he yet able to do so in his next group of poems, even though now he twisted his poetry into the violent and gasping thing it was to become for exactly this purpose—the strenuous effort to reform the lion and the wolf and to uproot the tree under which they roared and bled.

CHAPTER EIGHT

The Definition Dramatized

I

THREE FACTS had by now combined to make of William Blake what he was to become, a poet who went beyond the ordinary resources of poetry in order to "Create a System." These facts derive directly from three sources—his temperament, its operation on his tradition, and the place of his tradition in his time. The first was the original and mistaken sense of prophetic self-importance, a point of view that was reinforced by the newly developed rationalizations about reason, energy, genius, and the poetic character. The second was that what he had to say could be said only with great difficulty in the ordinary ways, but with relative ease in a system of mythological metaphor. The third was that it could be said clearly only with danger to himself, and that metaphor would conceal it and save him.

Between 1791 and 1795, Blake wrote the symbolical series that formalized what was to become his characteristic mode of expression, a group of eight poems that form a coherent narrative and of which only the conclusion is fragmentary. These poems embody in allegorical figures Blake's revolutionary doctrine as he had developed it through *The Marriage,* and they push back still further, or at any rate define more exactly, the boundaries of causation.

The second of these facts immediately complicates an exposition of the poems, for by the time Blake came to the first chapters of the story, *The Book of Urizen* and *The Book of Los* (and these were among the last parts to be written), he was no longer expounding a single, or even a double, but a triple doctrine, cosmogonal, historical, and psychological, in a single symbolism. It is impossible to separate one of these completely from the others, yet the historical and the psychological are more interesting than the cosmogonal, and we shall emphasize them. When we deal with cosmic meanings, it will be as much as possible in their representation of psychological material.

It is hard to know how literal Blake's cosmogonal intentions were. *Urizen* and *Los* deal with the separation of the Eternals, their fall from unity, and the subsequent creation of earth and of Adam; they also tell of the disruption of the individual's innocence and his subsequent confusion of spirit, his externalization of what is properly inner. The macrocosm is the microcosm in Blake's theory; yet the macrocosm is also Blake's method of exploring the microcosm. This is nowhere more clearly shown than in his use of the "fall." "The biblical fall of man presents the dawn of consciousness as a curse," Jung wrote. "And as a matter of fact it is in this light that we first look upon every problem that forces us to greater consciousness and separates us even further from the paradise of unconscious childhood." He was not thinking of Blake, yet he has stated as precisely as possible the value of Blake's symbol. One could not ask for a better explanation of the questions in the motto of Thel—who refused to "fall"—than this, that the "denial of a problem will not produce conviction; on the contrary, a wider and higher consciousness is called for to give us the certainty and clarity we need."

Blake's "fall" is the act whereby man moves from his pristine unconsciousness into the self-consciousness of experience. He finds himself in a situation in which he is aware of his separate impulses and of their conflicts; and the transcendence of experience lies in his reintegration, and in the achievement of a higher consciousness that is without the strife of the middle state but is also aware as the first was not. This theme Blake presents in cosmogonal terms, but he resolves it in historical terms.

These poems begin with the fall of angels, but they end with the French Revolution.

In them Blake formalizes his method. That method may be defined most simply as one that employs a form of the faculty psychology in order to overcome it. An easy representation of the method is in the lyric "My Spectre around me night & day," which was written about 1800. It is a useful introduction because all that is necessary to understand it is the knowledge that the "Spectre" is always the dominating rational part of the individual, and the "Emanation" is the outcast, imaginative portion.

> My Spectre around me night & day
> Like a Wild beast guards my way.
> My Emanation far within
> Weeps incessantly for my Sin.
>
> A Fathomless & boundless deep,
> There we wander, there we weep;
> On the hungry craving wind
> My Spectre follows thee behind. . . .
>
> Dost thou not in Pride & scorn
> Fill with tempest all my morn,
> And with jealousies & fears
> Fill my pleasant nights with tears? . . .
>
> When wilt thou return & view
> My loves, & them to life renew?
> When wilt thou return & live?
> When wilt thou pity as I forgive?
>
> "Never, Never, I return:
> Still for Victory I burn.
> Living, thee alone I'll have
> And when dead I'll be thy Grave.
>
> Thro' the Heaven & Earth & Hell
> Thou shalt never never quell:
> I will fly & thou pursue,
> Night & Morn the flight renew."

Till I turn from Female Love,
And root up the Infernal Grove,
I shall never worthy be
To Step into Eternity.

And, to end thy cruel mocks,
Annihilate thee on the rocks,
And another form create
To be subservient to my Fate.

This colloquy has something of the stark and sinewy beauty of the Gothic *débat,* whose logic, up to a point, it supports, and whose feeling it approximates in its description of the way the reason hounds and exhausts one. Its theme too, up to a point, is the old one, the tortured duality of men. But it departs from the old theme in its determination to "root up the Infernal Grove," which is to say that their duality is a condition into which men split themselves, and that they can "another form create."

This is the theme of all Blake's prophetic poems, and their method is in essence that of the debate between the warring, dual elements of man. For readers today all this is more complicated than it is complex. The fact to keep in mind as Blake amplifies his method is the importance of point of view. Everything that happens here happens in the universe as constructed under the necessities of Urizen, and therefore most assertions that are made in and about this universe are mistaken, or partial. The helpless confusion that Blake's reader sometimes feels comes not so much from the multiplicity of names and the rigmarole of events as from the reader's own neglect, even momentarily, to evaluate speaker and event, and to judge the extent and the significance of the error. Nothing in these poems can be taken at its face value.

The theme of the divisive life is stated at once in the "Preludium" to *Urizen:*

Of the primeval Priest's assum'd power,
When Eternals spurn'd back his religion
And gave him a place in the north,
Obscure, shadowy, void, solitary.

The "primeval Priest" is the original despot, the first restrainer, Nobodaddy, the reason. In the myth that begins here Blake gives this force the not very mysterious name of Urizen (your reason), and his opening description is a dramatic statement of the definition of reason already present in his earlier work:

> Lo, a shadow of horror is risen
> In Eternity! Unknown, unprolific,
> Self-clos'd, all-repelling . . .

Abstracted from the harmony of the whole, reason is uncreative, sees not infinity but self alone, and repels all that is not of self. Urizen, divided from the other Eternals when he attempts to usurp their power in order to "govern the unwilling," has lost his knowledge of infinity (and Blake therefore does not describe it), since he attains his separate consciousness only after he has already lost the sense of it. He is "A self-contemplating shadow," for, as Blake said in the second *Tractate,* seeing the "ratio" only, he "sees himself only." And this is original sin—so far as it exists in Blake at all—the selfish act of a portion of a whole, which is a disruptive act in any whole, individual, social, or cosmic, because it is the agent of isolation.

Yet the attempt at usurpation is Urizen's really well-intentioned error. He believes that through his laws he can improve life: "I have sought for a joy without pain," he declares, and:

> "Here alone I, in books form'd of metals,
> Have written the secrets of wisdom,
> The secrets of dark contemplation,
> By fightings and conflicts dire
> With terrible monsters Sin-bred,
> Which the bosom of all inhabit,
> Seven deadly Sins of the soul.
>
> Lo! I unfold my darkness, and on
> This rock place with strong hand the Book
> Of eternal brass, written in my solitude:
>
> Laws of peace, of love, of unity,
> Of pity, compassion, forgiveness;

Let each chuse one habitation,
His ancient infinite mansion,
One command, one joy, one desire,
One curse, one weight, one measure,
One King, one God, one Law."

"The Book Of eternal brass" is the book of false ethics, which, ignoring the precept that "One law for the Lion & Ox is Oppression," impoverishes man and gives birth to pity. Within the limitations of his separate state, Urizen's intentions are good enough. But the limitations are disastrous; for he does not see that by proclaiming one *right* pattern of conduct, he is himself creating those negations, the "Seven deadly Sins of the soul." The ideal of innocence—to snatch at joy as it flies but not to bind it—is lost; in its place is limitation, restraint, the dogma of right and wrong. Thus Urizen falls amid "fragments of life," and in the chaos of creation, he digs a cave for himself in earth and rock, and creeps into it—his world. Like Newton's God, he "formed matter in solid, massy, hard, impenetrable, moveable particles."

Chaos is marked by the fate of those powers whose place Urizen attempted to usurp. All eternity suffers a fall when a single part falls, all powers are weakened. As soon as Urizen falls, Urthona, spirit, falls too, and already in the secondary form of Los, "The Eternal Prophet." Los is poetry—

. . . howling around the dark Demon,
And cursing his lot; for in anguish
Urizen was rent from his side. . . .

But Urizen laid in a stony sleep,
Unorganiz'd, rent from Eternity.

It is a constant theme in Blake that error can be destroyed only after it has taken form, which is a perfectly orthodox revolutionary precept. It is the function of poetry, as Blake conceives it, to express the faults of men as well as to re-form them. Los is appalled by the proportions of his artistic task, and he howls in fright and rage—as Blake howls through his Prophecies —at "the formless, unmeasurable death" that his genius must circumscribe. Yet error must reach its most definite state and misery its severest if revolution is to begin, and Los, weakened as he is by his separation and fall, knows that he must work "the changes of Urizen." For this distasteful but necessary task, he moves from the sun into the ironworks:

> The Eternal Prophet heav'd the dark bellows,
> And turn'd restless the tongs, and the hammer
> Incessant beat, forging chains new & new,
> Numb'ring with links, hours, days & years.

Reason is bound and encumbered:

> Till a roof, shaggy wild, inclos'd
> In an orb his fountain of thought.

This is a modern brain, closed down on the spontaneous jet of intellect. A body, the kind that this brain can perceive, follows:

> . . . bones of solidness froze
> Over all his nerves of joy.

One by one, as external replaces organic form, the closed senses are beaten out on the forge, the narrow ways of perception from which reason (according to Locke) learns.

> All the myriads of Eternity,
> All the wisdom & joy of life
> Roll like a sea around him,
> Except what his little orbs
> Of sight by degrees unfold.
>
> And now his eternal life
> Like a dream was obliterated.

But Los, who has had to do this work, has suffered a similar fate—we become what we behold:

> . . . a cold solitude & dark void
> The Eternal Prophet & Urizen clos'd.

Separation breeds separation. The human divides into the sexual:

Thus the Eternal Prophet was divided
Before the death image of Urizen. . . .

At length in tears & cries imbodied,
A female form, trembling and pale,
Waves before his deathy face.

All Eternity shudder'd at sight
Of the first female now separate,
Pale as a cloud of snow
Waving before the face of Los . . .

At the first female form now separate.
They call'd her Pity, and fled.

But first they build a tent over the two,

"That Eternals may no more behold them." . . .

With infinite labour the Eternals
A woof wove, and called it Science.

Science is life as presented to the unorganized and fallen man, both a protection and a prison, and an act of obscuring.

Los, even though divided, is still the creative principle, poetry and the male. Enitharmon, "the first female form," is that sympathy which a brutal condition of life provides as the poet's inspiration, and the female principle. All the sins of inharmonious sexuality now begin:

. . . Los saw the Female & pitied;
He embraced her; she wept, she refus'd;
In perverse and cruel delight
She fled from his arms, yet he followed.

Cruel coyness, false modesty, hypocritical restraint, do not prevent generation. Enitharmon "Produc'd a man Child to the light," and eternity shrieks "At the birth of the Human shadow," sunken man. The new situation of father and son (Los and Orc) engenders jealousy, which enchains them both:

. . . O sorrow & pain!
A tight'ning girdle grew

Around his bosom. In sobbings
He burst the girdle in twain;
But still another girdle
Oppress'd his bosom. In sobbings
Again he burst it. Again
Another girdle succeeds.
The girdle was form'd by day,
By night was burst in twain. . . .

They took Orc to the top of a mountain. . . .
They chain'd his young limbs to the rock
With the Chain of Jealousy
Beneath Urizen's deathful shadow.

In the realms of Urizen, it is a fixed principle that the sins of the father are visited upon the sons.

Urizen, in the meantime, wanders through his universe and, like Newton, straightens it:

He form'd a line & a plummet
To divide the Abyss beneath;
He formed a dividing rule;

He formed scales to weigh,
He formed massy weights;
He formed a brazen quadrant;
He formed golden compasses,
And began to explore the Abyss;
And he planted a garden of fruits.

He explores his dens and sickens at the sight of his creations, "cruel enormities," "Portions of life, similitudes," and especially the four separated elementals, Thiriel (ethereal; air), Utha (water), Grodna (earth), and Fuzon (fire). He sees his error and like Tiriel he curses, but a curse can only multiply the error:

He in darkness clos'd view'd all his race,
And his soul sicken'd! he curs'd
Both sons & daughters; for he saw
That no flesh nor spirit could keep
His iron laws one moment.

He sees that under his legal provisions

> . . . life liv'd upon death:
> The Ox in the slaughter house moans,
> The Dog at the wintry door.

He resorts to a further device. If logic cannot support his law, superstition may. Out of the tragic sense of man's radical imperfections, religion grows:

> A cold shadow follow'd behind him
> Like a spider's web, moist, cold & dim,
> Drawing out from his sorrowing soul. . . .
>
> None could break the Web, no wings of fire,
> So twisted the cords, & so knotted
> The meshes, twisted like to the human brain.
>
> And all call'd it The Net of Religion.

Civilization starts up in Egypt, which is empire, and the inhabitants of this region feel the narrowing of their perceptions, the shrinking of sense:

> . . . till weaken'd
> The Senses inward rush'd, shrinking
> Beneath the dark net of infection;
>
> Till the shrunken eyes, clouded over,
> Discern'd not the woven hipocrisy;
> But the streaky slime in their heavens,
> Brought together by narrowing perceptions,
> Appear'd transparent air.

Only because they have suffered this decline do they continue to proliferate Urizen's error, mistaking Urizen himself for God:

> And their children wept, & built
> Tombs in the desolate places,
> And form'd laws of prudence, and call'd them
> The eternal laws of God.

One son, however, is unwilling to accept this bondage. He is the apocalyptic element, Fuzon, fire, or passion, whose powers are allied with those of the triad Urthona-Los-Orc, and will be identified with those of Jesus. At the end of the poem, Fuzon (the pillar of fire) leads the slaves out of Egypt.

II

The Book of Los tells the same story from the point of view of spirit. It opens with the song of Eno, the earth-mother, who looks back into eternity with nostalgic memory:

> "O Times remote!
> When Love & Joy were adoration,
> And none impure were deem'd:
> Not Eyeless Covet,
> Nor Thin-lip'd Envy,
> Nor Bristled Wrath,
> Nor Curled Wantonness;
>
> But Covet was poured full,
> Envy fed with fat of lambs,
> Wrath with lion's gore,
> Wantonness lull'd to sleep
> With the virgin's lute
> Or sated with her love;
>
> Till Covet broke his locks & bars
> And slept with open doors;
> Envy sung at the rich man's feast;
> Wrath was follow'd up and down
> By a little ewe lamb,
> And Wantonness on his own true love
> Begot a giant race."

In those remote and opulent times, none was *deemed* impure, because no desire was suppressed and no want left unfulfilled. Even when spirit is just becoming self-conscious in the fallen form of Los, Eno's lament is hopelessly elegiac. But Los is already at his forge, fashioning bodies for himself and for Urizen. Again, the senses are beaten into their closed forms, and the material world shrinks away from infinity in the symbolism of Eden and Adam, "Human illusion":

> Till his Brain in a rock & his Heart
> In a fleshy slough formed four rivers
> Obscuring the immense Orb of fire
> Flowing down into night: till a Form
> Was completed, a Human illusion
> In darkness and deep clouds involv'd.

Adam, Blake's "Human illusion," is born into a world already split up into duality, his own powers at war, as are his father's, reason in control of energy, false restraints his inheritance. Blake's drama is of the psychological conflicts of men in a world under tyranny. Except for occasional flashes of intuition, perceptions are limited to the reports of senses that have suffered a decline, and knowledge is the sum of these reports. And error is slippery. When it fails as logic, it slides into religion. Spirit too is degraded, but energy cannot be destroyed, and Orc, the power of revolt, finds a form, although in a world of conflict he is bound. Nevertheless:

> The dead heard the voice of the child
> And began to awake from sleep;
> All things heard the voice of the child
> And began to awake to life.

Fuzon takes up "the voice of the child" and rebels against his father. Reason, notwithstanding, continues his fatal rule, and man becomes weaker and weaker in the strife. Revolt must break loose to release the dead and to restore the balance of innocence, the original harmony.

Half the difficulty of Blake's Prophecies is solved if one remembers that their intention is to picture a world as seen in many mirrors, all slightly distorted, and all capable of only partial perspectives, an angle here or an angle there, from which inexact inferences are drawn about the whole.

III

The Book of Ahania carries on with Fuzon's revolt against his father:

> "Shall we worship this Demon of smoke,"
> Said Fuzon, "this abstract non-entity,
> This cloudy God seated on waters,
> Now seen, now obscur'd, King of sorrow?"

He fashions his wrath into a globe and hurls it at Urizen, who defends himself with the "broad Disk" of his rationalism, "forg'd in mills" of logic—

> . . . where the winter
> Beats incessant: ten winters the disk
> Unremitting endur'd the cold hammer.

This is not an adequate weapon against the onslaughts of passion and what passion has to teach. Now as he is struck in his loins, Urizen is suddenly aware that he still owns a "vulnerable part," his last claim to grace:

> Dire shriek'd his invisible Lust;
> Deep groan'd Urizen! stretching his awful hand,
> Ahania (so name his parted soul)
> He siez'd on his mountains of Jealousy.
> He groan'd anguish'd, & called her Sin,
> Kissing her and weeping over her;
> Then hid her in darkness, in silence,
> Jealous, tho' she was invisible.
>
> She fell down a faint shadow wand'ring
> In chaos and circling dark Urizen,
> As the moon anguish'd circles the earth,
> Hopeless! abhorr'd! a death-shadow,
> Unseen, unbodied, unknown,
> The mother of Pestilence.

This is pleasure, not joy, the delights of "self-contemplating" reason, and described, of course, in the imagery of sex. Blake's attitudes toward sexuality are not without ambiguity, but his essential distinction is between the innocent sexuality of a free and integrated impulsive life and the degraded sexuality of calculation and selfishness that develops under rationalism and its divisive sense of morality and law. When Urizen calls Ahania "Sin" and casts her out in suppression, she becomes at once "The mother of Pestilence," in the true Freudian transposition.

Once free of pleasure, as he thinks, Urizen seizes a snake, the "enormous dread Serpent" of sense and materialism, and from this fashions a bow that he loads with "A poisoned rock," the moral law. He draws it against Fuzon:

> His beautiful visage, his tresses
> That gave light to the mornings of heaven,
> Were smitten with darkness, deform'd
> And outstretch'd on the edge of the forest.
>
> But the Rock fell upon the Earth,
> Mount Sinai in Arabia.

Fuzon lies dying, and the heavy rock of the Decalogue weighs down the land in which the Israelite slaves wander. Freed from empire, they now submit to law of their own devising.

Fuzon, identified with Christ (who lived by passion, not by law), is crucified by Urizen on the contrived Tree of Error, of religious mystery, which has sprung up from the rock. There Urizen writes "his book of iron"; that is, of war. The tree—

> . . . bending its boughs
> Grew to roots when it felt the earth,
> And again sprung to many a tree.

In the wild maze that results, the slaves wander for forty years:

> Round the pale living Corse on the Tree
> Forty years flew the arrows of pestilence.
>
> Wailing and terror and woe
> Ran thro' all his dismal world;

Forty years all his sons & daughters
Felt their skulls harden; then Asia
Arose in the pendulous deep.

All the while the remote voice of Ahania wreathes itself in lamentation round the tree:

. . . "Ah, Urizen! Love!
Flower of morning! I weep on the verge
Of Non-entity; how wide the Abyss
Between Ahania and thee! . . .

Why didst thou despise Ahania
To cast me from thy bright presence
Into the World of Loneness?"

Like Eno, she remembers the fullness of life before self-consciousness split it into sterile fragments, the remote times:

"Where is my golden palace?
Where my ivory bed?
Where the joy of my morning hour?
Where the sons of eternity singing . . .

When he gave my happy soul
To the sons of eternal joy,
When he took the daughters of life
Into my chambers of love,

When I found babes of bliss on my beds
And bosoms of milk in my chambers
Fill'd with eternal seed.
O eternal births sung round Ahania
In interchange sweet of their joys! . . .

Then thou with thy lap full of seed,
With thy hand full of generous fire
Walked forth from the clouds of morning
On the virgins of springing joy,
On the human soul to cast
The seed of eternal science."

Then she returns to the theme of her present state, cast out by jealousy and fear, by that reason which is "Self-destroying," to wander in the regions of error, or death,

> Where bones of beasts are strown
> On the bleak and snowy mountains.

IV

In "Africa" and "Asia," the two parts of *The Song of Los,* the story carries on through the reign of Urizen until the first awakenings of the revolutions that will overthrow him. "Africa" deals with the promulgation of the false religions invented by Urizen to sustain the law, all of them weakened because passion has been crucified. The eternal forms of nature laugh at man, the slave of his disruption, lost in "dark delusion":

> (Night spoke to the Cloud:
> "Lo these Human form'd spirits, in smiling hipocrisy, War
> Against one another; so let them War on, slaves to the eternal
> Elements.")

But revolt is striving for release: "Orc on Mount Atlas howl'd, chain'd down with the Chain of Jealousy." Desire gives a message to Jesus:

> Then Oothoon hover'd over Judah & Jerusalem,
> And Jesus heard her voice (a man of sorrows) he reciev'd
> A Gospel from wretched Theotormon.

But this doctrine too decays, for even under Christianity love is bound by laws:

> The human race began to wither, for the healthy built
> Secluded places, fearing the joys of Love,
> And the diseased only propagated.

In this state of spiritual bondage, the arts, Har and Heva, enter their cage:

Creeping in reptile flesh upon
The bosom of the ground;
And all the vast of Nature shrunk
Before their shrunken eyes.

The imprisonment of man within his narrowed senses has brought him to the very nadir of life, but the triviality of even this existence has been rationalized into a philosophy:

Thus the terrible race of Los & Enitharmon gave
Laws & Religions to the sons of Har, binding them more
And more to Earth, closing and restraining,
Till a Philosophy of Five Senses was complete.
Urizen wept & gave it into the hands of Newton & Locke.

It is always at this point, when error has found its most precise statement, that revolution breaks out. Now when man is most completely bound, Orc's bondage becomes unendurable, and the prospect of his release is imminent in the unrest, the prophetic clouds of impending revolution:

Clouds roll heavy upon the Alps round Rousseau & Voltaire,
And on the mountains of Lebanon round the deceased Gods
Of Asia, & on the desarts of Africa round the Fallen Angels
The Guardian Prince of Albion burns in his nightly tent.

The impressive figure of the last line of "Africa" is a representation of none other than George III, whose historical insights here are somewhat sharper than they were in fact. The line supplies the proper transition to "Asia," the events of which are continuous with those of "Africa," but which present the spread of political, not of religious, tyranny. For the kings of Asia hear "The howl rise up from Europe" and are frightened "At the thick-flaming, thought-creating fires of Orc." They do not understand what is happening. They cry out to Urizen and question him "in bitterness of soul," for history is not fulfilling the philosophy of power in which they were instructed:

"Shall not the King call for Famine from the heath,
Nor the Priest for Pestilence from the fen,
To restrain, to dismay, to thin

The inhabitants of mountain and plain,
In the day of full-feeding prosperity
And the night of delicious songs?

Shall not the Councellor throw his curb
Of Poverty on the laborious,
To fix the price of labour,
To invent allegoric riches?"

From the "Schoolmaster of souls" they had learned that oppression and an enforced misery were the proper tools of life, and now they are bewildered:

"To turn the man from his path,
To restrain the child from the womb,
To cut off the bread from the city,
That the remnant may learn to obey,

That the pride of the heart may fail,
That the lust of the eyes may be quench'd,
That the delicate ear in its infancy
May be dull'd, and the nostrils clos'd up."

Urizen hears them but he is helpless to come to their rescue, for his laws are already being broken, his books of ethics, war, and commerce are melting in the flames that arise from Europe. And as soon as the laws are broken, Orc is free and takes up the work of Fuzon:

Orc, raging in European darkness,
Arose like a pillar of fire above the Alps,
Like a serpent of fiery flame!

Then, in the first of those apocalyptic occasions on which Blake was to rely more and more for the affirmation at the ends of his poems, the corrupted world is freed and life is rescued from apparent death:

Forth from the dead dust, rattling bones to bones
Join; shaking convuls'd, the shiv'ring clay breathes,
And all flesh naked stands: Fathers and Friends,
Mothers & Infants, Kings & Warriors.

The earth is seized in convulsive triumph and cries out ecstatically in the spasms of fulfillment.

> The Grave shrieks with delight & shakes
> Her hollow womb & clasps the solid stem:
> Her bosom swells with wild desire,
> And milk & blood & glandous wine
> In rivers rush & shout & dance,
> On mountain, dale and plain.

V

America: A Prophecy increases the overt historical meanings into which this myth has been moving. This is not to say that Blake has undertaken to imitate Barlow and write a *Columbiad,* or even that he is surveying history at all. As he drew psychological inferences from the myth of the creation and of the fall, so he draws them from the American Revolution. Indeed, the difference between the earlier poems in the series and this and the remaining poems is not so much that these later books are derived from recorded and contemporary history as it is that they deal with psychological effect during and after revolution, whereas the earlier books dealt with the psychological *causes* for revolution.

Blake is careful to tie *America* in with its predecessors. The episode of the "Preludium" restates the freeing of Orc as it was described in "Asia," and the first line of "A Prophecy," which follows, is the last line of "Africa." The poem as a whole expands and possibly makes more concrete the summary at the end of *The Song of Los*. It amplifies the vision of a freed life and of man's increase of stature in freedom.

The "Preludium" pictures Orc in his prison with the dumb female Nature (the joyous "Grave" at the end of *The Song of Los*) acting as slave to his captor: "His food she brought in iron baskets, his drink in cups of iron." Orc continues to struggle and at last "The hairy shoulders rend the links; free are the wrists of fire." Then he seizes "the panting, struggling womb" and again Nature, mute since Orc's imprisonment, is reanimated. She recognizes her salvation:

> "I know thee, I have found thee, & I will not let thee go:
> Thou art the image of God."

This event, with which the "Preludium" ends, duplicates that of joy and regeneration at the end of "Asia."

The "Prophecy" begins with the identification of reason and George III. His sullen fires, reaching across the Atlantic, torment "the souls of warlike men who rise in silent night," the heroes of the American Revolution—"Washington, Franklin, Paine & Warren, Gates, Hancock & Green"—who are meeting in a conclave of defiance. Washington warns his colleagues of increased tyranny:

> . . . "Friends of America! look over the Atlantic sea;
> A bended bow is lifted in heaven, & a heavy iron chain
> Descends, link by link, from Albion's cliffs across the sea to bind
> Brothers & sons of America till our faces pale and yellow,
> Heads deprest, voices weak, eyes downcast, hands work-bruis'd,
> Feet bleeding on the sultry sands, and the furrows of the whip
> Descend to generations that in future times forget."

England and America faint with weakness and the ocean swells between them, when suddenly Orc, freed, appears over the Atlantic, "a Wonder . . . a Human fire, fierce glowing," and terrorizes the king, who stands beside "the Stone of night." A voice that shakes the temple which houses the stone of law cries out, announcing liberation. It is a chant that draws its imagery from wide fields; first, from Biblical resurrection, representing the release from dogma:

> "The morning comes, the night decays, the watchmen leave their stations;
> The grave is burst, the spices shed, the linen wrapped up;
> The bones of death, the cov'ring clay, the sinews shrunk & dry'd
> Reviving shake, inspiring move, breathing, awakening,
> Spring like redeemed captives when their bonds & bars are burst."

Then from industry:

"Let the slave grinding at the mill run out into the field,
Let him look up into the heavens & laugh in the bright air."

Then from prisons, whose doors have burst open to free the politically oppressed at the same time that the "mind-forg'd manacles" fall off:

"Let the inchained soul, shut up in darkness and in sighing,
Whose face has never seen a smile in thirty weary years,
Rise and look out; his chains are loose, his dungeon doors are open;
And let his wife and children return from the oppressor's scourge.
They look behind at every step & believe it is a dream,
Singing: 'The Sun has left his blackness & has found a fresher morning,
And the fair Moon rejoices in the clear & cloudless night;
For Empire is no more, and now the Lion & Wolf shall cease.' "

The King hears his doom in this voice and knows that this is the end of "angels." He challenges Orc, with his antithetical character:

"Blasphemous Demon, Antichrist, hater of Dignities,
Lover of wild rebellion, and transgressor of God's Law . . ."

Orc replies and states his function:

"The times are ended; shadows pass, the morning 'gins to break;
The fiery joy, that Urizen perverted to ten commands,
What night he led the starry hosts thro' the wide wilderness,
That stony law I stamp to dust; and scatter religion abroad
To the four winds as a torn book, & none shall gather the leaves;
But they shall rot on desart sands, & consume in bottomless deeps,
To make the desarts blossom, & the deeps shrink to their fountains,
And to renew the fiery joy, and burst the stony roof;
That pale religious letchery, seeking Virginity,

May find it in a harlot, and in coarse-clad honesty
The undefil'd, tho' ravish'd in her cradle night and morn;
For everything that lives is holy, life delights in life;
Because the soul of sweet delight can never be defil'd."

In the alchemy of the millennial life, moral transmutations occur:

"Fires inwrap the earthly globe, yet man is not consum'd;
Amidst the lustful fires he walks; his feet become like brass,
His knees and thighs like silver, & his breast and head like gold."

The Angel of Albion, frightened by this lyric profusion, and weeping, warns the Angels of the Colonies, and now a somewhat more literal Lion than most of Blake's "lashes his tail!" The Colonies assemble on the infinite "Atlantean hills" to deliberate, until one of them, Boston, throws off the curb of authority and takes up the cry of Orc. Boston argues that the Revolution is in a just cause and assails the masks of tyranny:

. . . "Why trembles honesty, and like a murderer
Why seeks he refuge from the frowns of his immortal station?
Must the generous tremble & leave his joy to the idle, to the
    pestilence,
That mocks him? who commanded this? what God? what Angel?
To keep the gen'rous from experience till the ungenerous
Are unrestrain'd performers of the energies of nature;
Till Pity is become a trade, and generosity a science
That men get rich by; & the sandy desart is giv'n to the strong?
What God is he writes laws of peace & clothes him in a tempest?
What pitying Angel lusts for tears and fans himself with sighs?
What crawling villain preaches abstinence & wraps himself
In fat of lambs? no more I follow, no more obedience pay!"

The other Colonies follow Boston in a rushing flight down from their heights to inspire revolt in the patriots, Washington, Paine, and Warren. Then the English Governors convene at the house of Bernard, the Governor of Massachusetts, a notoriously avaricious man. But the flames of Orc drive them into flight, and when they tumble at the feet of Washington all the

British soldiers desert. These things happen somewhat more quickly in the spirit than they do in history.

All Americans arise:

The citizens of New York close their books & lock their chests;
The mariners of Boston drop their anchors and unlade;
The scribe of Pensylvania casts his pen upon the earth;
The builder of Virginia throws his hammer down in fear.

They hurl back England's plagues, which return upon the oppressors. Church and State ("London's Guardian, and the ancient miterd York") sicken, and official poetry ("the Bard of Albion"), with the tyrannies for which it habitually apologized, sickens. But the people feel freedom like a rush of Jacobin wind:

The doors of marriage are open, and the Priests in rustling scales
Rush into reptile coverts, hiding from the fires of Orc,
That play around the golden roofs in wreaths of fierce desire,
Leaving the females naked and glowing with the lusts of youth.

Urizen, too late, attempts to stifle the outbreak of energy by "Hiding the Demon red with clouds & cold mists from the earth." This he can manage for a short time only:

Till Angels & weak men twelve years should govern o'er the strong;
And then their end should come, when France receiv'd the Demon's light.

The kings of Europe, "Smitten with their own plagues," shudder in apprehension.

VI

THE *Visions of the Daughters of Albion* is a kind of interlude, descriptive of one aspect of life, "sexual strife," before "The doors of marriage are open"—in those years, perhaps, when Orc is still hidden in "clouds & cold mists from the earth." Middleton Murry has suggested that the poem is based on "the personal story of Mary Wollstonecraft," an implausible theory, since Mary Wollstonecraft was never involved in such a situation as Oothoon's; but the poem is a perfectly direct allegory of her doctrines.

The priests have come out of their "reptile coverts," and the enslaved Daughters of Albion know that they have, but Oothoon ("the soft soul of America"), like Mary of Blake's ballad, is an innocent, and does not know. She states the "Argument":

> I loved Theotormon,
> And I was not ashamed;
> I trembled in my virgin fears,
> And I hid in Leutha's vale!
>
> I plucked Leutha's flower,
> And I rose up from the vale;
> But the terrible thunders tore
> My virgin mantle in twain.

The poem begins with the lamentations of the Daughters drifting toward America while Oothoon wanders perilously through the vales of Leutha (puritan convention) and blithely picks the flower for which she has been searching. This is Blake's not very obscure way of saying that she yields to desire, here called Theotormon. But she is suddenly seized and ravished by Bromion, a form of Urizen, and is bewildered when he calls her his harlot and binds her to himself "back to back."

At the entrance of Bromion's cave, in which Oothoon endures her forced marriage, Theotormon sits weeping, his lament supplemented by the lamentation of other bondsmen:

> . . . beneath him sound like waves on a desart shore
> The voice of slaves beneath the sun, and children bought with money,
> That shiver in religious caves beneath the burning fires
> Of lust, that belch incessant from the summits of the earth.

Oothoon's tears are locked by sorrow but, remembering the past or expecting the future, she calls to Theotormon:

"I cry: arise, O Theotormon! for the village dog
Barks at the breaking day; the nightingale has done lamenting;
The lark does rustle in the ripe corn, and the Eagle returns
From nightly prey and lifts his golden beak to the pure east,
Shaking the dust from his immortal pinions to awake
The sun that sleeps too long."

Oothoon is bewildered by the doctrine that distinguishes between body and soul, which turns the first to a grave and the second to sick yearning, and by the rationalist dogma that impugns vision, a total perception:

"They told me that the night & day were all that I could see;
They told me that I had five senses to inclose me up,
And they inclos'd my infinite brain into a narrow circle,
And sunk my heart into the Abyss."

She develops the argument of the value of identity, and of individual impulse:

"With what sense is it that the chicken shuns the ravening
hawk?
With what sense does the tame pigeon measure out the expanse?
With what sense does the bee form cells? have not the mouse
& frog
Eyes and ears and sense of touch? yet are their habitations
And their pursuits as different as their forms and as their joys.
Ask the wild ass why he refuses burdens, and the meek camel
Why he loves man; is it because of eye, ear, mouth, or skin,
Or breathing nostrils? No, for these the wolf and tyger have."

All these questions lead to one: "How can I be defil'd when I reflect thy image pure?"

Theotormon breaks his silence in another series of questions, questions that only throw back the woolly rhetorical ball of bewilderment. He knows only that his life has vanished, and he can do little more than repeat in various guises the same question: ". . . where dwell the joys of old? & where the ancient loves?" Bromion answers for science, quoting the worn speeches of Urizen, but troubled, too. Is there warfare of intellect, sorrow of spirit, and sexual joy? These are obscure propositions to Bromion, who holds a simple and exclusive view.

"Ah! are there other wars beside the wars of sword and fire?
And are there other sorrows beside the sorrows of poverty?
And are there other joys beside the joys of riches and ease?
And is there not one law for both the lion and the ox?"

Oothoon, who hears the real voice in Bromion, expresses the familiar opposition of spontaneity and law:

"O Urizen! Creator of men! mistaken Demon of heaven! . . .
How can one joy absorb another? are not different joys
Holy, eternal, infinite? and each joy is a Love. . . .

Does he who contemns poverty and he who turns with abhorrence
From usury feel the same passion, or are they moved alike?
How can the giver of gifts experience the delights of the merchant?
How the industrious citizen the pains of the husbandman?
How different far the fat fed hireling with hollow drum,
Who buys whole corn fields into wastes, and sings upon the heath! *
How different their eye and ear! how different the world to them!

* Mr. Bronowski illuminates the two lines about the man with the drum: "The village worker on the farm and at his craft had hitherto kept some animals on the common, and had there cut his fuel. The village smallholders had farmed their land together, in strips. New ways of farming and of raising stock, and the dearth of corn, made these uses wasteful. The strips must be run together, and the common enclosed. In Blake's lifetime, parliament passed acts for more than three thousand enclosures. They would have been wise acts, had they also safeguarded those whom they dispossessed. Instead, they gave them into the hands of the large owner and large buyer. *The Deserted Village* of Oliver Goldsmith is a newly enclosed village, although it turns enclosure upside down; and Blake was following Goldsmith and Crabbe when he attacked the fat fed hireling."—Jacob Bronowski, *A Man without a Mask,* Secker and Warburg, 1944, p. 66.

With what sense does the parson claim the labour of the
farmer?
What are his nets & gins & traps; & how does he surround him
With cold floods of abstraction, and with forests of solitude,
To build him castles and high spires, where kings & priests may
dwell;
Till she who burns with youth, and knows no fixed lot, is bound
In spells of law to one she loaths? and must she drag the chain
Of life in weary lust? must chilling, murderous thoughts obscure
The clear heaven of her eternal spring; to bear the wintry rage
Of a harsh terror, driv'n to madness, bound to hold a rod
Over her shrinking shoulders all the day, & all the night
To turn the wheel of false desire, and longings that wake her
womb
To the abhorred birth of cherubs in the human form,
That live a pestilence & die a meteor, & are no more;
Till the child dwell with one he hates, and do the deed he
loaths?"

She catalogues the impulsive animals once more, pointing out that the whale does not follow a master, that the fly does not celebrate harvest festivals, and proceeds with a poeticization of the Wollstonecraft creed:

"Infancy! fearless, lustful, happy, nestling for delight
In the laps of pleasure: Innocence! honest, open, seeking
The vigorous joys of morning light; open to virgin bliss.
Who taught thee modesty, subtil modesty, child of night &
sleep?"

Her questioning lamentation is relentless; it continues when she points out in an impressive comment on sickly sexual reverie how desire is distorted:

". . . the youth shut up from
The lustful joy shall forget to generate & create an amorous
image
In the shadows of his curtains and in the folds of his silent
pillow.

Are not these the places of religion, the rewards of continence,
The self enjoyings of self denial?"

These are the distortions of Theotormon, who has yielded to Urizen's law. Oothoon upbraids the "Father of Jealousy" and defies him with her resolution:

"Oothoon shall view his dear delight, nor e'er with jealous cloud
Come in the heaven of generous love, nor selfish blightings bring."

But desire cannot free itself from the restraints of law and convention until Orc arises again and destroys the whole mold that encases life and which has so far only begun to crack. The poem ends, therefore, with the Daughters of Albion listening still to Oothoon's windy rhetoric, and echoing "back her sighs."

VII

THE NARRATIVE CONTINUES in *Europe: A Prophecy*. The action of its "Preludium" is exactly continuous with that of the "Preludium" to *America*, but it pauses, too, to make room in the whole myth for the interlude of *The Daughters*, by summarizing the psychological origins of the doctrine that "Woman's Love is Sin." But the "Preludium" is itself prefaced by a short section of whimsical verse that is charming in itself and has, as Mr. Damon first pointed out, a certain biographical interest. This preface opens with a fairy's song, which refutes Locke's evaluation of the senses. Blake captures the fairy, who offers to become his slave. "Then tell me, what is the material world, and is it dead?" Blake asks. The fairy replies:

"If you will feed me on love-thoughts & give me now and then
A cup of sparkling poetic fancies; so, when I am tipsie,
I'll sing to you to this soft lute, and shew you all alive
The world, where every particle of dust breathes forth its joy."

This fairy is a natural joy, a spontaneous expression of energy, a moment of desire immediately satisfied; such joys are described by Oothoon in the last speech of *The Daughters,* and the description provides the transition to *Europe:*

"Arise, you little glancing wings, and sing your infant joy!
Arise, and drink your bliss, for every thing that lives is holy!"

Coming in the content of *The Daughters,* these lines suggest a particular sexual emphasis, and the fact that the fairy in the new poem "sat upon the table and dictated EUROPE" supports in an almost bald fashion the speculation that Blake, leaving his wife's bed, did much of his writing late at night. Such circumstances of composition might suggest a tender lyric tone that is not at all characteristic of Blake. In the opening lines of *Europe,* however, that tone is present, and mixed with particular yearnings that the Blakes, who were childless, no doubt felt:

The deep of winter came,
What time the secret child
Descended thro' the orient gates of the eternal day:
War ceas'd, & all the troops like shadows fled to their abodes.

In these lines, reminiscent of Milton's *Nativity Ode,* Blake identifies Jesus and Orc, as earlier he had identified Jesus and Fuzon. In that earlier identification, he had dealt with the corruption of Christianity under law; and in "Africa," he had told how the message of Jesus decayed when men began to hide in "Secluded places, fearing the joys of Love."

Once more, in *Europe,* these things happen. At the birth of "the secret child," war ceases for a moment, in good omen, but begins again. In passages that amplify the psychological background of *The Daughters,* Enitharmon, the female principle, is separated from Los, the male, and the false dominion of woman, established by hypocritical arts, begins again:

". . . Who shall I send,
That Woman, lovely Woman, may have dominion? . . .
Forbid all Joy, & from her childhood shall the little female
Spread nets in every secret path."

Then again the plagues of restraint begin, and the errors of repression become the symbol for all European social corruption from the dawn of Christianity to the outbreak of the French Revolution. But this corruption, like all error, is negative, and for that reason Blake calls the whole period a dream in the sleeping consciousness of Enitharmon, the earth-mother:

> Enitharmon slept
> Eighteen hundred years. Man was a Dream!
> The night of Nature and their harps unstrung!
> She slept in middle of her nightly song
> Eighteen hundred years, a female dream.

A rapid summary of the action of *America* follows. Then Blake's familiar theme of the return of oppression upon tyranny itself, and the extension of oppression, appears again; then an account of reason's calculating code of charity "That Kings & Priests had copied on Earth." The theme of religious tyranny follows, and again, in the imagery of the prison, that of woman's dominion:

> Enitharmon laugh'd in her sleep to see (O woman's triumph!)
> Every house a den, every man bound: the shadows are fill'd
> With spectres, and the windows wove over with curses of iron:
> Over the doors "Thou shalt not," & over the chimneys "Fear"
> is written:
> With bands of iron round their necks fasten'd into the walls
> The citizens, in leaden gyves the inhabitants of suburbs
> Walk heavy; soft and bent are the bones of villagers.

But the flames of Orc, who is howling in captivity, are lapping at the Angel of Albion, and presently Newton, the limit of error, "siez'd the trump & blow'd the enormous blast!" Enitharmon, who awakens, does not know that she has been asleep, and goes on with the song that celebrates her triumph. There is a momentary return to the situation of *The Daughters:*

> "I hear the soft Oothoon in Enitharmon's tents;
> Why wilt thou give up woman's secrecy, my melancholy child?"

In her foolish confidence, Enitharmon summons and welcomes even Orc, "son of my afflictions," and he bursts forth at once:

. . . terrible Orc, when he beheld the morning in the east,
Shot from the heights of Enitharmon,
And in the vineyards of red France appear'd the light of his
fury.

The dominion of convention is at an end. Los, the poet-warrior, asserts himself:

> And with a cry that shook all nature to the utmost pole,
> Call'd all his sons to the strife of blood.

These lines, with which the poem closes, refer to poetry in general and to Blake's prophetic poetry in particular. Among his characters, he identified himself most frequently with Los, and he charged poetry, as a function of the imagination, with the love and praise of liberty.

VIII

THE MYTH COMES at last to the French Revolution, and for the first time Blake's imagination directly confronts the millennial event itself. Whether, in the terms he intended to employ, his imagination was staggered by the difficulties of the task, or whether it seemed the better part of wisdom to abandon it, or whether he in fact finished the poem and the greater part of it was lost through his carelessness or the negligence or circumspection of his publisher, Joseph Johnson, we cannot know. One book of the projected seven is preserved

Like *America, The French Revolution* is rooted in history, and it is nearly as free in its treatment. Blake's interest was in the psychic value of events rather than in events themselves, and even in this relatively early poem, whose characters are the real figures of history rather than the giant motives he devised a year or two later, it is these values that he pressed. It is possible that Blake intended to end his series with some other poem on this subject. But for some reason, perhaps the obvious one that by 1795 the history of the Revolution had distorted the motives for which it had once been such a favorite symbol, this other poem does not exist, and in its absence we must use the early *French Revolution* as the end of the myth. The justification for this procedure is that the whole series is clearly directed to that conclusion in eighteenth-century history. Without these effects, the carefully developed causes of the series and the movement of the whole lose their meaning.

In the Book the First of *The French Revolution,* Blake compresses the events of two months in the summer of 1789 into one day. That day opens on an ailing world, old systems brooding over Europe, and the King of France sick with self-corruptive tyranny:

The dead brood over Europe, the cloud and vision descends over chearful France;
O cloud well appointed! Sick, sick, the Prince on his couch, wreath'd in dim
And appalling mist, his strong hand outstretch'd, from his shoulder down the bone
Runs aching cold into the scepter, too heavy for mortal grasp, no more
To be swayed by visible hand, nor in cruelty bruise the mild flourishing mountains.

Nature faints under man-made encumbrances, the mountains are sick and the vineyards weeping. Such hope as remains rests in Necker, who brings the King into the council chamber to convene with the nobles, "Forty men, each conversing with woes in the infinite shadows of his soul." In another place, the National Assembly is gathered:

For the Commons convene in the Hall of the Nation. France shakes! And the heavens of France
Perplex'd vibrate round each careful countenance! Darkness of old times around them
Utters loud despair, shadowing Paris; her grey towers groan, and the Bastile trembles.
In its terrible towers the Governor stood, in dark fogs list'ning the horror.

In the prison are languishing human samples of the seven types that are the particular subjects of oppression. Blake's analysis of psychological states is more direct here than usual, but the relative clarity of his symbols has the advantage of showing us how exactly he defined the horrors that social institutions can work in the mind and the heart, and the extent to which he deemed them important in his estimate of the total human scene. The device he employs for this purpose is not unlike Dante's in his drama of the great forms of sin; for as the inhabitants of the *Inferno* are tormented by symbols of their crimes, so the oppressed in Blake's Bastille develop qualities that are representative of the oppression itself. The first of the seven prisoners is the poet whose inspiration has been corrupted by officialdom:

> . . . the den nam'd Horror held a man
> Chain'd hand and foot, round his neck an iron band, bound to the impregnable wall.
> In his soul was the serpent coil'd round in his heart, hid from the light, as in a cleft rock:
> And the man was confin'd for a writing prophetic.

In the tower of Darkness is an aristocrat whose natural virtue has been masked in iron and whose stature has shrunk:

> Pinion'd down to the stone floor, his strong bones scarce cover'd with sinews; the iron rings
> Were forg'd smaller as the flesh decay'd, a mask of iron on his face hid the lineaments
> Of ancient Kings, and the frown of the eternal lion was hid from the oppressed earth.

In the tower named Bloody is the radical dissenter, "a skeleton yellow . . . once a man who refus'd to sign papers of abhorrence." In the next tower is the victim of Religion, the diseased modern female, whose love convention regards as sin, "a loathsome sick woman" who "refus'd to be whore to the Minister, and with a knife smote him." In the tower of Order lies the venerable victim of censorship, breeder of poisons:

. . . his den was short
And narrow as a grave dug for a child, with spiders' webs wove, and with slime
Of ancient horrors cover'd, for snakes and scorpions are his companions; harmless they breathe
His sorrowful breath: he, by conscience urg'd, in the city of Paris rais'd a pulpit,
And taught wonders to darken'd souls.

In the tower of Destiny is the "friend to the favourite," the sycophant:

His feet and hands cut off, and his eyes blinded; round his middle a chain and a band
Fasten'd into the wall; fancy gave him to see an image of despair in his den,
Eternally rushing round, like a man on his hands and knees, day and night without rest.

In the last tower is a madman, the political radical, the true patriot whose unrewarded hopes have turned to a frenzy:

. . . In the seventh tower, named the tower of God, was a man
Mad, with chains loose, which he dragg'd up and down; fed with hopes year by year, he pined
For liberty; vain hopes! his reason decay'd, and the world of attraction in his bosom
Center'd, and the rushing of chaos overwhelm'd his dark soul. He was confin'd
For a letter of advice to a King, and his ravings in winds are heard over Versailles.

This is a translation into symbols, almost item by item, of the revolutionary catalogue of social abuse; Blake could not have been more comprehensive.

The prisoners know that their freedom is at hand. They "assay to shout; they listen, Then laugh in the dismal den" as "the triple forg'd fetters of times" are unloosed. The King knows, too, with the knowledge of Tiriel. The meeting of the Commons disturbs him, and he addresses his Nobles in terror:

"The nerves of five thousand years' ancestry tremble, shaking the heavens of France;
Throbs of anguish beat on brazen war foreheads, they descend and look into their graves.
I see thro' darkness, thro' clouds rolling round me, the spirits of ancient Kings
Shivering over their bleached bones; round them their counsellors look up from the dust,
Crying: 'Hide from the living! Our bonds and our prisoners shout in the open field,
Hide in the nether earth! Hide in the bones! Sit obscured in the hollow scull!
Our flesh is corrupted, and we wear away. We are not numbered among the living. Let us hide
In stones, among roots of trees. The prisoners have burst their dens.
Let us hide; let us hide in the dust; and plague and wrath and tempest shall cease.' "

Burgundy, the color of blood and the spirit of war, is not discouraged. He urges the use of force to support order and protect the sacred law:

"Shall this marble built heaven become a clay cottage, this earth an oak stool, and these mowers
From the Atlantic mountains mow down all this great starry harvest of six thousand years? . . .
And the ancient forests of chivalry hewn, and the joys of the combat burnt for fuel;
Till the power and dominion is rent from the pole, sword and scepter from sun and moon,
The law and gospel from fire and air, and eternal reason and science
From the deep and the solid, and man lay his faded head down on the rock
Of eternity, where the eternal lion and eagle remain to devour?"

Burgundy's lyric belligerence encourages the weak King, who dismisses Necker, the friend of the people, and calls for war.

The Archbishop of Paris, state religion at its most corrupt, who knows that his Church will fall with the throne, gives his blessing to war. He recounts a vision of "An aged form, white as snow, hov'ring in mist, weeping in the uncertain light"—the prefiguration of Urizen—who, "sighing in a low voice like the voice of the grasshopper," tells him his doom if revolution proceeds:

"They shall drop at the plow and faint at the harrow, unredeem'd, unconfess'd, unpardon'd;
The priest rot in his surplice by the lawless lover, the holy beside the accursed,
The King, frowning in purple, beside the grey plowman, and their worms embrace together."

The recommendation of Paris is forthright:

"Let thy soldiers possess this city of rebels . . . let the Bastille devour
These rebellious seditious; seal them up, O Anointed, in everlasting chains."

At this point in the Miltonic debate, Orleans, "generous as mountains," challenges Burgundy and Paris. At last the rhetoric catches fire, and Orleans utters the finest speech in the poem and one of the touchstones in Blake's poetry as a whole:

". . . O princes of fire, whose flames are for growth, not consuming,
Fear not dreams, fear not visions, nor be you dismay'd with sorrows which flee at the morning!
Can the fires of Nobility ever be quench'd, or the stars by a stormy night?
Is the body diseas'd when the members are healthful? can the man be bound in sorrow
Whose ev'ry function is fill'd with its fiery desire? can the soul whose brain and heart
Cast their rivers in equal tides thro' the great Paradise, languish because the feet,

Hands, head, bosom, and parts of love follow their high breathing joy?
And can Nobles be bound when the people are free, or God weep when his children are happy? . . .
But go, merciless man! enter into the infinite labyrinth of another's brain
Ere thou measure the circle that he shall run. Go, thou cold recluse, into the fires
Of another's high flaming rich bosom, and return unconsum'd, and write laws.
If thou canst not do this, doubt thy theories; learn to consider all men as thy equals,
Thy brethren, and not as thy foot or thy hand, unless thou first fearest to hurt them."

That nobility is a matter of character and that character is corrupted by chains is a proposition that Blake has already illustrated in his seven prisoners, but for the first and nearly the only time, he has allowed the proposition to push him into a statement almost as flat as any pamphleteer's: "Learn to consider all men as thy equals." Yet this is to remove the statement from the context of the passage and of Blake's development, wherein equality is based on the single universal, energy, and its multiple expressions, and the recognition of equality is an act of the imagination, of sympathetic identification of one individuality with another: ". . . go, merciless man! enter into the infinite labyrinth of another's brain Ere thou measure the circle that he shall run." And, "Go, thou cold recluse, into the fires."

Next, "the Nation's Ambassador," the representative of the people, enters the council. He begins his exhortations with a brief summary of past mythical action:

"The millions of spirits immortal were bound in the ruins of sulphur, heaven
To wander enslav'd; black, deprest in dark ignorance, kept in awe with the whip
To worship terrors, bred from the blood of revenge and breath of desire

In bestial forms, or more terrible men; till the dawn of our peaceful morning,
Till dawn, till morning, till the breaking of clouds."

The thought of the regenerative event that is at hand involves Blake in a catalogue of the encumbrances that it will destroy, the familiar grouping of monarchy and wars, priestcraft, and the oppression of classes, until "The mild peaceable nations" are "opened to heav'n, and men walk with their fathers in bliss." This speech concludes with a plea that the army be removed from the city. The King, speaking in the voice of Burgundy, refuses. His refusal is taken to the National Assembly, which votes that the army be forced to remove ten miles from Paris. Lafayette, guarded by the shades of Rousseau and Voltaire, issues the command. The army moves, and the King and the nobles are struck dumb and motionless with terror. Regeneration begins promptly:

. . . shaken the forests of France, sick the kings of the nations,
And the bottoms of the world were open'd, and the graves of arch-angels unseal'd:
The enormous dead lift up their pale fires and look over the rocky cliffs.

In the sky, morning breaks.

And the poem breaks off. The remaining six books, Johnson announced in his Advertisement, were "finished," and were to "be published in their Order." That they were not printed is certainly no great loss to poetry and no serious hindrance to our seeing the picture of Blake's work whole. One could not find a poem of greater "republican fervour," and one needs no further guide to the mode by which Blake expressed this fervor at its most republican. The intellectual essence here is as near as possible to the essence of Shelley's poems:

See a disenchanted nation
Springs like day from desolation;
To Truth its state is dedicate,
And Freedom leads it forth, her mate.

But the poetic essence is in sharp contrast. Shelley remained comfortable with the abstractions of political theory. "Truth" and "Freedom" even become characters in the drama. For these Blake's drama found no place, and for the conflict of mind and of political interest, he felt it necessary to devise new characters of his own when history did not provide them. That this invention had in some ways melancholy results is patent; but it had happier results as well. Blake's characters operate, if not as a wholly satisfactory means to poetic ends, as a reasonably exact mode of psychological analysis, and are therefore objective enough to prevent any merely personal reverie. Shelley's ideal world is a kind of sickened lyric fantasy that blurs the distinction between real and ideal and provides the poet's imagination with a means to feverish languishment. Blake's ideal world, founded on a more strenuous analysis of mind, is an imaginative reference that served not for the projection of neurotic rationalizations but for the statement of social ends that their more literal statement seemed to him actually to deny.

The distinction is perhaps most clear in the attitudes of the two poets toward love, which both thought must be "free." Shelley, who declared that he could "give not what men call love," offered instead:

> The desire of the moth for the star,
>   Of the night for the morrow.

This we may call Platonic love if the term pleases us, but, unlike Plato's love as usually understood, it leaps to a second love without reference to a first. Intellectual beauty was a private rationalization. In Blake, most of the rhetorical agony is to rescue physical love from the elements that retard it, and it is assumed that sexual love is a part, indeed the first part, of love of any kind at all, including brotherly love and divine love. Today this may be said somewhat more simply. If one is incapable of the most rudimentary love relationship, one can hardly be expected to achieve its more elaborate social forms without the distorting force of compensation. Blake stands squarely between Shelley and Lawrence, the first having dedicated himself to his own watered variety of Platonics, the second, to a blank naturalism. If Lawrence, so late as 1930, spent his talent in defending one against the other, it is not surprising that a hundred years earlier Blake became breathless when he declared that they were one and the same.

He tried to overcome the idea that it was desirable to separate one human faculty from another or necessary to abstract anything from its function. Because this intention sought for sources beneath politics, Blake's basic assumptions became deeper and his anarchism wider than those of his contemporaries. The function and the motive of reason, he insisted, were abstraction. Abstraction destroys individuality for the sake of generalization. In generalization lies law, which is the statement of ethical categories, the creation of evil.

All the radicals condemned many of the expressions of contemporary law; Godwin and Blake condemned law itself. Moral law is the basis of all legal expression. In the early books of his myth, Blake's Urizen promulgates the moral law. When he sees that it is impossible for man to obey it, he gives it other forms. As religion, it operates by superstition, which can enforce many restraints; and all religion, even Christianity, which was founded on a revolutionary faith in the integrity of the individual, becomes externalized and formalizes itself in law. Corruption is complete when religion, joining with government, seeks Establishment; then it helps to enforce a second kind of law, the political, which maintains itself by tyranny. "Asia" presents religious corruption and tyranny; "Africa," political corruption and tyranny. Political tyranny makes use of other tools than religion. It suppresses inquiry, destroys prophecy and poetry, reads its lesson out of three cold and inhuman codes: the idea of charity, the necessity of force, and the convenience of economic inequality. The various forms of restraint Blake expresses in appropriate varieties of imagery, but under them all, and dominating them all, is the imagery of sexual restraint, because he has chosen to present sex as the mainspring of all energy.

These early portions of the myth, which were the last to be written, express an avowal of anarchism; but *America, The Daughters, Europe,* and the fragment of *The French Revolution,* the last parts of the myth and the earliest to be written, express a relatively literal avowal of republicanism. As Blake pushes Godwin's ideas out of their rationalistic frame in the first group, so in the second group he pushes Paine's into a genuinely poetic principle, a principle not of politics alone but of life at large. Revolution, identified with imagination, becomes a constant principle of life; even when it is suppressed for ages, as Orc is, it lives, and must express itself. It can do so as the imaginative act of entering the labyrinth of another's bosom, or as the bloody act of force. Whatever the forms of its expression, Blake believed them necessary, inevitable, and just.

Any logical difficulty in Blake's symbolism is inherent in his curiously mixed tradition of religion and politics. The apocalyptic imagery that he found so useful to the resolutions of these poems—those "rattling bones to bones" joining, "The enormous dead" that "look over the rocky cliffs," and the constant background of a convulsive universe—suggest on the one hand the abrupt revolutionary achievement, but on the other they carry their older Biblical overtones, of a "world-judgment motif," which suggests the end of earthly things. Blake conjoins the faith of Thomas Paine in a social upheaval that would improve life in all its aspects with the medieval "illusion of finality," which would have ushered in that new "century" of the chiliasts, ancient and modern.

Both these possibilities are opposed to still a third that appears in Blake, the idea of progress as conceived by Godwin and many others, in which improvement is a gradual rather than a revolutionary event, and by which man is developed into a higher civilized condition rather than unraveled back to his natural condition. All three possibilities are confused in Blake by a fourth element, the regeneration of the individual in himself alone, either quickly or slowly. This is a difficulty that results from Blake's disinclination to separate the events of an individual life from those of its society and of the cosmos. And this difficulty presents yet one more. Is the development, in the individual life or in the social, sometimes conceived in the ancient terms of static cycles endlessly turning, and sometimes in the later sense of simple progress, and sometimes in the more modern sense of progressive cycles operating on the dialectical principle?

These are questions designed to raise logical difficulties that clearly did not exist in Blake's conscious mind, any more than they did in the minds of most of his contemporaries, but his "system," actually, seems to have been a device intended to overcome them. This suggests that they were problems which he sensed in his buried intuitional life, and which he attempted to shove aside if not quite resolve by an imaginative act. Yet the very elaboration of this act suggests that the difficulties were real in a way that Blake would not recognize. He could write it all out briefly and cryptically, as in the lyric "Morning" of 1800:

> To find the Western path
> Right thro' the Gates of Wrath
> I urge my way;
> Sweet Mercy leads me on:
> With soft repentant moan
> I see the break of day.
>
> The war of swords & spears
> Melted by dewy tears
> Exhales on high;
> The Sun is freed from fears
> And with soft grateful tears
> Ascends the sky.

But the very succinctness of statement in this poem would defeat the ends of the poem if it did not have as background Blake's own elaboration of his symbols, if, that is, the reader did not already know that the West, which is the direction of America, is synonymous with liberty; that Wrath is revolution; that Mercy is Jesus; that the repentant moan is the triumph of the imagination over selfishness; that physical conflict, war, then gives way to the rising Sun, which is poetry and art freed from corruption, and, in a larger sense, that "mental fight" which entertains Eternals.

These are among the central symbols that Blake's longer prophecies, like his shorter ones, amplify. In that amplification, rhetoric always threatens to drown out the poet's feeling and even his idea, with the result that in these poems there is a good deal of sound and fury, perhaps mainly that. Yet it is sound and fury signifying something. The significance is not only of a particular set of fresh ideas, or values, not only of an extraordinarily thorough regard for human liberty, but most poignantly, in the expression itself, of the instructive tragedy that overwhelmed a poet.

CHAPTER NINE

"I Must Create a System"

I

BLAKE HAD BECOME a curious figure engaged in a frantic struggle—a poet wrestling with his own monstrous poetic creation. Now he could not let the system go, nor the system, him; as a poet he was mercilessly caught in it. He is like Los in his rage and agony, and he is like him in that the binding of Urizen involves a "fall" for the poet too, but he is not quite like him in mastering the materials to be bound. For that, one finds a more eloquent representation in the picture "Binding of the Dragon," which suggests that at any moment the toils of the monster will lash round the angel, and that the chains which already encumber one of his arms may presently bind him helplessly to the beast itself. Blake's Prophecies are symbolic acts in many more ways than one; that is perhaps their chief interest.

In 1795 the system had not yet been closed, but was left in the unraveled state of *The French Revolution,* with which the narrative ended but in which the prophetic process had begun. In 1795 Blake started again from the beginning in the poem that he first called *Vala, or The Death and Judgement of the Ancient Man: A Dream of Nine Nights,* a title that by 1804, when he abandoned this work, had been changed to *The Four Zoas: The Torments of Love & Jealousy in the Death and Judgement of Albion, The Ancient Man.* In this poem, he completed the system, but at the expense of the poem, which he never finally finished; yet it solved the structural problem with which he had been wrestling as nearly as it could be solved.

The history of Blake's prophetic writings to this point is as follows: Discounting *The Book of Thel* and *Tiriel,* early experiments in method, and expansions of *Songs of Innocence* and *Songs of Experience* that really lie outside the central narrative content, one finds Blake beginning with the symbolic treatment of historical events—the French and American revolutions. But immediately he institutes his search for a method that will amplify these events and set them in a framework of psychological motive. Thus begin the experiments in cosmogonal metaphor, *The Song of Los* and *The Book of Urizen,* and works like *Europe* and the *Visions of the Daughters of Albion,* which are intermediary between these and those which recount history with relative literalness. The difficulty presented by this progress was that in dramatizing the psychological background, Blake was forced to abandon the social foreground. In separating the cosmogonal and the historical material, he gave an awkwardly equal narrative value as characters to the faculties and to men in history of whom they are only the parts. The result was that the regeneration of both men and their eternal powers failed to be accomplished. And the visionary temperament had likewise failed, thus far, to make its adjustment with the social insights that it was determined to express.

In *The Four Zoas,* Blake makes this adjustment. Here he organizes his powers more scrupulously, and he attributes them not to men in general, but to another psychological creature. Albion, the Ancient Man, has his own historical and political values, of course, but in him the explicit historical equivalents of the psychological drama are greatly diminished. Blake unifies his central framework of allegory, and the events of his poems are made to enact themselves within that framework alone. The considerable proliferation of characters and the extension of the whole mythological apparatus that result bring with them new strains on the poetry and additional difficulties in understanding it; but they do not diminish the intensity of Blake's observation, nor the role of contemporary allusion in imagery and attitude and tone. If we can accept Blake's poetic course at all, we should see that in *The Four Zoas* he has overcome a structural confusion in no merely mechanical sense, but has resolved his personal conflict in a mytho-dramatic framework that is itself expressive of the burden of his ideas.

The Four Zoas is a transitional poem in which Blake developed and expanded his earlier ideas through an elaboration and a deepening of that psychology of revolution with which he had been dealing almost from the first. Inevitably it was accompanied by a shift of emphasis from the earlier insistence on breaking the mold of social convention to a more anarchistic insistence than ever on breaking the selfish human heart. If the world is to be free, men as individuals must free themselves. This was the revision, along lines already laid down, of a simple political attitude that had presumably come to seem too barren to account for the observable and infinite complexities of human nature. Yet as Blake's chosen epigraph from Ephesians testifies, he was perfectly aware that here as before he was concerned with what he believed were the sources of misery in the world, dominion and authority. "For our contention is not with the blood and the flesh, but with dominion, with authority, with the blind world-rulers of this life, with the spirit of evil in things heavenly." Things heavenly are comprised of the spirit of man, which Blake continually showed was capable of conditions both of degradation and of triumph. *The Four Zoas* is an elaborate poetic diagram that charts the course of these conditions.

The symbolic device that Blake employs is again the Biblical "fall," and the character subject to this fall is that Grand Man derived from his esoteric reading. Albion, the universal giant, like every individual contained in his limbs, has four qualities, and these are Blake's Zoas. They derive, in the first place, from the "four living creatures" of Ezekiel ("They had the likeness of a man") and of Revelation. All these powers had been implied in Blake's writing before 1795, but not all of them had been differentiated or been given names. Now they are: Urizen, Luvah, Tharmas, and Urthona—reason, passion, body or sense, and spirit. Mr. Damon suggested that they have a certain analogy with the four occult "elements" of Paracelsus, which is possible, but a more interesting suggestion is that of Kerrison Preston, who proposes that they duplicate, in effect, "Jung's four basic functions of psychic activity, Thinking, Feeling, Sensation, and Intuition."

Mr. Preston suggests a further connection, that with Blake's "fourfold vision," and this is a connection of genuine importance. "Single vision belongs to Urizen, who sees primarily the material form . . . Luvah adds the emotions of the heart . . . giving an added meaning to form, which is the double vision of the artist. . . . Tharmas contributes the universality of the senses, touch, taste, all earthly and bodily feeling, the enriching orchestration of harmonious sex, which Blake calls Beulah and the threefold vision. . . . All this is raised to fourfold vision by Urthona, the prophetic imagination, transporting the beholder beyond Beulah to the very garden of Eden, which is still on Earth but where the pure in heart shall see God." The significant fact is one that Mr. Preston does not push on to, even though he connects the Zoas with the Jungian psychology of integration; that fact is that the value of the visionary experience increases as it becomes more and more full, as more of the faculties are called into an integral operation, until, "in my supreme delight," the four work together as one. This is the whole man, perceiving a total experience.

The concept of integration Blake himself underscores at once. He states his theme:

> Four Mighty Ones are in every Man; a Perfect Unity
> Cannot Exist but from the Universal Brotherhood of Eden,
> The Universal Man, To Whom be Glory Evermore. Amen.

These lines are accompanied by a marginal reference to John 17:21-23, verses which read: "That they may all be one; even as thou, Father, art in me, and I in thee, that they also may be in us: That the world may believe that thou didst send me. And the glory which thou hast given me I have given unto them; that they may be one, even as we are one; I in them, and thou in me, that they may be perfected into one; that the world may know that thou didst send me, and lovedst them, even as thou lovedst me." In Blake's context, the quotation has a double force: that "they," the Zoas, may operate harmoniously within men, who thus achieve the godlike condition; and that "they," the men in the world for whom Jesus is praying, may be as one among themselves, in "the Universal Brotherhood." A democracy of the faculties, the achievement of "identity," precedes and makes possible the brotherhood of men and of nations.

This is the theme of *The Four Zoas* and of Blake's remaining poems; it is likewise the means by which he finally welded into one his personal, or imaginative, and his social, or intellectual, necessities. The man of vision becomes, at last, the best man. It is not uncommon among poets to draw the social image in terms of purely personal impulsions, and in the nineteenth century and our own, when society itself has failed to provide a remotely satisfactory image, this procedure has become the great commonplace of literary history, as it has also become the source of so much wasted poetic energy and the scene of so many ruined monuments of poets. Blake was among the first, if he was not actually the first, to be confronted with this conflict, and he remains one of the very few poets who resolved the conflict in terms that, if by no means wholly applicable to the social man, yet favor and treasure him.

Near him if not like him in this was Whitman, whose personal impulses and social instincts were in some ways quite like Blake's own. Whitman too declared the equality of body and soul, yet even in his most visionary moments, it was an equality rather than an integration:

I believe in you my soul, the other I am must not abase itself
  to you,
And you must not be abased to the other.

Because of this rather simple psychological analysis, which ordinarily contented him, Whitman was free to direct his observation to the objects of the external world with stricter concentration than Blake, and to express humanitarian attitudes at once more obvious and less adequate, attractive as they may be to Americans who aspire still to realize even their limited demands. Blake, more concerned with *oneness* of personality than with a simple equality of its parts, recognized the enormous variety of ways in which personality could split asunder. Therefore he began with a fourfold man, and each of these four parts has a "place," and each part splits in two, and some have "sons" and some, "daughters," and the "sons" in turn may split. Yet the welter of Blake's Zoas, with their emanations and specters, and their confusing alternations of dominance and slavery, are really the expression of a complex analysis of human nature, cognizant of the multiple potentialities of human failure and of the difficulty of overcoming it even briefly. And the very complexity of Blake's analysis of man's interiors tended to turn his observation away from the objects of the external world, and to state social attitudes not capable of a broad fulfillment but, at least to our chastened generation, adequately complex for the complexity of the social situation itself.

II

BLAKE'S POEM is divided into nine parts, called "Nights" in imitation of Young's *The Complaint: or, Night Thoughts;* but in place of Young's melancholy, which flourished in a nocturnal atmosphere, Blake wishes to suggest the visionary state, even in its most habitual form of dreams, a meaning that his first title expressed. A line from the opening of Young's poem adequately describes the creative impulse behind Blake's:

> I wake, emerging from a sea of dreams
> Tumultous.

But that Blake's "dreams" were actually very different from the sort that Young had in mind—

> . . . where my wreck'd, desponding thought
> From wave to wave of *fancied* misery,
> At random drove, her helm of reason lost—

only the unsympathetic would deny. Blake's nine "dreams" are the already familiar diagram. One power revolts, then falls and divides; the others, inevitably implicated, fall and divide; man disintegrates; he wars against himself; the errors of authority grow like forests; the nadir of error is reached; then, in revolution, authority is cast off and the ascent begins; Albion is regenerate, and the new innocence has been wrested from experience.

"Night the First" begins after the fall has already taken place, for as we have seen, only then does separate consciousness exist. It opens amid the confusion of this separateness, with the familiar lament of the earth-mother, called Enion, since she has been separated from Tharmas, the body and its senses, the state of animal innocence. Enion tells what has happened:

"All Love is lost: Terror succeeds, & Hatred instead of Love,
And stern demands of Right & Duty instead of Liberty."

Blake's definition of liberty, the free expression of energy, involves no recognition of either rights or duties (the Rousseau-Burke, and for that matter the Paine-Godwin opposition), both of which imply restriction. With the creation of these concepts come fear and hatred, and for these Enion is herself partly responsible. In the fall of Tharmas, she denied the impulse by which she exists, the generative instinct. This denial is the creation of sin:

"I have look'd into the secret soul of him I lov'd,
And in the Dark recesses found Sin & cannot return."

Tharmas, pleading with her, states the old problem of spontaneity versus restraint, act versus analysis, love versus logic:

"Why wilt thou Examine every little fibre of my soul,
Spreading them out before the sun like stalks of flax to dry?
The infant joy is beautiful, but its anatomy
Horrible, Ghast & Deadly; nought shalt thou find in it
But Death, Despair & Everlasting brooding Melancholy."

Then the degraded senses create as much of earth as they can perceive, and in this "world of Tharmas" wander the fallen and divided forms of Urthona, Los and Enitharmon—time and space, male and female, poetry and its inspiration. They are already subject to the evils of sex division and restraint:

She drave the Females all away from Los,
And Los drave the Males from her away.

Los sees the sad state of the fallen man, and knows his error and the remedy:

"Refusing to behold the Divine Image which all behold
And live thereby, he is sunk down into a deadly sleep.
But we, immortal in our strength, survive by stern debate
Till we have drawn the Lamb of God into a mortal form.
And that he must be born is certain, for One must be All
And comprehend within himself all things both small & great."

But Enitharmon, beset with fear, denies this vision and rejects what Blake calls the "Human" for the sake of restraint. She appeals to Urizen and flees from the poetic power of Los:

"Descend, O Urizen, descend with horse & chariot!
Threaten not me, O visionary; thine the punishment.
The Human Nature shall no more remain, nor Human acts
Form the rebellious Spirits of Heaven, but War & Princedom,
& Victory & Blood."

Albion, "The Wandering Man," bows his "faint head" as Urizen, the restrainer, descends, announcing: "Lo I am God, the terrible destroyer, & not the Saviour." Los has already challenged him, and his wedding song describes the revolutionary strife that is to sunder men and the parts of men. Enion, in the following and complementary chorus, laments the cruelties of nature, the ruthless logic of animal survival, in the imagery of suffering birds, the cruelties of winter, "leafless bush or frozen stone," snowy wastes and "hungry wilds & sandy desarts." The answer to Enion's questions is contained in the close of "Night the First," where, at a counsel of Eternals, the previous action is reviewed, and the original revolt of Urizen is described. He attempted conspiracy with Luvah, who would not join him. Jesus, divine imagination, who is associated with Luvah as he is with Los, knows that he too will have to descend to reassemble man's scattered and conflicting parts.

"Night the Second" deals largely with the triumph of reason that follows upon Enitharmon's call to Urizen. It opens with the fallen man, "Turning his Eyes outward to Self, losing the Divine Vision," giving his power to Urizen, who thereupon builds his world. This world Blake describes again in the imagery of science and of industry, which, like his century, he associated with rationalism:

Some fix'd the anvil, some the loom erected, some the plow
And harrow form'd & fram'd the harness of silver & ivory,
The golden compasses, the quadrant, & the rule & balance.
They erected the furnaces, they form'd the anvils of gold beaten
  in mills
Where winter beats incessant, fixing them firm on their base.
The bellows began to blow, & the Lions of Urizen stood round
  the anvil. . . .
Rattling, the adamantine chains & hooks heave up the ore,
In mountainous masses plung'd in furnaces.

In the course of the externalization that this building represents, "Jerusalem came down in a dire ruin over all the Earth." Jerusalem, who is Albion's emanation, is Blake's symbol for liberty, the complete freedom that exists in love alone. With the fall of Jerusalem, men "behold What is within now seen without; they are raw to the hungry wind." All evils are involved. Once men lose the vision of harmony, the "divine image," justice is perverted, the sexes divide against each other and each is corrupted, and science and commerce spring up to express the division.

"What! are we terrors to one another? Come, O brethren, where-
  fore
Was this wide Earth spread all abroad? not for wild beasts to
  roam."
But many stood silent, & busied in their families.
And many said, "We see no Visions in the darksom air.
Measure the course of that sulphur orb that lights the darksom
  day;
Set stations on this breeding Earth & let us buy & sell."
Others arose & schools erected, forming Instruments
To measure out the course of heaven. Stern Urizen beheld
In woe his brethren & his sons.

Justice rent from the weak heart, impoverished love, is erected on a foundation of false rationalism; it is "fixed," that is, in legal concepts that are without love.

. . . the Sons of Urizen
With compasses divide the deep; they the strong scales erect
That Luvah rent from the faint Heart of the Fallen Man,
And weigh the massy Cubes, then fix them in their awful stations.

Urizen, "the Architect divine," builds his palace through earth and sky, but it is a joyless labor, for like Los he has been separated from his generous portion, Ahania, or pleasure. "Two wills they had, two intellects, & not as in times of old." The labors of Vala, who is nature, in the realm of Urizen are also joyless; she slaves like a woman in a factory, "mourning among the Brick kilns, compell'd To labour night & day among the fires," and as she works she protests against the misery of human slavery:

". . . We are made to turn the wheel for water,
To carry the heavy basket on our scorched shoulders, to sift
The sand & ashes, & to mix the clay with tears & repentance. . . .
Our beauty is cover'd over with clay & ashes, & our backs
Furrow'd with whips, & our flesh bruised with the heavy basket."

Through this travail, which exhausts the spirit of nature in the "year of dearth," "the Mundane shell," the mechanical universe of rationalism, is constructed.

In right lined paths outmeasur'd by proportions of number, weight,
And measure, mathematic motion wondrous along the deep . . .
In intricate ways, biquadrate, Trapeziums, Rhombs, Rhomboids,
Paralellograms triple & quadruple, polygonic
In their amazing hard subdu'd course in the vast deep.

The immediate effects of this universe are felt by Los and Enitharmon, who in their division suffer the Blakean agonies of sexual strife. This may also be read as meaning that under the strictures of science, the poet is no longer at one with his inspiration. Enitharmon, deserting the intuitional life that is truly hers, takes the form of earth or of pleasure at will, both inadequate sources of inspiration, and the poet languishes.

Enion has suffered no less a fall. "I have planted a false oath in the earth; it has brought forth a poison tree," she admits, and then, in the most sustained lamentation in the poem, one that apparently takes its start from the twenty-eighth chapter of Job ("Yea, the price of wisdom is above rubies") but which develops the typical Blakean imagery of human misery, she protests against experience:

"What is the price of Experience? do men buy it for a song?
Or wisdom for a dance in the street? No, it is bought with the price
Of all that a man hath, his house, his wife, his children.
Wisdom is sold in the desolate market where none come to buy,
And in the wither'd field where the farmer plows for bread in vain. . . .

It is an easy thing to laugh at wrathful elements,
To hear the dog howl at the wintry door, the ox in the slaughter house moan;
To see a god on every wind & a blessing on every blast;
To hear sounds of love in the thunder storm that destroys our enemies' house;
To rejoice in the blight that covers his field, & the sickness that cuts off his children,
While our olive & vine sing & laugh round our door, & our children bring fruit & flowers.

Then the groan & the dolor are quite forgotten, & the slave grinding at the mill,
And the captive in chains, & the poor in the prison, & the soldier in the field
When the shatter'd bone hath laid him groaning among the happier dead.

It is an easy thing to rejoice in the tents of prosperity:
Thus could I sing & thus rejoice: but it is not so with me."

Ahania, hearing Enion's lament, is doomed: "And never from that moment could she rest upon her pillow." She tries, as "Night the Third" begins, to make the best of her life with Urizen, and begs him to enjoy his creation. "Why wilt thou look upon futurity, dark'ning present joy?" His reply is that he foresees the birth of Orc and knows that ultimately he will have to serve him:

"I am set here a King of trouble, commanded here to serve . . .
All this is mine, yet I must serve, & that Prophetic boy
Must grow up to command his Prince."

Ahania remembers the eternal past, "those sweet fields of bliss Where liberty was justice, & eternal science was mercy," and she tells Urizen that in a vision she beheld Luvah's attempt to dominate Albion. Urizen, enraged, declares himself God and, not knowing that he is the cause of their present misery, casts Ahania away from him. In her fall Tharmas, the body, the innocent animal life, also falls, and in a scene of Boehmesque creation, generates a body. He casts Enion away from him, and in the mounting chaos of slavery and division, he cries:

"Rage, Rage shall never from my bosom: winds & waters of woe
Consuming all, to the end consuming. Love and Hope are ended."

In "Night the Fourth," Tharmas, in his rage, defies the "Sovereign Architect" and declares himself the ruler. He drives Los and Enitharmon apart, and calls Los his son, and yet he knows that his rule is only a device of desperation.

"O why did foul ambition seize thee, Urizen, Prince of Light?
And thee, O Luvah, prince of Love, till Tharmas was divided? . . .
Is this to be A God? far rather would I be a Man,
To know sweet Science, & to do with simple companions
Sitting beneath a tent & viewing sheepfolds & soft pastures."

His rule is as unsatisfactory as Urizen's, as all rule is unsatisfactory except that of the whole man himself, which is without rules. Tharmas commands Los to bind Urizen and his errors, and Los, working at his forge,

Link'd hour to hour & day to night & night to day & year to year,
In periods of pulsative furor; mills he form'd & works
Of many wheels resistless in the power of dark Urthona. . . .

Forgetfulness, dumbness, necessity, in chains of the mind lock'd up,
In fetters of ice shrinking, disorganiz'd, rent from Eternity,
Los beat on his fetters & heated his furnaces,
And pour'd iron sodor & sodor of brass.

Then follows the familiar description of the building of Urizen's brain and the series of the senses. With this externalization and solidification of impulse, the completion of separateness, society grows and spreads like a pestilent death:

The Corse of Albion lay on the Rock; the sea of Time & Space
Beat round the Rock in mighty waves, & as a Polypus
That vegetates beneath the Sea, the limbs of Man vegetated
In monstrous forms of Death, a Human polypus of Death.

Meanwhile Los, busy binding Urizen, has himself been bound. Here is an allegory of the Tolstoyan proposition that art is degraded by an unworthy subject matter:

. . . terrified at the shapes
Enslav'd humanity put on, he became what he beheld:
He became what he was doing: he was himself transform'd.

This is the familiar nadir of experience: ". . . mighty bulk & majesty & beauty remain'd, but unexpansive" to the closed sense. All life, like

. . . plants wither'd by winter, leaves & stems & roots decaying
Melt into thin air, while the seed, driv'n by the furious wind,
Rests on the distant Mountain's top.

Urizen, "the cold Prince of Light," is

. . . bound in chains of intellect among the furnaces;
But all the furnaces were out & the bellows had ceast to blow.

These, the opening lines of "Night the Fifth," provide the setting for the birth of Orc, the human protest against the stultifying condition of the world, the angriest expression of energy repressed:

The groans of Enitharmon shake the skies, the lab'ring Earth,
Till from her heart rending his way, a terrible child sprang
forth
In thunder, smoke & sullen flames, & howlings & fury & blood.

Orc, the son of severed spirit, is also an aspect of the passions, and now the cry arises that makes this identification: "Luvah, King of Love, thou art the King of rage & death." Luvah has already been identified with Jesus, who

. . . when Luvah sunk down, himself put on the robes of blood
Lest the state call'd Luvah should cease; & the Divine Vision
Walked in robes of blood till he who slept should awake.

The motive of Revolution is oppressed spirit, and it is the operation of love through rage.

Los, the father, self-divided and insecure, jealous and fearful, chains his son to the rock of law, only to repent his act once he has returned to his place, the city of imagination, Golgonooza. With Enitharmon, he goes back to the mountain to release their son only to find that Orc's body and his chains have rooted.

The suppression of revolution does not make Urizen happier. The book ends with Urizen's lament for his own bondage, and his false ministry in the realms of Urthona. He resolves to arise and explore his universe, to seek a remedy. Orc's protesting thunders have reached him. "When Thought is clos'd in Caves Then Love shall shew its root in deepest Hell."

"Night the Sixth" recounts his wanderings. Everywhere he meets "his Children ruin'd in his ruin'd world," but he persists in his errors. He falls again, "ending in death And in another resurrection to sorrow & weary travel," and still he carries with him his books of law, in which he continues to write his proscriptions:

> . . . nor can the man who goes
> The journey obstinate refuse to write time after time.

The rationalist's course is necessarily the lawmaker's, and it is an obstinate course because the promulgation of law means the proliferation of error. The net of religion springs up behind Urizen, and as he wanders, carrying his books, trailing this net, he comes even closer to the roarings of Orc, to his rising fires.

"Night the Seventh" has two versions. Both carry on the actions of "Night the Sixth," and it is not clear whether Blake intended to blend them or to abandon one. In the first, Urizen descends "to the Caves of Orc," where he "took his seat on a rock And rang'd his books around him." He writes in his book of iron, the Book of War, "While his snows fell & his storms beat to cool the flames of Orc Age after Age"; but wars of repression do not cool the fires. As he writes, his heel strikes a root into the rock, "the root of Mystery accursed." A tree springs up at once, almost enclosing Urizen in its meshlike branches. It is another form of oppression, of good and evil, the Church. Urizen himself escapes from the tree, but his Book of War is left behind, as militarism and clericalism collaborate against revolution. From a distance he taunts Orc, yet he senses the strength of purpose and the ideal of bliss that sustain Orc in his suffering:

> "Yet thou dost laugh at all these tortures, & this horrible place:
> Yet throw thy limbs these fires abroad that back return upon thee
> While thou reposest, throwing rage on rage, feeding thyself
> With visions of sweet bliss far other than this burning clime.
> Sure thou art bath'd in rivers of delight, on verdant fields
> Walking in joy, in bright Expanses sleeping on bright clouds
> With visions of delight so lovely that they urge thy rage
> Tenfold with fierce desire to rend thy chain & howl in fury
> And dim oblivion of all woe, & desperate repose."

Urizen's intuition of the power that supports Orc does not change his course. He summons his daughters to sing the words in the Book of War and then instructs them in the Book of Charity. This is an unusual passage in Blake, for its historical reference is rather more direct than usual. Not only does it caricature the eighteenth-century concept of benevolence, but it attacks the Malthusian theory of population. Malthus first published his *Essay on Population* in 1798; this was followed by the much expanded and considerably more brutal editions of 1803 and 1805. Blake's intention in these lines is underscored by his trio of pictures, "War," "Famine," and "Plague," executed in 1805. Of the several natural and necessary checks on population provided by vice and misery, such as dangerous and unhealthy employment, inadequate medical attention, and the most crushing forms of poverty, Malthus regarded war, famine, and pestilence as most important. In his later editions, he added "moral restraint"—the deferment of marriage and the practice of sexual abstinence. Whether Blake's "abstinence" and "Preach temperance" refer to this later doctrine, the unsettled facts of the composition of *The Four Zoas* make it impossible to know. We do know that this portion of the doctrine would have been even more repulsive to him than the rest. The lines are:

"Compell the poor to live upon a Crust of bread, by soft and mild arts.
Smile when they frown, frown when they smile; & when a man looks pale
With labour & abstinence, say he looks healthy & happy;
And when his children sicken, let them die; there are enough
Born, even too many, & our Earth will be overrun
Without these arts. If you would make the poor live with temper[ance],
With pomp give every crust of bread you give; with gracious cunning
Magnify small gifts; reduce the man to want a gift, & then give with pomp.
Say he smiles if you hear him sigh. If pale, say he is ruddy.
Preach temperance: say he is overgorg'd & drowns his wit
In strong drink, tho' you know that bread & water are all
He can afford. Flatter his wife, pity his children, till we can
Reduce all to our will, as spaniels are taught with art."

This philosophy enrages Orc, for he recognizes in it the kind of soporific that quells him for a time. Under the spell of reason's hypocrisy, Orc must become a hypocrite to express himself at all. In a corrupt world, all impulses are corrupted. And Orc's honest rage now takes the form of conspiracy and cunning in the materialist serpent, which Urizen will tolerate. When Orc rages honestly, his chains hold him down.

". . . Curse thy Cold hypocrisy! already round thy Tree
In scales that shine with gold & rubies, thou beginnest to weaken
My divided Spirit. Like a worm I rise in peace, unbound
From wrath. Now when I rage, my fetters bind me more.
O torment! O torment! A Worm compell'd! Am I a worm?
Is it in strong deceit that man is born? In strong deceit
Thou dost restrain my fury that the worm may fold the tree.
Avaunt, Cold hypocrite! I am chain'd, or thou couldst not use
me thus.
The Man shall rage, bound with this chain, the worm in silence
creep."

Urizen recognizes in Orc his ancient enemy, Luvah, who, materializing as the serpent, now twines his body around the tree of good and evil. One may read this as an involuted allegory of the French Revolution, of its theoretical operations through rationalism to overcome, as Blake viewed them, the very strictures of rationalism. What follows bears out this interpretation. For now Los, the poet, and Enitharmon appear again. Los laments his fading powers and the necessity of struggling with "secret monsters of the animating worlds" instead of singing of "the joys of love," as he had in his unfallen form. But Enitharmon does not hear him, and appears immediately as "the Shadow of Enitharmon," inspiration repressed, and Los, as "The Spectre of Urthona," logic without instinct. These two then re-enact the story of Eden under the tree. Enitharmon's selfish heart breaks; Los and his Spectre are reassembled ("If we unite in one, another better world will be Open'd within"), and presently Los sees a way to salvation:

". . . Now I feel the weight of stern repentance.
Tremble not so, my Enitharmon, at the awful gates

Of thy poor broken Heart. I see thee like a shadow withering
As on the outside of Existence; but look! behold! take comfort!
Turn inwardly thine Eyes & there behold the Lamb of God
Clothed in Luvah's robes of blood descending to redeem."

This figure ("the Lamb of God," or love) is the counterpart of revolution, who is wrathful. Under the sway of love, Los sees salvation:

"To form a world of sacrifice of brothers & sons & daughters,
To comfort Orc in his dire sufferings."

Los feels his old creativeness, which means that by love he has found his way back to imagination, the act of releasing the inner man from all the restraints of the self. Such "a world of sacrifice of brothers & sons & daughters" would be comfort to Orc indeed, and his rage could cease with his cunning. Now Los and Enitharmon together—like Blake and his wife in their collaborations—begin their works of creation:

And first he drew a line upon the walls of shining heaven,
And Enitharmon tinctur'd it with beams of blushing love.
It remain'd permanent, a lovely form, inspir'd, divinely human.

They build Golgonooza, the city of imagination, and they draw all spirits "From out the ranks of Urizen's war & from the fiery lake Of Orc," into the warfare of ideas. First to be drawn out are wrath and pity, and with their change, Orc is transformed:

First Rintrah & then Palamabron, drawn from out the ranks of war,
In infant innocence repos'd on Enitharmon's bosom.
Orc was comforted in the deeps; his soul reviv'd in them:
As the Eldest brother is the father's image, So Orc became
As Los, a father to his brethren, & he joy'd in the dark lake
Tho' bound with chains of Jealousy & in scales of iron & brass.

The transformation of Orc, from his enslaved condition in the realm of Urizen, is accomplished by the visionary poet. One need not press the allegory of his own relationship to revolutionary theory that, consciously or unconsciously, Blake was elaborating here.

In the imaginative life Los finds that even Urizen is transformed:

> Startled was Los; he found his Enemy Urizen now
> In his hands; he wonder'd that he felt love & not hate.
> His whole soul loved him; he beheld him an infant
> Lovely.

True imagination is selflessness and forgiveness. It is in this sense that Blake thought of all life as capable of the condition of true art. It is this that he meant when he said that Jesus was an artist whose works were destroyed by the Churches.

The alternate version of "Night the Seventh" returns to Urizen sitting triumphant under "the tree of Mystery in darkest night," believing himself "a Conqueror in triumphant glory" to whom "all the Sons of Everlasting shall bow down." His rule develops the most brutal forms of commercialism—slavery and the labor of children.

> First Trades & Commerce, ships & armed vessels builded laborious
> To swim the deep; & on the land, children are sold to trades
> Of dire necessity, still laboring day & night till all
> Their life extinct they took the spectre form in deep despair;
> And slaves in myriads, in ship loads, burden the hoarse sounding deep,
> Rattling with clanking chains; the Universal Empire groans.

In lines thickly sweet with his revulsion, Blake describes the counterpart of these evils in Urizen's world:

> . . . hid in chambers dark the nightly harlot
> Plays in Disguise in whisper'd hymn & mumbling prayer. The priests
> He ordain'd & Priestesses, cloth'd in disguises bestial,
> Inspiring secrecy.

Urizen has "divided day & night in different order'd portions," the white of moral pretension and the black of social horror,

"The day for war, the night for secret religion in his temple."

The shadow of Vala, nature in its most impoverished form, appears before Orc, and he, raging because she had

. . . become Urizen's harlot
And the Harlot of Los & the deluded harlot of the Kings of the Earth,

breaks loose and seizes her as his bride. This is a dramatization of the notion expressed in *The Marriage* that "the whole creation will be consumed and appear infinite and holy . . . by an improvement of sensual enjoyment." Vala has been degraded by the partial perceptions to which she has been subjected, and only an act of revolutionary force (characteristically symbolized as sexual) will renew her. But the immediate consequence of this released energy is war, and Luvah, Orc's other aspect of passion, is crucified for his defiance of restraint. This is the final triumph of Urizen, and life is at its blackest. To express this dark state, Blake turns again to industrialism:

Then left the sons of Urizen the plow & harrow, the loom,
The hammer & the chisel & the rule & compasses.
They forg'd the sword, the chariot of war, the battle ax,
The trumpet fitted to the battle & the flute of summer,
And all the arts of life they chang'd into the arts of death.
The hour glass contemn'd because its simple workmanship
Was as the workmanship of the plowman, & the water wheel
That raises water into Cisterns, broken & burn'd in fire
Because its workmanship was like the workmanship of the shepherd,
And in their stead intricate wheels invented, Wheel without wheel,
To perplex youth in their outgoings & to bind to labours
Of day & night the myriads of Eternity, that they might file
And polish brass & iron hour after hour, laborious workmanship,
Kept ignorant of the use that they might spend the days of wisdom
In sorrowful drudgery to obtain a scanty pittance of bread,

In ignorance to view a small portion & think that All,
And call it demonstration, blind to all the simple rules of life.

The Sons of Urizen call to Vala to side with them, but she is in Orc's hands.

Orc rent her, & his human form consum'd in his own fires
Mingled with her dolorous members strewn thro' the Abyss.
She joy'd in all the Conflict . . .
This was, to her, Supreme delight. The Warriors mourn'd disappointed.

Revolution, repressed too long, has entered the world of Urizen to destroy it; but the conditions of that world have forced him to use Urizen's tool, war, by which he breaks and renews the false forms of nature. Yet, in his form of the serpent, utilizing the means that he intends to destroy, Orc has not achieved the complete liberation of life; for at the very end of the book, faith and the "sweet labours of Love" are named as the content of the "Promise Divine," and at this point Satan himself, the very sum of error, appears.

"Night the Eighth" opens with Albion's awakening "In the Saviour's arms, in the arms of tender mercy & loving kindness." This is the "Promise Divine" mentioned at the end of the second version of the seventh part and discovered by Los at the end of the first version. The narrative continues the action of the first version, with Los. Now Enitharmon's "Obdurate heart was broken," and she assists Los in his task of imaginative reconstruction. But the wars of Urizen still rage, and Urizen himself is baffled to discover that Jesus and Luvah and Orc are all forms of the same condition:

When Urizen saw the Lamb of God clothed in Luvah's robes,
Perplex'd & terrifi'd he stood, tho' well he knew that Orc
Was Luvah.

Urizen, who is above all orderly, cannot understand that love and revolt are both functions of passion ("Love that hardens into hate," according to a modern poet in a brief mood of protest), and are complementary, the first eternal, the second, in its serpent form, temporal. The serpent twines himself in the tree of mystery, and at the order of Urizen fallen Nature feeds him poisoned bread, on which his serpent form thrives. But she also implores Urizen for release:

". . . When shall the dead revive?
Can that which has existed cease, or can love & life expire?"

Urizen "heard the Voice," which is to say that he recognizes his error, his false legal notions, all his corrupting restraints. Then "the direful Web of Religion" falls and in that moment freedom is born on earth—in the furnaces of imagination, "a Universal female form created . . . from the spectres of the dead."

And Enitharmon nam'd the Female, Jerusalem the holy.
Wond'ring, she saw the Lamb of God within Jerusalem's Veil;
The Divine Vision seen within the inmost deep recess
Of fair Jerusalem's bosom in a gently beaming fire.

Jesus and Satan confront each other, and Satan, "Being multitudes of tyrant Men in union blasphemous Against the Divine image," condemns Jesus to crucifixion. But Los knows that Jesus represents an eternal quality that cannot die and, rescuing Jesus' body, he voices one of Blake's most famous doctrines, that of "states" and individuals:

"There is a State nam'd Satan; learn distinct to know, O Rahab!
The difference between States & Individuals of those States.
The State nam'd Satan never can be redeem'd in all Eternity;
But when Luvah in Orc became a Serpent, he descended into
That State call'd Satan. Enitharmon breath'd forth on the Winds
Of Golgonooza her well beloved, knowing he was Orc's human
remains."

In this speech Blake arrives at his final theory of evil. The individuality, of which Jesus, who is love, is the very center, is pure and eternal. The "state," into which the restraints of circumstance, prejudice, and perception force the individuality, is most completely represented by Satan and is an external incrustation from which the individuality can step free. Revolution, in its aspect of hate, or war, is in the state of Satan, and destroys himself; its motive, Luvah, born of Los, is eternal.

Rahab, or moral virtue, is another such "state." Los rejects her, Urizen accepts her; and another fall takes place. Urizen sinks and petrifies as his individuality is further stifled by his error. Ahania, his long-departed emanation, laments his decline and thinks that "The Eternal Man" himself "sleeps in the Earth." Enion answers her in a wonderful song of affirmation, in which she tells how the spirit of man lives in all natural forms and in all the harshest forms of experience, and yearns in its travail.

Jesus is taken from the cross, and Jerusalem mourns over the sepulcher for two thousand years—roughly, until the end of the eighteenth century. Rahab, in the meantime, "triumphs over all," even over Jerusalem herself—

Captive, a Willing Captive, by delusive arts impell'd
To worship Urizen's Dragon form, to offer her own Children
Upon the bloody Altar.

Freedom has become the slave of reason and of self-righteousness, "the Harlot of the Kings of Earth," supplying from mystery, the tree of good and evil, the "food of Orc & Satan." But the lament of Ahania and the song of Enion disturb her, and she wavers between the two, Satan and Orc—

Sometimes returning to the Synagogue of Satan in Pride,
And sometimes weeping before Orc in humility and trembling.

This is "Satan divided against Satan," and the resolution is "To burn Mystery with fire & form another from her ashes." The old forms of theological oppression are replaced by a new form, no better, but nearer fulfillment. Once more Revolution is presented in its rationalist guise:

The Ashes of Mystery began to animate; they call'd it Deism
And Natural Religion.

"Night the Ninth" is an unusually sustained piece of impassioned rhetoric in which Blake, succeeding for the first time in describing regeneration, nearly bursts his poetic lungs. It opens with Los and Enitharmon struggling together for liberty in the building of Jerusalem, a city as well as a woman. Final revolution characteristically begins in the destruction of tyrants:

The thrones of Kings are shaken, they have lost their robes & crowns,
The poor smite their oppressors, they awake up to the harvest,
The naked warriors rush together down to the sea shore
Trembling before the multitudes of slaves now set at liberty. . . .
The oppressed pursue like the wind; there is no room for escape.

Orc, soon functionless, begins to consume himself in his own roaring flames in the tree. Revolution, wrapped round good and evil, destroys them with himself. Then, "when all Tyranny was cut off from the face of the Earth," Albion lifts his abject head from the rock. "When shall the Man of future times become as in days of old?" he cries, and lifting himself higher, demands that Urizen, "stony form of death," yield up his power:

My anger against thee is greater than against this Luvah,
For war is energy Enslav'd, but thy religion,
The first author of this war & the distracting of honest minds
Into confused perturbation & strife & horrour & pride,
Is a deceit so detestable that I will cast thee out
If thou repentest not, & leave thee as a rotten branch to be burned.

Albion's anger against Luvah-Orc is a lesser anger than that against Urizen; for Luvah-Orc's war is the necessary expression of energies that Urizen has repressed. He is the cause; Revolution is the effect. Urizen abdicates:

"Then Go, O dark futurity! I will cast thee forth from these
Heavens of my brain, nor will I look upon futurity more.
I cast futurity away, & turn my back upon that void
Which I have made; for lo! futurity is in this moment. . . .
Rage Orc! Rage Tharmas! Urizen no longer curbs your rage."

Renunciation of power is identical with casting off error. Urizen's pure energy immediately emerges from the state of Satan, and he is regenerate:

> . . . Then, glorious bright, Exulting in his joy,
> He sounding rose into the heavens in naked majesty,
> In radiant Youth.

Then Urizen's delimited universe explodes, life springs through the clefts in the dead mold, the oppressed turn on their oppressors:

> On rifted rocks, suspended in the air by inward fires,
> Many a woful company & many on clouds & waters,
> Fathers & friends, Mothers & Infants, Kings & Warriors,
> Priests & chain'd Captives, met together in a horrible fear;
> And all the marks remain of the slave's scourge & tyrant's Frown,
> And of the Priest's o'ergorged Abdomen, & of the merchant's thin
> Sinewy deception, & of the warrior's outbraving & thoughtlessness
> In lineaments too extended & in bones too strait & long.
> They shew their wounds: they accuse: they sieze the oppressor; howlings began. . . .
> "Rend limb from limb the warrior & the tyrant, reuniting in pain."

Urizen rests with his sons and daughters, watching "the flames Of Orc" and "the human harvest" spring up. The fires of Orc rage in the forms of nature until at last all are cleansed and "Orc had quite consum'd himself in Mental flames." Then both Orc and fallen nature, the Shadowy Female, are re-embodied in their pure forms of Luvah and Vala. Their temporary aspects, inharmonious and incomplete, have worked toward the restoration of harmony, which, when it comes, involves their own regeneration into eternal elements:

> "Luvah & Vala, henceforth you are Servants; obey & live. . . .
> If Gods combine against Man, setting their dominion above
> The Human form Divine, Thrown down from their high station
> In the Eternal heavens of Human Imagination, buried beneath
> In dark Oblivion, with incessant pangs, ages on ages,
> In enmity & war first weaken'd, then in stern repentance

An illustration from *Jerusalem*

By courtesy of the Houghton Library, Harvard University

"When Thought is clos'd in Caves Then love shall shew
its root in deepest Hell."

They must renew their brightness, & their disorganiz'd functions
Again reorganize, till they resume the image of the human,
Co-operating in the bliss of Man, obeying his Will,
Servants to the infinite & Eternal of the Human form."

All the Eternals now undergo a similar transmutation, reuniting in their original forms, sitting together at a "golden feast," where one of them states the ideal that they have reachieved:

". . . Man subsists by Brotherhood & Universal Love.
We fall on one another's necks, more closely we embrace.
Not for ourselves, but for the Eternal family we live.
Man liveth not by Self alone, but in his brother's face
Each shall behold the Eternal Father & love & joy abound."

Then follows what Blake calls the harvest of the nations, in which "all Nations were threshed out, & the stars thresh'd from their husks," an impressive allegory of the potential fullness of life, in which the winnowing fan blows away the husks of dominion, "Religion . . . Kings & Councellors & Giant Warriors," and all aspiration is freed and gathered.

"Let the slave, grinding at the mill, run out into the field;
Let him look up into the heavens & laugh in the bright air.
Let the inchained soul, shut up in darkness & in sighing,
Whose face has never seen a smile in thirty weary years,
Rise & look out: his chains are loose, his dungeon doors are open;
And let his wife & children return from the opressor's scourge."

This is the return to innocence, and "All the Slaves from every Earth . . . Sing a New Song . . . Composed by an African Black":

"Aha! Aha! how came I here so soon in my sweet native land?
How came I here? Methinks I am as I was in my youth
When in my father's house I sat & heard his chearing voice.
Methinks I see his flocks & herds & feel my limbs renew'd,
And Lo, my Brethren in their tents, & their little ones around
them!"

The familiar pastoral imagery of the early *Songs* is taken up by Albion in his rejoicing:

". . . from his mountains high
The lion of terror shall come down, & bending his bright mane
And crouching at their side, shall eat from the curl'd boy's white
lap
His golden food, and in the evening sleep before the door."

Then Luvah states the point of the poem and the basic theme of all of Blake: "Attempting to be more than Man We become less."

Two further symbolic events take place before the end: Luvah presses out the wine of humanity and casts off the lees, and Tharmas and Urthona make "the Bread of Ages." Now "The Expanding Eyes of Man behold the depths of wondrous worlds," and as in the first condition of innocence, he is able again to converse "with the Animal forms of wisdom night & day." But experience has intervened, and through the anguish of its fire and the torment of its machines, man has been relieved of error, and his essential purity, reclaimed, prevails:

"How is it we have walk'd thro' fires & yet are not consum'd?
How is it that all things are chang'd, even as in ancient times?"

The Sun arises from his dewy bed, & the fresh airs
Play in his smiling beams giving the seeds of life to grow,
And the fresh Earth beams forth ten thousand thousand springs
of life.
. . . & Urthona rises from the ruinous Walls
In all his ancient strength to form the golden armour of science
For intellectual War. The war of swords departed now,
The dark Religions are departed & sweet Science reigns.

III

The Four Zoas rests on this pattern, but the pattern is not easily extracted, since Blake did his best to conceal it; for it was an intellectual pattern, after all the fury a pattern of logic. Blake's visions are poetic intuitions up to a point; but beyond that point they are rationalizations, intellectual defenses that criticize an age. Insofar as they represent his intuitions in adequately expressive forms they make great poetry; insofar as they masquerade his ideas they are not poetry at all, but monstrous deceits of logic. But we are interested still in the *means* that Blake found to express himself in poetry, not yet with the success of his expression *as* poetry.

The Four Zoas, unfinished as it is, marks the crucial transition in Blake's development, because in it he found at last the means by which he could adjust his visionary temperament to the social insights that he wished to express, the means which brought together, in a single framework, the two persistent strains of evangelicism and humanitarianism. The method binds together in one semidramatic form—instead of in separate sets of lyrics of opposing mood or in mere prose assertion—the dialectic of innocence and experience. To make this adjustment, Blake had to shift his emphasis from the external to the internal, from the historical to the psychological, and by a considerable expansion of his mythological apparatus he was able to make this a shift of emphasis only, not a denial of the external and the historical. Now his two characteristic modes of imagery function side by side—the imagery of industrial, political, religious, and sexual slavery, imagery of a disjointed society, to express the trials of experience, and the imagery of a shimmering pastoralism, of a harmonious nature, to express the delights of innocence.

The shift of emphasis involved Blake in at least two important developments, which, although they appear to be unrelated, have their own subterranean connections. The first is that in moving deeper into man's interiors and in charting his categories, he becomes more and more careful not to commit Urizen's error of oversimplifying and fixing them. He employs abstractions to overcome the concept of the abstract, faculties to defeat the faculty psychology; but he strives constantly to remind himself and his reader that these are neither abstractions nor faculties in the usual sense. And this is one of the great failures in literature of a fresh and valuable imaginative insight to express itself.

No one would quarrel with Blake's intuition of the nature of mind, but even the most sympathetic must lament the form of expression which that intuition took. His insight was of the singleness of mind, and therefore of its appalling complexity. There is no dichotomy of reason and passion, sense and soul; these comprise a single fabric, and are inextricably woven. The possibilities of pattern are endless, but all the threads are involved in each; or the cloth can be torn, but then all the strands are severed. Yet this image does not express Blake's insight adequately, for threads, even when closely woven, are distinct. "How can we know the dancer from the dance?" That is too suave to express the vigor and the agony that are of the essence of Blake's insight into the drama. Either shows the difficulties that he faced.

His solution to these difficulties was an endless elaboration and complication of his drama, but hardly the unification that he sought. And who can tell him how he could have come by that? Yet the proliferation of characters, the splittings, the reproductions, the dislocations, that are so bewildering, even the confusions of identity whereby one character suddenly becomes another—all these serve rather to remind us of his insight than to express it. Blake's refusal to label and to fix, to systematize what is in itself without system, was intellectually sound. But as poetry, it was disastrous to take this way of showing that states of mind, involving the whole being, are in a constant flux involving perpetual external and organic interchanges, appearing now in one form with one activity and function, and now in another form with a subtly or utterly different activity and function. The possibilities are both too vast and too complex for form.

Blake's increasing awareness of the intricacy and subtlety of mind led him inevitably to the second important development that is apparent in *The Four Zoas*—his criticism of history. History is no more simple or mechanical than mind, but as an external reflection of mind it is involved in a drama no less organic. This perception Blake makes most clear in his criticism of the French Revolution—that is, in the development of Orc; for in that development he embodies his revision of revolutionary theory.

In earlier poems Orc had the function of destroying in order to create; now his function, while necessary, is destruction alone. His relations with other powers, however, are more complex. He is still the son of fallen spirit, and his energies are those of art, of the creative impulse; but they are repressed in Urizen's world, chained down by law and external form. They do not escape the force of corruption. Orc now submits to Urizen, uses the tools of reason itself—force and war—and the rational principle of deism in place of older orthodoxies. As natural religion denies the visionary life, so Orc "materializes" in the form of dissimulation, the serpent. He is fed by enslaved freedom, and the more he grows, the greater grows his rage, until at last he destroys the code of law and all it implies, ruins the narrowed forms of life and casts them out, and then expires in the form he was compelled to employ.

He is the son of Los, but once he is born, he is more closely associated with Luvah, who is in turn associated with Jesus. Orc is rage, passion divorced from love; Jesus is love, passion divorced from anger. While Orc destroys the false forms of the social order and breaks down external restraints, Jesus descends into man and breaks the gates of the selfish heart in the impulse of forgiveness. In that impulse even Urizen is forgiven; all individuality is seen as pure and as separate from the states into which it has been forced. To destroy the Satanic states, the mold of social convention, is one aspect of regeneration; to break the heart—that is, to destroy selfish impulses—in the great imaginative act that recognizes the integrity of all individuality is the other. Brotherhood is not easily come by. Political revolution cannot achieve it without the inward denial of self-righteousness. Yet it is significant that these two acts occur nearly simultaneously in Blake's poems, and are parallel. Social forms reach their most repressive before revolution breaks out; man's spirit endures to the bursting before he achieves his wisdom.

All this is, of course, only an extension of the challenge Blake had made as early as 1791:

"But go, merciless man! enter into the infinite labyrinth of
another's brain
Ere thou measure the circle that he shall run. Go, thou cold
recluse, into the fires
Of another's high flaming rich bosom, and return unconsum'd,
and write laws."

Yet it is an extension that contains a nearly explicit allegory worth analysis. When Orc, in the realm of Urizen, twines himself about the tree of error and is at last destroyed himself, Blake is, perhaps unconsciously, perhaps consciously, commenting on the three most basic defects in revolutionary theory as he had encountered it. The attack on rationalism is obvious; that he had assailed before, and for it he had substituted earlier his concept of human energy. But Orc's symbolic form of the serpent also represents Blake's recognition of the imperfection of all historical process. The doctrine of "states" is, in one sense, a repetition of this judgment; even the best impulses express themselves in forms that are corrupt with error. And this seems to be Blake's comment on the easy optimism of the idea of progress. Blake's third revision lies in his exaltation of individuality, and on its multitudinous and various forms, and this may be read as his comment on that atomistic view of man which was implicit in revolutionary rationalism. The theory preached an "individualism" that did not adequately recognize the individual, the enormous variety of human character, and its right to it.

In these three ways Blake corrects, without denying either their motives or their aspirations, both the republican and the anarchistic theorists. In doing so he deepens the political aims of both. The first expected to accomplish through social revolution alone an entire change in human nature; this, obviously, had not and cannot come about. The anarchists, trusting to reason, preached change through the release of that reason from all legal and institutional restraints and the chains of customary prejudice, and believed that revolution need play no part in the change. But obviously all men are not as rational as that, and Satan, at least, is immune to Godwinian "persuasion." The function of revolution is necessary to the destruction of the Satanic "states," and love, not reason, is the ingredient of brotherhood. Nor are they separate. Luvah and Orc are one; outer disorder reflects inner disorder, and outer restraint, inner restraint. When the outer is reordered, "rights" disappear; when the inner is reordered, "duties" disappear. In this both Godwin and Paine were mistaken. Love knows no duties and it does not ask for rights.

Yet old contradictions linger. If the doctrine of "states" is in one sense a recognition of the necessary imperfection of historical process, it is in the other Blake's most thoroughgoing and most paradoxical denial of evil. His concept of reordering the personality is at least as deficient of the tragic view of evil—even though wisdom is won only through the excruciating torments of experience—as the concept of adjustment in psychoanalysis, or that idyl of an ordered anarchy which is to follow upon "the dictatorship of the proletariat" in Marxism. And if we turn from the political implications of Blake's poem and glance at the religious, we find the same deficiency; for even though Blake's growing cosmogonal apparatus always threatens to and often does dominate the material it is intended to express, it is an inadequate cosmogony in the end. He may deny the materialist notion of progress, and yet at the close of his poem the old nagging hopes remain. And in the final vision of the millennial renewal of nature, he has given us, surely, no glimpse of heaven, but, once more, a vision of "this world made better," and not even on the other side of the stars.

CHAPTER TEN

The Devil's Party and the Part of Angels

I

AFTER *The Four Zoas,* neither Blake's method nor his message underwent further changes of importance. *Milton* follows with a precise consistency. *The Four Zoas* was Blake's criticism of his favorite historical event, the French Revolution, and a rewriting of its theory. *Milton* was a criticism of his favorite poet, and a reorganization of Milton's mind. The movement from one to the other is perfectly logical. He sympathized with the revolutionary aim of a liberated man in a free society, but he deplored the means and the rationalization. Likewise, he loved Milton's poems and the true impulses behind them—which he thought he understood more clearly than Milton—but he deplored the seventeenth-century emphasis on right reason and the Puritan concern with morality.

Milton was the most important single influence on Blake's poetry. The obvious debt, from the earliest lyrics to the final epic, is that of style, which appears in the persistent use of Miltonic diction, phrasing, imagery, poetic devices, even narrative episodes and actual quotations. This debt is the most painful of the several lumpish rocks that jut from the cliff of Blake's rhetoric, and which on the whole do more to hinder than to help him in his struggle for effects of grandeur. A less obvious influence, and one that Blake managed to assimilate in the framework of his own thinking, was that of Milton's themes and ideas. In many ways the lives of the two poets had a curious parallelism, none more evident than the double interest in revolutionary politics and Protestantism. And Blake found it easy to force Milton's ideas, which represent the beginning of a tradition, into the transformations and the inversions that represent its extreme, and its conclusion in one direction.

Mr. Damon has suggested * that it is not too much even to say that a number of Blake's works have a generic responsibility to a number of Milton's: *Songs of Innocence* and *Songs of Experience* are counterparts of "L'Allegro" and "Il Penseroso." *The Book of Thel* is a kind of rewriting of *Comus* (a beautiful inversion, really, when one considers their opposing attitudes towards chastity). *The Doctrine and Discipline* was a source of the *Visions of the Daughters of Albion,* and *Paradise Lost* caused *Milton.* One other debt remains, and that is a genuinely elusive one—Milton's influence in the sense that he was Blake's chief "ancestor," his spiritual father, who shared much of his moral being with the younger man. This is apparent in their common pride, their arrogance as artists, in the kind of flinty self-righteousness that both had and which arose from their absolute faith in themselves and from their sense of great and holy dedication to the task of art.

Yet there was never really a time when Blake did not chafe under the touch of the heavy ancestral hand upon him, and resist it. And there were, of course, central elements in Milton's thought, such as those summarized in Books Seven and Eight of *Paradise Lost,* that Blake found completely unacceptable. He expressed his resistance by criticizing these ideas, and from them he finally constructed his poem on the reform of Milton's character.

The original defect that Blake discovered was that Milton, in spite of everything to the contrary, had put himself on the side of the angels, the repressive forces, when in reality he was "of the Devil's party without knowing it," the party of the

* In correspondence with the author. Mr. Damon will develop this suggestion himself in his book on Milton's symbolism.

revolutionary prolific. The devourers exalt reason and law in order to deny energy and the impulsive life, and they remain devourers whether they appear in the guise of the timid and pious angels of *The Marriage* or in that of the boldly conspiratorial and accusatory Satan of the later poems, whether as Urizen challenging Luvah or as Jehovah denying Jesus. Milton submitted to the denial, and in doing so committed at least two gross errors that had always distressed Blake.

Milton's rationalism is curiously like Urizen's own. First it declares itself the superior power ("Love . . . hath his seat In Reason") and then, fearing to be "presumptuous," it admits its limitations.

> ". . . the rest
> From Man or Angel the great Architect
> Did wisely to conceal, and not divulge
> His secrets, to be scanned by them who ought
> Rather admire."

The "great Architect" is, in another sense, like Urizen, for his mind is legal, he accuses and he judges, and he is therefore both Jehovah and Satan, whose fault is "self-righteousness." "Satan thinks that Sin is displeasing to God; he ought to know that Nothing is displeasing to God but Unbelief & Eating of the Tree of Knowledge of Good & Evil. . . . In Hell all is Self Righteousness; there is no such thing there as Forgiveness of Sin; he who does Forgive Sin is Crucified as an Abettor of Criminals, & he who performs Works of Mercy in Any shape whatever is punish'd &, if possible, destroy'd, not thro' envy or Hatred or Malice, but thro' Self Righteousness that thinks it does God service, which God is Satan. . . . Forgiveness of Sin is only at the Judgment Seat of Jesus the Saviour, where the Accuser is cast out, not because he Sins, but because he torments the Just & makes them do what he condemns as Sin & what he knows is opposite to their own Identity."

The Satanic error of "self-righteousness" was the basis of Milton's rationalism, and his substitution of the individual "inner" law for the old external law was no improvement at all, but merely a change of name. It was the identical error that

Godwin made in his political terms, for while Godwin wished to rid the world of institutions and the forms of law, he put his trust in the impulse that underlies them, rational "duties," or "moral virtue." Their anarchism was incomplete, and as long as it remained incomplete, both real religion and genuine brotherhood were impossible. "The Moral Virtues are continual Accusers of Sin & promote Eternal Wars & Dominency over others."

To rescue Milton from "Satan's Labyrinth" meant that Blake had to correct this second error, the Puritan morality, and show moral virtue in its true and hideously self-righteous form, the "state" that Blake called Rahab. Milton had invited the correction. "I saw Milton in Imagination And he told me to beware of being misled by his Paradise Lost. In particular he wished me to shew the falsehood of his doctrine that the pleasures of sex arose from the fall. The fall could not produce any pleasure." It was that old mistake which Blake first noted in his reading of Lavater: ". . . all Act is Virtue. To hinder another is not an act . . . the origin of this mistake . . . is, They suppose that Woman's Love is Sin; in consequence all the Loves & Graces with them are Sins." This mistake made of Milton a self-divided man, a prolific who praised the devourer, and the division was dramatically expressed for Blake in Milton's hard and unhappy personal life, his relationship with his wives and daughters, his sixfold emanation. Like Urizen, he drove Ahania from him. It was an error that had overshadowed a century and corrupted an age; to save Milton would be to save mankind.

Yet the production of the poem waited upon a curious combination of circumstances in Blake's external life and his visionary life. He fell, first of all, into the intimate clutches of a devourer, William Hayley, the very worst kind of angel—pious, conventional, complacent, reasonable, sentimental, and absolutely bloodless—who, like Satan, had presented himself as a corporeal friend and then was revealed to be that most dangerous spiritual enemy, the well-intentioned. All this is merely to say that Hayley did not understand Blake's work, and insofar as he did not, hindered it. But from Blake's point of view it was the most immediate and deeply personal experience he had yet had of stupid restraints imposed upon a champing energy. And there was no escape. For three years Blake endured and chafed, and his only release was in savage epigrams dashed into a notebook. Hayley, unfortunately, for all that he represented, was too trivial a figure to become the subject of a poem. The most he earned in his own right was the role of a minor character called "Hyle."

Then vision came to Blake's assistance. Milton, like a meteor, dashed into his left foot as he was walking in his Felpham garden, and before him appeared the whole drama of Milton's salvation, replete with characters, some old, some new, with Hayley raised to the Satanic power and Blake as Los and the son of Los, Palamabron. It was all very convenient, and when Blake awoke from the faint into which he had fallen, he threw himself into what he later called his "Three years' Herculean Labours at Felpham" * and produced *Milton,* "the Grandest Poem that this World Contains."

Blake, who had always felt that in *The State of Innocence* Dryden had "degraded" Milton's chief poem, had no compunction about "rewriting" *Paradise Lost* himself in order to save the man, and men—and himself from the stifling grip of his indignation. The final lesson of art, that personality is only its first principle and is unacceptable as its last, Blake had forgotten. He "used" his art now in the way that all poets who attempt to substitute it for religion do "use" it, for solace and purgation, in an interchange as direct as the confessional. And no poem shows more clearly than *Milton* the irresponsibility into which direct inspiration can lead the artist who places an excessive value upon it.

One can view this, of course, as a real exhaustion of inspiration rather than as a too-willing submission to it. The two are probably the same. The central theme of *Milton* is not nearly adequate to fill the bloated structure of the whole, and one feels that Blake is now "enslaved" to his own system so com-

* An inaccurate description. The vision must have come late in his stay, and while the first version of the poem was apparently dashed off before he left Felpham, it was not engraved until 1804, after Blake had returned to London, and he continued to correct it and add to it until 1818.

pletely that it is the system that determines the theme and the handling of it rather than the theme which necessitates the system. Until *The Four Zoas,* and on the whole in *The Four Zoas,* the structure expressed the theme; in *Milton,* it depresses it and distorts it. This development is apparent at once in the repetition of old material; in the merciless involutions and extensions of previous symbols; in the widening Biblical and geographical allusions, arbitrary and functionless; in the new cryptography that Blake discovered to be possible in the manipulation of numbers—three's and four's, seven's and eight's, twenty-seven's and twenty-eight's; and most of all in the grave failure of objectivity that allowed him to superimpose the Hayley quarrel on the main portion of the poem, and to drop into it any other personal item of the Felpham years that interested him, including the rheumatism of his wife:

"Virgin of Providence, fear not to enter into my Cottage.
What is thy message to thy friend? What am I now to do?
Is it again to plunge into deeper affliction? behold me
Ready to obey, but pity thou my Shadow of Delight:
Enter my Cottage, comfort her, for she is sick with fatigue."

All this is the aesthetic failure. To readers whose sympathy Blake has won and whose intellect he has challenged, the poem has other rewards. These are, first of all, its revelations about the nature of his visionary experience and the insights it affords into the history and the operation of his mind; and second, the extent to which the poem develops his earlier themes and its relationship to the total structure of his ideas and poetic ambitions.

II

Milton is an elaboration of the revolutionary theme of *The Four Zoas* in terms of an individual. The fervor of Blake's expectations has not diminished. He regards his poems as the challenge of a new, aspiring world to an expiring and depraved one. "Rouze up, O Young Men of the New Age! set your foreheads against the ignorant Hirelings! For we have Hirelings in the Camp, the Court & the University, who would, if they could, for ever depress Mental & prolong Corporeal War." This dedication is followed by Blake's famous hymn, which, ironically, was used to help break the General Strike in 1926, and again, but more appropriately, one hopes, by the London crowds after the Socialist victory of 1945. It identifies the vision of Christ with the primitive pastoral past and the liberated future, and Satan with the tyrannies of the British present:

And did those feet in ancient time
Walk upon England's mountains green?
And was the holy Lamb of God
On England's pleasant pastures seen?

And did the Countenance Divine
Shine forth upon our clouded hills?
And was Jerusalem builded here
Among these dark Satanic Mills? . . .

I will not cease from Mental Fight,
Nor shall my Sword sleep in my hand
Till we have built Jerusalem
In England's green & pleasant Land.

The Industrial Revolution, like the philosophical revolution, had taken place since Milton's time; and they took place together, indeed, as Yeats pointed out in Blakean lines, because of one another:

Locke sank into a swoon;
The Garden died;
God took the spinning-jenny
Out of his side.

To this development Milton's errors had contributed considerably, and Blake's poem about him is written to reveal the imperfect poet returning to earth to redeem them. He must cast off his rationalism and free his essential humanity, his identity, by organizing it in all its parts:

Say first! what mov'd Milton, who walk'd about in Eternity
One hundred years, pond'ring the intricate mazes of Providence,
Unhappy tho' in heav'n—he obey'd, he murmur'd not, he was
    silent
Viewing his Sixfold Emanation scatter'd thro' the deep
In torment—To go into the deep her to redeem & himself perish?

Milton must return, recognize the emanation, destroy the selfhood, the restrainer that divides him, and embrace in love all his energies. In his own salvation, he will dramatize the salvation of mankind as Blake has already shown it operating in Albion. Thus the story of Milton is connected at once with the whole mythology that Blake had already constructed.

The poem opens, therefore, with a summary of familiar action, sung by a bard in eternity, and it is into this recapitulation that Blake weaves his allegory of Hayley. Milton listens to the song, which tells of the fall of Albion, the binding of Urizen, Los's own bondage, his separation from his emanation, the birth of Orc, Enitharmon's first child, and of Satan, her last, of Satan's interference with the harvest of the nations, and of the declension of mankind ("Ah weak & wide astray!") under these conditions. Los assails Satan, the rationalist error, for confounding identities in Urizen's legalistic vein:

"Every Man's Wisdom is peculiar to his own Individuality.
O Satan, my youngest born, art thou not Prince of the Starry
    Hosts
And of the Wheels of Heaven, to turn the Mills day & night?
Art thou not Newton's Pantocrator, weaving the Woof of
    Locke? . . .
Get to thy Labours at the Mills & leave me to my wrath. . . .

Thy Work is Eternal Death with Mills & Ovens & Cauldrons.
Trouble me no more; thou canst not have Eternal Life."

One cannot ignore here the deliberate confluence of imagery, the anarchistic assertion of the sanctity of individuality opposed to a figure that combines the mechanical view of the universe, the mechanical view of man (a pantocrator is an instrument for copying), and the actual blight of machinery on contemporary life.

Los has other sons, Palamabron and Rintrah, pity and wrath, and besides being new embodiments of Jesus and Orc, they are also aspects of Blake in his relation with Hayley. The cosmic difficulty at the moment is that Satan has usurped the work of Palamabron, and Palamabron is working in Satan's mills. This is to say that under Hayley's patronage Blake was compelled to perform unworthy tasks while Hayley pretended to be the serious artist, and also, in the larger drama, that when tyranny is triumphant, the best human energies are degraded.

. . . "You know Satan's mildness and his self-imposition,
Seeming a brother, being a tyrant, even thinking himself a brother
While he is murdering the just. . . .
But we must not be tyrants also."

Los assents to the dislocation of powers ("Mine is the fault! I should have remember'd that pity divides the soul And man unmans"), and Satan, declaring himself God, spreads sin by spreading laws:

He created Seven deadly Sins, drawing out his infernal scroll
Of Moral laws and cruel punishments upon the clouds of Jehovah,
To pervert the Divine voice in its entrance to the earth
With thunder of war & trumpet's sound, with armies of disease,
Punishments & deaths muster'd and number'd, Saying: "I am God alone:
There is no other! let all obey my principles of moral individuality."

This is an ancient usurpation, and Los recognizes it: Satan is Urizen. He appeals to Elynittria (a lower form of Enitharmon, who has been cast out, and opposed to Leutha, sex bound by convention) against the jealous strife in which the world struggles. Leutha, the ideal of chastity, admits her guilt, although it is Satan who has driven her from him:

"Wild with prophetic fury, his former life became like a dream.
Cloth'd in the Serpent's folds, in selfish holiness demanding purity,
Being most impure, self-condemn'd to eternal tears, he drove
Me from his inmost Brain & the doors clos'd with thunder's sound."

Leutha has recognized the basic evil, the impulse of self-righteousness, "making to himself Laws from his own identity," compelling "others to serve him." Therefore she now comes under the protection of the more generous Elynittria. Then the Bard's song breaks off, and the Eternals murmur, some in protest. "Pity and Love are too venerable for the imputation Of Guilt." But the Bard assures them that his wisdom is exact.

The Bard has really pictured only two events, the triumph of reason and the divisive effects in "moral virtue." In Blake's mind, the two comprised Milton's folly.

Milton, who had heard it all, knows at once that the Bard has represented to him the causes of his unfulfillment. He vows to redeem himself:

. . . "I go to Eternal Death! The Nations still
Follow after the detestable Gods of Priam, in pomp
Of warlike selfhood contradicting and blaspheming.
When will the Resurrection come to deliver the sleeping body . . . ?
I will arise and look forth for the morning of the grave:
I will go down to the sepulcher to see if morning breaks:
I will go down to self annihilation and eternal death,
Lest the Last Judgment come & find me unannihilate
And I be siez'd & giv'n into the hands of my own Selfhood. . . .
What do I here before the Judgment? without my Emanation?
With the daughters of memory & not with the daughters of inspiration?
I in my Selfhood am that Satan: I am that Evil One!
He is my Spectre!"

Milton falls and enters Blake, while the eternal Zoas watch his descent into the world. Orc, knowing Milton's revolutionary mission, struggles to free himself, and his bride, fallen nature, laments, and describes her garments, the errors that Milton will abolish—"The misery of unhappy Families," "dire sufferings, poverty, pain & woe Along the rocky Island," "the sick Father & his starving Family," "The Prisoner in the stone Dungeon & the Slave at the Mill."

"I will have Kings inwoven upon it & Councellors & Mighty
Men;
The Famine shall clasp it together with buckles & Clasps,
And the Pestilence shall be its fringe & the War its girdle . . .
And I will put on Holiness as a breastplate & as a helmet,
And all my ornaments shall be of the gold of broken hearts,
And the precious stones of anxiety & care & desperation & death
And repentance for sin & sorrow & punishment & fear,
To defend me from thy terrors, O Orc, my only beloved!"

Orc, knowing that he must only rend this garment of injustice and imposture, begs her not to put it on, but to wear "a Garment of Pity & Compassion like the Garment of God." The other powers tremble, too, until Los remembers "an old Prophecy,"

. . . often sung to the loud harp at the immortal feasts:
That Milton of the Land of Albion should up ascend
Forwards from Ulro from the Vale of Felpham, and so free
Orc from his Chain of Jealousy.

Ulro is the world of matter; Felpham was Blake's place of residence. Blake tells again how Milton entered his foot, which is his way of acknowledging his debt to Milton and also of expressing Milton's debt to him, for now Blake has become the spokesman for the erring poet. Los, the eternal prophet, seeing "the Cloud of Milton stretching over Europe," enters Blake too, inspiring him in the present poem to correct the errors of a hundred years. Then Ololon, the eternal form of the sixfold emanation, unredeemed in Ulro, follows Milton.

. . . "Let us descend also, and let us give
Ourselves to death in Ulro among the Transgressors.
Is Virtue a Punisher?"

The question is directed to Milton's theology and ethics, and it is the question over which in his last poems and during his last years Blake brooded most persistently. In his picture of "The Last Judgment," he included "Clergymen in the Pulpit, scourging Sin instead of Forgiving it," and a man, "strangling two women," who "represents a Cruel Church." His criticism had shifted from the old, blunter Jacobinical attack on "priestcraft" to an attack on the denial of the function of Jesus whereever it appeared. Rousseau and Voltaire are as guilty as Jehovah and Satan, or as Luther and Calvin. As *Milton* shows, they continue old error in new forms.

Regeneration begins in Golgonooza, the city of imagination, to which Los and Blake-Milton now go together. They are met at the gates by the sons of Los, Rintrah and Palamabron, who challenge them and prevent their entrance because "Milton's Religion is the cause" of the corruption of the world and the perversion of impulse.

"Milton's Religion is the cause: there is no end to destruction.
Seeing the Churches at their Period in terror & despair,
Rahab created Voltaire, Tirzah created Rousseau,
Asserting the Self-righteousness against the Universal Saviour."

Voltaire and Rousseau, enacting their historical role of secularizing Christianity, suggest the consequent revolutions, the unloosing of Orc:

"Awake, thou sleeper on the Rock of Eternity! Albion awake! . . .
Lo, Orc arises on the Atlantic. Lo, his blood and fire
Glow on America's shore. Albion turns upon his Couch:
He listens to the sounds of War, astonished and confounded . . .
How long shall we lay dead in the Street of the great City?"

Los, wiser than his sons, knows that another revolution is about to take place, to complete the political revolutions through which Orc is raging. The individual revolution of love and forgiveness, won in the city of imagination, will be accomplished by Milton, "the falling Death," which Los has "embrac'd."

"O when shall we tread our Wine-presses in heaven and Reap
Our wheat with shoutings of joy, and leave the Earth in peace?
Remember how Calvin and Luther in fury premature
Sow'd War and stern division between Papists & Protestants.
Let it not be so now. O go not forth in Martyrdoms & Wars!
We were plac'd here by the Universal Brotherhood & Mercy
With powers fitted to circumscribe this dark Satanic death . . .
And how this is as yet we know not, and we cannot know
Till Albion is arisen."

Then Los and Blake-Milton are admitted into the imaginative life,

Great Golgonooza, free from the four iron pillars of Satan's Throne,
(Temperance, Prudence, Justice, Fortitude, the four pillars of tyranny).

Their entrance is signified by the regenerative acts of Los, the harvest and the vintage of nations, and by a long passage to the end of Book the First in praise of the poetic faculty, that life of vision which is restorative. In the world of experience, man's senses cannot help him, for "the sun & moon & stars & trees & clouds & waters And hills" are all shut out from the optic nerve, which has hardened

. . . into a bone
Opake and like the black pebble on the enraged beach.

Still,

. . . the poor indigent is like the diamond which, tho' cloth'd
In rugged covering in the mine, is open all within
And in his hallow'd center holds the heavens of bright eternity.

To preserve the inward vision is the special function of poetry, and that is why Los struggles against Urizen and Satan, not to say Bacon, Newton, and Locke.

As to that false appearance which appears to the reasoner
As of a Globe rolling thro' Voidness, it is a delusion of Ulro.
The Microscope knows not of this nor the Telescope: they alter

The ratio of the Spectator's Organs, but leave Objects untouched.
For every Space larger than a red Globule of Man's blood
Is visionary, and is created by the Hammer of Los:
And every Space smaller than a Globule of Man's blood opens
Into Eternity of which this vegetable Earth is but a shadow.
The red Globule is the unwearied Sun by Los created
To measure Time and Space to mortal Men every morning . . .

Such is the World of Los, the labour of six thousand years.
Thus Nature is a Vision of the Science of the Elohim.

And thus, when vision is lost—or when a poet errs, as Milton had—the whole destiny of man is threatened.

Book the Second opens in Beulah, "where Contrarieties are equally True," the realm of happy sexual love "Where no dispute can come," the place where the faculties "rest," since body and soul are at peace. From this vantage point, the sons and daughters of Ololon observe the progress of Milton's fate and the strife below.

These are the Gods of the Kingdoms of the Earth, in contrarious
And cruel opposition, Element against Element, opposed in War
Not Mental, as the Wars of Eternity, but a Corporeal Strife
In Los's Halls, continual labouring in the Furnaces of Golgonooza.
Orc howls on the Atlantic.

Milton knows that he is himself Satan, but he is instructed now by "the Seven Angels of the Presence" in the doctrine of "states," and learns the difference between his essence, the permanent individuality, and the incrustations that form its corrupted exterior.

"Satan & Adam are States Created into Twenty-seven Churches . . .
Judge then of thy Own Self: thy Eternal Lineaments explore,
What is Eternal & what Changeable, & what Annihilable.
The Imagination is not a State: it is the Human Existence itself.
Affection or Love becomes a State when divided from Imagination.

The Memory is a State always, & the Reason is a State
Created to be Annihilated & a new Ratio Created.
Whatever can be Created can be Annihilated: Forms cannot."

The point of view moves again to Beulah, then to Ololon's descent and her appearance before Blake in his garden. The symbol of the visionary experience now is of a lark mounting in song through the heavens of the twenty-seven churches, a representation of that intuition which pierces through and transcends philosophical systems, preserving truth from the killing grip of dogma. In Blake's attempt to adjust such imagery to his system of characters, its increasingly mechanical operation is evident when the lark in its ascent encounters Ololon in her descent; and the translation of the visionary experience into an increasingly literal account, in Ololon's question to Blake:

> . . . "Knowest thou of Milton who descended
> Driven from Eternity? him I seek."

Ololon has hardly asked the question when Milton himself appears to Blake. Milton contains all the errors of men, and therefore Blake's vision is in reality of "Satan's Universe," in which Milton in his unregenerate form still exists. It is a world of "molten ore & fountains Of pitch & nitre," of "ruin'd palaces & cities & mighty works," of "furnaces of affliction," "stupendous ruins"; and "Here is Jerusalem bound in chains in the Dens of Babylon." To free her and himself is Milton's intention, which he now announces to Satan, the Spectre:

"... know thou, I come to Self Annihilation.
Such are the Laws of Eternity, that each shall mutually
Annihilate himself for others' good, as I for thee.
Thy purpose & the purpose of thy Priests & of thy Churches
Is to impress on men the fear of death, to teach
Trembling & fear, terror, constriction, abject selfishness.
Mine is to teach Men to despise death & to go on
In fearless majesty annihilating Self, laughing to scorn
Thy Laws & terrors, shaking down thy Synagogues as webs.
I come to discover before Heav'n & Hell the Self righteousness
In all its Hypocritic turpitude . . . & put off

In Self annihilation all that is not of God alone,
To put off Self & all I have, ever & ever. Amen."

Satan asserts himself:

. . . "I am God the judge of all, the living & the dead.
Fall therefore down & worship me, submit thy supreme
Dictate to my eternal Will, & to my dictate bow.
I hold the Balances of Right & Just & mine the Sword."

But the Seven Angels of the Presence, appearing round Milton, shout to Albion to awake and cast Satan out "into the Lake Of Los," and Albion rises. His Zoas strive with Milton in the act of self-annihilation. Milton beholds Ololon before him, and both are prepared for sacrifice.

"There is a Negation, & there is a Contrary:
The Negation must be destroy'd to redeem the Contraries.
The Negation is the Spectre, the Reasoning Power in Man;
This is a false Body, an Incrustation over my Immortal
Spirit, a Selfhood which must be put off & annihilated alway.
To cleanse the Face of my Spirit by Self-examination,
To bathe in the Waters of Life, to wash off the Not Human,
I come in Self-annihilation & the grandeur of Inspiration,
To cast off Rational Demonstration by Faith in the Saviour,
To cast off the rotten rags of Memory by Inspiration,
To cast off Bacon, Locke & Newton from Albion's covering,
To take off his filthy garments & clothe him with Imagination,
To cast aside from Poetry all that is not Inspiration,
That it no longer shall dare to mock with the aspersion of
Madness
Cast on the Inspired by the tame high finisher of paltry Blots
Indefinite, or paltry Rhymes, or paltry Harmonies,
Who creeps into State Government like a catterpiller to destroy;
To cast off the idiot Questioner who is always questioning
But never capable of answering, who sits with a sly grin
Silent plotting when to question, like a thief in a cave,
Who publishes doubt & calls it knowledge, whose Science is
Despair,

Whose pretence to knowledge is Envy, whose whole Science is
To destroy the wisdom of ages to gratify ravenous Envy. . . .
He smiles with condescension, he talks of Benevolence & Virtue,
And those who act with Benevolence & Virtue they murder time
on time.
These are the destroyers of Jerusalem."

With the saying the deed is accomplished. Satan disappears, and with him, rationalist restraints and the corruptions of moral law. Ololon divides into the sixfold emanation, the errors, which join with "Milton's Shadow" and fade from life; Milton is transformed into Jesus, the self within, and, wrapped in the garment of Ololon, history, which is the garment of God—

. . . a Garment dipped in blood,
Written within & without in woven letters, & the Writing
Is the Divine Revelation in the Litteral expression,
A Garment of War. I heard it nam'd the Woof of Six Thousand
Years—

he arises whole.

Then the lark breaks out in a triumphant song, and the wild thyme blows. Nature awaits the harvest of the nations, the declaration in universal act that innocence has been restored.

III

MILTON WAS "of the Devil's party without knowing it," and the immediate motive of the poem about him was Hayley's imposition of restraints on Blake's own daemonic energies. Yet it is significant that the poem says nothing of "devils" and that the agents of Milton's salvation are in fact the group called "Angels of the Presence." The significance lies in the shift of Blake's theme from his early praise of what he called "act," the energetic expressions of impulse, to his present denial of "self-righteousness." The two are not unrelated. Self-righteousness *is* the repressive force, the agent in the mind that checks impulse and divides the self, and the theology, the ethics, and the politics that perform equivalent tasks in society.

Yet, while one can point out that Blake's central attitudes have not changed, the shift in vocabulary and symbol does signify a difference in his own contemplation of those attitudes. As the two sides of a coin are wrought of the same piece of metal and yet exhibit different designs, so Blake's theme was capable of these two basic configurations, and in a considerable degree the quality of his style and of his thought may be tested in his preoccupation with one or the other. The gradual substitution of angelic for demonic figures marked the loss of the explosive vigor of *The Marriage of Heaven and Hell* and the incisiveness of *Songs of Experience;* but the increasingly involuted rhetoric of the last poems conceals a growth in wisdom. That style and wisdom are not the same is a humiliating lesson to those who prize art above all else or expect it to perform functions to which it is not fitted.

The shift in Blake's emphasis is no less clear in the functioning of his characters, and especially in the relation of Los and Orc and the relative importance of their roles. In *The Four Zoas,* regeneration was a responsibility shared between them, and was enacted simultaneously, but in *Milton* the burden rests almost entirely on Los. The part of Orc, indeed, is rather that of thematic amplification, or of restatement, than that of an organic segment in the narrative proper. Milton descends and Orc roars in wrath, which is to say that there is a relationship between the casting off of psychological and of social restraints. But the elaborate symbolism that Blake worked out in *The Four Zoas* to show the intricate connections of this relationship and the synthesis of the two terms once revolution in both quarters has taken place is now abandoned.

The difference may be explained in part by the subject matter of *Milton,* the salvation of the soul of a poet, which would naturally be subject to the operations of the eternal prophet, the creative imagination, rather than to those of social revolu tion. Yet this is but a partial explanation, for the increasing importance of Los is too much a matter of the whole tendency of Blake's development to be regarded as merely a structural necessity in a particular poem. The tendency represents at least as much his increased concern with change of heart, but the fact that he used Los rather than Luvah to dramatize this theme indicates, too, that the tendency represents even more his increasing valuation of art, and his final conclusion that the impulse of art is the fundamental value of life. The enormity of Blake's aesthetic rationalization is apparent when we remind ourselves that Los was the artist after Blake's kind: ". . . there is not much difference," T. S. Eliot has said, "between identifying oneself with the Universe and identifying the Universe with oneself." The progression from one to the other was nearly inevitable for Blake.

The real theme of *Milton* is the superiority of the visionary poet over other kinds. Los's function within the poem is to instruct Milton in the visionary way: the Blakean system of the universe is to be substituted for the Miltonic. To achieve this substitution it was necessary to abolish the rationalism of Puritanism. Once that was out of the way, it was easy enough to abolish the solid cosmology of Milton for Blake's mercurial cosmogony of interdependence. Immediately, the visionary life is established:

> . . . & the awful Sun
> Stands still upon the Mountain looking on this little Bird
> With eyes of soft humility & wonder, love & awe.

To the visionary in this universe, the instructions of the Angel Raphael in the seventh and eighth books of *Paradise Lost* are the instructions of Satan himself; for to the visionary, this universe presents nothing that is beyond the reach of perception, and therefore of conception. To say that it does is to set up as final truths the Satanic delusions of mechanism and materialism, or the no less Satanic delusion of deism; that is, the belief that God is to be understood in terms of these half-truths.

But precisely what is God, in Blake? God is the representation of the fullest visionary life, of the most complete unity of being. It follows in Blake's logic that when vision fails in man, God fails; and Jesus is man's enduring capacity for the visionary life, man's way of reasserting God in himself, hence God's way of reassertion. For Universal Brotherhood, the composite figure of Albion, is God himself, and when his powers fall, as Lucifer's did, God does not, as in Milton, remain in authority above, but falls too. This is, in the first place, to reject the kind of idealism represented by Plato, or by Spenser and Shelley, for the relative variety later represented by Yeats in his figure of the Rose, which he "imagined . . . as suffering with man and not as something pursued and seen from afar." And it is, in the second place, to limit the efficacy of Blake's Christianity except as a secular fact. It was precisely Milton's Christianity that Blake was intent on improving, yet apparently he lacked the historical sense necessary to understand that Milton had already gone as far with the antiauthoritarian position as it is possible to go without undermining completely the most serious claims of religion. Blake, determined to abolish authority, took the additional step. Like many more representative men of the eighteenth century, he took it because he loved man more dearly than he loved God.

As a Christian poet Blake was, for all his obscurity, rather too much than too little of his times. He carried up into his Christianity all those secular elements which he was once content to express in more purely secular terms; that is, after all his effort, his myth may be translated back—and too easily, perhaps, for the most genuine myth—into mundane terms. Myth supports logical structures, but it is not in itself a disguise for them. That is allegory.

As *The Four Zoas* rewrote the theory of the French Revolution, so *Milton* (and *Jerusalem* thereafter) continued the process by a transmutation of its institutional attacks. The condition of industrial labor, the worker bound to toil in mine and mill, becomes Blake's most familiar symbol for the enslaved self in a universe unilluminated by vision—barren, rocky, and hard, or a bewildering maze of wheels, unlovely and merciless in either case, and indifferent to life. Ecclesiastical authority and political tyranny have been elevated into a symbolism for dogmatic judgment and legalistic motives. By their disregard for individuality these create the divisive condition of conflict that is opposite to the integration of the visionary life. Marriage conventions and the condition of woman have been transformed into Blake's most precarious symbol, that concept of divisiveness drawn from the fact of sex itself, and opposed to the dubious integration of the "eternal" androgynous figure.

The transmutation of this institutional criticism into his mythical material has its counterpart in the framework of the action of Blake's central narrative as it has now been formulated and fixed, the fall and regeneration of man. For Blake's use of the "fall" is more nearly a psychological interpretation of Rousseau's primitivism than it is of the portions of Genesis from which, in a formal sense, it derives. The state of grace from which man falls and to which he aspires is not the original, but a latter-day Eden—liberty, fraternity, and equality compressed into their psychological equivalent, which Blake called forgiveness, an intensely positive version of our drearier and relatively negative concept of democratic tolerance. And the resurrection, which forgiveness accomplishes, is not the great Biblical drama, but an ideal statement of Godwin's anarchical perfection, where all authority has disappeared. Even those intellectual delights of Blake's Eternals, "the sports of Wisdom in the Human Imagination," have their equivalent in the purely rational delights and occupations that Godwin expected men in a properly conceived society to substitute for war and crime. Revolutions have become last judgments, the crises of the heart rather than of the state; but they satisfy the same fundamental human ambitions. They differ chiefly in their means of statement, which is to say that one of them also satisfies a visionary. That this is no minor difference Blake's revision of theoretical considerations shows. This revision enabled him to push what were for others external problems back into the realm of mind, the ground on which all human struggles begin and where at last they must be won.

His last long poem, *Jerusalem: The Emanation of the Giant Albion,* changes neither the theme nor the central narrative; but it continues the amplification of symbols and attempts the widest possible generalization of the problem that Milton had presented to Blake's mind. Milton's error was, after all, the world's error. It was remarkable in him only because he, a sublime poet, should of all men have been free of it. Having freed him, Blake moves on to the general problem, and minor differences in method result. They result perhaps as much from certain biographical circumstances that had intervened between the beginning of *Milton* and Blake's return to London. He had experienced genuine persecution at the hands of a drunken soldier whose accusations had brought Blake into a court of law on a charge of high treason. He was acquitted, but his discovery of actual legal procedure did nothing to change his feeling about the basic "Satanic" elements in human experience. Now all the errors of suffering mankind—rationalism, self-righteousness, natural religion, the delusions of materialism and mechanism, the multiformed devourer, repression and denial—all now are seen in the Satanic trinity of Accuser, Judge, and Executioner, who pit themselves against the individual integrity. It is the old Jehovah-Jesus conflict, expanded and from one point of view externalized.

Milton, as the account of a man who had really lived, involved historical suggestions. *Jerusalem,* an account of "the Giant Albion," is without any explicit historical considerations. This difference perhaps explains the fact that *Milton* again presented the episodes of Orc—his birth, bondage, and release in America—while in *Jerusalem* Orc is hardly mentioned. Yet, although Milton was a historical figure, his drama was internal, the relationship of mind and heart, body and soul. *Jerusalem* is an account of mankind, and the drama is in a sense external—not the social conflict of class interest, as in some of the early Prophecies, but the psychological relationship between individuals, "the Cruelty of Man to Man" in its primary vein.

The frame of the action is the same. Albion falls, Jerusalem is hidden, and Los is charged with the creative task of reconstruction in the "time of renovation." But for the particular purposes of the poem, swarms of new characters are announced. They are the sons and daughters of Albion, the men and women in this world, who come into separate being—that is, into a condition of strife—when the parent power falls. And now, having freed his system from direct temporal associations, Blake at once attempts to bring it back into a substantial framework by employing spatial associations, by pinning it down, in fact, to the map of Great Britain. The resulting cartography is the most baffling symbolism in Blake, and if it had for him a clear set of associations, except for certain fragmentary elucidations these remain unfathomed. Their general purport, however, is clear enough, and it is in their general purport that they are valuable to his total construction and that they were probably intended.

The symbolism is made both complex and operative through Blake's use of items selected from contemporary Celtomania, and especially his use of the curious theory of the Hebraic origins of Britain, which he inverted—for Blake, the most ancient Israelites were Druids. In *Jerusalem,* the twelve sons of Albion have strange English names, usually anagrams of the names of men who figured in the trial at Chichester; and their emanations, the twelve daughters, have names taken from the annals of British mythology. The twelve sons have a rough correspondence with another group of twelve figures, a mixture of the twelve sons of Israel and of the twelve tribes. Each of these twelve is in spiritual possession of a certain number of the counties in each of the four parts of Great Britain, and in turn, these have a vague equivalence with the cathedral cities, with the continents, and with the nations of the earth. Blake's search is for figures that will express his faith in the interdependence of experience and in his spiritual universalism. Albion, the universal man, has already been shown in his psychological organization, his internal conflicts, the war and peace of the Zoas. In the present poem, Albion is still the central figure, but he is shown in his external conflicts, the struggles of his sons and daughters, the psychological relationship *between* them. For this purpose, Blake not only retains the old metaphor of the "fall" and its debilitating divisions, but adds the implied metaphor of a vast and multipronged migration from a single place, "Albion, the high Cliff of the Atlantic." The new metaphor solidifies in a kind of literalness a symbol that Blake had already employed:

And was Jerusalem builded here
Among these dark Satanic Mills?

Jerusalem parts from Albion. Literally, this means that the Jews migrated from Britain in the primeval time, and symbolically, that liberty has been driven from the land. The new metaphor, then, has the double value of paradox. It expresses the present impoverished social condition ("Albion . . . is become a barren Land"), and it expresses with equal force the internationalism of love and the possibility of its ascendancy in universal peace. Blake's final poem is an effort to overcome all concepts of division—in individual psychology, in social institutions, in national interests and conflicts, in the physical and moral structure of the universe:

> Therefore I print; nor vain my types shall be:
> Heaven, Earth & Hell henceforth shall live in harmony.

It was his supreme effort and, the vigor of his assertion to the contrary, he apparently recognized in the scope of his ambition some need for introductory prayer: "dear Reader . . . love me for this energetic exertion of my talent."

IV

THE POEM OPENS with the voice of Jesus calling to the falling Man, urging him to "return":

> "I am not a God afar off, I am a brother and friend;
> Within your bosoms I reside, and you reside in me:
> Lo! we are One, forgiving all Evil, Not seeking recompense."

But "the perturbed Man," prisoner of self-absorption, has lost the vision:

> "Phantom of the over heated brain! shadow of immortality!
> Seeking to keep my soul a victim to thy Love! which binds
> Man, the enemy of man, into deceitful friendships,
> Jerusalem is not! her daughters are indefinite:
> By demonstration man alone can live, and not by faith.
> My mountains are my own, and I will keep them to myself."

Albion's rejection is fatal. He falls into sleep, the land shrinks into impoverished forms, "mountains run with blood, the cries of war & tumult Resound into the unbounded night," liberty "is scatter'd abroad like a cloud of smoke," and "the terrible sons & daughters of Albion" struggle to prevent Los from building the city of imagination. "From these Twelve all the Families of England spread abroad"—the family, that selfish social unit which Godwin scored and regarded as primary because it necessitates property. In Blake, one unit is more primary, the individual, and no individual escapes completely the assaults of self, not even Los in his prophetic building.

The Spectre of Los, "driv'n by the Starry Wheels of Albion's sons," stands over him "suggesting murderous thoughts against Albion," urging him not to build the city. But even in the midst of chaos Los understands the value of experience, and he refutes the Spectre:

"Pity must join together those whom wrath has torn in sunder,
And the Religion of Generation, which was meant for the destruction
Of Jerusalem, become her covering till the time of the End.
O holy Generation, Image of regeneration!"

He has a precise perception of the offenses to which generation is subject:

"I saw the limbs form'd for exercise contemn'd, & the beauty of
Eternity look'd upon as deformity, & loveliness as a dry tree.
I saw disease forming a Body of Death around the Lamb
Of God to destroy Jerusalem & to devour the body of Albion,
By war and stratagem to win the labour of the husbandman.
Awkwardness arm'd in steel, folly in a helmet of gold.
Weakness with horns & talons, ignorance with a rav'ning beak,
Every Emanative joy forbidden as a Crime
And the Emanations buried alive in the earth with pomp of religion,
Inspiration deny'd, Genius forbidden by laws of punishment,
I saw terrified."

From this material Los must form the instrument of salvation, "the spiritual sword," heat the metal in the forge of human misery and beat it out on the anvil of human cruelty, regenera-

"Angels Hovering over the Body of Jesus"
Courtesy of Esmond Morse, Esq.

"Gothic is Living Form"

tion from generation. His solution, desperate and simple, is Blake's own answer to the world:

> "I must Create a System or be enslav'd by another Man's.
> I will not Reason & Compare: my business is to Create."

But this business must be conducted in the world, and its purpose is to form a new world from the materials and the conditions of living in this one. "Los stands in London building Golgonooza." The point here, which Blake makes time and again, is basic to understanding the exact results of the confluence of ideas in his mind, to see, that is, how from a theological point of view politics corrupted his religion, or how from a social point of view politics gave religion meaning. Blake's attempt is to fuse sacred aspiration with secular objects.

The city of art is the city of Christian affections rather than of Christian dogma, a doctrine not of a supramundane but of a social salvation.

> What are those golden builders doing? where was the burying-place
> Of soft Ethinthus? near Tyburn's fatal Tree? is that
> Mild Zion's hill's most ancient promontory, near mournful
> Ever weeping Paddington? is that Calvary and Golgotha
> Becoming a building of pity and compassion? Lo!
> The stones are pity, and the bricks, well wrought affections
> Enamel'd with love & kindness, & the tiles engraven gold,
> Labour of merciful hands: the beams & rafters are forgiveness:
> The mortar & cement of the work, tears of honesty: the nails
> And the screws & iron braces are well wrought blandishments
> And well contrived words, firm fixing, never forgotten,
> Always comforting the remembrance: the floor, humility:
> The ceilings, devotion: the hearths, thanksgiving.

It is possible to build this city in the midst of London, transform the soldier's sigh and the harlot's curse into "love & kindness," through that negative view of evil which Blake accepted from his century even as he rejected its view of the universe. In *Jerusalem* he labors to show that his objection is not to matter but to a materialistic theory, and for this purpose he develops here a distinction that, although often submerged, has all along been present. It is the distinction between "the World of Generation," living material forms opening "like a flower from the Earth's center In which is Eternity," and the concept of Ulro, the Newtonian universe of inorganic matter, "the abstract Voids between the Stars," "the Satanic Wheels." This is the universe that does not exist at all, the abstract construction of scientific rationalism that closes its eyes to most of life, the fiction of a barren wasteland in a mathematical system, of a world (so beautiful to the senses and so novel in vision) devoid of qualities, reduced to colorless extensions that consist of extended atoms. And it is the acceptance of this bleak universe that involves man in all his cruel, but still remediable, errors:

There is the Cave, the Rock, the Tree, the Lake of Udan Adan,
The Forest and the Marsh and the Pits of bitumen deadly,
The Rocks of solid fire, the Ice valleys, the Plains
Of burning sand, the rivers, cataract & Lakes of Fire. . . .
The land of darkness flamed, but no light & no response:
The land of snows of trembling & of iron hail incessant:
The land of earthquakes, and the land of woven labyrinths:
The land of snares & traps & wheels & pit-falls & dire mills:
The Voids, the Solids.

The harshness of this bleak world is the counterpart of man's moral cruelty, and in terms of this landscape Blake recapitulates all his most familiar symbols for a depressed humanity: the cave of reason, the rock of law, the tree of mystery, the lake of the indefinite, the marsh and the pit of despair, the consumptive fires of aspirations that can find no forms. It is against the acceptance as realities of this view and these errors that Los's imaginative effort is directed, as

He views the City of Golgonooza & its smaller Cities,
The Looms & Mills & Prisons & Work-houses.

Yet even in this effort Los is compelled to struggle with his own dividing Spectre, to subdue it to his needs, and to pursue the unregenerate sons of Albion.

The sons, "Jealous of Jerusalem's children," gather in a counsel to plot her expulsion, and to plan, as a counteractivity to Los's building, the building of

"Babylon the City of Vala, the Goddess Virgin-Mother.
She is our Mother! Nature! Jerusalem is our Harlot-Sister."

The conflict of nature and liberty is a condition of the decline of man. Now "Vala produc'd the Bodies, Jerusalem gave the Souls." The false distinction and the conflict between the two is a result of the separation of Vala and Jerusalem themselves, a portion of the total degradation of things that Albion's fall involves.

Vala and Jerusalem, seeing Albion in his ruined state, "Seeking for rest and finding none," lament their ruin. Jerusalem reproaches Vala, who replies in a catalogue of miseries. Then Albion awakens and upbraids Vala, who replies with a further account of her devastation. But Albion persists in his error: "I brought Love into light, & fancied Innocence is no more." Then he turns on Jerusalem, who, in an image of wheels versus wings, begs to know why the condition of human existence should be brutal when it can equally well be idyllic:

"Why should Punishment Weave the Veil with Iron Wheels of
 War
When Forgiveness might it Weave with Wings of Cherubim?"

Momentarily, he glimpses his error when he turned his back on Jesus, the "Human Imagination," and entered "the Wastes of Moral Law," and he remembers the ancient concord of nations:

"In the Exchanges of London every Nation walk'd,
And London walk'd in every Nation, mutual in love & harmony.
Albion cover'd the whole Earth, England encompass'd the
 Nations,
Mutual each within other's bosom in Visions of Regeneration."

Can his errors be undone? Can the net of judgment, which at last ensnares even the judge, be destroyed?

". . . O my Children,
I have educated you in the crucifying cruelties of Demonstration
Till you have assum'd the Providence of God & slain your
Father."

Then as Albion falls into what he thinks is death, he has a vision of Jesus, whose principle is the liberal one of hating the sin but treasuring the sinner:

"Descend, O Lamb of God, & take away the imputation of Sin
By the Creation of States & the deliverance of Individuals
Evermore. Amen."

But the time is not yet at hand. Many are still unable to distinguish between the purity of individuals and the form it has taken. Chapter One ends with an address to the Jews. Blake reminds them of their parentage in Albion and of their part, which they would repudiate by a tribal segregation, in the universal religion of forgiveness.

And O thou Lamb of God, whom I
Slew in my dark self-righteous pride,
Art thou return'd to Albion's Land?
And is Jerusalem thy Bride?

Come to my arms & never more
Depart, but dwell for ever here:
Create my Spirit to thy Love:
Subdue my Spectre to thy Fear.

Spectre of Albion! warlike Fiend!
In clouds of blood & ruin roll'd,
I here reclaim thee as my own,
My Selfhood! Satan! arm'd in gold

Is this thy soft Family-Love
Thy cruel Patriarchal pride,
Planting thy Family alone,
Destroying all the World beside?

A man's worst enemies are those
Of his own house & family;
And he who makes his law a curse,
By his own law shall surely die.

Albion's seeming death is a further fall in which he loses his brief glimpse of error, and Chapter Two of *Jerusalem* opens at "his secret seat," where he declares himself "the punisher & judge" who, making "his law a curse," decrees "That Man be separate from Man." Here, in a landscape of petrified and frozen forms shrouded in Urizen's snows, where the only life is in the tree that grows like a banyan into "an endless labyrinth of woe," Albion erects twelve altars from the rocks and calls them Justice and Truth. His sons are to be the victims.

Jesus appears on the rocks and proposes a brief analysis of the situation. It is not Albion who must be exposed, but his Spectre, Satan:

"The Reactor hath hid himself thro' envy. I behold him,
But you cannot behold him till he be reveal'd in his System.
Albion's Reactor must have a Place prepar'd. . . .
. . . he admits of no Reply
From Albion, but hath founded his Reaction into a Law
Of Action, for Obedience to destroy the Contraries of Man.
He hath compell'd Albion to become a Punisher."

Los and his parts, his Spectre and his emanations, are free for their labors, but all others are enslaved. Los, protected by "the Divine Vision," follows "Albion into his Central Void among his Oaks." He prays that Jesus appear—

"Because of the Opressors of Albion in every City & Village.
They mock at the Labourer's limbs: they mock at his starv'd Children:
They buy his Daughters that they may have power to sell his Sons:
They compell the Poor to live upon a crust of bread by soft mild arts:
They reduce the Man to want, then give with pomp & ceremony:
The praise of Jehovah is chaunted from lips of hunger & thirst."

Then he searches out the "interiors of Albion's Bosom" to find the villains, but he cannot find them. He

. . . saw every Minute Particular of Albion degraded & mur-
der'd,
But saw not by whom; they were hidden within in the minute
particulars
Of which they had possess'd themselves, and there they take up
The articulations of a man's soul and laughing throw it down.

Taken together, these two passages express the culmination of Blake's insight into the double fact of evil—its obvious expression in the forms of social cruelty, and its obscure internal causes. Nothing can be easily separated from anything. The view is not essentially different from what Blake had been saying from the beginning, but it is now most expressly and sharply stated. At bottom, the second passage merely restates Blake's earliest attitude toward evil, that it is corrupted energy. The minute particulars that cannot be separated from the villainies within them are in themselves the evil fact. Satan is the impulse that restrains energy, but his multiple surrogates are the energies when they are restrained.

. . . Record the terrible wonder! that the Punisher
Mingles with his Victim's Spectre, enslaved & tormented
To him whom he has murder'd, bound in vengeance & enmity.

The actor becomes the reactor; action, reaction. Even the imputation of self-righteousness is self-righteous. To speak, therefore, of the expulsion of evil is not only inaccurate but it is to fall into Satan's very hands. That is why, in Blake's ethics, an act of love is the only remedy for the internal fault, and universal love the only one for even the most hideous social fact. And it is only in a figurative sense that an act of love *routs* Satan. What it really does is to reform him, and make *him* capable of love. Mysticism? Hardly. It is an intense and exceptional aesthetics operating as morals, and Los, the great poet, while he has an exact insight into the nature of his function, finds himself nearly desperate in the face of the confusing problem posed by this unlikely combination.

"What shall I do? what could I do if I could find these
Criminals?
I could not dare to take vengeance, for all things are so constructed
And builded by the Divine hand that the sinner shall always
escape,
And he who takes vengeance alone is the criminal of Providence.
If I should dare to lay my finger on a grain of sand
In way of vengeance, I punish the already punish'd. O whom
Should I pity if I pity not the sinner who is gone astray?
. . . What can I do to hinder the Sons
Of Albion from taking vengeance? or how shall I them perswade?"

Even Los's language—like Blake's—is subject to that basic inaccuracy which has corrupted Christianity and all religions. "What can I do to *hinder* . . . ?" That is precisely what he must not do, and he quickly finds other words: ". . . how shall I them perswade?" The difference is the whole difference.

Los, "the Demon of the Furnaces," hears Jesus answer from the fire:

"No individual can keep these Laws, for they are death
To every energy of man and forbid the springs of life.
Albion hath enter'd the State Satan! Be permanent, O State!
And be thou for ever accursed! that Albion may arise again.
And be thou created into a State! I go forth to Create
States, to deliver Individuals evermore! Amen."

The creation of "states" is the definition of error, its external expression in social forms, the mistaken attitude calcifying into mistaken act. Now Albion wears "death's iron gloves," and "The soul drinks murder & revenge & applauds its own holiness." All error is rampant, and Los, "furious, raging," cries out:

. . . "Why stand we here trembling around
Calling on God for help, and not ourselves, in whom God dwells,
Stretching a hand to save the falling Man?"

He groans over the Sons of Albion, who brood "in holy hypocritic lust, drinking the cries of pain From howling victims of

Law," who destroy friendship and benevolence and love, "every energy render'd cruel," who reduce "the two Sources of Life in Eternity, Hunting and War," to the bloody wars of nations, who perceive and thereby create a world that is in itself a "state":

". . . they accumulate
A World in which Man is by his Nature the Enemy of Man."

In this world, governments are "a pretence of Liberty To destroy Liberty," churches, "a pretence of Religion to destroy Religion." Only Los (only Blake), with his piercing insight through the surfaces of fact, is capable of the true revolutionary protest:

"I see America clos'd apart, & Jerusalem driven in terror
Away from Albion's mountains, far away from London's spires.
I will not endure this thing! I alone withstand to death
This outrage! Ah me! how sick & pale you all stand round me!
Ah me! pitiable ones! do you also go to death's vale?
All you my Friends & Brothers, all you my beloved Companions,
Have you also caught the infection of Sin & stern Repentance?
I see Disease arise upon you! yet speak to me and give
Me some comfort! why do you all stand silent? I alone
Remain in permanent strength."

Los's speech is persuasive, and, "on Cherub's wings," the Sons of Albion attempt "with kindest violence to bear him back Against his will thro' Los's Gate to Eden." But he resists, and suffers a further fall, and the individual life seems to wither under the burden of the "states" that encumber it.

An address "To the Deists" is interposed between Chapter Two and Chapter Three. Blake attacks the deistic view of human self-sufficiency and the attempt to reduce religion to morality, which is the substitution of "the Religion of Satan" for "the Religion of Jesus." For the ideal of moral virtue is the basis of self-righteousness, and self-righteousness has "accursed consequence to Man." It creates law, which ignores and scatters the sacred individual identity.

Early in Chapter Three, the "accurs'd consequence" is described:

In Great Eternity every particular Form gives forth or Emanates
Its own peculiar Light, & the Form is the Divine Vision
And the Light is his Garment. This is Jerusalem in every Man,
A Tent & Tabernacle of Mutual Forgiveness, Male & Female
Clothings.
And Jerusalem is called Liberty among the Children of Albion.
But Albion fell down, a Rocky fragment from Eternity hurl'd
By his own Spectre, who is the Reasoning Power in every Man,
Into his own Chaos, which is the Memory between Man & Man.

In its uncorrupted form, each individual thing differs, has "Its own peculiar Light," and the recognition of this "light" is in itself liberty. When law arises as reason, the distinction between individuals ceases, and liberty is lost; with it goes the beauty of the true anarchic order, and the attempt at enforced order brings psychological and social chaos. The agent of this destruction is the unreal Spectre, the negation, the force that denies individual impulse. It declares itself as follows:

. . . "I am God, O Sons of Men! I am your Rational Power!
Am I not Bacon & Newton & Locke who teach Humility to Man,
Who teach Doubt & Experiment? & my two Wings, Voltaire,
Rousseau?
Where is that Friend of Sinners? that Rebel against my Laws
Who teaches Belief to the Nations & an unknown Eternal Life?
Come hither into the Desart & turn these stones to bread.
Vain foolish Man! wilt thou believe without Experiment
And build a World of Phantasy upon my Great Abyss,
A World of Shapes in craving lust & devouring appetite?"

This is Blake's perpetual sermon to the reformers of the Enlightenment. They argued that because all men shared the gift of reason, all men were equal. But in founding concepts of social and political equality on reason, they ignored the quality that all men do share, energy; and they prevented genuine liberty, which is the beautiful flowering in all its variety and particularity of individual energy. The rationalism of the bourgeois revolutions proved to be the agent not of emancipation but of renewed tyrannies. Blake's buried argument is that if equality is granted to only a part of man rather than to the whole man, then liberty is granted to only a section of society rather than to the whole of it. Concepts of power on one level breed the practices of power on the other.

This is an axiom among the Eternals, who cannot understand the assertions of the negating Spectre:

"To be their inferiors or superiors we equally abhor:
Superior, none we know; inferior, none: all equal share
Divine Benevolence & joy; for the Eternal Man
Walketh among us, calling us his Brothers & his Friends."

Theirs is the wisdom of innocence, which exists before and after the divided state in which pity and mercy are necessities:

. . . "It is better to prevent misery than to release from misery:
It is better to prevent error than to forgive the criminal."

Then the "Great Voice of the Atlantic," the Divine Vision, finds a new way of expressing Blake's argument that authority makes those distinctions which sunder innocence:

"What is a Wife & what is a Harlot? What is a Church & What
Is a Theatre? are they Two & not One? can they Exist Separate?
Are not Religion & Politics the Same Thing? Brotherhood is Religion,
O Demonstrations of Reason Dividing Families in Cruelty & Pride."

The creation of prohibitions is the beginning of error. The false ideal of chastity produces the harlot; the repressions of the Church are the expressions of the theater. These are the fatal distinctions of experience. Mary Wollstonecraft had argued that in eighteenth-century society a wife was a prostitute with legal status. Blake pushed the notion further by pointing out that "Every Harlot was once a Virgin: every Criminal an Infant Love." The Church corrupts individuality through dogma; the theater, as Godwin had argued in one of his many moments of logical excess, ignores individual wisdom by making it mouth the wisdom of other individuals. Both compel mass attention through spectacle; are they not alike? "Every Man's Wisdom is peculiar to his own Individuality," as true religion and a genuine politics know very well. For they are identical: brotherhood, the condition of love in which every individual recognizes the need of every other individual to be precisely himself. The liberation of self can come about only through the repudiation of selfishness, an act of imagination that breaks down all barriers between men (the Godwinian "family," as well as the class and the nation) and thus for the first time allows men to become truly themselves. Without the imaginative act, love itself is a mere "state," the "Cruelty & Pride" of self-love. "Without Forgiveness of Sin, Love is Itself Eternal Death." This is the reason that the artist, Los, is the central character in Blake's drama of regeneration, building the city of imagination to rescue nature from the dark condition where imagination does not exist. To religion and politics we must add art, which includes them.

The Daughters of Albion confront Los in the single form of Vala, fallen nature.

Her Hand is a Court of Justice: her Feet two Armies in Battle:
Storms & Pestilence in her Locks, & in her Loins Earthquake
And Fire & the Ruin of Cities & Nations & Families & Tongues.

She weaves her garment with "the Flax of Human Miseries" as Los strives with his building, where they may be overcome. The Sons of Albion, abandoning "simple workmanship" for machine labor, illustrate in a passage that Blake repeats from *The Four Zoas* how Vala's "Human Miseries" thwart human fulfillment. And then they confront her:

"Now, now the battle rages round thy tender limbs, O Vala!
Now smile among thy bitter tears, now put on all thy beauty.
Is not the wound of the sword sweet & the broken bone delightful?
Wilt thou now smile among the scythes when the wounded groan in the field?
We were carried away in thousands from London & in tens
Of thousands from Westminster & Marybone, in ships clos'd up,

Chain'd hand & foot, compell'd to fight under the iron whips
Of our captains, fearing our officers more than the enemy."

In the press gang, Blake has found a single image to express that dual result of authority which is the substance of experience, slavery and conflict.

Mechanism, too, has its dual aspect—industrialization in work, scientific rationalism in the mind. The Sons of Albion turn from manufacturing "the Arts of Death" to the building of Natural Religion, "with chains"

Of rocks round London Stone, of Reasonings, of unhewn Demonstrations
In labyrinthine arches (Mighty Urizen the Architect) thro' which
The Heavens might revolve & Eternity be bound in their chain.
Labour unparallel'd! a wondrous rocky World of cruel destiny,
Rocks piled on rocks reaching the stars, stretching from pole to pole.

The building is constructed on Luvah's place, to destroy him, "For Luvah is France, the Victim of the Spectres of Albion."

As Orc, in the grip of Urizen, was transformed from the pure revolutionary energy into the materialist serpent of war, so Luvah, the revolutionary passion of France, is here buried under a naturalistic philosophy derived from Britain. Passion is not, of course, destroyed, but as it is degraded so are those sons who attempt to destroy it. "All who see become what they behold . . . as their Victim, so are they." And under the rule of Natural Religion, the tragedy of narrowed perception increases: ". . . as their eye & ear shrunk, the heavens shrunk away."

The rest of Chapter Three tells, in interminable catalogues, of the spreading errors until

. . . Albion is darkened & Jerusalem lies in ruins
Above the Mountains of Albion, above the head of Los.

But Los is still at his furnaces, demolishing with "his mighty Hammer . . . time on time In miracles & wonders" all the mistaken assertions of men. And Primrose Hill, where Blake "conversed with the Spiritual Sun," is "the mouth of the Furnace &

the Iron Door." With this warning, Blake takes over the narrative for the remainder of the chapter.

I behold Babylon in the opening Streets of London. I behold
Jerusalem in ruins wandering about from house to house.
This I behold: the shudderings of death attend my steps.
I walk up and down in Six Thousand Years: their Events are
present before me
To tell how Los in grief & anger, whirling round his Hammer
on high,
Drave the Sons & Daughters of Albion from their ancient mountains.

That Blake's visions of eternity appeared to him on Primrose Hill and in South Moulton Street is of great importance. It is the evidence for his belief that earth is not barred to paradise, that perception is everything.

. . . in your own Bosom you bear your Heaven
And Earth & all you behold; tho' it appears Without, it is
Within,
In your Imagination . . .

The function of Los in the Blakean myth is identical with the function of Blake in literary history as he conceived it: "I'll . . . shew you all alive The world"; and at the end of the third chapter of *Jerusalem,* Blake points out that this is likewise the function of one other:

. . . Jesus, breaking thro' the Central Zones of Death & Hell,
Opens Eternity in Time & Space, triumphant in Mercy.

The last part of *Jerusalem* begins with an address "To the Christians," and with the famous epigraph in which Blake tells his readers that his work is "a golden string" which if they wish will direct them to order, through liberty.

It will lead you in at Heaven's gate
Built in Jerusalem's wall.

The address consists of a statement of puritanical asceticism and the counterstatement of Blake's ethical aestheticism. "I know of no other Christianity and of no other Gospel than the liberty both of body & mind to exercise the Divine Arts of Imagination." For that "Labour in Knowledge" which alone builds Jerusalem, Blake invokes Jesus, "the bright Preacher of Life," the archetype of the visionary who never mistakes the individual for the "state": ". . . that which is a Sin in the sight of cruel Man is not so in the sight of our kind God." Blake's muse, a creature of vision, "a Watcher & a Holy-One," then repeats that divine commission which, at the end of Chapter Three of the poem, Blake had already ascribed to himself:

"Go therefore, cast out devils in Christ's name,
Heal thou the sick of spiritual disease,
Pity the evil, for thou art not sent
To smite with terror & with punishments
Those that are sick, like to the Pharisees
Crucifying & encompassing sea & land
For proselytes to tyranny & wrath;
But to the Publicans & Harlots go,
Teach them True Happiness, but let no curse
Go forth out of thy mouth to blight their peace;
For Hell is open'd to Heaven: thine eyes beheld
The dungeons burst & the Prisoners set free."

Then follows a prediction of that return to innocence, hell opening to heaven, which is the substance of the last chapter of the poem:

And now the time returns again:
  Our souls exult, & London's towers
Recieve the Lamb of God to dwell
  In England's green & pleasant bowers.

This is the poet's prophecy of triumph in the very time when error has sunk into its lowest forms, when Jerusalem lies in ruins, and Albion's individuality is being attacked on the rock where he sleeps. Blake, like Los, works most furiously toward regeneration when life is darkest; and Los, like Blake, keeps before him that communal idyl which is their object.

"When Souls mingle & join thro' all the Fibres of Brotherhood
Can there be any secret joy on Earth greater than this?"

Jerusalem and Vala struggle with one another, the daughters of Albion are in cruel conflict with the sons, and Los, at his furnaces, sings an unrewarded love song to Jerusalem. He is himself still divided from his emanation, who taunts him grimly with woman's most worldly cunning, but he persists in his task.

The blow of his Hammer is Justice, the swing of his Hammer Mercy,
The force of Los's Hammer is eternal Forgiveness.

He struggles to thrust the warring and refractory sons and daughters into his purging fires, belaboring them the while with "Demonstrations" of revolutionary wisdom.

". . . worshippers of a God of cruelty & law,
Your Slaves & Captives you compell to worship a God of Mercy!"

As his rage grows, Los's prophetic mood turns reminiscent, and in his next speech he includes three or four lines plucked from *The Marriage of Heaven and Hell:*

"It is easier to forgive an Enemy than to forgive a Friend.
The man who permits you to injure him deserves your vengeance:
He also will receive it; go Spectre! obey my most secret desire
Which thou knowest without my speaking. Go to these Fiends of Righteousness,
Tell them to obey their Humanities & not pretend Holiness
When they are murderers as far as my Hammer & Anvil permit.
Go, tell them that the Worship of God is honoring his gifts
In other men & loving the greatest men best, each according
To his Genius which is the Holy Ghost in Man; there is no other
God than that God who is the intellectual fountain of Humanity.
He who envies or calumniates, which is murder & cruelty,
Murders the Holy-one. Go, tell them this, & overthrow their cup,
Their bread, their altar-table, their incense & their oath,
Their marriage & their baptism, their burial & consecration."

This is Blake's social doctrine in essence, not very different now from what it was when first he expounded it; for no matter how his symbolism and his vocabulary developed, into what monstrous incumbrances, the attitude remained almost the same, the loyalty to "the Devil's party" unshaken. Like Los as regeneration comes into sight, because regeneration is always so tantalizingly near even when it can suddenly seem so far, Blake always fumed at the stultifying compromises of angelic piety. The problem is so simple, even though the achievement can be so agonizingly difficult.

"I care not whether a Man is Good or Evil; all that I care
Is whether he is a Wise Man or a Fool. Go, put off Holiness
And put on Intellect, or my thund'rous Hammer shall drive thee
To wrath which thou condemnest, till thou obey my voice."

That is Blake to the world, and Blake to his own impulses to compromise with the world, and Blake to *his* reason when it whispered that vision, and its nearly incredible consequences in a life, could be delusion. In *Jerusalem,* it is of course Los, "compelling" his Spectre, altering "every Ratio of his Reason . . . time after time," every fixity of judgment that would obstruct perception, forgiveness.

Such alterations *are* regeneration. The nations and the tribes begin their return to Albion's limbs. Los, active in the process of fulfillment, tells Enitharmon that she must lose herself in him. She is terrified, fearing the loss of her identity, but Los assures her that only in the destruction of falsely created sexual qualities can she release and develop her human qualities. It is Mary Wollstonecraft talking to the housewives of Europe, but now wholly in the symbols of the language of mind. Annihilation of selfishness is the creation of identity.

. . . "Sexes must vanish & cease
To be when Albion arises from his dread repose, O lovely
Enitharmon:
When all their Crimes, their Punishments, their Accusations of
Sin,

All their Jealousies, Revenges, Murders, hidings of Cruelty in Deceit
Appear only in the Outward Spheres of Visionary Space and Time,
In the shadows of Possibility, by Mutual Forgiveness for evermore."

The nadir of experience, "that Signal of the Morning which was told us in the Beginning," has been plumbed, and the ascent begins. "Time was Finished!" Feeling the "Breath Divine," Albion stirs on his cold rock. He joins his emanation and he beholds Jesus, who tells him of self-annihilation. "This is Friendship & Brotherhood: without it Man Is Not."

Albion reply'd: "Cannot Man exist without Mysterious
Offering of Self for Another? is this Friendship & Brotherhood?
I see thee in the likeness & similitude of Los my Friend."

Jesus said: "Wouldest thou love one who never died
For thee, or ever die for one who had not died for thee?
And if God dieth not for Man & giveth not himself
Eternally for Man, Man could not exist; for Man is Love
As God is Love: every kindness to another is a little Death
In the Divine Image, nor can Man exist but by Brotherhood."

One act of love slays the Spectre. At the end of the poem, Blake points this out in two ways. First, Albion plunges into "the Furnaces of affliction," which at once become "Fountains of Living Waters flowing from the Humanity Divine." He arises in the body of Jesus, he assimilates his cities and his sons, and the Four Zoas in their proper relationship. Second, with the bow and the arrows of Love, "in Wars of mutual Benevolence, Wars of Love," he annihilates the "Druid Spectre." It merely vanishes, insubstantial as smoke, as irrelevant as ghosts to daytime. No villain need be. Bacon and Newton and Locke appear in the heavens with Milton and Shakespeare and Chaucer. Urizen embraces and is embraced by his brothers, "And they conversed together in Visionary forms dramatic." The world is free, and "the Cry from all the Earth" as all identities discover what it is to "Humanize In the Forgiveness of Sins" is this:

"Where is the Tree of Good & Evil that rooted beneath the
cruel heel
Of Albions Spectre, the Patriarch Druid? where are all his
Human Sacrifice
For Sin in War & in the Druid Temples of the Accuser of Sin,
beneath
The Oak Groves of Albion that cover'd the whole Earth beneath
his Spectre?
Where are the Kingdoms of the World & all their glory that
grew on Desolation,
The Fruit of Albion's Poverty Tree, when the Triple Headed
Gog-Magog Giant
Of Albion Taxed the Nations into Desolation & then gave the
Spectrous Oath?"

V

In his last poems, in the articulation of his doctrine of love and forgiveness, Blake is concerned above all with an attempt to define Christianity as he understood it and wished it to be. Insofar as the later poems are different in their content from the earlier poems, it is in their increased concern with a religious rather than a political solution. Yet it is fatal to an understanding of Blake to separate these two except as the varying emphases of which the same theme is capable. He himself took pains to ask the question, "Are not Religion & Politics the Same Thing? Brotherhood."

Nearly everything in these poems centers in Blake's concept of the character and the significance of Jesus. The concept grows directly out of the characterization in *The Marriage of Heaven and Hell,* where a devil correctly points out to a mistaken angel that Jesus was a revolutionary genius who broke all his father's laws in the Mosaic tablet and, defying the standards of the eternal bourgeois, consorted with the lowliest sinners. In "The Everlasting Gospel," the fragmentary poem on which Blake was working at the same time as *Jerusalem,* this characterization is developed. Jesus had become Blake's main symbol for love, and he sharpened this symbol by insisting on an adulterous rather than an immaculate conception. The Son of God is the product of unrestrained desire, love unfettered, and these origins endow him with his antinomian proclivities. In *Jerusalem,* a long passage expands this interpretation of the nativity. Joseph reviles Mary as an adulteress. She begs for forgiveness, in the act of which he will free his own humanity.

". . . if I were pure, never could I taste the sweets
Of the Forgiveness of Sins; if I were holy, I never could behold the tears
Of love of him who loves me in the midst of his anger in furnace of fire."

Joseph repents, and in forgiving Mary he discovers that she, who has yielded to impulse, is actually "with Child by the Holy Ghost." The child is the embodiment of love, and because of the particular force that Blake gives to the idea of love, his Christianity is primarily ethical and his view of Jesus the basis of his picture of man in society. In his early Prophetic Books he pleaded for the external conditions of life in which the anarchy of love can thrive. In his late poems, he pleaded for the anarchy of love itself, which will create those conditions. In Blake's development it is not his terms that change but the relationship he imagines between them.

The change was not basic enough to make of him either a very good Christian or a poet with a real interest in practical politics. But it was quite adequate to the development of what was his interest, "the permanent politics of human nature"—the conflicts of mind and heart that develop between men in society and within the social man, the impulse to peace and the impulse to power, the tension between them, and the means to a resolution. In addressing himself to these problems, Blake declined from the beginning to accept as a necessary assumption the traditional view of good and evil, of the fixed relationship between God and man. He rejected the vocabulary of the philosophy of the Enlightenment in its declaration that God is rational and man likewise; but in the deepest sense he did not reject the view. The real significance of the incarnation in Christian dogma eluded him. That "Absolute Paradox" which Christ presents to the genuine Christian imagination, the insoluble mystery of a union of God, who is just and good, and man, who is damned and depraved, "as though fire were somehow also water"—it was not to accommodate this paradox that Blake denied the sufficiency of reason and asserted the necessity of faith.

Yet Jesus is the very keystone of Blake's thinking, and in that thinking he performs a paradoxical function, but it is a paradox perpetually capable of resolution. Its terms are aesthetic and ethical, and its basis in the history of European thought is political. Jesus is to Blake (as Baudelaire was to Rimbaud) *"le premier voyant,"* and he is usually content to designate him as "the Divine Vision," at once the archetype of the visionary and for that reason the main object of vision. Because of Jesus' perception that men are brothers and the example of his equal love, it follows that he should emerge as the ideal socialist. And in enacting the revolution of the heart, he solves the bitter riddle that the bourgeois revolutions of the eighteenth century thrust upon the world, that paradox of individualism in the conflict of liberty and equality.

Of liberty, equality, and fraternity, only the first was realized, and in a century that saw the most brutal developments of individualism in modern history, that was the privilege of a class, "the Monopolizing Trader," who was quick with his own rationalizations. "Obedience to the Will of the Monopolist is call'd Virtue." Blake had booksellers and picture-dealers in mind when he made this observation, but in a period of rapid capitalist expansion and the mushrooming of industrial power, it was axiomatic. The individualism developed in the nineteenth century was clearly not the individualism that eighteenth-century radicals had envisaged. Somehow, in less than fifty years it had developed tyrannies much more frightening than those of that monarchism and clericalism which the Revolution had diminished. In Blake we can see that the imagery of tyranny changes gradually from crowns and scepters to machines, and "The Serpent Bulk of Nature's dross" is clothed in gold, as in his last years money is opposed to art, commerce and empire to poetry and painting, and wheels to wings.

The mistaken individualist is the tyrant. He makes "to himself Laws from his own identity" instead of granting liberty to all identities. This is "moral individuality," and from it comes Albion's tragic decree "That Man be separate from Man" in conflict and slavery. But again—conflict *is* slavery. The mistaken individualist not only destroys the identity of those whom he oppresses, but also his own; for oppression works both ways, with equal devastation of spirit.

> . . . Record the terrible wonder! that the Punisher
> Mingles with his Victim's Spectre, enslaved & tormented
> To him whom he has murder'd.

A genuine individualism looks to others, not to self; and this is real liberty, not "a pretence of Liberty To destroy Liberty."

> In Great Eternity every particular Form gives forth or Emanates
> Its own peculiar Light, & the Form is the Divine Vision
> And the Light is his Garment. This is Jerusalem in every Man.

"The Divine Vision," or Jesus, in the lesson of love and forgiveness helps men see that brotherhood comes only from the act of imagination that recognizes in every identity its "peculiar Light." This is "self-annihilation," and the paradoxical function of Jesus in Blake's poems is to show men how liberty, equality, and fraternity, in spite of history, become compatibles in this act. Either you have them all or you have none of them.

It is history that induced Blake to put so much faith in vision, or fresh insight, and to denounce the role of memory. Albion is laid waste by a "deluge of forgotten remembrances," and when the Universal Man falls, it is "Into his own Chaos, which is the Memory between Man & Man." To achieve the pastoral peace of the mythical past, men must transcend the limitations of the historical past by a genuinely revolutionary perception of possibility. This is a complete rejection of the kind of institutional conservatism represented by Burke, and it is by no means a literal acceptance of the kind of primitivism taught by Rousseau. Both of these looked backward, to idealizations of a past, and Blake was impatient to spring beyond those six thousand years through which, he said, his imagination walked, to an ideal future. To this not memory but vision was essential, for "All who see become what they behold."

Yet if vision transcends history, it likewise transcends matter. It is in this that Blake is nearest Plato. There are perhaps more differences than similarities between their forms of idealism, but in at least one way Blake's life of vision is analogous to Plato's world of ideas. To both the ideal realm was a necessary source of refreshment for the material realm. Plato's admonition at the end of the *Timaeus,* "that we should not move the body without the soul or the soul without the body, that they will be on guard against each other, and be healthy and well-balanced," maintains the equipoise between matter and spirit, the relative validity of the material world together with the absolute validity of the ideal world. The result for Plato was an unusually happy system of ethics. Here Blake departs from Plato, for he failed to arrive at some comparable moderation between these opposites. Either he insisted that the life of vision alone was real, or he argued—more frequently—that the life of vision made matter real. Either position would have been tenable, but he wavered between them. When he was most insistent on the ideal values, he used Plato's images: the eternal Forms, of which "this Vegetable Glass of Nature," "this World of Mortality is but a Shadow," and the "cave" of reason ("The Caverns of the Grave"), which shuts men off from the light of vision in the bleakness of their own hampered perceptions.

Among Blake's favorite designs is the figure that is cramped tortured among rocks in total joylessness. Yet it is Blake's announcement, too, that "When Thought is clos'd in Caves Then love shall shew its root in deepest Hell." The concept to which he returned most often seems not to be that the material world is dead, but that reason makes it so. Ulro and generation are not identical. Vala is a fallen goddess only when she is at odds with Jerusalem. When her "veil" is penetrated by revolutionary or by poetic insights, she springs up in fruitfulness. In his aesthetics, Blake's own keen delight in the particularities of form and outline committed him to a love of the *embodiment* of spirit, and it followed in his philosophy that matter and the corporeal must be given their due. Most of the time, therefore, his idealism was less comprehensive than Plato's, a middle view that was well expressed by Swift in his quatrain:

> Matter, as wise Logicians say,
> Cannot without a Form subsist,
> And Form, say I, as well as they,
> Must fayl if Matter brings no Grist.

The increasing violence with which Blake tried to break through the boundaries of the mechanical universe was more often an attempt to give matter and bodily existence dignity than one to deny them. If his cosmogonal image implies that the "fall" is in itself the creation of the world, that the earthly life is a degradation of spirit, it is no less true that vision is "re-creation," an act that does not obliterate the natural life but lifts it into a more satisfying image. "Heaven, Earth & Hell henceforth shall live in harmony."

Yet there are these waverings and indecisions in Blake from the beginning, and they increase as he nears the end. The horror of life sometimes turned him against it; the very toughness of the world made him sometimes deny its existence. At the end his anarchy was more purely of the spirit, much less of the body, than at the start, and the enlightened naturalism of *The Marriage of Heaven and Hell* seems to come to us more and more in glimmerings, less and less steadily. Blake was not unwilling to invert his own propositions, as he inverted those of Godwin and Milton. The consequence is a genuine ambiguity in his millennial hopes, which seem to be neither exactly religious nor exactly political, and which leave one with an open question. Are they achieved after life, or in it? Perhaps the most that can be said of them is that they are no more ill-defined than any other millennial hopes, and that their meaning is in their force as aspiration rather than in their object.

Yet if they did not have an object in the world, much in Blake would be meaningless, particularly his unremitting attack on institutions and his enduring antinomianism. His triumphant declaration that "Time was Finished!" is probably like Hugo's phrase *"Ce monde est mort"* in his epic *La Légende des Siècles.* The time we have known is finished, the *old* world is dead, and before us are the "glorious and paradisaical" expectations we had been led to trust in. *"Regardez là-haut."* Blake's was not the theoretical kind of intelligence that would introduce a visionary poem with an explicit political statement in the manner of Shelley, declaring that "The cloud of mind is discharging its collected lightning, and the equilibrium between institutions and opinions is now restoring, or is about to be restored." Yet the political image, even in his last poems, is almost as clearly present in Blake's work as in Shelley's. There is, indeed, a curious verbal parallelism between much of the third act of *Prometheus Unbound* and the conclusion of *Jerusalem.*

> . . . Henceforth the many children fair
> Folded in my sustaining arms; all plants,
> And creeping forms, and insects rainbow-winged,
> And birds, and beasts, and fish, and human shapes,
> Which drew disease and pain from my wan bosom
> Draining the poison of despair, shall take
> And interchange sweet nutriment.

This is less cryptic than the closing lines of *Jerusalem,* but otherwise much the same.

> All Human Forms identified, even Tree, Metal, Earth & Stone; all
> Human Forms identified, living, going forth & returning wearied
> Into the Planetary lives of Years, Months, Days & Hours.

In Shelley, too, the part of women in the regenerative life is emphasized, again, of course, with the deadly literalness to which Blake would not reduce his poetry:

> And women, too, frank, beautiful, and kind
> As the free heaven which rains fresh light and dew
> On the wide earth, passed; gentle radiant forms,
> From custom's evil taint exempt and pure,
> Speaking the wisdom once they could not think,
> Looking emotions once they feared to feel,

And changed to all which once they dared not be,
Yet being now, made earth like heaven.

Shelley's "Thrones, altars, judgment-seats, and prisons . . . Sceptres, tiaras, swords, and chains, and tomes Of reasoned wrong," are identical with the imagery of vanquished tyranny in Blake, and for both the overthrow of these meant a whole renewal of nature.

The painted veil, by those who were, called life,
Which mimicked, as with colours idly spread,
All men believed and hoped, is torn aside;
The loathsome mask has fallen, the man remains
Sceptreless, free, uncircumscribed, but man
Equal, unclassed, tribeless, and nationless,
Exempt from awe, worship, degree, the king
Over himself; just, gentle, wise.

These similarities are not fortuitous. Blake and Shelley, for all the difference between a rugged and masculine temper that did not deceive itself about the difficulties and agonies involved in the politics of mind and an invertebrate effeminate temper that wrapped itself in the veils of a sickly reverie—for all this difference, they yet drank at the same springs of thought, and that thought flows through the work of both.

The very deep changes that Blake's imagination and intellect wrought on his sources are the mark of his greater force and sharper insight. His transformation and unification in what he called his system of a body of rather dreary political speculation and a body of esoteric religious thinking is one of the most extraordinary spectacles in the history of poetry. The system did not, of course, achieve all that he hoped for it. Its inadequacy as theology is the mark of its origins in revolutionary politics, and its deficiency as politics, its idealistic excesses, derives from its religious framework. Yet its value as an analysis of human nature is surely the consequence of the combination, its readiness to draw from both realms of experience, and indeed to declare that they are one and the same. The impulse to combine them is the expression of Blake's temperamental dilemma, his necessity to weld together the polar demands of his sensibility and his intellect, to synthesize a visionary and a social experience of life.

The man who achieves such a synthesis in a time when art and thought have grown stale is necessarily an eccentric, and the very spectacle of his achievement dooms him to dismissal and obscurity. He announces the future, yet he must wait upon it. "There have been men who loved the future like a mistress," Yeats said, "and the future mixed her breath into their breath, and shook her hair about them, and hid them from the understanding of their times. William Blake was one of these men." He called himself "a Mental Prince," and he thought of himself not as outside his time but as in its vanguard. "Rouze up, O Young Men of the New Age! set your foreheads against the ignorant Hirelings!" He could have said like Kierkegaard: ". . . when in a generation storms begin to gather, individuals of my type appear." These are geniuses.

A genius is one whose insights enable him to penetrate and sort out the materials of his times, to break up exhausted and stultifying patterns of myth and logic, and to forge new patterns that will prove to be more deeply expressive of life. A genius is not a tame man, nor a well-bred, pretty one. The first ingredient of his imagination is violence, the second, love. He is committed to an angry denunciation of the world in order to reassert a faith in the world. Blake's denunciation we have observed. His irrepressible faith was that the condition of life can approximate the condition of art. Nothing less. It was his sublime error—the triumph of his poet's ego, the folly of his love.

PART THREE

Art and Life

☼

"Oui, j'ai les yeux fermés à votre lumière. . . . Mais je puis être sauvé."

—ARTHUR RIMBAUD, *"Une Saison en Enfer"*

CHAPTER ELEVEN

The Decline of the Poet

I

ATTEMPTING TO BE more than Man We become less," and attempting to be more than poets, poets become at least something different.

Any effort to understand the degree to which Blake's anarchism determined the quality of his poetry, and ultimately corrupted it as poetry, brings one back at once to his private compulsion to be free, to the child who was shattered by whippings and outraged by the strictures of schools and churches, who read the prophets in the Old Testament as exemplars of free verse and discovered Jesus in the New Testament as the exemplar of free love. This is always the basic fact about him: that he did not need to seek grace through discipline and dogma. It came to him as naturally as his visions, which discipline and dogma would have crushed; it came, indeed, *because* of them, for he thought visions were revelations. Thus impulse and individual judgment must be asserted against the sanctions of social judgment, which express themselves in legal generalizations. The desire for freedom turned into a process that recognized no limits but those of the emancipated individuality itself.

Blake's antinomianism, beginning as a personal revolt against the normative values of reason, expressed itself most clearly in his criticism of organized religion. Even then "The stupendous failure of Christianity tortured history," and together with dissenters and deists it tortured William Blake. Like the criticism of Priestley and Paine, Blake's criticism was in a sense historical. He based his ideal of Christianity on the character of Jesus and the primitive Church. His view of Jesus as a revolutionary whose life was a perfect allegory of love was in line with the interpretation current among the radical critics of organized religion. Like Blake, they asserted that Jesus had opposed impulse to law. They declared, too, that the religion founded on his life had soon falsified its ideal in formalizations of ritual and dogma that had no relation to conviction, and in a hierarchical organization that defeated his republican teachings.

Barlow, declaring that the word religion had no connection with the word church, that true religion must be a private and not a corporate affair, expressed Blake's objections precisely. The Church, categorizing the religious impulse in dogma and standardizing religious worship in ritual, categorized and standardized the worshiper, and insofar as it did so, corrupted his individuality and with that, his religion: ". . . every one is King & Priest in his own House." It was a position of dissent that put no limits on the fractional possibilities.

The commonplace connection of king and priest reflected the argument of all eighteenth-century radicals that a political revolution would involve a religious revolution. Yet Blake, at least, was more profoundly concerned with religious than with political terms, with the issues of faith and doubt, the fellowship of love and the multiple forms of schism within the spirit. Aldous Huxley has said that "Political advice from even the most greatly gifted of religious innovators is always inadequate; for it is never, at bottom, advice about politics, but always about something else." The description is appropriate to Blake, whose advice was not really about politics but about what he believed lay behind political and all other human activity, the processes of the mind rather than the extension of these processes into the patterns of power. In a sense, Godwin is open to the same description, and not merely because his doctrine of necessity is derived from a Calvinistic background, but because his formulations, like Blake's, were not only directed toward but also founded on an ideal version of man. If Blake adumbrated a politics of vision, Godwin labored on a politics of reason less plausible to the degree that it excluded more of man's qualities. Therefore whatever the relative value of their idealized assumptions and aspirations, the quality of Blake's insight into the middle area, the world as it is, experience, is a good deal more valuable.

The two meet, of course, on many points. The general movement of Blake's thought, the inevitable compulsion, was from an early, moderately republican position to a position of anarchism related to Godwin's. The whole attack on political tyranny followed, and that on the tools of tyranny—religious superstition and war, marriage and the family, private property and capitalist charity. Yet there is always the difference that Blake's logic, much more piercing than Godwin's, struck deeper in each of these attacks. Nowhere is this more evident than in their different conclusions about benevolence, the concept that supported eighteenth-century ethics. Godwin did not see that if charity is attacked as hypocritical, benevolence itself must be. Blake saw that charity was hypocritical because benevolence was negative, a substitute for love, a social rationalization devised in the absence of brotherhood.

The same extension of insight can be observed in their different conclusions about the inequality of the sexes. Godwin and his wife were content to point out that in their society woman was man's slave. Blake, who knew that oppression takes the last and the mortal toll from the oppressor himself, saw that self-divided man became the slave, and woman the unwilling tyrant. "Women the comforters of Men become the Tormenters & Punishers."

The deepening shows again in their differing attitudes toward law. Their attitudes were founded on an identical antinomianism clearly expressed by Blake: "It does not signify what the laws of Kings & Priests have call'd Vice." The similarity continues in their attitudes toward crime and punishment; both believed that crime represents frustrated energy, not evil. "Every Harlot was once a Virgin: every Criminal an Infant Love." Punishment cannot cure what law has created. The difference appears in the third and final step, in Blake's rejection of those rational duties,

Godwin's inner law, as a substitute for the laws of Church and State. He regarded both rights and duties as evasions, the new source of the old errors, and insisted that for law there could be only the single exchange of love. It is never logic that fails in Blake, but patience.

Blake not only extended some but transformed other propositions of radical discussion, and he did so for the same reason, to sweep away *all* barriers to freedom. This is the root of his basic objection to revolutionary doctrine, his rejection of reason as the equation in human character and as the hope for social salvation. This rejection involved the entire Lockian series: sense, reason, logic, science. All of it was an enormous rationalization into apparent absolutes of man's qualities in a fallen state, in the condition of duality, which is of strife and bondage.

His rejection of experimental science as a means to knowledge goes immediately back to that quality which he substituted for reason as the human equation—energy, the genius of the individual, his identity. It is also the poetic impulse, and it retains its purity only when it is free to aim directly at and immediately achieve whatever it knows to be its need. When it has this freedom, it makes intuitive perceptions into the matter of life that are superior to scientific knowledge because they are complete; that is, particular, not abstract. "Every Man's Wisdom is peculiar to his own Individuality." And when Blake asked, "What is the Life of Man but Art & Science?" he had in mind another kind of science; namely, wisdom. This he distinguished from experimental science by examining the word "conscience." To answer Locke and Godwin on the theory of innate ideas, he split the word into its two parts: "Con-Science." This is wisdom, the knowledge that is the individual's own, peculiar to himself, the particular potentialities with which he is born, making him what he is, unique. Any abstraction from singularity is untruth.

The function that individuates is the basis of human equality, and a full recognition of the function is the only possible basis of human liberty. Anything short of a full recognition of the necessity of energy to express itself as its own power directs it is tyrannical, whether in the mind or out of it. The proposition has two important implications. It opposes unity to uniformity, and it opposes organic to mechanical form. The first opposition points to Blake's political and psychological content; the second, to his aesthetic creed and his poetic performance. Both are included in the central symbol of Jesus.

To most modern minds, Blake's interpretation of the character of Jesus is congenial. It is, for example, almost exactly like the interpretation of Carl Jung. "Are we to understand the 'imitation of Christ' in the sense that we should copy his life and . . . ape his stigmata; or in the deeper sense that we are to live our own proper lives as truly as he lived his in all its implications? It is no easy matter to live a life that is modelled on Christ's, but it is unspeakably harder to live one's own life as truly as Christ lived his. . . . Neurosis is an inner cleavage—the state of being at war with oneself. . . . What drives people to war with themselves is the intuition or the knowledge that they consist of two persons in opposition to one another . . . modern man has heard enough about guilt and sin. He is surely enough beset by his own bad conscience, and wants rather to learn how he is to reconcile himself with his own nature—how he is to love the enemy in his own heart and call the wolf his brother."

Whatever limitations theologians find in this doctrine, the modern version of eighteenth-century "natural virtue," one can say for it that it demands democratic peace between the human elements, not the divine right of one element to rule the others. Blake's vision of the integrated man, symbolized by Jesus, departs from the eighteenth century in precisely this way. The departure explains his attack on reason and his praise of energy, just as it explains his early refusal to submit to any dogma that preaches the separateness of body and soul, and his persistent discomfiture before separations of matter and spirit even when his own temperament and portions of his creed pushed him toward such separations. His praise was of wholeness, and of variety united. To this end, he was as enthusiastic about notions of "diversity" and "plenitude" as any eighteenth-century man, and yet at the same time derisive of classical concepts of beauty and of neoclassical theories of form. Thus while he abandoned the mechanical concepts of his own time as they were expressed by Sir Joshua Reynolds, he also avoided the extreme kind of aesthetic vitalism preached, for example, by Lawrence in our time. Paul Morel said: "Only this shimmeriness is the real living. The shape is a dead crust. The shimmer is inside reality." Blake sought the shimmer as it was expressed in the shape, the organic form.

"His gift is his fate," Huxley has said of the artist, "and he follows a predestined course, from which no ordinary power can deflect him." This is a partial truth, applicable only to artists of a certain temperament in certain centuries; but Blake was of these. His gift was his fate. It absolutely formed him, not only as a man among his fellows, but more particularly as an artist. His gift explains the ideas he chose to develop, and more than that, the way in which he chose to develop them. To say, with A. C. Benson, that he lacked "culture," or, with T. S. Eliot, that he lacked "education," is to state the obvious, but at the same time to ignore the fact that his gift did not permit him to pursue either culture or education as they were available in his time. Unless we would have no Blake at all, we must allow him the right (and the absurdity of insisting upon it) to be the only kind of Blake that he could be. For to insist, as he did, on the one true talent, on the validity of only one kind of imagination, is no doubt absurd, yet the insistence was a matter of artistic life or death to him. It was the necessary condition of his art. But it is also self-indulgence, and self-indulgence takes its toll from the artist more than from any other man.

II

As THE SPITALFIELDS WEAVERS broke their looms, so Blake was determined to break the machines of art. As the new machines in English mills were destroying the dignity of human labor, so the machinery of neoclassicism, derived from a concept of the machine of the universe, had destroyed the dignity of art. In his professional practice, Blake turned to the methods of the medieval bookmaker, and in the composition of his poems, he moved farther and farther away from the normal mechanical devices of poetic style. *L'esprit géométrique,* presumably correcting so much in the fantastic historical heritage that was merely barbarous falsehood, in many quarters had also "corrected" poetry, or at least the concept of poetry.

A prominent French theoretician like D'Alembert could propose that the stylistic ideal of the century recognize nothing as excellent in poetry that it could not consider excellent in prose. An obscure Englishman, in an *Essay on the Application of Natural History to Poetry,* could argue that poetry involved a specialist's knowledge of botany, zoology, and geology, and that poets could not write acceptably until they were as competent in observing nature as the scientists who made that their business. This writer, proposing the migration of birds as an ideal subject for a long poem, urged that "the poet should think it incumbent upon him to discover and investigate *new facts,* as well as to frame *new combinations of words.*" Such a theory of poetic content by no means expresses universal opinion in the eighteenth century, but it was an important element in the total aesthetic atmosphere. It was perhaps because Gray, for example, could not, in his content, accept this theory that he felt he "never could attain," and often did not try to do so, its equivalent in the ideal of lyric style—"extreme conciseness of expression, yet pure, perspicuous, & musical." Blake's style, like his content, developed in opposition to these notions, and one can observe the progress of this development not only in the mechanical categories of meter, rhyme, and rhetoric, but in such freer categories as imagery and structure.

Blake's earliest work, *Poetical Sketches,* reveals the presence not only of his characteristic double strain of mind—the pastoral and the humanitarian, the visionary and the social—but also that of a double style—the lyrical and what may be called the oracular.* The first style is developed in imitations of the Eliza-

* I speak of a double style from the point of view of Blake's later development, the two styles in which he continued to work. Actually, *Poetical Sketches* contains many styles—the dramatic imitations of Shakespeare and Thomson, the ballad imitations of Bishop Percy's collection and of Chatterton, one influence of Chatterton in the rhetorical prose and another in the

bethans, especially Shakespeare and Spenser, of Milton's lyrics, and of such diverse eighteenth-century poets as Thomson, Chatterton, and Collins. The second is contained in four prose passages called "Prologue to King John," "The Couch of Death," "Contemplation," and "Samson" (and in two, "Then She Bore Pale Desire" and "Woe, Cried the Muse," of the same date but not included in *Poetical Sketches*), in fitful imitations of Milton's long poems and in more deliberate imitations of the Bible, of the poeticized prose of Macpherson's Ossianic forgeries, and of the floreate rhetoric of James Hervey's now little known but then popular *Meditations and Contemplations.* Remembering that Blake's parents were probably associated with a Moravian congregation, it is of interest that both styles were contained in the eighteenth-century tradition of evangelicism. Hervey, with his "turgid, ejaculatory, Hebraic" strain, was as much a Methodist as Charles Wesley, with his simple, Wordsworthian piety, a quality that is exemplified even more satisfactorily in the work of his Nonconformist predecessor in hymnology, Isaac Watts. Blake's early style owes most to the naïve song of love and thanksgiving, his later style, most to the rhetorically charged adjuration.

Yet the use to which Blake put the pietistic song for children is preceded by his juvenile response to English poets in the more central lyric tradition. In pointing out that Blake, the boy poet, had an "immense power of assimilation" and was "very eighteenth century," Mr. Eliot performed a useful service in Blake criticism, yet one must not overlook the fact that even here he was "eighteenth century" with a difference, and that the difference marks the impulse of his talent and the direction it was to take. Eighteenth-century poets imitated Spenser, for example, in his antique vocabulary, his allegory, and his stanza form, but when we examine Blake's "Imitation of Spenser," we find the main interest in Spenser's verbal effects, no interest whatever in

lyrics, etc. The vexed problem of how Chatterton, whose first book of poems was not published until 1777, the year in which the last of the *Poetical Sketches* was written, could have influenced these poems at all has been satisfactorily settled by Miss Lowery in *Windows of the Morning* (Yale University Press, 1940).

his allegory, and a very wan interest in the Spenserian stanza. This last is the telling fact. In a poem of six stanzas, not one is wholly correct. Three times Blake troubles to set down the final alexandrine, but twice he does not manage its proper rhyme; of the total cadence that the stanza at its best achieves, there is, naturally, nothing. And the poem is perhaps of no consequence *except* as it shows the young poet's impatience, even when he is deliberately imitating a formal pattern, with the strictures of the pattern.

Poetical Sketches is a handbook of such unrecognized intentions. Collins's main influence on Blake may lie in the example of the unrhymed lyric "Ode to Evening." The first seven poems in *Poetical Sketches,* while broken into stanzas, are unrhymed, and their cadences, as in "To the Evening Star," are often more like those of the rhythmical prose passages at the end of the book than they are like the normal cadences of the iambic line they purport to emulate. In those poems which are rhymed, Blake's impatience is evident in his persistent use of half-rhymes and in his practice of shifting the rhyme pattern from stanza to stanza within the limits of a single poem.

The same impatience with metrical pattern is equally evident in his use of the freest possible Elizabethan lyric patterns. These last, "Mad Song," for example, and the song beginning "Memory, hither come," are his great early lyric triumphs, for, escaping the mechanical weight of the eighteenth-century lyric, they yet achieve an exquisite form of their own that is rare in this volume. "Memory, hither come" is, as a matter of fact, one of the most interesting illustrations in Blake of the influence of Milton, for the poem attempts to compress into two stanzas the content of Milton's companion poems, "L'Allegro" and "Il Penseroso," and yet it eludes, with lovely tact, Milton's somewhat thumping iambic tetrameter and achieves the ample grace of Elizabethan song. It looks forward, too, to the later productions of a poet who was not to be content with partial freedoms.

Of the rhetoric that these poems employ, the most impressive element is the strong infusion of neoclassical diction. They are sprinkled with conventional epithets—"dewy locks," "modest tresses," "noon upon his fervid car," "my vocal rage," "my pensive woe," "the pleasant cot" and "the innocent bow'r," "the watery glass" and the "flaming car"—and these sometimes come together in unexpectedly eighteenth-century clusters, such as these lines from "To Summer":

> Our bards are fam'd who strike the silver wire:
> Our youths are bolder than the southern swains:
> Our maidens fairer in the sprightly dance.

And the quatrain from "To the Muses":

> How have you left the antient love
>   That bards of old enjoy'd in you!
> The languid strings do scarcely move!
>   The sound is forc'd, the notes are few!

Even in their syntax such lines are hard to distinguish from the poetry of Collins or of Gray.

Yet at nearly every point one finds an admixture of the simpler diction and of the looser form of statement that was to characterize Blake's later poems. "The hills tell each other," "joy . . . roves round The gardens, or sits singing in the trees," "Like as an angel glitt'ring in the sky In times of innocence and holy joy," and

> I turn my back to the east,
> From whence comforts have increas'd;
> For light doth seize my brain
> With frantic pain—

these are examples of Blake's earliest impulse, even as he imitates the conventions of his contemporaries, to break through them to forms more suitable to a Biblical amplitude.

In his curious prose experiments, Blake expresses this impulse explicitly and purposefully. Biblical rhythms, Milton's diction and iambics, Hervey's brand of ejaculatory rhetoric, and Macpherson's melodramatic inflations that fill the gap of content—all are combined in these strange exercises in poetic license. The first two elements are obvious, the third and fourth perhaps less so. Blake writes as follows: " 'Parting is hard, and death is terrible; I seem to walk through a deep valley, far from the light of day, alone and comfortless! The damps of death fall thick upon me! Horrors stare me in the face! I look behind, there is no returning; Death follows after me; I walk in regions of Death, where no tree is; without a lantern to direct my steps, without a staff to support me.' Thus he laments through the still evening, till the curtains of darkness were drawn!" In Hervey's *Meditations,* one is asked to shudder through passages such as these: "Good heavens! what a solemn scene!—how dismal the *gloom!* Here is perpetual darkness, and night even at noon-day.—How doleful the *solitude!* Not one trace of chearful society; but sorrow and terror seem to have made this their dreaded abode. . . . They look backward, and behold! a most melancholy scene! Sins unrepented of; mercy slighted; and the day of grace ending!—They look *forward,* and nothing presents itself, but the righteous Judge, the dreadful tribunal; and a most solemn reckoning.—They roll *around* their affrighted eyes on attending friends." And in the companion essay, *Reflections on a Flower-Garden,* there are floriferous passages that more than match the graveyard prose in bombast. "Breathe soft, ye winds! O, spare the tender fruitage, ye surly blasts! Let the *pear-tree* suckle her juicy progeny, till they drop into our hands, and dissolve in our mouths. Let the *plum* hang unmolested upon her boughs, till she fatten her delicious flesh, and cloud her polished skin with blue." It was to prose so remote as this from the best eighteenth-century models that Blake turned for his early exercises in free forms, and this prose left its mark on him.

From Macpherson, Blake took elements that he might himself have isolated from the Bible and from Milton, but which were already concentrated in the Ossianic poems in what seemed to him to be the grand bardic manner.* It was for this manner

* One can overestimate the part Macpherson played in the formation of Blake's style and overlook equally significant contributions from more refined sources like Thomas Gray. An interesting essay in historical criticism could be based on a detailed analysis of the qualities in such a fashionable poem as "The Descent of Odin" which were to be picked up and developed in Blake's unfashionable work. The poem contains a thematic resemblance to Blake's poems in the descent of "the King of Men" into the "drear abode" of the realms of death; a structural resemblance in the defiant debate between

that he was uncertainly striving in his early prose fragments, and it was this manner, of course, that he was to cultivate in his Prophetic Books, when almost his whole stylistic ambition was to be directed toward effects of grandeur. The free and heavy cadences, the exclamatory and imperative syntax, and the device of repeating certain favorite epithets such as "dark" and "pale," "terrible," "lovely," and "mild," in all manner of combinations—these qualities were to serve their purpose in the development of a certain spaciousness of style that overcame the confines of eighteenth-century patterns. They were also, ultimately, to shut off the lyric impulse entirely.

Yet before that happened, Blake pushed all this stuff aside completely and produced his greatest lyrics. He put aside, too, the model of the eighteenth-century lyric, and to a considerable extent that of the Elizabethan. Nearly every influence he had felt before the *Songs of Innocence* was abandoned for the new influence of the pious hymn for children. There can be no question of Blake's intimacy with Watts's *Divine Songs Attempted in Easy Language,* or of his conscious imitation of their manner in *Songs of Innocence* and *Songs of Experience*. Actually, Watts's "Cradle Hymn" is the source of Blake's "A Cradle Song," and it seems likely that "London" took its start from "Praise for Mercies Spiritual and Temporal," which begins,

> Whene'er I take my Walks abroad,
> How many Poor I see!

the King and the Prophetess; a tonal resemblance in its cloudy, "prophetic" mood; a strong verbal resemblance, which includes some of Blake's rhyme words, to the particular debate in "My Spectre around me"; much the same kind of diction throughout that was to characterize the Prophecies; certain images, like Lok's "tenfold chain"; the relation between the apocalyptic vision at the end and the breaking of the chains of Lok, an Orc-like figure; the character of Hela, goddess of death, whose name appears in *Tiriel* as that of the sense of touch, or sex. If this is actually the source of the name for Blake, it suggests again that Elizabethan connection he seemed to make between the sexual act and "dying," between sex and experience as it appears in *Thel.* These striking resemblances show Blake, in his odd way, to have been so "very eighteenth century" that it is astonishing to find him persistently and vigorously disclaiming the fashions of his age..

In general, however, the influence is of a more pervasive kind. Watts's easy ballad stanza was exactly suited to the naïve attitudes expressed in *Songs of Innocence* and provided an ironic formal emphasis for the tortured wisdom of *Songs of Experience,* but more important, his attempts "in Easy Language" released Blake from the conventionalized diction of his first lyrics and helped him to a simplicity and homeliness of expression that had no precedent in English lyric tradition. Finally, Watts encouraged in Blake a device that he had already discovered in the Elizabethans, the suspended rhyme, the means by which Blake took the metallic edge off the rude stanza form and made the music subtle without the excessive elaboration of verbal effects that he had first imitated from the Elizabethans. The influence of these characteristics extends beyond the poems written in Watts's stanza form to those in forms of Blake's own devising.

"I have no name:
I am but two days old."
What shall I call thee?
"I happy am,
Joy is my name."
Sweet joy befall thee!

In such lines, Blake brings together in a perfect unity the directness of statement learned from Watts and his own perpetual impulse to elude rigid patterns.

Lacking the crystalline quality of *Songs of Innocence, Songs of Experience* yet represents a greater poetic achievement. Here, where the symbolical element has entered, where the intellectual content is much greater, and where the feeling is both more complex and more intense, he combines the lessons of Watts with a refined Ossianic element, the heavier adjectival quality and the more urgent rhetoric.

Hear the voice of the Bard!
Who Present, Past, & Future, sees;
Whose ears have heard
The Holy Word
That walk'd among the ancient trees,

Calling the lapsed Soul,
And weeping in the evening dew;
That might controll
The starry pole,
And fallen, fallen light renew!

Here, too, there is a further relaxation of formal strictures, but nevertheless a very exact sense of composition. A poem like "The Tyger," on the other hand, although written in quatrains, yet manages to utilize the hortatory antiphonal rhetoric of such a writer as Hervey and the balanced cadences of Macpherson together with the simplest diction in such a fashion that the poem seems to have no relation to any of them, but to Blake alone. In *Songs of Experience,* finally, emerges clearly what was to be one of Blake's most characteristic qualities, the ability to make intense verse out of abstractions, as in "Pity would be no more" and "Whate'er is born of mortal birth." The development of this quality of didactic lyricism one can attribute not only to the eighteenth-century poetic atmosphere in general, but, conceivably, to the specific source of the hymn, its persistent concern with the roster of the Christian virtues.

Yet the tradition of the hymn for children was not one that was capable of being fruitfully worked for very long by a secular poet, and even if it had been, it was not capable of developing the themes that it enabled Blake to introduce in *Songs of Experience*. In these poems, the intellectual content is coming into the ascendancy, and the treacherous allegorical element is about to become a necessity. This was to grow into a content that no lyric tradition would be able to express, and in a poem like "London," perfect and vastly original in its elisions and juxtapositions, Blake had pressed the lyric precisely as far as it could go. From that an explosion into larger forms was nearly inevitable, and the poem is so great for exactly the reason that it still manages, through its formal achievement, to hold the explosion back. But to hold it back longer Blake had no inclination. Revolution in one quarter involves revolution in others.

To look at Blake's early poems in this fashion is to predict his future—that inevitably he would write less and less in lyric forms. After *Songs of Experience* he attempted occasional lyrics, but most of them he left unfinished. In "Auguries of Innocence" and "The Everlasting Gospel," he wrote in octosyllabic couplets, but in the second ignored every demand of the couplet except the rhyme—and left both of them as fragments. Now and then, as in "And did those feet in ancient time" and "To the Accuser," he finished superb lyrics in the late, abstract manner of *Songs of Experience,* yet one may object to these poems on the ground that they are not really self-contained, that they are supplementary and posterior to the "system," and that a knowledge of the "system" is necessary to a full understanding of them. They are among the main poetic rewards that the grudging "system" yields, yet the encyclopedias that sprawl behind them belie their narrow and fastidious forms.

Blake had himself, intentionally, delivered various storm signals from the beginning. His return to prose during the composition of *Songs of Innocence* and *Songs of Experience* is indicative of his discomfiture with the lyric. It was a different kind of prose from his early pieces—taut and muscular in the three *Tractates,* and more purely intellectual, perhaps, than any other English prose of that century; easy and relaxed, as well as indignant and tough and wonderfully axiomatic in *The Marriage,* with that particular masculinity which always prevented his work from melting into the merely honeyed, the insipid, or the sanctimonious.* This prose was essential to the expansions that his content was now undergoing, and which in poetry would express themselves presently in such grossly expanded structures.

There were other signals. In one of his earliest poems, the "Imitation of Spenser," he referred to the "tinkling sounds . . .

* May one fairly concur with the sentiment in John Crowe Ransom's amusing couplet?

> Then there was poor Willie Blake,
> He foundered on sweet cake.
>
> (*Selected Poems,* Knopf, 1945, p. 62)

Blake said, "How wide the Gulf & Unpassable between Simplicity and Insipidity." (*Poetry and Prose,* p. 524; in mirror writing, at the top of the plate that introduces Book Two of *Milton*) I think he foundered on something sturdier than "sweet cake"—on something much more dangerous.

Sounds without sense" of modern poetry, to its "tinking rhimes, and elegances terse." "To the Muses" comments on the state of eighteenth-century poetic fashions and looks toward the revival of the bardic element. *Songs of Experience* and *The Marriage* both invoke "the Ancient Bard," and the *Tractates* propose a psychology that would enable bards again to raise their voices. And finally, in *Tiriel,* written between the two sets of songs and the first of the poems to employ the loose septenary that Blake at last hit upon as most suitable to his meanings, he states his rejection of conventional poetic forms in an allegory of eighteenth-century poetry and painting. Har is compelled to "sing in the large cage" of laws imposed from without; and he and his sister, Heva, are later described as

> . . . two narrow doleful forms
> Creeping in reptile flesh upon
> The bosom of the ground;
> And all the vast of Nature shrunk
> Before their shrunken eyes.

After *Tiriel,* Blake's prosody has only a small history. Between the heptameter of that poem, of *The Book of Thel,* the *Visions of the Daughters of Albion, America, Europe, The Four Zoas, Milton,* and *Jerusalem,* the octameter of *The French Revolution,* and the trimeter and tetrameter of the books of *Urizen* and *Ahania* and *Los,* there is small difference in effect. *Thel,* through its burden of pastoral imagery, achieves a crystalline quality that most of the Prophetic Books do not have. *The French Revolution,* with the longest line of all, is perhaps also the most windy. *Urizen, Ahania,* and *Los,* with their shorter lines, have a greater terseness than the others, even though a trimetric and tetrametric alternation gives one merely a heptameter again. The differences in effect of Blake's various unrhymed lines are at most differences of degree only, and it is fair to say of his Prophetic Books that when they gain most freedom and spaciousness they also lose most in musical force and variety.

Blake's line, whatever the number of stresses, was freely cadenced, and the number of stresses was not in the least regular. His rhythms and the syntax that contains them become more like the rhythms of certain books of the Bible—increasingly like the Book of Job—and less like the rhythms of Macpherson. The diction, too, becomes more truly Miltonic and Biblical and less Ossianic. What he achieved at last was a line less contrived in its rhythmic units than Macpherson's, and much looser and longer than Milton's. It was a line that, upon occasion, assimilated whole patches of his prose almost without change.* Even the loosest arrangements of the iambic and anapaestic feet that were his favorites often vanish completely in passages that defy all metrical system.

For the various Classes of Men are all mark'd out determinate
In Bowlahoola, & as the Spectres choose their affinities,
So they are born on Earth, & every Class is determinate:
But not by Natural, but by Spiritual power alone, Because
The Natural power continually seeks & tends to Destruction,
Ending in Death, which would of itself be Eternal Death.

Such passages attempt to push the abstract manner of the lyrics into a style that will accommodate prose, and their arrangement into lines is the merest irrelevance. Blake assuredly escaped from the prosodic cage. But the rights of poets, like those of men, involve their duties. He was freed to chaos.

Yet one knows what Blake's stylistic ambition is, and one respects it as a portion of his intellectual and aesthetic integrity. In the Preface to *Jerusalem,* he wrote: "When this Verse was first dictated to me, I consider'd a Monotonous Cadence, like that used by Milton & Shakespeare & all writers of English Blank Verse, derived from the modern bondage of Rhyming, to be a necessary and indispensible part of Verse. But I soon found that in the mouth of a true Orator such monotony was not only awkward, but as much a bondage as rhyme itself. I therefore have produced a variety in every line, both of cadences & number of syllables. Every word and every letter is studied and put into its fit place; the terrific numbers are reserved for the terrific parts, the mild & gentle for the mild & gentle parts, and the

* Compare the passage in *The Marriage* beginning "The worship of God is" (*Poetry and Prose,* p. 202) with the passage in *Jerusalem,* Bk. IV, beginning "Go, tell them that the Worship of God" (*Ibid.,* p. 736).

prosaic for inferior parts; all are necessary to each other. Poetry Fetter'd Fetters the Human Race. Nations are Destroy'd or Flourish in proportion as Their Poetry, Painting and Music are Destroy'd or Flourish!"

The two notable items in this passage are that Blake thought of himself not as a poet in the ordinary sense, but as a bard, "a true Orator," and that he had developed a theory of style, of organic form, on the principle of which he attempted to construct his poems.

Blake's hymnlike lyrics and his Prophecies have an important element in common. Both are meant to be uttered, and this is a quality that in the formation—or the dispersal—of Blake's later talent has gone unnoticed far too long. If, for example, one compares the rhetoric of the Prophecies with the rhetoric of such an eighteenth-century orator as Edmund Burke when his prose rises to the true declamatory pitch, Blake's writing seems much less strange. There is not a great difference between the quality of Burke's antirevolutionary wrath and that of Blake's revolutionary wrath. Burke's prose reads: "Out of the tomb of a murdered monarchy in France has arisen a vast, tremendous, unformed spectre in a far more terrific guise than any which ever yet have overpowered the imagination and subdued the fortitude of man. Going straightforward to its end, unappalled by peril, unchecked by remorse, despising all common maxims and all common means; that hideous phantom overpowered those who could not believe it was possible she should at all exist." In any of Blake's Prophecies, and particularly, perhaps, in *The French Revolution,* one discovers exactly the same kind of inflations—in diction, in imagery, even in the hortatory rhythms. Blake, with his faith in the prophetic function of poetry, needed only to return to the Hebraic tradition in the Old Testament—to Mosaic wrath and Jobian lamentation—to forge out a bardic poetry, but he had models much nearer at hand that brought together quite as easily the oratorical and the poetical. The kind of antiquarianism in which the century abounded, expressed by writers so different as Macpherson and Gray, was familiar to Blake. Attempting to renew that tradition of poetic utterance, he cultivated certain deficiencies of poetic style that their expression of it had already entailed. Among these is the concern with sound at the expense of sense, the use of proper names, often in catalogues, the alternations of exhortation and lamentation, and the consequent syntactical emphases. Blake's concern with these qualities threatened to make of him a somnambulist alone, and not, in Baudelaire's double demand of the poet, a hypnotist too; and he sacrificed, as Whitman did, the particular grip on the attention that more disciplined poetic styles obtain.*

In the theory of his style Blake most clearly extends his anarchy into a new aesthetic principle. He insists that poetry, like action, must have an inner, organic form, not merely an outer, mechanical structure. The first is the free expression of energy, the second is institutional bondage. The integrity and the beauty of the individuality of the poetic impulse, as of any other, require freedom from external restraint. Here Blake carried what was basically a political principle into the craftsmanship of poetry and the graphic arts. With the restrictions of feudal tyrannies and the bondage of church law and ritual went all the restrictions of the prosodic tradition. Yet Blake's concept of what a modern literary inquisitor has called "the fallacy of imitative form" is perhaps more successfully argued for in his theory than it is sustained in the practice of the poems themselves. His freedoms in practice provided him most frequently not with better forms but with none at all. It was on freedom that he foundered, and that is not quite "sweet cake."

III

BLAKE'S IMAGERY demonstrates an analogous relationship between his ideas and his art—the same doggedly independent ambitions, a reckless dependence on private associations or on associations without references beyond the limits of the private "system,"

* Mr. Matthiessen uses Baudelaire's distinction in his discussion of Whitman (F. O. Matthiessen. *American Renaissance,* Oxford University Press. 1941, p. 574).

and an original and individual conception of the nature and functions of imagery.

The controlling fact that his imagery is the product of his vision, the most private of all experiences, has two important consequences. At their best, his images are fresh and illuminating and embody brilliant insights, but at their worst, they are cloudy, vague, and perverse and obscure his meaning. With the double development of the sense of a prophetic function and of the idea of the uniqueness of all things, the imagery more and more consistently operated as symbolism. These two consequences are portions of the same general development, but they may be treated separately.

The *Poetical Sketches,* in their imagery as in their diction, are Blake's attempt to free himself from the conventional, and there is at least as much of early seventeenth-century and of eighteenth-century stock imagery as there is of the kind of original perceptions one associates with Blake in general. And among these "flaming cars" and "pale deaths" and "deeps of Heaven" one comes across his extraordinary innovations with a shock of discovery.

> . . . Let thy west wind sleep on
> The lake; speak silence with thy glimmering eyes,
> And wash the dusk with silver—

one of the most astonishing images in this volume—really represents a whole new way of *seeing* in poetry. It is a way that his visions enabled him to explore, for he derived such boldness in his pictorializations not from any traditional elements in poetry, but from his own early visionary experiences. They supplied him, too, with ready-made pictures. The lines in "To Autumn"—

> . . . joy, with pinions light, roves round
> The gardens, or sits singing in the trees—

may intend to comment on birds, but they are also reminiscent of that childhood experience recounted by Gilchrist, when Blake saw "a tree filled with angels, bright angelic wings bespangling every bough like stars." It is impossible to tell what proportion of Blake's images simply reproduce what he had beheld in vision, but that many of them did, not a few of his pictures and drawings corroborate. A striking example is to be found in *The Four Zoas,* lines that duplicate and explain a well-known picture:

. . . hovering high over his head
Two winged immortal shapes, one standing at his feet
Toward the East, one standing at his head toward the west,
Their wings join'd in the Zenith over head. . . .
. . . they bent over the dead corse like an arch,
Pointed at top in highest heavens, of precious stones & pearl.
Such is a Vision of All Beulah hov'ring over the Sleeper.

The content of Blake's vision is normally pastoral, with a Christian emphasis. In *Poetical Sketches,* even ships are sheep, and stars are already angels. From this primary inclination, Blake moves in two directions. The imagery of pastoralism includes animals, but animals are wild as well as mild, and the idyllic scene suggests its opposite.

. . . then the wolf rages wide,
And the lion glares thro' the dun forest:
The fleeces of our flocks are cover'd with
Thy sacred dew: protect them.

Even now, that is, the vision darkens from idyllic reverie to observation of natural fact. The Christian concern has its other side too, inevitably suggesting mortality and the melodrama of death. It is from this concern, through his imitations of the Gothic fashion and the graveyard poets, that Blake's apocalyptic imagery takes its start, and with that, his images of a convulsive universe.

The bell struck one, and shook the silent tower;
The graves give up their dead.

Such animation of earth suggests not only a lively nature in general, but a nature mingling with man, and a nature, finally, that is dominated by imagination. From all this Blake's particular and perpetual use of the pathetic fallacy proceeds, for in his poems the device represents not merely a rhetorical inflation, but a view of the universe.* Such a line as "And the vale darkens at my pensive woe" gives the clue to the real meaning of the imagery in the second stanza of "Mad Song," where a dislocation of mind results in a dislocation of nature:

Lo! to the vault
  Of paved heaven,
With sorrow fraught
  My notes are driven:
They strike the ear of night,
  Make weep the eyes of day;
They make mad the roaring winds,
  And with tempests play.

The ease with which Blake animated the inanimate and mixed the animate with the inanimate resulted in some of his happiest pictorial effects, but it was also the particular ingredient in his talent that passed most rapidly out of his control and which then resulted in turgid and cloudy rhetoric.

The imagery of pastoral vision was apparently without such dangers for Blake. Here something, perhaps the simplification inherent in all idealizations, kept the imagery pure and clear. Consequently *Songs of Innocence* and *The Book of Thel,* which expand this single strain of imagery, are works without a single infelicity. The *Songs,* however, have a defect of resonance, a kind of attenuation which indicates that the visionary experience requires an infusion of something from nearer home. That infusion comes in *Songs of Experience,* poems that are correspondingly richer. The visionary experience never ceases to operate but now it collaborates beautifully with intellect.

In what distant deeps or skies
Burnt the fire of thine eyes?

* ". . . in their worlds [Darwin's and Blake's] *everything* feels; they use the device not as bestowal by man on nature, but as activity in a different realm."—Josephine Miles, *Pathetic Fallacy in the Nineteenth Century,* University of California Press, 1942, p. 201. Miss Miles has inaugurated a valuable series of studies on the relationship between verbal techniques and thought, of which this is one. Her comments on Hopkins may be extended to include Blake and should be examined by students of Blake's development.

That is, one would think, a Blakean vision in the most exact sense. Likewise, "The Sun-flower":

> Where the Youth pined away with desire,
> And the pale Virgin shrouded in snow
> Arise from their graves, and aspire
> Where my Sun-flower wishes to go.

Yet in this last example, and throughout the *Songs of Experience,* there is a new intellectual element, observations on psychic friction and social pain that express themselves in the deliberately developed imagery of sex, and of commerce, industrialism, and science. These intellectual figurations lie outside the pastoral realm, and even outside the undiluted vision. They are Blake's most original contribution to the history of English poetry. They are poetry's debt to his determined independence—whole new fields of human experience relatively untouched by imagery before him; * and in these poems they sharpen his vision and weight it with meaning. Without this further element, he could not have written "London," certainly not those particular lines which are among his greatest:

> And the hapless Soldier's sigh
> Runs in blood down Palace walls.

And without them he could not have conjured up his "system." When, in his prophetic poems, these elements enter into his visionary experience, the imagery is successful, and when they are neglected and the visionary experience operates alone, the imagery is unsuccessful. For it is the intellectual element that keeps our general human experience in view, and that maintains the balanced relationship between the world and the particularities of identity that is even more essential to art than it is to happiness.

This distinction may be tested, certainly in Blake's more ambitious images and in many of the more fleeting, by the extent

* It is interesting to notice that Blake's entire range of industrial imagery has only a single line as predecessor in literature before him—Milton's "Eyeless in Gaza, at the mill with slaves."

of their associations, the degree to which the products of the private vision assimilate recognizable social or historical facts. Blake's many variations on "a Cave, a Rock, a Tree deadly and poisonous," all traditional in themselves but capable of fresh figurations, as his use of them shows, are eminently successful. Besides their past histories in philosophy and religion, all of them have a genuinely literal significance: the darkness of the cave, the solidity or the impenetrability of the rock, and the tree's subtle and nearly ineradicable spread of roots as well as the production of fruit. Blake's use of such familiar images was thoughtful and often extremely ingenious, as when the tree, already associated with original sin, becomes an oak, and is further associated with the Druids, men of darkness.

So too such esoteric images as "the Wicker Man of Scandinavia," "the Cities of the Salamandrine men," and "the Altars of Victims in Mexico" all have associative values that are effective for readers who do not assume that poetry involves no effort. And one may say the same for such more general images as "Human Thought is crush'd beneath the iron hand of Power," "on my hands, death's iron gloves," "blue death in Albion's feet," and "Thought changed the infinite to a serpent, that which pitieth To a devouring flame."

If we compare any of these with one of Blake's typical indiscretions in imagery, the difference is apparent. These lines from *The Four Zoas* will serve as an illustration:

. . . they took the book of iron & placed above
On clouds of death, & sang their songs, kneading the bread of
    Orc.
Orc listen'd to the song, compell'd, hung'ring on the cold wind
That swagg'd heavy with the accursed dough.

This dough serves no possible poetic purpose, for it suggests nothing but a weird confusion in the skies, wildly irrelevant both to nature and to mind, and rather foolish in its effect. It does serve to show, however, that vision is by no means wholly reliable as a pictorial source. Such excesses in his imagery are characteristic of the Prophetic poems, and they grow in number as Blake pursues his independent course. They are part and parcel of that earliest impulse to disrupt the universe, to penetrate the shell of matter by vision, to violate the mechanical. The impulse was capable of countless beautiful things, but when it was unguarded it often produced gross and bombastic follies.

The pathos of Blake's poetic development was that as he put more and more faith in vision, he felt less and less necessity to guard it. The result shows in another portion of the later imagery, his increasing pleasure in the poetic catalogue. This device is common in primitive poetry and in poetry imitative of primitive fashions. In Blake's early poems, even the early Prophecies, it had effective results, especially in his lists of animals and plants and their qualities. Later, when the device was employed merely to list proper names, of the twenty-seven churches and the innumerable cities, of the rivers and counties of England and the countries of Europe, of the multiple sons and daughters, it was turned into a perversely self-indulgent habit. These later catalogues may conceivably represent some grand panoramic spectacle in Blake's imagination, but they represent very little but an allegorical puzzle to the reader. Their exact meanings, if they had any, are nearly impossible to discover. Vision at its least successful became a matter of dark cryptography and mirror writing, of multiplication and amplification, as if Blake's content needed finally to be obscured and swollen to attain the grand Miltonic forms that were his ambition or even the exhalation of grandeur that he thought he detected in Macpherson.

Yet it would be a misrepresentation to let the matter stand there, Blake's aggressively independent imagination coming to such sad rest; for to the very end, when it allied itself with his equally aggressive social insights, it achieved imagery of the most penetrating kind. "We were carried away in thousands," he wrote in curiously modern lines that, commenting in general on human slavery and the toll of tyranny, yet had the objective core of comment on press gangs:

We were carried away in thousands from London & in tens
Of thousands from Westminster & Marybone, in ships clos'd up,

Chain'd hand & foot, compell'd to fight under the iron whips
Of our captains, fearing our officers more than the enemy.

In *Jerusalem,* too, are these lines, which present a general comment on the sources of human despair with a specific comment on absentee owners and the deadly monotony of piecework:

. . . The captive in the mill of the stranger, sold for scanty hire.
They view their former life: they number moments over and
over,
Stringing them on their remembrance as on a thread of sorrow.

In the same poem, his last, are many representations of that brilliant historical perception into the complex catena of abstract science, philosophy, techniques, and culture:

I turn my eyes to the Schools & Universities of Europe
And there behold the Loom of Locke, whose Woof rages dire,
Washed by the Water-wheels of Newton.

Blake's images are nearly always as surprising and as successful as these when he achieves his poetic ambition, the implausible synthesis of the visionary and the societal impulse. They are flat and unsuccessful when his anarchism forgets its function as social analysis and shoots off into the vision that is divorced from life. Yet that synthesis was achieved through a private mythology, an elaborate symbolical structure that was not only the product of an anarchistic imagination but was developed in order to elevate anarchy into public principle.

Blake was not, naturally, a symbolist in the sense of that term we have derived from France; but all the elements that the *symbolistes* isolated into a theory play a part in his more eclectic artistic purposes. Even more than Yeats, he overlaid his symbolism with a system of ideas, and he depended more than Yeats on explicit statement for the operation of this system. Yet the formal dislocation of Blake's poems, analogous to that derangement of the senses provided by his visionary experiences, and the visionary experience itself, which assumes the feasibility of discovering reality through the extrarational assertions of the ego, even the final tendency of finding sacred the very disorder of his mind—

all these qualities relate Blake more closely to certain poets of the late nineteenth century than to his contemporaries.

His visionary imagination seems to have contained a considerable injection of what has been called "empsychosis," a function that differs "from imagination . . . since the materials used for its products are drawn, not from the senses, but from our invisible life of sentiment and purpose." A modification of this definition would describe the symbolic imagination. It alters the process of metaphorical construction by regarding the objects of sensuous experience as projections of emotions and states of mind, and it constantly mingles matter and mind, sense and spirit, by representing emotions and attitudes as objects, or, less commonly, by representing objects as emotions and attitudes.

At its extreme, the tendency turns into surrealism. Blake differs from both surrealists and symbolists in that his visions are not generally set down as "free," the product of unanchored reverie or vagrant association, but emerge in his poetry as forms of "directed feeling," and take their place in a construction that is basically logical rather than hallucinatory, a product of the "social ego" with a purpose ultimately moral. His performance is not at all consistent. At one extreme he produces images such as that of the accursed dough swagging on the wind, which can only be described as surrealistic; at the other, his symbols stiffen into mere allegories not very different from Bunyan's, or Milton's of Sin and Death.

Between these extremes are the bulk of his figures, founded on a concept of the symbol as a means to knowledge and to power identical with the concept later developed by Mallarmé and Yeats. Yeats's comment, "Then I draw myself up into the symbol and it seems as if I should know all if I could but banish such memories and find everything in the symbol," expresses Blake's underlying ambition to turn art into ritual. "If the Spectator could enter into these Images in his Imagination, approaching them on the Fiery Chariot of his Contemplative Thought, if he could Enter into Noah's Rainbow or into his bosom, or could make a Friend & Companion of one of these Images of wonder, which always intreats him to leave mortal things (as he must know), then would he arise from his Grave, then would he meet the Lord in the Air & then he would be happy. General Knowledge is Remote Knowledge; it is in Particulars that Wisdom consists & Happiness too." The power of the symbol to transform matter and to expand mind lies in its representation of the uniqueness of every moment, the singularity of every thing, the identity of every individuality. Thus deviously eighteenth-century liberalism is transformed into an aesthetics.

The quality of Blake's symbols and the powers he ascribed to them are responsible for the strange character of his Prophecies, which are really forms of incantation. Yet he arrived at those symbols in the most mundane of literary ways. His evil gift in the *Poetical Sketches* is clearly also the evil gift of the poetry of his century—the facile device of personification; and from such devices spring even the grandest of his symbols. There is a process of foliation in the development of his imagery akin to that in Yeats, whose later poems, like Blake's, *seem* much more at variance with his early poems than they actually are. Thus, for example, one finds in the limp lines of *King Edward the Third* a blown-up description of "golden London," the "silver Thames," and an England "overflowing with honey," whose very inflations Blake will presently press into the metaphysical purposes of symbolism. Here, too, in a song sung by a minstrel, liberty is an eagle, time is a sea, and the Trojan ancestors of the British (including "Gothic Artists," no doubt) land "in firm array upon the rocks Of Albion." Here, as in "Gwin," real human creatures sit in real caves, and in "Fair Elinor" appears the grave—of such central importance in Blake's later symbolism—and it is at least as real as the graves in other eighteenth-century poems in the Gothic mood. The imagery of some primitivistic Edenlike time, when angels glittered in the sky for the edification of shepherds, occurs almost accidentally in "Fresh from the dewy hill," and the later concern with symbols of integration and unity finds its first faint suggestion in the conventional lines of "Love and harmony combine." Here, too, we may find the literary origins of Blake's gigantic mythological creatures. Urizen, for example, emerges quite complete in the personification of winter:

> O Winter! bar thine adamantine doors:
> The north is thine; there hast thou built thy dark
> Deep-founded habitation. Shake not thy roofs,
> Nor bend thy pillars with thine iron car.
>
> He hears me not, but o'er the yawning deep
> Rides heavy; his storms are unchain'd, sheathed
> In ribbed steel; I dare not lift mine eyes,
> For he hath rear'd his sceptre o'er the world.
>
> Lo! now the direful monster, whose skin clings
> To his strong bones, strides o'er the groaning rocks:
> He withers all in silence, and his hand
> Unclothes the earth, and freezes up frail life.
>
> He takes his seat upon the cliffs; the mariner
> Cries in vain. Poor little wretch! that deal'st
> With storms, till heaven smiles, and the monster
> Is driv'n yelling to his caves beneath mount Hecla.

The poem is worth quoting in its entirety because of its extraordinary prophecy of what is to come, not only in the literal details of snow and ice, dearth, desolation, steel and bones, cliffs and rocks, all of which become the symbolical equipment of reason later, but more particularly in the suggested narrative of a revolt from the proper "place" ("The north is thine"), the chaos which follows, and the final reachievement of a pastoral peace when the proper "place" is once more filled. This was to become the metaphor on which Blake's entire mythology rested, and which was to give his Prophecies such structure as they had.

The reader can follow the amplification and the specialization of Blake's symbols from these humble sources, and it is possible to detect in these sources the weakness as literary creations of those of his symbols which are also characters. As these characters derive from the popular device of personification, so also they suffer from the eighteenth-century habit of generalization. His mythological figures are totally devoid of the pictorial and particularized interest of the mythological figures of Spenser and Milton and Keats, all of whom we are made to feel as persons, or helped to visualize as creatures in a pageant, or both.

It is true that Blake's ambitions were very different from those of Spenser or Milton or Keats, but it is also true that the force of his characters is not at all that of particularities but of abstractions. As he personified the seasons in his first poems, so in his last he personified mercy, pity, peace, and love—and all other human qualities. He may have been, as various art critics have said, deficient in the descriptive imagination, but more than that, as his comments on Chaucer's characters and on his own kind of allegory suggest, he seems really to have submitted to that very tendency to generalize and idealize for which he never ceased to upbraid his contemporaries. He may have thought that he was expressing "essences," yet the fact is that his "essences" are at least as devoid of particularity as those fixed and final norms which the eighteenth century hoped to discover under the flux and shadows of temporal and local accident.

Among other poets who devised mythological characters, only those of Shelley are vaguer. Urizen, Urthona, Luvah, and Tharmas—how do we distinguish them? Are they not all the same loose-limbed giant in habiliments only so slightly different as not to be distinguishable at all except in wholly abstract terms? And is it not strange that an artist whose whole faith was in individuality produced hundreds of pictures filled with the same few recurrent physical types—the same old man, the same rather lumpish youth in his curious underwear, the gigantically muscled creature from Michelangelo, the rigid figure from Gothic tombs and columns (a very abstract model), and the airy females derived from a depraved popular art of Blake's own time? The point is that the individuality of these creations lies not in their rich diversity but in the outline that separates them from their backgrounds, and that outline, therefore, became the main item in Blake's aesthetic creed. This is not to deny his paintings any of their power or their beauty, but only to say what has always been known, that his was primarily a linear art.

Poetry, however, is a verbal art, without recourse to line, and the power of Blake's characters in the poems lies not in what they make us feel of themselves, as forms, but in their abstract utterances, and in the total meaning of which, taken together in the whole narrative pattern, they are the allegories. Does not Blake's individualism fail him, then, in the development of his symbols? In one sense, yes; but in another, no. For if it does not show itself in the creation of individuated forms, it does show itself in the value that Blake, as an individual, placed upon them. These creatures comprise a theogony, and they had real hypnagogic power for him, even when they do not compel us. His anarchism shows itself most clearly precisely here, in his eagerness to establish a private mythology and his willingness to submit his artistic fate to its characters, as some fervent laymen are willing to submit their fate to highly sectarian versions of God or to extremely fractional political groups. It is this that makes Blake's characters at once so flat and so terrible, so obscure and so portentous.

They are abstractions in a scheme designed to overcome abstraction, but in the poetry they retain the limitation that they transcend in the theory. Under Blake's protest against an isolated reason lies a framework of isolated reasoning that is not altered because he called it vision, and the result, prophecy.

IV

Blake's framework of reasoning, his poetic structures, emerge out of basic and buried images of harmony and disharmony, integration and disintegration, that seem to derive from the sectarian atmosphere in which he was raised. Of most of his lyrics and of a few of the early Prophecies, one can say with him that "they are organized and minutely articulated," and of many of them that the minute particulars are tightly contained in a kind of roundness, a pattern of turn and return like that of "To Winter." This he also employed with apparent enjoyment in many of his pictures, where an oval or an arch encloses the whole or marks off a portion from the whole. A typical thematic procedure in the early lyrics is to state a satisfactory situation, to dissolve it, and to resolve it.

This is, in essence, a reflection of the Christian pattern of Eden, the world of strife, and heaven; or of the political pattern of an ideal primitive past, the present of conflicting interests, and the revolutionary future. It is also an expansion of Blake's own dialectical pattern, presently developed, of innocence, experience, and the higher innocence, which attempted to include the terms of both religion and politics. In the *Poetical Sketches,* at least five of the lyrics, including such a trivial thing as "Blind Man's Buff," are built on this rounded structure, with its theme of disruption and resolution. "Memory, hither come" presents counterparts in balance, as many of the lyrics in *Songs of Innocence* and *Songs of Experience* were to do, and most of the others are built on a section, one arc or another, of the whole circle.

Songs of Innocence, Songs of Experience, and *The Marriage,* regarded as a whole, utilize this structure; and the refrain of Earth's *return* is not an accident, but a thematic expression of Blake's formal ambition in the large. The separate poems within the whole use one or another of the patterns already discovered in *Poetical Sketches:* the circular structure in such poems as "The Ecchoing Green," "A Cradle Song," and "Night"; and the segmented structure in most of them, depending on the volume in which they appear. These in turn have their counterparts, and taken together many pairs of the lyrics represent the balanced, antiphonal structure. That, again, appears in separate lyrics, such as "The Lamb," "The Little Boy Lost," "The Little Boy Found," and "The Clod and the Pebble." It is Blake's nearly mathematic scrupulosity in the handling of his structures that gives these poems their singular precision and much of their charm. These structures are maintained by the repeated use of certain kinds of imagery and of particular images, and from these Blake was to select two or three that would provide the structural apparatus of the long poems insofar as they were to have any.

With the Prophetic Books comes a narrative element, yet these poems, from *Tiriel* through *Jerusalem,* cannot properly be said to have a narrative structure, if one means by narrative structure an orderly temporal sequence of cause and effect. The structure of these poems is more nearly spatial, or pictorial, as one might expect from a poet who was both a visionary and a painter. They depend on a kaleidoscopic interplay of controlling images. These are metaphors for states of mind that are in a constant movement of focusing, shifting, and refocusing. They are generally metaphors of progression, and what may seem to be a dominating narrative element is actually their unfolding. One of these metaphors Blake derived from *Paradise Lost,* but he had no interest in emulating the orderly structure of the epic except in some of its superficial devices to which he trusted for associations of amplitude.

Tiriel uses the metaphor of revolt from "place"—the fall of the angels—and of a consequent dispersal and flight through increasing chaos, but it leaves the metaphor unresolved: ". . . now my paradise is fall'n & a drear sandy plain." *The Book of Thel* uses the metaphor of the grave, with the resurrection motif implicit although still unexploited; and here the circular pattern is achieved with all the precise charm of the *Songs,* but with a spaciousness of which they were incapable, and with the consequent increase in resonance and imaginative satisfactions. *Thel* is, as a result, a poem (and the only Prophecy) that combines with perfect poise Blake's two strains of the lyrical and the oratorical. It shows his talents in a structural unity in which subject and form collaborate exactly.

Yet in *Thel* no less than in *Tiriel* the trying rhetorical device that was to fill out between Blake's metaphors and provide for his transitions from one to another, the debate between opposing points of view, is already utilized. This derives from that antiphonal pattern which may be seen in so many of the lyrics, but it developed into swollen diatribe, often accompanied by mammoth physical struggles over which Blake increasingly relinquished his control. After *Thel,* the coalescence of styles was to give way to mere alternations between them, and these were increasingly usurped by the oratorical. With this, as form was more and more taxed with the inflations and the redundancies of subject, the collapse of the unity of subject and form followed.

The balance begins to break with the first of the poems to introduce historical elements—*The French Revolution.* Since this poem is fragmentary, one cannot properly speak of its structure, but it would seem that here Blake's intention was to write a poem more nearly in the conventional narrative tradition than any of his others. Yet here too metaphor dominates and breaks up the plain narrative line. Book the First is founded on images of death and resurrection, beginning with a withering landscape, proceeding through images of frost and stone and metal to the apocalyptic fire, and ending with the bursting grave. On this basic pattern is superimposed the debate of the nobles in conclave, a relatively literal rendering here of Blake's favorite device, and his persistent substitute for both genuine drama and genuine narrative. The poem indicates what is to happen to Blake's structures as his "system" begins to unfold. The antiphonal element expands more and more within the metaphorical and pictorial frame, the abstract discussion within the concrete symbolism, until it breaks its boundaries, flows over them and drowns them out.

The series of short Prophecies that Blake wrote before 1795 comprise in content a single whole, and exist within the single metaphor of the revolt and fall of the powers. Yet they have a degree of precision that the later, longer books lack, because each has its own frame, a segment of the total symbol. Thus, the *Visions of the Daughters of Albion* employs the metaphor of wandering and of imprisonment in a cave; *America* and *Europe,* of the millennial fires; *The Book of Urizen,* of his revolt from "place" and the desolation of the world he creates; *The Book of Ahania,* of the crucifixion; *The Book of Los,* of further "fall" in a convulsive universe and of creative "binding" to stop the fall; and *The Song of Los,* in "Africa," of the petrification of life, and in "Asia," of the fires again and of the bursting grave.

The Four Zoas orders, amplifies, and completes these metaphorical fragments, and the central, rounded structure of this long poem is perfectly clear: the revolt from unity and the fall; all the displacements, dispersals, and divisions of a world in conflict; the purifying fires that prelude "the bursting Universe;"

and the coda of harvest and vintage. But even as he achieves the total round, Blake begins to lose his control of the chaos it contains.

He was aware of his dilemma. *The Four Zoas* was not engraved, not even finished finally; and *Milton* and *Jerusalem,* maintaining the same frame, attempt to give its content more support and more line. In *Milton,* the general metaphor of the fall of the powers is duplicated within the frame by the descent of the mistaken poet and his divisions. The structural attempt is for a round within a round, as in such a picture as "Behold now Behemoth which I made with thee" in the "Job" group. But three elements conspire in Blake's formal defeat—the process of proliferation that seems to have become more and more a part of his vision; the attempt to dramatize directly, in imitative form, his intuition that the very singleness of mind entails an infinite complexity; and the failure of objectivity that allowed him to distort his structures with undigested lumps of personal experience. *Jerusalem,* like *Milton,* attempts to give the content of the encircling metaphor a certain objective underpinning. It constructs a spiritual cartography, a symbolical map of England with a vast network of associations and correspondences somewhat like the later effort in Joyce's *Finnegans Wake.* But again, the very complexity that Blake could not resist defeats him. His imagination no doubt achieved a sense of order from his great charts, but one has no reason to think that there was some single key to them that scholarship may one day discover, and in its absence the vast bulk of the poem remains chaotic. "A palace," Coleridge thought, "is more than a house, but it must be a house, at least."

Blake's structural ambition in his three long Prophetic poems was analogous to that in his pictures of "The Last Judgment" and "Meditations among the Tombs." These swarm with figures, rising and falling, separating and embracing, the landscape aflame, with tidy centers of symbolical interest around which groups of the multiple figures are ordered. The figures themselves are "organized and minutely articulated," and the whole is quite breath-taking in its achievement of a plastic balance undistorted by tremendous movement. But in words Blake could not achieve this balance, and the longer, the more full of figures, his poems become, the more he loses what he most wishes to attain, the plastic, spatial structure. His figures divide and multiply endlessly, but since they are characters in poems, not forms in a painting, they also argue, debate, plead, and wail, and the effect is doubly one of a nearly intolerable redundancy, in speech as in movement. In the paintings the effect is the impressive one of formal repetition in an exactly controlled design. Blake's long Prophecies are unwilling witnesses for Lessing's case against the notion of sister arts. Yet *ut pictura poesis* has had happier results. More needs to be said in defining Blake's structural failure.

There is, for example, the whole matter of the *order* of Blake's imaginative procedure, in which he seems to have hoped to achieve something like an inversion of the usual order. When Coleridge called for a "framework of objectivity" as a protection against moralistic verse on the one hand and thoughtless reverie on the other, he touched upon a central problem among poets, and the main problem in Blake. For Blake's method was to organize his long poems in terms of a subjective framework, metaphors representing states of minds alone, and then to fill them with a selection of objective material. Blake's visionary experiences were not wholly consistent, as we saw at the outset. He could see spiritual realities within natural objects and he could impose spiritual realities upon nature. In his development as a whole, if we may believe what he himself said, the second mode came to dominate, and this conclusion has some corroboration in the Prophetic Books, where he seems more and more to cram the detached vision with facts, less and less to illuminate facts by vision. That is the real difference between Prophecies like *Milton* or *Jerusalem* and lyrics like "London" or "The Sunflower."

One comes back to the question of what his visions really were, and a possible answer would seem to be that they were often private versions of literary conventions. The influence of Milton, merely in pictorial terms, is so obvious that it need hardly be mentioned; and nowhere is it more obvious than in Blake's cosmogonal metaphor of the revolt and fall of the angels, and all the consequent disaster. A metaphor derived from literary convention nearly as central to Blake's structure, but as yet largely unobserved, is that of the grave. Blake's earliest poems showed him imitating the subjects and the sentiments of the mortuary poets, as in "Fair Elinor" and some of the prose pastiches. These developed into symbolic lyrics such as "The Caverns of the Grave I've seen" and "The Door of Death is made of Gold," in which the grave is experience, as it is again in *Thel.* Their final use was in the picture of the bursting graves, the exploding universe with which his Prophecies conclude, and which completes the metaphor of the fall. "The Caverns of the Grave" and "The Door of Death" were both written with reference to Blake's illustrations to Blair's *The Grave,* which he no doubt studied closely, but these illustrations had been preceded years before by his illustrations to Young's *Night Thoughts,* and it is in Young's extremely sentimental pages that one finds some hints of Blake's intentions. *The Four Zoas* imitated the organization of *Night Thoughts* in its general proposition of *A Dream of Nine Nights,* but there is a subtler relationship than this between the two. Young's poem is a long reflective piece, with interpolated narratives of a highly hypothetical cast. Its main theme is the fact of death, explored through all the crude and grisly paraphernalia of the graveyard mode; but its main theme is constantly broken up by reflections on the social virtues and vices, especially friendship and love, benevolence and sincerity, ambition, avarice, and hypocrisy, and by attacks on deists and atheists and lengthy arguments for the immortality of the soul. All this appears in one way or another in Blake, and sometimes Young's sentiments, for all their crudeness of expression, are very much like Blake's.

> Joy is an import; joy is an exchange;
> Joy flies monopolists: it calls for two;
> Rich fruit! heaven-planted! never pluckt by one.
> Needful auxiliars are our friends, to give
> To social man true relish of himself.

In popular moralistic verse of this kind one can find one of the sources of Blake's ideas of universal love and brotherhood. From such abstractions he may have derived his visions of the depressed solitude of his Urizen figures, and of the joyous reunion and interchange of specters with their emanations, just as from the Ossianic poems he derived his images of cosmic struggle between gigantic characters. All of this is merely to suggest that we may find the clue to Blake's structures in such popular discursive poetry as Young's rather than in such coherent narrative as *Paradise Lost*. The *Night Thoughts,* like Blake's long poems, has a dominant imagery and theme, and within that packs a good deal of miscellaneous material. The chief structural difference is that Blake is intent on making his content concrete, that he dramatizes and pictorializes the reflections, and that instead of exhorting us himself, he enables his characters to exhort us and one another. There is a world of difference between the *quality* of their poetry and their ideas, yet in his basic patterns Blake is more nearly a mythological Young than he is a metaphysical Milton.

His purpose in using the mythological method was not only to satisfy the needs and resolve the contradictions of his own temperament, but to explore and extend the thought and encompass the contradictions in the thought of his age, even the dullest, like Young's. This method has been described by T. S. Eliot as "a step toward making the modern world possible for art, toward . . . order and form," and it was such a step for Blake. But it was also a way of making art possible again for a world that, as he thought, had exhausted it through obeisance to a too mechanical notion of order and form. The peculiar function of myth is to present to the imagination figures that are a direct expression of experience, not merely to put allegorical clothes on abstraction and thereby disguise theory. Blake did both, but with the single ambition of devising poetic forms more appropriate to the content of his experience and of the experience of a revolutionary age than the age itself had provided. This much he did, although with only partial success.

The paradoxical faith of eighteenth-century liberalism was in laissez faire and social order, the paradoxical faith of revolutionary theory was in liberty and fraternity, and the paradoxical faith of William Blake's art was in the free expression of energy and of outline, of anarchy and form. The structure of his long poems is an exact reproduction of this paradox in his thought. His forms encompass a chaos of symbols within the rounded metaphor of an initial and a final order. They are dramatizations of anarchy achieving its form, spectacles of utterly unleashed poetic energies coming together in unexpected moments of harmony. But if we argue that in this way Blake's long poems express an age, we are also saying that their poetic benefits exist not in their wholes but only in their coruscations.

That is the toll of Blake's faith in artistic freedom, in what Hopkins called the refinement of singularity, in "intellectual peculiarity, that must be myself alone shut up in myself, or reduced to nothing." His anarchy resulted in the dispersal rather than the organization of his talents. He trusted his intuitions completely, and more and more he was determined that they should be left unguarded. The violence of his later work, the windy rhetoric and the invertebrate metrics, the endless addresses and vexing exhortations, the perverse confusions, the dissipation of form, the redundancy, the repetition of theme, the unwillingness to find new embodiments for his intuitions—all these are one result. The exquisite occasional imagery, the lines that do express exactly the pulse of his perceptions, the deep penetration into the psychic and the cultural conflicts of his society, the rich abundance and the chilling axioms—these are another result. When personality gives way completely to itself, both its good and its bad emerge, and often in discouragingly unequal portions. "The poet," Coleridge said, "brings the whole soul of man into activity . . . a more than usual state of emotion with more than usual order; judgment ever awake and steady self-possession with enthusiasm and feeling profound or vehement." It is a definition that will not do for Blake. Having been at once dismissed by an audience, he dismissed self-criticism.

Self-criticism expresses itself in the austerities of technique, which is the means by which an artist's subject matter compels him to attend to it. As he was more and more dominated by vision, Blake relinquished his understanding of technique. His subjects presented themselves to him full-blown; his technique was to copy them. The wholly successful artist's technique is not separate in this way from his subject. It is the only means he has of exploring, developing, discovering, his subject, and finally, of conveying, through *all* the resources of poetry—the nerves of meter as well as the spectacle of image, the fixities of form as well as the privacy of vision—of *conveying* his perceptions. But Blake worked "without Labour or Study," which means that he had abandoned technique in this important sense. His material then spreads out, multiplies, begins to sprawl and grow lumpish, and it becomes increasingly obscure. Abandoning technique as the means of distilling his subject, Blake substituted repetitions, violent assertions, shrill pronouncements, and prolix persuasions. Yet his late prolixity does not at all represent a decline of passion, as prolixity usually does, but rather a decline of the means by which passion communicates itself without loss. We are as aware at the end as at the beginning of the force of his anger and his love, but we are less able to feel them as he felt them.

It is not Blake's difficulty to which one objects, but to the fact that it largely failed him. His perception of the singleness of mind revealed to him its vast complexities of pattern. There are no neat dichotomies, no separately parceled faculties; for every element in man involves every other, and the possible relationships are therefore endless. But to attempt to convey this by an ever-increasing complexity in verse, by a private system that became more and more ingrown and involuted and swollen, was a disaster. The system began as a means of expressing the theme, but before Blake had finished, the system dominated the themes and finally determined them. It is a tragic reversal of a noble poetic purpose. "Damn braces. Bless relaxes." But a blessing is not a plenary indulgence.

The fault lay in Blake's visionary talent, which also gives us what is greatest in him, and in his willingness to submit to it because even in its disorder he found it sacred. His visions transcended structure and number. They spilled out in a vast profusion, self-engendered, one exhaling another and that another, a spiritual kaleidoscope that operated as rapidly as the eye can wink. The dark, disordered profusions of Blake's last poems are the result. He was a slave to vision as other men are to cruelty or avarice or sensuality or opium, and the consequence for him was the same as it is for them—a narrowing of individuality and a final disregard for the order beyond one's own. We become what we behold.

CHAPTER TWELVE

The Triumph of Life

I

NONE OF the revolutionary theorists advanced any revolutionary principle of art, and in their expansive praise of life, none of them looked to art either as a form of social expression or as an ally. When they thought about art at all, it was almost inevitably from a static historical point of view, as in Godwin's schoolmasterish *Of English Style*. A few others reflected in the same dull way on literature, but not one was interested in deducing or capable of deducing a single original principle of aesthetics. This it remained for poets to do—Wordsworth with his theory of a democratized style, Coleridge with the organic principle, and Shelley with various notions about art and freedom. All these developments were worked out simultaneously or anticipated by Blake in his apparent isolation.

Many apostles of progress in the eighteenth century were considerably interested in art, however, and from the time of Thomson's "Liberty," the poetic tract devoted to the panorama of social progress was a commonplace, and in these epistles and odes, the arts and sciences took their place with morals and institutions. For minor poets from Thomson to Hayley, Greece became the home of a roast-beef version of liberty that provided them with an object for sentimental reflections as remote as possible from any view that one might regard as revolutionary. And among theorists who combined a faith in progress with revolutionary action, the interest was overwhelmingly in morals and institutions, and in the physical improvement of life.

This interest was so great that it served not only to separate science and art completely, but also to exclude art and letters from the total expectations held of life, until the Germans—Herder, for example—showed the nineteenth century how they were to be put solidly into the context of society, and helped poets of a revolutionary slant, like Shelley and Byron, to relate them more firmly than Thomson or Shaftesbury had managed, to notions of cultural character and change. The rift between knowledge and belief had, however, been accomplished, to the increasing vexation of poets from the beginning of that century into the depths of this one.

"Certainly we . . . have sold our birthright for a mess of facts," said Oscar Wilde at the end of the century, and pretended to repudiate facts for the sake of a febrile aestheticism. Feeling the same dilemma a hundred years before, Blake was able to decree an aestheticism under no necessity to sever itself from life, but the severance with fact was in its way nearly as complete. For Blake, facts were not "irreducible and stubborn," since he could either transcend or abolish them with vision. Never questioning the legitimacy of vision, he inverted "the modern man's intellectual attitude," as for example Mrs. Langer, following Whitehead, has described it. Quoting Wittgenstein—"The totality of atomic facts is the world" and "The world divides into facts"—she adds, "Our world 'divides into facts' because we so divide it. Facts are our guarantees of truth." Exactly, said Blake, and would *not* "so divide it." "Bring out number, weight & measure in a year of dearth." But one cannot challenge the current of one's age so utterly as this without strain.

The strain shows in Blake's life in the moments of crucifying doubt, and in his work in violence and shrillness. Yet as an individual if not always as an artist, he was able to rise above the strain, and he created for himself an account of the universe and an aestheticism that seem to have given him the deep satisfactions and the kind of serenity of which ancient and medieval men were capable but of which modern men are almost wholly deprived. He was striving against such a distinction as

De Quincey was later to make between a literature of knowledge and a literature of power; that is, he would not allow to the kind of material De Quincey had in mind the dignity of the word "knowledge." He identified knowledge and power as magicians do and as all Christians could do before the eighteenth century, and he reserved both terms for art.

Of the capacities of a genuine scientific imagination he had no understanding, and therefore he thought of its work as a relatively trivial accumulation of descriptive data. And to a scientific mind, Blake must seem to have fallen into the dilemma of Tennyson as Carlyle described it—"carrying a bit of Chaos about him . . . which he is manufacturing into Cosmos." What Carlyle—or, perhaps, the scientist—was not in a position to know was that this had become the dilemma of *all* genuine poets, and was to remain their dilemma. With the possible exception of Thomas Hardy, nineteenth-century naturalism could not produce a single poet; it destroyed many.

Some modern poets have been able to give their credence to older systems of unification, as T. S. Eliot has; a few, like Rimbaud, Yeats, and Crane, have been able to create—often at a price—such systems with a rich enough ground for poetry to grow in at least for a time. For the latter kind, Blake was the example in history. He refused to admit the cleavage between knowledge and belief. They were one. He strove to heal the breach between the functions of fact and the functions of faith, which the progressivists had accepted; therefore his view was of the entire improvement of life. A better life meant richer materials for the artist, hence a better art; and a better art, in turn, meant a better life, hence still better materials. Art is the ritual by which life can achieve the condition of art. This is the first relationship between Blake's aesthetics and his social views.

From Blake's faith in the dignity of the individual proceeds his faith in the divinity of the true artist, and vice versa. But the concept derives from a venerable tradition that in the eighteenth century had various representatives, and in the nineteenth, famous ones. Blake seized upon this tradition as a means of developing a theory of the imagination that released him from facts and enabled him to write "prophecy." This theory, in turn, resulted in a new set of ideas about the nature and the function of art.

When viewed historically, Blake's effort is in essence simple and obvious enough. Like many men in the Renaissance and later, he combined the Hebraic conception of prophets as poets of superior vision, able to transcend the corrupt universe (the world of fact) and seize upon the true revelation of things, with the Platonic conception of the enlightened seeker able to transcend a world of accident for that ideal realm of which it was but a poor copy. Neo-Platonism emphasized this element in Plato's thought, as in Plotinus, where imagination is named the first emanation of God, and Platonism is pushed into a form of absolute mysticism. The alchemical tradition, developing in a different direction, used the same idea as the basis of magic. The tradition of literary criticism in the Renaissance, developing in still a third direction, gave the superior powers to the artist, who like God was able to create in his works a superior nature. This tradition, expressing ideas in support of a generalized and idealized art, was first put forth in England by Sidney, who, with his belief in the poet as *maker,* stated exact equivalents for the two principal forms that one day William Blake's "vision" was to take: "making things either better then nature bringeth foorth, or quite a new, formes such as never were in nature."

It was an idea so loose as to include presently the inimical concepts of imitation and independent creation, of classic taste and original genius, and even in Blake both positions may be found in a mingled state. In the eighteenth century, in the theories of Sir Joshua Reynolds all these strains are still to be detected. But gradually, after the idea had sifted down through critics like Dryden, it had come more and more to the defense of independent creation and of original genius, the untrammeled spirit of the Godlike artist, and even in such pale expositors as Shaftesbury it begins to appear in this guise, one who "in a just sense deserves the name of poet" being "indeed a second *Maker;* a just Prometheus under Jove."

Blake's ideas look back over this entire tradition and give it a new vigor; for if Thomas Paine, in the naturalistic vein of deism, could discredit prophets because they were merely poets, Blake, while agreeing to the identification, could alter the emphasis and renew the dignity of poets by pointing out that formerly they had been respected as prophets.

This was also the attempt of Shelley in *A Defence of Poetry*, following the expansion of the entire tendency in Germany; but Blake had already pushed these ideas beyond Shelley before Shelley wrote. Blake could not, in fact, except in explication, have gone further than in his first statement on this subject: "If it were not for the Poetic or Prophetic character the Philosophic & Experimental would soon be at the ratio of all things, & stand still, unable to do other than repeat the same dull round over again." This is to say not only that art refreshes life but that it actually creates life's values, and the opposition that Blake had in mind is repeatedly dramatized in the figures of Los and Urizen, for Los gives Urizen his shape, "binds" him, and Los builds Golgonooza, the palace of art which is to supersede the rocky, wintry world of "the Philosophic & Experimental" character.

Blake believed quite as firmly as Shelley that poets and artists were "the institutors of laws and the founders of civil society, and the inventors of the arts of life, and the teachers"—albeit in his own terms. The rich and political protectors of the Royal Academy he advised as follows: "Foolish Men, your own real Greatness depends on your Encouragement of the Arts, & your Fall will depend on their Neglect & Depression. What you Fear is your true Interest. Leo X was advised not to Encourage the Arts; he was too Wise to take this Advice." "Degrade first the Arts if you'd Mankind Degrade" is a generalized anticipation of Shelley. "Empire follows Art & Not Vice Versa as Englishmen suppose" is a specific one.

In the intensity and the extremity of his sense of prophetic importance Blake is more like Rimbaud at the end of the century than he is like Shelley at its start. In Rimbaud one finds again the Blakean violence and the Blakean aesthetic concepts. Here the idea that the poet is a seer whose mind can penetrate fact for a higher reality, that the poet is the voice of God, and that to express this voice, he must abolish all egotism and prejudice, everything of the "selfhood"—plus that additional and fatal idea of the *"dérèglement de tous les sens"* that destroyed him. For this, Blake had what Rimbaud did not have, his rigid, Protestant self-righteousness which told him that, precisely as he was, he was equipped to speak for God. He did not need opium or vice, for he had "vision." Having been born a hundred years before Rimbaud, at a point when radical politics and dissenting religion were in an unusual congruence, he had no need to become God, for he felt, in effect, that he already was God. One may say this more attractively by pointing out the divergent ideas here of the nature of genius. One poet assumes that genius rests on personality abolished, the other, on personality wholly integrated. Rimbaud's mood comes from an utter despair of the world appropriate to the end of the nineteenth century, that monument to bourgeois failure. Blake's mood comes from an optimistic expectation of the world characteristic of if not entirely appropriate to the end of the eighteenth century, when the imposition of the bourgeois will on European life was not yet wholly apparent.

This difference means that as a poet Blake was able to retain a vivid interest in the world that he wished to rectify, and that he survived as a practicing poet, or nearly. The second depends on the first, and even in his most transcendental definitions of the imagination, other elements in Blake's aesthetics, and his practice itself, held him to the balance. The definition of imagination will be, of course, exactly as exalted as the concept of the artist, but this concept in Blake, being fairly loose, still allowed for degrees. Blake usually demanded more for the imagination in his definitions than he put into operation in his practice.

II

IMAGINATION, according to Blake, is not only the creative ego, it is the life force itself. This conception means that Blake disposed entirely of that favorite eighteenth-century metaphor of the imagination as a mirror held up to nature, and for two reasons. The first is that imagination is active and creative, not passive and reflective. The second is that nature itself is totally inadequate to art. "Nature has no Outline, but Imagination has. Nature has no Tune, but Imagination has. Nature has no Supernatural & dissolves: Imagination is Eternity." This is one of those definitions which exceed Blake's practice, yet it contains the item that the most mundane modern definition must contain—the formative power of imagination, its capacity for structure. "Nature has no Outline, but Imagination has." The sentence is reminiscent of a sentence in the *Hermetica,* with its Plotinian background: ". . . the incorporeal cannot be enclosed by anything; but it can itself enclose all things; it is the quickest of all things, and the mightiest." Indeed, the entire passage that opens with this sentence is illuminating, for it indicates the kind of religious basis on which Blake's doctrine of art rests, and also, in its suggestion that the "corporeal" is the unimaginative, the imprisoned, the selfish condition, its political implications. "Bid your soul travel to any land you choose, and sooner than you can bid it go, it will be there. Bid it pass on from land to ocean, and it will be there no less quickly; it has not moved as one moves from place to place, but it *is* there. Bid it fly up to heaven, and it will have no need of wings; nothing can bar its way, neither the fiery heat of the sun, nor the swirl of the planet-spheres; cleaving its way through all, it will fly up till it reaches the outermost of all corporeal things. And should you wish to break forth from the universe itself, and gaze on the things outside the Kosmos (if indeed there is anything outside the Kosmos), even that is permitted to you. See what power, what quickness is yours. And when you yourself can do all this, cannot God do it? You must understand then that it is in this way that God contains within himself the Kosmos, and himself, and all that is; it is thoughts which God thinks, that all things are contained in him. If then you do not make yourself equal to God, you cannot apprehend God; for like is known by like. Leap clear of all that is corporeal, and make yourself grow to a like expanse with that greatness which is beyond all measure; rise above all time, and become eternal; then you will apprehend God. Think that for you too nothing is impossible; deem that you too are immortal, and that you are able to grasp all things in your thought, to know every craft and every science; find your home in the haunts of every living creature; make yourself higher than all heights, and lower than all depths; bring together in yourself all opposites of quality, heat and cold, dryness and fluidity; think that you are everywhere at once, on land, at sea, in heaven; think that you are not yet begotten, that you are in the womb, that you are young, that you are old, that you have died, that you are in the world beyond the grave; grasp in your thought all this at once, all times and places, all substances and qualities and magnitudes together; then you can apprehend God. But if you shut up your soul in your body, and abase yourself, and say 'I know nothing, I can do nothing; I am afraid of earth and sea, I cannot mount to heaven; I know not what I was, not what I shall be'; then, what have you to do with God?"

This strange passage helps us to understand the several directions in which Blake applied his concept of the imagination; why, for example, he called Jesus "Divine Imagination," and why he thought that imagination was identical with liberty. Imagination, like God, creates all things, but it also understands all, encompasses all, sympathizes with all, and forgives all. This is, in its time, extraordinary. It is true that throughout the century aestheticians had tended to convert the traditional ethics of "sympathy" into a concept of the imagination as *Einfühlung,* which identified subject and object, but surely no one before Blake was so self-conscious in his pronouncements, or made claims so vast. Like God, imagination is slave to nothing, but is absolutely free. Therefore only men in the imaginative condition are free men and, concomitantly, only men imaginatively recognized by others are granted freedom. The term had for Blake both an exact aesthetic and a general moral significance. Imagination creates the particularities of art, and in life it treasures particularity, the mood on which true brotherhood can alone be founded. Blake's doctrine of the imagination is the aesthetic and moral equivalent of his political anarchism.

We are concerned now with the aesthetic rather than the moral implications. Did Blake's doctrine lead him to something like the young Keats's concept of "Negative Capability" and to its result in the idea of the imagination as essentially an instrument for the discovery of what already is, like Coleridge's wind harp? Or did it lead him to that other emphasis, also found in Coleridge, of the "esemplastic" force that actually creates, the emphasis toward which Keats was tending when he died? "Memory should not be called knowledge," Keats wrote in a Blakean moment. "Many have original minds who do not think it—they are led away by Custom. Now it appears to me that almost any Man may like the spider spin from his own inwards his own airy Citadel—the points of leaves and twigs on which the spider begins her work are few, and she fills the air with a beautiful circuiting. Man should be content with as few points to tip with the fine Web of his Soul, and weave a tapestry empyrean full of symbols for his spiritual eye, of softness for his spiritual touch, of space for his wandering, of distinctness for his luxury." The two modes are, of course, not separate, but are actually dependent on one another, and if we find them mingling in the theoretical speculations of Coleridge and Keats, we must surely expect to find them mingling in Blake's unsystematic observations.

Then too, there is always the fact of Blake's "vision," and of its several varieties. The illumination of natural objects by vision suggests the imaginative function as one of discovery. The substitution of visionary for natural objects suggests the imagination as purely creative, self-supporting, and autonomous. To assume, as Blake did, that vision is God-given and that he merely copied what God put before him abolishes both conceptions and returns him to the eighteenth-century notion of the imagination as mirror, although it is a different "nature" from theirs that he purports to reflect. Yet this assumption, while it discouraged a proper understanding of technique in Blake's practice, did not determine his theoretical reflections on the nature of imagination, although it helped him to pull together the two different ideas. Because he was divinely inspired, self-expression (creation) is the means of discovering the real order of things. In true poets the two are one; revelation and invention are the same.

"Memory should not be called knowledge." The attack on

"Memory" in Blake's aesthetics is the clearest indication of what he intended. Memory is the Satanic state, Albion's chaos; intuitions that escape the chains of sense provide the order of art. Recollections in tranquillity will not do for poetry. Wordsworth's "inward eye Which is the bliss of solitude" would doom art to the static imitation of dead things; therefore, for all his sense of an animated universe, Wordsworth was for Blake an "Atheist."

Nor could Blake ever subscribe to the idea of a "world memory" that fascinated Shelley, even though he was induced to toy with it. He revived the old theory of innate ideas, saying that "Man Brings All that he has or can have Into the World with him. Man is Born Like a Garden ready Planted & Sown" and that "Innate Ideas are in Every Man, Born with him; they are truly Himself." He thought of his symbols as having an eternal existence apart from and yet always available to the minds of enlightened men; and he was thus led to employ the Platonic doctrine of pre-existence as the metaphorical substructure of at least one poem, *The Book of Thel.*

Yet he could not admit the Platonic theory of reminiscence, which would have put these several ideas into a consistent order. The reason becomes clear in one of Shelley's juvenile outbursts: "How provokingly close are those new-born babes! . . . all knowledge is reminiscence: the doctrine is far more ancient than the times of Plato, and as old as the venerable allegory that the Muses are the daughters of Memory; not one of the nine was ever said to be the child of Invention!" Now for all their bright innocence, the children in Blake's poems do not come "trailing clouds of glory," but leap into a dangerous world with the challenge of a plastic energy, and if their minds are already "Planted and Sown," it is with capacities rather than with concepts.

Art is direct revelation, from the outside; and art is invention, from the inside. Both represent a potentiality of mind, but neither represents a body of ideas, and both exclude the Shelleyan proposition. "Reynolds's Opinion was that . . . all Pretence to Inspiration is a Lie & a Deceit . . . if it is a Deceit, the whole Bible is Madness. This Opinion originates in the Greeks' calling the Muses Daughters of Memory." To Blake, art could mean either innovation or renovation, but never reproduction. "Imagination has nothing to do with Memory"—

> . . . more than mortal fire
> Burns in my soul, and does my song inspire.

These are a late and an early statement of the same faith in the transcendental imagination.

The analogy with Rimbaud is again instructive. He too felt that the imagination could rise above all the trammels of the past, of memory and prejudice and even of personality. Baudelaire, *"le premier voyant, roi des poètes, un vrai Dieu,"* nearly achieved this condition, for he knew that "inspecting the invisible and hearing things unheard is entirely different from gathering up again the spirit of dead things," Blake's "deluge of forgotten remembrances." In their practice Rimbaud and Baudelaire came a good deal closer to the actual achievement of their ambition than did Blake, whose later poetry is shot through with personal reminiscence and whose characteristic imaginative operation was to place on the observations of his senses the value of symbols rather than to leap utterly beyond the order of the senses.

Yet the attempt at a transcendental imagination has a partial success in the equally characteristic tendency of Blake's imagery to shift away from the merely sensational, as in such images as a virgin "Cloth'd in tears & sighs," "all thy moans flew o'er my roof," "the fibrous roots Of every heart," and "the windows wove over with curses of iron." That he had no more conspicuous success in this direction, that, in fact, his poems tend to become allegories for historical conflicts rather than the kind of sustained visionary experience he hoped they were, is probably because of his particular attitude toward the personality of the artist, an attitude that differed radically from that of Rimbaud.

Poets in the nineteenth century lost a kind of pride that had been a characteristic of most great poets before them. Milton, humble as he was before his God and his task, as a poet among men was inflexibly *proud.* So, in their different ways, were Dryden and Pope. Pride is perhaps not quite the right word for men so amiable as Shakespeare. Spenser, and Chaucer, yet each of these was possessed of a kind of self-assurance that is no longer to be found in Wordsworth or Coleridge. Blake was perhaps the last poet who was as certain of himself as his great predecessors had been. We have called this quality in him "Protestant self-righteousness." It kept him from expressing for even a moment at least one prominent tendency of the nineteenth century—the desire for the dissolution of personality, a nearly universal atavism among poets.

Shelley and Byron and Keats and Wordsworth all yearned for absorption in the forms of nature, a yearning to lose identity that must have arisen from a common distaste for their identities, a common sense of their inadequacy. Coleridge's desperate need for a transmogrifying love is analogous: "Oh! that my spirit, purged by death of its weaknesses, which are, alas! my identity, might flow into thine, and live and act in thee and be thine." In the course of the century, the desire to abolish personality was developed into an aesthetic creed. Already in Keats, with the idea of "Negative Capability," of living by preference in a state of irresolution, the process has started, and one can trace it through Arnold and Tennyson and Rossetti to Rimbaud in France and Yeats in Ireland. Rimbaud crucified himself on the double motive of the impulse to assert his temperament and the impulse to destroy it utterly. His biography is a painful allegory of an aesthetic conviction. Yeats approved Keats's theory that "A Poet is the most unpoetical of any thing in existence; because he has no Identity—he is continually infor[ming] and filling some other Body—The sun, the Moon, the Sea and Men and Women who are creatures of impulse are poetical and have about them an unchangeable attribute—the poet has none; no identity—he is certainly the most unpoetical of all God's Creatures."

Art, like religion, has developed a *via negativa*. It was not Blake's way. If he had been a mystic, he would have anticipated this tendency both as an individual and as a theorist. But he was not a mystic, and while he believed that he was the passive instrument of God, his visions confirmed his sense of the importance of his personality rather than denied it, and one finds no trace in him of the later faith in the chameleon-like nature of the artist. The eager assertion of his own identity, his belief in the sacredness of every identity in the creation, and the place that "identity" came to have in his aesthetics are all expressions of his deep sectarianism and his political liberalism. He was the first and the last poet to declare, in all ways and with complete conviction, the absolute value of individuality.

His readiness to turn Edward Young's "conjectures" on original genius into noisy declarations is a result. Young warned against a too slavish imitation of the ancients, excellent as they were. Blake denounced them as warmakers and called their ideal of art a fraud. Young rather cautiously attempted to separate genius and learning: "I would compare genius to virtue, and learning to riches. As riches are most wanted where there is least virtue; so learning where there is least genius. As virtue without much riches can give happiness, so genius without much learning can give renown. . . . Learning is borrowed knowledge; genius is knowledge innate, and quite our own." Blake said that "There is no use in education," that it was "wrong," "the great sin," for it corrupted the individuality by custom and individual wisdom by the wisdom of others. To genius it was utterly irrelevant: "The Man who says that the Genius is not Born, but Taught—Is a Knave." Education, whose function is the preservation of tradition and the regulation of taste, is useless, for "Genius dies with its Possessor & comes not again till Another is Born with it." Young warned against "the too great indulgence of genius," the attempt to reveal divinity, but Blake pushed such reservations aside by declaring that "Genius has no Error" and that "Genius cannot be Bound."

Young denounced the doctrine of imitation on the basis of natural diversity: ". . . by a spirit of *Imitation* we counteract nature, and thwart her design. She brings us into the world all *Originals:* no two faces, no two minds, are just alike; but all bear nature's evident mark of separation on them. Born *Originals,* how comes it to pass that we die Copies? That meddling ape *Imitation* . . . snatches the pen, and blots out nature's mark of separation, cancels her kind intention, destroys all mental individuality." Blake, who advised young artists to copy the best models as mechanical exercises, nevertheless denounced imitation of style, and in Young's terms. "How ridiculous it would be to see the Sheep Endeavouring to walk like the Dog, or the Ox striving to trot like the Horse; just as Ridiculous it is to see One Man Striving to Imitate Another. Man varies from Man more than Animal from Animal of different Species." The folly of "walking in another man's style, or speaking, or looking in another man's style and manner" is that it is "unappropriate and repugnant to your own individual character," and that the imagination is "weakened" and "darkened." When genius "may soar in the regions of *liberty,*" why should it choose to "move in the soft fetters of easy *imitation*"? asked Young in a vocabulary that suggests the connection that Blake's politics later led him to attempt to forge between art and freedom.

The productions of unfettered genius have two distinguishing qualities. First, they are the expression of an uncorrupted individuality, and second, they are therefore truly expressive of their subject. "The Great Style is always Novel or New in all its Operations. Original & Characteristical are the Two Grand Merits of the Great Style," Blake wrote with reference to the first of these, and Young with reference to the second: "An *Original* . . . rises spontaneously from the vital root of genius; it *grows,* it is not *made: Imitations* are often a sort of *manufacture,* wrought up by . . . *mechanics.*"

Mechanization in art was as distasteful to Blake as mechanization in life, and the concept of "rules" and of artistic structures built and held together by "rules," as repellent as legal structures in society. D. H. Lawrence called machinery a "death product." Much earlier, Blake called machines "the arts of death," which destroyed "the arts of life." If we put this detestation of the mechanical together with Blake's conception of the transcendental imagination and his faith in inspiration, we might almost certainly expect an aesthetic preference for the merely suggestive and the indefinite. Yet this is precisely what he does not prefer, and the reason is the value he places on individuality. Exactitude, precision, outline—these were his demands of character as well as of art. "Truth has bounds, Error none" is the ethical statement of his creed. "The Infinite alone resides in Definite & Determinate Identity" is its aesthetic statement.

His trust in inspiration was complete, but it was inspiration very different from Shelley's, which was "as a fading coal . . . when composition begins, inspiration is already on the decline." Blake made no such distinction between the vast imaginative experience and the inadequate formal expression. "Grandeur of Ideas is founded on Precision of Ideas," he said, and "The Man's Execution is as his Conception & No better." His view of outline supports his entire view of art as the achievement of form, of expressing identity for artist and object alike. It is another equivalent for that anarchism which expects, from the free expression of individual energy, social order.*

Outline underlies Blake's theory of organic form. When he spoke of "determinate outline, or identical form," he meant that outline alone can express the individuality of the form in question; that is, the form of the identity. Identical form is particular form and is opposed to all generalization. "To Generalize is to be an Idiot. To Particularize is the Alone Distinction of Merit." In his professions if not in his practice, Blake was usually opposed to that neoclassic notion, so highly favored

* Blake's respect for outline probably began through his imitations of Gothic monuments and through his adolescent study of engravings and prints of antique statuary. It was developed almost certainly by a little book called *Thoughts on Outline* which his friend, George Cumberland, published in 1796. Cumberland declared that "There can be no art without it" (p. 8), the sentiment that underlies Blake's attack on the Venetian painters. Blake must have enjoyed Cumberland's criticism of the Royal Academy, and especially of the annual lecture, as destructive to art, and he later made the same connection between a healthy art and an influential society that Cumberland made: ". . . my sole motive for writing, is the desire that continually haunts me, of helping to give stability to the fine arts in this my native country; which alone can insure our future consequence in Europe and which, I sometimes flatter myself, will be the means of again extending them over the whole world" (p. 13). Blake had no interest in the commercial expansion of Britain, but he sometimes attempted to blackmail the British public by assuring them that if they did not encourage his art their commerce was doomed. This is perhaps the only strain in Blake's thinking that is pathetic. "The Value of this Artist's Year is the Criterion of Society: and as it is valued, so does Society flourish or decay."—*Poetry and Prose*, p. 807.

by Sir Joshua Reynolds, of art as the imitation of a generalized nature, a corrected "nature, which the Artist calls the Ideal Beauty," since "All Forms are Perfect in the Poet's Mind, but these are not Abstracted nor compounded from Nature, but are from Imagination." Here Blake argues from transcendental motives, the very motives that led *him* to generalize, but his theory of "identical form" led him just as frequently to argue against generalization from motives almost as naturalistic as Whitman's, in his effort to express the exact character of particulars.

Sir Joshua's ideal nature eliminated deformity with other accidents, and Blake said that "Leanness or Fatness is not Deformity, but Reynolds thought Character Itself Extravagance & Deformity"; ". . . rectify every thing in Nature as the Philosophers do, & then we shall return to Chaos." This is a considerable inconsistency, and perhaps his most conspicuous theoretical failure to link his visionary experience and his human interests. He drew angels with clearly articulated bodies, but still abstract, and he wrote poems in praise of the integrated individuality, and the only link between them is that cryptic one that "Spirits are organized men."

His announced preference for spiritual forms did not prevent Blake from describing in theory and struggling in practice for what he called "Living Form." In his poems, this intention is most clearly expressed in his attempts at metrical variation as he tells of them at the beginning of *Jerusalem*. Here he announces his intention to make his metrics directly expressive of his content, and to vary them accordingly. Somewhat more tamely, Pope had suggested the propriety of such a stylistic ambition, and after him, Hugh Blair in his *Lectures on Rhetoric* and Lord Kames in his *Elements of Criticism*. Kames, in fact, attempted to work out an exact relationship between accent and syllable length and various sensations and passions.

Blake is not singular, then, in having innovated a theory of style, but in the excesses to which this theory led him and in the particular way that it is tied in with the entire complex of his ideas. Of organic form in the sense of his total poetic structures, Blake shows little awareness and no deliberate pursuit; yet anarchy and a vision of order result in anarchy within a metaphor of order. In his paintings, his imitation of Gothic art gave him the kind of freedom and scope that he associated with "Living Form," and his beloved "outline" saved him from chaos as words and figures of speech could not.

Gothic, with its irregularity, its linear and vaulting effects, is what Blake meant by "Living Form," and this he opposed to "Grecian," or "Mathematic Form." More clearly than any other English poet who joined the Gothic cult, he reveals that the motives of that vogue lay in a reaction against the mechanistic philosophy and the Industrial Revolution, and that its ambition was a return to the ideal of individual craftsmanship and to a way of life in which the spinning wheel and the hourglass had not been changed to "the arts of death." His attack on the classics was an oblique expression of this reaction, for it was really an attack on neoclassicism, with its constant apotheosis of the ancients as models and with its mechanical notion of style, which it thought it had derived from them.

Blake's attitude toward Greece and classic art is by no means wholly consistent. His own art owed as much to classic as to Gothic art, and sometimes he expressly subscribed to classic theories, as in his comments on Chaucer, who, he said, "makes every one of his characters perfect in his kind; every one is an Antique Statue; the image of a class, and not of an imperfect individual." * Late in his life he took up the study of Greek. His closest associates among British artists, Fuseli and Flaxman, were leaders in the Hellenistic vogue, and his respect for "the hard and wirey line of rectitude" and his indifference to oil colors found as much encouragement in this source as in Gothic. Greek statues, like his own characters, were "spiritual exist-

* Such remarks, with their apparent inconsistency, do not prove that Blake eludes the labels of conventional literary history, that he is the exception which proves the rule, but rather that the labels are utterly inadequate to the facts of literary history. Blake shows us how the nineteenth century grew out of the eighteenth as well as how it revolted against it. In Blake, neoclassic generalization develops into nineteenth-century idealization. An expert discussion of this proposition may be found in the chapter on Blake in Stephen A. Larrabee's *English Bards and Grecian Marbles,* Columbia University Press, 1943, pp. 99-119.

ences," and Greek mythology as he understood it gave him the prerogative for creating his mythology.

Yet for all this, his final decision was that the root of the evil lay in the ancient past, even though its aggravations were entirely in the present. In his remarks "On Homer's Poetry" he observes the connection between the classic conception of unity and morality. As unity is the product of rules for art, so morality—in the detested sense—is the product of social convention and laws for man. Tyranny in art, mechanical and mathematical, is not separate from tyranny in life, legal and social. That is what Blake meant when he said "The Classics! it is the Classics . . . that Desolate Europe with Wars." This, like almost every other judgment he passed, took its rise from his love of, his demand for, freedom.

In our own time, another anarchist in the arts, Herbert Read, has amplified Blake's judgment, and clarified it: "Classicism . . . represents for us now, and has always represented, the forces of oppression. Classicism is the intellectual counterpart of political tyranny. It was so in the ancient world and in the medieval empires; it was renewed to express the dictatorships of the Renaissance and has ever since been the official creed of capitalism. Wherever the blood of martyrs stains the ground, there you will find a doric column or perhaps a statue of Minerva."

III

IMAGINATION IS FREEDOM, and art is the child of freedom. Here again Blake was not introducing a tradition so much as pushing it to its extremity. The theory that liberty and art go hand in hand, that the second is impossible without the first, takes its real start in England with Milton, and it was developed by a wide range of writers throughout the eighteenth century. Even such reserved spirits as Pope gave it passing attention, and such more impulsive ones as Thomson and Shaftesbury colored it, and such theoreticians as Hugh Blair developed it.

There is an irony in Blake's taking up this tradition, since his predecessors had looked to Greek political institutions as the ideal of freedom, and to Greek art as the beautiful consequence, whereas the barbarous Gothic ages, which Blake swore were not "Dark," represented political and artistic regression. To overcome this difficulty he created another difficulty for himself by denying the notion of progress to the arts: "If Art was Progressive We should have had Mich. Anegelos & Raphaels to Succeed & to Improve upon each other. But it is not so." His love of Gothic, indeed, drove him into another inconsistency, for it impelled him to declare that "Ages are all Equal. But Genius is Always Above The Age." He did not believe either of these propositions with his whole heart, and in other places denied both.

It was instinctive to Blake's genius to oppose poetry and art to brutality and barbarism, and this instinct reveals itself in his earliest efforts:

Such is sweet Eloquence, that does dispel
Envy and Hate, that thirst for human gore;
And cause in sweet society to dwell
Vile savage minds that lurk in lonely cell.

The entire content of his poetry develops, from one point of view, out of this idea, becomes a vast and continual dramatization of Yeats's belief that artists must "love most of all life at peace with itself and doing without forethought what its humanity bids it and therefore happily." Art is the function that comprehends the unity of things, "life at peace with itself." Law is the function that separates. Los, the eternal artist, the imaginative principle, is the hero of Blake's Prophecies, and his efforts are always directed against disunity, against Urizen's legalistic tyrannies, and he *constructs* the condition that overcomes them and all their savage consequences. Imagination is regeneration, and art is social.

"Now Art has lost its mental Charms
France shall subdue the World in Arms."
So spoke an Angel at my birth,
Then said, "Descend thou upon Earth.

Renew the Arts on Britain's Shore,
And France shall fall down & adore.
With works of Art their Armies meet,
And War shall sink beneath thy feet.
But if thy Nation Arts refuse,
And if they scorn the immortal Muse,
France shall the arts of Peace restore,
And save thee from the Ungrateful shore."

Blake repeatedly said that a corrupt political society is inimical to great art. "Empire against Art" was his briefest expression of the idea. At greater length he said, "Rome & Greece swept Art into their maw & destroy'd it; a Warlike State never can produce Art. It will Rob & Plunder & accumulate into one place, & Translate & Copy & Buy & Sell & Criticise, but not Make." And once again, for the point is central: "The wretched State of the Arts in this Country & in Europe, originating in the wretched State of Political Science, which is the Science of Sciences, Demands a firm & determinate conduct on the part of Artists to Resist the Contemptible Counter Arts Establish'd by such contemptible Politicians as Louis XIV."

Blake's poems are full of representations of this idea. The opposition of the honest man and the hypocrite in *The Marriage,* of the prolific and the devourer, of devils and angels, of Jesus and Satan, of Los or Orc and Urizen, of identity and specter—these are all oppositions of the artist to the "contemptible Politician." The point is made expressly in *The French Revolution,* in the portrait of the imprisoned poet:

. . . and the den nam'd Horror held a man
Chain'd hand and foot, round his neck an iron band, bound
to the impregnable wall.
In his soul was the serpent coil'd round in his heart, hid from
the light, as in a cleft rock:
And the man was confin'd for a writing prophetic.

America contains Blake's picture of the false poet who supports a tyrannical order:

Hid in his caves the Bard of Albion felt the enormous plagues,
And a cowl of flesh grew o'er his head, & scales on his back & ribs;
And, rough with black scales, all his Angels fright their ancient heavens.

Long before fascism taught a hesitant world the toll that it must, by its very nature, take in the products of mind, Blake prophesied it for us: "It will Rob & Plunder & accumulate into one place," but it cannot *"Make."* It cannot make because it has no freedom, and having no freedom, it knows neither love nor the love of life at peace with itself.

Yet if a corrupt society destroys art, art will also resist a corrupt society. This is one of Blake's most impressive insights. "The Arts & Sciences are the Destruction of Tyrannies or Bad Governments." True poetry, who is Los, comes to the aid of revolution.

Then Los arose: his head he rear'd in snaky thunders clad;
And with a cry that shook all nature to the utmost pole,
Call'd all his sons to the strife of blood.

That Orc was, indeed, the son of Los in Blake's enormous myth was not a genealogical accident. Blake believed that true poets are rare, and that as poets they are compelled to ally themselves with the cause that can establish a wise life, the condition of good poetry. That there have been great men in the history of poetry who refused to make this alliance is reason for lamentation. This is one of those defects in life which Blake would not admit into his artist's view of it. His own opposition, his partisanship, he felt keenly: "There cannot be more than two or three great Painters or Poets in any Age or Country; and these, in a corrupt state of Society, are easily excluded, but not so easily obstructed." His partisanship obscured him then, but we know now that it also saved him from historical obstruction.

The development of these ideas must be referred back again to Blake's anarchism. When he protested against the mediocrity of art and letters in the commercialized world of eighteenth-century England, he was really protesting against the loss or the obstruction of that imaginative view of life which was his own, which knew and continually insisted that "Every Man's Wisdom is peculiar to his own Individuality." The "Fiends of Commerce" are gods of bourgeois standardization, "for Commerce Cannot endure Individual Merit; its insatiable Maw must be fed by What all can do Equally well . . . Commerce is so far from being beneficial to Arts, or to Empires, that it is destructive of both, as all their History shews, for the above Reason of Individual Merit being its Great hatred." Godwin's anarchism was less complete. Both hoped for a world in which men would be entirely without money, Blake arguing that "Where any view of Money exists, Art cannot be carried on, but War only." Yet Godwin saw no necessary injustice and no inevitable standardization in an extensive commerce or even in machinery. To Blake, both were death to art, to that sacred integrity of the individual energy, the individual talent. To recognize the individuality is an act of identification that is the essence of imagination. To recognize it is likewise to establish the bond of brotherhood. When brotherhood is the first principle of social life, of governments and institutions, when life has blossomed into wisdom, the productions of the poetic or prophetic character will flourish universally. Then art in the narrow sense will be the product of art in the largest sense, of a whole life, harmonious and complete, so wisely conducted that art and life will begin to merge. Blake's only madness lay in the lingering of an inexhaustible hope.

Political impulses had thrust themselves into religious forms, and excesses were inevitable. Yet it is also true that Blake's most felicitous achievements sprang from this combination, and that the energy of his statements, that persistent vigor which is at the very center of his genius and for which one admires him most, also sprang from it. The combination reminds us how mistaken were the motives of those first men to rediscover him—the Rossettis and Swinburne, James Thomson, Wilde, Pater, and even, in part, Yeats—all of whom thought that they had found in his concept of the holiness of art the historical counterpart of their own aestheticism. Blake did not attempt a "pure" art. The holiness of art proceeds from the holiness of life. Life is the large art. Poetry and painting, music and architecture, are the specific products of time that express in special forms the best in that larger art. Imagination is not divorced from life, it is the best life. It does not isolate itself from life or isolate beautiful moments from the whole of it, but seizes upon the essence of life and expresses it in its totality.

Blake made a religion of art, but he also believed that religion was art: "The Mocker of Art is the Mocker of Jesus." The identification is important in any understanding of Blake's success and failure. Kierkegaard suggested that only religion can reconcile the two modes by which we tend to experience life, the aesthetic and the ethical, and this is what it did for Blake. We must remember the nature of Blake's religion, its extreme privacy, its heretical excesses, and expect from that to find that his ethical preoccupations would hardly be traditional. But the ethical element is there, sometimes predominantly, and it is inextricable from the aesthetic, although that too sometimes predominates. Blake varied, according to his emphasis on one or the other, between the Tolstoyan view that art is "simple, religious, and social" ("the realization of the brotherly union of mankind") and the view of a poet like Mallarmé, attacked by Tolstoy, that "there should only be allusion . . . the perfect practice of this mystery is the symbol. . . . There must always be enigma in poetry, and this is the aim of literature; there is no other, to evoke objects."

When his characters make their abstract speeches, when they preach of brotherhood and of the loss of selfhood, when they lament their sufferings in the express terms of social ailments, Blake writes in one way, and too baldly. When he flees into his system and attempts to convey the most elusive visionary experience, he writes in the other way, and too darkly. Both ways express his anarchistic faith, the first in its object, the second in its operation. The two ways come together when he is at his very best, as in the great lyrics and in fragments of the Prophecies. These are at once "simple, religious, and social" and as evocative as almost any poems in the language. In these moments of supreme achievement, when the several impulses of his talent are perfectly congruent, his poetry is neither bald nor dark. For the ambitious ethical purposes of his Prophecies, Blake's religion, his vision of spiritual regeneration, was too private to sustain the structure, but in his lyrics and in fragments of the Prophetic Books, where the ethical purposes were less expressed and less extensive and yet quite as sharp, he achieved an integration of his creative impulses that resulted in incomparable poetic triumphs.*

IV

WHY DID LANDOR, who prized formal achievement above all else, declare that Blake was "the greatest of poets"? Did he, whose art was so narrow although so lovely, read in Blake's work the lesson that there are qualities of vitality and grandeur that a too strict attention to formal effects may sometimes exclude, and that these too have their beauty and their bravery? Did Landor, viewing his own classic and nostalgic poems, wish that they had in them some infusion of the wild genius of Blake, whose heart was "full of futurity"?

If we put aside the question of a sustained formal achievement and view Blake, at almost any point in his work, as a historical phenomenon, the achievement is extraordinary. After a century in which sentiment and pathos had tried to substitute for passion in poetry, Blake returned passion to it, with the consequent elevation of style. He took the wan humanitarianism, sentimental and self-indulgent, of his time and forced it into a startling humanism, imaginative and profoundly social. He seized upon the abstract and bloodless conceptions of political radicalism and thrust them into their necessary habitat, the heart and the brain, the human fact. To a century that had been beguiled by a science which was later to prove both too mechanical and too rationalistic for the facts, Blake made the demand

* This evaluation was first suggested to me by Philip Horton, six or seven years ago, in a brilliant but still unpublished lecture on Hart Crane, which explained in similar terms the success of the lyrics in *White Buildings* and the structural failure of *The Bridge*.

that the organic and the irrational be recognized as anterior. Before Coleridge, but after a century of abstract and discursive poetry, he took up as his "darling studies" those "facts of mind" which Coleridge professed to love above all else, and he made of his poetry a vast and perhaps necessarily baffling mythology to express them. For this purpose, he felt it essential that he should not "be enslav'd by another Man's" system, and he created his own. His instinct was right. Other men's systems are suspect to the poet. Marx's friend, the poet Freiligrath, when he broke away from his party even though he was still in total political sympathy with it, declared: "My nature, like the nature of any poet, needs freedom. The party is a cage."

Blake's "system" was not manufactured out of air. He took over a cold and prosaic complex of *ideas* and turned it into characters for poetry, and then inferred a set of poetic principles, and these he called his system. A firm persuasion made the items of this theory *so*. They took on body, and in the heat of Blake's intuitions, they gathered meaning. And whatever deplorable results the system may have had in Blake's forms, it is still unexhausted as an imaginative complex, and will remain so. It is a system, to be sure, but it is not so closed that it prohibits further insights. It was a means, a poetic method, of relating concepts of universality and of individuality in such a way as to remind the world that the two are inextricable. Today, when the conflict of these two concepts has reached an almost total impasse, Blake's speculations are more relevant than ever.

William Blake provides the inspiring spectacle of a man who absolutely triumphed over his world; but as a poet, in the length and breadth of his career, the world was too much for him, his poetic genius could not beat it into forms that would not burst their seams. On the personal level he was that "Mental Prince" he called himself, one of his own Prolific, a hero of history. His work continues to challenge our attention largely for this reason, that as the monument to one of the great casualties in the history of poetry, perhaps the greatest, its hieroglyphs unlock the contradiction of his success and failure. In the end, the problem is very simple. He demanded too much of art because he hoped for so much from life.

Notes

The numerals at the left refer to page and line in this book. The phrase which follows is the beginning of a quotation or reference which appears or starts on the line indicated at the left, and comes from or refers to the work named at the right of the phrase. In the references, roman numerals refer to volume, and arabic numerals to pages.

CHAPTER ONE

3,22 "Attempting to be more . . ." *Poetry and Prose of William Blake,* ed. by G. Keynes, Random House, 3d ed., 1932, 454. Hereafter referred to as *PP.*

4,21 ". . . cannot the spirit . . ." *Letters,* ed. by R. L. Rusk, 6 vols., Columbia University Press, 1939, II:331

4,26 "I am convinced . . ." Newman Ivey White, *Shelley,* 2 vols., Knopf, 1940, I:309

4,27 "I hate scarce smiles . . ." *PP,* 904

4,31 "A man may lie . . ." *PP,* 904

4,37 "Did you ever see . . ." Allan Cunningham, *Life of Blake,* London, 1830, reprinted in Arthur Symons, *William Blake,* Dutton, 1907, 409

5,6 Now I a fourfold vision see . . . *PP,* 1068

5,20 . . . "with the eye." *PP,* 139 ("When you see with, not thro', the Eye")

5,25 For double the vision . . . *PP,* 1067

5,34 . . . "an Innumerable company . . ." *PP,* 844

6,3 My Eyes more and more . . . *PP,* 1051-52

6,16 . . . "Nature and Fancy . . ." *PP,* 1075

6,17 . . . "Natural Objects . . ." *PP,* 1024

6,19 ". . . I know that This World . . ." *PP,* 1039-40

7,2 . . . "clapping its hands." Alexander Gilchrist, *Life of William Blake,* ed. by Ruthven Todd, Dutton (Everyman's Library) 1942, 107. This is the most satisfactory version, a corrected text of the second edition, which appeared in 1880.

7,3 . . . "scaly, speckled, very awful" . . . *Ibid.,* 51

7,19 . . . "literalist of the imagination" . . . Marianne Moore, "Poetry," *Selected Poems,* Macmillan, 1935, 37; from Yeats's "a too literal realist of imagination, as some men are of nature," in "William Blake and His Illustrations to *The Divine Comedy,*" *Ideas of Good and Evil,* London, 1903, 182

8,2 "The connoisseurs and artists . . ." *PP,* 794-95

Notes

8,20 ("The Prophets Isaiah and Ezekiel . . ." *PP,* 195

8,22 "I am really drunk . . ." *PP,* 1110

8,30 ". . . & every Word . . ." *PP,* 749-50

9,1 "O Wordsworth! . . ." I prefer, for present purposes, the earliest version of this poem, as printed in a letter to Sotheby, July 19, 1802, *Letters,* ed. by E. H. Coleridge, 2 vols., Houghton Mifflin, 1895, I:382

9,25 "The mind is not a *tabula rasa* . . ." Milton O. Percival, *William Blake's Circle of Destiny,* Columbia University Press, 1938, 80

9,33 "1. The mind of the poet . . ." *Coleridge on Imagination,* Harcourt, Brace, 1935, 145

10,16 "The colours of Nature . . ." *Ibid.,* 152

10,19 "The subject is what it is . . ." *Ibid.,* 57

11,8 . . . "felt thought" . . . T. S. Eliot, "The Metaphysical Poets," *Selected Essays: 1917-1932,* Faber, London, 1932, 272

11,11 . . . "thinking visually . . ." Quoted by H. S. Bellamy, *The Book of Revelation in History,* Faber, London, 1942, 20-21

11,23 "Prayers plow not! . . ." *PP* 194

12,19 "And tho' I call them Mine . . ." *PP,* 1038

12,27 "I have written this Poem . . ." *PP,* 1073-74

12,33 "I may praise it . . ." *PP,* 1076

13,6 "Art has not wrote here . . ." Jakob Boehme, "Life," *Works,* tr. by William Law, 4 vols., M. Richardson, London, 1764-81, I:xiv-xv. All but one (63,11) of the references to Boehme are to the so-called Law translation in this edition, which Blake used.

13,17 "Intuition of truth . . ." *PP,* 907

13,18 "He knows himself . . ." *PP,* 927

13,22 ". . . if we fear . . ." *PP,* 1061

13,32 "My Beloved Reader . . ." "Threefold Life," *op. cit.,* II, 3:99

13,34 "Loving Reader . . ." "Three Principles," *Ibid.,* I, 7:1

14,1 "The Beauty of the Bible . . ." *PP,* 1028

14,3 "What is Grand . . ." *PP,* 1039

14,16 "I could not do otherwise . . ." *PP,* 1037

14,20 ". . . every genius, every hero . . ." *PP,* 918

14,22 ". . . prophecy never rendered the prophet . . ." "Tractatus-Theologico-Politicus," *Chief Works,* tr. by R. H. M. Elwes, 2 vols. G. Bell & Sons, London, 1883-84, I:27

14,24 "God, when he makes the prophet . . ." *Essay Concerning Human Understanding,* IV, xix, 14

15,9 "Every honest man is a Prophet . . ." *PP,* 961

15,17 . . . "to which later times . . ." "Age of Reason," *Writings,* ed. by M. D. Conway, 4 vols., Putnam, 1894-99, IV:36

15,20 . . . "dared so roundly to assert . . ." *PP,* 195-96

16,3 "You have said . . ." *A Vision,* Macmillan, 1938, 17

16,4 "Blake, be an artist . . ." Henry Crabb Robinson, *On Books and Their Writers,* ed. by E. Morley, 3 vols., Dent, London, 1938, I:330

16,15 The Vision of Christ . . . *PP,* 133

16,19 ". . . it was very enraging . . ." *Magnalia Christi Americana,* 2 vols., S. Andrus and Sons, Hartford, 1853, II:526

Notes

16,26 Thank God, I never was sent to school . . . *PP,* 854

17,11 . . . "Liberty Boy." Gilchrist, *op. cit.,* 80

17,26 "I attempted every morning . . ." *PP,* 1037-38

18,1 "I feel very sorry . . ." *PP,* 1038

18,10 ". . . send me your . . . opinion . . ." An unpublished letter now in the Houghton Library, dated April 30, 1803

19,16 . . . "I send you . . . a neat copy . . ." Another unpublished letter in the Houghton Library, about projected designs for Cowper's tomb, dated February 12, 1802

19,25 I Write the Rascal Thanks . . . *PP,* 853

19,28 Thy Friendship oft . . . *PP,* 850

19,30 . . . "I regard Fashion in Poetry . . ." *PP,* 1076

20,8 . . . "tho' [I] laugh at Fortune . . ." *PP,* 1042

20,15 "The hole of a Shit-house . . ." *PP,* 898

20,25 For meditations upon unknown thought . . . W. B. Yeats, "All Souls' Night," *Collected Poems,* Macmillan, 1933, 265

20,33 "This is to be understood . . ." *PP,* 939

21,3 ". . . the power of prophecy implies . . ." *Op. cit.,* I:19, 25

21,20 "All deities reside . . ." *PP,* 195

21,24 "Visions of these eternal principles . . ." *PP,* 788

22,7 "As the interest of man . . ." *PP,* 902

22,26 "The cistern contains . . ." *PP,* 193

22,27 . . . "Exuberance is Beauty" . . . *PP,* 194

22,28 "People who are always winning victories . . ." *Science and Poetry,* Norton, 1926, 43-44

23,20 F. O. Matthiessen . . . *American Renaissance,* Oxford University Press, 1941, 311

23,26 "Without Contraries . . ." *PP,* 191

23,31 . . . "a sixty-year-old smiling . . ." "Among School Children," *Collected Poems,* 249

23,37 . . . "all things must needs . . ." *Hermetica,* ed. and tr. by W. Scott, 4 vols., Oxford University Press, 1924, I:193-94

24,1 . . . "the friendship of contraries." *Ibid.,* I:213

24,24 . . . "the two contrary states of the human soul" . . . *PP,* 51

24,30 "I'll . . . shew you . . ." *PP,* 551

24,32 Of the Sleep of Ulro! . . . *PP,* 551

24,34 ". . . he did not believe . . ." *Op. cit.,* I:330

25,1 . . . "Man has no Body . . ." *PP,* 191

25,3 . . . "The Natural Body . . ." *PP,* 1023

25,5 . . . "Form must be apprehended . . ." *PP,* 1023

25,24 Tocqueville described . . . *L'Ancien régime et la révolution,* Bk. I, Ch. 3. See also Crane Brinton, *A Decade of Revolution: 1789-1799,* Harper, 1934, 158-63; Carl Becker, *Heavenly City of the Eighteenth-Century Philosophers,* Yale University Press, 1932, Ch. IV, especially 154-61; and Basil Wiley, *Eighteenth Century Background,* Chatto and Windus, London, 1940, Chs. X-XI

25,31 . . . "Christianity is not a negation . . ." By Robert Hall. Quoted by Anthony Lincoln, *Some Political and Social Ideas of English Dissent: 1763-1800,* Cambridge University Press, 1938, 20

26,3 . . . "the teleological suspension of ethics" . . . *Fear and Trembling*, tr. by R. Payne, Oxford University Press, 1939, 75

26,4 . . . "moral form of evil." "The Good and the Conscience," *Philosophy of Right*, Nos. 129-41

26,16 I made my song a coat . . . "A Coat," *Collected Poems*, 145

CHAPTER TWO

27,13 "The doctrines which men . . ." *History of English Thought in the Eighteenth Century*, 2 vols., Putnam, 1927, II:329

28,12 . . . "the very essence of myth . . ." "Poetry, Myth, and Reality," *The Language of Poetry*, ed. by A. Tate, Princeton University Press, 1942, 10

28,14 Durkheim pointed out . . . *The Elementary Forms of the Religious Life*, tr. by J. W. Swain, Macmillan, 1926, 36-42

28,22 . . . "the question of the human conscience . . ." "The War and the Future," *Order of the Day*, Knopf, 1942, 240

29,9 . . . "Speech is a storehouse of images . . ." *Modern Man in Search of a Soul*, Harcourt, Brace, 1934, 102

29,15 . . . "there is no such passion . . ." *Treatise of Human Nature*, Bk. III, Pt. ii, Sec. 1

29,22 ". . . we live in an intricacy . . ." "The Noble Rider and the Sound of Words," *The Language of Poetry*, 106

29,36 . . . "indispensable ingredient of all culture." *Myth in Primitive Psychology*, Norton, 1926, 92

30,11 "They know a body . . ." "The Bridge," *Collected Poems*, Liveright, 1933, 14

31,11 (The historical irony . . . See Cleanth Brooks, *Modern Poetry and the Tradition*, University of North Carolina Press, 1939, especially 39-53

32,6 . . . ("I love beauty . . ." Sonnet No. 60, "The Growth of Love," *Poetical Works*, Oxford University Press, 1936, 218

32,20 . . . "the expression not of one mind . . ." George Boas, *Philosophy and Poetry*, Wheaton College Press, 1932, 33

33,11 A recent series of lectures . . . *The Idiom of Poetry*, Cornell University Press, 1942, *passim*

33,35 The intelligible forms of ancient poets . . . *The Piccolomini, or, the First Part of Wallenstein*, II: iv, 123-31

34,8 Lo the Bat with Leathern wing . . . *PP*, 878

34,21 . . . "exploded." *Biographia Literaria*, ed. by A. Symons, Dutton (Everyman's Library), 1939, 203

34,22 Douglas Bush points out . . . *Mythology and the Romantic Tradition in English Poetry*, Harvard University Press, 1937, 35

35,1 . . . "Fair Nine." *PP*, 14

35,11 "Bloated Gods . . ." *PP*, 818-19

35,17 . . . "delicate conceits" . . . Kierkegaard, *op. cit.*, 4

35,21 ("The ancient Poets . . ." *PP*, 195

35,36 . . . "the mechanical system of philosophy" . . . *Op. cit.*, 203n

37,8 " 'Tis too true . . ." "Preface," *A Miscellany of Poems by Several Hands*, ed. by John Husbands, Oxford, 1731

37,25 . . . "esemplastic" . . . *Op. cit.*, Ch. XIII

37,33 "The gradual ebbing of an ancient faith . . ." *Op. cit.*, I:16

Notes

39,6 . . . "at top." Edward Young, *Conjectures on Original Composition,* ed. by E. Morley, Longmans, Green, 1918, 29

39,7 "Then tell me . . ." *PP,* 232

39,20 "*Vous criez 'Tout est bien'* . . ." Voltaire, *"Poème sur le désastre de Lisbonne," Œuvres Complètes,* 52 vols., Garnier, Paris, 1877-85, IX:474

39,31 . . . "To God": *PP,* 857

40,3 A Robin Red breast in a Cage . . . *PP,* 118

40,12 To be, or not to be . . . *PP,* 881

40,15 "Where man is not . . ." *PP,* 195

41,21 ("*Bacon* has broke that Scarcrow Deitie") . . . "To the Royal Society," Blake, *Poems,* ed. by A. R. Waller, Cambridge University Press, 1905, 449

44,1 "Genius has no Error." *PP,* 996

44,25 "In my picture of the world . . ." *Op. cit.,* 137

45,1 Tho' born on the cheating banks of the Thames . . . *PP,* 90

45,17 "There are always these two classes . . ." *PP,* 789

45,20 . . . "twin labourers"; "Prelude," V, ll. 42-44, *Poetical Works,* ed. by T. Hutchinson, Oxford University Press, 1929, 666

45,22 . . . "eternal principles . . ." *PP,* 788

45,29 "Let the Philosopher . . ." *PP,* 789

46,3 And 'tis most wicked . . . *PP,* 855

46,25 Yet, O my young man . . . "Spiral Flame," *Pansies,* Secker, London, 1929, 30

46,32 . . . "darkness of unknowing" . . . Dionysius the Areopagite, *On the Divine Names and the Mystical Theology,* tr. by C. E. Rolt, Macmillan, 1920, 194

47,2 Professor Helen White has demonstrated . . . *The Mysticism of William Blake,* University of Wisconsin Press, 1927

48,20 Professor Tillyard has said . . . *Poetry Direct and Oblique,* Cambridge University Press, 1934, 257

48,34 . . . admitting with Wordsworth . . . Robinson, *op. cit.,* I:85

49,4 "Cowper came to me and said . . ." *PP,* 1020

CHAPTER THREE

51,12 . . . "mystihood." Walter Hilton's word, used by P. E. More, "Christian Mysticism," *The Catholic Faith,* Princeton University Press, 1931, *passim*

51,12 "The art of mysticism . . ." *Interpretations of Poetry and Religion,* Scribner, 1900, 16

51,22 . . . "obstinate questionings . . ." Wordsworth, "Ode: Intimations of Immortality," ll. 145-46, *Poetical Works,* 589

51,23 . . . "deeply interfused" . . . "Lines Composed a Few Miles above Tintern Abbey," l. 96, *ibid.,* 207

52,1 . . . "disease" . . . *Op. cit.,* 297

52,16 . . . "Sr. Francis Bacon is a Liar." *PP,* 1132

52,18 . . . "the mischief began . . ." "Introduction," *Oxford Book of Modern Verse,* Oxford University Press, 1936, xxvii

52,30 . . . "between the materialistic mechanism of science . . ." *Science and the Modern World,* Macmillan, 1925, 116

53,10 . . . "an ungovernable yearning" . . . *Autobiography,* Macmillan, 1938, 227

53,11 "The Thing I have most at Heart . . ." *PP,* 1061

55,17 . . . "the imaginative use of fictions . . ." *Principles of Literary Criticism,* Harcourt, Brace, 1924, 266-67

56,28 . . . "helpless victims" . . . Charles A. Bennett, *A Philosophical Study of Mysticism,* Yale University Press, 1928, 8

57,6 "'No,' was the answer . . ." *A Vision,* 8

57,8 . . . "all metaphor" . . . "High Talk," *Last Poems and Plays,* Macmillan, 1940, 73

57,9 "I regard them . . ." *A Vision,* 25

57,28 I would be . . . "The Dawn," *Collected Poems,* 166

57,35 . . . "the whole creation . . ." *PP,* 197

58,12 Hands, do what you're bid . . . "The Balloon of the Mind," *op. cit.,* 177

58,17 ". . . in vain! the faster I bind . . ." *PP,* 1057

58,26 "I must Create a System . . ." *PP,* 564

59,7 ". . . they know very well . . ." *Theologia Germanica,* tr. by S. Winkworth, W. F. Draper, Boston, 1865, 127

59,12 . . . "singularity is a vice . . ." *Inner Life and Writings of Dame Gertrude More,* rev. and ed. by Dom Benedict Weld-Blundell, 2 vols., Benziger, 1910, II:27

59,14 With a few obvious and great exceptions . . . See White, *The Mysticism of . . . Blake,* 44-46

59,21 . . . "methodical elevation" . . . *Varieties of Religious Experience,* Longmans, Green, 1902, 406

60,11 "Is it not enough . . ." Porphyry's "On the Life of Plotinus," *Enneads,* tr. by S. Mackenna, 5 vols., Medici Society, Library of Philosophical Translations, 1917-39, I:1

60,17 . . . "passing of solitary to solitary." *Ibid.,* V:253

61,23 . . . "*magical, mystical, chemic* Philosophers" . . . "An Address to the Earnest Lovers of Wisdom," *Works,* I:viii

61,24 . . . "he has discovered . . ." *Ibid.,* I:vii

62,1 ". . . thou rulest over all Creatures . . ." "Dialogue between a Scholar and His Master," *ibid.,* IV, No. 75

62,7 . . . "the human will . . ." "Sermon for Whit-Sunday," *The History and Life of the Reverend Doctor John Tauler, with Twenty-five of His Sermons,* tr. by S. Winkworth, Smith, Elder, 1910, 329

62,12 "My writing . . ." "Three Principles," *op. cit.,* I, 3:3

62,14 ". . . there must be a contrary will . . ." "Threefold Life," *ibid.,* II, 1:33

62,32 Be shelled, eyes, with double dark . . . Gerard Manley Hopkins, *Poems,* ed. by R. Bridges, Oxford University Press, 1930, 8

62,35 . . . "if God reveals himself to man" . . . "Threefold Life," *op. cit.,* II, 10:10

63,11 . . . "there is nothing that is supernatural . . ." "The Spirit of Love," *Selected Mystical Writings,* ed. by S. Hobhouse, C. W. Daniel Co., Ltd., London, 1938, 173

63,28 "Be frank about our heathen foe" . . . "The Sea and the Mirror," *For the Time Being,* Random House, 1944, 10

64,3 "All deities reside in the human breast" . . . *PP,* 195

64,5 "The desire of Man being infinite . . ." *PP,* 148

64,15 He has observ'd the Golden Rule . . . *PP,* 848

64,18 "The worship of God . . ." *PP,* 202

64,24 "their Heavenly Father drew

them up . . ." "Threefold Life," *op. cit.,* 334

64,27 "Even though we have known Christ . . ." II Cor. 5:16

64,32 To man, that needs not worship . . . *Op. cit.,* 60

65,24 "a regress of visions . . ." Richards, *Coleridge on Imagination,* xiv

66,12 "Thy Saviour sentenc'd joy" . . . "The Size," *Works,* ed. by F. E. Hutchinson, Oxford University Press, 1941, 138

66,17 . . . "a Man may be happy . . ." *PP,* 1039

66,18 . . . "say that Happiness . . ." *PP,* 1085

66,21 "In the hands of theologians . . ." *Adventures of Ideas,* 40-41

67,14 . . . "the coil of sense" . . . "Paradiso," XXXI, *Divine Comedy,* tr. by M. B. Anderson, World Book Company, 1922, 438

67,16 . . . "hushing" . . . *Confessions,* IX, 25

67,16 . . . "the silencing of the faculties" . . . Dom Cuthbert Butler, *Western Mysticism,* Dutton, 1922, 44

67,21 . . . "soul . . . naughted of all things" . . . Juliana of Norwich, *Revelations of Divine Love,* ed. by Dom R. Huddleston, Burns, Oates, and Washbourne, London, 1927, 13

67,31 Was Jesus Humble? . . . *PP,* 136

67,33 "Pride may Love" . . . *PP,* 906

67,35 (". . . by humbling thyself . . ." *The Dialogue of the Seraphic Virgin Catherine of Siena,* tr. by A. Thorold, Newman Bookshop, Westminster, 1843, 32

68,1 If thou humblest thyself . . . *PP,* 136

68,6 "True humility . . ." *PP,* 926

68,14 But that which most I Wonder at . . . *Poetical Works,* ed. by G. I. Wade, P. J. and A. E. Dobell, London, 1932, 9

68,22 "Who are the saints . . ." *PP,* 915

68,31 . . . "ethical strenuousness" . . . White, *op. cit.,* 57

68,31 . . . "self-scrutiny" . . . Bennett, *op. cit.,* 10

68,33 . . . "all that is ignoble . . ." *Ibid.,* 191

68,35 . . . "infinite love and infinite grief" . . . Catherine of Siena, *op. cit.,* 30

69,3 "Wretched man that *I* am . . ." Rom. 7:24

69,9 . . . "a great hindrance unto me . . ." *The Book of the Divine Consolation of the Blessed Angelo of Foligno,* tr. by M. G. Steegman, Chatto and Windus, London, 1909, 5

69,15 "Bad men . . . rule . . ." *Hermetica,* II:22

69,20 ". . . from the moment your citizenship . . ." *Ibid.,* II:227

70,14 "Solomon says . . ." *PP,* 896

70,20 . . . in the sense of T. E. Hulme . . . *Speculations,* Harcourt, Brace, 1924, 46-72

71,13 Abstinence sows sand all over . . . *PP,* 99

71,18 The harvest shall flourish . . . *PP,* 98

71,25 "Chastity & Abstinence" . . . *PP,* 765

71,28 ". . . Enjoyment & not Abstinence . . ." *PP,* 1036

71,29 "The road of excess leads . . ." *PP,* 192

71,32 Was Jesus Chaste? . . . *PP,* 139

72,1 "The moment of desire! . . ." *PP,* 213

72,10 The Pilgrim with his crook & hat . . . *PP,* 877

72,17 ". . . in the school of the Spirit . . ." Tauler, *op. cit.,* 335

72,36 "We picture to ourselves . . ."

Op. cit., tr. by D. Lewis, Longmans, Green, 1928, 113-14

73,7 . . . "the darkness of unknowing." Dionysius, *On the Divine Names,* 194

73,29 "Man can have no idea . . ." *PP,* 934

74,10 "Self is death . . ." I quote this passage because Mr. Damon uses it twice to demonstrate similarities in *William Blake: His Philosophy and Symbols,* Houghton Mifflin, 1924, 74, 429.

75,2 "For in what measure . . ." *Op. cit.,* 3

75,4 ". . . he shall with great zeal . . ." *Adornment of the Spiritual Marriage,* tr. by Dom C. A. Wynschenk, Dent, London, 1916, 43

75,15 "If any man cometh unto me . . ." Luke 14:26

75,28 . . . never does my sister Rachel rise . . . "Purgatorio," XXVII, *Divine Comedy,* 266-67

76,6 Thou art a Man . . . *PP,* 136

76,32 "Here there begins an eternal hunger . . ." *Op. cit.,* 121

77,15 "The imaginative writer . . ." *Essays,* Macmillan, 1924, 354

77,28 Mr. Richards . . . contrasts . . . *Principles of Literary Criticism,* 249

77,30 F. O. Matthiessen . . . *American Renaissance,* 466

78,16 Much madness is divinest sense . . . *Complete Poems,* ed. by M. D. Bianchi, Little Brown, 1926, 9

78,19 "It is very true . . ." *PP,* 811

78,30 "Unto this Darkness . . ." Dionysius, *op. cit.,* 194

79,8 "Tuesday, Janry. 20 . . ." *PP,* 890

79,9 "23 May, 1810 . . ." *PP,* 893

79,16 "Suddenly . . . I was . . . enlightened . . ." *PP,* 1110

79,22 "I have indeed fought . . ." *PP,* 1111

80,25 *Feu. Dieu . . .* Quoted by practically all of his biographers. See Humfrey R. Jordan, *Blaise Pascal,* London, 1909, 189

81,7 . . . "World of Loneness" . . . *PP,* 264

81,7 . . . "the terrible desart of London" . . . *PP,* 1047

81,8 . . . "City of Assassinations." *PP,* 1104

81,14 . . . "a mighty & awful change . . ." *PP,* 1046

82,4 . . . "the crooked roads . . ." *PP,* 195

82,9 . . . "path of the serpent" . . . *Op. cit.,* 504

82,17 "Damn braces . . ." *PP,* 194

82,19 "There is an old sayng . . ." Yeats, *Discoveries,* Dum Emer Press, Dundrum, 1907, 32

82,37 . . . "increasing pessimism" . . . Damon, *op. cit.,* 6

84,5 . . . "intellectual War" . . . *PP,* 460

84,6 . . . "War & Hunting" . . . *PP,* 533

84,13 . . . "ravished above itself" . . . "A Very Devout Treatise, Named Benjamin," *The Cell of Self-Knowledge* . . . ed. by E. G. Gardner, Duffield, 1910, 33

84,14 . . . "holy oblivion" . . . *Op. cit.,* 248

84,15 . . . "seems to be God . . ." *Ibid.,* 80

84,17 . . . "swims in the Godhead . . ." Quoted by William R. Inge, *Christian Mysticism,* Methuen, London, 1899, 365

84,37 "Sin and destruction . . ." *PP,* 902

85,9 . . . Urizen laid in a stony sleep . . . *PP,* 247

85,18 "Unorganiz'd Innocence: . . ." *PP,* 460

86,25 I write in South Molton Street . . . *PP,* 621

86,30 I call them by their English names . . . *PP,* 625

86,33 "In language . . ." *Philoso-*

phy in a New Key, Harvard University Press, 1942, 103

87,3 Language is a perpetual Orphic song . . . *Prometheus Unbound,* IV, iiii, ll. 415-17

87,16 . . . "was caught up into paradise . . ." II Cor. 12:4

87,18 . . . "to many he spoke . . ." *Letters of William Blake,* ed. by A. G. B. Russell, Methuen, London, 1906, 229

87,28 . . . "spiritual bread" . . . The particular distinction between "spiritual" and "corporeal" food is made not by Blake but by the author of that "New Translation of the Lord's Prayer" which Blake so savagely attacked and parodied (*PP,* 1028-31). But Blake made the same distinction in other terms. See the stanzas beginning "Since all the riches of this world," p. 126; those beginning "I rose up at the dawn of day," p. 128; "We eat little, we drink less," and the following lines, p. 1068; and the final sentence of the *Descriptive Catalogue,* p. 806.

87,31 . . . "the Persons & Machinery" . . . *PP,* 1073

87,36 . . . "mirror" engraving . . . For example, *PP,* 627

88,21 "As the Eye . . ." *PP,* 984

88,21 . . . "they became what they beheld" . . . *PP,* 617

88,30 "What is now proved . . ." *PP,* 193

88,30 "Reason, or the ratio . . ." *PP,* 148

88,33 "A self-satisfied rationalism . . ." *Science and the Modern World,* 288-89

89,5 "I always thought . . ." *PP,* 1004

89,22 . . . "interior naturalist" . . . "Preface," *Songs of Innocence and Experience,* ed. by J. J. G. Wilkinson, London, 1839, vii: ". . . his immersion in that interior naturalism, which he was now beginning to mistake for spiritualism, listening, as he did, to the voices of the ground."

89,32 "Be assured, My dear Friend . . ." *PP,* 1063-64. Italics mine.

89,37 "I was a slave . . ." *PP,* 1110

90,8 . . . "Man has no Body . . ." *PP,* 191

90,11 . . . "were cleansed . . ." *PP,* 197

90,26 ". . . men may . . ." *The Amazing Marriage,* Scribner, 1895, 592

90,32 "Essential oils . . ." *Op. cit.,* 215

91,1 "I feel certain that man . . ." *Letters from the Underworld,* tr. by C. J. Hogarth, Dutton (Everyman's Library), 1913, 41

91,17 "The lie . . ." *Journals,* ed. by E. W. Emerson and W. E. Forbes, 10 vols., Houghton Mifflin, 1909-14, V:221

91,36 ". . . henceforth every man . . ." *PP,* 957

92,21 ". . . it is a part . . ." *PP,* 1059

92,33 "Without Contraries . . ." *PP,* 191

CHAPTER FOUR

93,11 . . . "the link between appearance and reality" . . . *Mysticism: A Study in the Nature and Development of Man's Spiritual Consciousness.* 12th ed. rev., Methuen, London, 1930, 75

93,15 . . . *"mystique manqué." Prière et poésie,* Bernard Grasset, Paris, 1926, 208

94,33 . . . "wings were not for such a flight" . . . "Paradiso," XXXIII, *Divine Comedy,* 448

95,5 Upon my flowery heart . . . "Obscure Night of the Soul," tr. by A. Symons, *Poems,* 2 vols., Heinemann, London, 1902, I:189

95,20 Poetry has been defined . . . See Cleanth Brooks, "The Language of Paradox," *The Language of Poetry,* 37-61

95,27 "Leave nothing of my Self in me." "The Flaming Heart," *Poems,* ed. by L. C. Martin, Oxford University Press, 1927, 327

96,12 . . . ("weariness") . . . *Works,* 160

97,4 (*"Du, nachbahr Gott . . ." "Das Stunden-Buch," Gedichte,* Insel-verlag, Leipzig, 1938, 11

97,4 "He of all . . ." "The Soldier," *Poems,* 61

97,5 "Sometimes I sit with thee . . ." "And do they so? have they a Sense," *Works,* ed. by L. C. Martin, 2 vols., Oxford University Press, 1914, II:432

97,6 "Having been tenant long . . ." "Redemption," *op. cit.,* 40

97,7 "And the astonished Wrestler found . . ." "A Little over Jordan," *Complete Poems,* 330

97,32 "Allegory addressed . . ." *PP,* 1076

98,3 "Copiousness of glance" . . . *PP,* 907

98,14 . . . were it not better . . . *PP,* 770

98,24 "compositions of a mythological cast" . . . *PP,* 780-81

98,32 "My picture is a History of Art . . ." *PP,* 839

99,5 ". . . the Venus, the Minerva . . ." *PP,* 794-95

99,18 . . . "these States Exist now . . ." *PP,* 831

99,26 "Fable or Allegory . . ." *PP,* 828-30

100,1 ". . . a system was formed . . ." *PP,* 195

100,7 . . . "the Antediluvians . . ." *PP,* 198

100,27 ". . . Chaucer makes every one . . ." *PP,* 787

100,33 "The Franklin is one . . ." *PP,* 787

101,2 "The reasoning historian . . ." *PP,* 797-98

101,22 "In the last Battle . . ." *PP,* 795

101,35 . . . "the human sublime . . .") *PP,* 796

102,1 "Antediluvians . . ." *PP,* 198

102,4 "The stories of Arthur . . ." *PP,* 797

102,10 "Mr. B. has done . . ." *PP,* 797

102,13 . . . "all containing . . ." *PP,* 781

102,20 "The antiquities of every Nation . . ." *PP,* 797

102,23 . . . "it ceases to be history . . ." *PP,* 959

102,27 "I do not believe . . ." *PP,* 913

102,30 "It ought to be understood . . ." *PP,* 832

102,33 "Two persons . . ." *PP,* 833

102,37 "I have given . . ." *PP,* 1074

103,13 "How he became divided . . ." *PP,* 797

103,18 "I have in these three years . . ." *PP,* 1073

103,38 . . . Mr. Damon explains . . . *William Blake,* 452-53

104,17 . . . "equilibrium between good and evil . . ." No. 45, "The Last Judgment," *Miscellaneous Theological Works,* American Swedenborgian Printing and Publishing Society, 1909, 456

105,3 . . . a Swedenborgian asserts . . . H. N. Morris, *Flaxman, Blake, Coleridge, and Other Men of Genius Influenced by Swedenborg,* New Church Press, London, 1915, 99. The evidence is given in a later work, a lecture printed in *The Quest,* Vol. XI (1920), 78-79.

105,7 ". . . a very sorrowful occurrence . . ." Marguerite Beck

Block, *The New Church in the New World,* Holt, 1932, 68

105,19 . . . "the Marriage hearse" . . . *PP,* 75

105,19 . . . "the cage." *PP,* 101

105,35 "The works of this visionary . . ." *PP,* 801

106,29 "Man is brought . . ." No. 440, *Heaven and Its Wonders and Hell, from Things Heard and Seen,* tr. by J. C. Ager, American Swedenborgian Printing and Publishing Society, 1909, 271

107,5 Mr. Damon . . . explains . . . *Op. cit.,* 203-04

107,10 As when a man dreams . . . *PP,* 489

108,1 "The whole natural world . . ." Nos. 89-90, *Heaven and Hell,* 58

108,5 "The world of Imagination . . ." *PP,* 830

108,18 "The animals of the earth . . ." *New Jerusalem Tracts: Selections from the Writings of Swedenborg,* Boston, 1830, Tract 3: I, 7. Quoted by White, *The Mysticism of . . . Blake,* 147

108,26 "Did he who made the Lamb make thee?" . . . *PP,* 73

109,11 To see a World in a Grain of Sand . . . *PP,* 118-21

110,20 . . . "Newton's Particles of light" . . . *PP,* 107

110,23 . . . "need not first put . . ." Boehme, "Threefold Life, *Works,* II, 3:29

111,11 ". . . without two Suns . . ." *PP,* 937

111,17 "The reason why a dead Sun . . ." *PP,* 937

111,23 ". . . all Things were created . . ." *PP,* 937

111,37 "All that we saw . . ." *PP,* 200

112,5 We eat little, we drink less . . . *PP,* 1068

112,27 ". . . astonishing indeed . . ." *PP,* 1072

113,1 . . . "his Version . . . of Genesis . . ." *Blake, Coleridge, Wordsworth, Lamb . . .* ed. by E. J. Morley, Manchester University Press, 1922, 12

113,3 . . . "world shall have . . ." *PP,* 202

113,26 "Every one who becomes an angel . . ." No. 739, *The True Christian Religion: Containing the Universal Theology,* 735

113,32 ". . . the angelic societies . . ." No. 94, *Heaven and Hell,* 59

113,36 ". . . the head signifies . . ." No. 97, *ibid.,* 60-61

114,7 "Beauty we call . . ." *PP,* 916

114,25 . . . in your own Bosom . . . *PP,* 692

114,30 "man's leading propensity . . ." *PP,* 931-32

115,12 Shewing the Transgressors in Hell . . . *PP,* 504-05

115,20 & Throughout all Eternity . . . *PP,* 106

115,30 . . . the points of the compass . . . No. 150, *Heaven and Hell,* 91-92

116,15 "*for* ALL LIFE IS HOLY." *PP,* 913

116,19 ". . . human form divine" . . . *PP,* 148-49

116,30 ". . . on my asking . . ." *Op. cit.,* 3

117,5 "The Spirit of Jesus . . ." *PP,* 550

117,14 . . . "to inquire into the mysteries of faith . . ." No. 136, *Arcana Coelestia: The Heavenly Arcana Contained in the Holy Scripture, . . .* ed. by the Rev. J. F. Potts, 12 vols., Swedenborg Foundation, Inc., 1928, I:62

117,18 ". . . if the love of God . . ." *William Blake: Poet and Mystic,* tr. by D. H. Conner, Chapman and Hall, London, 1914, 206

117,22 If the Sun & Moon should doubt . . . *PP,* 120-21

Notes

117,29 The end of love . . . No. 13, "Doctrine of Faith," *Four Leading Doctrines of the New Church,* American Swedenborgian Printing and Publishing Society, 1909, 176

117,33 . . . "charity" . . . See No. 535, *Heaven and Hell,* 345-46

117,36 "The Whole of Charity and Faith . . ." *PP,* 938

118,5 . . . "use to society . . ." Swedenborg, No. 422, *The True Christian Religion,* 452

118,32 . . . "sexual religion . . ." Robinson, *op. cit.,* 6

118,33 "Humanity knows not of Sex" . . . *PP,* 607

118,34 "In Eternity Woman . . ." *PP,* 840

119,13 Love seeketh not itself to please . . . *PP,* 66

119,26 ". . . where self and the world . . ." No. 233, *True Christian Religion,* 274-75

119,34 . . . "the Spectre . . ." *PP,* 612

120,4 . . . "have not the will . . ." No. 382, *True Christian Religion,* 407

120,13 . . . "everything is Atheism . . ." *Op. cit.,* 6

120,15 "Hence it may appear . . ." *PP,* 134

120,34 Let the Human Organs be kept . . . *PP,* 654

121,5 He attacked him . . . *PP,* 201

121,10 . . . his spiritual predestinarianism . . . *PP,* 944-48

121,11 . . . "divine teacher" . . . *PP,* 504

121,12 Swedenborg's own system . . . *PP,* 504-05; 539-41

121,21 . . . "a Mental Prince" . . . *PP,* 819

121,24 . . . "the time is arrived . . ." *PP,* 1045-46

121,25 "The Kingdoms of this World . . ." *PP,* 1058

122,4 O search & see . . . *PP,* 636

122,11 . . . "naturalized the spiritual . . ." *Songs of Innocence and Experience,* Preface, xvi

122,14 . . . "is not so much . . ." *Op. cit.,* 14

122,20 "Swedenborg had been . . . Symons, . . ." *William Blake,* 92

122,28 . . . "most accidental or partial kind." *Ibid.,* 92

124,14 "Whatsoever *strives* and contends . . ." "Mysterium Magnum," *Works,* III, 22:71

124,20 . . . "the resigned Ground of a Soul . . ." "Dialogue between a Scholar and His Master," Pt. II, *ibid.,* IV, 9:17

124,33 "God of This World" . . . *PP,* 763

125,11 ". . . that Image which . . ." "Three Principles," *op. cit.,* III, 16:37

125,22 "If we put our Imagination . . ." "Treatise of the Incarnation," Pt. II, *ibid.,* IV, 9:17

125,24 . . . "a beastial Nature . . ." "Dialogue between a Scholar and His Master," Pt. II, *ibid.,* IV, 75

126,9 ". . . if there were . . ." "Mysterium Magnum," *ibid.,* III, 29:7

126,11 "Without Contraries . . ." *PP,* 191

126,15 "For the Eternal Nature . . ." "Signatura Rerum," *op. cit.,* IV, 2:4

126,22 ". . . there are two Wills . . ." "Threefold Life," *ibid.,* II, 2:9

126,33 Earth was not . . . *PP,* 244

127,4 I have sought for a joy . . . *PP,* 244

127,6 "the indefinite . . ." *PP,* 429

127,7 . . . "petrific, abominable chaos." *PP,* 244

127,14 Creation in Boehme proceeds . . . See Howard H. Brinton, *The Mystic Will,* Macmillan, 1930, 135-38, for an admirable account of Boehme's doctrine of the seven forms; or Rufus M. Jones, "Jacob Boehme: His

Life and Spirit," *Spiritual Reformers in the Sixteenth and Seventeenth Centuries,* Macmillan, London, 1914, 180-82, for a briefer one.

127,26 "Seven Eyes of God" . . . *PP,* 301

127,36 . . . "fierce anguish" . . . *PP,* 246

127,36 "Pangs of Eternal birth" . . . *PP,* 344

127,37 . . . "universal shrieks" . . . *PP,* 362

128,22 . . . All were forth at sport . . . *PP,* 241

128,35 . . . "acted in no slight degree . . ." *Biographia Literaria,* 75-76

129,4 "Bring forth the New Jerusalem. . . ." "Treatise of the Incarnation," Pt. I, *op. cit.,* IV, 6:24

129,8 The morning comes, the night decays . . . *PP,* 219

131,3 "All Religions Are One." *PP,* 148

131,5 "The antiquities of every Nation . . ." *PP,* 797

131,6 "That the Jews assumed . . ." *PP,* 957

131,11 ". . . he eagerly assented . . ." *Op. cit.,* 10

131,17 "The Beauty of the Bible . . ." *PP,* 1028

132,2 "Truth is Nature" . . . *PP,* 944

132,3 "Natural Religion . . ." *PP,* 956

132,13 "The Bible tells me . . ." *PP,* 958

132,36 "There is no such thing . . ." *PP,* 1024

133,2 "Alas, in cities . . ." *PP,* 864

133,7 ". . . the Innocent civilized Heathen . . ." *PP,* 835

133,10 ". . . the Ancient Britons . . ." *PP,* 796

133,22 "Influx from above" . . . *PP,* 939

133,30 "Albion's Ancient Druid Rocky Shore" . . . *PP,* 597. For a full discussion of the influence of celtomania on Blake, see Denis Saurat, *Blake and Modern Thought,* Dial Press, 1929. For a brief discussion, see the chapter called "Vast Shady Hills" in James Bramwell's *Lost Atlantis,* Harper, 1938, especially pp. 214-27. Bramwell is himself indebted to Saurat, but his claims are in all ways more moderate.

133,34 "Read the Edda of Iceland . . ." *PP,* 957

134,4 "All had originally one language . . ." *PP,* 797

134,11 "That mankind . . ." *PP,* 956

134,27 . . . "simultaneous consciousness of a controlled universe . . ." "Introduction," *Poems of Gerard Manley Hopkins,* xiv

135,10 . . . "the Spirit of Prophecy" . . . *PP,* 149

135,12 "The world through its wisdom . . ." I Cor. 1:20

136,6 The Familists' faith . . . For this summary, see George H. Sabine, Introduction, *Works of Gerrard Winstanley,* Cornell University Press, 1941, 28

136,22 *"J'entends, par religion naturelle . . ." "Eléments de la philosophie de Newton," Œuvres Complètes,* XXII:449

136,24 "If Morality was Christianity . . ." *PP,* 1028

136,32 . . . Schleiermacher, asserted . . . See A. C. McGiffert, *Rise of Modern Religious Ideas,* Macmillan, 1922, 73

136,36 . . . "*expanded* benevolence" . . . *PP,* 919. The phrase belongs to Lavater, one of Schleiermacher's forerunners in the doctrine of religious feeling. Blake underlined it in his copy of the *Aphorisms*

137,18 "Others maintained . . ." John Lawrence Mosheim, *An Ecclesiastical History, Antient and Modern, from the Birth of*

Christ, to the Beginning of the Present Century, tr. by A. Maclaine, 6 vols., T. Cadell, London, 1782, I:87

137,21 "They also foretold . . ." *Ibid.,* I:133

137,29 . . . "the worship of the God of the Jews . . ." *Ibid.,* I:300

137,34 . . . "by the assistance of Jesus" . . . *Ibid.,* I:229

137,37 "For though they believed . . ." *Ibid.,* I:214

138,4 Was Jesus Chaste? . . . *PP,* 139

139,1 "Why did Christ come? . . ." *PP,* 954

139,6 . . . "the great mechanic of the creation . . ." Thomas Paine, "The Age of Reason," *Writings,* IV:193

139,9 "Man can have no idea . . ." *PP,* 934

139,11 . . . "man has closed himself . . ." *PP,* 197

139,23 "Listen! Every Religion . . ." *PP,* 647

139,26 "Love Is Life." *PP,* 916

139,27 "Ye are united . . ." *PP,* 597

139,30 "There can be no Good Will. . . ." *PP,* 933

139,37 "All Penal Laws . . ." *PP,* 963

140,14 Yet Milton's doctrine . . . See A. S. P. Woodhouse, *Puritanism and Liberty,* Dent, London, 1938, 65-66

140,19 Jesus was sitting in Moses' Chair . . . *PP,* 139

141,5 "The Whole Business of Man . . ." *PP,* 766

141,10 . . . "those writers" . . . "Hawthorne and His *Mosses," Representative Selections,* ed. by W. Thorp, Appleton (American Writers' Series), 1938, 339

141,33 The world an ancient murderer is . . . "Self-condemnation," *Works,* 170

142,12 "How is it that all things . . ." *PP,* 460

142,14 . . . "even Tree, Metal . . ." *PP,* 751

142,29 Turning from Universal Love . . . *PP,* 620

143,18 . . . "meer Nature or Hell." *PP,* 938

143,21 . . . "Universal Nature." *PP,* 647

143,23 That this pragmatical, preposterous pig of a world . . . "Blood and the Moon," *Collected Poems,* 274

143,34 . . . "an immanent *logos* principle" . . . Reinhold Niebuhr, *The Nature and Destiny of Man: Human Nature,* Scribner, 1943, 165

144,20 ". . . to think of holiness . . ." *PP,* 935

144,21 ". . . knaveries are . . . knaveries." *PP,* 924

144,36 What if the foot, ordain'd the dust to tread . . . *Essay on Man,* I, ix, ll. 259-64

145,6 Why has not man a microscopic eye? *Ibid.,* I, vi, ll. 193-94

145,8 "Deduct from a rose its redness . . ." *PP,* 923

145,12 "The roaring of lions . . ." *PP,* 193

145,19 . . . "Eternity is in love . . ." *PP,* 193

145,20 . . . "Time is the mercy of Eternity" . . . *PP,* 510

145,22 "God is in the lowest effects . . ." *PP,* 930

146,22 "There is no escape . . ." *Op. cit.,* 286

146,30 . . . "a stillness" . . . Boehme, "The Threefold Life," *op. cit.,* II, 10:10

148,14 Now as at all times I can see . . . W. B. Yeats, *Collected Poems,* 144

CHAPTER FIVE

151,1 . . . "the specious Liberal stuff . . ." *Further Letters,* ed. by C. C. Abbot, Oxford University Press, 1938, 238

Notes

151,16 "The error of poetry . . ." "The Artistic Future of Poetry," *New Republic,* Vol. LXXVIII, No. 1011 (April 18, 1934), 268-69

152,8 . . . the conventional view . . . The typical attitude as expressed by Alfred T. Story, for example, is this: ". . . on the outbreak of the Red Terror in the latter days of 1792, all his enthusiasm for the cause suddenly died, and he put on the red cap no more." (*William Blake: His Life, Character, and Genius,* S. Sonnenschein & Co., London, 1893, 18.) This was Story's invention, later elaborated in Edwin J. Ellis's piece of fantasy called *The Real Blake,* Chatto and Windus, London, 1907; and it persists still. Another view, first expressed by Irene Langridge in *William Blake: A Study of His Life and Art Work* (G. Bell and Sons, London, 1904), is that "this new philosophy which fired the imagination of Blake had a basis of materialism and violence which would have found no answering response in his soul, had he sought to investigate it." (page 18) This view also persisted, as, for example, in G. K. Chesterton's *William Blake* (Dutton, 1910), which refers to "the wild optimist Godwin and his daughter [sic] Mary Woolstonecraft [sic]." (page 30) The more careful study of Allardyce Nicoll (1922) checked these loose assertions, but it was not until 1924, with the appearance of the first systematic study of Blake's life and work, S. Foster Damon's *William Blake: His Philosophy and Symbols,* that readers of Blake were supplied with a balanced and over-all picture. After this, critics began to emphasize the "this-world" element in Blake's poetry. The first was Harold Bruce in his *William Blake in This World* (Harcourt, Brace, 1925) and a number of articles, especially "Beneath the Surface, 1800-1815," *Essays in Criticism,* by members of the Department of English, University of California Publications in English, Berkeley, 1934, Vol. IV, 201-21, which examined the impact of industrialism upon Blake. Others were C. H. Herford in 1928, Frederick E. Pierce in 1930, and Laurence Binyon in 1931. In 1933 appeared J. Middleton Murry's *William Blake* (Jonathan Cape). Mr. Murry, then in his Christo-Marxian mood, abjured the historical method for the sake of a pure study of Blake himself, with the nearly predictable result that his book, while concerned with Blake's social intuitions, makes of Blake a curiously Murryesque creature. In 1944 appeared Jacob Bronowski's *A Man without a Mask* (Secker and Warburg), an excellent book which overlaps the present work at a number of points, and which corrects most of the mistaken emphases in Blake criticism. These remarks would not be complete if I did not say that they do not touch on a number of very good books about Blake which, for one of two reasons, do not deal with the present matter at all. Such are Max Plowman's excellent but very general book and books which deal with a single problem or set of poems like those by Miss White, Miss Lowery, Mr. Wicksteed, and Professor Percival.

152,17 . . . "remarkable coterie" . . . Gilchrist, *Life of . . . Blake,* 79

154,15 "The literary exposition of freedom . . ." *Adventures of Ideas,* 84

154,33 "The task of the poet . . ." *Op. cit.,* 269

155,21 "All things Begin & End" . . . *PP,* 597

156,4 "I in Six Thousand Years . . ." *PP,* 503

156,19 . . . as a nerve o'er which do creep . . . *Julian and Maddalo,* ll. 449-50

157,30 . . . "in the very front rank . . ." Gilchrist, *op. cit.,* 10

157,36 "rioted with the rest." Ellis, *op. cit.,* 21

158,19 That Blake should have been engraving . . . For this early relationship, apparently not noted before, one need only compare Gilchrist, *op. cit.,* 46, and Elbridge Colby's *Bibliography of Thomas Holcroft,* New York Public Library, 1922, 41-43. The facts of Holcroft's life are given in Colby's introductory section, pp. 4-31. A fuller account, and an interesting one, is Holcroft's own unfinished *Life,* completed by Hazlitt, and re-edited by Mr. Colby in 1925. Harold Bruce, among the first Blake critics to attempt to relate Blake to his own times, yet seemed intent on the idea that Blake had nothing to do with these people. See his "William Blake and Gilchrist's Remarkable Coterie of Advanced Thinkers," *Modern Philology,* Vol. CI (February, 1926), 265-92, and his *William Blake in This World,* 29 n.

158,29 . . . printing of the *Poetical Sketches* . . . Margaret Ruth Lowery, in the second chapter of her careful study of the *Poetical Sketches* (Yale University Press, 1940) argues for the relatively small part the Mathews played in Blake's life at this time and the relatively large part played by Flaxman. Her argument is interesting but not at all conclusive.

159,10 . . . ("Fissie Follogy . . ." *PP,* 872

159,15 . . . "Pestilence" . . . *PP,* 883

159,18 "For now I have procur'd these imps . . ." *PP,* 874

160,2 ("I think that any natural fool . . ." *PP,* 873

160,4 ("I think the Ladies' discourses . . ." *PP,* 877

160,6 ("Matrimony's Golden cage"); *PP,* 881

160,7 ("The hungry poor enter'd the hall"); *PP,* 882

160,8 . . . ("a person may be as good at home") . . . *PP,* 870

160,9 ("A crowned king . . ." *PP,* 886

160,10 . . . ("a shameful thing . . ." *PP,* 868

160,16 "I'll hollow and stamp . . ." *PP,* 887

160,29 . . . "damned good to steal from" . . . Gilchrist, *op. cit.,* 45

161,1 The only Man that e'er I knew . . . *PP,* 855

161,5 . . . "her clothes . . . scarcely decent" . . . John Knowles, *Life and Writings of Henry Fuseli,* 3 vols., H. Colburn and R. Bentley, London, 1831, I:164

161,24 "O, why was I born . . ." *PP,* 115

161,25 . . . applied . . . to himself . . . *PP,* 1081; in a letter to Butts

161,27 "He says that from the Bible . . ." *Op. cit.,* 13
162,14 Such groups as . . . Crane Brinton, *op. cit.,* 170
163,14 "Thought is act" . . . *PP,* 968
163,21 . . . "an idea of the inflammatory eloquence . . ." Gilchrist, *op. cit.,* 81-82
163,38 "God has preserved him." *PP,* 951
164,3 "I say I shan't live five years. . . ." *PP,* 888
165,21 . . . "many years afterwards" . . . *Life of Percy Bysshe Shelley* (revised), ed. by H. B. Forman, Oxford University Press, 1913, 116
165,29 . . . Holcroft . . . was arrested . . . See Thomas Hardy's account of the affair, *Memoir . . . of the London Corresponding Society,* J. Ridgway, London, 1832
165,36 "To defend the Bible . . ." *PP,* 949
166,9 . . . "being a *seditious* . . ." *Memoirs of the Life of Gilbert Wakefield,* 2 vols., J. Johnson, London, 1804, II:134
166,13 "the Devil's party" . . . *PP,* 192
166,28 ". . . the common people . . ." *Anecdotes of the Life of Richard Watson, Bishop of Llandaff; Written by Himself . . . and Revised in 1814,* T. Cadell and W. Davies, London, 1817, 270. Wordsworth, like Blake, did not choose to print his attack.
166,35 . . . "with respect to the sincerity . . ." *Ibid.,* 304-06
167,7 . . . "glittering Dissimulation." *PP,* 951
167,9 "The Beast & the Whore . . ." *PP,* 949
167,12 "whatever was the beginning . . ." "An Essay on the First Principles of Government," *Theological and Miscellaneous Works,* ed. by J. T. Rutt, 25 vols., G. Smallfield, London, 1817-32, XXII:9
167,16 Bliss was it in that dawn to be alive . . . "Prelude," XI, ll. 108-09, *op. cit.,* 728
167,18 "AND NOW THE LION & WOLF SHALL CEASE." *PP,* 204
167,26 Now the sneaking serpent walks . . . *PP,* 190
168,2 . . . "State Trickster" . . . *PP,* 951
168,2 . . . "the Holy Ghost . . . in Paine . . ." *PP,* 955
168,4 . . . "would be as good an inquisitor . . ." *PP,* 952
168,6 . . . "English Crusade against France" . . . *PP,* 952
168,10 . . . "Kings & Priests . . ." *PP,* 962
168,13 . . . "State Religion" . . . *PP,* 963
168,16 . . . "blasphemous" . . . *PP,* 950
168,21 "It does not signify . . ." *PP,* 932
168,29 "A tyrant is the worst disease . . ." *PP,* 969
168,33 "hapless Soldier's sigh . . ." *PP,* 75
168,34 "What do these knaves mean by virtue? . . ." *PP,* 968
169,2 "Bacon calls intellectual arts unmanly . . ." *PP,* 969
169,4 "The increase of a State . . ." *PP,* 969
169,18 And My Angels have told me . . . *PP,* 1046
169,24 "Peace opens the way . . ." *PP,* 1058-59
169,34 They led their wild desires . . . *PP,* 978
170,9 Now Art has lost its mental Charms . . . *PP,* 857
170,23 . . . "Republican art" . . . *PP,* 1140
171,16 ". . . you cannot but recollect . . ." *Letters from William Blake to Thomas Butts: 1800-1803,* printed in facsimile with an Introductory Note by Geoffrey Keynes, Ox-

ford University Press, 1928, unpaged

172,2 ". . . thank you for your reprehension . . ." *PP*, 1051

172,20 . . . "uttered seditious and treasonable expressions . . ." Gilchrist, *op. cit.*, 172

172,28 . . . "used to declare" . . . *Ibid.*, 174

172,37 . . . Lamb's "Bitch" . . . Ford K. Brown, *Life of William Godwin*, Dent, London, 1926, 203 n

173,14 . . . "a certain free-thinking speculation . . ." Frederick Tatham, *The Life of William Blake*, printed in *Letters*, ed. by Russell, 26

173,21 . . . "interesting and eager . . ." *Ibid.*, 29

173,29 . . . "brisk, buxom, good-looking" . . . Brown, *op. cit.*, 202

173,31 . . . "on the following Sunday . . ." Tatham, *op. cit.*, 26

174,6 . . . "struggling men . . ." Conway, Introduction, Paine, *Writings*, III:viii. Actually, the suggestion seems unlikely when one considers Blake's habits of work as a graphic artist. Except for his own face and body and his wife's, he seems not to have used real-life models at all.

174,29 . . . the *Catalogue* . . . *PP*, 779-80

175,1 "The Times require . . ." *PP*, 804

175,26 "This Whole Book . . ." *PP*, 978

175,30 . . . "this President of Fools" . . . *PP*, 987

175,32 . . . "A Pretence of Art . . ." *PP*, 979

175,38 "The Rich Men of England" . . . *PP*, 979

176,2 . . . "royal liberality" . . . *PP*, 972

176,10 O dear Mother outline . . . *PP*, 1019

176,18 . . . "Hired Knave" . . . *PP*, 1002

177,23 "The wretched State of the Arts . . ." *PP*, 819

177,29 "I am really sorry . . ." *PP*, 819

177,37 "Now he had just before . . ." *William Blake*, 3

178,4 "Many Persons . . ." *PP*, 842-43

178,21 "The chief object . . ." Essay IV, "The Friend," *Complete Works*, ed. by Shedd, 7 vols., Harper, 1864, II:184-85

178,25 ". . . that government is good . . ." "Contributions to the *Morning Post* of 1799, 1800," *Essays on His Own Times*, ed. by his daughter, 3 vols., Pickering, London, 1850, II:331

179,3 "All Those who . . ." *PP*, 842

179,10 "Poverty is the Fool's Rod . . ." *PP*, 838

179,23 . . . the livelihood of engravers . . . Jacob Bronowski makes this fact the starting-point of his book.

179,30 "A Machine is not a Man . . ." *PP*, 823

179,36 ". . . so entire is the uncertainty . . ." Mona Wilson, *The Life of William Blake*, Robert O. Ballou, 1933, 219

180,3 ". . . you will not be surprised . . ." Brown, *op. cit.*, 249

180,7 "Leaving the delusive Goddess Nature . . ." *PP*, 1141

180,12 "Each Identity is Eternal," *PP*, 831

180,21 "Imagination & Visions . . ." *PP*, 1022

180,30 "I have never known . . ." Robinson, *op. cit.*, 26

180,33 "When I asked . . ." *Ibid.*, 9

181,1 . . . "King & Priest . . ." *PP*, 1141

181,3 "Down to his latest days . . ." Gilchrist, *op. cit.*, 80

Notes

181,21 . . . "intellectual peculiarity" . . . *PP,* 1138

181,26 . . . "Tory Translation" . . . *PP,* 1031

181,28 "Our Father Augustus Ceasar . . ." *PP,* 1031

181,36 . . . "just such a Tyrant . . ." *PP,* 1030

181,37 "Lawful Bread . . ." *PP,* 1029

182,11 "The True Christian Charity . . ." *PP,* 765

182,22 "Give us the Bread . . ." *PP,* 1030

182,25 "The Whole Business of Man . . ." *PP,* 766

183,31 This is to ask . . . See Kerker Quinn, "Blake and the New Age," *Virginia Quarterly Review,* Spring, 1937, 284, for illuminating suggestions on this matter, and for an instructive contrast with D. H. Lawrence, whom Blake sometimes perilously resembles.

184,3 Each outcry of the hunted Hare . . . *PP,* 118

184,8 The iron hand crush'd the Tyrant's head . . . *PP,* 118

184,14 ". . . the omission of act . . ." *PP,* 932

185,5 ("the MOST UNITED VARIETY"). *PP,* 916

185,24 It has been sugested . . . Newman White, *Shelley,* II:441-44

185,29 "I am hid" . . . *PP,* 970

186,1 . . . "a young Lark . . ." *PP,* 1137

187,14 The *Poetical Sketches* . . . All students of Blake are indebted to Margaret Ruth Lowery for her exacting study of Blake's early poems in her *Windows of the Morning,* Yale University Press, 1940.

187,17 "Blow, boisterous wind . . ." *PP,* 86

187,31 "I love the jocund dance" . . . See Tillyard, *Poetry Direct and Oblique,* 9-13

188,3 ("The Nobles . . . tear the poor man's lamb"). *PP,* 14

188,6 The husbandman does leave his plow . . . *PP,* 15

188,16 ". . . scatter thy pearls . . ." *PP,* 3

188,19 Cities shall sing, and vales in rich array . . . *PP,* 38

188,22 . . . if the heart is sick . . . *PP,* 25

188,26 The enemy fight in chains . . . *PP,* 22

189,4 He caught me in his silken net . . . *PP,* 9

189,14 My silks and fine array . . . *PP,* 9

189,26 Love and harmony combine . . . *PP,* 9

190,11 The Nobles of the land did feed . . . *PP,* 14, 17

190,32 . . . long a-gone . . . *PP,* 21

191,9 . . . sovereigns Of the sea . . . *PP,* 25

191,18 . . . "nets & gins & traps." *PP,* 211

191,30 O for a voice like thunder . . . *PP,* 39

192,5 Had I three lives . . . *PP,* 41

192,10 "The sword was bright . . ." *PP,* 47

CHAPTER SIX

194,15 "A revolution in the state of civilization . . ." "Agrarian Justice," *Writings,* III:342

195,5 "I early noticed . . ." *Life of Robert Owen by Himself,* G. Bell and Sons, London, 1920, 46

195,33 "Amongst these warlike machines . . ." Faujas de Saint-Fond, *Voyage en Engleterre,* . . . quoted by Paul Mantoux, *The Industrial Revolution in the Eighteenth Century,* tr. by M. Vernon, Harcourt, Brace, 1928, 313. I am considerably indebted to this book for parts of the general outline of the discussion of the Industrial Revolution.

197,17 . . . "unjust combinations" . . . *Poetical Works,* "Postscript," *op. cit.,* 962

197,30 ("It has been found . . ." Godwin, *An Enquiry Concerning Political Justice, and Its Influence on General Virtue and Happiness,* 2 vols., G. G. and J. Robinson, London, 1793, II:859. Hereafter referred to as *Political Justice.*

197,32 . . . in the novel . . . *Fleetwood: or, The New Man of Feeling,* 3 vols., R. Phillips, London, 1805, II:859

197,35 ". . . every human creature . . ." *Thoughts on Man, His Nature, Productions, and Discoveries,* E. Wilson, London, 1831, 53

198,1 . . . Godwin repeatedly insisted . . . *Ibid.,* 172; 175-78

198,4 . . . the monotony of his work . . . *The Enquirer. Reflections on Education, Manners, and Literature,* G. G. and J. Robinson, London, 1797, 16; 164-66; and *Fleetwood,* I:265-66

198,5 Mary Wollstonecraft . . . *An Historical and Moral View . . . of the French Revolution,* J. Johnson, London, 1794, 518-19

198,12 "A mechanic becomes . . ." *Fleetwood,* I:277

198,18 . . . "a sterilization of the self . . ." *Civilization and Technics,* Harcourt, Brace, 1934, 34

198,27 "Perhaps the most positive influence . . ." *Ibid.,* 81, 84

199,15 ("Commerce Cannot endure Individual Merit.") *PP,* 811

199,24 . . . "the poetical faculty . . ." "A Defence of Poetry," *Prose Works,* ed. by H. B. Forman, Oxford University Press, 1890, 135

200,4 "The superiority of the rich . . ." *Political Justice,* I:35

200,12 "The peer and the beggar . . ." "The Rights of Man," *op. cit.,* II:500-01

200,17 Pity would be no more . . . *PP,* 75

200,22 "Though I care . . ." "Agrarian Justice," *op. cit.,* III:337

200,33 "The rich are encouraged . . ." *Political Justice,* I:40

201,3 Paine said that . . . "The Rights of Man," *op. cit.,* II:465

201,6 . . . "the poor laws . . ." *Ibid.,* II:493

201,13 "When we look at the complicated machines . . ." *Political Justice,* II:845-46

201,29 "The way of life congenial . . ." "John Crowe Ransom," *Virginia Quarterly Review,* January, 1935, 99

201,31 Lewis Mumford argues . . . *Op. cit.,* 45 ff.

202,11 "Bring out number . . ." *PP,* 193

202,17 ". . . the *machine* of human society." *The Enquirer,* 10

202,19 "The Christian religion . . ." "Prospect Papers," *op. cit.,* IV:333

202,24 "The Almighty is the great mechanic . . ." *Ibid.,* 193-94

203,14 "Who, born within the last forty years . . ." "Reflections on the Revolution in France," *Works,* 12 vols., Little, Brown, 1865, III:349

205,4 . . . they are founded . . . This point, in connection with Traherne, is made by Professor Grierson in his essay "Blake and Gray," *The Background of English Literature,* Chatto and Windus, London, 1925, 129

205,19 "Jesus Christ was a Revolutionist . . ." Mark Wilks, *The Origin and Stability of the French Revolution: A Sermon*

Preached at St. Paul's Chapel, Norwich, July 14, 1791, 5

205,33 "As to the abuses . . ." "History of the Corruptions of Christianity," *Theological . . . Works*, V:482

206,2 "It is nothing . . ." *Ibid.*, V:504

206,7 ". . . the church has set up . . ." "The Age of Reason," *op. cit.*, IV:42

206,13 "The intellectual part of religion . . ." *Ibid.*, 249

206,25 "I consider no connection . . ." *Political Writings*, Mott and Lyon, New York, 1796, 35

206,30 According to Paine . . . "Worship and Church Bells," *op. cit.*, IV:250

206,33 Godwin pointed out . . . *Political Justice*, II:670-71

207,2 "Religion is in reality . . ." *Ibid.*, II:797

207,14 "All national institutions . . ." "The Age of Reason," *op. cit.*, IV:22

207,17 Church hierarchy . . . *Ibid.*, 324

207,24 . . . "a mere abortion . . ." *The Enquirer*, 232-33; see also *Political Justice*, I:61-62.

207,28 . . . "the object of the church . . ." "The Age of Reason," *op. cit.*, IV:171

207,35 "I saw the exceeding probability . . ." *Ibid.*, 22

207,38 ". . . perhaps we must wait . . ." "History of the Corruptions of Christianity," *op. cit.*, V:504

208,6 . . . "the proper office . . ." *The Evidence for a Future Period of Improvement in the State of Mankind with the Means and Duty of Promoting It Represented in a Discourse*, London, 1787, 23

208,12 "Respect a Parliamentary king . . ." "Institutes of Natural and Revealed Religion," *op. cit.*, II:xvii

208,16 "My own mind . . ." "The Age of Reason," *op. cit.*, IV:22

209,12 "We are all of us . . ." *Political Justice*, I:107

209,30 "From these reasonings . . ." *Ibid.*, I:18

210,6 . . . "consolation and luxury . . ." Godwin, *Thoughts Occasioned by Dr. Parr's Spital Sermon*, Taylor and Wilks, London, 1801, 82

210,9 "Man is perfectible . . ." Mary Wollstonecraft, *An Historical and Moral View*, 486

210,30 . . . "palpable to the mind." *Political Justice*, II:502

211,17 . . . "that men's interests . . ." *Modern Democratic State*, Oxford University Press, 1943, 142; see also 79-83

211,32 "a child is born . . ." *History of English Thought* . . . II:140

212,3 . . . Burke regarded as anarchical. *Ibid.*, II:223-24

212,8 "Willingly or unwillingly . . ." "Royalty," *op. cit.*, III:108

212,24 . . . "common deliberation" . . . *The Enquirer*, 149, 192

212,25 "To obey the committee . . ." Brinton, *op. cit.*, 160

212,34 . . . "sooner or later . . ." C. H. Driver, "William Godwin," *Social and Political Ideas of Some Representative Thinkers of the Revolutionary Era*, ed. by F. J. C. Hearnshaw, G. G. Harrap and Co., London, 1931, 164

213,4 "You know that I have always . . ." *Letters Written during a Short Residence in Sweden, Norway, and Denmark*, J. Johnson, London, 1796, 244

213,10 Finally, monarchy . . . *Political Justice*, I:5 ff. and II:511; also, *The Enquirer*, 235-36; also, Richard Price, *A Toast, Proposed by Dr. Price*, . . .

quoted by Rutt in Priestley, *op. cit.*, I, Pt. 2, 79-80n

213,13 . . . "the defense of our own liberty . . ." *Political Justice*, II:520

213,17 . . . exception of Paine . . . "Rights of Man," *op. cit.*, II:513

213,27 . . . "formal repetition . . ." *Political Justice*, II:847

213,33 "Instead . . . of endeavoring . . ." "First Principles of Government," *op. cit.*, XXII:46-47

214,14 How do you know but ev'ry Bird . . . *PP*, 192

214,19 "There is no maxim . . ." *Political Justice*, II:766-67

214,36 ". . . for to distribute . . ." "Prospect Papers," *op. cit.*, IV:324

215,10 "Excess of government . . ." "Of Legislative and Executive Powers," *op. cit.*, II:245

216,1 "A revolution . . ." "Agrarian Justice," *op. cit.*, III:342

216,33 . . . "the cement of society" . . . *A Vindication of the Rights of Woman; with Strictures on Political and Moral Subjects*, J. Johnson, London, 1792, 380

217,9 . . . "short-lived queens" . . . *Ibid.*, 116

217,14 "The shameless behaviour . . ." *Ibid.*, 275-76

217,22 "I wish to sum up . . ." *Ibid.*, 106

217,25 . . . "where love animates the behaviour" . . . *Ibid.*, 121

217,31 ". . . the sexual should not destroy . . ." *Ibid.*, 112

217,31 . . . "*arts* are employed . . ." *Ibid.*, 228

218,1 "The woman who has dedicated . . ." *Ibid.*, 278-79

218,18 . . . "the desire of exhibiting . . ." *Posthumous Works of the Author of A Vindication of the Rights of Woman*, 4 vols., J. Johnson, London, 1798, I, Preface, unpaged

218,24 "Marriage has bastilled me . . ." *Ibid.*, II:34-43

218,36 "To oblige them to act . . ." *Political Justice*, II:849

218,37 "Marriage is law . . ." *Ibid.*, II:850

218,38 . . . "an affair of property" . . . *Ibid.*, II:850

219,11 "We did not marry . . ." *Memoirs of Mary Wollstonecraft*, ed. by W. C. Durant, Constable, London, 1927, 101-02

219,31 "The only habit the child . . ." *Emile*, tr. by B. Foxby, Dutton (Everyman's Library), 1921, 30

CHAPTER SEVEN

221,14 "There is a strong objection . . ." *PP*, 932

222,31 How small, of all that human hearts endure . . . *The Traveller; or, a Prospect of Society*, ll. 429-30

223,15 "FIRST SERIES . . . SECOND . . ." *PP*, 147-48

225,4 ". . . the true rationalism . . ." *Science and the Modern World*, 288-89

225,19 "His 'single vision' . . ." Gilchrist, *Life of . . . Blake*, 408

225,31 "That the Poetic Genius . . ." *PP*, 148

226,20 "Every grain of sand . . ." *Essays on Physiognomy, Designed to Promote the Knowledge and Love of Mankind*, tr. by H. Hunter, 3 vols., J. Murray, London, 1789-98, I:13

227,14 Whatever stands in field or flood . . . Yeats, "Tom the Lunatic," *Collected Poems*, 308

228,1 . . . "fading in death" . . . *PP*, 150

228,3 "Look at my eyes . . ." *PP,* 151
228,11 Playing with flowers & running after birds . . . *PP,* 152
228,13 "For he is the king . . ." *PP,* 153
228,17 Thou art a very old old man . . . *PP,* 155
228,23 "Har sing in the great cage" . . . *PP,* 156
228,32 . . . all the sons & daughters of Tiriel . . . *PP,* 162
229,9 "Now, Hela, I can go . . ." *PP,* 162
229,11 . . . "the time of grace is past" . . . *PP,* 162
229,26 "Why is one law given to the lion . . ." *PP,* 166. Blake deleted the second line.
229,31 ". . . Such was Tiriel . . ." *PP,* 166-67
230,18 . . . "human nature has lost its antagonist." Quoted by Morton Downey Zabel, "The Thinking of the Body," *Southern Review,* Vol. VII (Winter, 1941), 588
231,2 "Piping down the valleys wild" . . . *PP,* 51
231,8 "How sweet is the Shepherd's sweet lot" . . . *PP,* 52
231,26 "Unorganiz'd Innocence . . ." *PP,* 460
232,23 Pitying, I drop'd a tear . . . *PP,* 62-63
232,33 . . . "our immortal day." *PP,* 60
233,4 . . . "pleasure which is personal . . ." Joseph Hone, *W. B. Yeats,* Macmillan, 1943, 296-97
233,8 . . . "the innocence of a child" . . . *PP,* 931
233,10 "Innocence dwells with Wisdom . . ." *PP,* 460
233,18 . . . the little ones weary . . . *PP,* 53
233,21 . . . "virtues of delight" . . . *PP,* 58
233,25 . . . "Heaven & Earth . . ." *PP,* 57
233,26 . . . intended counterpart . . . *PP,* 89
233,36 . . . "aged men, wise . . ." *PP,* 58
234,13 Then every man of every clime . . . *PP,* 58
234,27 . . . "to inherit" . . . *PP,* 60
234,28 "Joys impregnate" . . . *PP,* 193
235,2 Does the Eagle know what is in the pit? . . . *PP,* 168
235,18 . . . "Death is a veil . . ." *Prometheus Unbound,* III, iii, l. 113
235,23 . . . "fade away . . ." *PP,* 168
235,27 . . . "to be at death . . ." *PP,* 171
236,6 "O beauty of the vales of Har! . . ." *PP,* 172
236,11 Thel enter'd in & saw the secrets . . . *PP,* 173
236,20 "Why cannot the Ear be closed . . ." *PP,* 173
237,9 . . . "sexual strife." *PP,* 762
237,21 Struggling in my father's hands . . . *PP,* 76
238,3 . . . the Youth pined away with desire . . . *PP,* 73
238,16 "O Earth, O Earth, return!" . . . *PP,* 65-66
239,16 Love to faults is always blind . . . *PP,* 96
240,10 Remove away that black'ning church . . . *PP,* 96
240,15 The King & the Priest must be tied . . . *PP,* 98
240,19 I went to the Garden of Love . . . *PP,* 74
241,1 I saw a chapel all of gold . . . *PP,* 87
242,3 . . . "The invisible worm . . ." *PP,* 71
242,5 . . . "Love, free love . . ." *PP,* 91
242,9 A flower was offer'd to me . . . *PP,* 73
242,17 "As the shadow follows the body . . ." Aphorism 303. The change, trivial, to be sure, is not noted by Keynes.

The book is in the Huntington Library.

242,24 I asked a thief to steal me a peach . . . *PP,* 88

243,5 I told my love . . . *PP,* 86

243,11 I was angry . . . *PP,* 76

243,18 "grows . . . in the Human Brain." *PP,* 76

243,31 Mary moves in soft beauty . . . *PP,* 115-16

244,17 "I have . . . considered myself . . ." *Letters,* 15

244,29 Pity would be no more . . . *PP,* 75

245,17 Is this a holy thing to see . . . *PP,* 66-67

245,34 A little black thing among the snow . . . *PP,* 70

246,18 Fayette, Fayette, thou'rt bought & sold . . . *PP,* 102-03

247,1 "I die, I die," the Mother said . . . *PP,* 117-18

247,20 The Strongest Poison ever known . . . *PP,* 120

247,28 The Whore & Gambler, by the State . . . *PP,* 121

248,7 Why should I care for the men of thames . . . *PP,* 90

248,18 . . . "each dirty street" . . . *PP,* 92

248,22 I wander thro' each charter'd street . . . *PP,* 75

249,11 "It is very true . . ." *PP,* 811

249,16 . . . "beasts of prey" . . . *PP,* 68-70

249,33 The Gods of the earth and sea . . . *PP,* 76

250,5 Cruelty has a Human Heart . . . *PP,* 81

251,3 When the stars threw down their spears . . . *PP,* 73

251,22 . . . "futurity" . . . *PP,* 67

251,26 Hear the voice of the Bard! . . . *PP,* 65

252,17 Youth of delight, come hither . . . *PP,* 81

253,13 Once meek, and in a perilous path . . . *PP,* 190

254,12 "Without Contraries . . ." *PP,* 191

254,33 The body is not bruised to pleasure soul . . . "Among School Children," *Collected Poems,* 251

255,4 "Those who restrain desire . . ." *PP,* 191

255,17 The poet Milton . . . *PP,* 192

255,25 ". . . the bound or outward circumstance . . ." *PP,* 191

256,4 "He who desires but acts not . . ." *PP,* 193

256,9 "The whole of Freud's teaching . . ." "Psychology and Art," *The Arts Today,* ed. by G. Grigson, John Lane, London, 1935, 12

256,14 He who binds to himself a joy . . . *PP,* 99

256,20 "As the caterpiller chooses . . ." *PP,* 194

256,24 "Prisons are built . . ." *PP,* 193

256,36 "Prudence is a rich, ugly old maid . . ." *PP,* 193-94

257,15 "We know today . . ." *Socialism: Utopian and Scientific,* tr. by E. Aveling, International Publishers, 1935, 32

257,37 "Eternity is in love . . ." *PP,* 193

257,38 "Drive your cart . . ." *PP,* 192

258,1 . . . "The ancient tradition . . ." *PP,* 197

258,20 ". . . we must by reason . . ." Mary Wollstonecraft, *op. cit.,* 165

258,35 In the first chamber . . . *PP,* 197-98

259,20 "The mode of coalescence . . ." Whitehead, *Adventures of Ideas,* 59

259,22 "The Giants who formed this world . . ." *PP,* 198

259,33 . . . "the separatist's illusions" . . . *How to Read a Page,* Norton, 1942, 102

260,10 . . . "mankind . . ." *Op. cit.,* 99

261,1 . . . "the metaphysics of the Symbolists" . . . *Axel's Castle,* Scribner, 1931, 157

Notes

262,16 . . . old Nobodaddy . . . This figure occurs in several places, especially "To Nobodaddy," *PP,* 93. This expression of the idea that Jehovah is at most our wicked stepfather is one of Blake's best jokes, a Joycean portmanteau.

262,17 "the Devil's party." *PP,* 192

262,18 "The Devil answer'd . . ." *PP,* 202

262,32 "One Law for the Lion & Ox . . ." *PP,* 203

263,3 The Eternal Female groan'd! . . . *PP,* 203

263,26 . . . "Earth-Owner") . . . Kerrison Preston, *Blake and Rossetti,* Alexander Moring, Ltd., London, 1944, 24

263,27 . . . "promulgates his ten commands." *PP,* 204

264,11 "The new world citizens . . ." In a letter to Weydemeyer, 25 March 1852, quoted by Franz Mehring, *Karl Marx: The Story of His Life,* tr. by E. Fitzgerald, Covici Friede, 1936, 243

264,27 Nature, assuming a more lovely face . . . "Retirement," *Poems,* ed. by H. I'A. Fausset, Dutton (Everyman's Library), 1931, 296

264,34 I heard an Angel singing . . . *PP,* 88

266,2 . . . "when the activity of the Millerites . . ." Matthiessen, *American Renaissance,* 346

CHAPTER EIGHT

268,18 "The biblical fall of man . . ." *Modern Man in Search of a Soul,* 111

269,12 My Spectre around me night & day . . . *PP,* 105-06

270,34 Of the primeval Priest's assum'd power . . . *PP,* 243

271,7 Lo, a shadow of horror is risen . . . *PP,* 243

271,16 . . . "A self-contemplating shadow" . . . *PP,* 243

271,24 "I have sought for a joy without pain . . ." *PP,* 244-45

272,15 . . . "fragments of life" . . . *PP,* 246

272,18 . . . "formed matter in solid . . . particles." "Optics," *Opera Quae Existant Omnia,* ed. by S. Horsley, 4 vols., J. Nichols, London, 1779-85, IV: 260

272,24 . . . "The Eternal Prophet." *PP,* 248

272,25 . . . howling around the dark Demon . . . *PP,* 247

272,36 . . . "the formless, unmeasurable death" . . . *PP,* 247

273,3 . . . "the changes of Urizen." *PP,* 248

273,6 The Eternal Prophet heav'd the dark bellows . . . *PP,* 248

273,11 Till a roof, shaggy wild, inclos'd . . . *PP,* 249

273,15 . . . bones of solidness froze . . . *PP,* 249

273,20 All the myriads of Eternity . . . *PP,* 251

273,29 . . . a cold solitude & dark void . . . *PP,* 251

274,1 Thus the Eternal Prophet was divided . . . *PP,* 252

274,13 "That Eternals may no more behold them." *PP,* 253

274,23 . . . Los saw the Female & pitied . . . *PP,* 253

274,28 "Produc'd a man Child . . ." *PP,* 254

274,32 . . . O sorrow & pain! . . . *PP,* 154-55

275,17 He form'd a line & a plummet . . . *PP,* 255

275,27 . . . "cruel enormities" . . . *PP,* 256

275,31 He in darkness clos'd view'd all his race . . . *PP,* 256

276,2 . . . life liv'd upon death . . . *PP,* 256

276,8 A cold shadow follow'd behind him . . . *PP,* 257

276,18 . . . till weaken'd . . . *PP,* 257
276,28 And their children wept & built . . . *PP,* 258
277,9 "O Times remote! . . ." *PP,* 267
278,6 Till his Brain in a rock & his Heart . . . *PP,* 272
278,23 The dead heard the voice of the child . . . *PP,* 255
279,3 "Shall we worship this Demon of smoke . . ." *PP,* 259
279,8 . . . "broad Disk" . . . *PP,* 279
279,15 . . . "vulnerable part" . . . *PP,* 260
280,11 . . . "enormous dread Serpent" . . . *PP,* 261
280,26 . . . "his book of iron" . . . *PP,* 262
280,27 . . . bending its boughs . . . *PP,* 263
280,31 Round the pale living Corse on the Tree . . . *PP,* 263-64
281,6 "Ah, Urizen! Love! . . ." *PP,* 264
281,15 "Where is my golden palace? . . ." *PP,* 265-66
282,2 . . . "Self-destroying" . . . *PP,* 266
282,13 (Night spoke to the Cloud . . . *PP,* 273
282,17 "Orc on Mount Atlas howl'd . . ." *PP,* 273
282,20 Then Oothoon hover'd over Judah . . . *PP,* 273
282,25 The human race began to wither . . . *PP,* 273
283,1 Creeping in reptile flesh upon . . . *PP,* 274
283,8 Thus the terrible race of Los . . . *PP,* 274
283,18 Clouds roll heavy upon the Alps . . . *PP,* 274
283,28 . . . "The howl rise up from Europe" . . . *PP,* 274
283,31 . . . "in bitterness of soul" . . . *PP,* 275
284,8 . . . "Schoolmaster of souls" . . . *PP,* 428
284,11 "To turn the man from his path . . ." *PP,* 275
284,24 Orc, raging in European darkness . . . *PP,* 276
284,31 Forth from the dead dust . . . *PP,* 276
285,3 The Grave shrieks with delight . . . *PP,* 276
285,30 "His food she brought . . ." *PP,* 216
285,32 "The hairy shoulders rend the links . . ." *PP,* 217
286,4 "I know thee, I have found thee . . ." *PP,* 217
286,10 . . . "the souls of warlike men . . ." *PP,* 217
286,15 "Friends of America! . . ." *PP,* 218
286,24 . . . "a Wonder . . . a Human fire . . ." *PP,* 218
286,30 "The morning comes, the night decays . . ." *PP,* 219
287,2 "Let the slave grinding at the mill . . ." *PP,* 219
287,7 "Let the inchained soul . . ." *PP,* 219
287,21 "Blasphemous Demon, Antichrist . . ." *PP,* 220
287,24 "The times are ended; shadows pass . . ." *PP,* 220
288,7 "Fires inwrap the earthly globe . . ." *PP,* 220
288,12 . . . "lashes his tail!" *PP,* 222
288,17 "Why trembles honesty . . ." *PP,* 222-23
289,4 The citizens of New York . . . *PP,* 225
289,9 ("London's Guardian . . ." *PP,* 225
289,14 The doors of marriage are open . . . *PP,* 226
289,20 "Hiding the Demon red with clouds . . ." *PP,* 227
289,22 Till Angels & weak men . . . *PP,* 227
289,26 . . . "Smitten with their own plagues," . . . *PP,* 227
290,3 . . . "the personal story of Mary Wollstonecraft" . . . *William Blake,* 109
290,10 . . . ("the soft soul of America") . . . *PP,* 205

290,12 I loved Theotormon . . . *PP,* 205

290,27 . . . "back to back." *PP,* 206

290,31 . . . beneath him . . . *PP,* 206-07

291,3 "I cry: arise, O Theotormon! . . ." *PP,* 207

291,13 "They told me that the night & day . . ." *PP,* 207-08

291,19 "With what sense is it . . ." *PP,* 208

291,35 ". . . where dwell the joys of old? . . ." *PP,* 209

292,5 "Ah! are there other wars . . ." *PP,* 210

292,11 "O Urizen! Creator of men . . ." *PP,* 210-11

293,23 "Infancy! fearless, lustful, happy . . ." *PP,* 212

293,31 ". . . the youth shut up from . . ." *PP,* 213

294,4 . . . "Father of Jealousy" . . . *PP,* 213

294,6 "Oothoon shall view his dear delight . . ." *PP,* 214

294,12 . . . "back her sighs." *PP,* 215

294,23 "Then tell me . . ." *PP,* 232

295,3 "Arise, you little glancing wings . . ." *PP,* 215

295,7 . . . "sat upon the table . . ." *PP,* 233

295,14 The deep of winter came . . . *PP,* 234

295,30 "Who shall I send . . ." *PP,* 235

296,5 Enitharmon slept . . . *PP,* 236

296,13 "That Kings & Priests . . ." *PP,* 238

296,17 Enitharmon laugh'd in her sleep . . . *PP,* 239

296,27 . . . "siez'd the trump . . ." *PP,* 240

296,31 "I hear the soft Oothoon . . ." *PP,* 241

296,34 . . . "son of my afflictions" . . . *PP,* 241

297,1 . . . terrible Orc, when he beheld . . . *PP,* 241

297,7 And with a cry that shook all nature . . . *PP,* 242

298,13 The dead brood over Europe . . . *PP,* 174

298,26 "Forty men . . ." *PP,* 174

298,29 For the Commons convene . . . *PP,* 174-75

299,15 . . . the den nam'd Horror held a man . . . *PP,* 175

299,23 Pinion'd down to the stone floor . . . *PP,* 175

299,29 . . . "a skeleton yellow . . ." *PP,* 175

299,32 . . . "a loathsome sick woman" . . . *PP,* 175

300,1 . . . his den was short . . . *PP,* 176

300,9 . . . "friend to the favourite" . . . *PP,* 176

300,19 . . . In the seventh tower . . . *PP,* 176

300,32 . . . "assay to shout . . ." *PP,* 176-77

301,1 "The nerves of five thousand years' ancestry tremble . . ." *PP,* 177-78

301,22 Shall this marble built heaven . . . *PP,* 178-79

302,3 . . . "An aged form . . ." *PP,* 180

302,5 . . . "sighing in a low voice . . ." *PP,* 181

302,8 "They shall drop at the plow . . ." *PP,* 181

302,15 "Let thy soldiers possess this city of rebels . . ." *PP,* 182

302,19 . . . "generous as mountains . . ." *PP,* 183

302,23 ". . . O princes of fire . . ." *PP,* 183-84

303,29 . . . "the Nation's Ambassador" . . . *PP,* 184

303,32 "The millions of spirits immortal . . ." *PP,* 185

304,7 . . . "The mild peaceable nations . . ." *PP,* 186

304,17 . . . shaken the forests of France . . . *PP,* 189

304,24 . . . "finished" . . . See the facsimile of the title page in

Poetical Works of William Blake, ed. by J. Sampson, Oxford University Press, 1914, 262

304,32 See a disenchanted nation . . . *Prometheus Unbound,* I, ll. 567-70

305,21 . . . "give not what men call love" . . . "One Word Is Too Often Profaned," ll. 9-14

307,18 . . . "world-judgment motif" . . . Bellamy, *The Book of Revelation in History,* 10

307,21 . . . "illusion of finality" . . . J. B. Bury, *The Idea of Progress,* Macmillan, 1932, 351

308,13 To find the Western path . . . *PP,* 108

CHAPTER NINE

312,31 ("They had the likeness of a man") . . . Ezekiel 1:5

313,1 "Jung's four basic functions . . ." *Modern Man in Search of a Soul,* 16

313,6 "Single vision belongs to Urizen . . ." Preston, *Blake and Rossetti,* 15

313,25 Four Mighty Ones are in every Man . . . *PP,* 278

314,26 "I believe in you my soul . . ." "Song of Myself," *Leaves of Grass,* ed. by E. Holloway, Doubleday, Doran, 1929, 27

315,21 I wake, emerging from a sea of dreams . . . "Night I," *Poetical Works,* 2 vols., Pickering (Aldine Edition), London, 1844, I:2

316,10 "All Love is lost: Terror Succeeds . . ." *PP,* 279

316,20 "I have look'd in to the secret soul . . ." *PP,* 279

316,24 "Why wilt thou Examine . . ." *PP,* 279

316,34 She drave the Females all away from Los . . . *PP,* 287

317,3 "Refusing to behold the Divine Image . . ." *PP,* 289

317,12 "Descend, O Urizen . . ." *PP,* 290

317,17 . . . "The Wandering Man" . . . *PP,* 290

317,18 "Lo I am God . . ." *PP,* 291

317,24 . . . "leafless bush . . ." *PP,* 296-97

317,35 "Turning his Eyes outward . . ." *PP,* 302

318,4 Some fix'd the anvil . . . *PP,* 303, 305

318,15 . . . "Jerusalem came down . . ." *PP,* 304

318,18 . . . "behold What is now seen without . . ." *PP,* 304

318,24 "What! are we terrors to one another? . . ." *PP,* 307

319,4 . . . the Sons of Urizen . . . *PP,* 307-08

319,8 . . . "the Architect divine" . . . *PP,* 309

319,10 "Two wills they had . . ." *PP,* 310

319,13 "mourning among the Brick kilns . . ." *PP,* 311

319,17 ". . . We are made to turn the wheel for water . . ." *PP,* 311

319,25 In right lined paths . . . *PP,* 313-14

320,3 "I have planted a false oath . . ." *PP,* 318

320,10 "What is the price of Experience? . . ." *PP,* 318-19

321,1 "And never from that moment . . ." *PP,* 319

321,4 "Why wilt thou look upon futurity . . . ?" *PP,* 320

321,8 "I am set here a King of trouble . . ." *PP,* 320

321,11 . . . "those sweet fields of bliss . . ." *PP,* 321

321,20 "Rage, Rage shall never from my bosom . . ." *PP,* 328

321,23 . . . "Sovereign Architect" . . . *PP,* 331

321,27 "O why did foul ambition seize thee, Urizen . . ." *PP,* 335

322,3 Link'd hour to hour & day to night . . . *PP,* 336, 338

322,15 The Corse of Albion lay on the rock . . . *PP,* 340
322,22 . . . terrified at the shapes . . . *PP,* 340
322,25 ". . . mighty bulk & majesty . . ." *PP,* 341
322,28 . . . plants wither'd by winter . . . *PP,* 341
322,31 . . . "the cold Prince of Light" . . . *PP,* 342
323,5 The groans of Enitharmon shake the skies . . . *PP,* 342-43
323,10 "Luvah, King of Love . . ." *PP,* 343
323,13 . . . when Luvah sunk down . . . *PP,* 313
323,27 "When Thought is clos'd in Caves . . ." *PP,* 351
323,30 . . . "his Children ruin'd . . ." *PP,* 357
323,31 . . . "ending in death . . ." *PP,* 359
324,1 . . . nor can the man who goes . . . *PP,* 359
324,11 . . . "to the Caves of Orc" . . . *PP,* 365
324,13 . . . "While his snows fell . . ." *PP,* 366
324,16 . . . "the root of Mystery accursed . . ." *PP,* 366
324,23 "Yet thou dost laugh at all these tortures . . ." *PP,* 367-68
325,19 "Compell the poor to live upon a Crust of bread . . ." *PP,* 370
326,8 ". . . Curse thy Cold hypocrisy! . . ." *PP,* 371
326,27 . . . "secret monsters . . ." *PP,* 373
326,29 "the Shadow of Enitharmon" . . . *PP,* 374
326,33 "If we unite in one . . ." *PP,* 380
326,36 ". . . Now I feel the weight of stern repentance . . ." *PP,* 382
327,8 "To form a world of sacrifice . . ." *PP,* 383
327,17 And first he drew a line upon the walls . . . *PP,* 384
327,21 "From out the ranks of Urizen's war . . ." *PP,* 384
327,25 First Rintrah & then Palamabron . . . *PP,* 385
328,5 Startled was Los . . . *PP,* 385
328,14 . . . "the tree of Mystery . . ." *PP,* 386
328,19 First Trades & Commerce . . . *PP,* 386
328,29 . . . hid in chambers dark the nightly harlot . . . *PP,* 386
328,34 ". . . divided day & night . . ." *PP,* 387
329,4 . . . become Urizen's harlot . . . *PP,* 391
329,8 "the whole creation will be consumed . . ." *PP,* 197
329,18 Then left the sons of Urizen the plow & harrow . . . *PP,* 393
330,5 Orc rent her . . . *PP,* 394-95
330,16 . . . "sweet labours of Love" . . . *PP,* 398
330,19 . . . "In the Saviour's arms . . ." *PP,* 399
330,24 . . . "Obdurate heart was broken" . . . *PP,* 400
330,29 When Urizen saw the Lamb of God . . . *PP,* 401
330,33 ("Love that hardens into hate . . ." Archibald MacLeish, "Pole Star for This Year," *Public Speech,* Farrar and Rinehart, 1936, not paged.
331,5 "When shall the dead revive? . . ." *PP,* 405
331,7 . . . "heard the Voice" . . . *PP,* 405
331,9 . . . "the direful Web of Religion" . . . *PP,* 405
331,13 And Enitharmon nam'd the Female . . . *PP,* 405-06
331,17 . . . "Being multitudes . . ." *PP,* 408
331,23 "There is a State nam'd Satan . . ." *PP,* 413
332,7 . . . "The Eternal Man" . . . *PP,* 418

332,14 . . . "triumphs over all . . ." *PP,* 421
332,16 Captive, a Willing Captive . . . *PP,* 421-22
332,20 . . . "the Harlot of the Kings of Earth" . . . *PP,* 422
332,21 . . . "food of Orc & Satan" . . . *PP,* 422
332,24 Sometimes returning to the Synagogue of Satan . . . *PP,* 422
332,26 . . . "Satan divided against Satan" . . . *PP,* 422
332,27 . . . "To burn Mystery with fire . . ." *PP,* 422
332,31 The Ashes of Mystery began to animate . . . *PP,* 422
333,5 The thrones of Kings are shaken . . . *PP,* 423-24
333,14 . . . "when all Tyranny was cut off . . ." *PP,* 426
333,16 "When shall the Man of future times . . ." *PP,* 427
333,18 "stony form of death . . ." *PP,* 428
333,19 My anger against thee is greater . . . *PP,* 429
333,30 "Then Go, O dark futurity! . . ." *PP,* 430
334,4 . . . Then, glorious bright, Exulting in his joy . . . *PP,* 430
334,10 On rifted rocks, suspended in the air . . . *PP,* 432-33
334,22 . . . "the flames of Orc" . . . *PP,* 437
334,25 . . . "Orc had quite consum'd himself . . ." *PP,* 437
334,31 "Luvah & Vala, henceforth you are Servants . . ." *PP,* 438
335,6 . . . "golden feast" . . . *PP,* 450
335,8 "Man subsists by Brotherhood . . ." *PP,* 450
335,14 . . . "all Nations were threshed out . . ." *PP,* 451
335,19 "Let the slave, grinding at the mill . . ." *PP,* 452
335,25 "All the Slaves . . . Sing a New Song . . ." *PP,* 452-53
335,28 "Aha! Aha! how came I here . . ." *PP,* 453
336,3 . . . from his mountains high . . . *PP,* 454
336,9 "Attempting to be more than Man . . ." *PP,* 454
336,13 . . . "the Bread of Ages." *PP,* 459
336,14 . . . "The Expanding Eyes of Man . . ." *PP,* 459
336,20 "How is it we have walk'd thro' fires . . ." *PP,* 460
340,1 "But go, merciless man . . ." *PP,* 183

CHAPTER TEN

342,14 Milton was . . . This debt is summarized in Raymond D. Havens, *Influence of Milton on English Poetry,* Harvard University Press, 1922.
342,21 A less obvious influence . . . The influence of Milton's mind and the biographical parallels are summarized in Denis Saurat's *Blake and Milton,* first published in 1920, again by S. Nott, London, in 1935.
343,36 . . . "of the Devil's party . . ." *PP,* 192
344,10 ("Love . . . hath his seat In Reason") . . . *Paradise Lost,* VIII, ll. 589-90
344,13 ". . . the rest . . ." *Ibid.,* ll. 71-75
344,20 "Satan thinks that Sin . . ." *PP,* 842-44
345,6 "The Moral Virtues . . ." *PP,* 1022
345,13 "I saw Milton in Imagination . . ." Robinson, *Blake,* 9
345,18 ". . . all Act is Virtue . . ." *PP,* 932
346,15 "Three years' Herculean Labours . . ." *PP,* 810
346,16 . . . "the Grandest Poem . . ." *PP,* 1076

Notes

346,19 . . . "degraded" . . . *PP,* 820
347,16 "Virgin of Providence, fear not . . ." *PP,* 537
347,33 "Rouze up, O Young Men . . ." *PP,* 464
348,10 And did those feet in ancient time . . . *PP,* 464-65
348,26 Locke sank into a swoon . . . "Fragments," *op. cit.*, 247
349,1 "Say first! what mov'd Milton . . ." *PP,* 466
349,20 . . . ("Ah weak & wide astray!) . . . *PP,* 470
349,23 "Every Man's Wisdom is peculiar . . ." *PP,* 468-69
350,12 "You know Satan's mildness . . ." *PP,* 474
350,17 . . . ("Mine is the fault! . . ." *PP,* 476
350,21 He created Seven deadly Sins . . . *PP,* 478-79
351,1 "Wild with prophetic fury . . ." *PP,* 485
351,8 . . . "making to himself Laws . . ." *PP,* 481
351,12 "Pity and Love are too venerable . . ." *PP,* 487
351,20 "I go to Eternal Death! . . ." *PP,* 487
352,3 "The misery of unhappy Families . . ." *PP,* 493
352,17 . . . "a Garment of Pity . . ." *PP,* 494
352,19 . . . "an old Prophecy" . . . *PP,* 500
352,30 . . . "the Cloud of Milton . . ." *PP,* 501
352,34 . . . "Let us descend also . . ." *PP,* 502
353,4 . . . "Clergymen in the Pulpit . . ." *PP,* 833
353,18 . . . "Milton's Religion is the cause" . . . *PP,* 504
353,25 "Awake, thou sleeper on the Rock of Eternity! . . ." *PP,* 505
353,36 . . . "the falling Death" . . . *PP,* 506
354,1 "O when shall we tread our Wine-presses . . ." *PP,* 507
354,12 Great Golgonooza . . . *PP,* 523
354,20 . . . "the sun & moon . . ." *PP,* 520
354,26 . . . the poor indigent is like the diamond . . . *PP,* 520
354,32 As to that false appearance . . . *PP,* 522, 524
355,12 . . . "where Contrarieties are equally true" . . . *PP,* 524
355,18 These are the Gods of the Kingdoms of the Earth . . . *PP,* 526
355,29 "Satan & Adam are States . . ." *PP,* 529
356,15 "Knowest thou of Milton . . ." *PP,* 537
356,19 . . . "Satan's Universe" . . . *PP,* 541
356,26 ". . . know thou, I come to Self Annihilation . . ." *PP,* 541-42
357,4 . . . "I am God the judge of all . . ." *PP,* 542
357,9 ". . . into the Lake of Los" . . . *PP,* 542
357,13 "There is a Negation . . ." *PP,* 545-47
358,10 "Milton's Shadow" . . . *PP,* 548
358,13 . . . a Garment dipped in blood . . . *PP,* 548
360,8 ". . . there is not much difference . . ." "Shakespeare and the Stoicism of Seneca," *Selected Essays,* 140
360,22 . . . & the awful Sun . . . *PP,* 527
361,7 . . . "imagined . . . as suffering with man . . ." "Notes," *Collected Poems,* 442
362,19 . . . "the sports of Wisdom . . ." *PP,* 466
363,26 . . . "the Cruelty of Man to Man" . . . Damon, *William Blake,* 184
363,30 . . . "time of renovation." *PP,* 569
364,31 . . . "Albion, the high Cliff of the Atlantic." . . . *PP,* 614

365,3 . . . ("Albion . . . is become a barren land") . . . *PP,* 614
365,10 Therefore I print . . . *PP,* 551
365,14 . . . "dear Reader . . ." *PP,* 550
365,18 "I am not a God afar off . . ." *PP,* 552
365,21 . . . "the perturbed Man" . . . *PP,* 552
365,23 "Phantom of the overheated brain! . . ." *PP,* 552-53
365,30 . . . "mountains run with blood . . ." *PP,* 553
366,2 . . . "the terrible sons & daughters of Albion" . . . *PP,* 554
366,4 "From these Twelve . . ." *PP,* 554
366,10 . . . "driv'n by the Starry Wheels . . ." *PP,* 556
366,15 "Pity must join together . . ." *PP,* 559-60
366,22 "I saw the limbs form'd for exercise contemn'd . . ." *PP,* 562-63
366,35 . . . "the spiritual sword" . . . *PP,* 564
367,3 "I must Create a System . . ." *PP,* 564
367,7 "Los stands in London . . ." *PP,* 564
367,17 What are those golden builders doing? . . . *PP,* 568-69
368,3 . . . "the World of Generation" . . . *PP,* 569
368,3 . . . "like a flower . . ." *PP,* 571
368,6 . . . "the abstract Voids . . ." *PP,* 571
368,15 There is the Cave, the Rock, the Tree . . . *PP,* 571-72
368,32 He views the City of Golgonooza . . . *PP,* 572
369,1 . . . "Jealous of Jerusalem's children" . . . *PP,* 582
369,4 "Babylon the City of Vala . . ." *PP,* 582-83
369,7 "Vala produc'd the Bodies . . ." *PP,* 582
369,11 "Seeking for rest . . ." *PP,* 584
369,16 "I brought Love into light . . ." *PP,* 590
369,20 "Why should Punishment Weave the Veil . . ." *PP,* 591
369,24 . . . "Human Imagination" . . . *PP,* 594
369,26 "In the Exchanges of London . . ." *PP,* 594-95
370,1 ". . . O my Children . . ." *PP,* 595
370,8 "Descend, O Lamb of God . . ." *PP,* 596
370,17 And O thou Lamb of God . . . *PP,* 599-600
371,7 . . . "his secret seat" . . . *PP,* 600
371,8 . . . "That Man be separate from Man." *PP,* 601
371,11 . . . "an endless labyrinth of woe." *PP,* 601
371,17 "The Reactor hath hid himself . . ." *PP,* 602
371,26 . . . "the Divine Vision" . . . *PP,* 602
371,28 "Because of the Opressors of Albion . . ." *PP,* 606-07
372,1 . . . "interiors of Albion's Bosom" . . . *PP,* 607-08
372,21 . . . Record the terrible wonder! . . . *PP,* 639
373,1 "What shall I do? . . ." *PP,* 608-09
373,19 . . . "the Demon of the Furnaces" . . . *PP,* 611
373,29 . . . "death's iron gloves" . . . *PP,* 622
373,30 . . . "The soul drinks murder & revenge . . ." *PP,* 627
373,31 . . . "furious, raging" . . . *PP,* 631
373,35 . . . "in holy hypocritic lust . . ." *PP,* 631
374,1 . . . "every energy render'd cruel" . . . *PP,* 632
374,2 . . . "the two Sources of Life . . ." *PP,* 632
374,6 ". . . they accumulate . . ." *PP,* 633

374,8 . . . "a pretence of Religion . . ." *PP,* 632

374,13 "I see America clos'd apart . . ." *PP,* 634

374,23 . . . "on Cherub's wings" . . . *PP,* 634

374,31 . . . "the Religion of Satan" . . . *PP,* 647

375,3 In Great Eternity every particular form . . . *PP,* 650-51

375,20 "I am God, O Sons of Men! . . ." *PP,* 651-52

376,9 "To be their inferiors or superiors . . ." *PP,* 652

376,15 "It is better to prevent misery . . ." *PP,* 654

376,17 . . . "Great Voice of the Atlantic" . . . *PP,* 657

376,20 "What is a Wife & What is a Harlot? . . ." *PP,* 658

376,32 . . . "Every Harlot was once a Virgin . . ." *PP,* 668

377,2 "Every Man's Wisdom is peculiar . . ." *PP,* 468

377,12 "Without Forgiveness of Sin . . ." *PP,* 673

377,20 Her Hand is a Court of Justice . . . *PP,* 673

377,23 . . . "the Flax of Human Miseries" . . . *PP,* 674

377,25 . . . "simple workmanship" . . . *PP,* 675

377,29 "Now, now the battle rages . . ." *PP,* 676

378,8 . . . "the Arts of Death" . . . *PP,* 675

378,9 . . . "with chains . . ." *PP,* 678

378,18 "For Luvah is France . . ." *PP,* 679

378,24 "All who see become . . ." *PP,* 680

378,26 ". . . as their eye & ear shrunk . . ." *PP,* 680

378,32 ". . . his mighty Hammer . . ." *PP,* 698

378,34 . . . "conversed with the Spiritual Sun" . . . Robinson, *Blake,* 7

378,35 . . . "the mouth of the Furnace . . ." *PP,* 699

379,3 I behold Babylon . . . *PP,* 699-700

379,16 . . . in your own Bosom you bear your Heaven . . . *PP,* 692

379,21 "I'll . . . shew you all alive the world" . . . *PP,* 232

379,25 . . . Jesus, breaking thro' the Central Zones . . . *PP,* 702

379,29 . . . "a golden string" . . . *PP,* 703

379,34 "I know of no other Christianity . . ." *PP,* 703

380,3 . . . "Labour in Knowledge" . . . *PP,* 703

380,4 . . . "the bright Preacher of Life" . . . *PP,* 705

380,6 ". . . that which is a Sin . . ." *PP,* 704

380,8 . . . "a Watcher & a Holy One" . . . *PP,* 704

380,11 "Go therefore, cast out devils . . ." *PP,* 705

380,26 And now the time returns again . . . *PP,* 705

381,1 "When Souls mingle & join . . ." *PP,* 709

381,9 The blow of his Hammer is Justice . . . *PP,* 730

381,14 . . . "Demonstrations . . ." *PP,* 735

381,20 "It is easier to forgive an Enemy . . ." *PP,* 736-37

382,11 "I care not whether a Man . . ." *PP,* 738-39

382,19 . . . "every Ratio of his Reason . . ." *PP,* 738

382,31 "Sexes must vanish & cease . . ." *PP,* 739-40

383,7 . . . "that Signal of the Morning . . ." *PP,* 742

383,9 "Time was Finished!" *PP,* 743

383,9 . . . "Breath Divine" . . . *PP,* 743

383,11 "This is Friendship & Brotherhood . . ." *PP,* 745

383,13 Albion reply'd . . . *PP,* 746

383,24 . . . "the Furnaces of affliction" . . . *PP,* 746

383,28 . . . "in Wars of . . . Love" . . . *PP,* 747
383,29 . . . "Druid Spectre." *PP,* 748
383,33 "And they conversed . . ." *PP,* 749
383,35 . . . "the Cry from all the Earth" . . . *PP,* 750
385,9 ". . . if I were pure . . ." *PP,* 666
385,15 . . . "with Child by the Holy Ghost." *PP,* 667
386,2 . . . "Absolute Paradox" . . . E. L. Allen, *Kierkegaard: His Life and Thought,* Harper, 1935, 70
386,13 . . . *"le premier voyant"* . . . Enid Starkie, *Arthur Rimbaud,* Norton, 1939, 124
386,26 . . . "the Monopolizing Trader" . . . *PP,* 813
386,38 . . . "The Serpent Bulk of Nature's dross" . . . *PP,* 134
387,3 . . . "to himself Laws . . ." *PP,* 481
387,5 . . . "moral individuality" . . . *PP,* 479
387,6 . . . "That Man be separate from Man" . . . *PP,* 601
387,11 . . . Record the terrible wonder! . . . *PP,* 639
387,15 "a pretence of Liberty . . ." *PP,* 632
387,16 In Great Eternity every particular form . . . *PP,* 650
387,28 . . . "deluge of forgotten remembrances" . . . *PP,* 612
387,29 "Into his own Chaos . . ." *PP,* 651
388,4 "All who see become . . ." *PP,* 680
388,11 . . . "that we should not move the body . . ." *The Dialogues of Plato,* tr. by B. Jowett, intr. by R. Demos, 2 vols., Random House, 1937, II:65
388,24 . . . "this Vegetable Glass of Nature" . . . *PP,* 830
388,24 . . . "this World of Mortality . . ." *PP,* 692
388,25 . . . ("The Caverns of the Grave") . . . *PP,* 127
388,30 "When Thought is clos'd in Caves . . ." *PP,* 351
389,5 Matter, as wise Logicians say . . . "The Progress of Beauty," *Poems,* ed. by C. Williams, 2 vols., Oxford University Press, I:228
389,16 "Heaven, Earth & Hell . . ." *PP,* 551
389,37 . . . "Time was Finished! . . ." *PP,* 743
390,1 *"Ce monde est mort . . ." "Pleine mer," op. cit.,* ed. by P. Berret, 6 vols., Hachette, Paris, 1920-27, II:810
390,7 "The cloud of mind is discharging . . ." Author's Preface," *Prometheus Unbound, Complete Poetical Works,* ed. by G. E. Woodberry, Houghton Mifflin, 1901, 164
390,14 . . . Henceforth the many children fair . . . *Prometheus Unbound,* III, iii, ll. 90-96
390,23 All Human Forms identified . . . *PP,* 751
390,30 And women, too, frank, beautiful, and kind . . . *Op. cit.,* III, iv, ll. 153-60
391,3 . . . "Thrones, altars . . ." *Ibid.,* III, iv, ll. 164-67
391,8 The painted veil, by those who were, called life . . . *Ibid.,* III, iv, ll. 190-97
392,8 "There have been men . . ." "William Blake and the Imagination," *Ideas of Good and Evil,* London, 1903, 168
392,12 . . . "a Mental Prince" . . . *PP,* 819
392,13 "Rouze up, O Young Men . . ." *PP,* 464
392,16 ". . . when in a generation storms begin to gather . . ." *Journals,* ed. and tr. by A. Dru, Oxford University Press, 1938, 146

CHAPTER ELEVEN

395,1 "Attempting to be more than Man . . ." *PP,* 454

395,23 "The stupendous failure of Christianity . . ." Henry Adams, *The Education of Henry Adams,* Houghton Mifflin, 1918, 472

396,18 ". . . every one is King & Priest . . ." *PP,* 114

396,27 "Political advice . . ." Introduction, *Letters of D. H. Lawrence,* Viking Press, 1932, xxvii

398,28 "Women the comforters of Men . . ." *PP,* 696. In mirror writing, on the design at the bottom of the page.

397,32 "It does not signify . . ." *PP,* 932

397,35 "Every Harlot was once a Virgin . . ." *PP,* 668

398,23 "Every Man's Wisdom is peculiar . . ." *PP,* 468

398,24 . . . "What is the Life of Man . . ." *PP,* 703

398,29 . . . "Con-Science." *PP,* 986, 989

399,7 "Are we to understand . . ." *Modern Man in Search of a Soul,* 273-74

400,3 "Only this shimmeriness . . ." *Sons and Lovers,* Random House (Modern Library), 1922, 181

400,7 "His gift is his fate . . ." *Letters of . . . Lawrence,* x-xi

400,15 . . . "culture" . . . "William Blake," *Essays,* Macmillan, 1896, 181

400,16 . . . "education" . . . "William Blake," *Selected Essays, passim*

401,15 . . . "the poet should think . . ." J. Aiken, *op. cit.,* London, 1777, 132

401,22 . . . "never could attain" . . . *Correspondence,* ed. by P. Toynbee and L. Whibley, 3 vols., Oxford University Press, 1935, II:551

402,15 . . . "turgid, ejaculatory, Hebraic" . . . See Frederick C. Gill, *The Romantic Movement and Methodism,* Epworth Press, London, 1927, 35-38.

402,25 . . . "immense power of assimilation" . . . *Selected Essays,* 304

404,5 Our bards are fam'd . . . *PP.*

404,9 How have you left the antient love . . . *PP,* 3

404,17 . . . "joy . . . roves round the Gardens . . ." *PP,* 5

404,18 "Like as an angel . . ." *PP,* 12

404,21 I turn my back to the east . . . *PP,* 12

404,34 " 'Parting is hard . . . *PP,* 42

405,8 "Good heavens! . . ." *Meditations and Contemplations,* 2 vols., London, 1770, I:73-74

405,19 "Breathe soft, ye winds! . . ." *Ibid.,* I:125-26

406,24 Whene'er I take my walks abroad . . . *Divine Songs Attempted in Easy Language, for the Use of Children,* London, 1728, Song IV

407,16 "I have no name . . ." *PP,* 62

407,32 Hear the voice of the Bard! . . . *PP,* 65

409,29 . . . "tinkling sounds . . ." *PP,* 18

410,12 . . . "sing in the large cage" . . . *PP,* 156

410,14 . . . two narrow doleful forms . . . *PP,* 274

411,11 For the various Classes of Men . . . *PP,* 515-16

411,24 "When this Verse was first dictated . . ." *PP,* 551

412,19 "Out of the tomb . . ." Quoted by Stephen, *History of English Thought,* II:243

413,21 . . . "the fallacy of imitative form" . . . Yvor Winters,

Primitivism and Decadence: A Study of American Experimental Poetry, New Directions, 1937, 77

414,21 Let thy west wind sleep on . . . *PP,* 5-6

414,30 . . . joy, with pinions light, roves round . . . *PP,* 5

414,34 . . . "a tree filled with angels . . ." *Life of . . . Blake,* 6

415,4 . . . hovering high over his head . . . *PP,* 398-99

415,17 . . . then the wolf rages wide . . . *PP,* 6

415,28 The bell struck one . . . *PP,* 6

416,1 "And the vale darkens . . ." *PP,* 13

416,5 Lo! to the vault . . . *PP,* 11-12

416,29 In what distant deeps or skies . . . *PP,* 72

417,3 Where the Youth pined away with desire . . . *PP,* 73

417,20 And the hapless Soldier's sigh . . . *PP,* 75

418,3 . . . "a Cave, a Rock . . ." *PP,* 633

418,14 . . . "the Wicker Man . . ." *PP,* 538, 639

418,15 . . . "the Cities of the Salamandrine men" . . . *PP,* 572

418,15 . . . "the Altars of Victims in Mexico" . . . *PP,* 622

418,19 . . . "Human Thought is crush'd . . ." *PP,* 511

418,20 . . . "on my hands death's iron gloves" . . . *PP,* 622

418,20 . . . "blue death in Albion's feet" . . . *PP,* 619

418,21 "Thought changed the infinite . . ." *PP,* 237

418,26 . . . they took the book of iron . . . *PP,* 369

419,32 "We were carried away in thousands . . ." *PP,* 676

420,6 . . . The captive in the mill . . . *PP,* 586

420,13 I turn my eyes to the Schools . . . *PP,* 574

420,35 . . . finding sacred . . . See *"Alchimie du verbe"* in Rimbaud's *Une Saison en Enfer.*

421,4 . . . "empsychosis" . . . J. M. Stratton, *Psychology of the Religious Life,* G. Allen and Co., London, 1911, 247

421,19 . . . "directed feeling" . . . The vocabulary here is Christopher Caudwell's, from *Illusion and Reality,* Macmillan, London, 1927, 223. Compare these remarks with André Breton's in *Premier manifeste du surréalisme,* reprinted and expanded in *What Is Surrealism,* tr. by D. Gascoyne, Faber, London, 1936, 59-60.

421,30 "Then I draw myself up . . ." *A Vision,* 301

421,33 "If the Spectator could enter . . ." *PP,* 836

422,21 . . . "golden London" . . . *PP,* 23

422,26 . . . "Gothic Artists" . . . *PP,* 861

422,27 . . . "in firm array . . ." *PP,* 37

423,3 O Winter! bar thine adamantine doors . . . *PP,* 5

425,28 . . . "they are organized . . ." *PP,* 795

427,17 ". . . now my paradise is fall'n . . ." *PP,* 167

428,38 . . . "the bursting Universe" . . . *PP,* 432

429,27 "A palace . . ." "Table Talk" (May 9, 1830), *Complete Works,* VI:310

430,15 . . . "framework of objectivity" . . . "Notes and Lectures upon Shakespeare," *ibid.,* IV:21

431,31 Joy is an import . . . "Night II," *Poetical Works,* I:30

432,23 "a step toward . . ." *"Ulysses,* Order, and Myth," *The Dial,* Vol. LXXV (November 1923), 483

433,12 . . . refinement of singularity . . . In a letter to Robert

Bridges (September 25, 1888), quoted in Bridges' notes to Hopkins, *Poems,* 118

433,12 . . . "intellectual peculiarity" . . . *PP,* 1138

433,28 "The poet . . . brings the whole soul of man . . ." *Biographia Literaria,* 166

434,8 . . . "without Labour or Study" . . . *PP,* 1074

434,30 "Damn braces . . ." *PP,* 194

CHAPTER TWELVE

437,14 "Certainly we . . . have sold our birthright . . ." "The Decay of Lying," *Intentions,* Methuen (Fountain Library), London, 1934, 19

437,20 . . . "irreducible and stubborn" . . . Whitehead, *Science and the Modern World,* 3

437,22 . . . "the modern man's intellectual attitude" . . . *Philosophy in a New Key,* 273

437,28 "Bring out number . . ." *PP,* 193

439,5 Like many men . . . See E. M. W. Tillyard, *Elizabethan World Picture,* Macmillan, 1944, 19-20

439,23 . . . "making things either better . . ." "The Defence of Poesie," *Complete Works,* ed. by A. Feuillerat, 4 vols., Cambridge University Press, 1923, III:8

439,34 . . . "in a just sense . . ." "Advice to an Author," *Characteristics,* ed. by J. M. Robertson, 2 vols., Dutton, 1900, I:135-36

440,10 "If it were not . . ." *PP,* 147

440,21 . . . "the institutors of laws . . ." "A Defence of Poetry," *Prose Works,* III:104

440,24 "Foolish Men . . ." *PP,* 979

440,28 "Degrade first the Arts . . ." *PP,* 970

440,30 "Empire follows Art . . ." *PP,* 970

441,2 *"dérèglement de tous les sens"* . . . Starkie, *Arthur Rimbaud,* 125

442,3 "Nature has no Outline . . ." *PP,* 769

442,11 ". . . the incorporeal cannot be enclosed . . ." *Hermetica,* I:219-23

444,1 . . . "Negative Capability" . . . *Letters,* ed. by M. B. Forman, Oxford University Press, 1935, 72

444,6 "Memory should not be called knowledge" . . . *Ibid.,* 103. See Annie Edwards Dodds (Mrs. Powell), *Romantic Theory of Poetry,* Ed. Arnold and Co., London, 1926, 240-60, for a very able discussion of this distinction. She cites this passage from Keats, and the terms "discovery" and "creation" are hers.

445,5 . . . "inward eye . . ." "I Wandered Lonely as a Cloud," ll. 21-22, *Poetical Works,* 187

445,8 . . . "Atheist." Robinson, *Blake,* 15

445,12 . . . "Man Brings All . . ." *PP,* 1004

445,14 . . . "Innate Ideas . . ." *PP,* 989

445,23 "How provokingly close . . ." White, *Shelley,* I:84

445,28 . . . "trailing clouds of glory" . . . "Ode: Intimations of Immortality," l. 64, *op. cit.,* 588

445,36 "Reynolds's Opinion . . ." *PP,* 980

446,3 "Imagination has nothing . . ." *PP,* 1026

446,4 . . . more than mortal fire . . . *PP,* 12

446,12 . . . "inspecting the invisible . . ." The translation is Miss Starkie's, *op. cit.,* 123.

446,14 . . . "deluge of forgotten remembrances" . . . *PP,* 612

446,25 . . . "Cloth'd in tears & sighs" . . . *PP,* 110

446,25 . . . "all thy moans flew o'er my roof" . . . *PP,* 172

446,26 . . . "the fibrous roots Of every heart" . . . *PP,* 173

446,26 . . . "the windows wove over with curses of iron." *PP,* 239

447,14 "Oh! that my spirit . . ." *Anima Poetae,* ed. by E. H. Coleridge, Heinemann, London, 1895, 163

447,26 "A Poet is the most unpoetical . . ." *Letters,* 228

448,13 "I would compare genius to virtue . . ." *Conjectures,* 14

448,22 "The Man who says . . ." *PP,* 1003

448,25 . . . "Genius dies with its Possessor . . ." *PP,* 1003

448,26 . . . "the too great indulgence of genius" . . . *Op. cit.,* 18

448,28 . . . "Genius has no Error" . . . *PP,* 996

448,29 . . . "Genius cannot be Bound." *PP,* 1006

448,31 ". . . by a spirit of Imitation . . ." *Op. cit.,* 19-20

449,2 "How ridiculous it would be . . ." *PP,* 1003

449,7 . . . "walking in another man's style . . ." *PP,* 802

449,11 "may soar in the regions of liberty" . . . *Op. cit.,* 10

449,18 "The Great Style is always Novel . . ." *PP,* 1000

449,21 "An *Original* . . . rises . . ." *Op. cit.,* 7

449,28 "death product." *Apocalypse,* Viking Press, 1932, 48

449,29 "the arts of death . . ." *PP,* 393

449,37 "Truth has bounds, Error none." *PP,* 269

450,1 "The Infinite alone . . ." *PP,* 655

450,4 . . . "as a fading coal . . ." *Op. cit.,* III:137

450,7 "Grandeur of Ideas . . ." *PP,* 987

450,8 "The Man's Execution . . ." *PP,* 991

450,15 . . . "determinate outline . . ." *PP,* 890

450,18 "To Generalize is to be an Idiot . . ." *PP,* 977

451,2 . . . "nature, which the Artist . . ." *PP,* 988-89

451,11 "Leanness or Fatness . . ." *PP,* 990

451,13 ". . . rectify every thing in Nature . . ." *PP,* 923

451,19 . . . "Spirits are organized men." *PP,* 795

451,23 . . . "Living Form." *PP,* 768

451,30 Kames, in fact . . . *Elements of Criticism,* Ch. 18, Sec. 3

452,7 . . . "Grecian" . . . *PP,* 768

452,21 . . . "makes every one of his characters . . ." *PP,* 787

452,26 . . . "the hard and wirey line of rectitude" . . . *PP,* 806

452,29 . . . "spiritual existences" . . . *PP,* 794

453,11 "The Classics! . . ." *PP,* 767

453,16 "Classicism . . . represents . . ." Introduction, *Surrealism,* Faber, London, 1936, 23

454,5 . . . "Dark" . . . *PP,* 991

454,7 "If Art was Progressive . . ." *PP,* 1003

454,11 "Ages are all Equal . . ." *PP,* 991

454,17 Such is sweet Eloquence . . . *PP,* 18

454,23 . . . "love most of all life . . ." *Autobiography,* 93

454,33 "Now Art has lost its mental charms . . ." *PP,* 857

455,10 . . . "Empire against Art" . . . *PP,* 766

455,12 . . . "Rome & Greece swept Art . . ." *PP,* 768

455,16 "The wretched State of the Arts . . ." *PP,* 819

455,29 . . . and the den nam'd Horror held a man . . . *PP,* 175

456,1 Hid in his caves the Bard of Albion . . . *PP,* 225-26

Notes

456,14 "The Arts & Sciences . . ." *PP,* 970

456,17 Then Los arose . . . *PP,* 242

456,28 "There cannot be more . . ." *PP,* 777

457,2 . . . "Every Man's Wisdom is peculiar . . ." *PP,* 468

457,3 . . . "Fiends of Commerce" . . . *PP,* 857

457,4 . . . "for Commerce Cannot endure . . ." *PP,* 811

457,11 "Where any view of Money . . ." *PP,* 765

458,8 "The Mocker of Art . . ." *PP,* 1122

458,19 . . . "simple, religious, and social" . . . *What Is Art?* tr. by A. Maude, Crowell, n.d. 82, 212

459,9 . . . "the greatest of poets"? Edith J. Morley, *The Life and Times of Henry Crabb Robinson,* Dent, London, 1935, 80

459,16 . . . "full of futurity"? *PP,* 1074

460,3 . . . "darling studies" . . . *Letters,* I:181

460,7 . . . "be enslav'd by another Man's" . . . *PP,* 564

460,11 "My nature . . ." Mehring, *Karl Marx,* 317

460,32 . . . "Mental Prince" . . . *PP,* 819

Acknowledgments

Of the many publishers whose names appear in the text or the notes, special thanks are due to the following for their kind permission to quote from copyrighted material in their possession: J. M. Dent, Ltd., London; E. P. Dutton and Company; Faber and Faber, Ltd., London; Harcourt, Brace and Company; Harvard University Press; The Houghton Mifflin Company; Alfred A. Knopf, Inc.; Little, Brown and Company; The Macmillan Company; Manchester University Press, Manchester, England; John Murray, London; W. W. Norton and Company; Oxford University Press; G. P. Putnam's Sons; Random House, Inc.; Martin Secker and Warburg, Ltd., London; Swedenborg Foundation, Inc.

Indexes

NOTE—*Many topics treated in the text in connection with Blake and also in other connections will be found listed in both of the following indexes: in the first, as they touch him; and, in the General Index, in non-Blakean connections. If all page references to any given topic are sought, both indexes must then be consulted.*

WILLIAM BLAKE

I. LIFE

Index

II. CHARACTER AND TEMPERAMENT

III. AS VISIONARY

IV. AS MYTH-MAKER

V. AS THINKER

IDEAS, BELIEFS, ATTITUDES

Index

Index

VI. AS WRITER

VII. WRITINGS

Index

VIII. PAINTINGS, DRAWINGS, ILLUSTRATIONS

IX. SYMBOLIC CHARACTERS

A—Invented Characters and Places

B—OTHER SYMBOLS, MYTHS, ALLEGORIES

X. APHORISMS AND PHRASES

Index

GENERAL INDEX

Index

Index

Index

Index

Index

DESIGNER: Maurice Serle Kaplan

TYPE: Linotype *Baskerville* with display in *Bauer Text* and *Weiss* italic

TYPESETTING, ELECTROTYPING, PRINTING, AND BINDING: Quinn & Boden Co., Inc., Rahway, N. J.